THE RORSCHACH: A COMPREHENSIVE SYSTEM

Volume
1

WILEY SERIES ON PERSONALITY PROCESSES

IRVING B. WEINER, *Editor*
Case Western Reserve University

INTERACTION IN FAMILIES
by Elliot G. Mishler and Nancy E. Waxler

SOCIAL STATUS AND PSYCHOLOGICAL DISORDER: A Causal Inquiry
by Bruce P. Dohrenwend and Barbara Dohrenwend

PSYCHOLOGICAL DISTURBANCE IN ADOLESCENCE
by Irving B. Weiner

ASSESSMENT OF BRAIN DAMAGE: A Neuropsychological Key Approach
by Elbert W. Russell, Charles Neuringer, and Gerald Goldstein

BLACK AND WHITE IDENTITY FORMATION
by Stuart Hauser

THE HUMANIZATION PROCESSES: A Social, Behavioral Analysis of Children's Problems
by Robert I. Hamblin, David Buckholdt, Daniel Ferritor, Martin Kozloff, and Lois Blackwell

ADOLESCENT SUICIDE
by Jerry Jacobs

TOWARD THE INTEGRATION OF PSYCHOTHERAPY
by John M. Reisman

MINIMAL BRAIN DYSFUNCTION IN CHILDREN
by Paul Wender

LSD: PERSONALITY AND EXPERIENCE
*by Harriet Linton Barr, Robert J. Langs, Robert R Holt,
Leo Goldberger, and George S. Klein*

TREATMENT OF THE BORDERLINE ADOLESCENT: A Developmental Approach
by James F. Masterson

PSYCHOPATHOLOGY: Contributions from the Biological, Behavioral, and Social Sciences
edited by Muriel Hammer, Kurt Salzinger, and Samuel Sutton

ABNORMAL CHILDREN AND YOUTH: Therapy and Research
by Anthony Davids

PRINCIPLES OF PSYCHOTHERAPY WITH CHILDREN
by John M. Reisman

AVERSIVE MATERNAL CONTROL: A Theory of Schizophrenic Development
by Alfred B. Heilbrun, Jr.

INDIVIDUAL DIFFERENCES IN CHILDREN
edited by Jack C. Westman

EGO FUNCTIONS IN SCHIZOPHRENICS, NEUROTICS, AND NORMALS: A Systematic
Study of Conceptual, Diagnostic, and Therapeutic Aspects
by Leopold Bellak, Marvin Hurvich, and Helen K. Gediman

INNOVATIVE TREATMENT METHODS IN PSYCHOPATHOLOGY
edited by Karen S. Calhoun, Henry E. Adams, and Kevin M. Mitchell

THE CHANGING SCHOOL SCENE: Challenge to Psychology
by Leah Gold Fein

THE RORSCHACH: A COMPREHENSIVE SYSTEM
by John E Exner, Jr.

THE RORSCHACH
A COMPREHENSIVE SYSTEM
VOLUME 1

JOHN E. EXNER, JR., PH.D.

A WILEY-INTERSCIENCE PUBLICATION

JOHN WILEY & SONS, New York • Chichester • Brisbane • Toronto • Singapore

Library of Congress Cataloging in Publication Data

Exner, John E.
    The Rorschach.

    (Wiley series on personality processes)
    "A Wiley-Interscience publication."
    1. Rorschach test. I. Title. [DNLM: 1. Ror-
schach test. WM145 E96ra]

BF698.8.R5E87   155.2'842   74-8888

ISBN 0-471-24964-5

Printed in the United States of America

20   19   18   17   16   15   14   13

To My Sons and Daughter

John, Michael, Christopher, James, and Andrea

Series Preface

This series of books is addressed to behavioral scientists interested in the nature of human personality. Its scope should prove pertinent to personality theorists and researchers as well as to clinicians concerned with applying an understanding of personality processes to the amelioration of emotional difficulties in living. To this end, the series provides a scholarly integration of theoretical formulations, empirical data, and practical recommendations.

Six major aspects of studying and learning about human personality can be designated: personality theory, personality structure and dynamics, personality development, personality assessment, personality change, and personality adjustment. In exploring these aspects of personality, the books in the series discuss a number of distinct but related subject areas: the nature and implications of various theories of personality; personality characteristics that account for consistencies and variations in human behavior; the emergence of personality processes in children and adolescents; the use of interviewing and testing procedures to evaluate individual differences in personality; efforts to modify personality styles through psychotherapy, counseling, behavior therapy, and other methods of influence; and patterns of abnormal personality functioning that impair individual competence.

IRVING B. WEINER

Case Western Reserve University
Cleveland, Ohio

Preface

The decision to undertake this work evolved gradually. The nucleus of the idea was formed during the culmination of an earlier work, *The Rorschach Systems*, a comparative analysis of the various approaches to the test. There were many factors, however, arguing against this undertaking. First, the Rorschach is no longer in its youth. It is more than fifty years since the publication of Rorschach's classic monograph, and more than forty years since Beck, Klopfer, and Hertz began developing their respective approaches to the test. During those forty-plus years, several dozen texts and more than 5000 articles have appeared in the literature regarding its merits, or lack thereof. Second, there has been a decreasing emphasis on psychological testing, and projective methodology in particular, during the past ten to fifteen years. The Rorschach no longer holds the place of distinction as once was the case. This de-emphasis has occurred, in part, because of the expanding role of the clinician in the professional world. Therapeutic skills are afforded much emphasis in training, and assessment in general has often been relegated to a minor position. The end product finds the students subjected to less formal training in traditional methods of psychodiagnostics. Whether this de-emphasis is appropriate has been argued extensively, but its very existence seemed to mitigate against any new Rorschach approach. A third element arguing in favor of maintaining the "status quo" of the Rorschach is the fact that each of the approaches to the test appear to work quite well in the clinical situation. There are numerous empirical studies, some dating to the 1930s, supporting this position. The Rorschach has been the most frequently used instrument in the assessment situation since 1940. In that the methods work well, and the test is being used extensively, any new approach might seem both presumptuous and extraneous. Finally, a personal element has contributed to the ambivalence to undertake this work. During the period from 1962 to 1968, while compiling data for *The Rorschach Systems*, I was privileged to have many close contacts with most of the systematizers and have come to regard them with great affection. David Rapaport had, unfortunately, died before that work began; however, it had been his earlier warning to me to "know all the Rorschach" that stimulated the idea for the comparative analysis. During the six years of the *Systems* project, I had many interviews with Dr.'s Beck, Klopfer, Hertz, and Piotrowski. At times, I felt that the project could not be completed because of their substantial differences, and yet, at these very times, each, in his own way, offered words of encouragement and clarification, making it easy to continue. It seems important to emphasize that, during those years, none attempted to "sway" me to a particular position, and all encouraged as much objectivity as "I could muster." It was not only this form of encouragement that

caused me to become close to these Rorschach "giants," but more their willingness
to share with me very personal experiences which led to Rorschach events or
decisions. I have listened in amusement to Dr. Beck's tales of newspaper reporting,
and in awe of Dr. Klopfer's struggles to get to America during the Nazi era. I
shared some of the despair that Dr. Hertz suffered after learning that her Rorschach
manuscript had been inadvertently destroyed after the Brush Foundation closed,
and was privy to a recall of some of the sufferings of Dr. Piotrowski after his
beloved country of Poland was overrun by the Germans in 1939. These are not
experiences which one forgets, and admittedly, they played a significant role in
my determination not to offer judgements concerning any single system, while
working on the comparative analysis.

There have been many other factors leading to the final decision to seek out a
new system of the Rorschach, not the least of which has been the systematizers
themselves. Samuel Beck has consistently maintained that the Rorschach was
"incomplete" and has publically encouraged "young researchers" to continue its
investigation. In one of my last meetings with Bruno Klopfer, he encouraged a
"sequel" to the comparative analysis, suggesting that while the intersystem differences may have been acceptable, and even healthy, at one time, the obvious
proliferation of the test, "at the whim of the user," could only diminish the ultimate
usefulness of the inkblots. Zygmunt Piotrowski encouraged me to consider the
use of the computer to study the test, and Marguerite Hertz exudes an atmosphere
of enthusiasm for the Rorschach that is contagious to all around her. A second
major source of encouragement to the present undertaking has been from the
students of the test. Anyone who teaches the methodology of the Rorschach cannot
help but be impressed with the eagerness with which students approach the subject
matter, and the persistent questions that arise concerning differences in approach
or interpretive postulates. I have taught the Rorschach in the classroom, the
practicum, and the workshop, for about 15 years, and have often found myself
"apologizing" for the complexities of the test, and especially for the fact that the
systematizers of the test have not reconciled. For some time, I have required my
own students to learn at least two, and in some instances, all of the systems, so
as to able to use the test more wisely. The burden to the students is often overwhelming. The alternative, of course, is to teach only one method, as if it were
the "only Rorschach," and thus mislead the student. A third element, in the decision
to develop the Comprehensive System, is the fact that most "Rorschachers" solve
the dilemma of several systems privately, by intuitively adding a "little Klopfer,"
a "dash of Beck," a few "grains" of Hertz, and a "smidgen" of Piotrowski, to
their own experience, and call it *The Rorschach*. This personalized approach
frequently is very useful. In fact, when the work presented here, based largely on
empirical data, is compared with the judgements of those who "personalize," a
significant congruence is noted. Obviously, it is unfortunate that so many of those
personalized decisions have to evolve privately, in the clinical setting, rather than
in the teaching setting.

The goal of this work is to present, in a single format, the "best of the Rorschach."
This system draws from each of the systems, incorporating those features which,
under careful scrutiny, offer the greatest yield, and adds to them other components
based on more recent work with the test. The product, if successful, should be a
method which is easily taught, manifests a high interclinician reliability, and which

will stand well against the various tests of validity. It is not based on any particular theoretical position, and hopefully, can be useful to both the behaviorist and the phenomenologist. It is predicated on the notion that the Rorschach is one of the best methods available from which a useful description of the uniqueness of the person can be gleaned. It is not necessarily offered as a substitute for other systems, for no doubt, countless numbers of clinicians are perfectly well satisfied with the results of whatever method they currently employ. It may be criticized by some as too conservative and "score oriented," and by others as too "soft-headed." So be it. But it does not represent simply "another" Rorschach system. Rather, it hopefully represents an integration of the hard won wisdoms of those who have developed and researched the test.

Countless numbers of colleagues and students have contributed significantly to this project since its inception more than six years ago. It is impractical to attempt to list all by name; however, some recognition is in order. Several hundred members of the Society for Personality Assessment, and Division 12 of the American Psychological Association generously participated in surveys concerning their use of the test. More importantly, nearly 500 sent protocols from which a large pool of vital information was developed. More than 100 diplomates of the American Board of Examiners in Professional Psychology responded to an exhaustively lengthy questionnaire concerning their use of the test, and many contributed protocols. Nearly 100 colleagues who have researched the test have shared their ideas for needed research, and many have suggested very useful research designs. The feedback of more than 200 workshop participants has been especially valuable in gauging the usefulness of the system in the clinical setting. Nearly a dozen computer "experts" have helped me to understand the strange ways of that technology, and have assisted enormously in developing sorts and tallies. John Roger Kline has been the laboratory "General" in this operation, and his mastery of Rorschach concepts has clearly surpassed my understanding of his machinery. I owe him much.

One of the most important contributions for this work has come from students, interns, and postdoctoral fellows, who have actively collected protocols for the reference samples, and who, by their eagerness for knowledge, have often provoked important considerations during the various decision phases of the project. They include:

George Armbruster	Ralph Nicholson
Elaine Bryant	Michael O'Reilly
Francesca Cannavo	Felix Salomon
Mark Edwards	Barbara Seruya
Laura Gordon	Eva Stern
Dorothy Helinski	Robert Theall
Richard Kloster	Elizabeth White
Antonnia Leura	Joyce Wylie

Harry Fiss, Jeanne Knutson, and Raymond Meyers have been especially helpful with their constructive criticisms of the first two sections of the manuscript. Paul Kessel has also contributed significantly by "trying out" the system with his beginning Rorschach class.

I also owe a great deal to Irving Weiner, who has been a friend and colleague for many years. In co-directing many Rorschach Workshops, he has been a con-

tinuing source of encouragement, guidance, and criticism. He was directly responsible for the inclusion of a special scoring for Developmental Quality of Location
selections, and has been a sounding board for numerous ideas.

Finally, I owe an unpayable debt to my wife. She has been responsible for the
Form Quality Tables more than anyone else, to mention only a minor contribution.
She has taught me that there is such a thing as a comma, and has reconstructed
many of my very badly written sentences. If this work is readable, it is because of
her efforts. If it is not, it is because of my stubbornness.

JOHN E. EXNER, JR.

Bayville, New York
March 1974

Acknowledgments

Reproduction of the Rorschach Location Sheets for each of the protocols, and of the blots to illustrate Location areas is by permission of Hans Huber Publishers, Bern, Switzerland.

Reproduction of Tables 15, 22, C, and D, from Beck, S. J., Beck, A. G., Levitt, E. E., and Molish, H. B. *Rorschach's Test. I: Basic Processes.* New York: Grune and Stratton, 1961, showing weighted and estimated values for organization activity is by permission of Grune and Stratton, Inc., New York, New York and Samuel J. Beck, Professor of Psychology, Emeritus, University of Chicago.

Contents

PART I   FUNDAMENTALS

1. INTRODUCTION,   3

2. DECISIONS AND PROCEDURES,   20

   Procedures of Administration,   23
   Seating,   24
   Instructions,   26
   Free Association Period,   31
   Questions and Encouragement,   31
   Presentation of the Cards,   32
   Timing,   33
   Recording Responses,   33
   Inquiry,   35
   Direct Inquiry, Analogy, and Testing Limits,   38

3. SCORING: THE RORSCHACH LANGUAGE,   42

   Scoring Rationale,   45

4. LOCATION: SYMBOLS AND CRITERIA,   53

   The *W* Response,   54
   The *D* Response,   55
   The *Dd* Response,   56
   The *S* Response,   57
   The *DW* and *DdW* Responses,   57
   The *DdD* Response,   60
   Evaluation of Developmental Quality,   60

5. DETERMINANTS: SYMBOLS AND CRITERIA,   69

   The Form Determinant,   70
   The Movement Determinants,   73
   The Color Determinants,   76
   Achromatic Color,   83

The Shading Determinants, 86
The Form Dimension Response, 97
Pairs and Reflections, 99
Summary, 103

6. BLENDS, ORGANIZATIONAL ACTIVITY, AND
    FORM QUALITY, 106

The Blend Response, 106
Organizational Activity, 111
Form Quality, 117

7. CONTENT CATEGORIES, POPULARS, AND SPECIAL
    SCORINGS, 126

Content, 126
Popular Responses, 127
Special Scorings, 134

8. THE QUANTITATIVE SUMMARY, 138

Listing of Scores by Sequence, 138
Frequencies of Scores, 138

PART II   WORKING TABLES

9. FREQUENTLY USED TABLES, 153

Table A.   Figures Showing Common (D) and Unusual (Dd) Location
           Areas by Card, Plus Listings of Good and Poor Form
           Responses and Response Classes by Card and Location, 156

Table B.   Scoring Examples, by Card, of Good and Poor Form
           Responses, Differentiated Into the Four Categories of the
           Modified Mayman Scoring for Form Quality, 201

Table C.   Organizational (Z) Values for Each of the Ten Cards, 215

Table D.   Best Weighted ZSum Prediction When Zf Is Known, 215

Table E.   Popular Responses Used in the Comprehensive System, 216

Table F.   Group Means for Location Scores, Determinant Scores, Some
           Content Scores, Plus Various Summary Scores for Non-
           psychiatric Subjects Plus Three Psychiatric Groups, 217

PART III   INTERPRETATION

10. INTRODUCTION, 221

   The Rorschach Data, 221
   The Interpretive Process, 222
   Blind Interpretation, 225
   Interpretive Prerequisites, 230

11. *R*, LOCATION, ORGANIZATION, FORM QUALITY, AND
                              POPULARS, 233

   Number of Responses, 233
   Location Scores   234
   Developmental Quality Scores, 239
   The Organizational (*Z*) Activity, 241
   Form Quality, 243
   The Popular Response, 249

12. STRUCTURAL DATA: FORM, FORM DIMENSION, AND
                              MOVEMENT, 255

   The Pure Form Response, 255
   The Form Dimensional Response, 257
   The Human Movement Response, 259
   The Animal Movement Response, 263
   The Inanimate Movement Response, 265
   The Active–Passive Dimension of Movement Answers, 266

13. STRUCTURAL DATA: COLOR, SHADING, REFLECTIONS
                       AND PAIRS, 277

   Color Responses, 277
   Achromatic Color Responses, 281
   Texture Responses, 284
   Vista Responses, 286
   Diffuse Shading Responses, 288
   Reflection and Pair Responses, 290

14. STRUCTURAL DATA: CONTENT CATEGORIES AND REACTION
                       TIME, 300

   Content Categories, 300
   Reaction Time, 305

15. THE STRUCTURAL SUMMARY, 309

The Erlebnistypus, 309
The Experience Actual, 311
The Experience Potential, 313
The Experience Base, 315
Blend Responses, 317
A Review of the Structural Summary, 317
A Preliminary Summary of L. S., 325

16. ANALYSIS OF THE SEQUENCE AND VERBALIZATIONS, 328

Sequence of Scores, 328
Analysis of the Verbalizations, 330
A Summary of L. S., 344

PART IV CLINICAL APPLICATIONS

17. FALTERING RESPONSE STYLES, 349

Protocol #1. H. V.—The Internalizer, 349
Protocol #2. C. F.—The Externalizer, 361
Protocol #3. L. H.—The Impulsive, 375

18. SOME SYMPTOM PATTERNS, 386

Protocol #4. J. C.—An Obsessive with Somatic Features, 386
Protocol #5. B. N.—A Phobic with Depressive Features, 398
Protocol #6. H. J.—An Aggitated Depression, 408
Protocol #7. L. Y.—Multiple Suicide Attempts, 418

19. SCHIZOPHRENIA, 429

Protocol #8. V. M.—A Disintegrating Adolescent, 429
Protocol #9. D. C.—A Paranoid Schizophrenic, 442
Protocol #10. M. H.—A Question of Remission, 452

20. CHILDREN IN TROUBLE, 460

Protocol #11. R. J.—An Isolate, 460
Protocol #12. A. L.—Acting Out, 470

AUTHOR INDEX, 479

SUBJECT INDEX, 485

Tables

1 Comparison of 346 Rorschach Protocols Collected By Five Different Methods for Total R, W, D, Dd, F, and Multiple Determined Responses, 29

2 Abbreviations Commonly Used for Recording Rorschach Responses, 34

3 Symbols Used for the Scoring of Rorschach Location Responses, 54

4 Symbols and Criteria Used for the Differentiation of Location Responses, 63

5 Examples of Location Scoring, 64

6 Symbols and Criteria for Scoring Response Determinants, 71

7 Examples of Three Types of Movement Responses, 77

8 Examples of the Four Types of Chromatic Color Responses 82

9 Distribution of Texture Responses in 250 Protocols, 91

10 Examples of the Different Types of Texture and Vista Responses, 94

11 Examples of General-Diffuse Shading Responses, 98

12 Examples of Form-Dimensional Responses, 100

13 Examples of Reflection and Pair Responses, 102

14 Examples of Blend Responses, 109

15 Organizational (Z) Values for Each of the Ten Cards, 114

16 Examples of Z Score Assignment for Responses to Each of the Ten Rorschach Cards, 115

17 Symbols and Criteria for the Scoring of Form Quality, 120

18 Symbols and Criteria to be Used in Scoring for Content, 128

19 Popular Responses Selected for the Comprehensive System Based on the Frequency of Occurrence of at Least Once in Every Three Protocols Given by Nonpsychiatric Adult Subjects and Nonschizophrenic Adult Out-Patients, 132

20 Scoring Sequence for the Protocol of L. S., 144

21 Scoring Structure Summary Sheet for the Protocol of L. S., 145

22 Best Weighted ZSum Prediction when Zf Is Known, 146

23 Mean Percentages of $+$, o, w, and $-$ Scoring in the Protocols of Four Reference Groups, 248

24 Proportional Differences of a/p Answers in the Pre- and Posttreatment Protocols of Two Groups of Adolescents, 270

25 Mean Difference Scores and Shift Scores for Daydreams of Two Groups of Female Subjects, 271

26 Frequencies of C' Type Responses in Three Groups of Subjects, 283

27 Pre- and Posttreatment Reflection and Pair Responses for Three Psychiatric Groups, Subdivided on a Criterion of Change Versus Unchanged Based on Two Behavioral Ratings, 293

28 Structural Summary for the Protocol of L. S., 318
29 Sequence of Scores from the Protocol of L. S., 329
30 Structural Summary for Protocol #1—H. V., 356
31 Sequence of Scores for Protocol #1—H. V., 357
32 Structural Summary for Protocol #2—C. F., 368
33 Sequence of Scores for Protocol #2—C. F., 369
34 Structural Summary for Protocol #3—L. H., 381
35 Sequence of Scores for Protocol #3—L. H., 382
36 Structural Summary for Protocol #4—J. C., 393
37 Sequence of Scores for Protocol #4—J. C., 394
38 Structural Summary for Protocol #5—B. N., 404
39 Sequence of Scores for Protocol #5—B. N., 405
40 Structural Summary for Protocol #6—H. J., 414
41 Sequence of Scores for Protocol #6—H. J., 415
42 Structural Summary for Protocol #7—L. Y., 424
43 Sequence of Scores for Protocol #7—L. Y., 425
44 Structural Summary for Protocol #8—V. M., 437
45 Sequence of Scores for Protocol #8—V. M., 438
46 Structural Summary for Protocol #9—D. C., 448
47 Sequence of Scores for Protocol #9—D. C., 449
48 Structural Summary for Protocol #10—M. H., 456
49 Sequence of Scores for Protocol #10—M. H., 457
50 Structural Summary for Protocol #11—R. J., 466
51 Sequence of Scores for Protocol #11—R. J., 467
52 Structural Summary for Protocol #12—A. L., 475
53 Sequence of Scores for Protocol #12—A. L., 476

Figures

1 Format for Recording Rorschach Data, 35
2 Location Selection by L. S., 139
3 Common (*D*) and Unusual (*Dd*) Detail Areas for Card I, 155
4 Common (*D*) and Unusual (*Dd*) Detail Areas for Card II, 161
5 Common (*D*) and Unusual (*Dd*) Detail Areas for Card III, 166
6 Common (*D*) and Unusual (*Dd*) Detail Areas for Card IV, 171
7 Common (*D*) and Unusual (*Dd*) Detail Areas for Card V, 175
8 Common (*D*) and Unusual (*Dd*) Detail Areas for Card VI, 178
9 Common (*D*) and Unusual (*Dd*) Detail Areas for Card VII, 183
10 Common (*D*) and Unusual (*Dd*) Detail Areas for Card VIII, 187
11 Common (*D*) and Unusual (*Dd*) Detail Areas for Card IX, 191
12 Common (*D*) and Unusual (*Dd*) Detail Areas for Card X, 196

THE RORSCHACH: A COMPREHENSIVE SYSTEM

PART ONE

Fundamentals

CHAPTER 1

Introduction

It has been more than 50 years since the Rorschach test was first introduced in the postumously published monograph *Psychodiagnostic* (Rorschach, 1921). Since that time the test has stimulated great interest, extensive use, and considerable research. For at least two decades, the 1940s and 1950s, its name was almost synonomous with clinical psychology. While flourishing as an important tool of the practitioner, the technique often proved baffling to the researcher and irritating to those with strong allegiance to stringent measurement theory. Criticism of the test, both real and unreal, has been widespread. Many have judged its worth with contempt and have advocated its abandonment, while others have defended the technique, purporting it to be the most effective of the clinical instruments. The total effect of the criticisms leveled against the test is difficult to gauge. It does seem clear that as long as the primary role of the clinical psychologist has been defined as one focusing on assessment, the Rorschach has been afforded a high status. For instance, in 1947, the results of a survey of clinical testing practices showed the Rorschach to rank fourth in frequency of use when compared to 20 commonly used tests (Louttit and Browne, 1947). By 1959, the Rorschach had become the most frequently used instrument in clinical practice (Sundberg, 1961). The decade of the 1950s probably represents the "prime" years of the test in clinical psychology. Between 1950 and 1960, twelve major works were published on the Rorschach (Ames, 1952, 1959; Beck, 1950, 1952, 1960; Hertz, 1951; Halpern, 1953; Klopfer, 1954, 1956; Phillips and Smith, 1953; Piotrowski, 1957; Rickers-Ovsiankina, 1960; Schafer, 1954). By 1955 more than 3000 articles had appeared concerning the test and by 1957 each of the five major Rorschach systems (Beck, Hertz, Klopfer, Piotrowski, and Rapaport-Schafer) had crystallized fully.

Even though the Rorschach has prospered in the clinical setting, there has been no moderation in critical attacks. Quite the contrary, as its clinical status has increased, attacks against it have been even more serious and seemingly extreme. Those who advocate abandonment of the Rorschach usually cite any or all of three basic arguments. The first argument is that predictions made actuarially are equal or superior to those derived from the clinical method. The second argument is that a large number of publications have appeared concerning the Rorschach in which the findings have been negative. The third general argument is that assessment *per se* should not be a primary task for the clinician, especially if it is at all time consuming. Each of these positions is related to the others and, quite frequently, the same logic and/or supporting evidence is manifest in all three.

The key author in the clinical versus statistical prediction issue is Paul Meehl, who cited 20 studies comparing the two methods (1954). In all but one, the actuarial method yielded equal or better results than the clinical method. Subsequently, Gough (1963) and Sawyer (1966) published surveys of predictive studies which appear to support Meehl's contentions, although Gough did admit that "no fully adequate study of the clinicians forcasting skills has been carried out." Holt (1958, 1970) has produced two excellent rejoinders to the Meehl-Gough-Sawyer interpretations and conclusions. He points quite accurately to the fact that many of the studies cited in these reports use inadequate criterion measures or even contaminate criterion. He also invites attention to the fact that in many instances clinicians have been asked to predict behaviors which are not properly the subject matter of the assessment routine, such as school grades and compatibility of air crews, and that in numerous studies cited judges were not "clinicians" at all. Holt also makes a strong argument that prediction, as such, is not an end in itself. Rather, understanding is at least equally important as a scientific goal. Holt could have easily gone one step further to emphasize that understanding is the principal goal of the clinical assessment routine, and that prediction, in many instances, is of somewhat lesser importance. One of the broader implications of this controversy for the Rorschach is that the test is not, and cannot be, subjected to the traditional requisites in the interpretive process. In other words, a nomothetic basis for Rorschach interpretation has little practicality, and the bulk of data from which interpretations is derived are idiographic. This assumption is erroneous, for in fact, responsible Rorschach interpretation joins both the nomothetic and idiographic data revealed by the test protocol. But even in error, the argument has no doubt influenced the attitudes of novices in assessment and influenced some would be Rorschachers to another direction.

While arguments concerning the predictive effectiveness of the clinical method have also challenged the usefulness of the Rorschach, the criticisms of the test based on negative research findings may have had even greater impact on its credibility. Beginning with the late 1930s and continuing to the present, many such works have been published. An especially large number appeared in the literature during the 1950s and early 1960s. By sheer numbers they are impressive, and quantitatively exceed reports of positive findings considerably. As a result, almost every feature of the test has been declared unreliable, invalid, or suspect at one time or another. Possibly worse has been the fact that authors have been able to draw "selectively" from this literature to support any one of a variety of positions concerning the test. For example, Zubin, Eron, and Schumer (1965) use a relatively brief bibliography of approximately 250 books and related articles, most of which appeared earlier than 1955, to build a case for the conclusion that "the clinical status of the Rorschach technique, based on an evaluation of research evidence, is not wholly satisfactory, despite claims to the contrary," and to conclude that the Rorschach "is essentially an interview." The matter of selectivity of literature is by no means unimportant to many of the conclusions formulated concerning the worth of the Rorschach. Holt (1970) points to the fact that two reviews of studies concerning the issue of clinical versus statistical prediction occurred within 2 years of each other (Sawyer, 1966; Korman 1968). The Sawyer review yielded apparently negative findings while the Korman review yielded apparently positive findings. Holt found it "remarkable" that no overlap existed when the bibliographies of the two articles were compared. A somewhat similar phenomenon may be found to exist in review articles specific to the Rorschach. For instance, Cerbus and Nicholas (1963) offered a review of research relating to the responsiveness to color as correlated to personality variables. Most of the literature in their review concerned the

Rorschach. They cited approximately 70 articles, only 10 of which had appeared after 1955, and interpreted the overall data to suggest that little if any relation existed between color response and personality or behavior. They neglected at least 10 other articles published between 1955 and 1961 relevant to the issue all of which support the opposite conclusion.

Unfortunately, many of the publications summarizing Rorschach research, as well as many dealing with specific research endeavors, appear to yield misinterpretation of data. For example, Zubin, Eron, and Schumer noted that "global methods as well as content approaches have had somewhat more success than atomistic methods," yet still suggest the test to be suspect. Other such examples are quite commonplace in the Rorschach literature. For instance, Feldman and Graley (1954) published a work dealing with the "fakibility" of the test. They used a group administration of the technique with two groups of subjects. One group responded under "natural" instructions during a first administration and under instructions to simulate the record of an institutionalized patient in a second administration. The second group was given the test only once, under instructions to simulate serious illness. The results indicate that the protocols of Group I (natural instruction) differ significantly from Group II (simulate abnormality) for only two of 35 variables and that four judges were able to distinguish accurately 75% of the "normal" and "faked" protocols. Feldman and Graley also report that only "very few protocols resemble psychotic records" even though their instructions were to simulate psychotic-like records. These data would seem to make it difficult to conclude that psychopathology can be simulated on the Rorschach, yet this very conclusion is implied in the discussion of the data. They support this contention by the fact that Group I, which was administered the test twice under "normal" and "simulation" instructions respectively, did show a statistically significant change for 14 of the 35 variables. This conclusion obviously ignores the dangers of a test–retest method to study instruments involving stimulus ambiguity wherein the naiveté of the subject for the stimulus material is important. In all fairness to Feldman and Graley, it is important to emphasize that the test–retest methodology was very commonplace in Rorschach research during the 1940s and 1950s even though continually cautioned against (Swift, 1944; Macfarlane and Tuddenham, 1951; Gibby 1951; Kimble, 1945; Luchins, 1947; Holzberg, 1960). In fact, many seemingly credible conclusions about the test have been drawn from studies using the test–retest method. For example, four studies reported over a 3 year period indicate that the stimulus effects of color on the last three cards of the test, VIII, IX, and X, have no effect on the number of responses given to these cards (Sapenfield and Buker, 1949; Dubrovner, VonLackum, and Jost, 1950; Allen, Manne, and Stiff, 1951; Perlman, 1951). All four used a test–retest procedure varying an achromatic and standard series of the blots. Subsequently Exner (1962), using two groups of carefully matched subjects and administering the standard series to one group and an achromatic series to the other found that the color factor did increase frequency of response to these cards.

Other problems in methodology and/or data interpretation have been less obvious. For example, Little and Shneidman (1959) reported on a very complex study designed to evaluate the descriptive accuracy of each of four tests, MMPI, MAPS, TAT, and Rorschach, when each is used separately in a "blind" analysis situation. They used 48 test judges, 12 per test, each evaluating the records of 12 subjects. They found the accuracy level for each of the tests to be considerably poorer than the accuracy derived from anamesis data and the interjudge reliability to be disappointing. They asked each judge to *first* label each subject diagnostically and rate him for maladjustment, and then to complete a 76 item Q-sort and two lengthy true-false questionnaries concerning adjustment, behaviors, and such. No listing of diagnostic labels was provided for the judges; thus a wide variety of classifications occurred, some of which, scored as disagreements, might easily have been agreements if a forced-choice or more limited listing had been used. More importantly, however, there is no way of telling from the data presented how much the Q-sort and T-F responses were influenced by a set that may have been induced with the choice of a diagnostic label. The omission of that labeling process might have altered some of the other data in this premiere study. The subtlety of problems in data interpretation may also be exemplified by Baughman's two classic studies on Rorschach stimulus characteristics (1954, 1958). Both are very well designed and usually considered as "milestones" in this difficult area of study. His data discussions, especially 1954, were somewhat brief, superficial in terms of the wealth of data, and did not give adequate consideration to other related works (Baughman, 1967). The unfortunate product of this oversight has been for others to misinterpret frequently Baughman's findings even to the extent of suggesting that his data demonstrate that only the form qualities of the blots affect responses (Russell, 1967).

It would be unrealistic and quite inappropriate to lay the cause of negative Rorschach research findings at the door of design flaws or misinterpretation problems. While there have been many poorly designed or misinterpreted studies, the bulk of Rorschach research follows methodology which is scientifically acceptable and have produced data which have been honestly interpreted. But whether the data and conclusions are really applicable to the Rorschach has often been a matter for debate. As early as 1949 Cronbach pointed out that much of the contemporary statistical methodology was not truly useful for evaluating a test as complex as the Rorschach. Harris (1960) very neatly reaffirmed this problem emphasizing that the test was often evaulated against orthodox psychometric standards even though it is not designed or interpreted in that context. Wyatt (1968) has accented the fact that the great mass of Rorschach research has focused on "trait isolation" wherein minor segments of protocols are investigated in relation to specific behaviors. Some of the more commonly researched involve the relation of color responses to affect, movement responses to fantasy, shading responses to suicide, whole responses to intellect, and such. Almost surprisingly, many have yielded positive findings, even though all manifest the same problem inherent to this type research—namely, any Rorschach variable can only be interpreted in relation to other Rorschach variables. The meaningfulness of a particular class of responses is not simply determined by its presence or absence in a protocol but by its presence or absence *in relation* to the presence or absence of other classes of response. For example, two protocols, one from a normal and one from a schizophrenic, might both contain the same number of color responses, and those responses could even be of the same general characteristic. The Rorschach novice might be tempted to postulate that both subjects have similar emotions, basing this postulate on the color-affect hypothesis which appears frequently in the literature. This conclusion would be premature and probably very erroneous. Any interpretation of those responses requires a careful weighing of many other elements of the protocol such as its length, location factors, form quality, scored content, organizational features, and the occurrence of other classes of response such as movement, form, and shading before even the most tentative interpretive hypothesis can be formulated. The possible interdependence of Rorschach variables, which in some instances is highly complex, makes most of the data derived from trait research studies relatively useless, and the conclusions from these studies questionable or worse. At best, these kinds of data can only be used to formulate new questions, the answers to which might be obtained from research designs more compatible with the complexity of the test itself. In other words, designs which account for the fact that Rorschach data are used in a "global" or "configurational" context. Very few such studies have ever been published on the Rorschach, and unfortunately, when they have, their impact has been diminished significantly by the myriad of publications of findings from the more restricted designs. Most of the studies which deal directly with the configurational aspects of the Rorschach are summaries of research rather than specific investigations. For example, Weiner (1966) has neatly summarized the variety of clues leading to the differential diagnosis of schizophrenia. His work, which offers considerable support for the Rorschach in the differential diagnosis role, includes findings from many tests commonly used in the clinical setting. It clearly demonstrates that the Rorschach, used separately, or in the test battery, can provide substantial data from which the differentiation of schizophrenia can be made, data that stands up very well to validation demands. Goldfried, Stricker, and Weiner (1971) have drawn together a number of works exemplifying how the test may be used configurationally to identify and evaluate such factors as hostility, anxiety, body image, homosexuality, suicide potential, neurosis, and schizophrenia. In their presentation it is argued that the broad question, "Is the Rorschach valid" is somewhat inappropriate. Rather, they maintain that the question should be asked, "What is the Rorschach valid for," and proceed to demonstrate how the issue is really not as complex as has been implied when specific behavior patterns or behavioral features are studied.

The Rorschach "argument" centers mainly about validation problems and research failures, and has quite likely been confused even more by another phenomenon. Unfortunately, most of the discussions concerning the Rorschach, whether pro or con, give the impression that there is a single Rorschach orientation or system about which the controversy is centered. This is not exactly true. In fact, it is probably more false than true. It is true that there are the 10 Swiss inkblots about which Rorschach published his original treatise, and it is also true that many of Rorschach's postulates have formed the basis on which specific systems have been developed. But it is not true that the various Rorschach systems are highly congruent. Quite the contrary, they are substantially different. In the United States alone there have been at least five such methods or systems developed. These five systems, Beck, Hertz, Klopfer, Piotrowski, and Rapaport-Schafer, differ enormously—not so much so that each is completely discrete from each of the others, but enough so that five different Rorschach tests have been created. They differ in basic administrative procedures. They differ in scoring. And they differ in interpretive hypotheses. Where agreement between two or more of the systems does exist, it is usually because each has incorporated something from the original Rorschach, but these instances are considerably fewer in number than might be estimated at first glance (Exner, 1969).

The five different Rorschach systems evolved over a relatively short period of time. Between 1936 and 1945 three of the systems, Beck, Hertz, and Klopfer, had crystallized and the basics for the other two, Piotrowski and Rapaport-Schafer, had been formulated. By 1957 all five were fully developed and have remained reasonably static since that time. Additions and alterations have been minor, if they have occurred at all. It seems clear that none of the *systematizers* began with the intention of creating a Rorschach system which would be distinctly different from that of Rorschach himself, or different from other Rorschach authorities. But Rorschach had died in 1922, at an early age, after having devoted himself to a serious study of the inkblots for a comparatively brief period.[1] Although he did offer a variety of postulates concerning specific test features, especially form, color, and human movement, he did not formulate a global theory of the test and was quite conservative in discussing its potential usefulness (Rorschach, 1921). Many of Rorschach's contemporaries perpetuated the use of the test after Rorschach's death but none actually assumed the leadership necessary to perpetuate its development. For example, Oberholzer trained David Levy in the use of the technique. Levy, in turn, was the first to bring the Rorschach to the United States and later was instrumental in influencing Beck. But by the mid-1930s little had been accomplished concerning the test other than what Rorschach himself had done. And at that time, clinical psychology was developing at a fairly rapid pace. It was an appropriate time for almost any test to attract interest, and especially one like the Rorschach with its seemingly enormous potential. It would seem that Levy was the natural person to assume Rorschach leadership in the United States but his interests were not oriented in that direction. Both Beck and Hertz had completed dissertations on the Rorschach and Beck had also completed a year of postdoctoral study with Oberholzer in Switzerland. They had both become strongly committed to the Rorschach and were independently researching it, mainly concerned with establishing a credible normative base. It was about this same time that Bruno Klopfer emigrated to the United States. After leaving Germany in 1933 under the pressures of Nazism, he spent approximately one year working at the Zurich Psychotechnic Institute. It was there that he received his first formal training in the Rorschach, although he had some familiarity with it prior to leaving Germany. In 1934 he accepted an appointment at Columbia University, and shortly thereafter his presence as a teacher and organizer was clearly manifest on the American scene.

If the theoretical positions, toward psychology, of Beck and Klopfer had been similar, or if their orientations toward the Rorschach had been more alike, it is very doubtful that more than one approach to the test would have evolved in the United States. That was not the case. Their backgrounds in psychology and their Rorschach orientations were quite different. Klopfer received his doctorate at the University of Munich in 1922. His training, quite representative of the German psychology, was strongly oriented toward the phenomonological position. He had wanted to become an analyst and was particularly intrigued with the work of Carl Jung. He approached the Rorschach from this framework; he was prone to emphasize the qualitative and subjective and willing to change the Rorschach approach

[1] Although Rorschach first became interested in the use of inkblots to study psychopathology about 1911, it is doubtful that he undertook any serious investigation of their usefulness until 1917. In that he died in 1922, he probably spent no more than between 3 and 4 years working intensively with them.

on the basis of logic and clinical judgment. Beck was trained in a much more behavioristically oriented setting. He received his doctorate in 1932 from Columbia University where the fundamental commitment was to scientific methodology. He was also attracted by the psychoanalytic movement, particularly the Freudian position, but his orientation always reflected the influence of rigorous positivism. His approach to the Rorschach included considerable weight to nomothetic as well as idiographic data. He insisted on a cautious approach to any Rorschach change, arguing for data rather than simply logic or clinical judgment. It was almost inevitable that Beck and Klopfer were to disagree on many basic Rorschach issues. Even before any direct clash between them, Beck had already published an article expressing a feeling of distress that the Rorschach procedures used in Zurich were marked too much by the approach of the artist than the scientist (1936). These were the very procedures in which Klopfer had been trained.

While Beck was stressing the need for fixed standards in scoring and interpretation, Klopfer had begun a series of training seminars in the Rorschach and, in 1936, organized the *Rorschach Research Exchange*, which was to become an important journal for the dissemination of Rorschach information. In the second issue, he had added several scoring categories different from Rorschach, including two for shading responses and one for movement (K, c, m, all following mainly from Binder). In the fifth issue (July, 1937) he offered a very brief but somewhat critical discussion of Beck's newly published book, *Introduction to the Rorschach Method*. Beck replied in the next issue, a reply which was equally critical and again reaffirming his emphasis on caution and investigation before making modifications in the Rorschach approach. And so the schism developed between these two Rorschach authorities, focusing at first on differences in evaluating form quality and scoring movement and shading, and later encompassing many more Rorschach features. This divergence was to widen and never be reconciled. In fact, it was not even discussed very extensively after 1940 except as each would make an occassionally subtle reference to the other as they continued in their writings.

Hertz often found herself in the middle of the disagreement. She had received her doctorate in 1932 from Western Reserve University, which had a strong psychometric tradition. In that framework, she could more easily understand many of Beck's objections and warnings but was also sympathetic to Klopfer's eagerness to develop the test further. While proceeding in her own research, she often assumed the role of "evaluator", and it was not uncommon in the early literature to find her disagreeing with Beck and simultaneously cautioning Klopfer. She never worked with the specific intention of creating a "separate" Rorschach system but has found that she could not completely agree with any of the other systems. Her approach, based mainly on her own work with the test, includes such features as Binder's treatment of vista, Klopfer's approach to texture, and a method of evaluating form quality which is very similar to that used by Beck. She has argued the position that, although different scoring methods exist, there remains only one basic Rorschach system and that differences between Rorschach authorities are relatively minor (Exner, 1969).

Piotrowski was also involved with the Rorschach at the time of the first Beck-Klopfer clash. In fact, he contributed indirectly to it. Piotrowski had received his doctorate from the University of Poznan, Poland in 1927. His basic concentration was in experimental psychology. Subsequently, he came to the United States for post-doctoral work in clinical psychology at the Psychiatric Institute in New York City and at the Columbia University clinic in the College of Physicians and Surgeons. He was familiar with the Rorschach but had no formal training in it and thus joined Klopfer's first seminar. He published three articles in 1936, all concerning the applicability of the Rorschach to the study of organic disturbances. In 1937, in the *Rorschach Research Exchange*, he suggested the use of the symbol *m* to score responses involving inanimate movement. This suggestion was endorsed by Klopfer but rejected by Beck. Soon after this, Piotrowski found himself differing with Klopfer's test orientation, feeling that it focused too much on theory, Often at the expense of behavioral descriptions. By 1940, his own work with the test had moved him to a position significantly different than Klopfer's and also considerably different than Hertz or Beck. By 1957, he had developed a fully unique system of his own.

The fifth major approach to the Rorschach to be developed in the United States is that of Rapaport and Schafer. Their collective works generally focus on the use of the test battery for personality evaluation. While the Rorschach is perceived to have a nuclear role in such a test battery, neither Rapaport or Schafer has studied its usefulness with the specific intention of creating a separate system for it. However, such a system naturally evolved and is quite different from any of the other systems. Rapaport received his doctorate from the Royal Hungarian Petrus in 1938 and emigrated to the United States shortly thereafter. His orientation was very strongly psychoanalytic. He likened the test battery, including the Rorschach, to a structured interview wherein the method of association would be employed. While encouraging the accumulation of normative data, he was much more concerned with the idiographic features of the individual. He generally discouraged extensions of the Rorschach, except where indispensable, emphasizing that the test was already extremely complex. The basics of the Rapaport-Schafer approach were first presented in 1946 in a two volume work on the test battery, *Diagnostic Psychological Testing*. This system was later extended by Schafer's classic work, *Psychoanalytic Interpretation in Rorschach Testing* (1954). The totality of their works clearly achieved a unique approach to the Rorschach which is probably the least researched of any of the systems and the most heavily oriented toward psychoanalytic interpretation of the test data.

The total impact of the divergence of Rorschach methodology into at least five major systems or approaches is somewhat difficult to gauge. Certainly, the failure of the Rorschach community to concentrate on the development of a single system has penalized both the practitioner and the researcher. It may be suggested that the divergence has been healthy for the Rorschach, for logically based differences of opinion usually breed systematic research efforts. But this has not necessarily been the case with the Rorschach. The differences have been frequently disregarded or underplayed, usually in the broad context of many Rorschachers that regardless of which approach is employed, the results will be essentially the same. Most of the research published concerning the test has, at best, simply identified which scoring system was employed and, at worse, completely disregarded the issue or proceeded to intermix systems on the assumptions that differences between them were generally irrelevant or insignificant to the data. This latter position is predicated on the naive assumption that responses scored by one system will breed conclusions essentially identical to or highly similar with those scored by any of the other systems. This assumption has never really been tested and, in fact, the likelihood that it is even testable is, at best, remote. The difficulties in testing such a hypothesis lie in the considerable differences which exist across the five major systems. The five systems use 15 different scores for location alone, six of which were recommended by Rorschach. There is no single location score which is completely agreed to by all five systematizers, not even the criteria for scoring the *Whole* response. It is not uncommon to find a response which would be scored for location as *W* by the Piotrowski system, *W* in the Klopfer method, *D* by the Beck and Hertz systems, and *Dd* in the Rapaport-Schafer approach. Certainly, with such divergence, it is difficult to apply all of the research published on location scoring to all of the systems with equal applicability. Yet, research conclusions drawn from most of the research on location imply this to be the case.

The issue of scoring differences across systems becomes even more exaggerated as the complex problem of scoring for response determinants is considered. All five of the systems use the symbol *F* to denote "pure" form responses, and each provides some technique for judging the quality of the form used. Here, there is considerable variation from system to system. Rorschach had recommended that the scoring of plus or minus of form involved answers be based on the frequency of recurring answers. Beck and Hertz have followed this advice but have published different frequency distributions so that some responses regarded as good form by Beck are considered poor form by Hertz, and vice versa. Piotrowski established a "rule of thumb," indicating that responses produced by at least one-third of healthy subjects should be regarded as good form. But he offers no listing of such responses so that, in effect, the examiners subjective opinion and/or experience becomes an important determining factor. The Rapaport-Schafer method includes essentially the same approach. Klopfer attempted to go beyond the purely subjective but rejected the frequency distribution approach. In that system, form involved answers are evaluated against a "Form Level Rating" which may vary from $+5.0$ to -2.0 depending on the examiners evaluations of accuracy, organization, and specification.

The disagreements between Beck, Klopfer, and Piotrowski concerning the scoring of responses involving some sort of movement has already been mentioned. The end product of these and other such disagreements has been much diversity. For example, a single response might be scored as *F* by Beck and Hertz, *FM* by Rapaport-Schafer, $\rightarrow M$ by Klopfer, and *m* by Piotrowski. Another response might be scored *M* by Beck, *Ms* by Rapaport-Schafer, and *m* by Klopfer, Hertz, and Piotrowski. Sixteen different symbols are used in the five systems for the scoring of color responses. The lack of common criteria is striking, as much if not more so when compared to the diversity in scoring movement responses. The greatest disagreement across the systems occurs for the scoring of "light–dark" determined responses. This is an area about which Rorschach wrote almost nothing; thus each systematizer has apparently seen fit to develop his own criteria. The result is only very minor overlap between any two of the systems so that any single light–dark determined response could be expected to have at least three, more commonly four, and in some instances five different scorings when evaluated across all systems. It is very possible for one response to be scored *T* by Beck, *c* by Klopfer and Hertz, *c'* by Piotrowski, and *Ch* by Rapaport-Schafer. Another could be scored *Y* by Beck, *C'* by Klopfer and Rapaport-Schafer, *Cg* by Piotrowski, and *Ch''* by Hertz.

The problem posed by the use of different scoring symbols across the five systems would be relatively minor if the symbols could be equated but that is not the case. In some instances, the criterion for the use of a scoring symbol in one system has some overlap with the criterion for symbols in the other systems. The Beck scoring for "texture" responses (T) provides a good illustration. Both Klopfer and Hertz use the symbol c for such responses and to that extent the three systems agree. However, both Klopfer and Hertz also score other types of shading response with the symbol c which Beck would score with the symbol Y. Thus the categories of T and c are not really congruent. Piotrowski also used the symbol c for scoring shading responses but with a completely different criterion than used by either Klopfer or Hertz. In fact, Piotrowski and Rapaport-Schafer have no specific symbol for the scoring of texture responses. The same confusing lack of congruency exists when the scoring criterion for any one system is compared with the other systems, even in the outwardly superficial or fundamental scorings such as F for form and M for human movement. The confusion is accentuated even more where two or more systems use the same symbol, for the illusion is created that the criteria are identical but this is specious reasoning more often than not.

The differences that exist across the systems in scoring categories and their respective criteria magnify the differences across the systems in interpretive postulates and approaches. Each of the systematizers offers interpretive postulates for each of the scoring categories; thus where the categories are not congruent, neither are the postulates concerning them. But the intersystem differences in interpretation go well beyond scoring. In many instances interpretive concepts are specific to a system with no equivalent in the other systems. Beck's Experience Actual, Piotrowski's Principle of Interdependent Components, Hertz Interactionist approach, and the Rapaport-Schafer M percent are all illustrations of this phenomena. More commonly, concepts used in interpretation in the various systems, like many of the scoring categories, seem similar but in reality are not. The concept of introversion, usually associated with the M response, exemplifies the point. It is used as an interpretive postulate in all five systems but with little agreement regarding its meaning. Beck views introversion as an internalizing process or style. Klopfer and Hertz follow a Jungian position implying a greater avoidance response than does Beck.[2] Piotrowski de-emphasizes the internalization process altogether suggesting that M responses have a positive correlation with overt behavior. Rapaport-Schafer use the concept as one meaning resistance to spontaneity wherein internalization need not necessarily occur. These viewpoints are clearly different yet it is not uncommon to find the unskilled Rorschacher holding them to be identical, a position which is fallacious at best.

The Rorschach, as a test, would have probably fared much better had each of the systematizers divorced himself completely from the scoring symbols and interpretive postulates of other systematizers. At least, under that condition, each system might have become an attractive target of research. But that did not happen, mainly because each of the systematizers incorporated some of Rorschach's basics into his approach and often borrowed liberally from his fellow systematizer thereby making many of the differences less obvious. The result has been a penalty to the

---

[2] Rorschach specifically rejected the Jungian interpretation of introversion in his monograph *Psychodiagnostics* and Beck has maintained a position essentially identical to that of Rorschach.

test and to those who use it, be he teacher, researcher, or practitioner. Altogether too often, the Rorschacher has been faced with the problem of "pledging allegiance" to a specific system at the expense of discarding that which might be worthwhile in another system, or, more commonly, using his own experience and judgement to decide how best to intermix the systems. The result has been slightly less than chaos for those knowledgeable of the intersystem differences and a perpetuated naivete for those led to believe that the differences are only modest and inconsequential.

The manner in which the differences across Rorschach systems has affected the teaching of the test has been well documented by Jackson and Wohl (1966). They used an 81 item questionnaire to study the differences in practice and attitude among university faculty responsible for teaching courses in the Rorschach. The data that they obtained reflect the overall dilemma in Rorschach instruction. They found, possibly to no one's surprise, that the variability in methods of administration, scoring, and interpretation is quite remarkable. While most departments offer instruction in either the Beck or the Klopfer method, the variations on both are considerable with the final decision concerning approach being left almost exclusively to the instructor. Approximately 60% of these instructors have had little or no postdoctoral work in the Rorschach. Strikingly, 46% of those who teach the Rorschach would prefer to teach something else. A position defended by most of the respondents is that methods of administration, scoring, and interpretation should be sufficiently "flexible" to meet the needs of any given patient in almost any given situation. Consequently, uniform procedures are typically viewed as restrictive rather than instructional. Twelve percent actually teach their students not to score responses at all. It is implied from the Jackson-Wohl data that there may well be as many Rorschachs as there are Rorschachers. The implications of their study are quite important for the student of the Rorschach. First, there has been a significant failure to standardize the teaching approach to the test. Second, training programs are utilizing less well trained or qualified instructors to teach the Rorschach than has apparently been the case in the past. And third, a new generation of Rorschachers will be led to use the technique in ways that are substantially different from that of Rorschach and his intentions for the test.

In a related study, the actual methods employed by clinicians in their use of the Rorschach has been surveyed (Exner & Exner, 1972). A 30 item questionnaire was distributed to 750 members of the Society for Personality Assessment and the Division of Clinical Psychology of the American Psychological Association. Approximately two-thirds of the questionnaires were returned, the results from which lend substance to the implications from the Jackson-Wohl study and highlight the disarray which exists in the use of the test. Twenty-two percent of those responding do not score responses at all. Seventy-five percent of those who do score responses admit to some personalization of their scoring, that is, intermixing the scorings from different systems or adding scorings derived from personal experience. About 34% prefer the Beck system but nearly one in every six of those modify the Beck system with some other system, usually that of Rapaport-Schafer. Similarly, 54% prefer the Klopfer system but slightly more than one in six modify the Klopfer method with another approach, usually the Hertz or Piotrowski methods. The idiosyncratic proliferations that clinicians use are by no means simple, such as adding a few features from one system to another while continuing to use their "preferred" system intact. More often than not the clinician appears to have pieced together an assortment of features from several systems plus his own experience, *even though* maintaining some allegiance to a preferred system. The 166 respondents indicating that they use the Klopfer system serve as a good illustration. Seventy-one usually administer the test in a face-to-face situation (Piotrowski & Rapaport-Schafer); 63 instruct the subject to report all that he sees (Beck, Hertz, and Rapaport-Schafer); 31 score multiple determinant responses as blends (Beck); eight do not score additional determinants at all (personal); six use no inquiry whatsoever (personal); 81 score form quality as plus or minus (Beck, Hertz, Piotrowski, Rapaport-Schafer); and 32 do not score at all (personal). None of these procedures are endorsed by Klopfer and most have been cautioned against by him. The variety of amalgamations which have been created by a substantial number of those who use the Rorschach creates a clear obstacle to any acceptable level of standardization of the test as a single instrument.

How many Rorschachs are there really? No one can say but to guess gives rise to alarm. There are five reasonably distinct systems and so it can be argued that there are at least five reasonably distinct Rorschachs. But when the potential combinations of these systems are considered, the possibilities become astronomical. Even more intriguing is the salient fact that the Rorschach has flourished widely. The willingness of thousands of clinicians to use the test over a lengthy span of time cannot be ignored and suggests that it does provide data from which valid, or at least clinically valuable, conclusions may be drawn. Two factors have probably contributed largely to this phenomenon. First, no matter which system is employed, one of the basic products is the words of the subject, some generated during the free-association and more during the inquiry. Analysis of these verbalizations is always included in any Rorschach interpretation and special weight is frequently given the more unique or dramatic, both for actual content and for appropriateness to the blot. In this framework, the test can be likened to the interview, as has been suggested by both Rapaport and Zubin. But it seems likely that for most Rorschachers, the test structure also plays some role. Here, the second factor appears which has perpetuated the use of the test and given it a status well beyond that of the interview. All of the Rorschach authorities have emphasized the necessity to approach interpretation of the test material in a "global" manner, integrating all data before drawing firm conclusions. In this approach, the composite of structure plus content provides a rich data bank from which hypotheses are formulated, cross-checked, and finally accepted or rejected. It is in this complex methodology that the Rorschach has worked well for the practitioner, but it is this same methodology which has made it vulnerable to the critics. It is not a truly standardized methodology; thus much of the data to which it is applied can be suspect. A complete standardization has not been possible because of the many different approaches which have been employed with the test. Research concerning *the test* may actually be research concerning several tests which have the same stimulus figures in common.

The product of this situation has been the survival of the inkblots under the broad umbrella provided by the name Rorschach but a failure of the test, as a test, to reach the pinnacle of sophistication desired or predicted for it. Even though weathering a stormy history, the fragmentation of the technique into several systems and many approaches has precluded the compilation of the "hard" reliability and validity data and has instead, promoted the chronic *Rorschach problem*. This problem should have been faced squarely and resolved long ago by those most knowledgeable in Rorschach. At the very least, researchers in the Rorschach should have adjusted their approaches so as to provide data from which solutions could be formulated. But in an era where frequency of publication has often been rewarded more than scope of research, few have committed themselves to the task of studying the differences in Rorschach systems and the systematizers have each preferred to go his own way. The many approaches to the Rorschach are the result. It would still be easy to solve the Rorschach problem had each of the systematizers formulated his work on a solid research base but unfortunately most of the divergence in attitude and opinion came forth not from research but from different theoretical positions concerning all of psychology as well as theories specific to the test and how it might best be used. Much emotion was generated on this issue, emotion that cut deeply into the combatants and created a situation where reconciliation was unlikely or impossible. But the test, even with all of its mutations, survived because it was of obvious value to the diagnostician in his clinical routine.

Unfortunately, the survival of the Rorschach is no longer as certain as once was the case. Clearly, it is no longer synonomous with clinical psychology. The new synonym is psychotherapy. The seeds planted in Meehl's argument, that the actuarial method would provide more time for the important work of therapy, have taken firm root in clinical psychology during the 1960s. Emphasis on professional assessment has diminished in the midst of arguments against "diagnostic labeling" and medical models and the development of many new intervention approaches, some of which *appear* relatively independent of needs to "understand" the patient. It is a difficult time for all psychological tests and especially those such as the Rorschach which are difficult to learn, time consuming to administer, and complex to interpret. Two recently published surveys accent this point. Shemberg and Keeley (1970) have found that projective techniques are being emphasized less in the training of clinicians. They suggest that this reduced emphasis is a manifestation of the changing role of the clinician. More recently, Biederman and Cerbus (1971) report a significant decrease in the number of Rorschach courses being offered in clinical training programs. While the emphasis on teaching of Rorschach has apparently changed, the extent of its use apparently has not. Lubin, Wallis, and Paine (1971) reported a replication of the 1961 Sundberg survey concerning the use of tests in clinical facilities. They surveyed 251 clinical settings, compared to 185 surveyed by Sundberg, and found that the Rorschach is used in about 91%, compared with 93% reported by Sundberg. They also note that the actual proportion of patients who are administered the Rorschach has decreased somewhat, from 80% in 1961 to 60% in 1971. Weiner (1972) interprets these findings to suggest that the Rorschach is being used more selectively, but notes that the absolute number of Rorschachs administered has possibly increased. If this is in fact true, as seems the case, the de-emphasis on Rorschach training poses a serious problem concerning the qualifications of those using the test, and obviously, it will not help resolve the problems of the test.

If the collective wisdom of clinical psychologists over the past three decades is to be given any weight at all, then the role of the Rorschach has probably been greater than any other psychological test. If the goal of understanding the individual remains important to psychology, then the Rorschach will continue as a significant tool. Adding to its potential can make the test more accessible to the researcher and more productive for the user. One step which can add to this potential is to minimize the proliferations of the test into many different approaches—in other words, to provide some reasonable standardized base from which the Rorschach can be used and researched and further developed. This might have been done 35 years ago but it was not. Orientations, emotions, and a general lack of information and experience precluded such an endeavor and each of the Rorschach pioneers molded his own approach. It may seem that, after such a long period of time, the creation of any comprehensive approach to the Rorschach would be impossible. It is an arduous task but far from impossible. In fact, it is made considerably easier than might have been the case during the 1930s because there exists today a wealth of information concerning the test. Each of the systematizers has provided a thoroughly designed approach which can be evaluated. Adding to these systems is an enormous accumulation of research data plus the collective experience of psychologists using the test for more than 50 years. These data can be used to attack the questions which plague the student of the Rorschach systems. Which system is best, or which parts of each system are most appropriate to the technique? All of the systems are impressive, and each carries strong arguments for endorsement. Yet none are truly all inclusive, and none have accomplished the task of maximizing the full potential which the test presents.

What follows then is an attempt to incorporate the best of each into a comprehensive Rorschach system. A system is needed that would also include other developments in the test which are exclusive of any of the five systems. A system is needed that would strengthen the use of the test and make it better prepared to stand the tests of reliability and validation, and hopefully provide the greatest amount of descriptive information from which understanding can be gleaned.

The methodological format from which the comprehensive Rorschach system has been developed draws heavily from five sources. The first is a comparative analysis of the five major Rorschach systems. The results of that effort, which identifies the areas of agreement and disagreement across the systems, has been published in *The Rorschach Systems* (Exner, 1969). Second, in conjunction with the comparative analysis of the systems, many interviews and conversations occurred with the systematizers, providing rich information about their positions and attitudes toward different features of their respective systems. Third, there are the results of three surveys conducted especially for this purpose. One has been previously cited (Exner and Exner, 1972). It consists of a 30 item questionnaire concerning test practices with special focus on how each of the major systems are used. The second consists of a more elaborate 90 item questionnaire which was mailed to 200 Diplomates of the American Board of Examiners in Professional Psychology (ABPP). The mailings were randomly selected from a 1969 listing of Diplomates. The return yielded 131 completed questionnaires of which 20 were discarded because the respondents indicated that they use the Rorschach fewer than 20 times per year. The 111 remaining questionnaires represent practices and opinions of clinicians who use the Rorschach at least 20 times per year and who average 12 years of postdoctoral experience. The third survey consists of a 55 item questionnaire concerning Rorschach research methods and problems. It was mailed to 100 psychologists who have published on the Rorschach after 1960. The return yielded 71 usable replies. The fourth source from which the comprehensive system has been developed in a pool of 835 Rorschach protocols, contributed by more than 150 psychologists and graduate students in psychology. This does *not* provide a discrete normative base for the comprehensive system, for normative data are also available from other sources. Instead, these records, which include more than 200 from nonpsychiatric subjects, provide information useful in the study and cross-referencing of various normative baselines. They also provide a source for the study of specific issues where previously reported data are based on small numbers, or are incomplete. Finally, the data bank of published Rorschach research contributes in no insignificant way to the development of the comprehensive system. These data frequently provide clues, or direct answers, about methods or features of the test which have been controversial or ambiguous.

The structure of the comprehensive system closely parallels that of the traditional systems. It focuses on procedures, scoring, interpretation, and research problems and methodologies. It can be learned by the novice or adopted by the experienced Rorschacher as easily as most systems might be learned, and possibly easier than some. It borrows liberally from the other systems so that much of its content will not be new to the experienced clinician. Most important, it is designed to provide the Rorschach community with a common language and a common methodology. The realization of that goal will be no small tribute to the many who have devoted major portions of their professional lifetimes to the study of the inkblots.

REFERENCES

Allen, R. M., Manne, S. H., and Stiff, M. The role of color in Rorschach's test. *Journal of Projective Techniques*, 1951, **15**, 235–242.

Ames, L., Learned, J., Metraux, R., and Walker R. *Child Rorschach Responses.* New York: Paul B. Hoeber, 1952.

Ames, L., Metraux, R., and Walker, R. *Adolescent Rorschach Responses.* New York: Paul B. Hoeber, 1959.

Baughman, E. E. A comparative analysis of Rorschach forms with altered stimulus characteristics. *Journal of Projective Techniques*, 1954, **18**, 151–164.

Baughman, E. E. The role of the stimulus in Rorschach responses. *Psychological Bulletin*, 1958, **55**, 121–147.

Buaghman, E. E. The problem of the stimulus in Rorschach's test. *Journal of Projective Techniques and Personality Assessment*, 1967, **31**, 23–25.

Beck, S. J. Autism in Rorschach scoring: a feeling comment. *Character and Personality*, 1936, **5**, 83–85.

Beck, S. J. Introduction to the Rorschach method: A manual of personality study. *American Orthopsychiatric Association Monograph*, 1937, No. 1.

Beck, S. J. Some recent research problems. *Rorschach Research Exchange*, 1937, **2**, 15–22.

Beck, S. J. *Rorschach's Test. I: Basic Processes.* (2nd ed.) New York: Grune and Stratton, 1950.

Beck, S. J. *Rorschach's Test. III: Advances in Interpretation.* New York: Grune and Stratton, 1952.

Beck, S. J. *The Rorschach Experiment: Ventures in Blind Diagnosis.* New York: Grune and Stratton, 1960.

Biederman, L., and Cerbus, G. Changes in Rorschach teaching. *Journal of Personality Assessment*, 1971, **35**, 524–526.

Cerbus, G., and Nichols, R. Personality variables and response to color. *Psychological Bulletin*, 1963, **60**, 566–575.

Cronbach, L. J. Statistical methods applied to Rorschach scores: a review. *Psychological Bulletin*, 1949, **46**, 393–429.

Dubrovner, R. J., VonLackum, W. J., and Jost H. A study of the effect of color on productivity and reaction time in the Rorschach test. *Journal of Clinical Psychology*, 1950, **6**, 331–336.

Exner, J. E. The effects of color on productivity in cards VIII, IX, X of the Rorschach. *Journal of Projective Techniques*, 1962, **26**, 30–33.

Exner, J. E. *The Rorschach Systems.* New York: Grune and Stratton, 1969.

Exner, J. E., and Exner, D. E. How clinicians use the Rorschach. *Journal of Personality Assessment*, 1972, **36**, 403–408.

Feldman, M. J., and Graley J. The effects of an experimental set to simulate abnormality on group Rorschach performance. *Journal of Projective Techniques*, 1954, **18**, 326–334.

Gibby, R. G. The stability of certain Rorschach variables under conditions of experimentally induced sets: I. The intellectual variables, *Journal of Projective Techniques*, 1951, **15**, 3–26.

Goldfried, M. R., Stricker, G., and Weiner, I. B. *Rorschach Handbook of Clinical and Research Applications.* Englewood Cliffs, N. J.: Prentice-Hall, 1971.

Gough, H. G. Clinical versus statistical prediction in psychology. In Postman, L. (Ed.), *Psychology in the Making.* New York: Knopf, 1963.

Halpern, F. *A Clinical Approach to Children's Rorschachs.* New York: Grune and Stratton, 1953.

Harris, J. G. Validity: The search for a constant in a universe of variables. In Rickers-Ovsiankina, M. (Ed.), *Rorschach Psychology.* New York: Wiley, 1960.

Hertz, M. R. *Frequency Tables for Scoring Rorschach Responses.* (3rd ed.) Cleveland: Western Reserve University Press, 1951.

Holt, R. R. Clinical and statistical prediction: A reformulation and some new data. *Journal of Abnormal and Social Psychology*, 1958, **56**, 1–12.

Holt, R. R. Yet another look at clinical and statistical prediction: Or, is clinical psychology worthwhile. *American Psychologist*, 1970, **25**, 337–349.

Holzberg, J. D. Reliability re-examined. In Rickers-Ovsiankina, M., (Ed.), *Rorschach Psychology.* New York: Wiley, 1960.

Jackson, C. W., and Wohl, J. A survey of Rorschach teaching in the university. *Journal of Projective Techniques and Personality Assessment*, 1966, **30**, 115–134.

Kimble, G. A. Social influence on Rorschach records. *Journal of Abnormal and Social Psychology*, 1945, **40**, 89–93.

Klopfer, B., and Sender, S. A system of refined scoring symbols. *Rorschach Research Exchange*, 1936, **2**, 19–22.

Klopfer, B. The present status of the theoretical development of the Rorschach method. *Rorschach Research Exchange*, 1937, **1**, 142–147.

Klopfer, B., Ainsworth, M. D., Klopfer, W. G., and Holt R. R. *Developments in the Rorschach Technique. I: Theory and Development.* Yonkers-on-Hudson, N. Y.: World Book Company, 1954.

Klopfer, B. et al. *Developments in the Rorschach Technique. II: Fields of Application.* Yonkers-on-Hudson, N. Y.: World Book Company, 1956.

Korman, A. K. The prediction of managerial performance: A review. *Personnel Psychology*, 1968, **21**, 295–322.

Little, K. B., and Shneidman, E. S. Congruencies among interpretations of psychological test and anamnestic data. *Psychological Monographs*, 1959, **73** (whole No. 476).

Louttit, C. M., and Browne, C. G. Psychometric instruments in psychological clinics. *Journal of Consulting Psychology*, 1947, **11**, 49–54.

Lubin, B., Wallis, R. R., and Paine, C. Patterns of psychological test usage in the United States: 1935–1969. *Professional Psychology*, 1971, **2**, 70–74.

Luchins, A. S. Situational and attitudinal influences on Rorschach responses. *American Journal of Psychology*, 1947, **103**, 780–784.

Macfarlane, J. W., and Tuddenham, R. D. Problems in the validation of projective techniques. In Anderson, H., and Anderson, G. (Eds.), *An Introduction to Projective Techniques*. New York: Prentice-Hall, 1951.

Meehl, P. E. *Clinical versus Statistical Prediction*. Minneapolis: University of Minnesota Press, 1954.

Perlman, J. Color and the validity of the Rorschach 8-9-10%. *Journal of Consulting Psychology*, 1951, **15**, 122–126.

Phillips, L., and Smith, J. G. *Rorschach Interpretation: Advanced Technique*. New York: Grune and Stratton, 1953.

Piotrowski, Z. The Rorschach method of personality analysis in organic psychoses. *Psychological Bulletin*, 1936, **33**, 795.

Piotrowski, Z. On the Rorschach method and its application in organic disturbances of the central nervous system. *Rorschach Research Exchange*, 1936, **1**, 23–40.

Piotrowski, Z. The *M*, *FM*, and *m* responses as indicators of changes in personality. *Rorschach Research Exchange*, 1937, **1**, 148–156.

Piotrowski, Z. *Perceptanalysis*. New York: MacMillan, 1957.

Rapaport, D., Gill, M., and Schafer, R. *Diagnostic Psychological Testing*. Vols. 1 and 2. Chicago: Yearbook Publishers, 1946.

Rickers-Ovsiankina, M. (Ed.). *Rorschach Psychology*. New York: Wiley, 1960.

Rorschach, H. *Psychodiagnostics*. Bern: Bircher, 1921. (Transl. Hans Huber Verlag, 1942.)

Russell, E. W. Rorschach stimulus modification. *Journal of Projective Techniques*, 1967, **31**, 20–22.

Sapenfield, B. R., and Buker, S. D. Validity of the Rorschach 8-9-10%. *Journal of Consulting Psychology*, 1949, **13**, 268–271.

Sawyer, J. Measurement and prediction, clinical and statistical. *Psychological Bulletin*, 1966, **66**, 178–200.

Schafer, R. *Psychoanalytic Interpretation in Rorschach Testing*. New York: Grune and Stratton, 1954.

Sundberg, N. D. The practice of psychological testing in clinical services in the United States. *American Psychologist*, 1961, **16**, 79–83.

Shemberg, K., and Keely, S. Psychodiagnostic training in the academic setting: Past and present. *Journal of Consulting Psychology*, 1970, **34**, 205–211.

Swift, J. W. Reliability of Rorschach scoring categories with preschool children. *Child Development*, 1944, **15**, 207–216.

Weiner, I. B. *Psychodiagnosis in Schizophrenia*. New York: Wiley, 1966.

Weiner, I. B. Does psychodiagnosis have a future? *Journal of Personality Assessment*, 1972, **36**, 534–546.

Wyatt, F. How objective is objectivity? *Journal of Projective Techniques*, 1968, **31**, 3–19.

Zubin, J., Eron, L., and Schumer, F. *An Experimental Approach to Projective Techniques*. New York: Wiley, 1965.

CHAPTER 2

Decisions and Procedures

Before laying hand to the Rorschach cards, the assessor–diagnostician must make several important decisions. One of the most important of these decisions concerns the appropriateness of the Rorschach for the task at hand. Contrary to popular belief, the Rorschach *does not* provide data from which answers to all questions can be derived. The data which unfold from the Rorschach are essentially descriptive in substance. The data represent a report from the subject of what he has seen or imagined when confronted with 10 ambiguous figures. The report is a complex specimen of behavior which, when compared with other specimens and studied for its apparent idiosyncrasies, can be translated into a series of statements that describe the subject. The description may often be quite lengthy, converging on such features as response styles, affectivity, cognitive operations, motivations, preoccupations, and interpersonal-interenvironmental perceptions and response tendencies. Ordinarily, the description will include reference to both overt and covert behaviors, the characterization of either being mainly determined by the richness of the protocol. Some statements may be made with considerable sureness while others may be more speculative, but all represent the subject *as he is*, rather than as he was or will be. It is common for the description to include speculation concerning etiological factors and even to offer some predictions, but, generally, these kinds of statements are derived less directly from the data of the protocol and more likely from the process of inductive-deductive logic. Here, the accumulated knowledge regarding personality, response styles, and psychopathology are critically important. Some of these speculations are quite legitimate to the use of the Rorschach. For instance, piecing together the variety of assets and liabilities of the subject, *as manifest* in Rorschach data, can lead to logical recommendations about intervention alternatives. Similarly, an evaluation of the apparent strengths and relationships of certain response tendencies can generate logical speculation about the chronicity, or even the origins, of such tendencies. But speculation can be carried on *ad absurdum*. It would seem that, too frequently, clinicians have been enticed, by the intrigue of questions or by their own grandiosity, into issuing verdicts about people and their behaviors which have little relevance to data found in most Rorschach records. Descriptions of religious preference, hobbies, class standing, grade point average, supervisor ratings, job satisfaction, or frequency of intercourse are not items to which even the most experienced Rorschacher will address himself. They may all be intriguing questions, but most Rorschach data would be only very indirectly related to any of them. There are much better methods than the Rorschach to gain this kind of information. A good interview or social history should provide most of it. As these descriptions are inappropriate to the Rorschach, so too are certain classes of prediction such as success or attrition in some types of training, marital success, ultimate family size, length of hospitalization, and probability of parole violation or criminal recidivism. Most of these are intelligent questions, and the well equipped psychologist, given appropriate information and adequate criterion measures, might attack them with considerable success, but not from the Rorschach alone, and possibly not using the Rorschach at all.

There are other questions often asked of clinicians which may seem more compatible with the Rorschach method but are not necessarily so. These are questions concerning intellectual functioning and problems of organicity. Both have been considered in research with the Rorschach and results have generally been positive. Elements in the Rorschach correlate positively with other indices of intelligence, and some Rorschach features have been demonstrated to have a reasonably high probability of occurrence in some conditions of organic involvement. But there are many other tests and procedures which are specifically designed to evaluate these areas, and are generally much better suited to the purpose. Those instances where the Rorschach does correlate positively with these other instruments and procedures are interesting, but do not provide sufficient grounds on which to choose the Rorschach to assess these areas. Some of the data from the ABPP survey are of importance here. All 111 respondents indicate that they do not use the Rorschach where the prime purpose of assessment is the study of intelligence. All indicate a willingness to offer a broad estimate of intellectual functioning from Rorschach data, but where the specific issue of intelligence is concerned, the Rorschach is not the test of choice. Similarly, 89 of the 111 do not include the Rorschach in their methodology when the assessment issue is clearly one of organicity. Conversely, where the issue is one of organicity versus psychogenic involvement, all 111 do include the Rorschach in their methodology, but *not for* the purpose of deciding in favor of organic involvement. Rather, the Rorschach data are used to weigh the psychological aspects of the individual. This evaluation is, in turn, integrated with information from other testing more specifically designed to assess for organicity. At that point, the differential diagnostic conclusions are drawn. In this process, the traditional procedure of using a *test battery* is employed, the procedure that necessitates another important decision for the Rorschacher—namely, to what extent does the assessment question encourage the use of the Rorschach alone versus the use of multiple techniques.

In the historical framework of psychodiagnostics, the clinician typically has been inclined to use multiple procedures. The mainstay of the approach has been the interview and the test battery, the latter sometimes including as few as two or three tests but not uncommonly comprised of five or more. The rationale for the use of the test battery has been expounded considerably (Rapaport, Gill, and Schafer, 1946; Brown, 1948; Piotrowski, 1958; Harrower, 1965). The basic premises underlying the battery approach are essentially twofold. First, no test is capable of testing everything. Different tests focus on different dimensions or functions of the subject, thereby providing a broader data base from which to evaluate the *total* individual. Second, various tests do overlap to some extent, thus affording the possibilities of "cross validating" information derived from any single test. This procedure minimizes error and maximizes accuracy. It is a case of single versus multiple samples of related behavior wherein data from a single instrument might yield speculation, while similar data from several instruments provide for greater certainty. This issue has been challenged in several seemingly relevant studies (Sarbin, 1942, 1943; Kelly and Fiske, 1950; Gage, 1953; Kostlan, 1954; Giedt, 1955) which point to the fact that clinicians often do not use all of the data available to them, or, if they do, they are prone to weigh some segments inordinately. These critics also argue that a ceiling of predictive accuracy is usually reached quickly and adding more data provides only slight, if any, increase in the "predictive correlation." Also several studies demonstrate that the multiple methods technique works well in the clinical situation (Vernon, 1950; MacKinnon, 1951; Stern, Stein, and Bloom, 1956; Luborsky and Holt, 1957). In each, validity is increased as data are increased. The multiple methods technique has also been admirably championed by Holt (1958, 1970). He has demonstrated quite clearly how the additive process occurs, and how, for certain predictive tasks, it become essential.

Support for the test battery approach does not mean that it should be employed always; nor does it mean that the same test battery should be used when a battery is called for. The assessment decision must include which tests to use. This decision usually evolves from consideration of the question or questions which the assessor seeks to answer. But the decision does not always end there. Not uncommonly, the subject reacts to given test materials in an unpredicted manner, providing new questions or forcing the assessor to alter his "planned" battery. For example, the subject whose WAIS performance is extremely bizarre and psychotic-like probably need not be given a Rorschach if the basic question to be answered concerns the existence of psychosis. Similarly, the subject rendering 45 very rich Rorschach responses might not need to be administered the TAT unless there are clearly unanswered questions after the Rorschach data are examined. Unfortunately, there are far too many instances where a clinician perseverates in the use of a "standard" test battery no matter what the appointed task and no matter what data have become available as the testing progresses. Whether this procedure is due to faulty training, or because the assessor requires a "security blanket" as provided by great chunks of data, is not clear. It is clear that, in these instances, the amount of time con- sumed in test administration is disproportionate to the task, a fact made even worse when the clinician does not use all of the data obtained from this lengthy proce- dure. Hospital and clinic files have become filled with psychological test reports which range in length from one to three pages, much of which replay information given in the interview and provide for very little description from test data even though 5 to 10 hours of testing occurred. No clinician should insult the dignity of his subject with such a piece of work. If a test battery is used, then all of the data obtained should be interpreted.

Still another decision must be made should the assessor decide on the test battery; that is, the element of "placement" of a test in the framework of a battery. There is work suggesting that the administration of one test affects the responses given to tests administered subsequently. For instance, Van de Castle, (1964) discovered that test order could alter the incidence of human content responses in the Rorschach. Grisso and Meadow (1967) found that differences in WAIS performance occur when the test is given after the Rorschach versus being administered prior to the Rorschach. While the consequences of these findings are not devastating, they do indicate the need for caution in selecting the serial order in which a test battery will be administered. The tradition of clinicians using the Rorschach has been to place it last, or next to last, in the battery. This seems logical in that the Rorschach is probably the most ambiguous, and therefore possibly the most threatening, of the instruments commonly used. The Grisso and Meadow results clearly suggest that the Rorschach should not precede the WAIS. In the ABPP survey, 94 of the 111 respondents indicate that they prefer to give the Rorschach last in the test battery, although all indicate that they modify this procedure in specific situations.

It also seems important to emphasize that when a test battery is selected, it need not involve a lengthy process. Careful selection of the tests to be used can frequently reduce the time involvement to less than 3 hours. For example, Weiner (1966) has presented an exceptionally fine summary of those indicators important to the differential diagnosis of schizophrenia. His work centers mainly on the use of three instruments, the WAIS, Draw-A-Person, and Rorschach. In such a battery, which should ordinarily require less than 3 hours to administer, the primary diagnostic decisions are made from Rorschach data. The WAIS and DAP are used to add information concerning intellectual operations and self-concept. Both also provide information for "cross-checking" Rorschach findings.

None of the foregoing should be misinterpreted to mean that whenever the Rorschach is used, it should always be part of a test battery. The Rorschach can stand quite well alone and provide much data concerning the subject. These are data which generate description of the subject going well beyond that ordinarily afforded from other tests. Quite commonly, the major portion of the "personality description" included in a psychological report is based on Rorschach results. One need only to review the many teaching cases which have been published to gauge the wealth of information which may be obtained from the test data. Extensive descriptions have been provided by Beck (1937, 1945, 1952, 1960, 1967), Klopfer (1954, 1956 1962), Hertz (1969), Piotrowski (1957, 1969), and Schafer (1954). Early Rorschach literature is filled with similar material, especially the *Rorschach Research Exchange* and the first several volumes of the *Journal of Projective Techniques*. The Beck 1960 presentation is particularly relevant in that he demonstrates how the test data may be used, not only when it is the only test administered, but when the interpreter works "in the blind." In this context, the assessor should not be averse to considering the use of the Rorschach alone. The final decision should be made on the basis of the question to be answered. Some questions are probably unanswerable, whether the Rorschach, interview, observations, or other tests are used. These questions should be rejected by the assessor. Other questions, such as evaluating intelligence, or the extent of organic damage, are answerable but the use of the Rorschach can be perceived only as "supplementary," and even questionable. Likewise, where predictions are involved, the Rorschach may or may not be of value, and the assessor may be hardpressed in his decisions concerning method selection. If however, the question concerns a description of the subject, the Rorschach is probably the best of the instruments available, assuming that it is used intelligently. This decision, sometimes not rendered easily, must be weighed with care, taking advantage of all information available concerning the subject, and evaluating the issues to which answers are sought. It is in the pressure of this surrounding that the assessor/diagnostician manifests his true worth.

PROCEDURES OF ADMINISTRATION

Once the decision to use the Rorschach in the assessment process has been made, it is vitally important that the test be used appropriately. Factors such as seating, instructions, recording of responses, timing, and Inquiry all become manifest. These items may seem somewhat incidental to the task at hand, but they are not. The procedures employed with the inkblots can often dictate whether a protocol is a truly representative sample of the subject's behavior and response style. Alteration in procedure can influence such elements as number of responses, content of responses, use of the stimulus, and characteristics of the response as reported. The composite of these factors can minimize the ultimate data available to the interpreter, and, in the instance of the more naive user of the test, create some alterations in the final description rendered.

SEATING

The issue of seating has been neglected generally by those who have researched the test. The Rorschach systematizers have varied considerably in their recommendations. Both Rorschach and Beck have advised the examiner to sit behind the subject. Klopfer and Hertz suggest that the examiner sit to the side of the subject. Rapaport-Schafer favor a face-to-face arrangement, and Piotrowski stresses using the most "natural" position (Exner, 1969). In light of this disagreement, the Rorschach novice might believe that the Rorschach seating arrangement has considerable flexibility. And to some extent this is true. However, some conditions and principles should be weighed. First, there is a clear rationale for each of the methods prescribed by the systematizers. Rorschach, Beck, Klopfer, and Hertz all express concern that the examiner avoid undue influence on the responsiveness of the subject and, more important, that the examiner be in a position to see those features of the blot referred to by the subject. Klopfer and Hertz disagree with the Rorschach-Beck positioning in that it is unique to the typical testing position, expressing the hypothesis that the side-by-side position is more compatible with natural testing procedures. Piotrowski emphasized this even more. He indicates that the side-by-side position is preferable but should not be used if it necessitates a change in the regimen that has been used in prior testing. Rapaport deviates most sharply from the rest. He assumes that the natural testing-interviewing procedure is face-to-face. In this respect, Rapaport should not be faulted, for the typical testing posture of the 1940s was to sit the subject at a desk opposite the examiner. But both Rapaport and Beck are probably too rigid with regard to testing practice. It may be that some settings require the examiner to use a desk whereby the subject is on the opposite side. But even this can be modified by the creative examiner. There is no psychological test that absolutely requires a desk or a face-to-face procedure. Even where materials must be laid before the subject, as in some of the intelligence test subtests, the examiner could as easily sit side-by-side. This seating arrangement has potential advantages which are far more reaching than simply providing the examiner a better view of the blots as the subject describes them. It is an arrangement which controls some of the impact that the examiner may have on the subject's responsiveness.

The problem of examiner influence has been studied extensively, but by no means conclusively. As early as 1941, Coffin demonstrated that the ambiguity and novelty of the Rorschach situation, factors intended to evoke projection, seem to heighten the subjects susceptibility to influence or suggestion. Schachtel was among the first to provide a major conceptual position regarding this element (1945). He stressed the problem of the subject in reacting to the total test situation, which includes apparent freedom yet simultaneous control, compounded by the relationship between examiner and subject. Schachtel argued that the subject creates a "subjective definition" of the situation. Schafer (1954) has extended these ideas, emphasizing the interaction between the individual and the situational dynamics. He suggests that factors such as the level of communication required, the violation of privacy, the lack of situational control, and the danger of premature self-awareness arouse anxiety and defensiveness from which specific reactions to the examiner evolve. Neither Schachtel nor Schafer believe that the Rorschach performance can be *completely* altered by the examiner–subject relationship, but both warn that many of the test variables can be affected. Research on the examiner influence has covered a wide range of independent variables, including the impact of the waiting room, instructions, method of administration, Inquiry, and the examiner *per se*. In this latter category, four studies are of particular importance to a decision concerning seating arrangements.

The first is generally considered a classic work in the area of examiner influence and experimentally induced variations in test performance. It was reported by Lord in 1950. She used three female examiners to test 36 male subjects. Her design called for each subject to be tested three times, once by each of the examiners. The instructions for each administration of the test were essentially identical, all apparently following the Klopfer method, but the "affective" climate varied for each administration. In one administration, the subject was made to feel accepted and successful. In a second administration, the subject was made to feel rejected and a failure. In the third model, the more "typical" procedure was followed wherein the subject was not deliberately given cues to make him feel either accepted or rejected. The time between tests ranged from 4 to 6 weeks. The order for the "rapport" model was counterbalanced so that 12 subjects were examined in the neutral model first, 12 in the positive model first, and 12 in the negative model first. The second and third testings were varied similarly. The examiners were also counterbalanced for rapport models so that each administered 12 tests under neutral conditions, 12 under positive conditions, and 12 under negative conditions. Lord's results, even though clouded by the complex retest design, are impressive. As expected, many significant differences were created by the different rapport models; however, the largest and most frequent differences occurred across the examiners, regardless of the rapport models that they used. Subsequent studies offer substantial confirmation of differences in examiner influence, and provide some hints as to how this occurs. Baughman (1951) studied the protocols obtained by 15 examiners from 633 subjects. He found that the records obtained by some examiners are highly comparable, but records obtained by others continually deviate markedly. He suggests that these differences may be due to procedure, or more likely, to the relationship effected by the examiner. Gibby, Miller, and Walker (1953) also found substantial differences between examiners for the length of protocols, and for certain classes of determinants, especially pure Form, color and shading. Masling (1965) speculated that unintentional reinforcement by examiners could be a major factor underlying the observation that subjects produce different responses for different examiners. He created an especially clever design to test this hypothesis. He used 14 graduate students, naive to the Rorschach, who volunteered for "special" training in the test, which allegedly would be quick and efficient. Divided into two groups of seven each, all received identical instruction except that one group was given the set that experienced examiners always elicit more human than animal responses. The second group was given the opposite set. Each student tested two subjects. The sessions were recorded with the expectancy of finding evidence for verbal conditioning by the student examiners. The two groups of examiners did differ in the predicted direction for the ratio of human to animal responses, but *no evidence* was found for verbal conditioning. Masling logically concludes that the examiners influenced subjects with postural, gestural, and facial cues.

It would be folly to assume that side-by-side seating eliminates all examiner influence, but it should be used in the comprehensive system as it would reduce considerably the prospect of the subject being "bombarded" by nonverbal cues from the examiner, especially during the Free Association portion of the test, as contrasted with the face-to-face approach. A basic caution is possibly in order here. While side-by-side is a preferable method, it seems inappropriate for the examiner to suddenly alter seating arrangements during an examination. In other words, it is probably best to administer the Rorschach in the confines of whatever seating arrangement the examiner chooses initially. Hopefully, this will be a side-by-side order. Interestingly, 82 of the 111 respondents in the ABPP survey use the side-by-side seating for all interviewing and testing which they do. Conversely, only 107 of the respondents in the Exner and Exner (1972) survey avoid the face-to-face arrangement, while 288 endorse it. It would seem that the accumulated information concerning behavior modifying techniques has made considerably less of an impact on assessment procedures than should logically have been the case. If nonverbal cues from the examiner influence the subject to specific kinds of Rorschach responses, the same influence is highly probable on most other kinds of techniques employed in the clinical setting. The assessor who does not weigh the potential impact of his behaviors in the assessment situation only makes his own task more difficult and may even provide a disservice to his subject.

INSTRUCTIONS

Assuming that the seating arrangement of examiner and subject has been properly considered, and that the general physical setting is reasonably conducive to the assessment process, the administration of the Rorschach can proceed. The main order of business at this point is to introduce the test and provide the subject with instructions appropriate to his task. The cards, of course, should not be within reach of the subject. If the test is being used as part of a test battery, there is little need for a specific explanation other than the basic instructions. In that situation, the subject has already discussed his presence in the test situation with the assessor, and already has test experience. When the Rorschach is used alone, it is reasonable for the examiner to offer some information concerning the technique, but should avoid creating a unique set. Most subjects are probably "test-wise," for testing has become an integral part of the culture, and have been tested for many different purposes such as job placement and academic achievement. Likewise, most subjects will have some familiarity with the inkblot method, whether through news media, educational experience, games, or relationships with others who have been administered the Rorschach. A simple statement, such as that suggested by Schafer (1954), to the effect that the test is designed to study personality, should suffice. Ninety of the 111 respondents in the ABPP survey do not say anything specific about the Rorschach when it is used in a test battery. Surprisingly, the remaining 21 who do make specific mention of the fact that it is a test of personality, also include in their introduction a comment to the effect that there are no "right or wrong" answers. Such a comment is technically true and is consistent with the procedure recommended by Hertz. The issue of whether such a statement is influential has not been tested, and, no doubt, most of the Rorschach systematizers would endorse it in response to a question from the subject. But it may be misleading to the particularly naive subject and probably is best avoided whenever possible.

The basic instructions to the subject provide another issue which has not been resolved previously. There are notable differences across the Rorschach systems concerning how the task should be formulated for the subject. Rorschach merely specified handing the subject the first card and asking, "What might this be?" Possibly, had he said no more on the subject, the systematizers would have been more prone to agree, but he added that in some instances the subject might be told how the blots are made if this appeared to enhance cooperativeness or alleviate anxiety. In attempting to develop a system compatible with Rorschach, the systematizers have seen fit to interpret his flexibility in different ways. Only Klopfer persisted in using the original Rorschach instructions. Beck has extended these to include mention that the subject may keep the card as long as he wants and that he should tell *everything* that he sees on the card. Piotrowski has maintained Rorschach's instructions but adds that it is permissible to turn the card. Hertz follows the Beck procedure but also introduces the test using a trial blot wherein the subject is provided encouragement and additional information concerning the test. Rapaport-Schafer also use Rorschach's basic instructions but, after the free association to the first card has been completed, use reinforcement and encouragement for the subject to "tell everything they might be." In the early days of the Rorschach there was some controversy over the differences in instructional procedure. Klopfer (1942) was particularly critical of instructions encouraging the subject to tell everything he perceived, suggesting that such instructions emphasize quantity thereby creating some distinct restrictions to the task.

Research concerning the effects of different types of instructions has generally focused on sets or procedures which are quite deviant from typical Rorschach practice. Some of the earliest work in this area was reported by Fosberg (1938, 1943). He was concerned with faking on the Rorschach and used a very complex retest design with psychologically "sophisticated" subjects. All were administered the Rorschach first under Beck instructions. In a second administration, the subjects were asked to make their "best" impression, and in a third administration to make their "worst" impression. Finally, the test was administered a fourth time using a testing-of-limits procedure. He found that subjects did change their protocols under the various retest sets, but not so much that the basic configuration "of the personality" was concealed. In a related work, Carp and Shavzin (1950), also using a retest design, asked subjects to make a good impression in the first administration, and a bad impression in the second administration. They found marked individual changes but no consistent group shifts. In another study using the retest design,

Hutt, Gibby, Milton, and Pottharst (1950) obtained a 100% gain in M where the second administration included instructions to see human movement.

Studies which have avoided the pitfalls of the retest design have also yielded data that encourage caution in the selection of instructions and the circumstances of their application. Coffin (1941) and Abramson (1951) both found some differences between groups for location and determinants when the test is introduced as one to which persons in "prestige" occupations respond in specific ways. Cox and Sarason (1954), however, found no differences under "standard" versus allegedly "ego involving" instructional sets. Williams (1954) failed to find differences when subjects were told to respond as quickly as possible. Henry and Rotter (1956) report that when the Rorschach is introduced as a test to detect serious emotional disturbance, significantly more Form, animal, and popular responses occur. Peterson (1957) used Klopfer instructions with one group, and instructions emphasizing that the test measures imaginative ability to a second group. She found no differences between the groups. Phares, Stewart, and Foster (1960) used instructions similar to Klopfer's with one group, while telling the second group that it is a test with specific right and wrong answers. They found no differences between the groups but did find differences between examiners.

While these results vary in demonstrating the susceptibility of the Rorschach to change under unusual procedural or instructional sets, none have squarely faced the problem created by intersystem differences in instructions. Goetcheus (1967) did, at least partially, approach this problem using 16 examiners to test 64 subjects. Each examiner tested four subjects, using Beck instructions for two, and Klopfer instructions for two. She counterbalanced the procedure so that eight examiners used the Beck method first, and eight the Klopfer method first. She found that the Beck instructions did produce significantly more responses. Her analysis of protocol configurations indicates that the Beck-instructed group produced significantly more small and unusual detail responses and tended to give more Whole responses while the Klopfer instructed group tended to give more pure Form responses. There were no significant differences between the groups for determinants, content, or the frequency of popular responses. While the Goetcheus data support Klopfer's contention that the instructions which include a directive to "tell everything" will produce a more lengthy record, they do not support his hypothesis that "restrictions" to the task will occur.

Because the Goetcheus study is the only one which makes a direct approach to understanding the potential impact of intersystem instructional differences, it seemed appropriate to analyze the 835 protocols collected as an aid to the development of the comprehensive system for possible differences. These protocols were submitted by 153 examiners in response to a mailing request to 600 members of the Division on Clinical Psychology of the American Psychological Association, and a specific request to instructors of Rorschach courses at eight universities. The 835 were selected from more than 1300 submitted.[1] Each was accompanied by a

[1] The protocols were solicited in a mailing to 600 psychologists throughout the United States and Canada who are members of Division 12 of the American Psychological Association and whose place of work was shown in the *Directory* of the American Psychological Association to be a hospital or clinic; and from instructors of Rorschach courses at eight universities. A total of 1342 protocols were submitted, but 507 were discarded because of illegibility, no completed data sheet, or no inquiry, or because the procedures used in taking the protocol were grossly different than those recommended by any of the five Rorschach systems.

data questionnaire concerning the demographic features of the subject, place, and purpose of the examination, and relevant personal information concerning the subject and the procedures of examination. Classification of the records reveals that 204 are from nonpsychiatric subjects where the purpose of the examination was employment or academic counseling, industrial consultation, or, in many instances, the development of a nonpsychiatric control group for research purposes. The remaining 631 protocols were obtained from a variety of psychiatric populations, both in-patient and out-patient. A breakdown of the total pool concerning system procedures employed (including instructions) reveals: Klopfer, 329; Beck, 310; Rapaport, 78; Piotrowski, 66; and Hertz, 52. All protocols were reviewed for accuracy of scoring appropriate to the system used, and all were rescored using the comprehensive system.

The evaluation of intersystem differences in instruction was accomplished by using all of the protocols collected which had been administered via the Rapaport, Piotrowski, and Hertz methods, plus a randomly selected group of 150 protocols, 75 each from the Beck and Klopfer pools. The resulting 346 protocols were then analyzed, using an analysis of variance, for total number of responses, Whole, Large Detail, Unusual Detail responses, pure Form responses,[2] and the number of multiple-determined responses. The result of that analysis are shown in Table 1.

Table 1. Comparison of 346 Rorschach Protocols Collected by Five Different Methods for Total R, W, D, Dd, F, and Multiple Determined Responses

Item	Beck $(N/X = 75)$	Hertz $(N/X = 52)$	Klopfer $(N/X = 75)$	Piotrowski $(N/X = 66)$	Rapaport $(N/X = 78)$
Total R	31.2	32.9	23.9[a]	33.8	36.4[b]
W responses	6.2	5.7	7.1[b]	5.9	7.9
D responses	21.3	23.3	15.1	25.8	24.8
Dd responses	3.7	3.9	1.3[b]	2.1	3.9
F responses	18.1	16.8	11.6	18.4	16.7
Multiple determinants	5.3	6.7	5.4	7.1	9.8[a]

[a] Statistically significant difference from all other groups at .05.
[b] Statistically significant difference from 3 other groups at .05.

It will be noted from examination of the data in Table 1 that the Klopfer records yield the lowest mean number of responses and that the Rapaport protocols give the highest number. The analyses for location, pure Form, and multiple determined responses were all done using proportions, as related to the total number of responses. Here, the Klopfer records provide the greatest proportion of Whole responses, but not significantly greater than in the Rapaport protocols. Similarly, the Klopfer records give the smallest mean number of unusual detail responses, but not significantly fewer than the Piotrowski records. The Rapaport records clearly give the significantly highest mean number of multiple determined responses.

[2] Beck and Rapaport protocols were translated so that FM and m responses were not counted as pure Form.

It is very important to emphasize here that any conclusions drawn from these kinds of data, especially with regard to differences in instructions *per se*, must be tempered considerably, as variations in seating undoubtedly occurred within groups, and most particularly because of the possibility of examiner influence. It might even be more appropriate to discuss the differences in terms of examiner differences, as they relate to preferences for one system versus the others, rather than differences created by specific features of a system. In any event, these data, plus that from the previously mentioned studies, have all contributed to logical consideration regarding which, if any, of the Rorschach instructions are most appropriate for the comprehensive system. The final decision then has been to select the Klopfer methodology, which, in effect, is the same methodology and instruction originally used by Rorschach. The rationale for this selection is reasonably simple. First, it will generally produce the shorter record at no apparent expense to the configuration. Second, and more important, the instructions are brief, and neatly set forth the task. They maintain ambiguity and yet are quite specific. Third, they avoid the possible complications which go hand-in-hand with asking the subject to "tell everything" he sees, or using a trial blot for practice, or suggesting that the cards may be turned. Any or all of these messages can be interpreted differently, a phenomenon which can breach the necessary goal of using a "reasonably standardized" set.

The basic *instructions recommended for use in the comprehensive system are*, on handing the subject the first card, asking, *"What might this be?"* This is a rather simple instructional procedure which hopefully maximizes the ambiguity of the task.

Some words of caution are in order. It would obviously be inappropriate for the examiner to lead a subject into a testing room, be seated next to him, and hand him the first Rorschach card together with the instructional question, "What might this be?" Some pretest preparation is definitely necessary. Where a test battery is being used, this will have already been accomplished, but where the Rorschach is the only tool being used, some examiner–subject dialogue is essential. But equally essential is that the examiner avoid any discussion or description of the Rorschach which will provoke an unusual or distorted set concerning the task. The specific content of any pretest dialogue will depend largely on the age, experience, and sophistication of the subject. The word "inkblot" can be used freely, and is probably much more preferable than "ambiguous figures." In a few instances, the actual construction of inkblots might be discussed, and in other instances it may seem important to mention that people see all sorts of things in the blots. This kind of commentary should be minimized or avoided whenever possible, and most specifically, it *should not* include reference to card turning, right and wrong answers, timing, or any statement that might emphasize quantity of responses. The ultimate characteristics of the instructional phase of administering the Rorschach must be left to the judgements of the examiner. No two subjects or testing situations will be identical; however, it behooves the examiner to uphold controls that are as stringent as possible within the realities of the situation.

These procedures, at least hypothetically, should reduce substantially the potential influence of the examiner and his words. Side-by-side seating removes the examiner from the subject's direct line of vision, thereby making the impact of nonverbal cues less likely. Brief and ambiguous instructions that are also specific to the task eliminate more possibilities for examiner influence or unique set by the subject. Adequate preparation of the subject also permits the task to proceed with-out unusual sets or conditions. It is in this circumstance that the Free Association Period begins.

FREE ASSOCIATION PERIOD

As the test begins with the handing of the first card to the subject, the examiners responsibilities become even more complex than in the pretest phase. He must time and record responses quickly and efficiently, field questions on occasion, and in some instances provide a very nondirective form of encouragement. It is not an easy or simple function, yet it must be carried forth smoothly without injecting bias, set, direction, or some other form of influence into the situation. Silence, by the examiner, is of paramount importance and should be interrupted only when absolutely essential. Any verbalizations from the examiner should be deliberate and formulated with care. It is the perfunctory utterance that carries the potential to impinge on the ambiguity of the situation. Wickes (1956), Gross (1959), and Dinoff (1960) have all demonstrated the effectiveness of verbal conditioning and perfunctory nonverbal acts in altering the frequency of human, animal, and move-ment responses, Dinoff, for example, has shown that the simple reinforcement of "mmm-hmm" can operate as a significant influence without any awareness by the subject.

QUESTIONS AND ENCOURAGEMENT

It is not uncommon for subjects to ask a variety of questions concerning the pur-poses and procedures of the test. The response from the examiner generally should be nondirective, conveying the notion that people respond to the blots in different ways. The following are some examples of questions commonly asked, and re-sponses which would ordinarily be appropriate.

S: "Can I turn the cards?"
E: "Its up to you."
S: "Should I use the whole thing?"
E: "Whatever you like. Different people see different things."
S: "Do you want me to show you where I see these things?"
E: "That's not necessary." (It is probably best at this point not to make note of the inquiry.)
S: "Should I just use my imagination?"
E: "Yes, just tell me what you see." (It seems more appropriate to use the word see rather than "what it reminds you of" to questions of this sort, stressing perception versus association.)
S: "Should I see more than one thing?"
E: "Most people usually see more than one thing."

This last question raises another issue concerning methodology about which the various systematizers have differed. Namely, to what extent should the subject be encouraged after giving only one response to a card. Klopfer suggests that a comment such as "Some people see more than one thing in the cards," should be used if only one response is given to the *first* card, but not to subsequent cards. Beck, whose instructions include a request to tell everything seen, employs similar encouragement ("But most people see more than one thing. Look at it a bit longer.") not only to the first card, but through the *first five* cards. Piotrowski is apparently willing to accept one "scoreable" response per card but is quite liberal with general encouragement, especially at the onset of the test. Hertz does not encourage *per se* during the Free Association but uses extensive instructions, which include a request for everything seen, plus the trial blot. She encourages extensively during the trial blot. Rapaport-Schafer request that the subject pursue the task further if only one response is given to the first card. Subsequently, they reinforce the subject before presenting the second card and at that time ask him to report everything seen. These differences in encouragement procedures probably contribute in some way to the differences in the length of records derived using the various systems. In the Exner and Exner survey, 166 of the 385 respondents encourage on Card I if only one response is given, but not thereafter. An additional 134 respondents use encouragement on both Cards I and II if only one response is given to either. Only 85 encourage beyond Card II, 42 of who encourage throughout the entire test. The results of the ABPP survey also show diversity, but not quite as extreme. Fifty-four of the 111 respondents encourage only on Card I when one response is given, while 49 encourage through Card V under those circumstances. The remaining eight encourage beyond Card I but not to Card V. Unfortunately, research efforts have not attacked this issue directly. Logically, the task should remain as ambiguous as possible, and in that context it seems less appropriate to continually remind the subject that quantity is of importance. It has already been mentioned that the shorter protocol, as apparently yielded by the Rorschach-Klopfer type instructions, is acceptable, particularly in that the overall configuration is essentially the same as found in the longer protocols. To this end, the Klopfer procedure of encouraging *only* on Card I, when the subject gives but one response, is most consistent with the format for the comprehensive system.

In a very small number of instances, the subject may reject completely one or more of the cards. If this happens, the examiner may have erred in his preparation of the subject, or even in selecting the Rorschach as the instrument of choice. When rejection occurs on the first or second cards, the examiner might do well to rethink his procedures and choices. If the rejection occurs late in the protocol, as for example with Card IX, which apparently has the highest rejection rate, it must be accepted but not before sufficient encouragement is provided. Comments such as, "Try and see something in it," or "There's no hurry, most everyone can find someting there," are not only permissible, but esential. It is also important for the subject to keep the card for an adequate amount of time before being permitted to reject it completely. Beck and Hertz both suggest a minimum of 2 minutes while Piotrowski indicates that as much as 5 minutes would not be extraordinary. The 2 minute minimum seems reasonable, with the final decision to go beyond that time a matter for the examiner's judgement.

PRESENTATION OF THE CARDS

The cards should, of course, be presented in consecutive order *and* with the top side up. The examiner will do well to inspect the deck of cards before the examination to make sure that none are accidentally inverted. They should *always* be kept out of reach of the subject. Each card should be *handed to the subject* rather than placed before him on a table or desk. If the subject asks how long he is expected to keep the card, the standard response is, "As long as you like." Extremely compulsive subjects have been known to respond endlessly which may warrant interruption by the examiner. Beck recommends permitting the subject to retain the card for as much as 10 minutes, while Piotrowski suggests 5 minutes as a reasonable maximum. The final decision in this matter must be left to the examiner, but it is probably reasonable to stop the subject after 10 or 12 responses to a card if that pattern of response persists card after card. A protocol of 200 responses probably offers little more information concerning the subject than a protocol of 30 to 50 responses.

Beck, Hertz, and Rapaport-Schafer all advise that the instructions include a directive for the subject to return the card to the examiner when he is "finished" with it. Klopfer and Piotrowski do not mention this to the subject. It seems advisable to keep instructions to a minimum, therefore the directive to return the card is not included in the procedure for the comprehensive system. It is, of course, a permissible response to a question from the subject.

TIMING

The timing of the test can be quite important in revealing some of the characteristics of the subject, such as his approach to each card, the length of time that he retained each card, and particularly, the cards that seemed to require unusually long times before a response was verbalized. Therefore, the examiner should record the time elapse between presentation of the card and the first response, plus the total time the subject retains the card. It is very important, however, that the timing be accomplished in a manner which does not disrupt the procedure, or create any implications for the subject that time is of essence. In the early days of psychological testing the stopwatch was a standard part of the "examiners kit" and efforts to record responses to different tasks with much precision, even to a fifth of a second, were made. While reasonably precise timing is important to tasks such as the testing of intelligence, it is less so with the Rorschach. In fact, it would probably be best not to time at all if the only available method involved starting and stopping a stopwatch. Fortunately, adequate Rorschach timing can be accomplished by other means. Most examiners will find it a relatively simple process by using the sweepsecond hand on a wristwatch, desk, or wall clock. Hopefully, timing will be accurate within 1 or 2 seconds, but that is less important than the set that the subject may interpret if he knows that he is timed. Timing is probably best accomplished by recording the minute and second shown on a watch or clock when each card is presented, such as 4'15'', a similar notation when the first response is given, and a final notation when the card is returned or the subject states that he is finished.

RECORDING RESPONSES

All responses should be recorded *verbatim*. This may seem like a difficult feat, especially to the Rorschach novice, but it is not as arduous as may seem. Most

Rorschachers use a relatively common scheme of abbreviations which combines the use of phonetics, the scoring abbreviations for response content, and some logically derived abbreviations not unlike many of those found in speed writing. Some of the most common abbreviations used are shown in Table 2.

Table 2.   **Abbreviations Commonly Used for Recording Rorschach Responses**

Phonetically Derived		Logically Derived		Derived from Scores	
Abbreviation	Meaning	Abbreviation	Meaning	Abbreviation	Meaning
b	be	a.t.	anything	h	human
c	see	bc	because	a	animal
g	gee	cb	could be	cl	cloud
o	oh	ll	looks like	ls	landscape
r	are	ss	some sort	hh	household
u	you	j	just	bl	blood
y	why	w	with	fi	fire
		st	something	cg	clothing
		wm	woman	fd	food
		-g	ing	na	nature

The object of recording the responses verbatim is essentially twofold. First, the examiner will be able to read them later, and second others can also read the record and know *exactly* what the subject said. The latter cannot be overestimated in importance. In many instances, especially those for evaluating progress in therapy, a second administration of the test will occur. If the responses to the first administration are illegible, or not recorded verbatim, the comparison of the two records becomes at best difficult, and more commonly impossible.

It is also important for the examiner to record the position of the card when the response is given. The symbols used for recording card direction are fairly standard throughout the Rorschach world. They were developed by Loosli-Usteri (1929), ∧, <, >, ∨, with the peak of each angle representing the direction of the top of the card. Most examiners use no symbol at all when the card is upright. A circle (○) may also be used to denote instances where the subject has rotated the card *without stopping*, but should not be confused with the more common behavior of deliberately turning the card to each side and examining it before giving a response, <, ∨, >.

The format for recording responses seems to vary considerably from examiner to examiner and system to system. One which seems easiest to work with is shown in Figure 1. It will be noted that the format shown in Figure 1 provides space for the card number, the reaction times, the card turning, the response in the Free Association period, the Inquiry, and a scoring of the response. Whatever format is selected, it is probably most important that space be provided near the Free Association response for the material obtained from the Inquiry.

Free association	Inquiry	Scoring

I 4″6″
4′11′ 1. Ths lla bat 2 me

<, V, >

| | *E:* You said this ll a bat 2 me. *S:* Yea, thts rite, it ll it hs wgs out here & som feelers or feet in frnt. *E:* I'm not quite clear @ wht prt of the blot u'r using. *S:* O, the W thg, c here r the wgs & her's the bdy. | |

2. U kno, this c.b a wm 2. It ll she's got her hands up

5′26″

| | *E:* You said this c.b. a wm 2. It ll she's got her hands up. *S:* Yea, rite in the middl, I don't c no head tho, mayb its tossed back. *E:* I'm not sure I c it as u do. *S:* Wel, its jst kina shaped lik that, sorta curvy & these r her hand up here. | |

II 5′30″
5′37″ 1. Wow, ths ll ss of a's fiting w. e.o

○

| | *E:* You said ths ll ss of a's fit-g w e.o. *S:* Yea, lik a coupl of bears stnd-g on their legs w their paws touch-g, c thes r their heads & their paws, theyv got bl on em 2. *E:* Bl? *S:* this red c.b. bl. | |

2. Ths cntr prt c.b. a space ship

6′30″

| | *E:* U said the cntr prt c.b. a spac ship *S:* Yea, ths white prt. *E:* Wh is ther that maks it ll a spac ship. *S:* Its shap, w wgs & the nose tht way. | |

Figure 1.   Format for recording Rorschach data.

INQUIRY

The issue of the Inquiry has been a knotty one among the Rorschach systematizers. Four of the five, Beck, Hertz, Klopfer, and Piotrowski, all agree that it should be conducted after the Free Association period has been completed. The Rapaport-Schafer system calls for the Inquiry to be conducted after each card, and with the card out of sight from the subject. Rapaport defends this procedure on the premise that delayed questions about the response will create a situation wherein memory is weighed too heavily. In some respects, Rapaport is quite correct, especially if the interpreter tends to regard the inquiry material heavily in his interpretations. Possibly however, Rapaport overemphasized the Inquiry. The basic purpose of the Inquiry is to provide whatever information necessary to score the response accurately. While the verbalizations of the subject, given during the Inquiry, may seem important, especially to the psychoanalytically oriented interpreter, *they do not represent* a continuous thought operation, even if done in the Rapaport method. Quite the contrary, they ordinarily will follow an interruption of thought, even if only one response per card is given, because between the response and the first question is the procedure of removing the card from the subject's line of vision and offering the first question. Rapaport was possibly being a bit self-deceptive here. If the Rapaport derived protocols used in the comprehensive system pool are a realistic guideline, this procedure yields longer protocols marked by an increase in multiple determined responses. In other words, the Rapaport procedure exaggerates the number of responses required, and precipitates a greater tendency, by the subject, to provide statements concerning elements of the blots which caused the response to be formulated. This process might easily be translated into a simple instrumental conditioning procedure in light of findings in contemporary psychology. Rapaport should not be faulted completely however for his concerns with the Inquiry procedure. It is quite true that the perceptions of the subject can be markedly different in the Inquiry than occurred during the Free Association. Levin (1953) has called attention to this fact, suggesting that the Rorschach is really two tests rather than one. His criticism of the testing procedure provoked commentary by both Walter Klopfer (1953) and Beck (1953) concerning the issue. Both conceded that "overuse" of the Inquiry data breeds considerable subjectivity, and Beck reemphasized Rorschach's original implication that all responses need not be inquired.

The extent to which Inquiry questions are formulated must be left to the decisions of the examiner, but the purpose of the inquiry should not be distorted. The object remains the collection of data necessary for the scoring of responses. Nevertheless, the Inquiry proceeds under difficult decisions. The more familiar the examiner is with scoring possibilities, the easier the procedure. Excessive questioning can yield complex scores to simple responses. For example, Gibby and Stotsky (1953) demonstrated that the number of pure Form responses will decrease, and color and shading increase as a function of the number of questions used. This fact caused Baughman (1958) to develop a "paired-comparison" method for Inquiry. He used a variety of Rorschach-like cards, with the stimulus modified. Subsequently, reporting on the results of this procedure (Baughman, 1959), he found that color responses did not alter significantly, but there were striking differences in the frequencies of shading responses. Zax and Stricker (1960) compared the standard Inquiry methods with one providing subjects descriptions of determinants beforehand. They paralleled a procedure used earlier by Klingensmith (1956), who reported that texture, vista, and general shading responses all increased with a more structured Inquiry. The Zax and Stricker data generally agree with that reported by Klingensmith, except that they found little difference in reports of vista responses. Their data did reveal that the various determinants tend to be elicited in different phases of the total test. Most movement responses are scorable simply from the information provided in the Free Association, while color and shading responses are generally only scorable after some form of Inquiry. Zax and Stricker unfortunately used a test–retest type design for their 75 subjects, a method previously described as questionable for Rorschach research. However, Reisman (1970) reported on a replication of their work using two groups of subjects, one group under relatively standard inquiry and the second group under the structured conditions. He found that the "direct" Inquiry had no significant effect for any of the basic Rorschach determinants, including shading.

In light of the various research findings concerning the Inquiry procedures, it seems most appropriate for the comprehensive Rorschach system to include the more "traditional" inquiry method, *provided* certain basic principles are followed. First, it must be noted that the inquiry will be valuable *only* to the extent that the examiner develops appropriate questions. There is no cookbook list of questions which should be asked for all responses. As Rorschach, Beck, and Klopfer have each pointed out, some responses occur in the free association for which no Inquiry is needed. This would be the case, however, only where clear information has also been developed in the free association concerning the location of the response. When the examiner is in doubt concerning location, an Inquiry, at least for that purpose should evolve. Second, the Inquiry questions *need not* test for the existence of every possible determinant. Most responses are not generated by multiple-determinants, and excessive questioning will serve only to distort the issue. Even in instances where it seems obvious that a determinant other than that specified by the subject has been favored, it should not be pursued excessively, for the value of the Rorschach is, at least in part, dependent as much on what the subject verbalizes as what he sees and is aware of. It has been demonstrated for example, by both Baughman (1954, 1959) and Exner (1959), that the achromatic features of Card I are quite essential for the response of "a bat" to be given. Nonetheless, most subjects do not report the influence of the achromatic color as a factor in their selection of that particular response. In fact, when a subject does report that the achromatic features of Card I were influencial in determining his responses of a bat, it is generally considered highly important. It is this very argument that makes the usefulness of the Baughman paired-comparison method of inquiry least appealing, not ·to mention its unwieldy nature. A third important Inquiry principle is that *brevity is the rule*. Questions should not be asked simply out of routine. Instead, each question asked should be carefully formulated and based on the hypothesis that the answer will contribute added vital information from which the scoring of the response can be developed. It is true that, in some instances, questions may be formulated for some purpose other than accurate scoring, such as determining the sex of human figures perceived or clarifying the use of a seemingly unique word. The fourth, and probably most important principle of the Inquiry, is that it *must* be kept nondirective. Questions such as "Did the color or shading help you see it that way?" are taboo, as are questions such as "Which side of the skin is up?" The restrictions necessitated by nondirective questions are often frustrating to the examiner, but they must be followed or the record will be made vulnerable.

Usually, no more than one or two questions will be required. The first should not even be a question, but rather a restatement of the subjects response. The onset of the Inquiry should be prefaced with a statement by the examiner regarding its purpose, such as, "I would like to go through the cards with you once again. This time, I'm concerned with making sure that I understand where it is on the blot that you have seen something, and I would like to try to see it as you did." This statement should suffice, for most subjects, as an introduction to the inquiry. Questions from the subject should be answered but, as with the earlier segments of the test, the answers should not induce sets.

As the Inquiry begins, the examiner should have a "location" sheet readily available so that he can make a permanent recording of the areas used by the subject. The beginning of each response inquiry should be started by repeating for the subject, verbatim, the response which he gave. If, after he responds to that stimulus, the location of the response is not clear, it should be requested, "Could you show me where you saw that?" If the determinants for the response are not clear from the Free Association and/or the first comments of the subject in the Inquiry, further questioning is permissible but should follow the four basic principles. A request such as, "Could you tell me what makes it look like that to you," is appropriate but more directive questions are not. *One of the best* Inquiry comments is, "I'm not sure I see it as you do." Some examples of Inquiry dialogue are shown in the Figure 1 format. It will be noted from those few examples that direct questions are avoided. Instead, the subjects task remains ambiguous.

DIRECT INQUIRY, ANALOGY, AND TESTING OF LIMITS

Rorschachers frequently find themselves a bit frustrated after some inquiries. Responses may have been given by the subject about which the examiner is virtually certain concerning scoring, yet the subject has not articulated the predicted determinants. For instance, the response of "a flower" to a card which contains color is likely determined in part by the fact of the color. Where the subject makes no mention of color, either in the Free Association or the Inquiry, *it cannot be scored.* Whether to satisfy curiosity, or gain added clinical input, it is reasonable that the examiner ultimately ask the subject directly, "Did the color on this card help you to see it as a flower?" Many subjects, when the question is posed in this direct fashion, will acknowledge that the color was a factor in the decision to give that particular response. This is, of course, clinically useful information, but it is *still not scored* because of the possibility of examiner influence. Even though the response is not scored for color, the fact that the subject did admit to its importance is useful information. Likewise, many other bits and pieces of "subjective" data can be gained if the examiner decides to review the cards a third time asking specific questions. To this end, it seems wise to include in the comprehensive system some endorsement of these procedures. Either the directive inquiry method of Zax and Stricker, the paired-comparison technique of Baughman, or the analogy or testing-of-limits procedures described by Klopfer may suffice, depending on the specific information desired. The Zax and Stricker method of directive inquiry is very similar to Klopfer's analogy period, wherein the subject may be asked directly whether color or shading helped to form the percept or whether movement may have been involved. The Baughman technique is a more subtle form of this approach. In testing-of-limits, the subject is advised that "people sometimes see . . ." and are asked if anything about the blot reminds them of that. Testing-of-limits seems most useful when the responses of the subject have been quite unique, containing few, if any, common or popular responses. The more directive forms of inquiry may be most useful to gauge the extent to which problems of defensiveness, or in some cases, articulation, may have led to an unusual record. The use of directive inquiry methods, or testing-of-limits will probably be the exception rather than the rule for most Rorschach protocols. The overwhelming number of subjects seem to provide considerable information in the Free Association and/or nondirective Inquiry from which adequate scoring and interpretation can evolve.

REFERENCES

Abramson, L. S. The influence of set for area on the Rorschach test results. *Journal of Consulting Psychology*, 1951, **15**, 337–342.

Baughman, E. E. Rorschach scores as a function of examiner differences. *Journal of Projective Techniques*, 1951, **15**, 243–249.

Baughman, E. E. A comparative analysis of Rorschach forms with altered stimulus characteristics. *Journal of Projective Techniques*, 1954, **18**, 151–164.

Baughman, E. E. A new method of Rorschach inquiry. *Journal of Projective Techniques*, 1958, **22**, 381–389.

Baughman, E. E. The effect of inquiry method on Rorschach color and shading scores. *Journal of Projective Techniques*, 1959, **23**, 3–7. (a)

Baughman, E. E. An experimental analysis of the relationship between stimulus structure and behavior on the Rorschach. *Journal of Projective Techniques*, 1959, **23**, 134–183. (b)

Beck, S. J. *Introduction to the Rorschach Method: A Manual of Personality Study*. American Orthopsychiatric Association Monographs, 1937, No. 1.

Beck, S. J. *Rorschach's Test. I: Basic Processes*. New York: Grune and Stratton, 1944.

Beck, S. J. *Rorschach's Test. II: A Variety of Personality Pictures*. New York: Grune and Stratton, 1945.

Beck, S. J. *Rorschach's Test. III: Advances in Interpretation*. New York: Grune and Stratton, 1952.

Beck, S. J. Comments on "The two tests in the Rorschach." *Journal of Projective Techniques*, 1953, **17**, 475–476.

Beck, S. J. *The Rorschach Experiment: Ventures in Blind Diagnosis*. New York: Grune and Stratton, 1960.

Beck, S. J., and Molish, H. B. *Rorschach's Test. II: A Variety of Personality Pictures*. (2nd ed.) New York: Grune and Stratton, 1967.

Brown, F. The psychodiagnostic test battery: Use of the test battery for psychodiagnostic appraisal. In Brower, D., and Abt, L. E. (Eds.), *Progress in Clinical Psychology*. Vol. 3. New York: Grune and Stratton, 1958.

Carp, A. L., and Shavzin, A. R. The susceptibility to falsification of the Rorschach diagnostic technique. *Journal of Consulting Psychology*, 1950, **3**, 230–233.

Coffin, T. E. Some conditions of suggestion and suggestibilty: A study of certain attitudinal and situational factors influencing the process of suggestion. *Psychological Monographs*, 1941, **53**, Whole No. 241.

Cox, F. N., and Sarason, S. B. Text anxiety and Rorschach performance. *Journal of Abnormal and Social Psychology*, 1954, **49**, 371–377.

Dinoff, M. Subject awareness of examiner influence in a testing situation. *Journal of Consulting Psychology*, 1960, **24**, 465.

Exner, J. E. The influence of chromatic and achromatic color in the Rorschach. *Journal of Projective Techniques*, 1959, **23**, 418–425.

Exner, J. E. *The Rorschach Systems*. New York: Grune and Stratton, 1969.

Exner, J. E., and Exner, D. E. How clinicians use the Rorschach. *Journal of Personality Assessment*, 1972. **36**, 403–408.

Fosberg, I. A. Rorschach reactions under varied instructions. *Rorschach Research Exchange*, 1938, **3**, 12–30.

Fosberg, I. A. How do subjects attempt fake results on the Rorschach test. *Rorschach Research Exchange*, 1943, **7**, 119–121.

Gage, N. L. Explorations in the understanding of others. *Educational and Psychological Measurement*, 1953, **13**, 14–26.

Gibby, R. G., Miller, D. R., and Walker, E. L. The examiner's influence on the Rorschach protocol. *Journal of Consulting Psychology*, 1953, **17**, 425–428.

Gibby, R. G., and Stotsky, B. A. The relation of Rorschach free association to inquiry. *Journal of Consulting Psychology*, 1953, **17**, 359–363.

Giedt, F. H. Comparison of visual, content, and auditory cues in interviewing. *Journal of Consulting Psychology*, 1955, **19**, 407–416.

Goetcheus, G. The effects of instructions and examiners on the Rorschach. Unpublished M. A. Thesis, Bowling Green State University, 1967.

Grisso, J. T., and Meadow, A. Test interference in a Rorschach-WAIS administration sequence. *Journal of Consulting Psychology*, 1967, **31**, 382–386.

Gross, L. Effects of verbal and nonverbal reinforcement on the Rorschach. *Journal of Consulting Psychology*, 1959, **23**, 66–68.

Harrower, M. Differential diagnosis. In Wolman, B. (Ed.), *Handbook of Clinical Psychology* New York: McGraw-Hill, 1965.

Henry, E. and Rotter, J. B. Situational influence on Rorschach responses. *Journal of Consulting Psychology*, 1956, **20**, 457–462.

Hertz, M. A Hertz interpretation. In Exner, J. E. *The Rorschach Systems*. New York: Grune and Stratton, 1969.

Holt, R. R. Clinical and statistical prediction: A reformulation and some new data. *Journal of Abnormal and Social Psychology*, 1958, **56**, 1–12.

Holt, R. R. Yet another look at clinical and statistical prediction. *American Psychologist*, 1970, **25**, 337–349.

Hutt, M. Gibby, R. G. Milton, E. O., and Pottharst, K. The effect of varied experimental "sets" upon Rorschach test performance. *Journal of Projective Techniques*, 1950, **14**, 181–187.

Kelly, E. L., and Fiske, D. W. The prediction of success in the V. A. training program in clinical psychology. *American Psychologist*, 1950, **4**, 395–406.

Klingensmith, S. W. A study of the effects of different methods of structuring the Rorschach inquiry on determinant scores. Unpublished Ph.D. dissertation, University of Pittsburgh, 1956.

Klopfer, B., and Kelley, D. M. *The Rorschach Technique*. Yonkers-on-Hudson, New York: World Book Company, 1942.

Klopfer, B., Ainsworth, M. D., Klopfer, W. G., and Holt, R. R. *Developments in the Rorschach Technique. I: Technique and Theory*. Yonkers-on-Hudson, New York: World Book Company, 1954.

Klopfer, B., et al. *Developments in the Rorschach Technique. II: Fields of Application*. Yonkers-on-Hudson, New York: World Book Company, 1956.

Klopfer, B., and Davidson, H. H. *The Rorschach Technique. An Introductory Manual*. New York: Harcourt, Brace, and World, 1962.

Klopfer, W. G. Comments on "The two tests in the Rorschach." *Journal of Projective Techniques*, 1953, **17**, 473–474.

Kostlan, A. A method for the empirical study of psychodiagnosis. *Journal of Consulting Psychology*, 1954, **18**, 83–88.

Levin, M. M. The two tests in the Rorschach. *Journal of Projective Techniques*, 1953, **17**, 471–473.

Loosli-Usteri, M. Le test de Rorschach applique a differents groupes d'enfants de 10-13 ans. *Archives de Psychologie*, 1929, **22**, 51–106.

Lord, E. Experimentally induced variations in Rorschach performance. *Psychological Monographs*, 1950, **60**, While No. 316.

Luborsky, L., and Holt, R. R. The selection of candidates for psychoanalytic training. *Journal of Clinical and Experimental Psychopathology*, 1957, **18**, 166–176.

MacKinnon, D. W. The effects of increased observation upon the accuracy of prediction. *American Psychologist*, 1951, **6**, 311 (abstract).

Masling, J. Differential indoctrination of examiners and Rorschach responses. *Journal of Consulting Psychology*, 1965, **29,** 198–201.

Peterson, L. C. The effects of instruction variation on Rorschach responses. Unpublished M. A. thesis, Ohio State University, 1957.

Phares, E. J., Stewart, L. M., and Foster, J. M. Instruction variation and Rorschach performance. *Journal of Projective Techniques*, 1960, **24,** 28–31.

Piotrowski, Z. A. The psychodiagnostic test battery: Clinical application. In Brower, D., and Abt, L. E. (Eds.), *Progress in Clinical Psychology.* Vol. 3. New York: Grune and Stratton, 1958.

Piotrowski, Z. A. A Piotrowski interpretation. In Exner, J. E. *The Rorschach Systems.* New York: Grune and Stratton, 1969.

Rapaport, D., Gill, M., and Schafer, R. *Diagnostic Psychological Testing.* Vol. 1. Chicago: The Yearbook Publishers, 1946.

Sarbin, T. R. A contribution to the study of actuarial and individual methods of prediction. *American Journal of Sociology*, 1942, **48,** 593–602.

Schachtel, E. G. Subjective definitions of the Rorschach test situation and their effect on test performance. *Psychiatry*, 1945, **8,** 419–448.

Schafer, R. *Psychoanalytic Interpretation in Rorschach Testing.* New York: Grune and Stratton, 1954.

Stern, G. G., Stein, M. I., and Bloom, B. S. *Methods in Personality Assessment.* Glencoe, Ill.: Free Press, 1956.

Van De Castle, R. L. Effect of test order upon Rorschach human content. *Journal of Consulting Psychology*, 1964, **28,** 286–288.

Vernon, P. E. The validation of civil service selection board procedures. *Occupational Psychology*, 1950, **24,** 75–95.

Weiner, I. B. *Psychodiagnosis in Schizophrenia.* New York: Wiley, 1966.

Wickes, T. A. Examiner influence in a testing situation. *Journal of Consulting Psychology*, 1956, **20,** 23–26.

Williams, M. H. The influence of variations in instructions on Rorschach reaction time. *Dissertation Abstracts*, 1954, **14,** 2131.

Zax, M., and Stricker, G. The effect of a structured inquiry on Rorschach scores. *Journal of Consulting Psychology*, 1960, **24,** 328–332.

CHAPTER 3

Scoring: The Rorschach Language

The full value of the Rorschach is realized only from the sum of its parts. A neglect of any available Rorschach data, whether "quantitative" or "qualitative," is an abuse of the text and a disservice to the subject. This principle has been emphasized consistently by the Rorschach systematizers. Beck (1945, 1967), Klopfer (1942, 1954), and Rapaport-Schafer (1946, 1954) have each stressed the importance of using the *total* configuration of the record Hertz (1952, 1963) has accented the same principle in her "interactionist approach" and Piotrowski (1957) has elaborated on it in his "principle of interdependent components." In essence, the concept of *total* Rorschach acknowledges that few, if any, single test variables, such as a particular class of scores, a specific kind of content, or a special type of response, will have a consistently high relationship with any internal or external behavior. Instead, the concept insists that an understanding of any feature of an individual can only be useful when it is judged against other features. In other words, an understanding of the complex interrelationships of characteristics that "make up" the person yields a reasonable understanding of the person.

A part of the richness of information available in the Rorschach is derived from the scoring and scoring summary. The procedure of scoring is very critical to the total test. Once the protocol has been obtained from the subject, the scoring process converts the responses into a logical and systematic format so that they may be studied both individually and collectively. Rorschach (1942) perceived the need for such a procedure and devised a system of symbols and abbreviations to be used for the coding of each response. In effect, the scoring or coding process reduces each response to a special Rorschach language which identifies its characteristics and components. It provides a kind of "shorthand" description of the record. The scoring and scoring summary might best be described as the *basic structure* of the protocol. While some of the substance of the response is lost in this translation from words to symbols, the coding makes possible an evaluation of responses and response styles which otherwise would not be possible.

Rorschach's scheme for scoring consisted of four basic categories: (1) Location (to which area of the blot did the response occur), (2) Determinant(s) (what features of the blot contribute to the formation of the percept), (3) Content (what is the class of content of the response), and (4) Popularity (is the response common to the general population). All of the Rorschach systematizers have maintained the same basic format of scoring categories in their respective systems, and Hertz (1940) and Beck (1937) each added a fifth category, Organizational Activity, to account for the extent to which the percept has organized various features of the blot in a meaningful way.

The issue of scoring and the symbols to be used have been topics of much discussion in the literature. In fact, it was this very issue that formed the original seeds of divergence among the various systematizers and ultimately led them in different directions (Exner, 1969). It has also been on this issue that the major critique of the Rorschach has unfolded, and because so much of the Rorschach research has centered on single variables rather than on configurations of variables, it has provoked some such as Zubin (1965) to suggest that the test should not be considered in the "measurement" framework. And to *some* extent, the critics such as Zubin have been correct in assuming that the Rorschach "scores" do not always meet stringent psychometric principles. It is probably unfortunate that the procedure of translating Rorschach words into Rorschach symbols has been called scoring. The very use of the word score, in the realm of psychology, carries with it the concepts of measurement which are not always useful or even appropriate to the Rorschach. Scoring usually implies specific nomothetic bases, summations, wrong versus right answers, standard deviations from a mean, conversions to standard scores, and even the well-known psychogram. These psychometric tenets, while not totally alien to the Rorschach, have only limited usefulness when applied to the classification of responses. The procedure of Rorschach scoring is much more similar to coding data for entry into a computer than to scoring in the usual sense of the word, and several features of the test make it highly unlike the typical psychometric instrument.

First, there are no absolutely right or absolutely wrong answers in the Rorschach. At best, responses can be classified on some form of continuum ranging from exceptional to very poor, but exceptional responses may be found in the protocols of the very disturbed and, conversely, very poor responses may be found in the records of the well adjusted. Neither situation necessarily detracts from the ultimate description of the individual as derived from the total Rorschach. Second, there is no absolutely best Rorschach protocol. Subjects of exceptional adjustment differ extensively in their own response styles, preoccupations, symptoms, assets, liabilities, and so on. Similarly, very maladjusted people also differ substantially in their response styles, assets, liabilities, and so on. Just as no two people are exactly alike, no two Rorschach protocols are exactly alike. Thus unlike the format common to many psychometric instruments such as intelligence tests and "self-report" inventories, there is no particular profile or psychogram of scores which is average, above average, or below average. The configuration of Rorschach scores used in interpretation is much more complex than can be represented in the simple two dimensional psychogram, although it is possible to compare some classes of Rorschach scores and score configurations with a nomothetic base. In this context, it is important to re-emphasize that, even though undesirable features of personality have been conceptualized and validated, no class of Rorschach response can be discretely identified as consistently representing those features. When a nomothetic base is applied against Rorschach scores and score configurations, ranges and interrelationships of scores are typically involved rather than fixed numbers. Isolated interpretation of Rorschach scores is relatively meaningless. For example, five human movement responses in a brief record that contains no color responses will be interpreted quite differently than five human movement responses in a lengthy protocol which also contains many color responses. Most of the series of comparisons required for interpretation of the "quantitative" data of the Rorschach are complex and usually involve evaluations of response components and configurations against many other components and configurations in the record. The extensive complexity of this process constitutes part of the richness of the test.

There is still another reason why basic measurement principles are not always appropriate to the Rorschach. This is related to the open-endedness of the test itself. All protocols are not of the same length. Even where the total number of responses for two records is identical, it is unlikely that the distribution of responses to each of the 10 cards will be the same. This is both an asset and a liability for the test. Numerous critics of the Rorschach have cited this factor of open-endedness as a severe liability in that it serves to restrict the full usefulness of normative comparisons and obviously makes for greater difficulty in the establishment of norms. Cronbach (1949) concluded that the open-ended nature of the test seriously limits the applicability of many standard statistical evaluations. Holtzman et al. (1961) has accurately pointed out: "Providing a subject with only ten inkblots and permitting him to give as many or as few responses to each card as he wishes characteristically results in a set of unreliable scores with sharply skewed distributions, the majority of which fail to possess the properties of even rank-order measurements." The validity of the Holtzman criticism is undeniable, and, to be sure, the nomothetic usefulness of the test would be increased if all protocols were of equal length with the same number of responses given to each card.[1] The potential cost for such a Rorschach model, however, would be extremely high in loss of idiographic information, which is probably the greatest asset of the test.

The fact that the Rorschach does not meet all of the stringent principles of measurement theory does not detract seriously from the usefulness of the "quantitative" data in interpretation. It does however, make the interpretation of these data a complex task and requires that the process of scoring be accomplished in a precise and standardized manner. The major advantage of the kind of scoring language devised by Rorschach is that it establishes a base from which a variety of frequency distributions can be developed. These distributions, in turn, are the foundation for the derivation of several important ratios and percentages. The frequencies, ratios, and percentages are the crux of information used in normative comparisons of a protocol with groups and subgroups and constitute a critical mass of data representing the relationships of features within the protocol. It is in the framework of this special scoring language that the interpreter begins his analysis of the record. The constancy of the language permits several interpreters to recognize the same characteristics in a single record and across records with comparative ease. Using the quantitative data first in the interpretive process avoids direct use of the subject's words, thereby permitting the formation of "interpretive hypotheses" free of unusual sets based on dramatic verbalizations. This procedure does not replace the words, for they too are ultimately used in the interpretation. Instead, it offers, at the onset of interpretation, a broad portrayal of the individual and his manner of response. The normative comparisons identify the extent to which characteristics of the record are similar to, or different from, other classes of protocols. The internal comparisons render a wealth of information concerning the

---

[1] In fact, Holtzman has devised a new inkblot test comprised of 45 cards in which subjects are permitted to give only one response per card. This attempt to overcome some of the limitations of the Rorschach has been quite successful in that normative data have been easily compiled and the use of the psychogram employed. The extent to which idiographic information, as yielded by the Rorschach may have been sacrificed by this format is not accurately assessable at this time.

manner of functioning of the subject, and highlight strengths, weaknesses, preoccupations, and response tendencies or styles. In addition, examination of the scores in the order of their occurrence in the record reveals much information concerning the approach of the subject to complex stimulus situations, and offers a representation of variations in his functioning under these conditions.

Thus working only with this unique language of Rorschach scoring the interpreter is able to form many hypotheses concerning the individual. These hypotheses focus on both internal and external behaviors, and collectively form an elaborate, although tentative, description of a unique person. This description is ultimately added to and/or modified as the qualitative analysis of the verbalizations ensues and the total Rorschach has been used.

SCORING RATIONALE

Because scoring is a significant portion of the total Rorschach, it has been natural that much discussion has evolved concerning its complexity and goal. Rorschach conceived of his method of scoring to identify the *Free Association* responses of the subject. His vagueness on the matter of Inquiry[2] stimulated the various systematizers to develop comprehensive Inquiry methods which do not always agree in scope or technique. All of the systematizers agree that the basic purpose of the Inquiry is to clarify the Free Association response and all have stressed the necessity of inquirying "nondirectively." Unfortunately, the definitions and examples of nondirective inquirying appear to vary considerably among the systematizers. For example, both Beck and Hertz are prone to ask, "Is there anything else?", while Klopfer endorses the use of such questions as, "Did the color help?", or "Did you use the upper part?". Any of these questions, which are quite suggestive, can generate a new response process through which the subject *adds to, rather than clarifies*, that which he perceived during the Free Association. Unfortunately, instances occur where the unwitting scorer draws on this newly developed information in his scoring decision. The end product is a score which does not really represent that which was perceived during the Free Association, but instead one that represents a consolidation of two responses—the one which occurred in the Free Association and the one developed by the suggestion of the Inquiry stimulus question. These kinds of scoring errors can be highly detrimental to the full evaluation of the Rorschach structure.

The *cardinal rule* of Rorschach scoring is that the score should represent that which was perceived in the Free Association. The importance of scoring *only* the Free Association response cannot be emphasized enough, particularly to the Rorschach novice. The scorer–interpreter must resist the temptation to consider the Free Association and the Inquiry as a continuous thought process or a single perception, for this is an illogical assumption. Many events transpire between the time that the subject gives the Free Association response and the onset of the Inquiry to that response. This is obviously true when the Inquiry is conducted after the Free Association to all 10 cards has been completed and probably true even

---

[2] Rorschach did not write specifically about a technique of Inquiry but implied that there is a need to determine the location of responses and to clarify whether movement or color might be included in the percept.

when the Inquiry is conducted after the Free Association to each card, as in the Rapaport-Schafer system. A similar kind of error is often committed by the interpreter who is inauspiciously prone to study the "perceptual-cognitive" functioning of the subject by reading the protocol "horizontally," that is, reading from Free Association to Inquiry, and generating a stream of hypotheses while doing so. If the scorer or interpreter is interested in studying the manner of perceptual-cognitive functioning of the subject, the approach must be "vertical" rather than horizontal, in other words, reading down through the Free Association responses and then downward through the Inquiry. Levin (1953) has quite accurately pointed out that this material may in fact represent two different test taking processes. One, the Free Association, represents perceptions developed under considerably ambiguous conditions and which has the open-ended features of the Rorschach. Conversely, the Inquiry occurs under considerably more structure which tends to build even more with the cumulative effects of questioning.

If logic and reasoning are consistently employed, the pitfalls of translating material developed in the Inquiry into the scoring of the Free Association can be avoided, but this is not always an easy task and caution must be exercised. On the issue of whether or not a component, clearly stated in the Inquiry, was in fact involved in the Free Association, the scorer must take a conservative posture. Some examples may be useful here in clarifying this point. Each involves a relatively common response to Card III, and all are real responses and inquiries, gleaned from the 835 protocols collected in conjunction with the development of the comprehensive Rorschach system.

FREE ASSOCIATION	INQUIRY
III Ths cld b 2 wm stirring s.t. in a pot	*E:* (Repeats *S*'s response verbatim)
	S: Thats rite, thyr here (points) & this is the pot

In this example, the subject provides most of the information required for scoring the response. He perceives what might be assumed to be the "popular" human figures and includes in the Free Association and frequently reported human movement. The Inquiry, which begins with the examiner's simple restatement of the original response, is designed to verify the location of the response. No other questions by the examiner are needed in light of the subject's response. Some examiners are interested in developing more information and use such questions as, "Why do they ll women?" or "What might they be stirring?" The response of the subject to these types of questions can be of considerable qualitative interest, but do not contribute to accurate scoring and, in fact, are probably of greatest value if left to a more directive Inquiry such as Testing-Of-Limits or an Analogy Period. In other instances, information developed *spontaneously* at the onset of the Inquiry should be included in the scoring of the Free Association. The same Free Association response serves a useful example.

FREE ASSOCIATION	INQUIRY
III Ths cld b 2 wm stirring s.t. in a pot	*E:* (Repeats *S*'s response)
	S: Yeah, they ll 2 African broads rite here in the middle & ths is the pot
	E: African?
	S: Sure, thy'r black like Africans

In this response, the subject offers seemingly new information in his spontaneous reply to the examiner's restatement of the response. The word "African" constitutes a clue for the examiner to follow. His inquiry concerning the word reveals that the subject did use the black-gray features of the blot as color. Thus a multiply-determined answer appears to have occurred, and the color factor should be included in the scoring. The decision to do so is based on the fact that the information was developed spontaneously and was not precipitated by any questions from the examiner (either in this response or in prior responses). In still other instances, the examiner finds himself in a difficult judgement position regarding whether to include material developed in the Inquiry into the scoring of the original response. Another answer to Card III provides a good example.

FREE ASSOCIATION	INQUIRY
III Ths cld b 2 wm	*E:* (Repeats *S*'s response)
	S: Yeah, rite here (points)
	E: Cld u tell me wht maks them ll 2 wm?
	S: Well, thy just ll tht
	E: I'm not sure I'm seeing thm as u do
	S: Look, ths r the heads, & ths is the bodies & the arms r going dwn here
	E: Going dwn?
	S: Yeah, like thy were stirring s.t. in ths her pot

In this response the subject has been cautious and/or inarticulate forcing the examiner to probe more than ordinarily should be the case. Ultimately, the Inquiry has yielded a human movement response, but the lateness of its occurrence in the Inquiry process raises the question as to whether the movement was perceived in the Free Association or whether it was provoked by the questioning in the Inquiry. Many times, subjects fail to report movement in the Free Association when they have actually perceived it; yet the probing required here, which finally focuses on what may be a form description (Going down), may have provoked a new perception. The general rule of being conservative in scoring applies here, and possibly the best guideline for the scorer will be the remainder of the protocol. If other human movement responses occur in the record, *and* the pattern of brief articulation during the Free Association is commonplace, the scoring for human movement should be included. Conversely, if the record is void of human movement responses, it is probably best not to score it and, instead, note it in the qualitative evaluation of the record. There are still other situations where the alertness of the examiner to the verbalizations of the subject will be important. Another response to Card III offers a fine example.

FREE ASSOCIATION	INQUIRY
III Wow, ths cld be 2 wm stirring s.t. in a pot	*E:* (Repeats *S*'s response)
	S: Well, they r rite her (points)
	E: I'm interested about the wow that u said before u described them

> *S:* Well u kno, it struck me tht thy were witches or s.t. in a den stirring bld or s.t. in that pot. U c all this red thgs her cld really b pieces of meat or s.t. like an A or H all cut up & waitin to be cookd
>
> *E:* Pieces of meat?
>
> *S:* Yeah and theyr all bloddy & e.t., just like thy was hung up ther & ths witches was gonna cook em

In this response, there is no indication in the Free Association, other than the comment "Wow," that the percept had struck the subject so intensively. Quite wisely, the examiner has inquired about the "Wow," and subsequently has developed considerable information, including the fact that the subject has used the entire blot rather than just the grey-black areas and that color has been used in the total percept, a factor which had not been hinted in the Free Association. If the "Wow" had not occurred in the Free Association, the scorer would not be justified in including the color component in the scoring of the response, if the conservatism rule regarding scoring is to be followed.

If the cardinal rule of the Rorschach scoring language is to score only the Free Association, the second most important rule for scoring is to include *all* of the components which appear in the response. Rorschach did this, although his system of scoring symbols is far less elaborate than has been ultimately developed by each of the systematizers.[3] Each of the Rorschach systems, formulated subsequent to Rorschach's death, makes some form of provision to include and weigh all components in a response equally. Klopfer has deviated from this pattern, preferring to identify only one component for each of the scoring categories as "main," and including the remaining components as "additional" scores. For example, if more than one determinant of a response occurs, such as the concurrent existence of human movement and color, Klopfer somewhat arbitrarily designated one as the "main" determinant and the other as an "additional." This is possibly the most important major error in Klopfer's formulation of a Rorschach system, not so much because of the methodology of scoring employed, but because of the differential interpretations assigned to main versus additional scores. The assignment of different weights to main scores versus additional scores causes the Klopfer approach to interpretation to differ significantly, in some respects, from that of the other systems. Interestingly, the Exner and Exner (1972) survey of Rorschach practitioners reveals that slightly more than half follow the Klopfer routine of scoring

---

[3] Rorschach's system of scoring is relatively more brief than that offered by any of the systematizers. For the most part, this is due to the fact that the original plates with which Rorschach worked contained no shading components. The kinds of chiaroscuro components which exist in the contemporary plates were first created through a printing error, not long before Rorschach's death. He was intrigued with the possibilities inherent in these new stimuli but had little time to consider or write of them. Interestingly, the greatest differences among the Rorschach systematizers have evolved around the issue of scoring shading responses.

mains and additionals, while more than 90% of the ABPP clinicians surveyed report agreement with the practice of scoring and weighing all components of the response equally. The logic of scoring and weighing all components equally is clearly supported by the empirically demonstrated fact that no single score can be interpreted by itself with confidence, and, of course, by the very principle which Klopfer strongly endorsed, that of using the *total* Rorschach.

In the following chapters, the symbols and abbreviations which have been adopted for scoring in the comprehensive system are described and defined. They have been selected from the composite offered by the five major Rorschach systems plus the original suggestions of Rorschach. The criteria for selection of each have been essentially fourfold. First, Rorschach's original arguments have been considered, and, for the most part, they remain logical and realistic. Second, the empirically based data relating to Rorschach's arguments and those of the various systematizers have been reviewed in the hope of finding information that might lead to some reconciliation of differing points of view. Ordinarily, this has not proved to be the case, and in such instances, the symbol and its criteria which have been most clearly supported by research findings have been selected. Third, consideration has been afforded to the arguments posed by the systematizers themselves. In some instances, even though not supported by research finding (mainly because such research has not been accomplished) these arguments are impressive as well as consistent with other decisions. Finally, the opinions expressed by the two samples surveyed, practicing clinicians and ABPP diplomates have been included. These opinions have seemed particularly important where the two groups agree with near unanimity. In addition to these four basic criteria, samples have been drawn frequently from the 835 protocols solicited for this project to test specific hypotheses which still remained vague after the other criteria had been applied. The comments and suggestions accumulated from the survey of Rorschach researchers proved especially useful in drawing attention to unresolved questions and to methodological problems. These samples proved particularly useful in comparing the components of two or more systems and permitted study of the alteration in configurations under different scoring criteria.

The premise underlying the selection of this language for the Rorschach has been to avoid ambiguity, maximize use of the wisdoms of others, and develop a system useful to both the practitioner and researcher which offers some resolution to the annoying differences that have persisted among systematizers and have often handicapped the Rorschach community.

The general scoring format selected for the comprehensive system consists of five basic categories: (1) Location, (2) Determinant(s), (3) Content(s), (4) Popularity, and (5) Organizational Activity. As has been mentioned, the first four were suggested by Rorschach and subsequently incorporated into all other systems developed. The fifth category represents a factor which was implicit in Rorschach's work but not fully exploited by him. Every response is scored for the first three categories, while the applicability of the remaining two is contingent on the characteristics and content of the response. Thus the scoring of a response can be relatively simple and uncomplicated, especially if only one determinant and one content are involved, or it can be substantially complex in instances all where five categories are involved and multiple determinants and/or contents are included. Two responses, each involving the use of the entire blot on Card I serve to illustrate the variations in scoring complexity that occur.

FREE ASSOCIATION	INQUIRY
1 It ll a bf to me	*E:* (Repeats *S*'s response)
	S: Yes, the whole thg ll that 2 me
	E: Cld u tell me what makes it ll a bf?
	S: Sure, ths r the wgs & this is the body & ths cld b antennae

The Inquiry has verified the use of the whole blot and that the percept has been based exclusively on the form or shape of the blot. This particular response to Card I is Popular (very high frequency of occurrence), and because the parts of the whole blot have been organized into a single percept, a score for Organizational Activity will be included. In other words, all five scoring categories are represented in this response, which is scored: *Wo Fo A P* 1.0. Each of the symbols has a specific meaning.

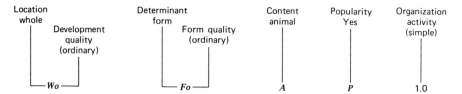

FREE ASSOCIATION	INQUIRY
1 It ll a wm tied to the stake w her arms reaching up & smoke is all around her & 2 thgs r whirling around her	*E:* (Repeats *S*'s response)
	S: Well the wm is in the cntr, u can c her outline w her hands reaching up in the air
	E: U said ther was smoke
	S: Its all dark & hazy like smoke
	E: U also mention thgs whirling around her
	S: Yeah, thy ll big birds with thr wgs outstretched like thy were flying around her, rite here are the wgs & ths is the hds

This response is much more complex than the first, although both represent each of the five basic scoring categories. Here, the whole blot has been used; a complex kind of organizational activity has been involved; three determinants are included, human movement (arms reaching up), shading (smoke all around), and animal movement (birds flying around her); two contents are used (human and animal);

and a part of the response is Popular (woman in the center area). The score for this response is: $W+$ $M.FM.Y+$ H, A P 4.0.

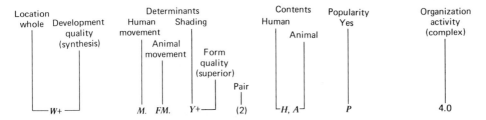

Most responses are not this complex, but some may be even more so. The goal of the scorer is to accurately code the response based on the verbalizations of the subject, *not* on the inferences of the examiner-scorer. Obviously, the verbatim recording of the protocol is essential for scoring accuracy.

Those familiar with any given Rorschach system or systems will find that the comprehensive system borrows considerably from both Beck and Klopfer, but will also find that features of the other major Rorschach systems (Hertz, Piotrowski, and Rapaport-Schafer) have also been included. This composite has not been by design or intent. Rather, the comprehensive system has hopefully evolved from the "best" of each.

REFERENCES

Beck, S. J. *Introduction to the Rorschach Method.* American Orthopsychiatric Association Monograph No. 1, 1937.

Beck, S. J. *Rorschach's Test. II: A Variety of Personality Pictures.* New York: Grune and Stratton, 1945.

Beck, S. J., and Molish, H. B. *Rorschach's Test. II: A Variety of Personality Pictures.* (2nd Ed. rev.) New York: Grune and Stratton, 1967.

Cronbach, L. J. Statistical methods applied to Rorschach scores: A review. *Psychological Bulletin*, 1949, **46**, 393–429.

Exner, J. E. *The Rorschach Systems.* New York: Grune and Stratton, 1969.

Exner, J. E., and Exner, D. E. How clinicians use the Rorschach. *Journal of Personality Assessment*, 1972, **36**, 403–408.

Hertz, M. R. *Percentage Charts for Use in Computing Rorschach Scores.* Brush Foundation and the Department of Psychology, Western Reserve University, 1940.

Hertz, M. R. The Rorschach: Thirty years after. In Brower, D., and Abt, L. E. (Eds.), *Progress in Clinical Psychology.* New York: Grune and Stratton, 1952. Pp. 108–148.

Hertz, M. R. Objectifying the subjective. *Rorschachiana*, 1963, **8**, 25–54.

Holtzman, W. H., Thorpe, J. S., Swarz, J. D., and Herron, E. W. *Inkblot Perception and Personality.* Austin: University of Texas Press, 1961.

Klopfer, B., and Kelley, D. M. *The Rorschach Technique.* Yonkers-on-Hudson, N. Y.: World Book Company, 1942.

Klopfer, B., Ainsworth, M. D., Klopfer, W. G., and Holt, R. R. *Developments in the Rorschach Technique. I: Technique and Theory.* Yonkers-on-Hudson, N.Y.: World Book Company, 1954.

Levin, M. M. The two tests in the Rorschach. *Journal of Projective Techniques*, 1953, **17,** 471–473.

Piotrowski, Z. *Perceptanalysis*. New York: Macmillan, 1957.

Rapaport, D., Gill, M., and Schafer, R. *Diagnostic Psychological Testing: The Theory, Statistical Evaluation, and Diagnostic Application of a Battery of Tests*. Vol. II. Chicago: Yearbook Publishers, 1946.

Rorschach, H. *Psychodiagnostics*. Bern: Verlag Hans Huber, 1942.

Schafer, R. *Psychoanalytic Interpretation in Rorschach Testing*. New York: Grune and Stratton, 1954.

Zubin, J., Eron, L. D., and Schumer, R. *An Experimental Approach to Projective Techniques*. New York: Wiley, 1965.

CHAPTER 4

Location: Symbols and Criteria

The first, and possibly easiest, of the scoring decisions concerns the location of the response; that is, to which part of the blot did the response occur. In some instances this information may be given in the Free Association, as in the response which begins, "Well, the whole thing looks like . . . ," or "If I use only this upper part . . . ," and requires only a brief verification in the Inquiry. In most cases, however, the subject does not spell out the area of the blot that he is using, and this matter becomes one of the major targets of the Inquiry. Ordinarily, it is information easily derived, especially when the general introduction to the Inquiry includes some mention of this goal. It is also important for the examiner to record the blot area used in the response on a *location sheet* to maintain a permanent record.[1]

The symbols and criteria used in the comprehensive system for the scoring of location are essentially those described in the Beck methodology. This decision has been based on a variety of factors which are described as each of the symbols are defined and discussed. Overall, however, the Beck method seemed preferrable to the other systems for four reasons. First, it is reasonably clear and concise, avoiding some of the arbitrary or overinclusive features of the other methods. Second, it is relatively well known. Third, it is generally based on sound empirical data, and fourth, it seems very consistent with Rorschach's basic intentions. The comprehensive system also adds to the basic Beck methodology by including an evaluation of the "developmental quality" of the location selection. This technique was first suggested by Rapaport (1946) and studied by Meili-Dworetzki (1956) and Friedman (1952, 1960, 1971).

As previously mentioned, the scoring for location is one of the least complex aspects of the scoring process. The open-endedness of the test permits either of two approaches in forming a percept. The subject may use the entire blot, or he may select only a portion of it. When the former occurs, it is a *whole* response and the scoring is simple and straightforward. In the latter case, the symbol for scoring will be selected on the basis of whether the area used is one *commonly* used. In this context, there are three primary scoring classifications for location, plus four other special scoring symbols and abbreviations that are used for unusual location descriptions. These seven scoring symbols are shown in Table 3 which also gives the essential criterion for each.

---

[1] The formal use of a "location sheet" for the permanent recording of response locations dates to the middle 1930s having apparently been suggested by both Beck and Klopfer. Prior to that time examiners were accustomed to making tracings of the locations on a thin sheet of paper.

Table 3.   Symbols Used for the Scoring of Rorschach Location Responses

Symbol	Definition	Criterion
W	Whole response	Where the blot is interpreted as a whole. All portions of the blot must be used.
D	Common detail response	A frequently identified area of the blot.
Dd	Unusual detail response	An infrequently identified area of the blot.
S	Space response	A white space area is used in the response (scored *only* with another location scoring).
DW or DdW	Confabulated whole response	The blot is interpreted as a whole secondarily, the primary answer being based on a detail feature of the blot.
DdD	Confabulated detail response	A commonly perceived detail area is interpreted secondarily, the primary answer being based on an unusual detail area.

THE *W* RESPONSE (WHOLES)

The criteria for the scoring of *W* is essentially the same as that provided by Rorschach and generally adopted by the Rorschach systematizers. It constitutes an either-or phenomenon wherein the subject uses the entire blot or he does not. The guidelines of this criterion make the scoring of *W* relatively simple. Two of the systematizers, Klopfer (1942) and Hertz (1942), added a second type of *W* response to their respective systems, that of the cut-off whole, which uses the symbol *Ẁ* for scoring. The rationale for the cut-off whole has been based on the fact that Rorschach scored a *W* for some responses to Card III even though the red portions were omitted. Klopfer ultimately defined the cut-off whole as applicable to responses in which at least two-thirds of the blot is used, *with the intent* of using the entire blot. Beck (1944) has taken an opposite position concerning *W*, arguing that either the response is *W* or it is not. The decision to exclude the cut-off *W* from the comprehensive system is based on three data inputs. First, the issue of scorer reliability was considered. Since there are no published data concerning the scorer reliability for the cut-off *W*, a sample of 20 protocols were selected from the protocol pool, each of which contains a minimum of three responses which might be scored *Ẁ*. These records were scored (naively) by three groups of three scorers each. Two of the scorer groups consisted of postdoctoral clinicians trained in the Klopfer system, and the third was comprised of third year graduate students who had been trained in the Klopfer methodology. The correlation coefficients for the cut-off *W* scoring were .74, and .68 for the postdoctoral scorers, and .69 for the graduate students. Since all of these coefficients seemed low, the scorers were asked to recheck their scorings giving special attention to the use of the cut-off whole, and emphasizing the Klopfer definition. Under these instructions, the coefficients increased to .86, .81, and .78, none of which are especially overwhelming in light of the instructions provided. A discussion among the scorers concerning their differences in identification of cut-off whole responses indicates that the criterion of "intent" makes a major impact, with various scorers interpreting intention in different ways. A second factor leading to the exclusion of the cut-off *W* from the comprehensive system is that the research literature makes little mention of it, or of its interpretive significance. Finally, only 17% of the 111 ABPP survey respondents rank the cut-off whole as an important interpretive variable. In the context of these findings, it was decided to adopt the more conservative Beck position concerning whole responses. It is definitely clear and leaves little room for scorer judgements in a protocol that has been adequately recorded.

The criterion for scoring *W* requires only that the examiner verify that the entire blot has been used. It is highly important however, that this affirmation be made, and the examiner–scorer should *never* assume the *W* simply because the response sounds like the whole blot has been used. For example, the response of "a bat" to Card I most frequently uses the whole blot. But there are instances when the subject may exclude the side projections, or may even form his percept using only the upper half of the card. Under the routine conditions of test administration, there should be no reason for a misidentification of the whole answer.

THE *D* RESPONSE (COMMON DETAILS)

The criteria for the scoring of *D* is also essentially the same as that suggested by Rorschach. He referred to these areas as "Normal" details of the plates. He suggested that the differentiation between these and other areas of the blots should be based on the frequency with which subjects referred to them in reporting answers. During the early history of the Rorschach, several efforts were made to codify the variety of obvious detail areas with numerical designations so as to provide easy identification of the areas. These efforts did not always use the same format for decision-making, nor did those involved always agree on Rorschach's intent. The result has been several systems for identification of the different areas of the blots. Both Beck and Hertz have used a frequency distribution method as the basis for their respective decision-making. Each has published lists and charts of usual and unusual detail areas (Beck, 1937, 1944, 1961; Hertz, 1936, 1938, 1942, 1951, 1970). While the designations have changed slightly as each of these authors has "updated" his work, the two systems have continued to differ somewhat significantly concerning a few of the blot areas. Piotrowski (1957) has also followed a frequency distribution approach, but less extensively than either Beck or Hertz. The Rapaport-Schafer system relies more on the judgements of the examiner–scorer in determining whether the area used is "common" or "uncommon." This approach can be considered consistent with Rorschach's comments, on the subject in that he suggested that "Normal" details of the plates are "most striking," suggesting that they stand out by reason of their position and contour. Rapaport (1946) has followed this lead and defines *D* as an area "which is conspicuous by its size, its isolation, and the frequency of response it draws." Klopfer (1936, 1942, 1954) has been the most elaborate in describing different kinds of detail answers. In doing so, however, he generally avoided the preciseness of statistical frequencies used by both Beck and Hertz and, instead, followed Rorschach's suggestion that usual details stand out because of their "general properties of relatively independent sub-wholes . . . ." The Klopfer system identifies two types of usual details, differentiated on the basis of size (*D* for large usual areas; *d* for small usual areas).

Hertz (1970) has made a detailed comparison of her own designations of blot areas with those suggested by Beck, Klopfer, and Piotrowski. She notes that she and Beck agree on 90 of 97 areas which she has designated as appropriate for the scoring of *D*, while her range of agreement with Klopfer is slightly less (87 of 97) and with Piotrowski even more so (83 of 97). This level of agreement between Hertz and Beck has been important in the decision regarding which system of coding *D* areas of the blots would be most appropriate for the comprehensive system.

The Beck method of detail area coding has been adopted in the comprehensive system for three important reasons. First, as has been noted, there is considerable agreement between Hertz and Beck on which areas constitute usual details. This seems important in that both are based on frequency distributions. The Beck scheme is somewhat preferable to the Hertz designations because it includes 25 additional areas which Hertz does not consider. Second, in the Exner and Exner (1972) survey of practicing clinicians, it has been noted that nearly half had been trained in the Beck method, versus only 10% who had been trained in the Hertz system. Half of those responding expressed competence in using the Beck system, versus only 9% expressing competence in the Hertz method. Third, only two of the 111 respondents to the ABPP survey indicated that they use the Hertz system for identifying detail areas of the blots, while 71 report using the Beck system. Thus while both systems are empirically based, the Beck method has gained substantially wider recognition and use and seems to correlate well with the Hertz data. The Klopfer differentiation of usual detail areas into large and small was considered, but decided against, mainly because that differentiation is somewhat arbitrary and frequently disagrees with the Beck and Hertz designations, and also because the research literature contributes little information regarding the interpretive significance of one versus the other.

Scorers using the comprehensive system will, in effect, be using the designations for *D* as described by Beck. The numbering of these areas is shown for each of the ten cards in figures included in Table A in Part II of this work.

THE *Dd* RESPONSE (UNUSUAL DETAILS)

The *Dd* response is one given to a blot area which is *not* used frequently. The majority of *Dd* responses are formed using small areas of the blots, but size is not necessarily an important factor. Some small areas of the blots are commonly used, and thus scored *D*. Conversely, some large blot areas are scored *Dd* because of their infrequent use. Beck has provided numerical designations for some *Dd* areas. These are also shown in Table A. Obviously, they do not represent all of the possible *Dd* areas. The logical rule which the scorer must use is to score *Dd* for any areas which are neither *W* or *D*. Some of the systems, particularly Klopfer (1942, 1954) have included special scores to identify the type of *Dd* area chosen, such as *dd* for "tiny" areas, *dr* for "rare" areas, *di* for "inside" areas, and so on. While there is no doubt that the interpreter should attend to these kinds of differentiations, it seems impractical to include special symbols for their scoring for three reasons. First, there is no research base to justify such a differentiation. The limited amount of research published concerning *Dd* type responses makes no differentiation regarding type of *Dd*. Second, the frequency of any one type of *Dd* response is ordinarily very small and contributes little to a scoring summary. Third, and possibly most important, is the tendency for scorers to disagree on the specific type of *Dd*. For example, a response can be both tiny and rare and thus could be scored either *dd* or *dr*. Some "inside" detail responses are not uncommon among the relatively small frequency of *Dd* responses overall, whereas other inside detail responses are extremely rare and unusual. One type probably could be scored *di* and the other *dr*, or both could be scored *di*. Whether the scoring is by rule or by judgement, the decision becomes somewhat arbitrary and the end product is a failure to make the refined kinds of differentiations originally intended. Thus in the comprehensive system, all *Dd* areas are scored *Dd* and interpretations based on the kind of *Dd* are left to the qualitative analysis of the interpreter.

THE *S* RESPONSE (WHITE SPACE DETAILS)

The symbol *S* is included in the scoring for location whenever a white space area of the blot is included in the response. The *S* is never scored alone, but instead is always used in conjunction with one of the three primary location scores such as *WS*, *DS*, or *DdS*. The rationale for using *S* only with another location symbol is to maintain consistency in evaluating the three primary types of location answers. Some space areas, particularly on Cards II, VII, and IX, are responded to with considerably greater frequency than space areas on other cards. If the *D* versus *Dd* criteria are applied, some *S* answers are clearly *D*, while others are *Dd*. Rorschach did not make this differentiation, and considered all space responses to be "rare." Some of the systematizers have followed Rorschach's assumption concerning *S* percepts, recommending that *S* be scored separately when only space is used in the percept, and combining *S* with another location symbol when space is used in some combination of the blot proper. The *S* responses scored separately are not included in the *D* or *Dd* totals in these systems, although one (Hertz, 1970) does use two symbols for space (*S* for frequently given space answers; *s* for infrequently given space answers).

  Since the configuration of *W* to *D* to *Dd* is quite important to the analysis of the quantitative data, each of these totals must reflect accurately the location selections of the subject and thus the separate scoring for space complicates the system unnecessarily. Obviously, space answers have considerable interpretive importance and require careful evaluation. The total number of *S* responses is entered in the scoring summary, and analysis of the type of *S* (common, uncommon, separate, or combined) can be noted in that summary and/or in the qualitative evaluation of the protocol.

THE *DW* AND *DdW* RESPONSES (CONFABULATED WHOLE)

The confabulated whole is a very unusual, and ordinarily pathognomic, response. The *DW* or *DdW* is scored when the subject attends *only* to a detail area of the blot, but then generalizes from that detail to the entire blot. For example, a subject might specify the upper (*D*1) projections on Card I as, "Claws, so I guess it's a lobster." The Inquiry must also verify that *only the detail area* has been discretely conceptualized. If the subject, without provocation from the examiner, articulates other areas of the blot as also being representative parts of a lobster, *DW would not* be scored. The confabulated whole probably represents some perceptual-cognitive impairment rather than "lazy" articulation, and for the this reason the scorer must exercise caution in applying the *DW* or *DdW* symbols. The issue should be reasonably clear that the subject has not differentiated various areas of the blot to form the percept, but instead has generalized from a single detail. Resistive and/or inarticulate subjects sometimes appear to have given *DW* or *DdW* responses, but in fact have not, and usually this can be clarified by careful inquirying, or where the matter remains in doubt, through a nondirective kind of testing-of-limits *after* the formal Inquiry has been completed. Two examples, taken from Card IV, serve as good illustrations of a *DW* and a poorly articulated *W*.

FREE ASSOCIATION	INQUIRY
IV Hey, thrs feet here, it must be a person	*E:* (Repeats *S*'s response)
	S: Yeah, like feet here (Points to *D6* area)
	E: U said it must b a person
	S: Yeah, well it ll feet to me & if there's feet there must b a person
	E: I'm not sure how u'r seeing it
	S: Rite here see! Ths ll feet

This response sounded like it was the relatively common percept of a human figure to the whole blot from the Free Association; however, the persistence of the subject to focus only on the Popular "feet" portion of the blot renders the distinct possibility of a *DW* answer. In this example, the examiner wisely did not pursue the Inquiry further so as to avoid unnecessary sets. After the Inquiry has been completed the examiner returned to Card IV and used a nondirective testing-of-limits.

POSTINQUIRY

E: I want to take another look at this one to make sure that I have seen the person as u have

S: O.K.

E: Cld u show it to me

S: Well u see ths r the feet here so it must be a person

E: I'm no sure what u mean when u say it must be a person

Ss Well, if there's feet thr must b a person, like all the rest of this

Here, the examiner has clearly verified that the subject has not differentiated other features of the blot in forming the percept, and the *DW* scoring is justified. The examiner, out of curiosity, might wish to be more directive with the subject at this point and ask that other parts of the person be identified. The *DW* scoring would not be changed, however, regardless of further articulations from the subject as they would be derived under directive rather than nondirective conditions. In the second example a similar response is noted.

FREE ASSOCIATION	INQUIRY
IV I guess ths cld b a boot here, maybe a person	*E:* (Repeats *S*'s response)
	S: Rite here (Points to *D*6). Ths is the front part & hers the heel
	E: U said mayb a person
	S: Yeah, mayb
	E: I'm not sure how u'r seeing it
	S: Well, if ths is a boot, that other one cld b a boot too & ths would b the rest of the person

As in the preceding example, the response appears to meet the criterion for *DW* scoring as the Inquiry ends. Postinquiry testing-of-limits offers additional clarification.

POSTINQUIRY

E: I want to take another look at this one to make sure that I hav seen the person as u hav

S: Well ths two thgs ll the boots & ths cld b a head I suppose & this cld be arms altho they'r awful skinny

At this point, no further information is necessary unless the examiner is interested in added verbalization for qualitative evaluation. The subject has, without directive provocation, articulated other areas of the blot consistent with his percept and the response should be scored *W*.

These examples probably represent unusual extremes in which the examiner is forced to clarify this important scoring issue. Most confabulated whole responses are more easily identified by the rare and/or unusual generalizations which the subject makes. It is highly important, however, that the examiner–scorer not confuse a "lazy" *W* with the confabulated whole. This criterion is more stringent than that used by Beck, but hopefully reduces the degree of scorer subjectivity that may be involved. The final decision, however, will often be made more subjectively than for other location scoring, and the scorer will find it useful to include in the decision process some evaluation of the cooperativeness of the subject. It may also be useful to evaluate the other location selections; that is, if other responses are clearly *DW* or *DdW*, then one which is questionable could be scored as a confabulatory whole with justification. Conversely, if no other *DW* or *DdW* responses occur, then a conservative approach is probably more appropriate. Three of the systematizers, Klopfer, Hertz, and Piotrowski, stress the need for conservatism by recommending that the scoring of confabulatory location response be used only when the form quality of the response is also poor. While it is true that the majority of confabulatory location responses will be of poor form quality, this recommendation is not adopted in the comprehensive system, because there are instances, such as the example to Card IV, where form quality is adequate but the response is still a true confabulatory process. These latter types of response are not uncommon among some organics, and especially among younger subjects with perceptual learning disturbances.

THE *DdD* RESPONSE (CONFABULATED DETAIL)

The confabulated detail response is one in which the subject interprets an unusual detail of the blot and then generalizes from that interpretation to a common detail area. The criterion for scoring *DdD* is exactly the same as for the *DW* and *DdW* type responses and conservatism continues to provide the basic guideline. The *DdD* type response occurs much less frequently than *DW* or *DdW*, and, because of this, has even greater significance in the total evaluation of a record than either *DW* or *DdW*.

EVALUATION OF DEVELOPMENTAL QUALITY OF LOCATION SCORES

The full interpretive value of scoring for location can be increased substantially if some added differentiation is made regarding the "quality" of the area specification. All whole responses are not selected or organized in the same manner. Neither are the specifications involved in the selection of common or unusual details, or the use of space in forming a percept. Rorschach recognized these differences and discussed them as "Apperceptive" approaches (Erfassungstypen), suggesting that some subjects manifest a keen imagination in forming answers, while others approach the blot in a more simple and concrete manner. For example, most of the systematizers have described the different kinds of *W* response, ranging from the *simple* or *unorganized*, to the *combinatory*, *organized*, or *superior* whole answer. The former seems to occur, somewhat spontaneously to the entire blot as in, "a bat," "a skin," "a mask for Halloween," and so on. The latter clearly integrates the variety of stimuli presented by the blot in a combined or organized manner such as, "two people at a cocktail party," "a submarine, gliding through the water and reflected in the moonlight," or "a woman running after a child up a small hill with their shadows being cast on the ground." Where the simple unorganized answer occurs, the superior organized response is created. This same process is also noted in the use of common detail areas. Some are exceptionally well defined and integrated into a percept, while others manifest an ordinary, or almost mediocre, quality.

There have been several approaches to the problem of distinguishing these different kinds of answers through the scoring of the protocol. One has been the special category developed by both Beck and Hertz to denote the Organizational Activity involved in the percept. This score, however, does not pertain exclusively to the location selections and, instead, involves the total complex of the percept. While the score for Organizational Activity is critical to the total Rorschach, it fails to capture the differences which occur specifically in the selection of location areas. Meili-Dworetzki (1939, 1956) appears to have recognized the potential in the Rorschach for differentiating of mental complexity and flexibility through the study of location responses. She studied levels of location area selection in children of various ages, creating the design of her investigations on the assumptions of Rorschach, Beck (1933), and Piaget (1924). She found a general "enrichment" of approach in location selection and integration with increasing age levels and suggested the possibility of studying cognitive development through a differentiation of types of location responses. Rapaport obviously perceived the same potential in the Rorschach and recommended, as an experimental approach to this kind of study, a differentiation of location scores. His scheme focused mainly on the whole response, suggesting a differentiation of W's into $W+$, Wo, Wv, and $W-$ depending on the extent to which a sharp integration of the blot features has occurred. The $W+$, in this system, represents the integrations of separately perceived details; Wo is defined as the more gross perceptual impressions; Wv is used for the "haphazard," hastily responded to, whole where the final response implies "little or no articulation"; and $W-$ is assigned to those selections which are arbitrary and have a limited or "minimum" inclusion of the actual perceptual features of the blot. Rapaport maintained that the Wv and $W-$ types of responses occur most frequently in instances of psychopathology.

Unfortunately, Rapaport did not follow through on his differentiations concerning W responses, not did he extend this system of differentiation to other kinds of location selections such as D or Dd.[2] Friedman (1952, 1953) has developed a method for differentiating location selection based on Werner's (1948, 1957) theory of cognitive development. It is similar to, but more inclusive than the Rapaport approach, being applicable to both Whole and Detail responses. Friedman recommends six criteria for location evaluation, three of which denote "developmentally high" scores, while three others represent "developmentally low" scores.

$++$: A unitary blot, or blot area is perceptually articulated and then reintegrated into a well differentiated percept. The analysis–synthesis process must be obvious; thus Friedman restricts this scoring for Whole responses *only* to those given to the unitary of "unbroken" blots (I, IV, V, VI, and IX). Similarly, where a Detail response is involved, the area used must be unitary in its stimulus features.

$+$: Discrete portions of a blot are combined into a single percept. Where the $++$ scoring requires both analysis and synthesis, the $+$ score emphasizes the synthesis operation. It is applicable to Whole responses (but ordinarily only to the differentiated or "broken" blots, II, III, VII, VIII, and X) and to Detail responses in which two or more discrete areas are used.

m : A "mediocre" selection in which the gross outline of a blot or blot area is used and articulation *of the content* is adequate and appropriate for the blot area. In other words, the form quality used must be appropriate to the percept.

v : A "vague" response in which a diffuse impression of the blot or blot area is given. Some form element may be present but the form demands are relatively "nonspecific" such as in maps, clouds, rock formations, and such.

---

[2] Rapaport was less interested in the Rorschach as a test than in the use of the test battery as a form of structured interview. Consequently, after the publication of Diagnostic Psychological Testing, he concerned himself very little with the further development of the Rorschach per se, and instead concentrated most of his efforts on the theoretical foundations of ego psychology.

a   :   an "amorphous selection in which the shape of the area plays no determinable role, such as in paint, night, and blood.

—   :   A response in which the content requires a specific form; however, that form does not exist in the blot area selected.

The research on the Friedman method has been considerable and appears to establish that the technique can be useful for the study of "developmental levels"[3] and cognitive functioning. For example, Hemmendinger (1953, 1960) reports a decrease of undifferentiated and diffuse responses with increasing age in children. Becker (1956) and Wilensky (1959) have suggested a weighting formula for the scoring categories to provide greater "developmental" differentiation. A variety of other studies such as Siegel (1953), Frank (1952), and Lebowitz (1963) have related different levels of scores to psychiatric disabilities. Goldfried, Stricker, and Weiner (1971) have summarized the work with the Friedman method as a useful research technique which appears to differentiate children at different levels as well as normal adults from neurotics, aged, brain damaged, and schizophrenics.

The Friedman method has apparently had little appeal for the practicing Rorschacher. Only eight of the 111 respondents in the ABPP survey report an attempt to use it, and only three of those continue to do so. Nine of the 71 respondents who have published research on the Rorschach have considered the usefulness of the method, but none had pursued it in depth. Six of those nine commented that the method was possibly "overelaborate," citing the fact that most of the studies which show effective discrimination between groups use *summations* of the "developmentally high" versus the "developmentally low" scores rather than differentiate on the basis of the separate scoring categories. In other words, a total frequency or percentage of + +, +, and *m* is compared with the frequency or percentage of *v*, *a*, and —. This approach seems necessary since some of the categories, especially + + and *a*, occur with very low frequency in some groups. It would also appear that, while the method takes into account both the structural and organizational aspects of the percept, parts of the scoring criteria weigh the "form" and "content" adequacy more heavily than occurs in other scoring criteria.

Considering the limitations of the Friedman method, it seemed inappropriate to incorporate the technique into the comprehensive system as is, yet it also seemed inappropriate to neglect the valuable contribution which this approach offers. In this context, the Rapaport approach to differentiating Whole responses was reviewed to study the possibility of extending it to all responses, and including in that extension, the assets of the Friedman method. The result provides four categories for the differentiation of location selection, the criteria for which are generally consistent with the intentions of both Friedman and Rapaport. The scoring symbols and criteria for these four categories are presented in Table 4.

It will be obvious, from examination of the criteria offered in Table 4, that the "Synthesis" category represents a combination of Friedman's + + and + scorings. It also generally agrees with the Rapaport criterion for scoring *W*+. The "Ordinary" classification is comparable to Friedman's scoring of *m* and Rapaport's use of *o*. The "Vague" scoring represents a condensation of the Friedman *v* and *a*

---

[3] While the method does distinguish differences in children, as identified by chronological and "mental" age, it probably deals more specifically with general cognitive operations. Thus the concept of development, as has been used traditionally in the study of children, is not directly applicable.

Table 4. Symbols and Criteria Used for the Differentiation of Location Responses

Symbol	Definition	Criteria
+	Synthesized response	Unitary or discrete portions of the blot are perceptually articulated and integrated or combined into a single percept.
o	Ordinary response	A discrete area of the blot is selected and articulated so as to emphasize the gross outline and obvious structural features of the area selected.
v	Vague response	A diffuse or general impression is offered to the blot or blot area in a manner which avoids the necessity of articulation of specific outlines or structural features.
−	Arbitrary response	Articulation of the blot or blot area is inconsistent with the structural limitations of the blot.

scorings, and is also consistent with Rapaport's concept of *v*. The "Arbitrary" category is essentially unchanged from that defined by Rapaport and Friedman. Thus the + and *o* categories would represent Friedman's concept of "developmentally high" locations and the *v* and − categories represent the "developmentally low" responses.

While the four categories used for evaluating location in the comprehensive system do not avoid completely the use of content and form adequacy, the extent of involvement of these factors is less than in the Friedman approach. In addition, these symbols can be used for responses which might occur to any of the 10 cards. Under the Friedman method, restrictions existed for the scoring of the higher developmental categories in Whole responses. The ++ score could be used only on five cards, the + score on the remaining five, and the *m* score on six. Two other factors have been important in the decision to use four categories to evaluate location. The first involves the evaluation of Form adequacy. Friedman has used the Beck system as a base for determining whether a location selection should be scored −, or should be assigned a different score. Thus a *D* response could be discrete and well articulated but scored −, because it is so represented in Beck's listing of Poor Form responses. The comprehensive system includes a method for evaluating Form adequacy which is derived from Beck, Hertz, and Mayman, which does not necessarily advocate discrimination based soley on a normative frequency of responses. This methodology is described in considerable detail in Chapter 6; however, it seems important to stress here that the evaluation of location should be compatible with, but not necessarily dependent on the evaluation of Form adequacy. A second factor important to the selection of the four category method is that of scorer reliability. Several studies are cited by Goldfried, Stricker, and Weiner which report interscorer reliabilities for the Friedman method to range from .89 to .96, all of which are obviously high. Each of these reports is based on two or three independent scorers, while another report (Margolis et al., 1960) which used five scorers yields only a 70% agreement. In an effort to evaluate the interscorer reliability of the Friedman method versus the four category scheme adopted in the comprehensive system, two groups of five scorers each were used. Each of the groups was comprised of three clinicians in postdoctoral clinical training plus two fifth year graduate students who had recently completed their clinical internship. All had completed at least two formal courses in the Rorschach. Both groups were provided with 2 hours of special training, either in the Friedman method, or the four category method, during which 35 responses were collectively scored. Subsequently, they independently scored the same 200 responses which had been selected randomly from the protocol pool, one group scoring the Friedman method, the second group scoring the four category method. The correlation coefficient for the group scoring the Friedman method was .93, while the coefficient for the group scoring the four category method was .98. The difference, while not satistically significant, does favor the four category method. The differences which occurred among the group scoring the Friedman method were generally between $++$ and m, or between v and a. Differences among the group scoring the four category method were generally between o and $-$, and always occurred to Dd type responses.

SCORING EXAMPLES

The location component of the responses will be scored twice in the comprehensive system. One symbol is used to designate the actual area selected (W, D, Dd, S, DW, DdW, or DdD), and one symbol is used to evaluate the Developmental Quality of the selection ($+$, o, v, or $-$). Examples of the various types of responses are shown in Table 5.

Table 5. Examples of Location Scoring

Card	Response	Scoring
I	Two witches dancing around a woman	$W+$
	A bat	Wo
	A halloween mask (spaces used as eyes)	WSo
	A cloud formation	Wv
	A fish	$W-$
	Two people with their arms around each other ($D4$)	$D+$
	A woman standing with her arms in the air ($D4$)	Do
	Coral ($D2$)	Dv
	A human heart ($D3$)	$D-$
	Robed figures ($DdS30$) climbing up a hill ($Dd24$)	$DdS+$
	A man's face ($Dd25$)	Ddo
	Mountains ($Dd22$)	Ddv
	A broken heart ($Dd27$)	$Dd-$
II	Two bears dancing in a circus act	$W+$
	A colorful butterfly	Wo
	Some sort of design	Wv
	A prize winning rose	$W-$
	Two bears rubbing their noses together ($D6$)	$D+$
	A dog head on each side ($D6$)	Do
	Some sort of map ($D1$)	Dv
	Morley's ghost ($DS5$)	$DS-$
	Intercourse during menstruation ($Dd24$ is penis and $D3$ is vaginal area)	$Dd+$
	Icicles ($Dd25$)	Ddo
	∨ Like in the painted desert ($Dd22$ plus $Dd23$)	Ddv
	President Eisenhower ($Dd31$)	$Dd-$

Table 5. (Continued)

Card	Response	Scoring
III	Two people bowing to each other at a party	W+
	∨A magnified insect with his markings	WSo
	Pieces of a picture puzzle	Wv
	∨Christ in prayer	W−
	A person leaning over seeing his reflection in a mirror (D1)	D+
	A pelvis (D1)	Do
	Blood (D3)	Dv
	A catfish (D2)	D−
	∨Two birds (Dd22) flying up out of a cave (D3)	Dd+
	A penis (Dd26)	Ddo
	An ocean or lake (DdS23)	DdSv
	An unborn child (Dd28)	Dd−
IV	A man sitting on a tree stump	W+
	A bearskin	Wo
	Seaweed	Wv
	A spider	W−
	<A dog barking (D6) at a snake (D2)	D+
	A couple of boots (D6 on each side)	Do
	∨A storm cloud (D6)	Dv
	An intestine (D1)	D−
	∨Two people talking to each other (Dd26)	Dd+
	A nail (Dd30)	Ddo
	A lake (DdS29)	Ddv
	A jailhouse (center of blot)	Dd−
V	Two people sitting back to back	W+
	A butterfly	Wo
	A fungus growth	Wv
	A map of the United States	W−
	Two people standing with their arms up (D7)	D+
	A person dressed up in a rabbit suit (D7)	Do
	A cloud (D4)	Dv
	A shark (D2)	D−
	The heads of two people kissing (Dd30)	Dd+
	An arrow (Dd22)	Ddo
	The limb of a tree (Dd26)	Ddv
	The brain of a man (midline)	Dd−
VI	An indian totem pole sitting up on a carved stone	W+
	∨A bearskin rug	Wo
	Some sort of micro-organism, like a cell	Wv
	A lobster dinner	W−
	<A submarine cruising in the night and being reflected in the moonlight (D4, both sides)	D+
	A totem pole (D3)	Do
	A snowflake (D1)	Dv
	A whale (D4)	D−
	∨Two birds (Dd21) looking into their nest (Dd28)	Dd+
	Claws (Dd21)	Ddo
	A harbor (DdS30)	DdSv
	A person waving (Dd25)	Dd−

Table 5. (Continued)

Card	Response	Scoring
VII	∨Two girls dancing the can-can	*W+*
	A necklace	*Wo*
	Clouds	*Wv*
	∨A bird	*W−*
	Two girls talking to each other (*D1*, both sides)	*D+*
	<A scotty dog (*D2*)	*Do*
	An ocean (*DS7*)	*DSv*
	Smoke (*D1*)	*Dv*
	A preying mantis (*D4*)	*D−*
	A bird (*Dd25*) gliding toward his nest (*D11*)	*Dd+*
	A thumb, like a hitch-hiker holds it (*Dd21*)	*Ddo*
	A peninsula (*Dd21*)	*Ddv*
	Christ giving the sermon on the mount (*Dd25*)	*Dd−*
VIII	Two animals climbing up an unusual rock formation	*W+*
	A very elaborate chandelier	*Wo*
	The parts of a dissected animal	*Wv*
	An evergreen tree	*W−*
	A frog (*D4*) leaping over a rock (*D5*)	*D+*
	A rodent (*D1*)	*Do*
	Some human tissue (*D2*)	*Dv*
	A bird flying along (*D1*)	*D−*
	Two nuns (*Dd24*) standing on a hill (upper *D4*)	*Dd+*
	∨A milkbottle (small center space)	*DdSo*
	A tree branch (*Dd22*)	*Ddv*
	A butcher knife (*Dd30*)	*Dd−*
IX	∨Two birds (*D3*) sitting beneath some sort of unusual plant that has big green leaves and a pink flower	*W+*
	∨An atomic explosion with the fire (*D3*) and the cloud (*D6*)	*Wo*
	Colored rocks	*Wv*
	Someone's lungs	*W−*
	<A woman running after a child (*D1*)	*D+*
	A man's head (*D4*)	*Do*
	Landscape reflected in the water (*D12*, both sides)	*Dv*
	A cow (*D3*)	*D−*
	Two ku-klux-klan members (lower space above *D9*) waving to each other	*Dd+*
	Fingers (*Dd21*)	*Ddo*
	Blood stain, dried up (*Dd28*)	*Ddv*
	A little sailboat (*Dd26*)	*Dd−*
X	An aquarium with crabs and little fish and some coral and pretty plants	*W+*
	∨Fireworks that are designed to look like a tropical display	*Wo*
	An abstract painting	*Wv*
	The face of Fu-Man-Chu	*W−*
	Two insects struggling to carry a stick (*D11*)	*D+*
	∨Two seahorses (*D4*)	*Do*
	Coral (*D9*)	*Dv*
	A rocking chair (*D2*)	*D−*
	Paint that just landed on a dog (*Dd33* and *D2*)	*Dd+*
	A Buddha (*DdS29*)	*DdSo*
	An amoeba (*Dd33*)	*Ddv*
	A basketball (*Dd34*)	*Dd−*

It seems important to stress the need for accuracy in the scoring for location. While the criteria are reasonably "straightforward," the process may sometimes seem to be more simple than is actually the case and caution is always in order. The overall interpretive "impact" of the location scores is considerable and hypotheses involving a variety of features are generated from these data. These hypotheses often concern intellect, perceptual and cognitive operations, environmental, awareness, and needs for achievement, to mention a few. The location scoring also contributes significantly to the interpretations gleaned from other Rorschach scores. It is also important that the scorer not confuse the scoring for Form Quality with the criteria for evaluating the Developmental Quality of location selections. Some "overlap" does exist, however, the two evaluations are by no means congruent.

Each of the scores which have been selected for use in the comprehensive system contribute important information. They have been selected with regard to the relative importance of this information and in consideration for interscorer reliability, a factor which should lend itself to greater interinterpreter reliability.

REFERENCES

Beck, S. J. Configurational tendencies in Rorschach responses. *American Journal of Psychology*, 1933, **45,** 432–443.

Beck, S. J. *Introduction to the Rorschach Method: A Manual of Personality Study*. American Psychiatric Association Monograph, 1937, No. 1.

Beck, S. J. *Rorschach's Test. I: Basic Processes*. New York: Grune and Stratton, 1944.

Beck, S. J., Beck, A., Levitt, E., and Molish, H. B. *Rorschach's Test. I: Basic Processes*. (3rd ed.) New York: Grune and Stratton, 1961.

Becker, W. C. A genetic approach to the interpretation and evaluation of the process-reactive distinction in schizophrenia. *Journal of Abnormal and Social Psychology*, 1956, **53,** 229–236.

Exner, J. E., and Exner, D. E. How clinicians use the Rorschach. *Journal of Personality Assessment*, 1972, **36,** 403–408.

Frank, I. H. A genetic evaluation of perceptual structurization in certain psychoneurotic disorders by means of the Rorschach technique. Unpublished doctoral dissertation, Boston University, 1952.

Friedman, H. Perceptual regression in schizophrenia: An hypothesis suggested by use of the Rorschach test. *Journal of Genetic Psychology*, 1952, **81,** 63–98.

Friedman, H. A note on the revised Rorschach developmental scoring system. *Journal of Clinical Psychology*, 1960, **16,** 52–54.

Friedman, H. Perceptual regression in schizophrenia: An hypothesis suggested by use of the Rorschach test. *Journal of Projective Techniques*, 1953, **17,** 171–185.

Goldfried, M. R., Stricker, G., and Weiner, I. B. *Rorschach Handbook of Clinical and Research Applications*. Englewood Cliffs, N. J.: Prentice-Hall, 1971.

Hemmendinger, L. Perceptual organization and development as reflected in the structure of the Rorschach test responses. *Journal of Projective Techniques*, 1953, **17,** 162–170.

Hemmendinger, L. Developmental Scores. In Rickers-Ovsiankina, M. (Ed.), *Rorschach Psychology*. New York: Wiley, 1960.

Hertz, M. R. *Frequency Tables to Be Used in Scoring the Rorschach Inkblot Test*. Brush Foundation, Western Reserve University, Cleveland, Ohio, 1936.

Hertz, M. R. *Code Charts for Recording Rorschach Responses*. Brush Foundation and the Department of Psychology, Western Reserve University, Cleveland, Ohio, 1938.

Hertz, M. R. *Frequency Tables for Scoring Rorschach Responses*. (2nd ed.) Cleveland: Western Reserve University Press, 1942.

Hertz, M. R. *Frequency Tables for Scoring Rorschach Responses*. (3rd ed.) Cleveland: Western Reserve University Press, 1951.

Hertz, M. R. *Frequency Tables for Scoring Rorschach Responses*. (5th ed.) Cleveland: The Press of Case Western Reserve University, 1970.

Klopfer, B., and Sender, S. A system of refined scoring symbols. *Rorschach Research Exchange*, 1936, **1**, 19–22.

Klopfer, B., and Kelley, D. *The Rorschach Technique*. Yonkers-on-Hudson, N. Y.: World Book Company, 1942.

Klopfer, B., Ainsworth, M. D., Klopfer, W. G., and Holt, R. *Developments in the Rorschach Technique. I: Technique and Theory*. Yonkers-on-Hudson, N.Y.: World Book Company, 1954.

Lebowitz, A. Patterns of perceptual and motor organization. *Journal of Projective Techniques*, 1963, **27**, 302–308.

Meli-Dworetzki, G. Le test Rorschach et l'evolution de la perception. *Archives of Psychologie*, 1939, **27**, 111–127.

Meli-Dworetzki, G. The development of perception in the Rorschach. In Klopfer, B., et al. *Developments in the Rorschach Technique. II: Fields of Application*. Yonkers-on-Hudson, N.Y.: World Book Company, 1956.

Piaget, J. *Le Judgement et le Raisonnement chez l'Enfant*. Neuchatel: Delachaux and Niestle, 1924.

Piotrowski, Z. *Perceptanalysis*. New York: MacMillan, 1957.

Rapaport, D., Gill, M., and Schafer, R. *Diagnostic Psychological Testing*. Vol. 2. Chicago: Yearbook Publishers, 1946.

Siegel, E. L. Genetic parallels of perceptual structuralization in paranoid schizophrenia: An analysis by means of the Rorschach technique. *Journal of Projective Techniques*, 1953, **17**, 151–161.

Werner, H. *Comparative Psychology of Mental Development*. (Rev. ed.) Chicago: Follett, 1948.

Werner, H. The concept of development from a comparative and organismic point of view. In Harris, D. B. (Ed.), *The Concept of Development*. Minneapolis, Minn.: University of Minnesota Press, 1957.

Wilensky, H. Rorschach developmental level and social participation of chronic schizophrenics. *Journal of Projective Techniques*, 1959, **23**, 87–92.

CHAPTER 5

Determinants: Symbols and Criteria

The most important, and possibly the most complex, of the scoring decisions concerns the response determinant, that is, the blot features that have contributed to the formation of the percept. The object of determinant scoring is to provide information concerning the complex perceptual-cognitive process which has produced the response. There are many stimulus characteristics in the blots, each of which generally falls into one of three descriptive classifications: (1) those involving form, (2) those involving color, and (3) those involving the shading features. Determinant scoring would be a relatively easy task if all responses could be discretely identified as falling into one of these three categories, but that is not ordinarily the case. In many instances, more than one of the three categories is involved as in, "a yellow rose with a long stem," or "a man in the shadows." The first involves both form and color while the second involves both form and shading. In other instances, a broad classification of stimulus characteristics fails to differentiate the ways in which the stimulus is used. For example, form features can be used to create the impression of movement as in "a person bowing," or "a bat flying." Sometimes the symmetrical form of the blot is used as a reflection as in, "a woman seeing herself in a mirror." In still other instances the form may be used simply for purposes of identification as in, "It looks like a bat because of the shape of the wings and the body."

The numerous ways in which the stimulus characteristics of the blots can be used to create responses has continually posed a challenge to those seeking to offer a systematic scoring for the test. Recommendations for determinant scoring have varied considerably from system to system and have often been focal points of Rorschach controversy. Rorschach had originally suggested five symbols for the scoring of determinants, one for form (*F*), one for human movement (*M*), and three for color (*FC*, *CF*, and *C*), two or which were selected to indicate the relative importance of form in the color answer (1921). It was a relatively simple scoring system which discounted the importance of separate scorings for responses marked by animal or inanimate movement, perceived dimensionality, reflections, or the use of the achromatic coloring as color. It obviously contained no scoring for shading type responses. The latter appears to have been the case, because the blots with which Rorschach did most of his work *did not* contain shading but were, instead, of a single hue. He did begin working with shaded blots shortly before his death, and introduced a sixth scoring symbol (*C*) in his last, postmously published, paper (1923), to be used for "chiaroscuro" responses. The six scoring symbols provided the base from which others continued to study and refine the test. Unfortunately, each Rorschach systematizer has preferred to use symbols and criteria for their scoring, which, more often than not, are different than those selected by another systematizer, and in some instances even different than those that Rorschach had suggested. The end product is an astonishing lack of agreement. Even where the same symbol appears in two or more systems, the criterion for the use of that symbol probably differs. In fact, there is no single symbol, the criterion for which is agreed upon by all five American Rorschach systems, and there are only a few determinant symbols, the criteria for which are agreed upon even by two of the systems (Exner, 1969). For example, 16 different symbols, representing 12 different types of color response have been suggested. An even greater number of symbols have been recommended for the scoring of shading responses.

The selection of the symbols and criteria for scoring determinants in the comprehensive system would be relatively uncomplicated if any one system could be demonstrated as clearly superior to the others, but that is not the case. Some seem overly elaborate, including components without the logic of a sound empiric base or providing "subscorings" that tend to misrepresent summary data. Others appear to have omitted important components, or have altered component criteria in such a way as to be inconsistent with symbol definitions. Consequently, the symbols and criteria selected for the comprehensive system constitute a composite of several systems. Each of the possibilities from each system has been considered and evaluated against research findings, the results of the three questionnaires, and in many instances, a testing of specific hypotheses using the protocol pool. The result of this process has yielded 24 symbols, representing nine determinant categories. These nine categories are: (1) Form, (2) Movement, (3) Color (chromatic), (4) Color (achromatic), (5) Texture (shading), (6) Dimensionality (shading), (7) General Shading, (8) Dimensionality (form), and (9) Pairs and Reflections. The symbols used in each of these categories, plus the criterion for the symbol, are presented in Table 6.

It will be obvious to the experienced Rorschacher that, in addition to including the five original Rorschach symbols (F, M, FC, CF, C) and his criteria for them, many of the symbols are drawn from the Beck and Klopfer systems. The familiarity of the symbol, however, does not necessarily mean that the criterion is identical. This is not the case in some instances, particularly where a symbol has been used in two or more systems with different criteria. This matter is clarified as each of the symbols, its criterion, and reason for selection is discussed more extensively.

THE FORM DETERMINANT (F)

The selection of the symbol F for the scoring of Form answers should require little explanation. It was used by Rorschach to denote answers based on form and has been incorporated into all subsequent systems, using essentially the same criterion. The Form answer has been the focus of some intersystematizer disagreements, but the issues have not concerned the basic criterion. Rather, these disagreements have centered on methods of evaluating form quality (which are discussed in the next chapter), or have related to other determinant criteria, the inclusion or exclusion of which determines what is a "Pure" Form answer. For example, Beck has been quite adamant in his stand against a separate scoring for either animal or inanimate movement. His position is very similar to that stated by Rorschach; thus in the Beck system, responses involving animal or inanimate movement are ordinarily scored simply as F, or Pure Form. Klopfer, Hertz, and Piotrowski have all adopted the position that such responses are not Pure Form, and have developed separate scoring criteria for them. This issue is described in more detail in the sections dealing

Table 6. **Symbols and Criteria for Scoring Response Determinants**

Category	Symbol	Criteria
Form	F	*Form answers.* To be used separately for responses based exclusively on the form features of the blot, or in combination with other determinant scoring symbols (except *M* and *m*) when the form features have contributed to the formulation of a percept.
Movement	M	*Human movement response.* To be used for responses clearly involving a kinesthic perception, the content of which involves behavior restricted to humans, or, in animals, is human-like.
	FM	*Animal movement response.* To be used for responses involving a kinesthetically marked movement involving animals. The movement perceived must be congruent to the species identified in the content. Animals perceived in movement *not* congruent to their species should be scored *M*.
	m	*Inanimate movement response.* To be used for responses involving the movement of an inanimate, inorganic, or insensate object.
Color (chromatic)	C	*Pure color response.* To be used for responses based exclusively on the chromatic color features of the blot. No form is involved.
	CF	*Color-form response.* To be used for responses which are formulated because of the color features of the blot or blot area and the form involved is of secondary importance.
	FC	*Form-color response.* To be used for responses which are formulated because of the form of the blot area, and in which color is used secondarily for purposes of clarification and /or elaboration.
	Cn	*Color naming response.* To be used when the colors of the blot or blot area are identified by name with no form involved and with the intention of presenting a response.
Color (achromatic)	C'	*Pure achromatic color response.* To be used when the response is based exclusively on the grey-black-white features of the blot or blot area, as they are identified as color. No form is involved.
	C'F	*Achromatic color-form response.* To be used when the response is based primarily on the grey-black-white features of the blot or blot area, as they are identified as color, and where form has been involved secondarily.
	FC'	*Form-achromatic color response.* To be used when the response is based primarily on form and the achromatic coloring of the blot, or blot area, is used for purposes of elaboration and /or clarification.
Texture (shading)	T	*Pure texture response* To be used for responses where the shading components of the blot are interpreted as representing a textural phenomenon with no involvement of the form of the blot.

Table 6 (Continued)

Category	Symbol	Criteria
	TF	*Texture-form response.* To be used for responses where the shading features of the blot or blot area are interpreted as texture and form is used secondarily for purposes of elaboration and/or clarification.
	FT	*Form-texture response.* To be used for responses in which form is a primary determinant and the shading is interpreted as textural for purposes of clarification and/or elaboration.
Dimensionality (shading)	*V*	*Pure vista response.* To be used when the shading features of the blot or blot area are interpreted as depth or dimensionality with no form involvement.
	VF	*Vista-form response.* To be used for responses in which the shading components of the blot or blot area are interpreted as depth or dimensionality and the form features are used for purposes of clarification and/or elaboration.
	FV	*Form-vista response.* To be used for responses in which form is the primary determinant and the shading features are included secondarily to represent depth or dimensionality.
Shading (general-diffuse)	*Y*	*Pure shading response.* To be used for responses based exclusively on the light-dark features of the blot which are completely formless and do not involve either reference to texture or vista.
	YF	*Shading-form response.* To be used for responses based primarily on the light-dark features of the blot or blot area, in which the form features are used for purposes of clarification and/or elaboration.
	FY	*Form-shading response.* To be used for responses which are based primarily on the form of the blot or blot area in which the shading features are used for purposes of elaboration and/or clarification.
Dimensionality (form derived)	*FD*	*Form based dimensional response.* To be used for responses which are identified as having depth or dimension based exclusively on the form features of the blot or blot area. No shading is involved.
Pairs and Reflections	(2)	*Pair response* To be used for responses in which the content includes two objects identified and which is based on the symmetrical features of the blot or blot area. The objects identified must be "equivalent" in all respects but must not be identified as "reflected" or "mirror images."
	rF	*Reflection-form response.* To be used for responses in which the blot or blot area is perceived as a reflection (because of the symmetry), and the content or object reflected has no specific form requirements.
	Fr	*Form-reflection response.* To be used for responses in which the blot or blot area is identified because of its form and is also perceived as reflected or "mirrored" because of the symmetry features.

72

with movement responses. For the moment, it seems appropriate to reaffirm the criterion for scoring F. Namely, that F is scored for any response which includes Form as one of the determinant features, and is scored separately when no other determinant is involved.

Generally, the inclusion of Form as a response determinant is easily identified. Subjects frequently use the words "form" or "shaped," or, in some cases, describe the details of the object perceived so as to emphasize the form features. For instance, in elaborating on the response of "a bat" to Card I, the subject may add, "These outer parts look like wings and the center looks like the body part." Even without further elaboration it seems clear that the Form features of the blot have been used. Responses based exclusively on the Form features usually comprise the largest single determinant category in a record, and ordinarily Form features will be included in more than 95% of all responses given.

THE MOVEMENT DETERMINANTS

Three kinds of movement responses may occur in the Rorschach, (1) those involving humans or human-like behaviors, (2) those involving animals, and (3) those involving inanimate or inorganic objects or forces. Rorschach scored for only one type of movement, that involving humans or human behaviors. He specifically discounted animal movement as having the same meaning as human movement, and thus, provided no scoring for it. Beck (1937, 1944, 1961) has vigorously defended Rorschach's position, and also excludes any formal scoring for animal or inanimate movement in his method. Klopfer (1936, 1942, 1954), Hertz (1942, 1951, 1970), and Piotrowski (1937, 1947, 1957) have each taken the opposite position and include scorings for animal and inanimate movement, using the same scoring symbols but with differing criteria for the scoring of inanimate movement.

An examination of each of these positions seems to indicate that both are at least partially correct. Thers is very little empirical evidence to suggest that the three types of movement all represent different levels of the same psychological process as has been implied by Klopfer and Piotrowski. Quite the contrary, that work which has been reported (which is discussed fully in the chapters on interpretation) encourages the notion that the three types of responses represent relatively different psychological operations. In that context, Rorschach and Beck have been correct in discouraging separate scorings for animal and inanimate movement so as not to confuse the interpretation of human movement responses. On the other hand, animal and inanimate responses do occur, the former with considerable frequency. Research findings indicate that, just as they are different from human movement responses, they are different from answers based only on form. Both Rorschach and Beck score them as F responses, although Beck clearly does interpret them somewhat differently than pure F answers in his overall interpretation of the protocol. The decision to include the three symbols for the scoring of the different types of movement answers in the comprehensive system has both a logical and empirical basis. First, the goal of providing a separate score or code for each type of response that is distinct from other types of responses logically argues for three movement scores. Second, and possibly even more important, practicing Rorschachers, regardless of their respective training and/or orientation, use separate scorings for animal and inanimate movement. The 1972 Exner and Exner survey reveals that 94% score for these types of answers, even though nearly half of those responding prefer the Beck system. The survey of APBB Rorschachers yields similar results. One hundred-two of the 111 respondents score for both animal and inanimate movement.

HUMAN MOVEMENT (*M*)

The symbol *M*, and its criterion, is derived from Rorschach's original work. Each of the systems developed after Rorschach include this symbol for the scoring of human movement answers and three of those ((Beck, Klopfer, and Hertz) use Rorschach's criterion. The Piotrowski (1947, 1957) and Rapaport-Schafer (1946) systems each include modifications of Rorschach's criterion. Piotrowski restricts the scoring of *M* to responses occurring to an area sufficiently ambiguous as to make any type of movement or posture equally plausible. It is a caution designed to avoid scoring *M* falsely, as in responses where movement is injected to explain form features. Rapaport restricts the scoring of *M* to responses which include complete, or nearly complete, human figures. Neither of the arguments for these criterion restrictions follows from an empirical base, nor is the logic strongly persuasive. The Piotrowski position appears to depend excessively on the subjective judgments of the scorer concerning the intent of the subject in his use of movement. The Rapaport restriction appears to eliminate the scoring of *M* in some instances where *M* does occur. It is quite true that movement perceived to whole human figures is interpreted differently than in movement perceived in partial human figures, but in each, the movement has been perceived and should be scored.

The *M* is scored for human activity. The movement may be active such as in running, jumping, fighting, and arguing, or it may be passive, such as in sleeping, thinking, smiling, and looking. In either instance *M* is scored; however, it is worthwhile to include a superscript to denote whether the movement is active or passive (^{a} for active, ^{p} for passive). Rorschach suggested that it was important to evaluate *M* answers in terms of "Flexion" and "Extension." All of the systematizers have reaffirmed the importance of such an evaluation, and Beck (1961) has called attention to a third *M* stance, that is a static one. In an attempt to quantitatively weigh the differences in types of movement, the categories of active–passive seem most appropriate. Empirical findings regarding the interpretation of *M* indicate this distinction to be important. Thus "Two people struggling with a heavy object, trying to lift it up" would be scored M^a, while "two people resting back to back" would be scored M^p.

The symbol *F* is *not used* when *M* is scored. The *M* assumes form, even when the content is abstract such as "Depression," or "Happiness." The existence of *M* should not be assumed simply because human figures are perceived. The movement itself must be articulated for a response to be scored *M*. In *most cases*, the movement is reported during the Free Association. In *fewer instances*, the movement is not reported in the Free Association, but instead is reported *spontaneously* at the onset of the Inquiry to the response. For example, a subject might respond to the Free Association to Card III, "It looks like two people here." This response appears to be based on form only and would not be scored *M*. If, however, after the examiner begins the Inquiry to the response by simply restating *S*'s response and *S* offers, "Yes, they are right here, it looks like two people doing something," it seems logical to assume that movement had been perceived during the Free Association but had not been articulated. Spontaneity must be the guideline and *M should never be scored* if there is reason to believe that the movement was provoked by the Inquiry questioning of the examiner. This rule holds true for all determinants.

While most *M* responses involve human figures, *M* may also occur where the content is animal, but only when the movement described involves a human activity which is not common to the animal species. For example, "two beetles arguing" would be scored *M*, as would "two bears playing gin rummy." Conversely, "Two beetles fighting over something," or "Two bears playing together," *would not* be scored *M*, but instead would be scored using the symbol for animal movement, *FM*.

ANIMAL MOVEMENT (*FM*)

This scoring was originally suggested by Klopfer (1936). His justification for the use of *FM* was based primarily on Rorschach's 1923 article, in which Rorschach referred to a special scoring consideration for responses which are essentially form based but which also tend toward the use of movement or color. Since some of Rorschach's examples included animals in movement, it was natural for Klopfer to include the designation of animal movement in this category. By 1942, Klopfer had decided to use a different symbol to represent "tendencies toward" ($\rightarrow$), and selected the *FM* scoring for use exclusively in animal movement responses. The criterion selected for use in the comprehensive system, is that of Klopfer. It is to be scored for any response involving animals in activity which is common to the species, such as "a dog barking," "a bat flying," and "a leopard stalking its prey." In extremely rare instances, an animal will be perceived in an activity which is not common to its species, such as "a snake flying along in the air." In these cases, assuming that the nonspecies behavior is not human-like, the scoring of animal movement should still be employed but parenthesized (*FM*). As with the scoring of *M*, the ^{a} and ^{p} superscripts should be included to denote whether the movement is active or passive.

While most *FM* answers include a whole animal, some will involve only a partial animal figure such as "two animals scampering behind a bush, you can only see their legs," on Card V. Occasionally, the content of the animal movement response will be a mythological animal such as a dragon or a unicorn. The scoring in these unusual types of responses continues to be *FM* and the uniqueness of the animal is accounted for in the Content scoring. The scoring of *FM*, like that of *M*, is contingent on the spontaneous reporting of movement by the subject.

INANIMATE MOVEMENT (*m*)

The third type of movement response which may occur in the Rorschach involves inanimate, inorganic, or insensate objects. The symbol *m*, which has been selected to denote such responses, was first suggested by Piotrowski (1937) during a time when he was closely identified with Klopfer's efforts to develop the Rorschach. Klopfer and Hertz have continued to use the symbol in their systems of the test, but with a substantially broader criterion than is used by Piotrowski. They use the category somewhat idiomatically, including in it phallic forces, facial expressions, and human abstracts. Klopfer and Hertz also combine the symbol F with m to indicate the relative importance of form in the response, so that some inanimate movement responses are scored Fm, some mF, and some m. Piotrowski does not follow this logic, instead preferring to score m for any inanimate movement, regardless of form involvement.

It is essentially the Piotrowski criterion and method which have been selected for the scoring of inanimate movement in the comprehensive system. The criterion is reasonably precise and does not overlap with either the M, or FM categories, as does the broader criterion of Klopfer and Hertz. Thus m is scored for any movement perceived which involves nonhuman and nonanimal objects. The most common types of inanimate movement responses include fireworks, explosions, blood dripping, water falling, and trees bending. Some other types of inanimate movement which occur with considerably less frequency include, skins stretched tightly, a leaf floating, seaweed drifting, a bullet smashing, and such. The m is scored for any of these or similar responses. In very rare cases, inanimate objects are perceived in human-like activity, such as "trees dancing a waltz." In this kind of response the scoring should be M, rather than m.

Some examples of the three types of movement responses (M, FM, and m) are provided in Table 7. Most of these examples show only the Free Association material, although the critical parts of the Inquiry are included in parentheses when that information has been essential to the scoring decision.

Some responses require special consideration in the scoring of the "active–passive" dimension. They involve instances where the movement reported is perceived as *static*. The static feature of the response is usually created by qualifying the percept so as to make it an *abstract*, a *caricature*, or a *picture*. All such responses should be scored *passive* (p) regardless of the description of the movement reported. Most static responses involve inanimate movement such as "an abstract of fireworks exploding to represent the 4th of July" (Card X). The described movement, "exploding" is clearly active but it is qualified by the word "abstract" and thus would be scored m^p. The static feature of movement may, less commonly, occur in either human or animal responses such as "a caricature of two people who are struggling to lift something" (Card III), or "a painting of a lion leaping over something" (Card VIII). These responses would be scored M^p and FM^p, respectively, even though the described movement is active, as each has been qualified as static. The examiner–scorer should be cautious in this type of scoring decision, making sure that the subject has qualified the response rather than simply used a qualifying word as a manner of articulation. It is not uncommon for children and some adults of limited intelligence to use the words "picture" or "painting" in their responses. Differentiation between the static response and the articulation style is sometimes difficult but in most cases of articulation style, the qualifying word will also be used in responses not involving movement.

THE COLOR DETERMINANTS (CHROMATIC)

The scoring criteria for the chromatic color determinants are essentially those of Rorschach. He observed that subjects frequently use color as a factor in their re-

Table 7. Examples of the Three Types of Movement Responses

Card	Location	Response	Scoring
I	D4	A wm stndg w her arms raised	M^p
I	W	Two witches dancing arnd some symbol	M^a
I	W	A bf glidding along	FM^p
I	W	A bat zoomg in to strike	FM^a
I	Dd24	A church bell ringing (Dd 31 is clapper)	m^a
I	W	A fallen leaf disintegrating (S: Ths little pieces out to the sides r prts fallg off)	m^p
II	W	Two clowns dancing in a circus	M^a
II	D3	Menstruation	M^p
II	D6	Two dogs fighting	FM^a
II	D4	An erect penis	M^a
II	DS5	A top spinning	m^a
III	D1	Two people leaning over something	M^p
III	D1	Two people picking something up	M^a
III	D3	A bf flyg between two cliffs	FM^a
III	D2	A bat hanging upside down, asleep	FM^p
III	D2	Blood running down a wall	m^p
IV	W	A man sitting on a stump	M^p
IV	W	A giant looming over you	M^a
IV	D1	A caterpillar crawling along	FM^a
V	W	A bf floating along	FM^p
V	W	Someone dressed up like a bunny doing a ballet dance	M^a
V	W	Two people resting against each other	M^p
VI	D3	An erect penis	M^a
VI	< D4	A ship passing silently in the night	m^p
VI	D11	A speedboat racing up a river	m^a
VII	D2	A little boy looking in the mirror	M^p
VII	∨ W	Two wm dancing	M^a
VIII	Dd	(Half of blot including D1) An animal climbing up something	FM^a
VIII	D4	A frog leaping over something	FM^a
VIII	D5	Two flags waving in the breeze	m^a
IX	W	Intercourse (D9 male, remainder of blot female)	M^a
IX	> D1	A wm running after a child	M^a
IX	∨ W	An atomic explosion	m^a
IX	DS8	A waterfall	m^p
X	D1	A crab grabbing something (D12)	FM^a
X	D2	A collie dog sitting down	FM^p
X	Dd	(Upper D9 each side) Two boys talking to each other	M^a
X	∨ D10	Someone swinging in a swing (D5 is the person, D4 is the swing)	M^a
X	∨ D6	Two people reaching out to each other	M^a
X	W	Fireworks	m^a
X	D7	A deer jumping	FM^a
X	D3	A seed dropping to earth	m^p
X	W	A lot of seaweed floating along	m^p
X	Dd	(Center parts including D9, D3, D6, and D10) A flower that is opening up to the sun	m^p
X	D11	Two animals trying to climb a pole	FM^a

sponses to the five cards which contain chromatic features. He differentiated these responses into three basic categories, (1) those based exclusively on the color features (C), (2) those based primarily on the color features but also involving form (CF), and (3) those based primarily on form but also involving color (FC). He also used a special scoring (CC) in one of his example protocols to note an instance of color naming. Each of the Rorschach systematizers has incorporated Rorschach's three basic scoring categories for chromatic color responses into their respective systems and have generally maintained the same criteria. Klopfer has deviated to some extent from Rorschach's criteria by requiring that C, the pure color response, be used only when the response is "repetitive." This requirement, which is much more stringent than Rorschach's or any of the other systematizers, excludes the use of C for many responses which would be scored C in the other systems. Consequently, Klopfer scores CF in many instances where others would score C. Klopfer also restricts the scoring of FC to responses that include objects of a specific form; thus some responses that the other systems would score FC are scored CF in the Klopfer method.

Each of the systematizers, except Beck, has also proliferated the chromatic color scoring categories somewhat extensively. Special scorings for "color projection," "color denial," "crude color," "color description," "color symbolism," "arbitrary color," and "forced color" are found in the various systems. All of the systems except Beck also include a scoring for color naming, although the criterion varies from system to system with two, Piotrowski and Hertz, requiring that the subject make it known that no further interpretation is intended to those areas of the blot named. Klopfer and Rapaport simply require that the color naming be intended as a response.

The decision to include only four scoring categories for chromatic color responses in the comprehensive system is based on three factors. First, there is no substantial research to support special scorings for the variety of proliferated categories. There is some work concerning the incidence of "crude" color responses in the protocols of seriously disturbed subjects, however, similar findings have been reported when the same types of response are scored C. Second, 94 of the 111 ABPP survey respondents report that they do not differentiate chromatic color responses beyond the four categories selected. Finally, a sampling of 300 protocols, taken and scored by the Klopfer, Hertz, Piotrowski, or Rapaport methods, yields an extremely low frequency of scores for the proliferated categories. This sample contained more than 8000 responses and only two of the categories show a frequency greater than 10 (color symbolism = 19; arbitrary color = 13). Obviously, the types of color response represented by the proliferated categories are important, but their interpretive significance can be incorporated into the qualitative evaluation of the record quite easily, thereby avoiding unnecessary scorings in the quantitative summary.

THE PURE COLOR RESPONSE (C)

The C response is based exclusively on the chromatic features of the blot. It occurs with least frequency of any of the three basic types of color answers and is identified by the complete lack of form. The decision to score pure C is usually based on the fact that color alone has been specified or implied in the Free Association with no attempt to articulate form features. Among the more common examples of the pure *C* response are blood, paint, water, and ice cream. Any of these might be articulated in such a manner as to include form, such as "blood running down" (Card III), and when such an articulation occurs the scoring is *CF* rather than *C*. In that the clarification of the use of color is not commonly offered during the Free Association, it is especially important that the Inquiry be nondirective. It is unfortunate, but not uncommon among careless examiners, when Inquiry questions preceding those to an apparent pure *C* response shape a subject's answers to form; therefore, when the pure *C* response is inquired, some form is included with the subject's clarification. The examiner–scorer must rely on the "spontaneity" of the Inquiry material and, for responses such as "blood" given in the Free Association, the *C* should be scored unless a form clarification is spontaneously offered *at the onset of the Inquiry*. Ordinarily, when a pure color response has been given in the Free Association, the subject simply verifies the location of his answer at the onset of the Inquiry. Conversely, where form has also been involved, the subject usually concentrates on the form features at the onset of the Inquiry. Two similar responses, extracted from the protocol pool, serve as good examples. Both are whole responses to Card X.

FREE ASSOCIATION	INQUIRY
X Gee, a lot of paint	*E:* (Rpts *S*'s response)
	S: Yeah, all over like somebody thru a lot of paint there
	E: Why paint?
	S: All those colors, that's like paint

In this response the absence of form is implied in the Free Association and confirmed immediately in the Inquiry, and a score of *C* is appropriate. The second example is somewhat different even though the Free Association is extremely similar.

FREE ASSOCIATION	INQUIRY
X Oh, a lot of paint	*E:* (Rpts *S*'s response)
	S: Yes, all of it ll an abstract of some sort
	E: An abstract?
	S: Yes, it's the same on both sides as if to give each of the colors a double meaning, as if the painter was trying to convey s.t. by the design that he selected which is very pretty by the way

In this response the subject spontaneously injects the form features of the blot at the onset of the Inquiry. In most instances, the form quality of the blot would have been implied in the Free Association such as "oh, an abstract painting," but this particular subject did not do so. Assuming that there has been no set offered by the examiner during the Inquiry which would produce a form orientation, this response would be scored *CF* rather than *C*. It has been suggested previously that questionable *M* responses might best be decided in light of the overall record. This principle also holds for the scoring of questionable *C* responses; namely, if other pure *C* responses have occurred, the questionable response should probably be scored *C* and vice versa.

THE COLOR-FORM RESPONSE (*CF*)

The *CF* response is one based primarily on the color features of the blot and which also includes reference to form. These are very often answers, the content of which does not require a specific form. In many instances, the presence of form articulation differentiates them from pure *C* responses as in "two scoops of ice cream sherbet" (Card VIII), or "orange flames from a forest fire" (Card IX). In other responses, the vagueness of form articulation differentiates them from the *FC* type answer as in "a lot of flowers" (Card X). Most flower responses are *FC* because the form characteristics such as petals, leaves, and stems are mentioned. In the example above, however, the subject offers no further form differentiation in the Inquiry ("Yeah, just a lot of different colored flowers). The distinction of *CF* from *FC* is often difficult for Rorschach scorers because of the vagueness or inarticulation of subjects. A seemingly large number of *CF* responses involve objects which have ambiguous form requirements such as lakes, maps, meat, foliage, minerals, or underwater scenes. Any of these contents can be scored *FC* if the subject provides sufficient justification by his emphasis on form. Conversely, many responses, such as the example used to Card X, which carry specific form requirements, and which usually will be scored *FC* when color is used, might be scored *CF* if form is deemphasized by the subject.

Some Rorschach authorities, such as Klopfer and Hertz, have suggested a more definitive criterion for differentiating *FC* from *CF* by using the form requirements of the content as a guide. Thus all flowers, which have a relatively common form are scored *FC*, while all lakes, which have only ambiguous form requirements, are scored *CF*. While the intent of these scoring differentiations is clearly worthwhile, the logic is not altogether sound, for it assumes that all subjects interpret color equally if they use the same content. This is probably no more the case for differentiating *CF* from *FC* than it would be for differentiating *C* from *CF*. Consequently, the articulation of the subject must be weighed carefully and a cautious but nondirective Inquiry is always in order. Where doubt remains, the examiner may choose a testing-of-limits or, more preferably, use the remainder of the protocol as a basis for decision making.

THE FORM-COLOR RESPONSE (*FC*)

The *FC* response represents the most controlled use of color. It involves an answer where the form features of the blot are primary in forming the percept and color is also used for purposes of elaboration or clarification. The overwhelming majority of *FC* responses have specific form such as in "a red butterfly" (Card III), "an anatomy chart with the lungs (*D*1), the rib cage and the lower organs" (Card VIII), or "daffodils" (Card X). These form features are also given considerable elaboration, either in the Free Association or in the Inquiry. Some inarticulate subjects do not offer much elaboration regarding form features but do mention color. Here, as with decisions about other determinants, the total protocol proves a useful guide and the limited articulation will be noted in noncolor responses. If the issue remains in doubt, a conservative approach to scoring *CF* versus *FC* is in order, since one is generally interpreted to mean a more limited affective control than the other. In either instance, it is quite important that the *FC* score *not be rejected* simply because the content reported does not have a specific form requirement. Numerous contents of ambiguous form requirement such as anatomy, foliage, sea animals, and even blood cells can be offered in a manner which emphasizes the form features while also including reference to color. In such cases, the score is *FC*.

THE COLOR NAMING RESPONSE (*Cn*)

Rorschach gave little attention to color naming other than to score it *CC* and to note that he observed it in the records of deteriorated epileptics. Piotrowski (1936) introduced the use of the symbol *Cn* for color naming in his studies of the protocols of organics. He does not consider it to be a genuine color response but rather an acknowledgement of the presence of color. The research which has been reported on color naming suggests that it can be an important diagnostic clue and that it does occur with sufficient frequency among the more severely disturbed to warrant special scoring. The criterion adopted for *Cn* in the comprehensive system follows Klopfer and Rapaport; that is, that it is intended as a response. The added qualification suggested by Piotrowksi and Hertz that the subject makes no further attempt at meaningful interpretation to the blot areas named seems too restrictive and, in some instances, prohibits a *Cn* scoring when *Cn* has actually occurred. Naturally, it is important that *Cn*, as is the case with any other unique or dramatic response, be interpreted in the context of the total configuration of the protocol. Thus, a *Cn* response followed by a *CF* response, using the same or nearly the same blot areas, will be interpreted differently than will be a *Cn* which is the only response given to a card. In either instance, the *Cn* should be scored, provided that the subject actually identifies one or more chromatic areas by name (red, green, blue, etc.) and intends that identification as a response. The examiner–scorer should not confuse occasional spontaneous comments which some subjects give when presented with chromatically colored cards, with color naming. Comments such as "Oh, how pretty," or "My, look at all the colors," *are not* color naming. They are interpretively important comments but should not be considered as the same, or even similar, to the *Cn* answer. Most *Cn* responses are given with an almost mechanical or detached flavoring manifesting the difficulties which the subject has in cognitively integrating the complex stimulus material.

Some examples of the four types of chromatic color responses are provided in Table 8. The Inquiry material included consists *only* of that which is relevant to the scoring decision, so that in some instances, the Inquiry is omitted and in other instances only a portion of the Inquiry is shown.

The decision to score color is sometimes complicated by the approach of the subject to the test. Under ideal conditions, subjects will identify color responses by a statement, such as "It looks like that because of the color." Unfortunately, many subjects are not that cooperative or articulate. For example, a subject may give a response such as "blood" to the D3 area of Card III. When the response is inquired he may state, "Yes, here in this red part." The question is legitimately raised concerning the necessity to inquire further to verify the actual use of color. It is indeed, a rare subject who would give a blood response to a red area and then deny that color was influencial; however, it does happen occasionally. These rare instances do necessitate some inquiry approach by the examiner to establish the fact that color is used. It is *not*, however, necessary for the examiner to repeat the same Inquiry routine to evoke the word "color" to every response which apparently involves color. The skilled examiner will detect the pattern of articulation early in the Inquiry, and it is appropriate for him to use that information wisely in forming subsequent Inquiry questions. The use of good judgement by the examiner will save both time and probably avoid some irritation to the subject. Thus if a subject gives several color responses in a protocol but does not articulate the word color easily in the Inquiry, the examiner should rely on the consistency of articulation as a guide once the color element has been established as being important. This is not to imply that color should be automatically assumed in one response because it has been used in another response for that should never be the case. It is, however,

Table 8. **Examples of the Four Types of Chromatic Color Responses**

Card	Location	Free Association		Inquiry	Scoring
II	D3	This red ll blood	S:	Its all redish	C
II	D3	A red bf			FC
II	D2	A fire, like a bonfire	S:	Well its all red like a bonfire sort of blazing upward	CF
II	W	Two clowns, in a circus	S:	I thought of a circus because of the red hats	FC
III	D2	Bad meat	S:	The color makes it look spoiled to me	C
III	∨D2	Blood running down a wall or s.t.	S:	Its red & u can c it like its running down	CF
III	D3	A hair ribbon	S:	Its a pretty red one	FC
VIII	W	A dead animal	S:	It looks like the insides, all decayed	CF
			E:	Decayed?	
			S:	Yes all the different colors ll decay & u can c some bones	
VIII	D5	Two blue flags			FC
VIII	W	Pink and orange & blue			Cn
VIII	D4	A frog	S:	Well the legs r out & it has a froggy like body & it has a froggy like color to it	FC
VIII	D2	An ice cream sundae	S:	It ll orange & raspberry ice cream, like two scoops	CF
IX	W	A forest fire	S:	Well the fire here (D3) is coming up over ths trees & stuff	CF
			E:	Trees & stuff?	
			S:	C, the green here cld b trees & ths other cld b bushes	

Table 8 (Continued)

Card	Location	Free Association		Inquiry	Scoring
IX	D9	Pink here	S:	Right down here	Cn
IX	D4	A newborn baby	S:	U can c the head, that's all, it must b newborn because its pinkish	FC
IX	∨ W	An atomic explosion	S:	The top prt is the mushroom cld & dwn here the orange is the fire blast & the green area cld b smoke	FC
X	∨ D4	A seahorse	S:	It has that shape & its green	FC
X	D9	Coral	S:	Its colored like coral	C
X	W	Some sort of really neat abstract	S:	Well the artist has taken pains to make it the same on both sides & then he's represented his different thoughts with different colors, really neat	FC
X	W	An abstract painting of some kind	S:	Just a lot of colors to represent an abstract thought I guess, its pretty good	CF
X	D13	A potato chip	S:	Well it's kind of shaped like a potato chip & it has the same color as one	FC
X	D15	A flower	S:	I don't kno what kind, it is a pretty yellow, there isn't much of a stem tho u can only c the flower part itself, like the petals and that	FC
X	D12	A leaf	S:	Its green like a leaf	CF

necessary for the examiner to manifest some flexibility in his communications with the subject. The inflexible examiner takes the risk of creating a "color set" for the subject so that, as the questioning is repeated and prolonged, the tendency to articulate color to the last three cards is exaggerated, and color may be offered as an elaboration when, in fact, color was not used in the Free Association.

The examiner–scorer must also be careful not to assume the use of color simply because the subject identifies a location area by its color, as in "This red part looks like a butterfly," or "This blue reminds me of a crab." These *are not* color responses as they stand. Naturally, if there is reason to believe that color might be used, it should be inquired, however, the use of color to specify location should not be confused with the use of color as a response determinant.

THE COLOR DETERMINANTS (ACHROMATIC)

Rorschach did not suggest a special scoring for responses which include the use of achromatic color as color in determining a response. The first formal scoring for these kinds of responses was devised by Klopfer (1938), using the symbol *C'*.

Klopfer's decision to create a separate scoring for the achromatic color response was, at least in part, based on Rorschach's apparent disregard of the determinant, plus the subsequent writing of Binder (1932), who proposed an elaborate system for evaluating "chiaroscuro" responses. Binder, like Rorschach, did not suggest a separate scoring for the achromatic color response, but did imply that they are interpretively different than responses using the light-dark features as "shading." Klopfer defined the C' response as one in which the black, grey, or white areas of the blot are actually used as color. The same scoring and criterion was adopted by Rapaport and variations of it are in the Piotrowski and Hertz systems, each of which has a special scoring depending on which achromatic color is used. Beck has avoided a special scoring for achromatic color responses and instead, includes them in his scoring for shading.

Information from three sources has contributed to the decision to incorporate a separate scoring for achromatic color responses in the comprehensive system. First, 91% of the practitioners reporting in the Exner and Exner (1972) survey, and 101 of the 111 ABPP respondents, use the Klopfer C' symbol and criterion. Second, Campo and de de Santos (1971) offer a strong logical argument for the C' type of score in their excellent review of the various approaches to scoring responses which include the light-dark features of the blots. Third, and possibly most important, is a small but positive accumulation of research findings which indicate that the C' type response, as differentiated from shading responses, does have diagnostic and evaluative importance. The symbols and criteria selected are essentially those of Klopfer and follow on a form related continuum similar to that used for the scoring of chromatic color.

THE PURE ACHROMATIC COLOR RESPONSE (C')

The C' response is one based exclusively on the achromatic features of the blot. It is very uncommon and is identified by the complete absence of form. In some instances, the achromatic color will be used directly in the Free Association, as in "white snow" ($DS5$ area of Card II). In most cases, a formless content is offered in the Free Association and elaborated as having been perceived by the achromatic color in the Inquiry. Two responses, both to Card V, serve as good examples.

FREE ASSOCIATION	INQUIRY
V It ll mud to me	E: (Rpts S's response)
	S: Yeah, it's black
	E: I'm not sure I c it as u do
	S: All of it here, its black just like mud
V Some coal	E: (Rpts S's response)
	S: Its black
	E: Im not sure I c it as u do
	S: It must b coal, its black

In each of these responses the subject has made no effort to develop the form characteristics and, in each case, has offered achromatic color spontaneously. If the second response had been "a piece of coal," accompanied by some attempt at form differentiation, the scoring would not be *C'* but rather *C'F*.

THE ACHROMATIC COLOR-FORM RESPONSE (*C'F*)

The *C'F* response is one based primarily on the achromatic color features and form is used secondarily for purposes of elaboration or clarification. In almost all of these responses it is clear that the answer would not have been formulated without the achromatic features of the blot being involved and the form features are vague and often undifferentiated.

FREE ASSOCIATION	INQUIRY
I A black sky with white clouds	*E:* (Rpts *S*'s response) *S:* Its all black & ths thgs r like white clouds (*DdS* 26)
VII Pieces of black coral	*E:* (Rpts *S*'s response) *S:* There r 4 of them, thyr black like pieces of coral, black coral, they mak jewlry out of it

In the first example the differentiation, by content, of the blackness of the whole blot from the white spaces is a vague form use, sufficient to warrant scoring *C'F* rather than *C'*. In the second example, the differentiation of blot into "pieces" also justified the inclusion of *F* in the scoring. Occasionally, subjects will perceive "smoke" because of the achromatic color and, depending on the extent of form use, the scoring will be *C'* or *C'F*. Most "smoke" responses, however, are perceived because of the shading features rather than the achromatic color and the scoring decision must be formulated carefully, with regard to the report of the subject. It is not uncommon for subjects to use the word "color" to articulate shading features, and, in even more frustrating circumstances for the scorer, subjects may include the specific achromatic element, such as "the blackness of it." This is not necessarily an achromatic color answer and the examiner needs to ensure that it is not simply a way of describing the shading features.

THE FORM-ACHROMATIC COLOR RESPONSE (*FC'*)

The *FC'* response is one in which form is the primary determinant and achromatic color is used secondarily, for elaboration or clarification. It occurs most frequently in the achromatic color responses and is usually easy to identify because of the emphasis on specific form features offered by the subject. Among the more common *FC'* responses are "a black bat" (Cards I and V); "Halloween figures in ghost costumes" (*DdS* 26 area of Card I), clarified as ghost costumes because they are white; "african figures" (Card III), elaborated as being African because they are black; and "a milk bottle" (Center Space area on Card VIII inverted), which is specified to look like a milk bottle because it is white.

The key words on which any of the achromatic color scorings are based are black, white, or grey, as they are used to explain why the object is perceived. In any instance where these words have not been used to specify location or to imply shading, the scoring will be one for achromatic color.

THE SHADING DETERMINANTS

The scoring of responses in which the light-dark features of the blot are used as a determinant has been one of the most controversial aspects of the Rorschach. Although discussed extensively, it has been the least researched of the major determinant categories. It has been previously noted that Rorschach made no mention of shading or "chiaroscuro" features in his original monograph because the cards on which his basic experiment was based contained no variations in hue. These characteristics of the blots were created through a printing error, and according to Ellenberger (1954), Rorschach immediately perceived the possibilities created by the new dimension. Rorschach, during the brief period in which he worked with shaded cards, scored all references to shading as (C) to denote the *Hell-Dunkel* interpretations. Binder (1932) was the first to systematically develop a more extensive scoring for the shading features, following from some of the inferences which had been offered by Rorschach. The Binder approach differentiates four basic types of shading responses but suggests scorings for only two of these. The two which Binder scores are Helldunkel (scored using the symbol *Hd*), which includes answers based on "the diffuse total impression of the light and dark values of the whole card," and *F(Fb)* responses in which shading is differentiated within the blot area used. Binder also noted that subjects sometimes use the shading contour as form-like, or use the light dark features as achromatic color. Since neither meet his criteria for *Hd* or *F(Fb)*, he offers no special scorings for them.

Binder's work has been quite influencial to the decisions of the systematizers in their respective approaches to shading answers. Piotrowski, in addition to scoring for achromatic color, uses two scoring categories for shading responses. One category, scored *c* or *Fc* depending on the degree of form involvement, is used for shading and/or texture responses prompted by the light shades of grey. The second, scored *c'* or *Fc'*, is used where the dark nuances of the blot are involved, or when a dysphoric mood is expressed in the interpretation. The Rapaport system also includes two scoring categories for shading, in addition to scoring for achromatic color. The first category, scored *Ch*, *ChF*, or *FCh*, represents all shading responses except those falling into the second category. The second category, scored *(C)F* or *F(C)*, depending on the use of form, is used for the chiaroscuro answer in which the shading components specify important inner details, or for Color-Form responses which include reference to texture.

The Hertz system also uses the symbols *Ch* and *(C)* but with a considerably different criterion for each than that suggested by Rapaport. Hertz includes three categories of shading response, in addition to scorings for achromatic color. The first, scored *c*, *cF*, or *Fc*, is for responses in which the shading features produce a textural, surface, or reflective quality. The second, employing the symbols *(C)*, *(C)F*, and *F(C)*, is for answers where shading precipitates the interpretation of a three dimensional effect. The third, scored *Ch*, *ChF*, or *FCh*, depending on form involvement, is used for all other shading responses. Beck also uses three scoring categories for shading responses. One category, scored *T*, *TF*, or *FT* depending on form involvement, denotes answers in which the shading features create the impression of texture. The second, scored *V*, *VF*, or *FV*, is for responses in which shading contributes to the interpretation of depth or distance, and the third, scored *Y*, *YF*, or *FY* is used for all other types of shading responses and is also used when achromatic color is involved.

The Klopfer approach to shading is the most complex. Klopfer was actually the first, after Binder, to formulate multiple categories for the scoring and interpretation of shading responses. In addition to creating the *C'* scoring for achromatic color, Klopfer formulated four categories of shading. The first category, scored *c*, *cF*, or *Fc*, is used for responses in which shading is interpreted to represent textural, surface, or reflective qualities. It is the same scoring and criterion incorporated by Hertz into her system and the criterion is nearly the same as used by Beck in his scoring of *T*. The second utilizes the symbols *K* and *KF* to note responses in which the shading is perceived as diffuse. It is very similar to Binder's *Hd*, the Rapaport and Hertz *Ch*, and the Beck *Y*. The third, scored *FK*, represents instances where shading is used for vista, linear perspective, reflections and landscapes. Some components of this criterion are similar to the Hertz use of (*C*) and the Beck *V*. These three shading categories appeared in Klopfer's original 1936 work on scoring. In 1937, Klopfer added a fourth category, scored *k*, *kF*, or *Fk*, and defined as a three dimensional expanse projected on a two dimensional plane. The *k* category, as used in the Klopfer system, applies to x-ray or topographical map responses. The Klopfer approach to the scoring of shading responses is made considerably more complex by a number of idiomatic rules for specific types of responses. The product of these rules is that some responses are provided a shading score, even though the response determinant does not meet the criterion for the scoring category. The majority of these idiomatic rules require the use of the *Fc* score, although some call for the use of *FK*. For example, "transparencies" are scored *Fc*, as are answers in which achromatic color is interpreted as "bright" color. Similarly, most responses which emphasize "roundness" are scored *Fc* rather than *FK*, and *Fc* is also used when the "fine differentiations" in shading are designated to specify parts of objects. The *FK* idioms include both vista and reflection responses *even though* shading is not mentioned.

The selection of scoring symbols and criteria for the coding of shading responses in the comphrehensive system is based on several considerations. The first concerned the possible use of the Klopfer method because it is the most comprehensive. Campo and de de Santos, in their evaluation of the various approaches to the scoring of shading, make a strong logical argument favoring the Klopfer method, but they neglect the complications created by the variety of idiomatic scorings. These scoring idioms not only tend to violate the scoring criteria but also imply the feasibility of interpreting relatively different types of responses as the same. The empirical data available concerning shading responses are somewhat complex, because it is difficult to translate findings derived by one method of scoring to another scoring approach. It is clear, however, that reflection answers are interpretively different from vista responses, and that percepts which include an emphasis on roundness are different from transparencies. A notable lack of empirical support for the separate *k* scoring category also argues against the Klopfer approach.

Data which have been reported suggest that the kind of shading perceived in x-ray responses is different than that used in topographical maps, the former being either achromatic color or diffuse shading, the latter involving the use of shading as vista.[1]

The factors which argue against the Klopfer system also argue in favor of an approach in which the criteria are distinct, which avoids idiomatic scorings, and which neatly differentiates the various types of shading responses. None of the systems accomplish these tasks completely, although the Beck and Hertz approaches to the shading problem are closer to an optimal method than any of the others. Both Beck and Hertz use three basic categories for scoring shading, one for texture, a second for vista, and a third for the general type of shading answer. The three category approach appears clearly preferable to the two category method of Binder, Piotrowski, and Rapaport. The symbols selected for the comprehensive system are those of Beck (T, V, and Y), but the criteria for two of these three is *more restricted* than that suggested by Beck. The V category includes *only* responses in which shading is present, and the Y category *excludes* achromatic color responses. Reflections are also *excluded* from the V scoring. The Beck symbols, rather than those used by Hertz, have been chosen for two reasons. First, most practitioners are familiar with the Beck symbols whereas this is not the case for the Hertz symbols (C) and Ch. Approximately half of the practitioners responding to the Exner and Exner survey expressed competence in the Beck approach versus only 9% who expressed competence in the Hertz system. Similarly, the ABPP survey reveals that approximately 85% understand the Beck criteria for shading responses while only 32% expressed familiarity with the Hertz criteria. Second, the symbol (C) can be confusing, especially to the novice because of its similarity to C and C'. It seems important to emphasize that the two methods are very similar, and in fact, the criteria used in the comprehensive system approximate those of Hertz as much as Beck, possibly even more so.

THE TEXTURE DETERMINANTS

The shading features of the blots are often interpreted to represent "tactual" stimuli. In these types of answers the subject elaborates on the composition or texture of the object. The elaboration carries with it, explicitly or implicitly, the conceptualization that the object is differentiated by its tactual stimulus features such as soft, hard, smooth, rough, silky, grainy, furry, cold, hot, sticky, and greasy. Texture is scored when the shading components of the blot area are used to justify or clarify these kinds of associations. Texture *should not* be assumed simply because words such as those listed above are used. They are legitimate clues to the probability that shading is involved but this is not always the case; thus Inquiry skill of the examiner is often extremely important. It is not uncommon, for example, to obtain responses in which words such as "rough," "shaggy," or "furry" are used as form elaborations, with no concern for shading features. Similarly, objects may be

[1] Klopfer remarked during a 1964 interview with me that he had been continuously dissatisfied with the various criteria for the scoring of shading responses in his system, especially the k category. He quickly added, however, that he felt his own approach was superior to others developed, and expressed the belief that it would be unrealistic to attempt to change his own system in that it had been in use for 30 years by that time.

perceived as "hot" or "cold" because of color. In the optimal situation the subject will reveal his use of shading in the Free Association but this seems to be the exception rather than the rule. All types of shading are the least commonly articulated by subjects in the Free Association. More often than not, the subject will give some clue in the Free Association which should be pursued by the examiner in the Inquiry. As with other determinants, the examiner must remain nondirective. If the articulation of shading does not occur in the Inquiry, a Testing-of-Limits may be advisable for those responses in which the examiner "feels" certain that shading was used, but decisions to score shading reported in the Testing-of-Limits should be made *only* under exceptional circumstances. Above all, the examiner must avoid the use of "leading" questions in the Inquiry, such as "Which side of the skin is up?", which often provoke revelations of texture when in fact, texture was not perceived in the original association. The texture response will be scored in one of three ways depending on the degree of form involvement.

THE PURE TEXTURE RESPONSE (*T*)

The *T* response is the least common of the three kinds of texture scorings. It is used for answers in which the shading components of the blot are represented as "textural" with no form involvement. The criterion for differentiating a *T* from a *TF* answer is essentially the same as for differentiating *C* from *CF*. In other words, no effort is made by the subject to use the form features of the blot, even in a secondary manner. Responses such as "wood, flesh, ice, fleecy wool, grease, hair, and silk" all represent examples which *might* be scored *T* provided shading is involved and has been perceived as texture, *and* no form is used. Where the form configuration of the blot area is included, even though it is relatively ambiguous or formless, the scoring should be *TF* rather than *T*.

THE TEXTURE-FORM RESPONSE (*TF*)

The *TF* response is one in which the shading features are interpreted as texture and form is used secondarily for purposes of elaboration and/or clarification. In most instances the object specified will have an ambiguous form such as "a chunk of ice," "an oily rag," "a piece of fur," or "some very hard metal." Less commonly, a specific form is used but it is clear, from the Free Association or information offered spontaneously in the Inquiry, that the shading features precipitated the response; for example, "Something breaded, like a,—well like shrimp, yeah, that's it, fried shrimp" (Card VII). Usually this response will be scored *FT*, as most subjects giving it emphasize the form features and mention the texture as a clarification. In this example, however, the subject, responds first to the texture and then integrates the form in a meaningful way. The scoring of *TF* for objects of specific form must meet the criterion requirement that the interpretation of shading as texture is primary in the response, and that the form features have been used secondarily in the percept. In most cases, the issue is clarified by the Free Association material, and that must be considered before information given in the Inquiry is weighed. In some situations, the first information given in the Inquiry elaborates shading. This should not automatically be interpreted by the examiner–scorer to mean that shading was perceived as the primary feature in forming the response, particularly if the Free Association is such to suggest that the response might have been form determined. Three very similar responses to Card VI provide examples of how form and texture may vary in importance.

FREE ASSOCIATION	INQUIRY
VI Gee, ths is a funny one, I guess it could b a skin, like an A skin	E: (Rpts S's response)
	S: Well, yeah its all kinda fuzzy like an A skin, ths here cld b legs

In this example, there is no indication in the Free Association material that form has been primary. Quite the contrary, the subject is somewhat vague in the response formulation and uses the word "skin" first, and then clarifying it as an animal skin. In addition, the first material offered in the Inquiry concerns shading ("kinda fuzzy"), and only after that is some reference to form injected. The appropriate scoring for this response is *TF*. In a second example, the response is similar but the scoring is different.

FREE ASSOCIATION	INQUIRY
VI It ll an A skin to me	E: (Repeats S's response)
	S: Well it has a very furry appearance to it and the edging is very rough like an A skin wld b & there is the distinct impression of legs and & the haunch part too

The appropriate scoring for this response is *FT*, even though the shading features are mentioned first in the Inquiry. The decision to score *FT* rather than *TF* is based on the fact that the Free Association is reasonably definitive and *could be* form dominated, and the bulk of the *spontaneously given* Inquiry material is form oriented. The necessity of weighing the possibility of form domination in the Free Association response is demonstrated by a third example.

FREE ASSOCIATION	INQUIRY
VI Well, it cld b an A skin	E: (Rpts S's response)
	S: Yes, its not very well done either, it ll the skinner didn't get as much of the front prt as he could have
	E: I'm not sure what u see that ll an A skin
	S: Well all of it except ths top part looks that way, here r the rear legs & I suppose ths r the ft legs
	E: (Testing-of Limits after all of Inquiry is completed) I'd like to go back to this one. U said an A skin & I'm still not sure I see it the way u did.
	S: Well its very irregular as a skin would be, especially one that wasn't done too well. U see ths r legs (points).

This response involves no shading, or at least the subject has not articulated shading. The total emphasis of the subject is on the form features and the scoring must be *F*. The Rorschach skeptic may argue that, since most animal skin responses to Card VI do involve the use of shading as texture, the scorer would be justified in scoring *FT*, even though it is not articulated. Empirical findings argue against such a procedure. Baughman (1959) obtained animal skin responses to cards presented in silhouette form and to those in which shading features had been eliminated. It has also been demonstrated (Exner, 1961) that the frequency of "skin" responses to Cards IV and VI is not altered if the grey-black features of the cards are made chromatic.

THE FORM-TEXTURE RESPONSE (*FT*)

The *FT* scoring is used for responses in which form is the primary determinant and the shading features, articulated as texture, are used secondarily for purposes of elaboration and/or clarification. Most responses scored as *FT* will involve objects which have specific form requirements. For example, the commonly perceived animals on Cards II and VIII are sometimes elaborated as "furry" because of the light-dark features. Similarly, the human figure often reported to Card IV is frequently perceived as wearing a "fur coat." There is, however, a glaring exception to the guideline that *FT* will ordinarily involve objects of specific form requirement. This occurs in the scoring of animal skin responses to Cards IV and VI. In these instances, the form requirement is much more ambiguous, and yet they represent the most frequently reported "texture" answer. This fact has been determined through the examination of 250 records, randomly selected from the protocol pool. These records contain 5778 responses, of which 375 include a scoring for texture. The frequency of these responses to Cards IV and VI versus the remaining eight cards is shown in Table 9. The responses are sub-divided into two categories, one representing contents of "animal skin" or a close variation, and the second representing other kinds of texture responses.

Table 9. **Distribution of Texture Responses in 250 Protocols**

Scoring	Card IV		Card VI		Other Cards	
	Skin-Like	Other	Skin-Like	Other	Skin-Like	Other
FT	91	4	133	7	9	30
TF	2	7	8	18	5	49
T	1	2	0	1	0	8
Totals	94	13	141	26	14	87

It will be noted that the *FT* score constitutes nearly three-fourths of all the texture answers; however, 224 of the 274 *FT* responses are for animal skins, or similar variations, on Cards IV and VI. Interestingly, if those responses are excluded from the sample, the incidence of *TF* answers is greater than *FT* answers. Similarly, *TF* responses occur to Cards I, II, III, V, VII, VIII, IX, and X with a greater frequency than *FT* responses.

THE SHADING-DIMENSIONALITY DETERMINANTS (VISTA)

The least common use of the light-dark features of the blot involves the interpretation of depth or dimensionality. These responses are marked by the use of the shading characteristics to alter the flat perspective offered by the blot stimulus. The most frequent type of vista response is one in which the contours created by the shading are used as a form dimension, such as in a contour map or an aerial photograph. Less commonly, the shading is used more diffusely to convey the general impression of depth. An example of the "infrequency" of the vista type response is found in a comparison of types of shading responses in the 250 records noted in Table 9 concerning texture responses. Those protocols, representing 5778 responses, contain 375 texture answers, 344 general shading responses, and only 186 vista responses. Three scorings are used for the vista responses.

THE PURE VISTA RESPONSE (V)

The pure V answer is extremely rare. The scoring of V requires that the subject reports depth or dimensionality based exclusively on the shading characteristics of the blot, with no form involvement. These responses, when they occur, are somewhat dramatic because they ignore the form qualities of the stimulus. Some examples are "depth," "perspective," "deepness," and "It's sticking out at me." Any of these or similar responses might have some elaboration which involves the form features of the blot. When this occurs, the scoring is VF rather than V.

THE VISTA-FORM RESPONSE (VF)

The VF responses include primary emphasis on the shading features to represent depth or dimensionality and incorporate the form features of the blot for clarification and/or elaboration. Most VF responses have contents of nonspecific form requirement, such as "one of those maps like you use in a geography class with the mountains and plateaus shown," "rain clouds, one behind the other," or "a deep canyon with a river running in there." If the topographical map were to be more specifically defined, such as "a topographical map of the western part of the United States," or the canyon and river were more specifically defined, as in "an aerial view of the Colorado River," wherein the form features are given greater emphasis, the scoring would be FV rather than VF. The VF score, like the TF score, is contingent on the primary emphasis being given to the shading features.

THE FORM-VISTA RESPONSE (FV)

The FV response is one in which form is the primary feature and the shading component is used to represent depth or dimensionality for purposes of clarification and/or elaboration. Most FV responses will have contents with a relatively specific form requirement but that is not necessarily an adequate guideline for differentiating the FV and VF answers. For example, "a well" has a reasonably specific form requirement, yet most "well" responses are VF rather than FV, the differentiation being based on whether primary emphasis is given to the form characteristics or the shading. The response which is scored *FV* will generally include considerable emphasis or elaboration on form. Almost any content, ranging from frequently perceived human or animal figures to very unusual answers, may involve vista. Bridges, dams, and waterways are among the more frequently given *FV* responses; however, the vista component may be reported in almost any form dominated response. For example, the popular human figure often reported to the center *D* of Card I is sometimes perceived as "behind a curtain" because of the shading differences, or the lower center *D* area of Card IV is often perceived as a worm or caterpillar "coming out from in under a leaf." Both are scored *FV, provided* shading contributes to the percept. The *FV* answer is the most common of the three types of vista. The 186 vista responses tallied from the previously mentioned sample of 250 protocols included 128 *FV*'s, 53 *VF*'s and only 5 pure *V* answers.[2]

Some examples of the different types of texture and vista responses are provided in Table 10. The Inquiry material included consists *only* of that which is directly relevant to the scoring decision; therefore, in some instances the Inquiry is omitted, and in other instances, a portion of the Inquiry is presented.

The differentiation between texture and vista answers is not always precise and can make for difficult scoring decisions. For example, a response such as "the convolutions of the brain" to the center area of Card VI will ordinarily be scored *VF* because of the emphasis on dimensionality. The same response, however, might be elaborated as "It looks bumpy, like if you touched it you could feel the bumps." This elaboration, which emphasizes the tactual interpretation, meets the criterion for the scoring of *TF*. The guideline which should be used for the scoring decision requires consideration of the "interpretive emphasis" offered by the subject. If, in the example cited, the elaboration on "bumpy" features appears to have been injected for purposes of clarification, the scoring remains *VF*. Conversely, if the tactual emphasis is injected in the Free Association, or is offered spontaneously *at the onset* of the Inquiry, the scoring should be *TF*. Fortunately, in most cases, the subject provides material from which the "interpretive emphasis" can be identified easily. For example, "rough mountain peaks" (vista) is easy to differentiate from "a rough piece of sandpaper" (texture). The word "rough" occurs in each, but mountain peaks are not associated tactually, and sandpaper is not perceived dimensionally. In those few responses where doubt may remain after the Inquiry has been completed, the examiner should include a Testing-of-Limits to obtain further information concerning the interpretive emphasis. If that procedure fails to clarify the issue, a second guideline should be employed. This consists of reviewing the remainder of the record with concern for the occurrence of other texture or vista answers. If the record contains no other vista responses but does have texture answers, the texture scoring should be used, and *vice versa*. Accurate scoring of vista and texture is quite important as each carries significantly different interpretive assumptions.

---

[2] The average number of vista responses in these records (.74) is considerably lower than that found by Beck in a sample of 155 adult records (1.84). The difference is apparently created by the fact that many responses scored by Beck as *FV* are scored in the comprehensive system as *FD*. Similarly, Beck includes some types of reflection answers in his *FV* score which are scored separately in the comprehensive system. A difference also occurs in the average reported by Beck for general shading responses in that the comprehensive system includes the *C'* category for achromatic color answers which Beck scores as general shading.

Table 10. Examples of the Different Types of Texture and Vista Responses

Card	Location	Free Association	Inquiry	Scoring
I	W	A dried up leaf	S: Pts r missing & fallg off & its crinkly E: Crinkly? S: It looks rough, the way the colors are there	FT
I	D4	A wm behind a curtain	S: U can't c all of her, just the lowr prt of her body (D3) & ths is like a curtain u can c thru	FV
I	W	An old torn rag w oil spots on it	S: Its all black and oily looking to me	TF
II	D4	A circumcised penis	S: U can c the folds left thr in the cntr	FV
II	D1	A teddy bear	S: It has that shape & it has all that fur ther	FT
II	DS5	Somethg deep, lik a hole mayb	S: U can c the round edges ther, like a bottomless pit, at least I don't c any bottom	VF
III	D1	Two gentlemen in velvet suits	E: U mentioned velvet suits S: Yes, it looks velvet to me, dark shiny velvet	FT
III	D3	A bow tie	S: It has a big bulging knot ther in the middl of it	FV
IV	W	Hunters boots prop'd up against a post	S: The post is behind them u can tell bec it looks further away E: Further away? S: Well u c where they come together the color is different like the post was further back	FV
IV	W	An old bearskin	S: It looks like the fur is pretty well worn	FT
IV	Dd30	A red hot spike	S: Its a lot lighter on the outside like very hot metal	FT
V	W	A person in a fur cape	S: U c mostly the cape, it looks like fur to me (rubs fingers on card)	FT
V	W	It looks sticky if u touched it	S: Ugh, it just ll a sticky mess	T
V	W	The rite half is lower than the left	S: Thers a deep crack rite dwn the cntr & it ll the rite side is lower	V
V	W	A rabbits head behnd a big rock	S: Its here (D6), u can't c much of it, just the outline, the drkr prt is the rock in frt	FV
VI	D1	An irrigation ditch	S: Its dwn in the cntr ther U can c how the diffrnt amounts of waterg have effected the land @ it	FV

Table 10 (Continued)

Card	Location	Free Association	Inquiry	Scoring
VI	D4	A chunk of ice	S: Its cold lookg like ice wld b, all grey	TF
VI	W	A skinned A, the head is still on	S: Most of it ll the furry skin & u can still c the head prt here (points)	FT
VI	∨Center Dd	A deep gorge	S: Ths prt (D12) is the bttm & u can c the sides comg up to the top	VF
VII	>D2	A scotty dog	S: He has more fur on his chin & ft legs, where its drkr	FT
VII	W	Rocks	S: It just ll 4 rocks next to e.o., u can c that they r round, especially the bottom 2	VF
VII	Dd25	It ll a dam back in there	S: Well the dam is here, ths liter prt (Dd25 ceter) & the frt prt is like the water-fall part, or mayb a river comg ths way	FV
VII	∨W	Hair, a lot of hair	S: It all looks hairy to me	T
VIII	D5	An aerial view of a forest	S: Yeah, thes drkr prts wld be the bigger trees stckg up	VF
VIII	D2	Ice cream sherbet	S: It looks grainy like sherbet is grainy	TF
IX	D6	Cotton candy, its al fluffy	S: It has like rolls, like it was fluffy like cotton candy is fluffy	VF
IX	DS8	There's a plant inside a glass	S: U can just c the stem (D5) & it looks hazy like u were seeg it inside the glass or bowl	FV
IX	DS8	Like u were lookg into a cave or s.t.	S: It ll an opening & u can c back into it, like the cave mouth	VF
X	D9	Ths pink part ll a map of a chain of mts	S: Its like a map that is used in schls or s.t. to show the way mts r formed, some r higher than others	VF
X	D13	A piece of leather	S: Its rough, like it hasn't been tanned E: Rough? S: U c the different colors there, they make it ll that	TF
X	D3	A maple seed	S: The pods r a drkr color, like they r thicker, round like	FV

THE GENERAL-DIFFUSE SHADING DETERMINANTS

The second most frequent use of the shading features of the blots is in a nonspecific, more general manner than is the case in either vista or texture answers. It is this type of shading response with which Rorschach concerned himself in developing the scoring of (C). The shading features may be used in this way as primary to the formation of a percept, or secondary to provide greater specification to a form answer. The scoring for general-diffuse shading incorporates all shading answers which are neither vista or texture.

THE PURE SHADING RESPONSE (Y)

The scoring of Y is used for percepts based exclusively on the light-dark features of the blot. No form is involved, and the content used typically has no form feature as in mist, fog, darkness, and smoke. A response in which pure Y is the only determinant is quite rare. It is more common for the contents ordinarily scored pure Y to be integrated into a percept which also contains some form. For example, "A woman standing with her arms raised, and there is smoke all around her" (Card I) contains both M and Y and is scored as a *blend* ($M.Y$). The blend scoring is described in more detail in the next chapter. In this example it denotes that a pure Y response was given in association with a form oriented answer. The scoring of pure Y, as such, indicates that the shading features were used exclusive of the form in the response. Two separate contents, Woman, and Smoke, have been included, and *no effort has been made* to assign form features to the smoke. When form features are assigned to the shading characteristics, the scoring is not pure Y.

THE SHADING-FORM RESPONSE (YF)

The YF response is one in which the light-dark features of the blot are primary to the formation of the response and form is used secondarily for purposes of elaboration and/or clarification. The content of the YF answer ordinarily has an ambiguous or nonspecific form requirement as in clouds, shadows, nonspecific types of x-rays, and smoke associated with a specific form object such as "smoke coming out of this fire." The main factor which differentiates YF from pure Y is the intent of the subject to delineate form features, even though vague, in the response. Similarly, the YF response is usually differentiated from the FY answer by the lack of specificity or emphasis on form. Contents having a specific form requirement are rarely scored YF, occurring only in those cases where the shading features are clearly of primary importance to the formation of the percept.

THE FORM-SHADING RESPONSE (FY)

The FY score is used for responses in which form characteristics are primary to the formation of the percept, and shading is used for purposes of specification and/or elaboration. Silhouettes, specific content x-rays, and elaborations concerning characteristics of form specific objects, such as dirty face or dark suit, are among the more commonly reported *FY* responses. Ordinarily, the *FY* response can be identified by the fact that the content could be given as a pure form response, whereas this is not usually the case in the *YF* or pure *Y* answer. A notable exception to this rule is the "cloud" response *which can be* based purely on form. When the shading features are associated with the cloud answer, the scoring is usually *YF*, but in some instances, such as "cloudiness," the scoring may be pure *Y*, and in other cases where form is strongly emphasized, the scoring may be *FY*.

Some examples of the various types of general-diffuse shading responses are provided in Table 11. The Inquiry material included consists only of that related to the scoring decision.

It is important to emphasize that, at times, the shading features of the blots are used as form contour. For example, the *D3* area of Card I is sometimes perceived as the lower part of a person and delineated by "these dark lines." Similarly, the frequently perceived animal in the *D1* area of Card VIII is sometimes identified as a raccoon because the dark ring around the eye area is noticeable. These *are not* shading responses *per se* and should be scored as form answers. They do have interpretive importance because the subject has chosen to respond to the "internal" form features of the blot, but they should not be confused with the shading answer.

THE FORM-DIMENSIONAL RESPONSE (*FD*)

This is a new scoring category, developed out of the research related to the formation of the comprehensive system. There is no scoring comparable to it in the other Rorschach systems, although both Beck and Klopfer have noted the existence of such answers. Klopfer had idiomatically included such responses in the *FK* category, even though no shading is involved. Beck has been prone to score these answers *FV*, but only in instances where the unarticulated use of shading seems very probable. Beck specifically avoids the scoring of *FV* for perspective or dimensionality based on size discrimination.

The potential usefulness of a separate scoring for dimensional responses based exclusively on form was first noted during some system related research concerning the meaningfulness of vista answers. This research, which is presented in detail in the chapters on interpretation, included examination of 60 protocols obtained from subjects prior to suicide or a suicidal gesture. It was noted that a significant number of form determined dimensional-perspective responses occur in this group when compared with a nonpsychiatric group. A closer inspection of an additional 150 protocols reveals that the *FD* type of answer occurs with considerable frequency in the records of a variety of subjects, both psychiatric and nonpsychiatric. The total number of *FD* answers, tallied from 250 records, is greater than the total number of vista answers (186 vista answers and 243 *FD* answers). Subsequently, a more detailed evaluation of these records, plus an additional 30 protocols collected specifically to investigate the interpretive usefulness of the *FD* scoring, yielded data suggesting that the *FD* response may be quite meaningful. When it is interpreted in the context of other information in the protocol, it appears related to factors such as introspectiveness, distanciation, and self-awareness. In view of these findings, the separate scoring of *FD* has been selected for use in the comprehensive system.

Table 11. Examples of General-Diffuse Shading Responses

Card	Location	Free Association		Inquiry	Scoring
I	W	An x-ray of a pelvis			FY
I	<D8	A Xmas tree at night	S:	Its dark like it wld b at night	FY
I	W	Ink	S:	It's just all dark like ink is dark[a]	Y
II	D3	A very delicate bf	E:	U mentioned that it is delicate	FY
			S:	You can c the differnt colors, their shades I guess, in the wgs	
II	D4	A church steeple	S:	It looks like light is in the top, it's lighter there as if the sun was shining on it	FY
III	D7	Some sort of x-ray	S:	It is different colors like an an x-ray	YF
IV	W	Darkness	S:	It just ll darkness to me, I can't tell u why	Y
IV	D3	A multi-colored flower	S:	It has different colors in it, like the petals r a different color fr the middle part	FY
V	W	A piece of rotten meat	S:	Some of it is more rot'd than the rest	YF
			E:	More rotted?	
			S:	The colors r different	
VI	D2	A highly polished bedpost	S:	Its very shiny lookg	FY
VI	D4	It ll a sailing ship cruising in the nite	S:	Its all dark so it must be in the nite	FY
VII	W	It could be clouds I guess	S:	Its pretty irregular like clouds would be & it has sort of a lite color to it like clouds, mayb like cumulus clouds	FY
VII	W	Storm clouds	S:	They'r dark like a storm cloud formation is dark	YF
VII	D2	A granite statue	S:	Its dark like granite	FY
VIII	D1	An animal with dirt all over its face	S:	This drkr part is the circle around the eye like dirt, ther's more there too, more dirt	FY
IX	∨W	A lot of smoke and fire	S:	The orange part is the fire & the rest is the smoke, u can see how the colors go together	CF.YF
X	D11	Some bones that r drying out	S:	It ll bones drying up, ths prt is lighter so it must be drier	YF

[a] Had the subject indicated that it is *black* like ink the scoring would be C'.

The *FD* is scored for responses which include perspective or dimensionality based *exclusively* on form, interpreted by size or in relation to other blot areas. The most common *FD* is the Card IV human figure, seen as "leaning backward," or "lying down." The elaboration to this response usually includes mention that the "feet" portion is much larger; thus the head must be further away. While the *FD* response occurs most frequently to Card IV, it has been noted in every card. In some answers, such as "leaning backward" on Card IV, another determinant is involved, but in most instances only the form features are used. Some examples of *FD* responses are provided in Table 12.

Many of the examples offered in Table 12 are of responses in which the dimensionality or perspective is based on the size of the blot area used. In other instances, the relationship between two blot areas creates the effect, wherein the "absence" of features is interpreted to support a percept of dimensionality or perspective. For example, the response to Card V, shown in Table 12, notes the leg of an animal is showing while the larger portion of the blot is interpreted as a bush. The interpretation is of an animal jumping behind a bush because only the leg is obvious. Whether or not this is the same type of percept as "a person lying down" to Card IV is still open to investigation. At this time, it seems appropriate to score both responses as *FD* because both imply perspective. Additional research, however, is obviously necessary before the full importance of these kinds of responses is understood, and before the criterion adopted for the scoring of *FD* is finalized.

PAIR AND REFLECTION RESPONSES

Another scoring category incorporated in the comprehensive system, which is not found in any of the other Rorschach systems, is related to the reflection response. This category, like the *FD* scoring, was somewhat accidentally discovered during and investigation regarding "acting out" which was conducted during 1966 and 1967. In that investigation, which included the collection of a large number of protocols from patients in an installation for the "criminally insane," it was noted that overt homosexuals and "psychopaths" tend to offer a significantly greater number of reflection responses than do other psychiatric subjects or nonpsychiatric subjects. Originally, these data were interpreted as an index of "narcissism" (Exner, 1969, 1970); however, because of the complexity of the concept narcissism, it seems more appropriate to use the concept of "egocentricity." A sentence completion test, patterned after one developed by Watson (1965), was developed to study the characteristic of egocentricity in greater detail, and to relate those findings to the occurrence of reflection answers in the Rorschach. This work has confirmed a high correlation between a high "self-centeredness" score on the sentence completion blank and the reflection answer in the Rorshach. A variety of independent measures of egocentricity, or self-centeredness have been used, and the results seem to clearly indicate that subjects who are highly egocentric or self-focusing tend to give significantly more reflection responses than do subjects who are not highly egocentric. These types of reflection answers are based *on the symmetry of the blot*, and are different from the extremely rare reflection answer which does not use symmetry. The nonsymmetrical reflection ordinarily involves shading, and thus is usually scored either *V* or *Y*.

Table 12. Examples of Form-Dimensional Responses

Card	Location	Free Association		Inquiry	Scoring
I	$<D2$	A tree off on a hill	S:	Its a lot smaller so it must be far off	FD
II	$D4 + DS5$	Some sort of temple at the end of a lake	S:	This ($DS5$) is the lake & here ($D4$) is the temple, u have to thk of it in perspective	FD
III	$\vee D12$	Two trees off on a hill with a path leading up to them	S:	These ($D4$) r the trees & this ($D11$) is the path	FD
			E:	U said off on a hill	
			S:	It doesn't hav to b a hill, its just that they'r small & the path is pretty wide so they r off a ways	
IV	W	A person laying down	S:	His feet r out in front, like toward me & his head is way bk there, like he was flat on his back	$M^p.FD$
V	$D4$	An animal jumping behnd a bush, u only c his leg	S:	Well here is where the bush ends & ths is the leg so it has to be behind	$FM^a.FD$
VI	W	A religious statue on a hill-top	S:	Well its a lot smler so it wld b off in the distance like ths cld b a hill here if u stretch u'r immagin	FD
VII	$D8$	A city off in the distance	S:	U can c the bldgs there	FD
			E:	U said off in the distn.	
			S:	Its so small, it must b a long ways off	
VIII	$D4$	Two people stndg off on a hill	S:	U can c the people here ($Dd24$) & this wld b the hill	$M^p.FD$
IX	$<Dd26$	A person stndg out on a ledge	S:	Yeah, here's a ledge (most of $D3$) & there's this person way out there, leaning up against a tree or s.t., its quite far out there	$M^p.FD$
			E:	Quite far?	
			S:	He's so small, it's fairly hard to even see him	
X	$\vee D6$	Two men pushing s.t. out in front of them	S:	Their bodies r shaped like they were bending forward & their arms r extended outward like they were pushing this thing in front of them	$M^a.FD$

Numerous studies have been completed to validate the usefulness of the sentence completion blank as an index of egocentricity (Exner, 1973), and to investigate the reflection answer in more detail. During the course of these investigations, which are described in detail in the chapters on interpretation, a second Rorschach phenomenon was discovered which appears to be related to the reflection answer. This is the *pair* response, in which the perceived object is reported as two identical objects because of the card symmetry. The pair type of response occurs with considerable frequency in most records, usually including about one-third of the responses. The pair frequency increases significantly in the more egocentric subjects and is almost nonexistent in the protocols of subjects who have little regard for themselves.

The selection of appropriate scoring symbols to record the reflection and pair answers created some problem for, like the *FD* answer, they are based on the form of the blot, and yet the form is used somewhat differently than in selection of content. Beck and Klopfer had each suggested that reflections be scored as a type of vista answer, although Beck cautioned against scoring reflections based on card symmetry as *FV*. Hertz, like Beck, scores reflections based on shading as a shading response, and those based on symmetry as form answers. Obviously, the symmetry reflection requires a different scoring symbol than is used in the shading answer. The symbol *r* seems a logical choice. The symbol selected for scoring the pair response is the Arabic numeral 2. Since the pair answer occurs with considerable frequency, it was decided that the scoring should be entered apart from the regular determinant scoring and in parentheses, so as to avoid "cluttering" the determinant scoring and also to make the number of pair answers easy to tabulate for the scoring summary. There is only one scoring for the pair answer (2), while two scorings are used for different types of reflection answers.

THE REFLECTION-FORM RESPONSE   (*rF*)

The *rF* scoring is used for responses in which the symmetry features of the blot are primary in determining the answer, and form is used nonspecifically, or ambiguously, as an object being reflected. The *rF* type of reflection is very uncommon, and always involves content with nonspecific form requirements such as clouds, rocks, shadows, and rain. In some instances, the subject may select a content which is nonspecific in form requirements, but provides sufficient articulation of the perceived object to warrant the scoring of *Fr* rather than *rF*. The most common example of this is when landscape is perceived as being reflected in a lake or pond. In almost all of these cases the appropriate scoring is *Fr*.

THE FORM-REFLECTION RESPONSE (*Fr*)

The *Fr* is scored for responses in which the form of the blot is used to identify specific content, which, in turn, is interpreted as reflected because of the symmetry of the blot. In many cases, movement is also associated with the reflection as in "a girl seeing herself in the mirror." The critical issue in scoring either *rF* or *Fr* is that the subject *uses* the concept of reflection. This may be manifest directly through the use of the word "reflection" or it may be implied by other wording such as "mirror image," and "seeing himself in the lake." The identification of "one on each side" or "there is two of them" *is not a reflection* answer and is scored simply as a pair response.

THE PAIR RESPONSE (2)

The scoring symbol (2) is used whenever the symmetry features of the blot precipitate the report that "two" of the perceived object are present. The pair is independent of form specificity or the form quality used in the answer. The pair scoring of (2) *is not* used when the object is interpreted as being reflected, as the reflection scoring already denotes that two of the object are being seen. The articulation of pairs varies considerably among subjects. Some will actually use the word "pair," but more commonly the word "two" is used, and in many responses, the subject comments, "There is one here and one here." The pair scoring is used *only* when the symmetry is involved; thus clarification of the location areas used is important. It is not uncommon, for example, for a subject, looking at Card X, to report, "A couple of bugs." The response appears to be a pair but, the Inquiry reveals that he is using the upper *D*1 area as one bug, and the side *D*7 area as a second bug.

Some examples of pair and reflection responses are provided in Table 13. It will be noted that either the reflection or pair answers can occur in responses which have other determinants as well.

Table 13.   **Examples of Reflection and Pair Responses**

Card	Location	Free Association	Inquiry		Scoring
I	<*D*2	A couple of donkeys, there's one on each side			$F(2)$
I	*D*1	Two little birds who r peeking their heads out of a nest			$FM^a (2)$
II	<*D*6	A rabbit sliding on an ice pond, he's being reflected in the ice	S:	Ths white is the ice & u can c his reflection in it	$FM^a.Fr$
II	*W*	Two bears doing a circus act	S:	They have red hats on like a circus act & they have their paws touchg	$FM^a.FC (2)$
III	*D*1	Two people picking s.t. up			$M^a (2)$
III	*D*1	A person inspecting himself in the mirror	S:	He's bending forward like he's looking at himslf	$M^p.Fr$
IV	<*W*	If u turn it ths way it ll a reflection of s.t., mayb a cloud	S:	Well all of ths on one side is being reflected here, its like a cloud I guess	$YF.rF$
			E:	I'm not sure how u c it as a cloud	
			S:	Well its all dark like a cld at nite. There's not much shape to it	

Table 13 (Continued)

Card	Location	Free Association	Inquiry	Scoring
IV	D6	A pair of boots		F (2)
V	W	Two people laying back to back		M^p (2)
VI	>W	All of ths is the same down here	S: I don't kno what it is, mayb rocks of s.t., it's the same on both sides like a reflection	rF
VI	<D1	It ll a submarine in the nite being reflected in the water	S: Its all black like nitetime, u can c the conning tower & the hull & here its all reflected	FC'.Fr
VII	D2	Ths ll a little girl, there's one on each side		F (2)
VII	D2	A little girl looking in the mirror		M^p.Fr
VIII	D5	A pair of flags		F (2)
VIII	<W	An A crossing over some rocks or s.t. like in a creek, u can c his reflection there, he's looking down at it		FM^a.Fr
IX	<D5	Its like u r out in the water & u can c ths coastline off in the distance	S: Well, its being reflected in the water, c here is the waterline (points to midline), its all so small it must b way off in the dist. U really can't make much out, mayb some trees or s.t. like that	FD.rF
IX	D3	Two halloween witches	S: They r colored like for halloween, all orangish & they'r leaning back like they r laughing	M^a.FC (2)
X	D1	A couple of crabs	S: There's one on each side, they'r the same on both sides	F (2)
X	D7	Deer, like they'r jumping	S: One here & one here, they'r the same, w. their legs outstretched like they were jumpg	FM^a (2)

SUMMARY

The 24 scoring symbols representing the nine scoring categories constitute the basis of the comprehensive system. Each represents a particular type of cognitive-perceptual organization of the stimulus features of the blots, and each appears to be related to particular response features or styles of the person. Evaluated separately, none provide exacting correlations with behavior or personality characteristics; however, studied in configuration, they represent a composite caricature of the preferences for behavioral response. Among the several goals considered relevant to the selection of these categories and scoring symbols is the premise that each can be subjected to further investigation and evaluation, separately and collectively. One of the more interesting areas of study, which has generally been neglected in Rorschach research, is that of the response which contains multiple determining characteristics, as these kinds of answers occur with considerably greater frequency than had been implied by Rorschach, or than has been discussed by the various systematizers. A second, and possibly even more important area of study which has been generally neglected in the Rorschach research efforts, encompasses the "perceptual" relationships which may exist between determinants. Hopefully, the selection of criteria for each of the nine scoring categories and the 24 scoring symbols provides a discriminant base from which such studies can evolve. In this context, the conscientious scorer will manifest a high reliability with other scorers. The end product of this process is an accurate "scoring summary" from which the interpreter is able to make useful and valid statements concerning the subject.

REFERENCES

Baughman, E. E. An experimental analysis of the relationship between stimulus structure and behavior on the Rorschach. *Journal of Projective Techniques*, 1959, **23**, 134–183.

Beck, S. J. *Introduction to the Rorschach Method: A manual of Personality Study*. American Orthopsychiatric Association Monograph, 1937, No. 1.

Beck, S. J. *Rorschach's Test: Basic Processes*. New York: Grune and Stratton, 1944.

Beck, S. J., Beck, A. G., Levitt, E. E., and Molish, H. B. *Rorschach's Test. I: Basic Processes*. (3rd ed.) New York: Grune and Stratton, 1961.

Binder, H. Die Helldunkeldeutuntungen im psychodiagnostischen experiment von Rorschach. *Schweizer Archiv fur Neurologie und Psychiatrie*, 1932, **30**, 1–67; 233–286.

Campo, V., and de de Santos, D. R. A critical review of the shading responses in the Rorschach I: Scoring problems. *Journal of Personality Assessment*, 1971, **35**, 3–21.

Ellenberger, H. The life and work of Hermann Rorschach. *Bulletin of the Menninger Clinic*, 1954, **18**, 173–219.

Exner, J. E. Achromatic color in Cards IV and VI of the Rorschach. *Journal of Projective Techniques*, 1961, **25**, 38–40.

Exner, J. E. *The Rorschach Systems*. New York: Grune and Stratton, 1969.

Exner, J. E. Rorschach responses as an index of narcissism. *Journal of Projective Techniques and Personality Assessment*, 1969, **33**, 324–330.

Exner, J. E. Rorschach manifestations of narcissism. *Rorschachiana*, 1970, **IX**, 449–456.

Exner, J. E., and Exner, D. E. How clinicians use the Rorschach. *Journal of Personality Assessment*, 1972, **36**, 403–408.

Exner, J. E. The self focus sentence completion: A study of egocentricity. *Journal of Personality Assessment*, 1973, **37**, 437–455.

Hertz, M. R. *Frequency Tables for Scoring Rorschach Responses*. Cleveland, Ohio: The Press of Western Reserve University, 1942.

Hertz, M. R. *Frequency Tables for Scoring Rorschach Responses*. (3rd ed.) Cleveland, Ohio: The Press of Western Reserve University, 1951.

Hertz, M. R. *Frequency Tables for Scoring Rorschach Responses*. (5th ed.) Cleveland, Ohio: The Press of Case Western Reserve University, 1970.

Klopfer, B., and Sender, S. A system of refined scoring symbols. *Rorschach Research Exchange*, 1936, **1,** 19–22.

Klopfer, B. The shading responses. *Rorschach Research Exchange*, 1937, **2,** 76–79.

Klopfer, B., and Miale, F. An illustration of the technique of the Rorschach: The case of Anne T. *Rorschach Research Exchange*, 1938, **2,** 126–152.

Klopfer, B., and Kelley, D. *The Rorschach Technique*. Yonkers-on-Hudson, N.Y.: World Book Company, 1942.

Klopfer, B., Ainsworth, M., Klopfer, W., and Holt, R. *Developments in the Rorschach Technique. I: Theory and Technique*. Yonkers-on-Hudson, N.Y.: World Book Company, 1954.

Piotrowski, Z. On the Rorschach method and its application in organic disturbances of the central nervous system. *Rorschach Research Exchange*, 1936, **1,** 23–40.

Piotrowski, Z. The M, FM, and m responses as indicators of changes in personality. *Rorschach Research Exchange*, 1937, **1,** 148–157.

Piotrowski, Z. A Rorschach compendium. *Psychiatric Quarterly*, 1947, **21,** 79–101.

Piotrowski, Z. *Perceptanalysis*. New York: Macmillan Company, 1957.

Rapaport, D., Gill, M., and Schafer, R. *Diagnostic Psychological Testing*. Vol. 2. Chicago: Yearbook Publishers, 1946.

Rorschach, H. *Psychodiagnostik*. Bern: Bircher, 1921.

Rorschach, H., and Oberholzer, E. The application of the form interpretation test. *Zeitschrift fur die Gesamte Neurologie und Psychiatrie*, **82,** 1923.

Watson, A. Objects and objectivity: A study in the relationship between narcissism and intellectual subjectivity. Unpublished Ph.D. Dissertation, University of Chicago, 1965.

CHAPTER 6

Blends, Organizational Activity, and Form Quality

Three very important elements, for which all Rorschach responses must be evaluated, are (1) the blend, wherein two or more determinants have been used for an answer, (2) the organizational activity, which represents those responses in which some synthesis of the blot stimuli has occurred, and (3) the form quality, which is an evaluation of the "fitness" of the blot features to the object described. Each of these response characteristics carries considerable interpretive significance, especially because they are *not common* to all responses. A relatively small proportion of the answers in most records have multiple determinants. Similarly, it is unusual to find a large proportion of the responses marked by the synthesis features of organizational activity. Conversely, most responses can be evaluated for form quality. These response features often yield important data concerning the idiographic dimensions of the subject; thus accurate evaluation of responses for their presence is vital.

THE BLEND RESPONSE (.)

The term "blend" signifies that more than one scorable determinant has been used in the formulation of a response. When this occurs, each determinant should be entered in the determinant scoring, separated from each other by a dot (.), as in, $M.YF$ which represents the answer containing both human movement and a shading-form component. The frequency of blend responses varies considerably from record to record. A sample of 200 protocols, for example, shows that slightly more than 15% of the responses are blends, but the variance is considerable, with some records yielding nearly 50% blends and others containing no blend answers. Any combination of determinants is theoretically possible in a percept, and each should be scored. The majority of blend answers contain two determinants, but in very unusual instances three, and even four, separate determinants may be noted.

There has been some disagreement among the Rorschach systematizers concerning the appropriate method for scoring and evaluating the blend answer. Most have followed Rorschach's lead in the scoring procedure. He simply scored multiple determinants together when they occurred, as in MC (1921). The protocols published by Rorschach contain relatively few blend responses, mainly because his basic work was accomplished using blots which contained no shading features. Klopfer (1942, 1954) has deviated most from Rorschach's approach to the multiple determined responses. He has postulated that only one determinant can be "primary" to the formation of a percept, and recommends that the scoring be subdivided so as to represent the "Main" or primary determinant, with other determinants being scored as "Additional." Accordingly, Klopfer weighs the interpretive importance of the Main determinants differently than Additionals. This procedure is possibly one of the major limitations to the Klopfer system, and is compounded by the fact that a somewhat arbitrary "hierarchical" scheme is presented to distinguish Main from Additional determinants in answers where the relative importance is not clear. Klopfer suggests that human movement (*M*) be given preference in these situations, with chromatic color, texture, and achromatic color ranked in that order of importance. Klopfer did not begin his Rorschach system with the Main–Additional distinction. Quite the contrary, he originally followed Rorschach's technique of entering multiple scores, but, as his recommended technique of Inquiry became more elaborate, and as the number of scoring categories were proliferated, he perceived the fact that large numbers of multiple determinant scores would create much difficulty in interpretation. In addition, he became convinced that determinants relevant only to a part of a concept, or those given somewhat reluctantly in the Inquiry, were not as important to the "basic" personality as the "primary" determinant. By this time (1938), he began scoring some of the "questionable" determinants as Additional, although he continued to use multiple determinant scores where the issue seemed clear. Subsequently, however, he decided that it was impractical to expect all scorers to be consistent in these decisions and by the time that his first text on the Rorschach was published (1942), he had settled on the principle of giving only one score for the Main determinant.[1]

The other systematizers differ only slightly from each other, and from Rorschach, in scoring multiple determined answers. Piotrowski (1957) and Rapaport (1946) use a scoring procedure identical to that of Rorschach. Hertz (1970) uses a similar procedure, but also frequently evaluates each determinant for form quality. Beck (1937) introduced the use of the dot (.), as a convenient method of identifying and tabulating the blend response. In each of these systems, unlike Klopfer's, all determinants are given equal weight in forming interpretive postulates. Unfortunately, there are no empirical data of substance available from which the usefulness of the Main–Additional procedure can be compared with the Blend approach. Interestingly, the clinicians responding to the Exner and Exner survey (1972) are almost equally divided on the issue, with 54% scoring Main–Additional, 43% scoring Blend, and 3% scoring only one determinant. The ABPP respondents are somewhat more favorable toward the Blend, with 59% endorsing it and 41% preferring the Main–Additional method.

The decision to include the Blend method of scoring in the comprehensive system is based on two elements. First, four of the five Rorschach systems endorse this approach. Second, and more important, is a series of three studies completed to gather more data concerning the multiple determinant answer. The first of the three was designed to evaluate the relationship of the multiple determinant response to intelligence. The protocols of 43 nonpsychiatric subjects, for whom Otis Intelligence Test scores were also available, were rescored using the comprehensive system by

[1] In a private interview in 1965 at Asilomar, California, Klopfer expressed some regret concerning that decision. He alluded to the fact that the interpreter, relying "too heavily" on the psychogram, could be misled in some instances. He maintained, however, the belief that the Main–Additional dichotomy in determinant scoring did, in fact, preclude the interpreter from "overemphasis" of determinant scores which might be developed in the Inquiry.

one of three scorers. These subjects were selected because the I.Q. scores manifest a considerable range 84 to 122, with a median of 103. The Rorschach protocols were divided on the basis of an I.Q. median split, with the midranking protocol discarded, thus creating two groups of 21 each. The mean I.Q. for the upper half is 113.4, and for the lower half 93.7. The number of blend responses was tallied for each protocol and the data subjected to chi square analysis, which indicates that subjects in the upper half give significantly more blend answers than do subjects in the lower half. In fact, 15 of the 21 protocols of subjects in the upper half contain at least one blend, while only eight of the 21 protocols in the lower half contain at least one blend. The number of blends in a given protocol does not correlate highly with I.Q. ($r = .32$), but the tendency to give a blend answer apparently does require at least average intellectual ability. In view of these findings, a second study was undertaken using 28 psychiatric out-patients for whom WAIS I.Q. scores were also available. These I.Q.'s ranged from 97 to 132, with a median of 110. Using the same procedure of a median split and tallying the number of blend answers for upper and lower half, the resulting chi square *was not* significant. Twelve of the subjects in the upper half gave blend answers, while 10 of the 14 protocols in the lower group contained blends. An interesting by-product of these two investigations is the fact that the psychiatric group tended to give proportionally more blends per protocol than did the subjects in the upper half of the nonpsychiatric group (11 versus 6%). This finding generated a third study, using two protocols from each of 21 "psycho-neurotic" out-patients. The first protocol from each subject was collected at the onset of intervention, while the second was taken at intervention termination, which varied from 9 to 17 months later. A comparison of the pre- and posttreatment protocols for total number of blends *is not* significantly different, although there is a tendency toward decrease. Conversely, when the actual number of pre- and post-treatment records containing blend answers are compared, a significant difference is discovered. Twenty of the 21 pretreatment protocols contain blend responses as contrasted with 11 of the 21 posttreatment records. It is possibly of even greater interest to note that the kinds of determinants used in the blend answers change substantially when the pre-and posttreatment records are compared, the former containing more shading blends, and more determinants in which form is secondary such as *CF* and *TF*. The latter records yield fewer shading blends, more *FD* type determinants, and more determinants in which form is primary. These data appear to indicate that the blend, while somewhat related to intellect, is very possibly a useful index of the complexity of the subject's psychological process. This interpretation is generally consistent with Beck's hypothesis concerning the blend (1944, 1961), and argues for a method of scoring multiple determinant answers which gives equal weight to each of the determinants involved. Thus it is essentially the Beck procedure which has been incorporated into the comprehensive system.

The scoring symbols entered in the blend *are the same* as would be used if any of the determinants were scored separately. Some examples of blend responses are shown in Table 14.

The majority of blend responses are found in the more complex answers, and quite frequently, the whole blot or a large segment of it is involved. The least common type of blend answer is one which includes pure form (*F*) as a determinant. These are responses in which two *seemingly separate contents* are included in the single answer such as, to Card III, " It ll some bones here [*D7*] and there is a butterfly [*D3*] flying over them." The Inquiry establishes the fact that the "bones" are

Table 14. Examples of Blend Responses

Card	Location	Free Association	Inquiry	Scoring
I	W	A wm stndg in the cntr w her arms raised w a lot of smk around her	E: (Rpts S's resp) S: Rite here, ths r her arms & ths is her body & all ths (points to each side) is all dark & hazy like smoke	$M^p.YF$
II	W	Two bears fitg, they'v got ther paws togethr & ther's bld on ther heads & feet	E: (Rpts S's resp) S: C, heads, paws, bodies, feet & the red ll bld	$FM^a.CF$
III	W	Ths ll 2 butlers bowing to e.o.	E: (Rpts S's resp) S: Its like at a party, thes red thgs cld b s.s. of decoration & ths r the butlers in their formal suits sort of bending frwd like they were bowing E: Formal suits? S: Yes, they'r black, like a tuxedo.	$M^a.FC.FC'$
IV	∨W	Ths ll a snake or a worm crawling out from in under a leaf	E: (Rpts S's resp) S: Well u can just c the head, I thk its a snake bec it has the different markgs on it E: And the leaf? S: Yeah, all the rest of it ll a leaf, its dead and dried up E: Dead & dried up? S: Yeah, its all black like dead leaves get after a while E: U said it was crawling out from in under the leaf S: Yeah, the way it is there he must be under it bec u can only c the head	$FM^a.FY.C'F.FD$
IV	W	A guy sitting on a stump in a fur coat, like an old raccoon coat	E: (Rpts S's resp) S: He's leaning backward, like he was laughg or s.t., c heres the feets, big feets & his head & little arms E: U mentioned a fur coat, like an old raccoon coat S: Yeah, it looks all furry to me	$M^p.FT.FD$
VI	D1	Its a deep gorge with a river I guess, it must b cause it overflowd not too long ago	E: (Rpts S's resp) S: This cntr looks really deep, c how dark it is & yet all the land around it looks differnt colors like it was partly water	$FV.YF$

Table 14 (Continued)

Card	Location	Free Association	Inquiry		Scoring
VII	D2	A cpl of kids w mud or dirt on their faces like they r makg faces at e.o.	*E:*	(Rpts *S*'s resp)	$M^p.FY$
			S:	U just c the upper part of 'em, 2 little girls I guess stickg their lips out like makg a face	
			E:	U mentioned that they hav mud or dirt on their faces	
			S:	Its all dark like dried mud or dirt wld b	
VIII	D2	Down here it ll some strawberry & orange Italian ices	*E:*	(Rpts *S*'s resp)	$CF.TF$
			S:	See here is the pink like strawberry & the orange	
			E:	U said they ll ices	
			S:	Rite, I did. They look icy to me, not like real ice cream, more like ice chips	
IX	∨ *W*	Wow, an explosion w a lot of fire & smoke	*E:*	(Rpts *S*'s resp)	$m^a.CF.YF$
			S:	Yeah, its all shootg up & u c the fire here, its orange & all ths green ll the smoke	
			E:	I'm not sure why it ll smoke	
			S:	Well u c how the diff colors come togethr, like fire & smoke all mixed together	
X	D9	Ths ll bld thats dryg	*E:*	(Rpts *S*'s resp)	$C.Y$
			S:	Well its blood o.k., there's no question about that & u can tell that its drying because these outside parts r darker	

perceived because of the form and the "butterfly" is also seen as a form dominant object. The correct scoring for this kind of answer is $F.FM^a$. The scorer should exert much caution, however, before including pure F as a determinant in a blend score. In the example of "bones" and "butterfly" given above, the relationship between the two objects is established (flying over) but there is no implication of *immediate* proximity, nor is there the inference of any *direct* relationship as in, "a woman standing with smoke all around her" to Card I. In this response, both proximity and direct relationship are present. Here the scoring is $M^p.YF$, and if the response had been "a woman with smoke all around her," with no inference of movement being offered in the Free Association or spontaneously in the Inquiry, the scoring would be simply YF. The most common, but still unusual, type of blend answer which involves pure F is to Card III and includes the $D3$ "butterfly" which is generally not perceived as having any direct relation or immediate proximity to other content.

One further scoring caution concerning the blend answer seems important, particularly for the novice scorer. This concerns the scoring of shading determined responses. The light-dark features of the blot, when used to delineate a feature of a percept, are usually perceived as only one of the three types of shading. Responses containing multiple shading determinants are quite unusual, and, when they do occur, a vista component is frequently involved. When shading blends occur, they are identifiable by the fact that different contents, or different characteristics of a single content, are articulated, for example, "muddy fields on each side of a deep gorge" (Card VI). In this response two contents, muddy fields and deep gorge, are offered, each of which includes a shading determinant, yielding a scoring of *YF.FV*. Obviously, the possibilities exist for any combination of shading determinants to be given in a single response so that blends such as *FV.FY*, *V.T*, *FT.YF*, or even *YF.TF.VF* are noted occasionally. It is quite important, however, that the scorer not confuse the shading blend with the sometimes complex articulation of a single shading determinant; for instance, "These dark differences in the shading make it look bumpy, like velvet. Its all very soft looking like it is the soft folds in a blanket" (Card IV). Even though the articulation is complex, including words relevant to each of the three types of shading (dark differences, bumpy like velvet, soft looking), the content is essentially singular and only one perceptual use of the shading is manifest. Thus the response is scored only once, for texture. A similar response is, in fact, a shading blend: "This looks like a piece of material, something very fuzzy, that has been bunched together, like it was pleatted, these lies here are the folds." The Inquiry to this answer confirms that the subject perceives both texture (fuzzy) and vista (folds) and the scoring is *TF.VF*.

ORGANIZATIONAL ACTIVITY (Z)

The scoring for organizational activity has, possibly, been one of the most neglected of the Rorschach components. A mere 12% of the practitioners responding in the Exner and Exner survey indicate that they score organizational activity. Slightly less than half, 47%, of the ABPP respondents include some form of organizational scoring. There are at least three factors which appear to contribute to the general lack of interest among Rorschachers in this type of scoring. First, the various systems differ considerably in approaching this feature. Beck was the first to introduce an organizational score (1933), using a scheme of weighing organized responses depending on the type of organization and the complexity of the stimuli involved, (Z score). Hertz uses a method in which all organized responses are weighed equally (g score, 1940), while Klopfer (1946) includes some recognition of organizational activity in his Form Level Rating but also includes other elements in this score; thus it does not represent organizational activity *per se*. The other Rorschach systems do not include a formal scoring for organization activity, nor did Rorschach, although he appears to have offered some description of the process in his discussion of *Assoziationsbetrieb*. Second, most of the literature concerning a scoring for organizational activity focuses on the Beck Z score, the procedure for which sometimes appears to be much more complicated than is really the case. Third, and possibly most important, is the *misconception* that the clinical utility of a scoring for organizational activity is mainly centered on estimates of I.Q. Unfortunately, Beck's own words, "These totals (ZSums) vary directly as the intelligence of S," (1945), plus the fact that a considerable segment of the research on organizational activity scores has concerned the relationship to intelligence test performance, seems to have encouraged this misconception.

There is no question but that organizational activity scores, whether weighed as in Beck or unweighed as in Hertz, do correlate positively with some components of intelligence testing. A variety of positive correlations have been reported for both types of scoring, some of which are statistically significant well beyond the .01 level. Wishner (1948) reports a .536 correlation between Wechsler-Bellevue I.Q. and the weighted Z score. Sisson and Taulbee (1955) obtained correlations of .43 and .52 between Wechsler I.Q. and weighted and unweighted ZSums, respectively. Blatt (1953) found correlations of .49 and .46 between weighted ZSums and the verbal and reasoning sections of the Primary Mental Abilities Test. The Wishner findings seem especially important to understanding the kind of relation which seems to exist between organizational activity and intellect. He reports correlations for each of the individual subtests in the Wechsler-Bellevue, including data both for the regular weighed Z scores and using a method which eliminates Z scores for the so-called unorganized Whole answers such as the Bat response on Cards I and V. The standard Beck z sum correlates significantly with two verbal subtests (vocabulary .605 and information .365) and two performance subtests (picture completion .346 and digit symbol .308) with other correlations ranging as low as .102 for block design. The modified ZSum correlates quite differently with the Wechsler subtests, ranging from a high of .306 for similarities to $-.059$ for object assembly. In other words, these data seem to suggest that the weighted method of assigning Z scores, as used by Beck, does correlate significantly with some types of intellectual operations but not with others. Even this issue is cast in some doubt when it is noted that Wishner's data are collected from only 42 psychiatric (neurotic) cases. Hertz (1960) has reported substantially lower correlations between the Beck z sum and Otis I.Q. (.174) and Stanford-Binet M.A. (.113) for 12 year olds. She also reports low positive correlations between her g score and I.Q. and M.A. (.256 and .249). At the lower end of the intellectual spectrum, Jolles (1947) using "feebleminded" subjects found correlations of .08 between weighted ZSum and Binet I.Q. and .15 with Wechsler I.Q. Kropp (1955), in reviewing most of the studies on the Z score, concluded that it relates highly to W, and to M, but that it does not relate to intelligence as operationally defined by intelligence tests.

Obviously, intelligence appears to have some relationship to organizational activity, but this relationship apparently varies with certain response styles, a variation which is especially notable in some instances of psychopathology. Schmidt and Fonda (1953) have shown that Z scores are significantly higher in manics than in schizophrenics. Varvel (1941) and Hertz (1948) both report lower levels of organizational activity in depressed patients, while Beck (1952) and Molish (1955) find high organizational activity in patients prone to "project conflicts" in a systematized delusional operation. It would seem that intelligence is prerequisite to organizational activity, but other factors influence the frequency and characteristics of the organizing activity.

The variety of empirical data seems to argue in favor of including some form of organizational activity scoring in the comprehensive system. A major question appears to be whether such a scoring should include weighing different kinds of responses as suggested by Beck, or considering all organized responses equally as purported by Hertz. An interesting work, published by Wilson and Blake (1950), appears to support the Hertz approach. They correlated Z scores, as weighed in the Beck method, using a count of *one* for each organized response, with the weighed ZSums for 104 subjects and derived a .989 correlation. The Wilson and Blake sample, however, included 81 "normals" and only 23 psychiatric cases of which only eight were psychotic. The sample limitations in their study appeared to suggest that a larger psychiatric group would be worthwhile to study. In this context, two groups of 60 protocols each were randomly selected from the protocol pool, one representing nonpsychiatric subjects and the second a psychiatric group comprised of 26 schizophrenics and 34 nonschizophrenics. Each of the protocols were rescored using the Beck weighted Z score method and also with the Wilson-Blake method of assigning a value of 1 to each response manifesting organizational activity. The correlation for the "normal group" was consistent with the Wilson-Blake findings, .984; however, the correlation for the psychiatric group was considerably lower, .708. A closer examination of the data from the group of psychiatric protocols revealed that in approximately 25 % of the cases, the sum of Z differed from the Wilson-Blake estimated sum of Z by four or more points. In fact, using an arbitrary cut-off value for a difference score (d) of 3.0, nearly one-third (32 %) of the psychiatric group is identified while only two of the "normal" subjects fall in this range. Evaluation of the "kinds" of patients who have an actual ZSum at least 3.0 greater or less than the predictive ZSum reveals that many are "depressives" and the difference is in the negative direction. It is important, however, to emphasize that in seven of the 21 differences greater than 3.0, the subject was diagnosed either as paranoid schizophrenic, hypomanic, obsessive-compulsive, or psychopathic personality, each of which would be generally consistent with the earlier research findings or the postulates of Beck or Molish.

These data are, of course, somewhat tentative, and still subject to the criticism of small samples. Nonetheless, they argue against discarding a weighted scheme of scoring for organizational activity. If it is true, as suggested by both Beck and Hertz, that organizational activity is indicative of the use of intellect as *directed toward adaptation*, the importance of including a scoring for organizational activity is of paramount importance. And if the use of a d score, derived from the difference between an actual weighted Z sum and an estimated weighted ZSum can be derived, it should be included in any new approach to the test. It is in this framework of logic that the Beck approach to scoring organizational activity has been adopted in the comprehensive system. This decision is contingent upon further evaluation and investigation, and it may be that other data sources will promote a better method for this type score. The question concerning the relevance of scoring Z for "unorganized" Whole answers needs to be resolved and the manner of assignment of weights, with regard to stimulus complexity, should be evaluated more extensively than has been the case thus far. Until these tasks are accomplished, it seems reasonable to include the Beck approach to organizational scoring in the comprehensive system.

As previously mentioned, the Beck weighted scoring for responses manifesting "organization" sometimes seems more complex than is actually the case. In reality, the method may be applied easily to any response which meets *at least one* of the following criteria: (1) it is a *W* response; (2) it is a response which *meaningfully* integrates two or more adjacent detail areas; (3) it is a response which *meaningfully* integrates two or more nonadjacent detail areas; or (4) it is a response in which white space is *meaningfully* integrated with other details of the blot. Form *must always* be involved to score *Z*; thus pure *C, T, Y,* or *V* answers *are never scored Z.* The specific *Z* score assigned to an organized response will depend on which of the scoring criteria have been met, and to which card the response has been given. The weighted *Z* values for each of the four types of organizational activity are shown, by card, in Table 15.[2]

Table 15.   Organizational (*Z*) Values for Each of the Ten Cards

| | | Type of Organizational Activity | | |
| | | Adjacent | Distant | White Space |
Card	*W*	Detail	Detail	with Detail
I	1.0	4.0	6.0	3.5
II	4.5	3.0	5.5	4.5
III	5.5	3.0	4.0	4.5
IV	2.0	4.0	3.5	5.0
V	1.0	2.5	5.0	4.0
VI	2.5	2.5	6.0	6.5
VII	2.5	1.0	3.0	4.0
VIII	4.5	3.0	3.0	4.0
IX	5.5	2.5	4.5	5.0
X	5.5	4.0	4.5	6.0

Whenever a response meets two or more of the criteria for scoring *Z*, the higher of the values is assigned. For example, a *W* response to Card I is ordinarily assigned a *Z* score of 1.0; however, if the whole blot is used in a manner so that adjacent detail areas are specifically organized as in "a woman standing in the center with two creatures dancing around her," the value of 4.0 (Adjacent Detail Weighted score) would be assigned.

The issue of meaningfulness of organization in responses is critically important to the decision to score *Z*, in both whole and detail responses. It should be obvious that the component parts of the blot used in the response are related to each other in some meaningful way. For instance, "two figures, pointing in different directions" on Card VII is not scored *Z*, since the response does not manifest any *meaningful* relationship. The same two figures, ". . . arguing about which way to go," is scored *Z* in that a meaningful relation does obviously exist. Some examples of organizational activity scores are provided in Table 16. Inquiries are included only where they are relevant to the decision concerning the *Z* score.

---

[2] This table is taken directly from Beck, S. J., Beck, A., Levitt, E., and Molish, H. *Rorschach's Test*, Vol. 1. New York: Grune and Stratton, 1961. Those familiar with the Beck system will note that Beck's special *z* scoring for *W* with Adjacent Detail, which Beck uses for some responses to Cards III, VI, and VII, has been omitted in preference for criteria which are consistent across all cards.

Table 16. Examples of *Z* Score Assignment for Responses to Each of the Ten Rorschach Cards

Card	Free Association	Inquiry	Z Scoring
I	A bat	(Confirms *W*)	1.0
I	A halloween mask	*S:* The white parts are the eyes & mouth so the rest is a mask	1.0[a]
I	A dead leaf lying on the snow	*S:* U can c the snow thru the holes in the leaf	3.5
I	Two big birds, thy'r lookg at a couple of mountains off in the distance (*D2* = Birds; *Dd22* = Mountains)		6.0
II	Two clowns kicking e.o.	[The lower (*D3*) area represents the kick]	4.5
II	Two dogs rubbing noses		3.0
II	A rocket ship taking off w the fire coming out	(Confirms *DS5* + *D4* is rocket, *D3* is flame)	4.5
II	Two hens getting ready to fite, lik fiting cocks	(*D2*)	5.5
III	Two witches brewing s.t. in their den w trophies hung all over	(*W*)	5.5
III	Two wm pickg up a basket	(*D1*)	3.0
III	Two wm looking at e.o.	(*D9* only, *D7* not includ)	4.0
IV	A big giant sitting on a stump	(*D1* is stump)	4.0
IV	A bear hide	(*W*)	2.0
IV	∨Two witches arguing w e.o.	(*Dd26*)	3.5
IV	∨Like Hansel & Gretel taking a bite off a candy tree	(*DdS24* are Hansel & Gretel, *D1* is the candy tree)	5.0[b]
V	A butterfly	(*W*)	1.0
V	An alligator's head, there's one on each side		No *Z* score
VI	Ths ll a totem pole sitting high up on a mountain	(*D3* is totem, the rest of the card is the mt)	2.5
VI	I c a submarine being reflectd	(*D4* is the submarine)	No *Z* score
VI	∨There r 2 littl birds in a nest	(*Dd28*)	2.5
VI	∨There r 2 birds calling to e.o.	(*Dd21*)	6.0
VI	Ths whole thg cld b an island in the sea	(*W* is the island, all white space is sea)	6.5
VII	Two wm smiling at e.o.	(*D1*)	3.0
VII	Two wm talkg to e.o. standg behind ths rock	(*W*, *D2* are wm, *D4* is rock)	1.0
VII	∨Two can-can dancers	*S:* Their heads r touchg here & u can only c one leg bec the other is kicked out:	3.0[c]
VII	A mountain range and a lake	*S:* Ths white part (*DS7*) is the lake & the rest r mountains, like u were lookg thru them to see the lake down below	4.0
VIII	Two rats climbing up a garbage heap of s.s.	(*W*)	4.5

115

Table 16 (Continued)

Card	Free Association	Inquiry	Z Scoring
VIII	Two animals, one on each side		No Z score
VIII	A bear climbing a tree	(D1 is a bear, D4 is tree)	3.0
VIII	∨ A milk bottle balanced on a log	(Center small white space is milk bottle, D5 is the log)	4.0
VIII	Somebody splattered paint here	(W) Names colors	No Z score[d]
IX	∨ The whole thg ll an atomic explosion	(W, with D6 being the cloud, the green area being smoke, & the orange area being fire)	5.5
IX	A man playing a saxaphone	(D1, with the man being the major portion of the area used and the saxaphone the remaining part):	2.5[e]
IX	Two witches having a good joke together	(D3) S: They are leaning backward as if they are laughing about a joke	4.5
IX	Like an explosion on the sun where gas is shot off	(Top of D8 is sun, Dd25 is the gas shooting off) S: U can c the space in between the sun and where the gas rises (DdS32)	5.0
X	An artist's abstract, its symmetrical with each pair of object having a special significance	(W)	5.5
X	A lot of paint, like s.b. thru alot of paint on it	(W)	No Z score[f]
X	A fraternity paddle	(D11 is the handle, upper DdS30 is the paddle, D3 is a design on the paddle)	6.0
X	Two dogs, they'r each sitg up	(D2)	No Z score
X	Two dogs, they'r both sitg w their heads raised as if they r howling at the moon	(D2)	4.5
X	Two creatures trying to climb a pole	(D8 are animals, D14 is the pole)	4.0
X	A lot of undersea things, I c 2 crabs and 2 lobsters & 2 fish:	(D1 are crabs, D7 are lobsters, D13 are fish)	No Z score[g]

[a] In this response the subject used the whole blot and the white space; however, the z value ordinarily assigned for space with detail (3.5) is not assigned here in that the subject does not offer a "meaningful" integration of the dark portion of the blot. In other words, it would appear that the response is to the white areas, the dark area being included by necessity.

[b] Hansel and Gretel alone would be assigned the value for distant detail (3.5); however, the fact that they are related meaningfully to the "candy tree" requires the value of 5.0 (space integrated with detail).

[e] The Z value for distant detail is assigned here because the figures are not perceived as adjacent even though the portions of the blot used actually do touch.

116

Table 16 (Notes Continued)

d No *Z* score is assigned as no basic form is used.

e This is an example of an organizational activity which involves a break-up and synthesis of a single *D* area. In this instance the *Z* value for "adjacent detail" is assigned.

f In the first example to Card X the response clearly includes reference to meaningful relationships of the component detail. In the second example no such reference occurs.

g This response, although similar is basic content to *W* responses of "an underwater scene" which would have a *Z* score of 5.5, is essentially three separate detail responses. The whole blot is not used nor is there any indication of a meaningful synthesis of the pairs of "undersea things" identified.

An accurate scoring of organizational activity in the Rorschach protocol, both in terms of frequency of *Z* and the sum of *Z* scores, can provide very useful data from which some aspects of cognitive activity can be evaluated. It is a feature of the test which should be researched more thoroughly than has been the case, especially in relation to some of the more contemporary developments in the psychology of thinking.

FORM QUALITY

The issue of "goodness of fit" of the response to the area of the blot used was, during the time of the development of the five major Rorschach Systems, a major point of contention. Each of the systematizers has agreed that form quality or "fit" is one of the most important of the "quantifiable" elements of the test. They have also generally agreed that responses can be differentiated into two basic categories, those with good form, and those with poor form. This is consistent with Rorschach's recommendation. Beyond these two basic points of agreement, the systematizers differ to some extent among themselves concerning the "best" method of evaluating the appropriateness of the form used in the response. Beck (1961) and Hertz (1970) have followed Rorschach's suggestions most closely. They, like Rorschach, use the symbol + for good form answers, and the symbol − for poor form answers. The assignment of the plus or minus symbols is, essentially, based on the statistical frequency with which any given type of response occurs to specific location areas. In these systems, elaborate tables have been developed, by card, location areas, and content showing which responses are + and which are −. The two systems differ slightly in that they do not always use the same location areas and the fact that the statistical frequencies are based on different samples of records, although both used a large number of protocols. They also differ in that Beck allows that some responses may not be scoreable as + or − where statistical data are insufficient, while Hertz has preferred to include the "subjective agreement" of at least three judges.

Piotroswki (1957) and Rapaport (1946) both endorse the concept of statistical frequency in determining form quality, but neither have actually developed a frequency distribution for use. Piotrowski suggests that any responses produced by at least "one third of healthy subjects" should be regarded as +. Rapaport includes the more subjectively evaluative symbols ± and ∓ where responses appear to have both qualities. In the early Klopfer system, he too used the symbols + and − but was generally opposed to statistical frequency as a determining criterion. Rather, he preferred to defend the appropriateness of the subjective evaluation of the examiner in determining the quality of the form. Ultimately, he discarded the use of these symbols and developed a method of Form Level Rating (Klopfer & Davidson, 1944). The Form Level Rating includes a subjective evaluation of form accuracy, plus evaluation of organization and specification, so that each response is given a numerical score which may range from $+5.0$ to -2.0.

The decision concerning the method adopted in the comprehensive system to evaluate form quality was derived from several considerations. First, most all responses include some use of form; thus any technique requires broad applicability and high interscorer reliability. While the Klopfer Form Level Rating assures the applicability, the element of interscorer reliability is somewhat questionable. Interestingly, only 148 of the 213 respondents in the Exner and Exner (1972) survey who prefer the Klopfer system use Form Level Rating, while the remaining 65 use either the Beck or Hertz tables. Similarly, only 26 of the ABPP respondents prefer the Form Level Rating, while 69 use the Beck tables and 16 the Hertz tables. Thus it was decided not to include the Form Level Rating in the comprehensive system. A method based on statistical frequency, such as that of Beck and Hertz, also assures broad applicability and appears to be effective in assuring high interscorer reliability. This seems especially important in that the proportion of good and poor form answers in a protocol is often an important clue in some differential diagnoses (Weiner, 1966). Statistical frequency methods are, however, somewhat limited by the fact that all $+$ responses are not of equal quality, nor are all $-$ answers equally poor in form fit. Rapaport (1946) noted this in his work, and suggested that form quality might be differentiated into six categories (plus, ordinary, vague, minus, special plus, and special minus). Rapaport argued that such a differentiation of form quality would provide a clearer understanding of the "reality testing" operations of the subject.

Mayman (1966, 1970), following from Rapaport's basic suggestion, has developed a method of evaluating form quality which has six categories ranging from exceptionally good form to exceptionally poor form. The categories and criterion for each are as follows:

F+ (highest level): Representing a successful combination of imagination and reality congruence.

Fo (ordinary level): Representing the obvious, easily noticed answers, requiring little or no creative effort. This category includes most all responses which would be considered commonplace.

Fw (weak level): Representing a significant shift away from the reality adherence characteristic of the *F+* or *Fo* answers. Mayman suggests that some *Fw* answers border on the adequate (scored *Fw+*) when the general contours do not clash with the answer, while other *Fw* answers are less than adequate (scored *Fw−*) when some of the blot area used makes the form fit somewhat incongruous.

Fv (vague level): Representing answers in which the content avoids the necessity of specific shape.

Fs (spoiled level): Representing an essentially adequate use of form which has been spoiled by an oversight or distortion.

F− (minus level): Representing the wholly arbitrary percept where there is substantial disregard for the structural properties of the blot areas used.

Mayman has been able to demonstrate, quite convincingly, that this method of differentiation of form quality yields data of substantially greater diagnostic usefulness than does the simple plus and minus differentiation. He reports very respectable correlations with ratings of health, tolerance for anxiety, motivation, ego strength, and quality of interpersonal relations. He also reports a reasonably high level of agreement between scorers for most of the six categories.

At first glance it appeared that the Mayman method for evaluating form quality might be appropriate for the comprehensive system, especially if it could be integrated with a format based on statistical frequency. A pilot study concerning its usefulness was conducted in which four predoctoral clinical psychology interns were given approximately 90 minutes of instruction in the Mayman method, plus preinstructional readings, and asked to independently score 20 protocols randomly selected from the protocol pool. Their scorings were only for form quality, and they were also permitted to use the Beck Tables of Good and Poor Form as a guideline. The results were somewhat disappointing in that the levels of agreement among the four scorers ranged from 41 to 83%. Checking the levels of agreement among only three of the four scorers yielded only slightly higher percentages. An analysis of the discrepancies rendered some insight into the low reliability problem. First, there was considerable disagreement in the scoring of responses as $Fw+$ or $Fw-$. Second, there was substantial disagreement in the use of the Fv category, partly because some of the responses which might be scored Fv in the Mayman scheme are listed as $+$ by Beck while others are listed $-$ by Beck, and partly because the levels of articulation varied considerably in these types of responses. Mayman has also reported the lowest level of agreement between his scorers for this category. Third, there was considerable disagreement for the scoring of Fs versus $F-$. As a consequence of these findings, it was decided to investigate a modification of the Mayman method, in which Fv and Fs would be eliminated from the format, and all Fw answers would be considered as a single score rather than attempt to differentiate $Fw+$ and $Fw-$.[3] The same four predoctoral interns independently scored a second set of 20 randomly selected protocols using this modified format. The results of this scoring were quite encouraging. The percentage of agreement among all four scorers ranged from 87 to 95%. It was even more encouraging to discover that most all instances of disagreement occurred either between the scoring of Fw or $F-$, or between the scoring of $F+$ or Fo. In other words, if the $F+$ and Fo answers are all considered as representing "good" form, the scorers agreed in 99% of the responses. Similarly, if the Fw and $F-$ answers are all considered as representing "poor" form, the scorers agreed in 98% of the responses. These high levels of agreement were generated essentially through the use of Beck's Tables of Good and Poor Form, with instances of disagreement occurring where the response in question did not appear on the Beck listing.

These findings prompted a decision to select a method of form quality evaluation for the comprehensive system which utilizes the frequency distribution method favored by Beck and Hertz, and which *also* permits some differentiation regarding the goodness or poorness of the form used in the response. This format consists of four categories, derived from Mayman's work, two of which represent form which is used appropriately with good fit, and two of which represent form which

---

[3] Mayman, in personal communication (1973), indicates that he is studying the usefulness of a modification of his method in which the scoring of v (vague) has been dropped.

is used inappropriately, with poor fit. The four categories, and the criterion for each, are shown in Table 17.

Table 17.   Symbols and Criteria for the Scoring of Form Quality

Symbol	Definition	Criterion
+	Superior	The unusually well developed and articulated use of form in a manner that enriches the quality of the percept without sacrificing the appropriateness of form involved. The + answer need not involve an "original" percept, rather should be unique by the manner in which the form is used and specified.
o	Ordinary	The obvious, easily developed use of form, wherein the content and blot areas are congruent. The answer is generally commonplace, and easy to see, with no enrichment to the quality of the answer by the manner in which the form is used and specified.
w	Weak	The unconvincing, ill-conceived use of form manifesting a shift away from a congruence between the blot area and the content. Form fit is not grossly distorted, yet fails to meet the criterion of being easily perceived.
−	Minus	The distorted, arbitrary, unrealistic use of form as related to the content offered, where an answer is imposed on the blot area with total, or near total, disregard for the structure of the area.

Three steps have been involved in developing the format for scoring form quality for the comprehensive system. The first concerned the establishment of a listing of answers, by location area for each card, representing good and poor form fit. While both Beck and Hertz have published such lists, it seemed more appropriate to establish a new listing which could be evaluated against their findings for agreement, rather than to attempt to extrapolate from their works. In this context, the responses contained in the 835 records in the protocol pool formed a base from which to work. Subsequently, 365 additional records were collected using the methodology of the comprehensive system. The total of 1200 protocols contain slightly more than 26,000 responses which were ultimately used to create the listing of good and poor form scorings. The methodology by which this listing was established involved the separation of the protocol into "general" categories from which frequency distributions were developed. Four such categories were employed, the number of protocols for each, and the source, is shown below.

	PROTOCOL POOL	NEW PROTOCOLS
Nonpsychiatric	200	115
Out-patient (nonpsychotic)	364	130
In-patient (nonschizophrenic)	125	50
In-patient (schizophrenic)	146	70

It was decided to "collapse" the records of the nonpsychiatric and nonpsychotic out-patients into one basic grouping. The logic here, following from Beck, is that subjects in either of these groups, while occasionally offering poor form answers, generally give responses which show a good form fit. Therefore, a listing of "good form" answers could be developed from these 809 records. It was also assumed that the in-patient population, comprising 391 records (of which 216 are from schizophrenics) would be an excellent source of the highly idiographic, poor form answers.

The 809 protocols from the nonpsychiatric and out-patient samples yielded nearly 17,500 responses, which, when subdivided by card location areas into "general class of content," rendered approximately 4100 *classes* of response. A class of response is defined as "contents which are not identical but similar to each other occurring to the same location area of a given card." In other words, the responses of bat, eagle, butterfly, moth, and so on, to the whole of Card I are considered as a single class of response. Caution was exercised in developing the classes of response so as to ensure that the objects did have a relatively common shape, so that at no time, for example, would a deer and a rodent be considered in the same class of response, even though both would be scored for content as "Animal."

Frequency distributions of response classes were developed for each location area, by card. Criteria were then selected from which responses and classes of response could be judged as good or poor form, using different frequency "cut-off" points for the unusual (*Dd*) detail areas than for the whole (*W*) or common (*D*) locations. Where responses were to a *W* or *D* area, any frequency of 20 or greater was considered adequately indicative of "good" form use. Where the frequency fell between 10 and 19, the form quality of the response or response class was judged as "questionable," and if the frequency were less than 10 the response was judged as "poor" form use. When the responses were to a *Dd* area, a frequency of 10 or greater was considered adequate for the judgement of good form use. Responses or response classes with frequencies between 5 and 9 were considered "questionable," and frequencies of less than 5 were judged as poor form use.

The second step in establishing this form quality scoring format included a decision procedure for those responses judged strictly on frequency as "questionable," plus a "subjective" reevaluation of those responses judged on the basis of frequency as poor form use. The latter seemed especially important so as to avoid "misidentifying" the very unique and creative answer which employed good form. It was decided to use the Beck and Hertz listings of good and poor form answers as a guideline for decisions concerning the questionable responses, and concurrently to have three judges review all answers listed as poor form. The end product of these procedures was that approximately half of the 513 questionable responses or response classes were determined as good form from the Beck and Hertz tables, and approximately half were designated as poor form, and 16 responses that had been designated as poor form on the basis of frequency were changed to the good form listing.

At this point then, two listings were available, one for good form and one for poor form, by card and location area. Approximately 85% of the more than 4100 responses and response classes studied appear on the good form listing, while the remaining 15%, or slightly more than 600 responses appear on the poor form listing.[4] The next step was to "rescore" for form quality, the 391 protocols which had been taken from the in-patient sample, and to calculate the percentage of responses which

[4] Both the Beck and Hertz listings of good and poor form responses are longer than that offered in Table A. The Beck listing contains approximately 5500 responses while the Hertz listing contains nearly 10,000 designations. Some scorers may wish to use either of these listings to supplement or clarify that offered in Table A.

would be judged by the new listing as good form. The rationale for this procedure is that, as Rorschach suggested and which since has received considerable empirical support, the more seriously disturbed subjects, especially schizophrenics, tend to distort or disregard the reality demands of form in the test more extensively than do nonpatients of the less severely disturbed. These records contained slightly more than 9200 responses, which, when judged against the listing of good form answers yielded an $F+\%$ (all responses in which form was the only determinant) of 69% and an extended $+\%$ (all responses in which form was involved) of 72%. Nearly 1700 of the responses in these protocols were highly unique and generally manifesting an inappropriate use of form. In the context of most any clinical judgement they would be considered as poor form answers and thus were added to the listing of poor form responses or classes of response.

The third step in developing the format for the evaluation of form quality focused on extending, in a practically useful manner, the listings of good and poor form responses and response classes so as to permit a broader differentiation into the four categories taken from the Mayman method ($+$, o, w, $-$). Such a differentiation is obviously somewhat subjective, in that any percept which could be classified as ordinary (o), might by the nature of the specification and articulation become plus, and similarly, minus answers vary from those which offer a slight distortion of form to those in which form features are almost completely disregarded. Mayman's data, and the pilot work previously mentioned, support the notion that the experienced or seasoned Rorschacher can make these subjective differentiations, provided adequate guidelines are available. Two studies were undertaken to test this hypothesis. In the first, three clinicians were given approximately 2 hours of training in this procedure of differentiation, plus pretraining readings taken from Mayman, and subsequently asked to score for form quality, using the modified Mayman method, 700 responses. The responses were near equally divided, so that 375 were taken from the good form listing and 325 from the poor form listing. The instructions were that answers taken from the good form listing should be differentiated into $+$ or o, while those taken from the poor form listing should be differentiated into w and $-$. The results of this scoring indicate that a unanimous agreement was obtained for 87% of the responses tested. A second test of the methodology utilized 13 second and third year graduate students in clinical psychology, each of whom independently scored four protocols selected specifically for this purpose. The students had been previously trained in the comprehensive system and had received supervision in the scoring of at least 10 records. They were instructed that, in instances where a response might not occur exactly on the listings of good and poor form answers, they were to use a logical process of extrapolation (checking for similar types of answers), and that ultimately they should differentiate all responses into the four categories of $+$, o, w, and $-$. Each had completed or was in the process of completing a year of Rorschach training. The four protocols selected contained 94 responses. The student scorers agreed unanimously on the form quality score for 85 of the 94 answers. In the case of the remaining nine responses, several of which were quite unusual, there was general agreement among the scorers concerning the adequacy of form fit; that is, four were good form and were scored by all scorers as $+$ or o, and five were poor form and were scored by all scorers as w or $-$. These findings suggest that trained scorers do use available data accurately for the scoring of form quality, and even when the data available are not specific to the case, their judgements concerning good and poor form are consistent and clinically logical.

The Mayman technique for scoring form quality, and the modification of it included in the comprehensive system, are necessarily subject to additional investigation. This is primarily important because of the potential interpretive yield rather than interscorer reliability, although that too remains open to investigation. Mayman's validation data, using six categories, are impressive. The four category modification included here will hopefully provide an interpretive input similar to Mayman's findings. Some data concerning this methodology are included in the chapters on interpretation. It should suffice to emphasize at this point, that while the methodology injects a degree of subjectivity into the scoring for form quality, the interpretive gains appear to outweigh any limitations.

The assignment of the appropriate form quality symbol is placed at the end of the determinant scoring. For instance, responses based exclusively on form features will be scored as $F+$, Fo, Fw, or $F-$. Similarly, where determinants other than form are used, the placement of the form quality scoring symbol remains the same, as in the examples of M^po, TFw, $M^a.CF+$, or such. The $+$ and o scorings are used only for responses judged as using good form, and the w and $-$ scorings are used only for responses where the form has been used inappropriately.

Mayman (1970) has provided a very worthwhile statement which should caution all Rorschach scorers, especially with regard to the scoring for form quality. He states, "Many clinicians seem to feel that there is little they can learn from form-level scores that they do not already know from their impressionistic scanning of Rorschach protocols. Those who do score form quality often settle for a rough-and-ready classification of responses as either "acceptable" or "poor" . . . . The form quality of Rorschach responses indicates in microcosm the attitude with which a person maintains his hold on his object world." Presumably, the modification of Mayman's technique for scoring form quality included in the comprehensive system goes well beyond the "rough-and-ready" classifications to which Mayman alludes, and will provide a more sophisticated glimpse into the world of the subject and his object relations than does the more simplified method of "good-form–poor-form" differentiation based strictly on statistical frequencies.

The listings of good and poor form responses and response classes are provided in Table A in Chapter 9. These listings, which are by card and location area, should be followed carefully by the scorer where possible. In instances when a response or response class is *not shown* in the listing, the scorer should *seek to extrapolate* from scorings for similar responses, or in the final analysis, use good clinical judgement. Table B in Chapter 9, contains examples by card of responses which are subjectively differentiated into the four scorings of the modified Mayman method ($+$, o, w, $-$). They are provided to aid in establishing guidelines for scorers in differentiating good form answers into the $+$ and o scorings, and poor form answers into the w and $-$ categories.

REFERENCES

Beck, S. J. Configurational tendencies in Rorschach responses. *American Journal of Psychology*, 1933, **45**, 433–443.

Beck, S. J. *Introduction to the Rorschach Method: A Manual of Personality Study*. American Orthopsychiatric Association Monograph, No. 1, 1937.

Beck, S. J. *Rorschach's Test. I: Basic Processes*. New York: Grune and Stratton, 1944.

Beck, S. J. *Rorschach's Test. II: A Variety of Personality Pictures*. New York: Grune and Stratton, 1945.

Beck, S. J. *Rorschach's Test. III: Advances in Interpretation*. New York: Grune and Stratton, 1952.

Beck, S. J., Beck, A., Levitt, E., and Molish, H. *Rorschach's Test. I: Basic Processes*. (3rd ed.) New York: Grune and Stratton, 1961.

Blatt, H. An investigation of the significance of the Rorschach z score. Unpublished Ph.D. dissertation, University of Nebraska, 1953.

Exner, J., and Exner, D. How clinicians use the Rorschach. *Journal of Personality Assessment*, 1972, **36**, 403–408.

Hertz, M. *Percentage Charts for Use in Computing Rorschach Scores*. Brush Foundation and Department of Psychology, Western Reserve University, 1940.

Hertz, M. Suicidal configurations in Rorschach records. *Rorschach Research Exchange*, 1948, **12**, 3–58.

Hertz, M. Organization Activity. In Rickers-Ovsiankina, M. (Ed.), *Rorschach Psychology*. New York: Wiley, 1960. Pp. 25–57.

Hertz, M. *Frequency Tables for Scoring Rorschach Responses*. (5th ed.) Cleveland: Case-Western Reserve University Press, 1970.

Jolles, I. The diagnostic implications of Rorschach's Test in case studies of mental defectives. *Genetic Psychology Monographs*, 1947, **36**, 89–198.

Klopfer, B., and Tallman, G. A further Rorschach study of Mr. A. *Rorschach Research Exchange*, 1938, **3**, 31–36.

Klopfer, B., and Kelley, D. *The Rorschach Technique*. Yonkers-on-Hudson, N.Y.: World Book Company, 1942.

Klopfer, B., and Davidson, H. Form level rating: A preliminary proposal for appraising mode and level of thinking as expressed in Rorschach records. *Rorschach Research Exchange*, 1944, **8**, 164–177.

Klopfer, B., Ainsworth, M., Klopfer, W., and Holt, R. *Developments in the Rorschach Technique. I: Technique and Theory*. Yonkers-on-Hudson, N.Y.: World Book Company, 1954.

Kropp, R. The Rorschach "Z" score. *Journal of Projective Techniques*, 1955, **19**, 443–452.

Mayman, M. Measuring reality-adherence in the Rorschach test. American Psychological Association Meetings, New York, 1966.

Mayman, M. Reality contact, defense effectiveness, and psychopathology in Rorschach form-level scores. In Klopfer, B., Meyer, M., and Brawer, F. (Eds.), *Developments in the Rorschach Technique. III: Aspects of Personality Structure*. New York: Harcourt, Brace, Jovanovich, 1970. Pp. 11–46.

Molish, H. Schizophrenic reaction types in a naval hospital population as evaluated by the Rorschach Test. Bureau of Medicine and Surgery, Navy Department, Washington, D.C., 1955.

Piotrowski, Z. *Perceptanalysis*. New York: Macmillan, 1957.

Rapaport, D., Gill, M., and Schafer, R. *Diagnostic Psychological Testing*. Vol. 2. Chicago: Yearbook Publishers, 1946.

Rorschach, H. *Psychodiagnostics*. Bern: Bircher, 1921 (Transl., Hans Huber Verlag, 1942).

Schmidt, H., and Fonda, C. Rorschach scores in the manic states. *Journal of Projective Techniques*, 1953, **17**, 151–161.

Sisson, B., and Taulbee, E. Organizational activity of the Rorschach Test. *Journal of Consulting Psychology*, 1955, **19**, 29–31.

Varvel, W. The Rorschach Test in psychotic and neurotic depressions. *Bulletin of the Menninger Clinic*, 1941, **5,** 5–12.

Weiner, I. *Psychodiagnosis in Schizophrenia*. New York: Wiley, 1966.

Wilson, G., and Blake, R. A methodological problem in Beck's organizational concept. *Journal of Consulting Psychology*, 1950, **14,** 20–24.

Wishner, J. Rorschach intellectual indicators in neurotics. *American Journal of Orthopsychiatry*, 1948, **18,** 265–279.

CHAPTER 7

Content Categories, Populars, and Special Scorings

The final task in the formal scoring of the Rorschach response involves two steps. First, an appropriate symbol must be selected to represent the content of the response. Second, the response should be checked against a listing of "Popular" answers, that is, those given quite frequently in Rorschach records. Neither of these procedures is complex, but both are quite important for the interpretive process. It is also important to mention other possible scoring methods which may have clinical utility, but which have not been incorporated into the comprehensive system for various reasons.

CONTENT

All responses are scored or coded for content. The symbol used for the content score should be reasonably representative of the object or of the class of objects reported in the response. Rorschach (1921) used only six different symbols for content scoring. They are *H* (Human), *Hd* (Human Detail), *A* (Animal), *Ad* (Animal Detail, *Ls* (Landscape), and *Obj* (Inanimate Objects). In the early development of the test it became obvious that these six categories did not provide adequate differentiation of many frequently reported classes of objects. Therefore, each of the Rorschach systematizers has expanded Rorschach's original listing considerably, so as to provide for a greater discrimination among responses. There is considerable agreement among the systems concerning the scoring for the more commonly appearing contents; however, the agreement is far from unanimous. The lists of scoring categories vary considerably across the systems, differing notably in length. Beck uses the longest (35 categories), and Klopfer (1962) the shortest (23 content categories). Slight variations also occur across the listings regarding the actual symbol to be used. For instance, Beck uses the symbol *An* to score anatomy content, while Klopfer uses the symbol *At* for the same category.

The list of content scoring symbols to be used in the comprehensive system was developed in three phases. First, a random sample of 300 protocols was selected from the protocol pool. These records constituted 7411 responses, each of which was scored for content using the Beck listing of symbols, as that list is the longest for any of the systems. A frequency tally was then derived for each of the 35 content scores, and any category which did not show a frequency of 10 or more was deleted from the list. This procedure reduced the length of the Beck listing from 35 to 20 content categories.[1] The rationale for this procedure is that any content occurring with very limited frequency is probably quite "idiographic" when it does occur; thus it is better represented in a scoring or summary of scores in written out form. For example, contents such as a test tube, a candle, the Sun, a milk bottle, ice tongs, and snow appear in Rorschach records very infrequently. While each could be scored in a general category, such as scoring a test tube as *Sc* (Science), the full uniqueness of the content would not be readily evident in a summary of scores as it would be in written out form.

The second phase, in developing the list of content scorings, was comprised of a reexamination of the 20 remaining content categories to determine if any one might be including two or more frequently occurring, but relatively different, classes of objects. Two such categories were discovered. The scoring of Anatomy (*An*) included 83 responses of anatomy and 97 x-ray responses. Although Beck had decided to score both under the single rubric of *An*, it was decided to create a separate scoring for x-ray. Similarly, the scoring of Fire (*Fi*) included two relatively separate kinds of answer. The most frequent was "explosion" ($N = 159$), approximately half of which included reference to fire. A somewhat different kind of response, also scored *Fi*, is "fire," involving no explosion ($N = 46$). These findings seem to warrant a separate content scoring for explosion answers. These decisions increased the number of content scoring categories to 22.

Finally, the responses obtained in the ABPP survey were also considered. That questionnaire has asked if any special problems were experienced in scoring content appropriately. Most respondents answered this item negatively; however, approximately 20% of the sample included some comment about the scoring of fictional and mythological humans and animals, such as witches, giants, unicorns, and devils, with a majority of those who commented reporting the use of a parenthesis with the appropriate content symbol, such as (*H*). This procedure is already recommended in some of the Rorschach scoring systems, that is, Klopfer, Piotrowski, and Rapaport, and it has seemed logical to include it in the comprehensive system as a supplementary category for *H*, *Hd*, *A*, and *Ad*. The final listing selected for the comprehensive system is therefore comprised of 22 basic content scoring categories, plus four parenthesized supplementary scorings. These categories, the symbols and criterion for each, are shown in Table 18.

POPULAR RESPONSES

Rorschach made no mention of the commonly given, or Popular, answers in his original work (1921). He did, however, call attention to these types of responses in his posthumously published 1923 paper, referring to them as "Vulgar" answers. Rorschach defined the Vulgar or Popular responses as those occurring at least once in every three protocols, suggesting that they represent the capability for conventional perception. Each of the Rorschach systematizers has included the Popular, or *P* scoring as an important feature of the test; however, there exists considerable

---

[1] The 15 Beck Content scorings eliminated by this procedure are *Aq* (Antiquity), *Ar* (Architecture), *As* (Astronomy), *Dh* (Death), *Im* (Implement), *Mn* (Mineral), *Mu* (Music), *My* (Mythology), *Pr* (Personal), *Rc* (Recreation), *Rl* (Religion), *Ru* (Rural), *Sc* (Science), *Tr* (Travel), and *Vo* (Vocational).

Table 18. Symbols and Criteria to be Used in Scoring for Content

Category	Symbol	Criterion
Whole Human	*H*	Involving or implying the percept of a whole human form.
Whole Human (fictional or mythological)	*(H)*	Involving or implying the percept of a whole human form of a fictional or mythological basis, that is, gnomes, fairies, giants, witches, King Midas, Alice in Wonderland, monsters (human like), ghosts, dwarfs, devils, and angels.
Human Detail	*Hd*	Involving the percept of an incomplete human form, that is, a person but the head is missing, an arm, fingers, two big feet, and the lower part of a woman.
Human Detail (fictional or mythological)	*(Hd)*	Involving the percept of an incomplete human form of a fictional or mythological basis, that is, the hand of God, the head of the devil, the foot of a monster, the head of a witch, and the eyes of an angel.
Whole Animal	*A*	Involving or implying the percept of a whole animal form.
Whole Animal (fictional or mythological)	*(A)*	Involving or implying the percept of a whole animal form of a fictional or mythological basis, that is, unicorn, flying red horse, black beauty, Jonathan Livingston Seagull, the horse of Napoleon, and a magic frog.
Animal Detail	*Ad*	Involving the percept of an incomplete animal form, that is, the hoof of a horse, the claw of a lobster, the head of a fish, the head of a rabbit.
Animal Detail (fictional or mythological)	*(Ad)*	Involving the percept of an incomplete animal form of a fictional or mythological basis, that is, the wing of the bird of prey, Peter Rabbit's head, the head of Pooh Bear, the head of Bambi, and the wings of Pegasus.
Abstraction	*Ab*	Involving the percept which is clearly an abstract concept, that is, fear, depression, elation, and anger. Abstract paintings *are not* included in this scoring.
Alphabet	*A*1	Involving percepts of arabic numerals, that is, 2, 4, and 7, or the letters of the alphabet, that is, A, M, and X.
Anatomy	*An*	Involving the percept of anatomy (internal organs) of either human or animal content, that is, a heart, lungs, stomach, a bleached skull of a cow, a brain of a dog, and the insides of a person's stomach.
Art	*Art*	Involving percepts of paintings, either definitive or abstract, plus other art objects, that is, a family crest, the seal of the president, and a sculpture of a bird.
Anthropology	*Ay*	Involving percepts which have a specific cultural relationship, that is, a totem pole, and a helmut like those used by Romans.
Blood	*B*1	Involving the percept of blood, either human or animal.
Botany	*Bt*	Involving the percept of any plant life, that is, flowers, trees, bushes, and seaweed.
Clothing	*Cg*	Involving the percept of any clothing ordinarily associated with the human, that is, hat, boots, jacket, trousers, and tie. Articles of clothing associated with fictional or mythological characters, that is, the seven league boots, a witches hat, should be scored as *(Cg)*.

Table 18 (Continued)

Category	Symbol	Criterion
Clouds	Cl	Involving the percept of clouds. Variations of this category, such as fog, mist, and so on, should be scored either as Na (Nature) or written out in full.
Explosion	Ex	Involving percepts of an actual explosion, occurring most commonly to Card IX, as an atomic explosion or blast. The scoring determinant for inanimate movement (m) should always accompany this scoring. Percepts of an explosion "aftermath" such as, "A blast has just occurred and things are lying all over the place," should be scored for other content, or written out in complete form.
Fire	Fi	Involving percepts of actual fire, smoke associated with fire, burning candles, flame given off from a torch, and such. These percepts will ordinarily involve the determinant scoring of m to denote the inanimate movement of the "fire" association, but, unlike the "Explosion" content score, this will not always be the case. In other words, fire might be perceived as fire without movement being involved. The most common example of this occurs to the upper red areas ($D2$) of Card II, seen as "fire," with neither movement or form reported.
Food	Fd	Involving the percept of any edible, such as ice cream, fried shrimp, chicken legs, a piece of steak, that is. The intent or meaning of the association must be clearly associated with "everyday" consumer produce, as in the instance of lettuce, cabbage, carrots, fried foods, etc., or must be presented in such a manner as to suggest that the object perceived is identified as a food substance, that is, "looks like a chicken like we used to have for Sunday dinner."
Geography	Ge	Involving percepts of any maps, specified or unspecified, that is, a map of Sicily, or a map of an island, peninsula, and continent. The percepts of Ge do *not* include the actual percept of definite or indefinite land masses which are "real" rather than representations. These type of percepts are scored as Ls (Landscape) or written out in rare instances.
Household	Hh	Involving percepts of interior household items, that is, chairs, beds, bedposts, plates, silverware, and rugs. The scorer should be cautioned not to score "highly idiographic" percepts Hh, as for instance "a butcher knife," rather to write out the full content so as to manifest the idiographic meaningfulness in the scoring.
Landscape	Ls	Involving percepts of landscapes or seascapes, neither of which would be scored as Bt or Ge. A tree or a Bush, might legitimately be scored as Bt, whereas "trees," or "a bunch of shrubs" are more ordinarily scored Ls. This category includes some underwater scenes where specific animals are not identified, or in some instances as a secondary score as in Card X where a few specific animals may be cited but the bulk of the percept is left vague.

Table 18 (Continued)

Category	Symbol	Criterion
Nature	*Na*	Involving percepts of a wider natural scope than are included in *Bt*, *Ge*, or *Ls*, usually including sky, snow, water, raging sea, a storm, night, ice, rainbow, and such. In some responses, the idiographic representation of the content is intense or peculiar, as in "a tornado sweeping everything up in its path." The content score here is legitimately *Na*; however, a written out content scoring of Tornado may be more appropriate.
Sex	*Sx*	Involving percepts of sex organs or activities related to sex function, that is, intercourse, erect penis, menstruation, vagina, testes, and breasts.
X-ray	*Xy*	Involving percepts of x-ray, most of which pertain to bone structure, that is, the x-ray of a pelvis, the x-ray of some bones, but may also involve x-rays of organs or organ like structures, that is, an x-ray of the stomach and an x-ray of the intestines. *Shading is always* involved in these percepts.
Vocational (supplementary)	*(Vo)*	Involving percepts which *may* be interpreted as related to the occupation of the subject. This scoring is *never* used as the primary or main content score but may be included as secondary or additional so as to alert the interpreter of a vocational or occupational percept.

variation across the systems concerning the listings of responses to be scored *P*. These intersystem differences have generally been created by disagreements concerning the criterion of *P*, although in some instances sampling differences have contributed to the variations. Most of the systematizers have chosen to broaden Rorschach's criterion of limiting the *P* scoring to answers occurring at least once in three records. Rapaport (1946) recommends the scoring of *P* for responses occurring once in every four or five records. Beck (1961) lists as Popular, responses occurring at least three times as frequently as the next most commonly occurring answer to a blot, provided that it is given not less than once by at least 14% of his adult sample. Piotrowski (1957), while cautioning that any listing of Popular answers will vary with sampling differences, includes responses given at least once in every four records. Hertz (1970) uses the broadest criterion, defining as Popular, any answer which occurs at least once in six protocols, and thus presents the longest listing of Populars, although not substantially longer than that developed by Beck. The Klopfer (1962) listing of Populars has considerably fewer answers, having been developed from "clinical experience," using Rorschach's guideline of responses occurring once in three protocols.

The suggestions of three respondents to the "Researchers Questionnaire" contributed significantly to the method used for the selection of a "Populars list" for the comprehensive system. Each of these three had cited the need to study the "*P* Deficiency" in the records of the more seriously disturbed schizophrenics. This absence or deficiency of Popular answers has been noted in several empirical works (Rickers-Ovsiankina, 1938; Rapaport, 1946; Beck, 1954; Bloom, 1962), and is probably the most consistent finding across systems. There are many other interpretive conclusions, empirically based, in the literature concerning the incidence of high or low numbers of *P* answers; however, they are often "system-specific" and not easily generalized across systems. It was decided to use the "*P* Deficiency" findings among chronic schizophrenics as a comparative baseline. In other words, responses given with high frequency by nonpsychiatric subjects, and low frequency by chronic schizophrenics might best represent the Popular listing. Accordingly, 300 protocols were collected using the methodology of the comprehensive system, 200 of which were obtained from nonpsychiatric subjects, and 50 from each of two psychiatric groups, one comprised of nonschizophrenic out-patients, and the second of chronic schizophrenic in-patients.[2] These protocols yielded 6983 responses which were coded and entered in computer storage for frequency analysis. Each group was evenly divided for male and female subjects, so that the analysis of response frequencies was available by group and by sex. All subjects were 17 years of age or older, with the mean age for each group at about 29 years.

Two frequency distributions were drawn for each group. The first contains responses occurring in at least one-third of the records, the second responses occurring in at least one-fourth of the records. A listing of responses derived using the "one-in-three" criterion shows 13 answers for both the nonpsychiatric and nonschizophrenic groups. The schizophrenic population yielded only four responses meeting the criterion, three of which occurred in the other two groups. The listing of responses derived using the "one-in-four" criterion yielded 17 answers for the nonpsychiatric group, 18 answers for the nonschizophrenic group (which include all 17 for the nonpsychiatric group), and seven for the schizophrenic sample, which includes six from each of the other two listings.[3] These findings appear to give support to the adoption of the "one-in-three" criterion for the definition of the Popular response in the comprehensive system in that absolute agreement occurs between the nonpsychiatric and nonschizophrenic groups, and concurrently, schizophrenic subjects do manifest a statistically significant "*P* Deficiency."

The adoption of the one-in-three criterion and the corresponding list of 13 Popular responses also avoid a problem of sex differences which occurs when the one-in-four criterion is applied. Some sex differences do exist using the one-in-three criterion, but they occur within a class of response rather than actually manifesting different contents. For example, by either criteria, female subjects tend to give the response of "butterfly" to Card I more than do male subjects. This is also true in responses to Card V. A more extensive difference between males and females is found when the one-in-four criterion is used. In that instance, the response of a human, or human-like creature, becomes "Popular" to Card IV, but with female

---

[2] The criterion used in selecting "chronic" in-patient schizophrenics was threefold; (1) at least two independently derived diagnoses of schizophrenia, (2) at least two hospitalizations equal to at least 30 months total hospitalization time, and (3) current hospitalization to have lasted no less than 9 months. The nonschizophrenic out-patients represent a variety of diagnostic categories, including reactive and neurotic depression, psychosomatic, obsessive-compulsive neurosis, and a variety of characterological disorders.

[3] Interestingly, 28 of the 50 chronic schizophrenics (56%) gave the response "blood" to the upper detail areas of Card II. Technically, this frequency meets the criterion for popularity, within that group. Obviously, it occurred with considerably less frequency in the other groups, and thus is not scored *P*.

subjects generally reporting "a man" or variation thereof, and male subjects more commonly reporting "a monster." The most distinct sex difference occurs on Card IX when the one-in-four criterion is applied. Both males and females report a human head in the lower $D4$ area, but females report a witch or variation thereof almost twice as frequently as males to the upper $D3$ area of the card.

The 13 Popular responses designated for the comprehensive system are shown in Table 19, which also includes the percentage reporting the P in the nonpsychiatric and schizophrenic groups. It seems important to note that this listing is based on an adult population, 17 and older, and thus does not necessarily hold true for the child or young adolescent. The scoring of P should be used only for these responses, however, if the comprehensive system is employed. Some scorers will wish to "further refine" their scoring by using the symbol (P) for percepts which are similar, but not identical, to those listed as Popular. For example, "an eagle" in response

Table 19. **Popular Responses Selected for the Comprehensive System Based on the Frequency of Occurrence of at Least Once in Every Three Protocols Given by Nonpsychiatric Adult Subjects and Nonschizophrenic Adult Out-Patients**

Card	Location	Criterion	% Nonpsychiatric Reporting	% Schizophrenic Reporting
I	W	Bat or butterfly. The response always involves the whole blot and alterations in location or content have not been found to be Popular.	86	32
I	$D4$	Human figure, ordinarily reported as female. The figure is described as a whole human or headless human. No other variations are P, nor is the lower half of this area ($D3$) described as a part of a human found to be P. Where the percept to $D4$ is of a male figure, the scoring of (P) may be most appropriate.	48	13
II	$D1$	Animal forms, usually the heads of dogs or bears, however the frequency of the whole animal to this area is sufficient to warrant the scoring of P. If the content does not specify a dog or bear, the (P) score may be more appropriate. (*Note.* The percept of whole humans or whole animals using the entire blot does not meet the P criterion but does approach that level (26%) and may be scored as (P).	39	9
III	$D1$ or $D9$	Two human figures, or representations thereof, such as dolls and caricatures. The scoring of P is also applicable to the percept of a single human figure to area $D9$. Human movement, as a determinant, is frequently associated with, but not necessary for the scoring of P.	82	50

Table 19 (Continued)

Card	Location	Criterion	% Nonpsychiatric Reporting	% Schizophrenic Reporting
III	D3	Butterfly, designated by reason of form but sometimes involving color as a determinant.	44	12
IV	W, or W minus D1	Animal skin, or human figure dressed in animal skin or an appropriate variation thereof, such as "in a fur coat." This category of Popular also includes the large "furry" animal. The proof of the P rests with the designation of the "furry" pelt or pelt-like covering.	38	16
IV	D6	Shoe or boot, seen separately or in association with an animal or human figure. The designation of the shoe or boot in the D2 area has not been discovered to be P.	44	12
V	W	Bat or butterfly, the apex of the card upright or inverted. Variations of the content, such as moth, vulture, and eagle, are probably best scored as (P).	91	28
VI	W, or D1	Animal skin, hide, rug, or pelt.	68	24
VII	D1	Human heads or faces, ordinarily perceived as women or children. A W response involving the human percept typically notes the lower D4 portion of the blot as a content separate from the Hd, such as, a rock, pedestal, and bush. Where the D4 is reported as part of the human figure, the scoring might better be (P).	54	9
VIII	D1	Whole animal figure. This is the most frequently perceived common answer, the content varying considerably, such as bear, dog, rodent, fox, wolf, and coyote. All are scored as P. The P is also scored when the animal figure is reported as part of a W percept as in a family crest, seal, and emblem.	95	37
IX	D4	A human face or head, usually reported as male and frequently identified as T. Roosevelt, or perceived as an infant. This percept occurs with the least frequency of all Popular answers.	34	6
X	D1	Crab, lobster, or spider. In some instances the object has greater specificity as in sand crab, daddy long legs, and crawfish. Other variations of multilegged animals are not P.	57	26

to Card I is not a Popular answer, yet it is usually specified in a manner very much like that used by subjects who give the Popular "bat" or "butterfly" responses. The meaningfulness of the (P) scoring is still somewhat conjectural and is discussed in comparison to the "true" P answers in the chapters on Interpretation. It is also important to reaffirm Piotrowski's caution that some variation of the listing of Popular answers seems inevitable when different cultures are compared; however, as discussed in detail later, the intercultural differences apparently must be substantial for the listing to be altered significantly.

The mean number of P answers given by the 200 nonpsychiatric subjects is 6.7 (SD = 1.8). The mean number of P answers given by the nonschizophrenic outpatient group is 7.2 (SD = 2.1), and the mean P for the schizophrenic group is 2.4 (SD = 2.2). Beck (1961) has reported that the average number of Popular answers varies with the length of the record, ranging from a mean of 4 to 5 for the 10 to 19 response protocols, to a mean of 9 to 10 for the 50 to 79 response record. This is not generally the case in the comprehensive system, partly because the absolute number of Popular answers is considerably less than Beck's listing, but also because the variation in protocol length is less than derived in the Beck system, apparently due to the differences in instruction and extent of encouragement.

SPECIAL SCORINGS

A variety of other types of scoring are reported in the literature which have been considered for inclusion in the comprehensive system, but which have not been adopted. The exclusion of these scorings does not necessarily imply a lack of utility, for this is clearly not the case. In some instances, the decision not to adopt a scoring methodology is derived from an unconvincing empirical literature. In other instances, it appeared that scoring methodologies included in the system encompassed the bulk of that which the special scoring represents. Finally, in some instances, it is obvious that the special scoring might overextend an already complex methodology without offering clinically helpful information to the everyday Rorschacher. Nevertheless, It seems important to make note of these special approaches to the scoring of responses, as they may be invaluable to some researchers and/or practitioners.

ORIGINAL RESPONSES

Rorschach (1921) suggested that a scoring should be included to represent the Original (*Originalantwort*) answer. He defined the Original, scored as O, as the response which occurs no more than once in 100 records. He also indicated that some O responses would be quite creative and would involve good form quality (scored $O+$), whereas others, involving a poor form selection, might be more indicative of pathology (scored $O-$). Each of the Rorschach systematizers, except Beck, has attempted to include this scoring in their respective systems, but with various qualifications and only limited success. Rapaport (1946), for example, cautions that only the very experienced Rorschacher (having given 400 to 500 records) should attempt to score for O. Piotrowski (1957) wisely notes that the scoring of O will be much more subjective, depending on the experience of the examiner, than will other Rorschach scores. As Klopfer (1942) points out, "Any attempt to list representative samples of O responses would be a hopeless enterprise, since the number of original responses is by definition unlimited." Beck defends his decision to exclude the formal scoring of O partly on the basis that some O answers are simply a product of unique location selections, which are different than the qualitatively rich, creative answer. The Hertz (1970) scoring of O probably is closest to Rorschach's intent, developing listings of $O+$ and $O-$ responses from statistical frequencies. She adds the caution that Original answers cannot automatically be interpreted as representing a rich "creativeness or inventiveness." The complications created by such statistical frequencies, plus the fact that the empirical support for a scoring of O is extremely limited, seemed to argue in favor of exclusion of an O scoring in the comprehensive system. This decision seems strengthened further by the fact that the scoring format used in the comprehensive system includes several elements from which the rich, creative answer is easily identified, such as the scoring for developmental quality, form quality, organizational activity, and the complexity of the blend.

BODY-IMAGE BOUNDARY SCORING

The development of a special coding of some Rorschach responses, which are seemingly related to the Body-Image Boundary concept, has been one of the most interesting of the experimental approaches to the test. This work, initiated by Fisher and Cleveland (1955) in a study of arthritic patients, and leading to a scoring system (1958), attempts to differentiate the "firm" body boundary from the "weak" or easily "penetrable." Two basic scores or codes are employed. One is the Barrier score which is applicable to contents which have a definiteness to the structure or surface. The second is a Penetration score which is afforded those percepts in which the boundary of the object reported is weak or lacking in substance. The scoring is derived exclusively from content, regardless of whether elicited during the Free Association or in the Inquiry. A sizable literature has developed concerning the significance of the B and P scores which has recently received a thorough review (Goldfried, Stricker, and Weiner, 1971). It seems clear from this review that many questions concerning the scoring and meaningfulness of the scores remain unresolved although some findings, particularly those regarding the Barrier scores, are quite encouraging.

CODING OF UNUSUAL VERBALIZATIONS

Most Rorschachers give significance, in their interpretations, to answers which include unusual verbalizations. Rapaport (1946) attempted to formally "schematize" a series of categories which could be used, in conjunction with the formal scoring, to denote their presence. These categories include the Fabulized response, Fabulized Combinations, Confabulations, Contaminations, Autistic Logic, Peculiar verbalizations, The Self-Reference Response, and such. These categories attempted to formalize, and thereby differentiate, different kinds of "idiographic" displays that frequently occur in the test. Unfortunately, as Rapaport cautions, some of the discriminations overlap, and the issue of scorer–interpreter subjectivity in the assignment of categories is extremely difficult if not impossible to resolve. Obviously, any unusual verbalizations occurring in a response are important to the interpreter, but a formal and objectively useful coding of them can become unwieldy, especially if the definitions of categories are not extremely precise and avoid overlap. It is for this reason that no effort is made at this time to provide special codings of verbalizations in the comprehensive system. The assumption here is that the astute clinician will note the more unusual verbalizations in the protocol, particularly contaminations, and peculiar phrases, and include these notations into his overall interpretation. Such use of unusual verbalizations is demonstrated in detailed case studies by Schafer (1954) and Weiner (1966). Some of these scorings are also shown in Protocol #8 of this work.

In a similar, but much more sophisticated procedure, Holt (1966, 1970) has been developing special codings of content which also include the formal scoring properties of the test. This procedure is referred to in the literature as the scoring for primary process (PRIPRO), and is designed to provide information concerning many of the basic cognitive operations, such as flexibility, adaptive regression, and defense effectiveness. At this time Holt's work is still incomplete, however, data which have been published concerning its usefulness are quite encouraging, especially in that it appears useful as a companion scoring to any of the current Rorschach methodologies, including the comprehensive system.

REFERENCES

Beck, S. J. *The six schizophrenias*. American Orthopsychiatric Association, Research Monograph No. 6, 1954.

Beck, S. J., Beck, A. Levitt, E., and Molish, H. B. *Rorschach's Test. I: Basic Processes.* (3rd ed.) New York: Grune and Stratton, 1961.

Bloom, B. L. The Rorschach Popular response among Hawaiian schizophrenics. *Journal of Projective Techniques*, 1962, **26,** 173–181.

Fisher, S., and Cleveland, S. E. The role of body image in psychosomatic symptom choice. *Psychological Monographs*, 1955, **69,** Whole No. 402.

Fisher, S., and Cleveland, S. E. *Body Image and Personality*. New York: Van Nostrand Reinhold, 1958.

Goldfried, M. R., Stricker, G., and Weiner, I. B. *Rorschach Handbook of Clinical and Research Applications*. Englewood Cliffs, N.J.: Prentice-Hall, 1971.

Hertz, M. R. *Frequency Tables for Scoring Rorschach Responses*. (5th ed.) Cleveland: The Press of Case Western Reserve University, 1970.

Holt, R. R. Measuring libidinal and aggressive motives and their controls by means of the Rorschach Test. In Levine, D. (Ed.), *Nebraska Symposium on Motivation*. Lincoln, Neb.: University of Nebraska Press, 1966.

Holt, R. R. Artistic creativity and adaptive regression. In Klopfer, B., Meyer, M., and Brawer, F. (Eds.), *Developments in the Rorschach Technique*. New York: Harcourt, Brace, and Javanovich, 1970.

Klopfer, B., and Kelley, D. *The Rorschach Technique*. Yonkers-on-Hudson, N.Y.: World Book Company, 1942.

Klopfer, B., and Davidson, H. *The Rorschach Technique. An Introductory Manual.* New York: Harcourt, Brace and World, 1962.

Piotrowski, Z. *Perceptanalysis.* New York: MacMillan, 1957.

Rapaport, D., Gill, M., and Schafer, R. *Diagnostic Psychological Testing.* Vol. 2. Chicago: Yearbook Publishers, 1946.

Rickers-Ovsiankina, M. The Rorschach Test as applied to normal and schizophrenic subjects. *British Journal of Medical Psychology*, 1938, **17,** 227–257.

Rorschach, H. *Psychodiagnostics.* Bern: Bircher, 1921 (Transl. Hans Huber Verlag, 1942).

Rorschach, H., and Oberholzer, E. The application of the interpretation of form to Psychoanalysis. *Zeitschrift fur gesamte Neurologie und Psychiatrie*, 1923, **82,** 240–274.

Schafer, R. *Psychoanalytic Interpretation in Rorschach Testing.* New York: Grune and Stratton, 1954.

Weiner, J. B. *Psychodiagnosis in Schizophrenia.* New York: Wiley, 1966.

CHAPTER 8

The Quantitative Summary

The quantitative summarization of the protocol is developed after each of the responses has been scored. The summary procedure consolidates the scores or codings so that they may be reviewed as a total configuration and so that comparisons of scoring components may be accomplished with ease. The summary represents a structural composite of the test in which the accumulation of scores, frequencies, ratios, percentages, and such form the basis for the beginnings of interpretation. Many important postulates may be drawn from this structure which, when integrated subsequently with information obtained from the "content," or qualitative analysis of the record, renders a highly idiographic description of the "psychology" of the subject. The summary or structure consists of three component parts, (1) a listing by chronological sequence of each of the scorings in the record, (2) the compilation of frequency tallies, one for each of the scoring elements in the protocol, and (3) the calculation of several ratios and percentages.

L. S. 26 YEAR OLD MALE, MARRIED, ONE CHILD (MALE 1 YEAR), HIGH SCHOOL TEACHER

The protocol of L. S., a 26 year old male, is included here to illustrate each of the three components of the structural summary as they are described in more detail.

LISTING OF SCORES BY SEQUENCE

The first step in the summarization is the listing of scores in the order of their occurrence in the record. The scores are shown by card, and with the reaction time for the first response to each card also entered. This sequence of scores becomes the basis for several operations. It is a simple task of transferring the scores from the protocol to a separate sheet. The scoring sequence for the protocol of L. S. is shown in Table 20. This consolidation makes the scores easier with which to work in the various calculations necessary, and provides an important data base of information concerning the approach of the subject to the test.

FREQUENCIES OF SCORES

The second step in developing the structural summary is the tallying of the frequency with which each type of score occurs. Table 21 shows a Scoring Structure Summary

138

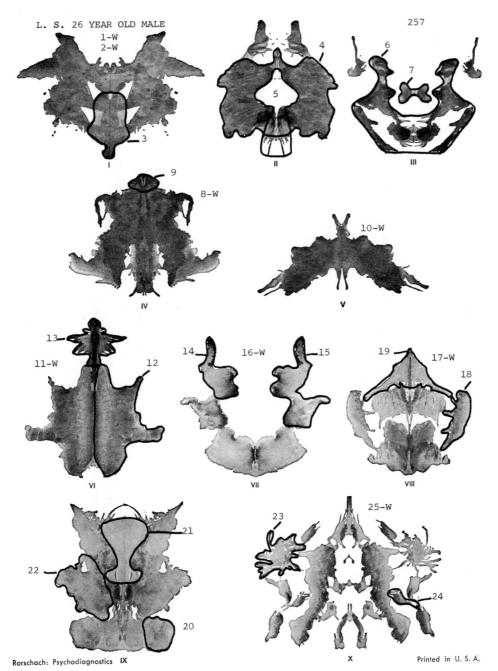

L. S. 26 YEAR OLD MALE
1-W
2-W
3
I

257
4
5
II

6
7
III

9
8-W
IV

10-W
V

13
11-W
12
VI

14
16-W
15
VII

19
17-W
18
VIII

21
22
20
Rorschach: Psychodiagnostics IX

25-W
23
24
X
Printed in U. S. A.

Figure 2. Location Selections by L. S.

139

L. S. 26 YEAR OLD MALE, MARRIED, ONE CHILD (MALE 1 YEAR), HIGH SCHOOL TEACHER

Card		Free Association	Inquiry	Scoring
I	4″	1. ll a bat gliding along	E: (Rpts S's resp) S: It has the outstrchd wgs & the small ft feet & ths cntr part wld b the body	Wo FM^po A P 1.0
		2. It cld also b a modrn dance of s.s. w a wm in the cntr w her hands in the air & 2 creatures dancg around her	E: (Rpts S's resp) S: Yes, it ll her hands r raised in sort of supplication & ths creatures on the side reprsnt s.t. symbolic of whatever she's doing E: Symbolic S: They rem me of those wgd A's in Greek mythology, I can't rem the name.	$W+$ M^a+ (2) $H, (A)$ P 4.0
		3. Say, ths lowr prt c.b. a bell	E: (Rpts S's resp) S: It has a pretty good shape of one w the clapper here	Ddo Fo Bell
II	6″	4. It cld b a cpl of dogs touchg noses	E: (Rpts S's resp) S: Its ths drkr areas (points), it ll the upper prts of dogs, thr noses r touchg, ths wld b the ear E: Upper parts? S: Its just the neck & head, u can't c the rest of the body	$D+$ FM^po (2) Ad P 3.0
		5. The cntr cld b a rocket ship taking off & ths red cld b the exhaust fire	E: (Rpts S's resp) S: It has a delta shape & the way the color is there u get the impression of firey exhaust & upward motion	$DS+$ $m^a.CFo$ Rocket, Fi 4.5
III	5″	6. A cpl of men bendg ovr to lift s.t. up	E: (Rpts S's resp) S: U can c the gen outlns of thm, it ll thy'r about to lift s.t. up but I can't tell what it is	$D+$ M^ao (2) H P 3.0

140

Card	Time	No.	Response	Inquiry	Loc & DQ	Determinant(s)	Content	P	Z
		7.	The cntr red area c.b. a bowtie	E: (Rpts S's resp) S: Well, the red attracted my attention to it, made me thk of those big red bowties that clowns wear sometimes	Do	FCo	Cg		
IV	7″	8.	It cld b a gorilla sittg on a stump	E: (Rpts S's resp) S: Yeah, it looks all furry lik a big A, lik a gorilla w the feet here (points), sorta lik he's leaning bkward bec the ft r so much bigger E: U said it looks furry S: Yes, all of the color variation makes it ll that	W+	FMp.FT.FDo	A	P	4.0
		9.	A delicate flower	E: (Rpts S's resp) S: I don't kno the name, my wife grows them, they almost ll velvet w ths contour & coloring effect E: Coloring effect? S: Yes, all the different shades in there	Do	FYo	Bt		
V	4″	10.	It cld b a bat or a bf, I thk more a bf now that I look at it bec I said bat before.	E: (Rpts S's resp) S: Well it has the wgs & antennae & the split tail lik som bf's hve E: I'm not sure where u see it S: All of it I suppose, the W thg	Wo	Fo	A	P	1.0
VI	3″	11.	Wld u believe an A skin?	E: (Rpts S's resp) S: I don't kno what kind of A, prob from the cat family bec of the stuff around the head E: The stuff around the head? S: Well actually, the W thg looks furry & spotted, lik from a tiger or s.t. & ths r whiskers	Wo	FTo	Ad	P	2.5

141

Card	Free Association	Inquiry	Scoring			
	<12. Ths c.b. a submarine crusg along in the drkness	E: (Rpts S's resp) S: It has a pretty good shape of a sub, & the fact its all blk makes me thk of drknss, like at night, the blackns is like a shadowy effect, lik a nite, u get a good effect of the superstructure, the conning tower part here (points) & the long bow (points)	Do	m^p.FY+		Ship
	13. U kno, tht c.b. a totem too	E: (Rpts S's resp) S: The gen form of it rem me of kind of carving u mite c on a totem, usually a wgs effect like ths has to it	Do	Fo		Ay
VII	14. A cpl of kids	E: (Rpts S's resp) S: Just the heads, lik they hav feathers in their hair E: I'm not sure why they ll tht S: U can c the gen features, chins, noses, foreheads, that sort of thg	Do	Fo	(2)	Hd P
	<15. Ths way the side ll a scotty dog	E: (Rpts S's resp) S: It has the blunt nose, thes r the short legs, & here's the tail	Do	Fo		A
	V16. Ths way it ll a cpl of wm doing the can-can	E: (Rpts S's resp) S: Thy hav big hairdos & r dancg on one leg, sort of throwg their heads backward	W+	M^a+	(2)	H 3.0
VIII	17. The W thg cld b an emblem	E: (Rpts S's resp) S: Yes, its like a family crest of s.s., beig symmetrical & quite colorful	Wo	FCo		Art 4.5
	18. Ths thg on the side c.b. A's of s.s.	E: (Rpts S's resp) S: There's 2 of 'em, one on each side E: Can u tell me how u c them S: Well thy c.b. mice or s.t. of the ro-	Do	Fo	(2)	A P

142

dent family, c (points) here r the legs & head & tail

19. U kno, ths top prt c.b. a sand crab, lik it was leapg forward, going away from u

E: (Rpts S's resp)
S: The pincers r here (points) & the area where the eyes r & it has the legs extended lik it was leaping out, prob going away fr u the proportions give that effect

Do FM^a.FDo A

IX 19"

20. Ths ll T. Roosevelt's head

E: (Rpts S's resp)
S: Rite here in the pink, its got the mustache & the flat forehead, its just the head, it really ll tht

Do Fo Hd P

21. Tht cntr prt c.b. a vase

E: (Rpts S's resp)
S: Its just shaped lik a vase to me

Do Fo Hh

<22. U kno, ths way it ll a person on a motorcycle or bike

E: (Rpts S's resp)
S: Ths W green prt, most of it ll the person, I guess a heavy set man, & he's holdg the handlebars. The bike isn't too clear but the way his head is formed there u can get the impression of his hair flying bk in the breeze

D+ M^a+ H 2.5

X 8"

23. Ths blue thg ll crabs

E: (Rpts S's resp)
S: Thy just giv tht impress w all the legs

Do Fo (2) A P

24. Ths brwn c.b. a deer jumpg

E: (Rpts S's resp)
S: The legs r outstrtchd & u can c the antlers here (points)

Do FM^{a}o A

√25. Ths way it ll a floral scene, w a huge flower in the cntr & smaller flwrs around it

E: (Rpts S's resp)
S: Well, the cntr flwr made me thk of it & I stretched it abit about the other thgs
E: I'm not sure what u were seeing
S: Its very colorful, the pink c.b. a daffodil & the blue pom poms but I can't really identify the rest. Its very pretty tho like a floral display

W+ FC+ Bt 5.5

Table 20.   Scoring Sequence for the Protocol of L.S.

Card	RT	No.	Location	Determinant(s)		Content(s)	Pop	Z Score
I	4″	1.	Wo	FM^po		A	P	1.0
		2.	$W+$	M^a+	(2)	$H, (A)$	P	4.0
		3.	Ddo	Fo		Bell		
II	6″	4.	$D+$	FM^po	(2)	Ad	P	3.0
		5.	$DS+$	$m^a.CFo$		Rocket, Fi		4.5
III	5″	6.	$D+$	M^ao	(2)	H	P	3.0
		7.	Do	FCo		Cg		
IV	7″	8.	$W+$	$FM^p.FT.FDo$		A	P	4.0
		9.	Do	FYo		Bt		
V	4″	10.	Wo	Fo		A	P	1.0
VI	3″	11.	Wo	FTo		Ad	P	2.5
		12.	Do	$m^p.FY+$		Ship		
		13.	Do	Fo		Ay		
VII	5″	14.	Do	Fo		Hd	P	
		15.	Do	Fo		A		
		16.	$W+$	M^a+	(2)	H		3.0
VIII	7″	17.	Wo	FCo		Art		4.5
		18.	Do	Fo	(2)	A	P	
		19.	Do	$FM^a.FDo$		A		
IX	19″	20.	Do	Fo		Hd	P	
		21.	Do	Fo		Hh		
		22.	$D+$	M^a+		H		2.5
X	8″	23.	Do	Fo	(2)	A	P	
		24.	Do	FM^ao		A		
		25.	$W+$	$FC+$		Bt		5.5

Sheet which was developed for use with the comprehensive system. The frequency tallies of scores from the L.S. protocol are shown to illustrate how the sheet is used.

Locations Features: Each of the types of location scores are tallied separately. A frequency of the incidence of S is also shown, although in the formal scoring S is always included with another location score. A frequency tally is also entered for the Developmental Quality scores, disregarding the type of location used. Some scorers may wish to further subdivide the DQ scores by location used so as to compute high and low W and D percentages as suggested by Rapaport (1946) and Friedman (1953). The High $W\%$, for example, is derived by determining the proportion of $+$ and o W's used out of all W locations selected. In the L.S. protocol, the High $W\%$ would equal 100 as all W's used are either $+$ or o.

Determinants: Each of the determinant scores are tallied separately, except when occurring in a Blend. Each Blend is entered in its basic form and determinants included in Blends *are not* counted again as each of the frequencies for the single determinants are obtained.

Form Quality: Two distributions are entered concerning Form Quality. The first, shown by the heading on the Summary Sheet as FQx (Form Quality Extended), includes all responses in the protocol in which Form is used. In other words, all

Table 21. Scoring Structure Summary Sheet for the Protocol of L.S.

$R = 25$ $Zf = 12$ $ZSum = 38.5$ $P = 11$ $(2) = 7$

Location Features			Determinants (list blends first)		Contents		Contents (idiographic)	
W	$= 8$	DQ			H	$= 4$		
			$FM.FT.FD$	$= 1$	(H)	$=$	Bell	$= 1$
D	$= 16$	$+ = 8$	$FM.FD$	$= 1$	Hd	$= 2$		
			$m.CF$	$= 1$	(Hd)	$=$	Rocket	$= 1$
Dd	$= 1$	$o = 17$	$m.FY$	$= 1$	A	$= 8$		
					(A)	$= 0,1$	Ship	$= 1$
S	$= 1$	$v =$	M	$= 4$	Ad	$= 2$		
			FM	$= 3$	(Ad)	$=$	———	$=$
$DW =$		$- =$	m	$=$	Ab	$=$		
			C	$=$	Al	$=$	———	$=$
			CF	$=$	An	$=$		
			FC	$= 3$	Art	$= 1$	———	$=$
			C'	$=$	Ay	$= 1$		
FORM QUALITY			$C'F$	$=$	Bl	$=$	———	$=$
			FC'	$=$	Bt	$= 2$		
FQx		FQf	T	$=$	Cg	$= 1$	———	$=$
			TF	$=$	Cl	$=$		
$+ = 5$		$+ =$	FT	$= 1$	Ex	$=$		
			V	$=$	Fi	$= 0,1$		
$o = 20$		$o = 9$	VF	$=$	Fd	$=$		
			FV	$=$	Ge	$=$		
$w =$		$w =$	Y	$=$	Hh	$= 1$		
			YF	$=$	Ls	$=$		
$- =$		$- =$	FY	$= 1$	Na	$=$		
			rF	$=$	Sx	$=$		
			Fr	$=$	xy	$=$		
			FD	$=$				
			F	$= 9$				

RATIOS, PERCENTAGES, AND DERIVATIONS

$ZSum/Zest = 38.5/38.0$	$FC/CF + C = 3/1$	Afr	$= 0.56$		
$Zd = +0.5$	$W/M = 8/4$	$3r + (2)/R$	$= 7/25 = .28$		
$EB = 4/2.5$ $EA = 6.5$	$W/D = 8/16$	$Cont/R$	$= 10/25$		
$eb = 7/4$ $ep = 11$	$L = .56$	$H + Hd/A + Ad = 6/10$			
$Blends/R = 4/25$	$F + \% = 100$	$H + A/Hd + Ad = 12/4$			
$a/p = 7/4$	$X + \% = 100$	XRT Achrom	$= 4.6''$		
$M^a/M^p = 4/0$	$A\% = 40$	XRT Chrom	$= 9.0''$		

responses except those which are *exclusively* Pure Color or Pure Shading. The second, headed on the Summary Sheet as FQf (Form Quality-form) is a distribution of the Form Quality scores of responses in which Pure Form, F, is the only determinant.

Organizational Scores: Two entries are required concerning the scores for organizational activity. The first, Zf, is the number of times a Z response has occurred in the record. The second is the $ZSum$, which represents the summation of the weighted Z scorings assigned in the protocol.

Content Scores: The frequency with which each of the formal content categories has occurred in the record is entered by the respective scoring abbreviation. A special column of blank spaces is also included for the entry of idiographic contents, that is, those for which no formal scoring category is available.

Pairs and Populars: The number of pair responses and the number of Popular responses are entered in the spaces provided.

RATIOS, PERCENTAGES, AND SPECIAL DERIVATIONS

The final step in preparing the structural summary involves the calculation and entry of 24 ratios, percentages, and special score derivations. These are obtained by using the data in the frequency tallies, or from the sequence of scores. They constitute a nucleus of the summary structure and are the source from which most of the interpretive postulates, derived from the structural summary, originate. The 24 ratios, percentages, and derivations are entered in the lower portion of the Summary Sheet, as shown in Table 21. Some of these were suggested by Rorschach, while others have been created in the various Rorschach systems. Several have evolved in the development of the comprehensive system.

ZSum/Zest: This is a comparative ratio which shows the obtained sum of weighted Z (ZSum) versus the best weighted Z prediction (Zest) using the Wilson and Blake (1950) method. The Zest is a value taken from Table 22, corresponding

Table 22. Best Weighted ZSum Prediction When Zf is Known[a]

Zf	Zest	Zf	Zest
1	*	26	88.0
2	2.5	27	91.5
3	6.0	28	95.0
4	10.0	29	98.5
5	13.5	30	102.5
6	17.0	31	105.5
7	20.5	32	109.0
8	24.0	33	112.5
9	27.5	34	116.5
10	31.0	35	120.0
11	34.5	36	123.5
12	38.0	37	127.0
13	41.5	38	130.5
14	45.5	39	134.0
15	49.0	40	137.5
16	52.5	41	141.0
17	56.0	42	144.5
18	59.5	43	148.0
19	63.0	44	152.0
20	66.5	45	155.5
21	70.0	46	159.0
22	73.5	47	162.5
23	77.0	48	166.0
24	81.0	49	169.5
25	84.5	50	173.0

[a] Taken from, Beck, S. J., Beck, A., Levitt, E., and Molish, H. *Rorschach's Test I: Basic Processes* (3rd ed.) New York: Grune and Stratton, 1961.

to the *Zf* obtained in the protocol. For example, the L.S. protocol has a *Zf* of 12, which corresponds to a predicted weighted *Z*Sum (Zest) of 38.0.

Zd: This is a difference score, obtained by subtracting the Zest from the *Z*Sum. In the L.S. protocol the *Z*Sum/Zest is 38.5/38.0; thus the *Zd* = +0.5.

EB (**Erlebnistypus**): This is a basic ratio suggested by Rorschach (1921). It represents a comparison of the sum of human movement responses in the record to the weighted sum of color responses given. It is used in all of the Rorschach systems and is generally considered to be one of the most important elements in the quantitative summary. It has been variously referred to as the Experience Type, Experience Balance, and *M* to Sum *C* ratio. It is entered as Sum *M*/Sum Weighted *C*. The Sum weighted *C* is obtained by assigning the following values to each chromatic color determinant, *FC* = 0.5, *CF* = 1.0, *C* or *Cn* = 1.5. All human movement and chromatic color responses are included in the Erlebnistypus, regardless of whether they appear as the only determinant of a response, or appear in a blend.[1] The L.S. protocol contains 4 *M* determinants, 3 *FC* determinants, and 1 *CF* answer, yielding an *EB* = 4/2.5.

EA (**Experience Actual**): This is a derivation, suggested by Beck (1960) which is obtained from the data in the Erlebnistypus. It is the Sum *M* plus the Sum weighted *C*, or in other words, an adding together of the components appearing in the Erlebnistypus.

eb (**Experience Base**): This is a ratio developed from research with the comprehensive system. It follows from a similar ratio suggested by Klopfer (1954) and represents a comparison of all nonhuman movement determinants with all responses involving the use of shading or achromatic features of the blots. It is entered as, Sum *FM* + *m*/Sum *Y* + *T* + *V* + *C′*. In the L.S. protocol, for example, there are 5 *FM* and 2 *m* responses, plus 2 *FY* and 2 *FT* answers, yielding an *eb* = 7/4.

ep (**Experience Potential**): This is a derivation obtained from the data in the Experience Base, representing the Sum *FM* + *m* + Sum of *Y* + *T* + *V* + *C′*. It is related to the Experience Base as the Experience Actual relates to the Erlebnistypus.

Blends/*R*: This entry in the structural summary represents the number of blends in the record as contrasted with the total number of responses.

a/p (**Active/Passive**): The ratio contrasts the actual numbers of active and passive movements in the record. It represents *all types* of movement answers, *M*, *FM*, and *m*.

M^a/M^p: This entry is similar to the *a/p* ratio but includes *only* human movement responses.

FC/CF + *C*: This ratio shows the absolute number of form dominated chromatic color responses as compared with the absolute number of color dominant chromatic answers. Each of the chromatic color determinants are weighed equally in this

---

[1] Klopfer, although using the same computational method as suggested here for arriving at the Sum weighted *C*, does not include determinants scored as "Additional" in the basic calculation. Thus the *EB* derived by most of the Rorschach systems, including the comprehensive system is often different than that shown in a Klopfer system summary.

ratio, as contrasted with the weighed Sum C used in the EB and EA. Cn determinants are included as color dominant answers.

W/M: This entry represents a comparison of the number of W location selections to the absolute number of numan movement answers.

W/D: This ratio is a comparison of the number of Whole responses with the number of responses involving Common Detail areas.

L (**Lambda**):   The Lambda represents the computation of the ratio of Pure F responses to non-Pure F responses. Most of the Rorschach systems express the relationship as a percentage ($F\%$), calculated as Sum F/R; however, Beck (1950) has offered a logical argument favoring a ratio index (Lambda) which avoids some of the problems of interpreting percentages where R is varied. In this context, the Beck Lambda Index has been adopted in the comprehensive system to represent the F:non-F relationship. Lambda is calculated as Sum Pure F R's/Sum non-Pure F R's. In the L.S. protocol there are nine Pure F responses and 16 non-Pure F responses, yielding $L = .56$.

$F+\%$:   This is basic feature of the structural summary which was originally suggested by Rorschach to denote the proportion of Pure F responses manifesting an appropriate use of the form characteristics of the blot. It is calculated as Sum $(F+)$ + (Fo)/Sum Pure F R's. This percentage includes *only* Pure Form responses.

$X+\%$:   This percentage represents the proportion of good form usage throughout the record. It is a modification of a calculation originally suggested by Rapaport (1946) and elaborated on by Schafer (1954), as the Extended $F+\%$. Rapaport had recommended that, in addition to the regular $F+\%$, a second calculation be included involving the appropriateness of form in all responses in which form is the dominant feature (M, FC, FY, etc.). Investigation concerning the usefulness of Rapaport's Extended $F+\%$ reveals that a more precise evaluation of appropriateness of "form fit" is derived if all responses in the record containing form are included, regardless of whether form is dominant or secondary. In view of this finding, the $X+\%$ (Extended $+\%$) has been adopted for use in the comprehensive system. It is calculated as Sum $(+)$ + (o) R's/R. The rationale for using R as the denominator, rather than Sum (w) + $(-)$ R's, is to include the "form absent" responses, such as Pure Color or Pure Shading answers, wherein the disregard of form can be interpreted as inappropriate usage of the stimulus.

$A\%$:   This percentage, originally suggested by Rorschach, represents the proportion of animal content response in the protocol. It is calculated as $A + Ad/R$.

Afr (**Affective Ratio**):   This is an index derived from the ratio of the number of responses given to the last three cards of the test as compared with the number given to the first seven cards of the test. The Affective Ratio was suggested by Beck (1944) as a more accurate representation of the proportion of responses given to the last three cards than a percentage, such as the VIII, IX, X$\%$ which had been recommended by Klopfer (1939). The Afr is calculated as Sum R (VIII + IX + X)/ Sum R (I − VII).

$3r + (2)/R$ (**Egocentricity Index**):   This entry represents the proportion of reflection and pair responses in the total record, wherein the reflection answers, because of their relative "scarcity" in most records, are weighed as being equal to three pair answers. The weight afforded the reflection response is based on research using the comprehensive system and the Self-Focus Sentence Completion Test with a wide variety of psychiatric and nonpsychiatric subjects in which the criterion for egocentricity has been both behavioral and judgemental measures (Exner, 1973). The calculation of the this ratio is $3(Fr + rF) + (2)/R$.

Cont/R: This entry represents the number of different contents in the protocol as compared with the total number of responses. In determining the number of contents in the record, H and Hd are combined as one category (human), and A and Ad are combined as a single category (animal). All other content categories appearing in the summary, whether formal scorings or written out idiographic contents, are counted as one category each. In the L.S. protocol there are seven formal content category scorings and three idiographic contents yielding a Cont/R = 10/25.

$H + Hd/A + Ad$: This ratio represents the proportion of human to animal contents in the record. Interestingly, while several of the Rorschach systematizers have offered normative information concerning the respective percentages of human and animal content expected in the protocols of both patients and nonpatients, none have found it useful to enter the actual frequencies for each of these categories in ratio form, although Piotrowski (1957) does compute an $H\%$. In constructing the comprehensive system it seemed realistic to enter these data as a ratio which could more easily be interpreted against "normative" standards. The method of calculation of the ratio appears obvious from the formula.

$H + A/Hd + Ad$: This is also a ratio concerning the use of human and animal contents in the protocol, however, unlike the $H + Hd/A + Ad$ ratio, the focus is on the occurrence of whole versus detail. It was first suggested by Klopfer (1936) following the earlier interpretive suggestions of Rorschach.

XRT **Achrom:** This entry represents the mean reaction time for the first response to the five cards of the test which are exclusively achromatic (I, IV, V, VI, VII).

XRT **Chrom:** The entry represents the mean reaction time for the first response to the five cards of the test which contain chromatic color (II, III, VIII, IX, X).

REFERENCES

Beck, S. J. *Rorschach's Test. I: Basic Processes.* New York: Grune and Stratton, 1944.

Beck, S. J. *Rorschach's Test. I: Basic Processes.* (2nd ed.) New York: Grune and Stratton, 1950.

Beck, S. J. *The Rorschach experiment. Ventures in Blind Diagnosis.* New York: Grune and Stratton, 1960.

Exner, J. E. The Self Focus Sentence Completion: A Study of Egocentricity. *Journal of Personality Assessment*, 1973, **37,** 437–455.

Friedman, H. Perceptual regression in schizophrenia: An hypothesis suggested by use of the Rorschach Test. *Journal of Projective Techniques*, 1953, **17,** 171–185.

Klopfer, B., and Booth, G. Personality studies in chronic arthritis. *Rorschach Research Exchange*, 1936, **1,** 40–51.

Klopfer, B., Burchard, E., Kelley, D., and Miale, F. Theory and technique of Rorschach interpretation. *Rorschach Research Exchange*, 1939, **3,** 152–194.

Piotrowski, Z. *Perceptanalysis*. New York: MacMillan, 1957.

Rapaport, D., Gill, M., and Schafer, R. *Diagnostic Psychological Testing*. Vol. 2. Chicago: Yearbook Publishers, 1946.

Rorschach, H. *Psychodiagnostics*. Bern: Bircher, 1921 (Transl. Hans Huber Verlag, 1942).

Schafer, R. *Psychoanalytic Interpretation in Rorschach Testing*. New York: Grune and Stratton, 1954.

Wilson, G., and Blake, R. A methodological problem in Beck's organizational concept. *Journal of Consulting Psychology*, 1950, **14**, 20–24.

PART TWO

Working Tables

CHAPTER 9

Frequently Used Tables

This chapter contains six tables, each of which have special importance to the comprehensive system, and each of which are used frequently in scoring and interpreting the test. The first, Table A, includes figures of each of the 10 blots showing the location numbering system, as derived from Beck, for all of the common and unusual detail areas. The bulk of Table A is comprised of listings, by card and location area, of good and poor form responses as determined by frequency distributions. This procedure has been described in greater detail in Chapter 6. These listings are somewhat less extensive than those offered by either Beck or Hertz. Possibly this is due to the fact that nearly 25% of the protocols used in establishing the frequencies were obtained using the methodology of the comprehensive system. This methodology generally produces fewer responses than do most of the other systems, especially to unusual detail areas. The brevity of this listing may also be a product of a less extensive extrapolation from responses, particularly as compared with the Hertz listing in which the itemization is much more specific than in either the Beck or Comprehensive systems. It is also important to note that numerous instances occur in which the designation of the form quality, as good or poor, disagrees with either or both the Beck-Hertz judgments. These differences are apparently due to criterion differences across the three systems, especially those used to designate poor form answers, but the differences may also be a function of different populations. Table A also differs from those of Beck and Hertz in that judgments are given as "good" or "poor" rather than the traditional plus (+) or minus (−). The reason for this, as has been described in Chapter 6, is that those symbols, + and −, are used in the more subjective modified Mayman scheme for evaluating form quality, which is included in the comprehensive system. In this system, the scorer will refer to Table A to determine if the response is good or poor form, and then differentiate good form answers into the plus (+) and ordinary (*o*) categories, and poor form responses into the weak (*w*) and minus (−) categories. It is also important to emphasize that some of the responses, listed in Table A, *may occur without reference to form*, and thus *are not accorded a form quality designation*. Examples of these are blood, flesh, smoke, and snow. They are listed because of the frequency with which they occur, and the fact that in many instances they are associated with form and, therefore, assigned a form quality designation.

Table B contains scoring examples, by card, in which responses judged as good and poor form from Table A have been differentiated into the four categories of the modified Mayman scoring system, plus (+), ordinary (*o*), weak (*w*), and minus (−), using the criteria described in Chapter 6. These examples, obviously, do not represent all possible differentiations, or even the differentiations of the responses listed in Table A. They are included to provide guidelines from which the scorer can develop this semi-subjective skill. It is important to note that the elements of specification and articulation can often convert a very ordinary kind of percept, such as a bat to Card I, into a very striking answer which would be judged as plus instead of ordinary. Conversely, a seemingly very poor form use can be made less inappropriate, and thus scored weak rather than minus by the same factors. The examples which have been selected for inclusion in Table B are taken from a larger sampling of responses which were independently scored by at least four examiners, trained in the comprehensive system. There has been unanimous agreement among the scorers concerning each of the examples shown in Table B, a phenomenon which suggests that substantial interscorer reliability can be obtained using this method of evaluating the form quality of the answers.

Tables C and D, taken from Beck and Wilson and Blake, provide the weighted Z values for each of the 10 blots, and the estimated weighted ZSum. These tables have been shown earlier in this work as tables 15 and 22 in Chapters 6 and 8, respectively. They are included here for the convenience of the scorer who will generally refer to them often for the scoring of specific responses and for the calculation of the Zd score in the Structural Summary.

Table E is a listing of the 13 responses which have been designated as Popular in the Comprehensive System. These Populars have also been listed previously in Table 19 in Chapter 7. As with the tables referring to Z scores, this listing of Populars is included in this section for the convenience of the scorer who may find cause to refer to them with considerable frequency.

Table F provides normative data from 495 protocols obtained using the methodology of the Comprehensive System. These records are presented for four different groups. The first includes 200 nonpsychiatric subjects who have no known history of psychiatric disability. These subjects represent a variety of socioeconomic and educational levels and are almost equally distributed by sex. The age range is from 18 to 57 and approximately 65 % of the group are married. The second includes 100 out-patients, none of whom have evidenced psychotic features or behaviors. These records have generally been collected at the onset of intervention. Approximately 60 % of the sample are female, about half of the sample are married. The age range is 18 to 54 and, like the nonpsychiatric subjects, a variety of socioeconomic and educational levels are represented. The third includes 70 nonschizophrenic in-patients, all of whom are first admissions. Forty-eight of these patients have been identified as various kinds of depressive reactions, while the remaining 22 subjects have been diagnosed as a form of characterological disturbance. The age range is 19 to 59, and the group is evenly divided by sex. The fourth includes 125 in-patient schizophrenics, ranging in age from 18 to 55, about 75 % are first admissions. The group represents a variety of educational levels and socioeconomic backgrounds. These protocols were collected during the first week after admission.

It seems important to caution that the data in the reference samples are presented as general guidelines. The drawing of excessive generalizations from any of these samples is obviously unwarranted. The samplings are relatively small, and have not been subdivided by special age groups, educational levels, socioeconomic patterns, private versus public clinics or hospitals, intellectual levels, and such, so as to maintain reasonably useful numbers. *No data* are provided for children, nor are subjects included in any of the groups who would be considered as severe intellectual defectives.

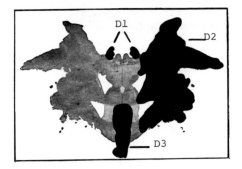

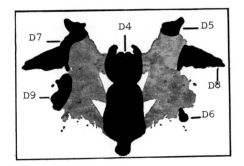

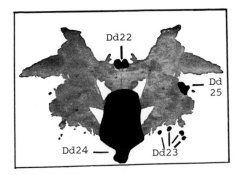

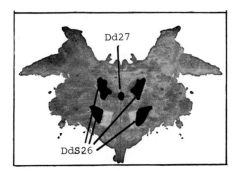

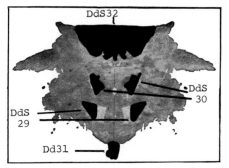

Figure 3. Common (*D*) areas and unusual (*Dd*) areas for Card I.

Table A.   Figures Showing Common (*D*) and Unusual (*Dd*) Location Areas by Card, Plus Listings of
Good and Poor Form-Responses and Response Classes by Card and Location

Loca-tion	Form Quality	Category	Loca-tion	Form Quality	Category

CARD I

Loca-tion	Form Quality	Category
W	Poor	Abalone
	Poor	Abdomen
	Poor	Airplane
	Poor	Amoeba
	Poor	Anchor
	Good	Angel
	Good-Poor	Animal

(This class of response is judged good
form when the outer areas (*D*2) are
identified as flappers, wings, etc., as in
marine, prehistoric, or flying animals.
When the *D*2 areas are not so identified,
as in bear, cat, dog, lion, etc., the response is judged poor form)

Good		Bat
Good		Beetle
Good	V	Bellows
Good		Bird
Poor		Body (split)
Poor	V	Bookmark
Good		Bone (skeletal)
Good		Brain (cross-section)
Good		Breastbone
Good		Bug (winged)
Good		Butterfly
Poor	V	Butterfly
Poor		Cactus
Good	V	Castle

(This class of response includes churches,
pagodas, temples, etc.)

Good		Cave
Good		Chandelier
Poor	V	Chest (human)
Poor	V	Cheveron (military)
Good		Chinese Art
Good		Clouds
Poor		Cocoon
Good		Coral
Good		Crab
Good		Crawfish
Good	V	Crown
Good		Dancer (with cape)
Good		Design

(This class of response includes reference to the symmetry of the blot)

Poor		Dirt
Poor		Dragonfly

Good		Eagle
Good		Emblem

(This class of response includes badges,
coat of arms, family crest, seals, etc.)

Poor	V	Explosion
Good-Poor		Face

(This class of response is judged good
form when the face is abstract or symbolic, as in, face of evil, mask of death,
halloween mask, etc., or if it is the face
of an animal wherein the outer detail
areas are specified as ears, as in the face
of a cat, wolf, etc. When the *W* is reported as a human face (not mask), the
form quality is judged poor)

Good		Figurehead
Poor		Fly
Good		Fossil
Good	V	Fountain
Good		Fountain (with side carvings)
Poor		Frog
Poor		Fur
Good		Girls (dancing in a circle)
Good	V	Hat

(This class of response includes a variety
of headdress and hair stylings, as in
chinese hairdo, fancy tribal headdress,
funny hat)

Poor	Head

(This class of response includes any
head, *H* or *A*, which is not described as
a face. See Face also)

Good-Poor	Human(s)

(This class of response is considered
good form if the center figure is reported
as a human, or if two humans or human-like figures are perceived in the
outer detail areas. If the entire blot is
reported as a single human, with the
outer detail areas used as arms, clothing,
etc., the form quality is judged as poor)

Good	Insect (winged, unspecified)

Table A (Continued)

Location	Form Quality	Category	Location	Form Quality	Category
	Poor	Insect (not winged, unspecified)			structures, i.e., chest, pelvis, rib cage. X-rays of anatomy, i.e., heart and lungs, are poor form)
	Good	Island			
	Poor	Jellyfish			
	Poor	Kidneys	D1	Good	Antennae
	Good	Landscape		Good	Birds (heads)

(This class of response includes foliage, rocks and trees, rough terrain, bushes being reflected, etc.)

(This class of response often includes the Dd22 area as a nest)

Location	Form Quality	Category	Location	Form Quality	Category
	Good	Leaf (torn)		Good	Claws
	Good	Map (nonspecific, usually topographic)		Good	Crab
				Good	Feelers
	Poor	Map (specific, i.e., Australia, Asia, Europe, U.S.)		Good	Fingers
				Poor	Fork
				Good	Hands
	Good	Mask (see Face also)		Poor	Heads (animal except bird)
	Good	Monster (Face)			
	Good	Moth		Good	Horns
	Good	Mythological creatures (on each side)		Poor	Humans
				Good	Mittens
	Poor	Nest		Good	Pincers
	Good	Ornament (X-mas)		Poor ∨	Roots
	Poor	Owl		Poor	Tooth
	Good	Pelvis (skeletal)		Good	Vulture (head)
	Poor	Pot		Poor	Waves
	Poor ∨	Printing Press			
	Poor ∨	Rocket	D2	Good	Acrobat
	Poor	Rug		Good	Angel
	Good	Sea Animal		Good- ∧ <	Animal
	Poor ∨	Ship		Poor	
	Poor	Shrimp			
	Good	Skull (skeletal)			(This class of response is considered
	Poor	Sky			good form if the animal is unspecified,
	Poor	Snowflake			or if the specified type of animal is des-
	Poor	Spider			ignated as "long-eared" as in donkey,
	Poor	Sponge			elephant, etc. referring to the D8 pro-
	Good	Statues (2 or 3)			jection. If the "long-eared" specification
	Poor ∨	Steps			is not included, or the type animal se-
	Good	Stone (carved)			lected has form which is inappropriate
	Good	Totem (winged)			for that specification, as in bear, cat,
	Poor ∨	Tree			pig, etc., the form quality is judged as
	Poor	Tuning Fork			poor)
	Poor	Turtle			
	Poor	Wasp		Poor	Bat
	Good	Witches (2 or 3)		Poor	Beetle
	Good	Woman (see Human)		Good	Bird
	Poor	Wood		Poor	Bug (winged)
	Good- Poor	X-ray		Poor	Chicken
				Good	Cloud
				Poor <	Dog (see also Animal)

(This class of response is good form for nonspecified x-rays and some specific

Good <	Donkey
Poor	Dragon

Table A (Continued)

Location	Form Quality	Category	Location	Form Quality	Category
	Good	Elephant (see also Animal)		Poor	Skeleton
	Good	Face		Poor	Snake
	(This class of response includes human, human-like, monster, and caricature faces, where the D8 detail area is identified as the nose)			Good	Spinal cord
				Good	Statue (human)
				Good	Vase
	Poor	Fish	D4	Poor	Alligator
	Good	Head (bird)		Poor	Animal (unspecified)
	Good	Head (Human, see also Face)		Poor	Ant
				Good	Beetle
	Good	Human(s)		Poor	Bone structure
	(This class of response includes human and human like figures, as in girls, people, witches, etc. The D8 area is usually identified as clothing or as an arm when rapid movement is implied)			Poor	Cat
				Good	Cello
				Poor	Centipede
				Good	Crab
	Good ∧ < Landscape			Poor	Fish
	(This class of response includes cliffs, mountains, rocks, rough terrain, shrubbery, etc.)			Poor	Frog
				Good	Gorilla
				Good	Human
	Good	Map (unspecified)		(This class of response generally includes the use of the D1 area as hands or arms and may be reported as headless or a whole human. In some instances the D3 area is specified as the lower portion excluding the remainder of Dd24)	
	Poor	Map (specified)			
	Good	Pegasus			
	Poor	Pig			
	Poor	Rodent			
	Poor	Skin (furry)			
	Poor	Sky		Good	Human figures (two, facing each other)
	Good	Trees (see also Landscape)		Good	Insect (unspecified, with D1 as antennae or feelers)
	Good	Wings			
	Poor	Wolf		Good	Jack-in-box
	Good	Woodpecker (profile)		Poor	Lobster
	Poor	X-ray		Good	Monument
D3	Good	Alligator (reflection)		Poor	Reptile
	Good ∨ Bowling Pin			Poor ∨ Rocket	
	Poor	Brain Stem		Good	Scarab
	Poor ∨ Candle holder			Poor	Spider
	Good	Human (lower half)		Good	Statue (human)
	(This class of response includes several variations of the lower half of the human form as in child's legs, nude form, woman's features, etc. The form quality is good only when the incomplete human is reported. Whole human figures perceived in this area are poor form)			Poor ∨ Tree	
				Good	Urn
				Good	Vase
				Good	Violin
			D5	Poor	Arrowhead
				Poor	Bird (whole)
				Good	Hat
	Good	Legs		Good	Head
	Good	Mummy case		(This class of response includes animal, bird, and human heads, all reported in profile)	
	Poor ∨ Penis			Poor	Shoe

Table A (Continued)

Loca-tion	Form Quality	Category	Loca-tion	Form Quality	Category
D6	Poor	∨ Head (animal)			Heads of other animals, specified or un-specified, or birds, are judged as poor form)
	Good	∨ Head (human)			
	Good	∨ Mushroom			
	Good	Tail (poodle)			
	Good	∨ Tree	Dd22	Poor	Breasts
D7	Good	Animal (winged)		Good	Boulders
	Good	Bird		Poor	∨ Buttocks
	Good	Eagle		Good	Heads (human)
	Good-Poor	Head		Good	Hills
				Good	∨ Labia
		(This class of response includes animal, bird, and human heads provided the D8 area is used as the beak or nose, as in comic bear, collie dog, fox, woodpecker, etc. If the D8 area is not so specified, the form quality is poor)		Good	Mountains
				Poor	Trees
			Dd23	Poor	Dots
				Poor	Flies
				Poor	Insects
	Good	Landscape		Good	Islands
		(This class of response frequently in-cludes mountains, rocky terrain, trees, etc.)		Poor	Math symbols
				Good	Notes (musical)
				Good	Question mark (below the D6 area)
	Good	Map (unspecified)			
	Poor	Map (specified, as in Africa, South America)	Dd24	Good	Bell
				Poor	Bug
				Good	Cello
	Good	Sphinx		Good	Emblem
	Good	Wing(s)		Good	Human figure (lower half, transparent)
D8	Good	Arrowhead			
	Poor	Blade (knife)		Good	∨ Lantern
	Good	Cliff		Poor	∨ Plant
	Poor	Face (animal or human)		Poor	X-ray
	Good	< Fin (shark)			
	Good	< Ghost	Dd25	Poor	Animal
	Poor	Head (animal or human)		Good	Face (human)
	Poor	Insect			(This class of response includes human and human abstracts, as in old man winter, the face of the north wind blow-ing, etc.)
	Good	< Mountain			
	Good	Nose (animal or human)			
	Good	Rock			
	Good	< Seal			
	Good	Shrub	DdS26	Good	Clouds
	Good	< Tree (fir)		Good	Eyes
	Poor	< Tree (unspecified)		Good	Ghosts
	Poor	< Umbrella (closed)		Good	Mask details
D9	Good	Cloud		Good	Snow
	Good	Face (human)			
	Good-Poor	Head	Dd27	Poor	Boat (with midline)
				Good	Buckle (belt)
		(This class of response is good form when the head is human, human like, or of the specific animals, ape, cat, dog, monkey, or those of a similar variety.		Poor	Elevator (with midline)
				Poor	Heart
				Good	Top (with midline)
				Poor	Ulcer

Table A (Continued)

Location	Form Quality		Category	Location	Form Quality		Category
DdS29	Poor		Eyes		Good		Snow
	Poor	V	Heads (animal)		Good	∧ V	Windows
	Good		Mouth (pumpkin)				
	Good		Snow	Dd31	Good		Feet
	Poor	V	Tents		Poor		Hammer
	Good	V	Windows		Good	V	Head (animal)
	Good		Wings		Poor	V	Nose (bird)
					Poor		Root
DdS30	Good		Eyes		Poor	V	Skull (animal)
	Good		Ghosts				
	Good		Human (in costume or nightshirt)	DdS32	Good		Bay (inlet)
					Good		Canyon
	Poor		Lungs		Poor		Vase

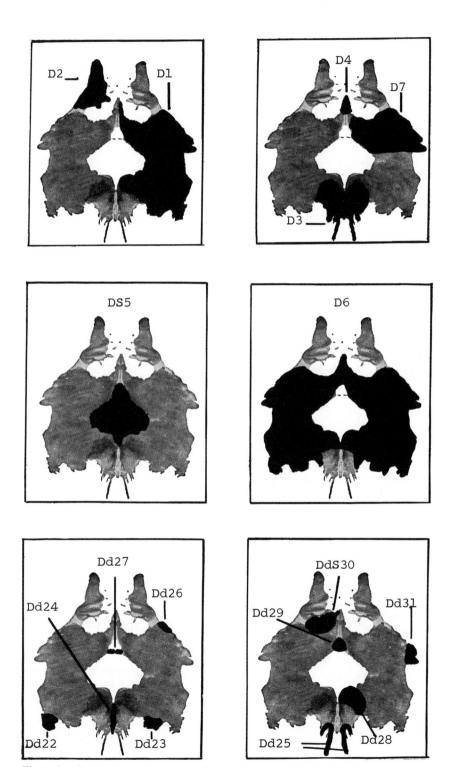

Figure 4. Common (*D*) and unusual (*Dd*) areas for Card II.

Table A (Continued)

Loca-tion	Form Quality	Category	Loca-tion	Form Quality	Category

CARD II

Loca-tion	Form Quality	Category
W	Good	Anatomy (unspecified)
	Poor	Bat
	Good	Bears
	Good	Bookends
	Good	∨ Butterfly
	Good	Cave (DS5 represents entrance)
	Good	Design (carved)
	Good	Devils
	Good	∨ Emblem
	Good	∨ Explosion
	Poor	Face

(This class of response includes animal and human faces with the DS5 area ordinarily reported as the mouth, and the space area around the D4 area reported as eyes)

	Good	Fire & Smoke (with some form)
	Poor	Fly
	Poor	Gorillas
	Poor	Heart
	Good	Humans

(This class of response is good form when two human or human-like figures are reported, one on each side of the blot, with the D2 area representing a hat, head, or mask. Numerous variations occur as in clowns clapping or dancing, people fighting, kneeling, praying, struggling, etc. The percept of a human (singular) to the whole blot is poor form)

	Poor	Insect

(This class of response includes the percept of an insect to the whole blot, or two insects, one on each side)

	Poor	Intestines
	Poor	Kidneys
	Poor	Lungs
	Poor	Map
	Poor	Mask
	Good	∨ Moth
	Poor	Mouth (open)
	Good	∨ Ornament (Xmas)
	Poor	∨ Pelvis
	Poor	∨ Plant
	Poor	Rectum
	Good	Statues

Loca-tion	Form Quality	Category
	Poor	Stomach
	Poor	Throat
	Poor	∨ Torches (generally with smoke)
	Poor	Vagina
	Good	∨ Volcano (red areas usually as fire or lava)
	Poor	X-ray
D1	Good	Animal

(This class of response includes many varieties of animal. When the card is upright, this area is often perceived as bear, dog, elephant, lamb, monkey, etc., either as a whole animal or the upper portion of the animal. When the card is turned, percepts such as buffalo, cat, dog, rabbit, etc. are among the more common, generally perceived as a whole animal)

	Poor	∨ Animal
	Good	Bear
	Poor	∨ Bear
	Poor	Bird
	Good	< Buffalo
	Good	< Cat
	Poor	Clouds
	Poor	∨ Clown
	Good	∨ Coat
	Good	Cow (see also Animal)
	Good	Dog
	Poor	∨ Dog
	Good	Elephant (see also Animal)
	Poor	Fish
	Poor	∨ Gorilla
	Poor	Heart
	Poor	Human (either whole or part)
	Good	∨ Human

(This class of response includes both human and human like figures, usually seen in an active posture as in boxing, dancing, fighting, etc. When the apex of the card is turned to the side, a human is often perceived on hands and knees (mostly by younger subjects).

	Good	Lamb (see also Animal)
	Poor	Map

Table A (Continued)

Loca-tion	Form Quality		Category	Loca-tion	Form Quality		Category
	Good		Mountain range		Poor		Tooth
	Poor		Monument		Good		Torch
	Good	<	Rabbit	D3	Poor		Anemone (sea)
	Good		Rocky terrain		Poor		Anus
	Poor	V	Tree		Good		Beetle
	Poor		Turtle		Good		Blood
	Poor		Wing (unless specified with W as a winged animal)		Good		Bug (winged)
					Poor		Bug (nonwinged)
					Good		Butterfly
D2	Good		Bird		Poor		Coral
	Good		Blood		Good		Crab
	Poor		Boot		Poor		Crawfish
	Poor		Bug		Good	V	Explosion
	Good		Butterfly (sideview)		Good	∧ V	Fire
	Good		Cap		Poor		Fish
	Poor		Candle		Poor		Flower
	Poor		Cells (blood)		Poor		Fly
	Poor		Chicken		Good		Genitals (female)
	Good		Creature (cartoon)		Poor		Head (animal)
	Poor		Devil		Poor		Head (human)
	Poor		Finger painting		Poor		Heart
	Poor		Finger print		Good		Insect (with Dd25 as antennae or feeler)
	Good		Foot print				
	Poor		Hand		Poor		Jellyfish
	Good		Hat		Poor		Kidney
	Good-Poor		Head		Poor		Lobster
					Poor		Lungs

(This class of response includes all human and human-like heads, and some specific bird heads, as in chicken, rooster, etc. All animal heads are judged as poor form quality)

					Good		Manta ray
	Good	V	Holster (gun)		Poor		Mask
	Good	V	Italy (map of)		Poor		Meat
	Poor		Kidney		Good		Menstruation
	Good	V	Lantern		Good		Moth
	Good		Lava		Poor		Octopus
	Poor	V	Leg		Good		Paint (splattered)
	Good		Mask (human-like)		Poor		Plant
	Poor		Mitten		Good		Snail (head)
	Poor		Penis		Good	V	Sun (rising or setting)
	Good		Puppet (hand)		Good	V	Torch
	Good		Rabbit		Poor		Uterus
	Poor		Rat	D4	Good		Arrow
	Good		Seal		Poor		Bell
	Poor		Shoe		Poor		Bottle
	Good		Snail		Good		Bullet
	Good	V	Sock		Poor		Candle
	Good	V	South America (map of)		Good		Castle
	Poor		Tongue		Poor		Crucifixion
					Good		Dome
					Good	V	Drill
					Poor		Face (animal or human)
					Good		Hands (prayer-like)
					Poor		Hat

Table A (Continued)

Location	Form Quality	Category	Location	Form Quality	Category
	Poor	Head (animal or human)		Good	Ornament
	Poor	Helmet		Good	Pendant
	Poor	Knife		Good	Rocket (may include $D3$ and/or $D4$)
	Good	Missile		Good	Steeple
	Good	Monument		Poor	Sting-ray
	Poor	Mountain		Poor	Stomach
	Poor	Nose (animal or bird)		Good ∧∨	Top
	Good	Penpoint		Good	Tunnel (entrance)
	Poor	Penis		Good	Vagina (may include $D3$)
	Good	Pliers		Good	Vase
	Good	Pyramid			
	Good	Rocket			
	Poor	Snake (head)	$D6$ (see	Poor	Anatomy
	Good	Spear (tip)	also $D1$)	Poor	Animal
	Good	Steeple		Poor	Bat
	Poor	Tail		Poor	Bird
	Good	Temple		Good	Butterfly (includes $DS5$)
	Good	Tower		Poor	Clouds
	Good	Tree (pine)		Poor	Insect
	Poor	Vase		Poor	Island
$DS5$	Good	Airplane (may include $D3$ and/or $D4$)		Poor	Lungs
				Poor	Map
	Good	Basket		Good	Moth (includes $DS5$)
	Poor	Bat		Good ∨	Pelvis
	Poor	Bell		Poor	Rug
	Poor	Bird		Good	X-ray
	Poor	Boat			
	Good	Bowl		(This class of response includes chest, pelvis, ribs, etc.)	
	Poor	Butterfly			
	Good	Castle (may include $D4$)	$D7$	Poor	Beak
	Good	Cave (entrance)		Poor	Bird
	Good	Chandelier (may include $D3$ and/or $D4$)		Poor	Ear
				Good	Head (animal)
	Good	Church (may include $D4$)		Poor	Head (bird)
	Good	Crown		Good	Head (fish)
	Good	Dome (may include $D4$)		Good	Head (human)
	Poor	Dress		Good <	Mountain
	Good ∧∨	Fountain (may include $D3$ and/or $D4$)		Poor	Seal
				Poor	X-ray
	Good	Goblet			
	Poor	Hat			
	Poor	Heart	$Dd22$	Good ∨	Bush
	Good	Hole		Good ∨	Chicken
	Poor	Island		Poor	Head (animal)
	Poor	Kite		Good	Head (human)
	Good	Lake		Good ∨	Rock
	Good ∧∨	Lamp (may include $D4$)		Poor ∨	Tree
	Good	Light (electric)			
	Poor	Mask	$Dd23$	Poor ∨	Frog
	Good	Missile (may include $D3$ and/or $D4$)		Poor ∨	Head (animal or human)
				Good ∨	Mountain
	Poor	Mouth		Poor ∨	Shrubbery

Table A (Continued)

Location	Form Quality		Category	Location	Form Quality		Category
Dd24	Good		Anus	Dd27	Good		Bridge (draw)
	Poor		Bowling pin		Poor		Claw
	Poor		Candle		Poor		Tail
	Poor		Face				
	Good		Genitals (female)	Dd28	Good		Bloodstain
	Poor		Human		Good		Head (monster)
	Poor		Penis		Poor		Turtle
	Poor	∨	Tooth		Poor		Varnish
	Good		Totem		Poor		Wood (stained)
	Good		Vagina				
	Poor		Waterfall	Dd29	Good		Dome
					Good		Entrance (cave)
Dd25	Good		Antennae		Good	∨	Goblet (may include D4)
	Good		Antlers		Good	∨	Pottery
	Good		Feelers (insect)				
	Good		Horns	DdS30	Poor		Eyes
	Good		Icicles		Poor		Head (monster)
	Good		Spear		Poor		Oyster
	Poor		Stick				
	Poor		Tail	Dd31	Good		Beak
	Poor		Tusk		Poor		Claw
					Good	<	Ears (animal)
Dd26	Good		Caterpillar		Poor		Head (animal)
	Good		Fire (forest)		Good		Head (human)
	Good		Sunset		Good		Head (prehistoric)
	Poor		Walrus		Good	<	Mountains

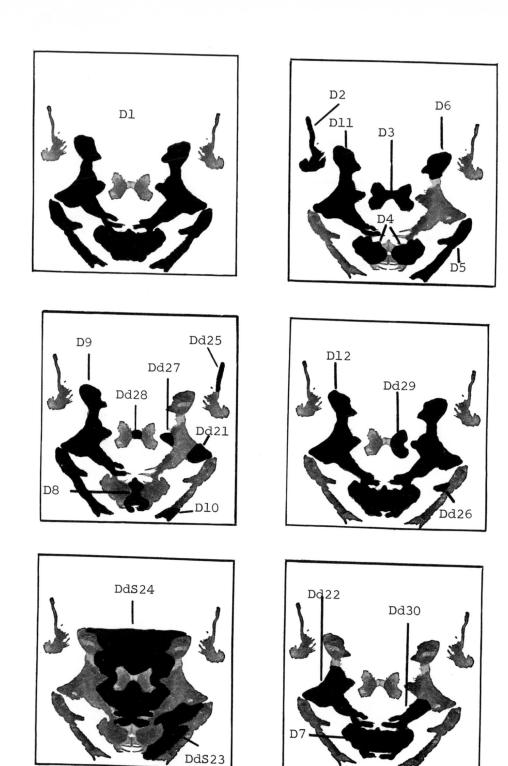

Figure 5. Common (*D*) and unusual (*Dd*) areas for Card III.

Loca-tion	Form Quality		Category	Loca-tion	Form Quality		Category

CARD III

Location	Form Quality		Category
W	Poor		Anatomy
	Poor	∨	Ant
	Good		Bowl
	Poor	∨	Bug
	Poor	∧ ∨	Butterfly
	Poor		Cat
	Poor	∧ ∨	Crab
	Poor	∧ ∨	Face (animal or human)
	Good		Emblem
	Poor		Flower
	Good	∨	Fly (D4 as eyes)
	Poor	∨	Frog
	Poor		Human
	Good	∨	Human (D5 as arms)
	Poor		Insect
	Poor		Map
	Good	∨	Monster
	Poor		Skeleton
	Poor		Spider
	Good		Vase
D1	Poor		Animal
	Poor	∨	Ant
	Good		Birds

(This class of response includes several variations, as in cocks fighting, ducks, large birds by a nest, roosters, etc.)

Location	Form Quality		Category
	Good		Bone structure
	Poor	∨	Bug
	Good		Dolls
	Good	∨	Human (D5 as arms)
	Good		Humans (two)

(This class of response applies if it is reported as *two* human figures, frequently seen in movement. The figures may be reported as either sex)

Location	Form Quality		Category
	Poor		Insect
	Poor		Lobster
	Poor		Map
	Good		Monkeys
	Good	∨	Monster
	Poor		Skeleton
	Poor	∨	Skull
	Poor		Spider
	Good		Vase
	Good		X-ray (pelvis)
	Poor		X-ray (unspecified)
D2	Good		Amoeba
	Good-Poor		Animal

(This class of response is good form for the variety of long tailed animals, as in monkey, or for animals falling, hanging, or swinging where the Dd25 area is realistically included. Animal responses not meeting these requirements are poor form)

Location	Form Quality		Category
	Poor	∨	Animal
	Poor		Artery
	Good	< ∨	Bird
	Good		Blood
	Good		Chicken (hanging)
	Poor		Club
	Poor		Devil
	Poor		Dog
	Poor		Dragon
	Poor		Duck
	Good		Embryo
	Good		Esophagus (usually with stomach)
	Good		Fire
	Poor		Flesh
	Poor		Flower
	Good		Germ
	Good		Hat (clown or costume)
	Good-Poor		Head

(This class of response is good form only when it is reported as human-like or mythological. Animal or human heads are poor form)

Location	Form Quality		Category
	Poor		Heart
	Poor		Hook
	Good	∧ ∨	Human

(This class of response includes many variations of the human figure. When the card is upright, it is most commonly reported as an acrobat, child, or gymnast. When the card is inverted, the response may be of a real human, as in person bowing, or a mythological or unusual human-like figure as in dwarf, elf, imp, etc.)

Location	Form Quality		Category
	Poor		Insect
	Poor		Intestine
	Poor		Island
	Good		Kidney
	Poor		Lung(s)
	Poor		Meat
	Good	∧ ∨	Monkey
	Good		Neuron

Table A (Continued)

Loca-tion	Form Quality		Category	Loca-tion	Form Quality		Category
	Poor		Note (music)		Good		Ball
	Good	V	Parrot		Good		Basket
	Good	<	Pipe		Good		Bones
	Poor		Plant		Poor		Breastbone
	Good	V	Puppet		Poor		Bust
	Poor		Rabbit		Good	<	Child
	Poor		Sea horse		Good	<	Dog
	Poor		Snail		Poor		Earmuffs
	Poor		Snake		Poor		Embryo
	Poor		Stick		Poor		Eyes
	Good		Stomach		Good	V	Face (human)
	Good	V	Tree		Good		Gourd
	Good		Umbilical cord		Good		Hat
	Poor		Vase		Poor	V	Head (animal)
D3	Poor		Antlers		Good	V	Head (human)
	Poor		Bird		Good	V	Head (skeleton)
	Good		Blood		Good		Kettledrums
	Good		Bone		Poor		Lamp
	Good		Bow		Poor		Lungs
	Good		Bowtie		Good		Mittens
	Poor		Brassiere		Poor		Mountains
	Poor		Breastbone		Good		Pots
	Good		Butterfly		Good		Skeletal
	Poor		Dam				

(This class of response includes the skull, joints, pelvis, etc.)

Loca-tion	Form Quality		Category	Loca-tion	Form Quality		Category
	Good		Dumbbell		Good		Stones
	Poor		Eyeglasses		Good	V	Trees
	Good		Fire		Poor		Turtles
	Poor		Fly		Poor		Womb
	Poor		Heart				
	Poor		Human (one or two)				
	Poor		Insect	D5	Poor		Arm
	Poor		Intestine		Good	V	Arm
	Good		Kidney		Poor		Bird
	Good		Lung(s)		Poor		Bug
	Poor		Mask		Good	∧ V	Claw
	Good		Moth		Good		Club
	Poor		Mouth		Good		Fish
	Poor		Nose		Poor		Gun
	Poor		Oranges		Poor		Hand
	Good		Pelvic structure		Poor		Island
	Good		Ribbon		Good		Leg (animal, hoofed)
	Poor		Skeleton		Good		Leg (human)
	Good		Spinal cord (cross-section)		Good		Log
	Poor		Testicles		Good		Limb (tree)
	Good		Wings		Poor		Map
	Poor		Wishbone		Poor		Peninsula
D4	Poor		Anatomy		Good	<	Shark
					Good		Stick

(This class of response includes all internal organs as in kidneys, lungs, stomach, etc.)

					Poor		Torpedo
					Poor		Tree
					Poor		Vine

Table A (Continued)

Location	Form Quality	Category	Location	Form Quality	Category
D6	Poor	Animal		Good	Bird (large)
	Poor	Coconut		Good	Chicken
	Poor	Egg		Poor	Clouds
	Poor	Eye		Good	Doll
	Poor	Head (animal)		Good	Duck (human-like)
	Good	Head (bird)		Good	Fowl
	Good	Head (human)		Poor	Ghost
	Good	Mask		Good ∧ V	Human
	Good	Rock		Poor	Insect
				Good <	Landscape
D7	Poor	Anatomy		Good	Monster
	Poor	Butterfly		Good <	Mountain
	Good	Cauldron		Poor	Parrot
	Poor	Crab		Poor	Root
	Good	Drum		Good	Skeleton
	Poor	Eyeglasses		Poor V	Spider
	Poor	Face (animal or human)		Poor	Tree
	Good	Fireplace		Poor	X-ray
	Good	Gate			
	Poor	Head (animal, human or insect)	D10	Good V	Finger
				Poor	Foot (webbed)
	Poor	Kidneys		Good V	Hand
	Poor	Lungs		Poor ∧ V	Head (animal or human)
	Good V	Mushroom		Good	Hoof
	Good	Nest		Poor	Penpoint
	Good	Pelvis		Good	Shoe (heeled)
	Good	Shadows		Poor	Spear
	Good V	Smoke	D11	Poor	Animal
	Poor	Vagina		Good V	Bird
	Good	Vertebrae		Good V	Chicken
	(This class of response includes a variety of skeletal references, usually reported in association with the Popular human figures)			Poor < V	Dog
				Poor	Fish
				Poor	Insect
	Good	X-ray (bone structure)		Good	Human (upper part)
D8	Good	Bones		Poor	Landscape
	Poor	Brain stem		Good <	Mountains
	Good	Chest		Poor	Skeletal
	Good ∧ V	Crab	D12	Good V	Arch
	Poor	Genitals (female)		Good	Bones
	Poor	Hourglass		Good	Bowl
	Good	Lamp		Poor V	Crab
	Poor	Pumpkin		Poor	Frog
	Good	Ribs		Poor	Landscape
	Good	Skeletal		Good	Mountains (aerial view)
	Poor	Vagina		Good	Pelvis
	Good V	Vase		Poor V	Trees
	Good V	Wineglass	Dd21	Good V	Bird
	Poor	X-ray		Poor V	Dog
D9	Poor	Anatomy		Poor	Head (animal)
	Poor	Animal		Poor <	Head (human)
				Good <	Mountain

Table A (Continued)

Location	Form Quality		Category	Location	Form Quality		Category
Dd22	Poor	∧ ∨	Animal		Good		Penis
	Good	∨	Bird		Poor		Stump
	Poor		Rodent	Dd27	Good		Breast
DdS23	Good		Bird (in (flight)		Good		Head (animal or bird)
	Poor		Ghost		Poor		Head (human)
	Poor		Head (animal)		Poor		Mountain
	Good		Water		Poor		Nose
DdS24	Good		Bowl	Dd28	Poor		Corset
	Poor	∧ ∨	Face (animal or human)		Good		Doors (swinging)
	Poor		Lake		Poor		Face
	Good	∨	Lamp		Poor		Tooth
	Good	∨	Mushroom	Dd29	Poor		Arrow
	Good	∨	Snow		Poor		Fetus
	Good	∨	Statue (carved)		Poor		Head (animal or human)
Dd25	Good		Esophagus		Poor		Insect
	Poor		Root		Poor	<	Valentine
	Poor		Stick	Dd30	Good		Arm
	Good		Tail		Poor		Foot
	Good		Umbilical cord		Good		Hand
Dd26	Good		Fin		Poor		Icicle
	Poor		Leg		Poor		Weapon

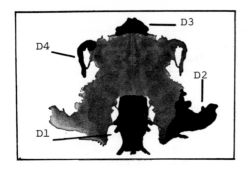
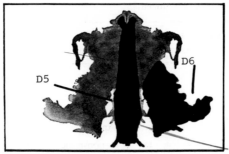
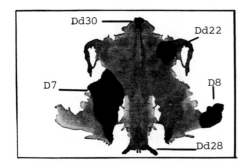
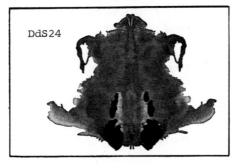
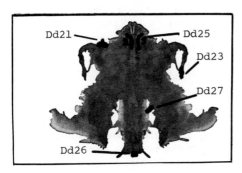
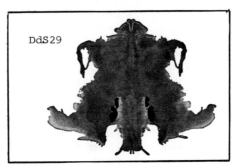

Figure 6. Common (*D*) and unusual (*Dd*) areas for Card IV.

Table A (Continued)

Location	Form Quality		Category	Location	Form Quality		Category

CARD IV

Location	Form Quality		Category
W	Poor		Amoeba
	Good	∨	Anchor
	Good		Animal

(This class of response includes the variety of large animals as in bear, gorilla, etc., and unspecified types of animals when the extremities are identified in a manner consistent with the blot)

	Form Quality		Category
	Good	∨	Bat
	Good		Bell
	Good		Boots (hanging on a pole)
	Poor		Bull
	Good	∧ ∨	Bushes

(This class of response is often reported with the card inverted as including an animal head (D1), behind or looking through)

	Form Quality		Category
	Good	∧ ∨	Butterfly
	Poor		Candle
	Good		Carcus (animal)
	Poor	∨	Chandelier
	Good	∧ ∨	Clouds
	Good		Coat
	Poor		Coral
	Poor		Crab
	Good		Design (carved)
	Poor	∨	Eagle
	Good	∨	Emblem
	Poor		Embryo
	Poor		Face (animal or human)
	Good	∧ ∨	Flower
	Good		Fossil
	Poor		Frog
	Good		Giant
	Good		Gorilla
	Good		Human

(This class of response includes a variety of human and human-like figures, sometimes excluding the D1 area. These responses generally identify the figure as masculine, and emphasize the large size)

	Form Quality		Category
	Poor	∨	Human
	Poor	∧ ∨	Insect
	Poor		Island
	Poor		Jellyfish
	Good		Kite
	Good	<	Landscape (reflected)
	Good		Leaf (torn)
	Poor		Lobster

	Form Quality		Category
	Poor	∨	Lung
	Good		Map (topographic)
	Good	∨	Moth
	Good		Mountain
	Good	∨	Pelvis
	Good		Plant
	Good		Robe
	Poor		Root
	Good		Rug
	Good	∧ ∨	Sea animal
	Good	∨	Seaweed
	Good-Poor	∧ ∨	Skin

(This class of response is good form only when it is a hide, pelt, or skin of a fur bearing animal. If the description is of human or reptile skin the form quality is poor)

	Form Quality		Category
	Good		Smoke
	Poor		Snail
	Poor	∧ ∨	Snowflake
	Good		Squid
	Good	∨	Sting-ray
	Good	∧ ∨	Temple
	Good		Tree
	Good	∨	Urn
	Good	∧ ∨	X-ray

Note. In many of the responses shown as W, the form quality will remain the same if the D1 area is omitted. Exceptions are percepts where D1 is an essential component.

Location	Form Quality		Category
D1	Poor		Alligator
	Good	∧ ∨	Animal

(This class of response is good form only for those animals with antennae, feelers, horns, etc. where the Dd28 area is so specified)

	Form Quality		Category
	Good		Bug
	Good	∨	Bush
	Good	∨	Cactus
	Good	∧ ∨	Candle
	Good	∨	Castle
	Good		Caterpillar
	Good	∨	Crab
	Poor		Crawfish
	Good	∨	Crown
	Poor		Fish

Table A (Continued)

Location	Form Quality	Category
	Good-Poor	Head (animal)

(This class of response is good form only for those animals for which the Dd28 area can be appropriately used as ears, horns, etc. as in goat, ram, etc. All other animal heads, such as cat, dog, horse, etc. are poor form)

Location	Form Quality	Category
	Poor	∨ Head (human)
	Good	∧∨ Head (insect)
	Good	∨ Head (monster)
	Poor	∧∨ Head (reptile)
	Poor	∧∨ Human
	Good	Hydrant
	Good	Insect
	Poor	Intestines
	Good	∨ Lamp
	Good	∨ Lighthouse
	Good	Medulla
	Good	∧∨ Owl
	Poor	Penis
	Poor	Shell
	Good	∧∨ Shrub
	Poor	Snake
	Good	∧∨ Spinal cord
	Good	Stool
	Good	Stump
	Good	Tail
	Good	∨ Totem
	Good	Tree trunk
	Good	Vertebrae
	Poor	X-ray
D2	Good	< Bear
	Poor	Boat
	Poor	Bone
	Good	Cloud
	Poor	< Cow
	Good	< Dog
	Poor	Emblem
	Good	Foot
	Good-Poor	< Head (animal)

(This class of response is good form when the animal specified has a short or stubby snout, as in bear, dog, pig, seal, etc. Other types of animals, such as cat, horse, lion, etc. are poor form)

Location	Form Quality	Category
	Poor	< Head (bird)
	Good	< Head (human)
	Good	Map
	Good	Peninsula

Location	Form Quality	Category
	Good	< Rock
	Good	Shoe
	Good	< Sphinx
	Good	< Totem
	Good	Wing
	Poor	X-ray
D3	Poor	Anus
	Good	Bud (flower)
	Good	∧∨ Butterfly
	Good	Cabbage
	Poor	Clam
	Good	Crown
	Poor	Face (animal, bird, or human)
	Poor	Fan
	Good	Flower
	Good-Poor	Head (animal)

(This class of response is good form only when the animal specified is "flat-faced" as in cat, monkey, owl, etc. When the facial features of the animal specified are substantially different as in dog (most breeds), fox, horse, etc., the form quality is poor)

Location	Form Quality	Category
	Good	Head (human)
	Good	Insect (winged)
	Good	Leaf
	Poor	Shell
	Poor	Shellfish
	Good	Vagina
D4	Poor	Animal
	Good	Arm
	Poor	Arrow
	Good	Branch (tree)
	Good	Cap (stocking)
	Good	Claw
	Poor	Ear
	Good	Eel
	Poor	Fish
	Good	∧∨ Handle
	Poor	Head (animal)
	Good	Head (bird)
	Good	Horn (animal)
	Good	Human (bending)
	Good	Icicle
	Poor	Leg
	Good	Lizard
	Good	Peninsula
	Poor	Penis
	Good	Root

Table A (Continued)

Location	Form Quality		Category	Location	Form Quality		Category
	Good		Snake		Good		Head (human)
	Poor		Tail		Good		Landscape
	Good		Trunk (elephant)		Good		Temple
	Good		Vine (hanging)		(This class of response includes all buildings which have a peak or spire)		
D5	Good		Column				
	Poor		Crawfish		Poor		Tree
	Poor		Fish	Dd22	Poor		Eye
	Good	∧∨	Fountain		Poor		Head (animal)
	Poor		Insect		Good		Head (human)
	Good		Pole				
	Good		River	Dd23	Good		Beak
	Good	∧∨	Rocket	(see also	Poor		Head (animal)
	Good		Spinal cord	D4)	Good		Head (bird)
	Good		Statue				
	Good		Totem	DdS24	Good	∨	Ghosts
	Poor		Tree		Good		Head (bird)
	Good		Vertebrae		Poor	∨	Head (human)
	Good		Waterway		Good	∨	Head (monster or mythological)
	Good		X-ray				
D6	Good		Boat		Good		Snow
	Good		Face (human)	Dd25	Good		Carving
	Good		Foot		Good		Face (animal or human)
	Good	<∨	Human		Poor		Vegetation (aerial view)
	Good		Italy				
	Good		Leg	Dd26	Poor		Clitoris
	Poor		Map (unspecified)		Good		Feet
	Poor	∨	Seahorse		Good		Fingers
	Good		Shoe		Good	∨	Humans (two)
	Good		Smoke		Good		Legs
	Good		Wing		Poor		Teeth
D7	Poor		Animal		Poor		Udder
	Poor		Bird	Dd27	Poor		Foot
	Good		Ghost				
	Poor		Head (animal)	Dd28	Good		Antennae
	Good	∨	Head (human)		Poor		Feet
	Good	∨	Human		Good		Horns
	Poor		Rock		Poor		Legs
	Poor		Root		Poor		Roots
	Good	∨	Seal				
	Good	∨	Statue	DdS29	Good	∨	Ghosts
	Poor		Tree		Good		Water
D8	Good		Dog	Dd30	Good		Flower
	Good	<	Head (animal)		Poor		Heart
	Good	<	Head (human)		Poor		Human
	Poor		Rock		Good	∨	Rocket
Dd21	Good		Face (human)		Good		Tack
	Poor		Head (animal)		Good		Tee (golf)
					Poor		Tooth

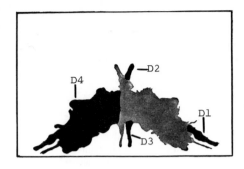
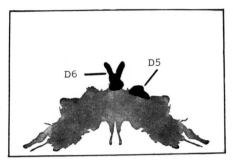

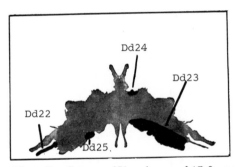
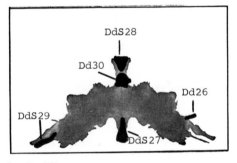

Figure 7. Common (*D*) and unusual (*Dd*) areas for Card V.

Table A (Continued)

Location	Form Quality		Category	Location	Form Quality		Category
			CARD V				
W	Good		Airplane	D1	Poor		Arm
	Poor		Anatomy		Good		Bone
	Good		Angel		Poor		Fish
	Poor		Animal		Good		Foot (animal)
	(This class of response includes any whole animal (non-winged), animal split open, or animal squashed)				Poor		Head (animal)
					Good		Head (reptile)
					Good		Leg (animal or human)
	Good		Animals (butting heads)		Good		Muscle
	Good	∧ ∨	Bat		Good		Nose (alligator)
	Poor		Bee		Good		Root
	Poor		Beetle		Poor		Spear
	Good	∧ ∨	Bird	D2	Good		Bone
	Good		Bookends		Good		Ear (animal)
	Good		Bug (winged)		Good		Elf
	Good		Cape		Poor		Finger
	Poor		Cloth		Poor		Foot (animal or human)
	Good		Clouds		Poor		Head (animal or human)
	Good		Dancer		Good		Human
	Good		Devil (caped)		Good	∧ ∨	Leg
	Good		Eagle		Poor		Penis
	Poor		Flower		Poor		Tree
	Poor		Fly		Poor		Worm
	Poor		Grasshopper				
	Poor		Head (animal or bird)	D3	Good		Antennae
	Good		Hill (with trees)		Good	<	Beak
	Good		Human		Good		Bone
	(This class of response is good form only when the center (D7) is used as the basic human form and the side projections (D4) are identified as parts of a costume, clothing, wings, or landscape surrounding the human)				Good		Club
					Poor		Finger
					Good	<	Head (bird)
					Poor		Match
					Poor		Root
					Good	< ∨	Snake
	Good		Humans (back to back)		Good	< ∨	Swan
	Good		Insect (winged)				
	Good		Landscape	D4	Good		Animal (with head at D7)
	Poor		Leaf		Good		Animal (carcus)
	Poor		Map		Good		Blanket
	Poor		Microorganism		Good		Bushes
	Poor		Mosquito		Good		Cloud
	Good		Moth		Poor		Driftwood
	Good		Ostrich		Poor		Head (animal)
	Poor		Pump		Good		Head (human)
	Poor	∨	Sailboat		(This class of response is often reported as a male face, bearded, in profile or semi-profile)		
	Poor		Smoke				
	Poor		Spider				
	Good		Stole (fur)		Good		Human (reclining)
	Poor		Tent		Poor		Kangaroo
	Good		Vampire		Good		Landscape
	Good		Vulture		Poor		Leg
	Good		Wings		Poor		Skin
	Good		Woman (dancing)		Good	∨	Smoke

Table A (Continued)

Loca-tion	Form Quality		Category	Loca-tion	Form Quality		Category
	Poor		Tree		Poor		Vagina
	Good		Wing		Good		Wishbone
D5	Poor		Breast	D10	Poor		Head (animal)
	Good		Head (human or human-like)		Good		Head (bird)
					Good		Head (reptile)
	Good		Hill		Good		Legs (animal or human)
	Good		Mountain		Good		Peninsula
	Poor		Shrubbery		Good		Roots (tree)
					Poor		Sticks
D6	Good	∨	Elves	D11	Poor		Breast
	Good		Face (animal, long eared)		Poor		Head (animal)
	Good		Face (human)		Good		Head (human)
	Good-Poor		Head (animal, insect)		Good		Human (sitting)
					Good		Mask
			(This class of response is good form for animal and insect heads which include appropriate reference to D8 as antennae, ears, or horns. All other animal or insect heads are poor form)		Good		Mountains
					Good		Nose
					Good		Stone (natural)
				Dd22	Good		Arrow
	Good		Head (human)		Good		Bayonet
	Good	∨	Human (lower half)		Good		Crutch
	Good		Pliers		Poor		Finger
	Good		Scissors		Poor		Head (bird)
	Good		Slingshot		Good		Limb (tree)
	Good		Wishbone		Poor		Leg (animal)
D7	Good		Animal (when D9 are legs)		Good		Leg (bird)
					Good		Reptile
	Good		Devil		Good		Spear
	Good		Human		Good		Tail
	Good		Humans (two)	Dd23	Poor	∧∨	Head (animal)
	Poor		Fish		Good	∧∨	Head (human)
	Good		Insect (D6 as antennae)	Dd24	Poor		Breast
	Good		Rabbit		Poor		Human
	Poor		Tree stump		Good		Nipple
D8	Good		Antennae	Dd25	Good	∨	Cannon
	Good		Bones		Poor	∨	Rock
	Good	∧∨	Humans (two)	Dd26	Good	∨	Bird (in flight)
	Good	∨	Legs (animal or human)		Good		Branch (tree)
	Good	<	Mouth (animal or bird)		Poor		Reptile
	Good		Pliers	DdS27	Good		Inlet
	Good		Scissors		Good		Tower
	Good	∨	Stool	DdS28	Poor		Helmet
	Poor		Trees		Good		Inlet
D9	Good	<	Beak		Poor		Vase
	Good		Chopsticks	DdS29	Good		Inlet
	Good		Feet (animal, bird, or human)		Poor		Snake
	Good		Legs (animal, bird, or human)	Dd30	Poor		Ball
					Good		Face (human)
	Good		Tail		Good		Head (human)
	Good		Tweezers		Poor		Skull

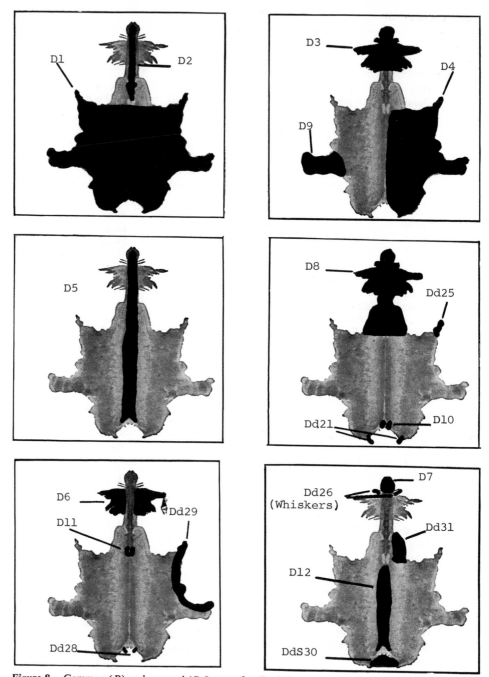

Figure 8. Common (*D*) and unusual (*Dd*) areas for Card VI.

Table A (Continued)

Loca-tion	Form Quality	Category	Loca-tion	Form Quality	Category

CARD VI

Loca-tion	Form Quality	Category
W	Poor	Airplane
	Poor	Amoeba
	Good- ∧∨	Animal
	Poor	

(This class of response includes several variations such as carcus, flattened, hung-up, pelt, skin, or stretched. In most instances the type of animal specified is canine (dog, fox, wolf, etc.), or feline (cartoon cat, lynx, etc.). All such responses imply that the animal is not in natural form. Percepts which imply an animal in natural form are poor form)

Loca-tion	Form Quality	Category
	Poor ∧∨	Animal (sea)
	Poor ∨	Artichoke
	Poor	Bat
	Poor	Bear
	Good ∨	Bears (two)
	Good ∨∧	Bearskin
	Poor	Beetle
	Poor	Bird (reflected)
	Good ∧∨	Bug (winged)
	Poor ∧∨	Butterfly
	Good	Candle (with D1 as base)
	Good	Cat (see also animal)
	Poor	Crab
	Good <	Cliff (reflected)
	Poor ∨	Club
	Good ∨	Coat rack (with coat hanging)
	Good	Dog (see also animal)
	Good ∨	Doll
	Good ∧∨	Duster (with handle)
	Good ∧∨	Emblem
	Good	Explosion
	Good ∨	Fan
	Poor <	Fish
	Poor ∨	Flag
	Poor	Flower
	Poor	Fly
	Good	Fountain
	Poor	Genitals (male)
	Good	Guitar
	Poor ∨	Hair style
	Good <	Iceberg (reflected)
	Good	Insect
	Poor	Island
	Poor ∨	Lamp
	Good <	Landscape (reflected)
	Good ∧∨	Leaf

Loca-tion	Form Quality	Category
	Good	Leather
	Poor	Lungs
	Poor ∨	Mirror (hand)
	Poor ∨	Moth
	Poor	Pan (frying)
	Good	Pelt (animal)
	Poor ∨	Plant
	Good	Rug
	Good ∨	Scarecrow
	Poor ∨	Shield
	Poor ∨	Shrimp
	Good ∧∨	Skin (see also animal)
	Poor	Snail
	Poor	Spider
	Good ∨	Statue
	Good	Totem (on hill or rock)
	Good ∨	Tree
	Good ∧∨	Waterway

(This class of response is good form only when the center (D5) is specified as the waterway (canal, ditch, river, stream) and the other areas of the blot are reported as landscape)

Loca-tion	Form Quality	Category
	Poor	X-ray
D1	Poor	Anatomy
	Poor ∧∨	Animal
	Good ∨	Animals (back to back)
	Poor	Artichoke
	Good	Bookends
	Poor	Bug
	Good	Clouds
	Good ∨	Coat
	Good	Doors (swinging)
	Poor	Face (animal or human)
	Poor	Flesh
	Poor	Flower
	Poor	Gate
	Good	Heads (human)

(This class of response includes human and human-like heads, in profile, back to back. Dd25 is often reported as a crown or hat in these responses)

Loca-tion	Form Quality	Category
	Good <	Iceberg (reflected)
	Poor	Island
	Good ∨	Jacket
	Good <∨	Landscape (aerial view or reflected)
	Good	Leaf
	Poor	Lungs

Table A (Continued)

Location	Form Quality	Category	Location	Form Quality	Category
	Good	Map (topographic)		Good	Butterfly
	Good	∨ Monkeys (back to back)		Good	Crucifix (abstract
	Good	Pot (cooking)			representation)
	Good	Rock		Good	Emblem
	Poor	Shell		Good	Flower
	Good	< Ship (reflected)		Poor	Fly
	Good-Poor	Skin		Poor	Flying fish
				Good	Goose
		(This class of response is good form only for pelts, rugs, skins, etc. from fur bearing animals. Human or reptile skins are poor form)		Good	Head (animal, with D6 as whiskers)
				Poor	Head (insect or reptile)
	Poor	Smoke		Poor	Human
	Poor	Starfish		Good	Insect (winged)
	Good	Waterway (with landscape)		Good	Lamp
	Poor	X-ray			(This class of response is good form when the D6 area is used as a lampshade, light rays, etc.)
D2	Good	< Alligator (reflected)		Poor	Owl
	Good	Banister		Good	Penis (with D6 omitted or as wings)
		(This class of response includes a variety of wood carvings associated with the general household category as in chair rungs, bedpost, etc.)		Good	Reptile (with D6 omitted or as wings)
	Good	Bone		Good	Rocket
	Good	∨ Candle		Good	Scarecrow
	Good	Candlestick		Good	< Shrubbery (reflected)
	Poor	Caterpillar		Good	Totem
	Good	Club		Good	Tree
	Poor	Drill		Good	Wasp
	Poor	Fish	D4	Poor	∧ ∨ Animal
	Good	Human		Good	< Animal
	Poor	∧ ∨ Knife			(This class of response includes D9 as animal and the remainder of D4 as an object on which the animal is sitting or standing)
	Good	Lamp (ornamental)			
	Good	Lamp (street)		Poor	< Building
	Good	Lamppost		Good	Cloud
	Poor	Needle		Good	∧ ∨ Head (animal or human)
	Poor	Penis		Poor	Insect
	Poor	Piston		Good	Landscape
	Good	Reptile		Poor	Map
	Good	Statue (human-like)		Good	∧ ∨ Mask
	Good	∨ Sword		Good	< Mountain
	Good	Thermometer		Poor	Rock
	Poor	Vertebrae		Good	< Ship
	Good	X-ray (esophagus)		Good	< Tank (army)
D3	Good	Airplane	D5	Good	Backbone
	Poor	Anatomy		Good	Bone
	Poor	Animal		Good	Canal
	Good	Animal (winged)		Good	Caterpillar
	Good	Bird		Poor	Fallopian tube
	Good	Bug (winged)			

Table A (Continued)

Loca-tion	Form Quality	Category	Loca-tion	Form Quality	Category
	Good	Gorge		Poor	Spinal cord
	Poor	Knife		Good	Statue (human-like)
	Poor	Paddle		Good	Totem
	Poor	Pole (carved)		Good	Tree
	Good	Reptile		Poor	Turtle
	Good	River		Poor	X-ray
	Good	Road	D9	Poor	< Boot
	Good	Shaft		Good	< Castle
	Good	Spinal cord		Good	Cliff
	Good	Thermometer		Good	< Head (canine)
	Poor	Tree		Good	< Head (bird)
	Good	Worm		Good	< Leg (animal)
				Good	< Paw
D6	Poor	Arms		Good	Peninsula
	Good	Birds		Good	Rock
	Good	Branches		Good	< Seal
	Poor	< Cactus		Good	< Smokestack
	Good	Feathers		Good	< Statue (carved)
	Poor	Flags		Good	< Walrus
	Good	Flames			
	Poor	< Flowers	D10	Poor	Anatomy
	Good	Geese (flock)		Poor	Buttocks
	Poor	< Ice		Good	Eggs
	Good	Light (rays)		Good	Eyes (insect)
	Poor	Pelts		Good	V Heads (bird or insect)
	Good	< Shrubbery		Poor	V Heads (human)
	Good	< Trees		Poor	Testicles
	Good	Whiskers (animal)		Poor	Vagina
				Poor	V Waterfall
D7	Good	Bug			
	Poor	Eyes	D11	Good	< Boat (reflected)
	Good	Fist		Poor	Brain
	Good	Hands (clasped)		Good	Butterfly
	Good	Head (animal, bird, or reptile)		Good	Eggs
				Good	Flames
	Poor	Heads (two)		Poor	Kidneys
	Poor	Human		Poor	Lungs
	Poor	Knob (door)		Good	Shell (clam, opened)
	Poor	Nose		Poor	Tonsils
				Poor	Waterwings
D8	Poor	Animal			
	Good	Bird (statue)	D12	Good	Burner (Bunsen)
	Good	Bug (crawling from object)		Good	Candle
				Good	Canal
	Good	Crucifix		Poor	Human
	Good	Dragonfly		Good	Missile
	Good	Flower		Poor	Needle
	Good	Fountain		Poor	Penis
	Poor	Head (animal)		Poor	Rectum
	Good	Insect (winged)		Good	Road
	Good	Lighthouse		Good	River
	Poor	Map		Good	Rocket
	Good	Scarecrow		Good	Shaft (mine)

Table A (Continued)

Loca-tion	Form Quality	Category	Loca-tion	Form Quality	Category
	Poor	Spear		Poor	Penis
	Good	Spinal cord		Good	Shoe
	Poor	Vagina			
	Good	Waterway	Dd26	Good	Antennae
				Poor	Sticks
Dd21	Good	Claws		Good	Whiskers
	Poor	Hands			
	Good	Heads (bird or reptile)	Dd28	Good	Claws
	Good	Horns		Good	∨ Heads (bird)
	Good	Pincers		Poor	Stalagmites
	Good	Tongs	Dd29	Good	Coastline
				Good	Profile (human)
Dd25	Good	Carving (wood)			
	Good	Foot (human)	DdS30	Good	Inlet
	Good	Head (human)		Poor	Mouth
	Good	Human		Poor	Vase
	Poor	Mountain	Dd31	Poor	Iceberg
	Good	Paw		Poor	Nose (reptile)

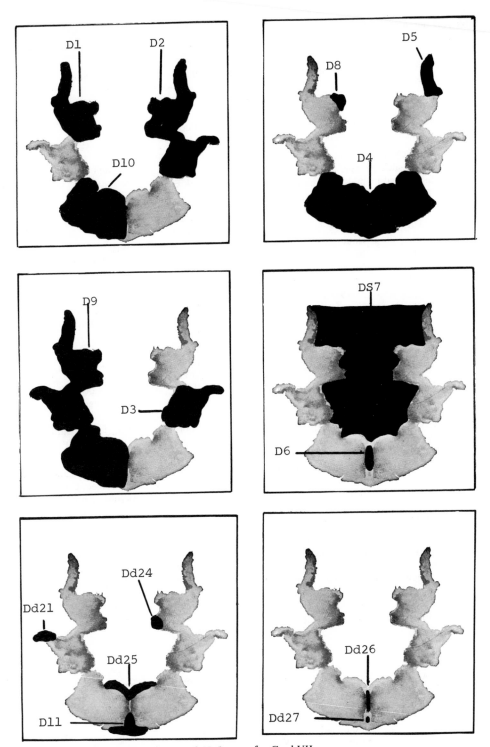

Figure 9. Common (*D*) and unusual (*Dd*) areas for Card VII.

Table A (Continued)

Location	Form Quality	Category	Location	Form Quality	Category
		CARD VII			
W	Poor	Animal		Poor	Puzzle
	Good	Animals (two)		Good	Reef
				Good	Rocks
		(This class of response includes anthropoids such as ape, monkey, etc. and long eared animals such as rabbit, etc. They are reported as D2 with D4 as a rock, platform, etc. or as all of D9)		Poor	Sea animal
				Good	Sculpture
				Poor	Shrubbery
				Good	Smoke
	Good	∨ Arch		Good	∨ Stool
	Poor	Bones		Good	Vase
	Poor	Bug		Poor	∨ Wig
	Poor	Butterfly		Poor	Womb (open)
	Good	Canyon (includes use of DS7) D1		Poor	X-ray
	Poor	∨ Cap (fur)		Poor	Anatomy
	Good	Carving		Poor	∨ Art (abstract)
	Good	∨ Cave (entrance)		Good	Art (sculpture)
	Good	∨ Chair (includes use of DS7)		Poor	∨ Cat
	Good	Clouds		Poor	Chair
	Poor	∨ Crown		Poor	Chicken
	Good	Dogs (two)		Good	Clouds
	Good	Dolls (two)		Poor	Commode
	Good	Food (fried)		Good	Doll (head)
	Poor	∨ Frog		Poor	Fish
	Good	∨ Gate		Poor	Fist (finger pointing)
	Good	Harbor (includes use of DS7)		Good	Head (animal)
	Good	Horseshoe		Good	Head (human)
	Poor	∨ Human			(This class of response includes many variations such as cameo, child, indian, etc. plus numerous human-like and mythological figures as in elf, gnome, snow white, etc.)
	Good	∨ Humans (two)			
		(This class of response includes several variations for human and human-like figures. Frequently, with the card in the upright position, the figures are identified only as D2 with D4 as a separate object. When the card is inverted the entire D9 area is reported as the human, usually female)		Poor	∨ Horse
				Poor	Map (specific)
				Good	Map (unspecified)
				Good	Mask
				Poor	Mountain
				Good	∨ Rabbit
				Good	Statue
				Poor	∨ Tree
	Poor	∨ Insect D2		Good	Ape
	Good	Islands		Good	Angel
	Good	Lamp (ornamental)		Poor	∨ Cat
	Poor	Leaf		Poor	Chicken
	Poor	∨ Legs (animal)		Good	< ∨ Clouds
	Good	Map		Poor	∧ Clouds
	Good	Monument		Poor	Cow
	Poor	∨ Moth		Good	< ∧ Dog
	Poor	Mouth		Poor	Donkey
	Good	Necklace		Good	Dwarf
	Poor	Plants		Good	∨ Elephant

Table A (Continued)

Location	Form Quality	Category	Location	Form Quality	Category
	Poor	Fish		Good	∨ Bowtie
	Poor	Fox		Poor	Bowl
	Poor	∨ Frog		Poor	Bridge
	Good	Head (human) (see also *D1*)		Good	∨ Butterfly
				Poor	Buttocks
	Poor	Horse		Good	Clouds
	Good	Human (see also *W*)		Poor	Cushions
	Good	Islands		Good	∨ Doors (swinging)
	Good	Lamb		Poor	Fly
	Poor	Lion		Good	Head (animal, reflected)
	Good	Map		Good	∨ Insect (winged)
	Good	Mountains		Poor	Landscape
	Good	Rabbit		Poor	Map
	Good	Sculpture		Poor	Mountains
	Good	∨ Shrimp		Good	Paper (torn)
	Good	Snowman		Good	Pelvis
	Good	Statue		Good	Rocks
	Poor	Tiger		Poor	Rowboat
	Poor	Trees		Poor	Shell
				Poor	Shrubs
D3	Poor	∨ Animal		Good	Wings
	Poor	Animal (sea)		Poor	X-ray
	Poor	Beard			
	Good	Candy (cotton)	*D5*	Poor	Arrow
	Poor	Cap (stocking)		Good	Blade (knife)
	Poor	Cleaver (meat)		Good	Caterpillar
	Good	Cliff		Poor	Claw
	Poor	Cup		Good	Comb (ladies)
	Poor	Dog		Good	Feather
	Poor	Ham		Good	Hair (styled)
	Good- Poor	∨ Head (animal)		Good	Headdress
				Poor	Horn
				Poor	Leg

(This class of response is good form for bear, dog, and similar varieties when the card is upright. Horned animals such as deer, goat, ram, etc. are poor form. When the card is inverted, long nosed animals such as anteater, elephant, etc. are good form)

Location	Form Quality	Category	Location	Form Quality	Category
				Poor	Penis
				Poor	Plant
	Good	Head (human)		Poor	Reptile
	Good	Island		Poor	Sausage
	Good	Mask		Poor	Saw
	Good	Rock		Poor	Smoke
	Poor	Sack		Poor	Stalagmite
	Poor	Shrub		Poor	Sword
	Good	Stone (carved)		Good	Tail
D4	Poor	Anatomy		Good	Trunk (elephant)
	Poor	Animals (small)		Poor	Wing
	Good	∨ Arch	*D6*	Good	Anus
	Good	∨ Bat		Good	Canal
	Good	∨ Bird		Poor	Caterpillar
	Good	∨ Bow		Good	Dam
				Good	Doll
				Good	Gorge
				Good	Hinge (door)
				Good	∨ Human

Table A (Continued)

Loca-tion	Form Quality	Category	Loca-tion	Form Quality	Category
	Poor	Insect		Good	Rocks (piled or balanced)
	Poor	Missile		Poor	V Tree
	Poor	Penis	D10	Poor	Animal (small, crouching)
	Good	River			
	Poor	Spine		Poor	Brick
	Poor	Tower		Good	Cloud
	Poor	Tree		Poor	V Hat
	Good	Vagina		Good	Head (animal)
	Good	Waterway		Poor	V Head (animal or human)
DS7	Poor	Anatomy		Poor	Landscape
	Good	V Arrowhead		Good	Pillow
	Poor	Bell		Poor	Stool
	Good	Bowl			
	Poor	Cloud	D11	Poor	V Bird
	Good	V Entrance (cave)		Poor	Buttocks
	Poor	Face (animal or human)		Good	V Emblem
	Good	Harbor		Good	Humans (two)
	Good	Hat (historical)		Good	V Parachute (with D6 as person)
	Poor	V Head (animal)			
	Good	V Head (human)		Poor	Plant
	Good	V Helmet		Good	Statues
	Good	Lake		Good	Water
	Good	V Lamp		Good	V Waterfall
	Poor	V Mushroom	Dd21	Good	Arm
	Good	V Pagoda		Good	Caterpillar
	Good	Pot		Poor	Face (animal or human)
	Good	V Sphinx		Good	Finger
	Poor	V Tree		Poor	Head (animal or human)
	Good	Vase		Good	Horn
D8	Good	City (in distance)		Good	Paw
	Good	Cliffs		Poor	Peninsula
	Poor	Dragon		Good	Tail
	Good	Forest		Good	Thumb
	Poor	Hair		Good	Trunk (elephant)
	Poor	Head	Dd24	Poor	Cloud (rain)
	Good	Humans		Poor	V Head (animal)
	Good	V Icicles			
	Poor	Sea monster	Dd25	Poor	Gull
	Good	Snail		Good	Landscape (with waterfall)
	Good	Stalagmites			
	Good	Towers (for electric cables)	Dd26	Good	Human
	Good	Whale		Good	River
				Good	Vagina
D9 (see also W)	Good	V Animal			
	Good	Clouds	Dd27	Good	Anus
	Good	V Elephant		Poor	Teeth
	Good	V Human		Good	Vagina
	Poor	Landscape		Poor	Window

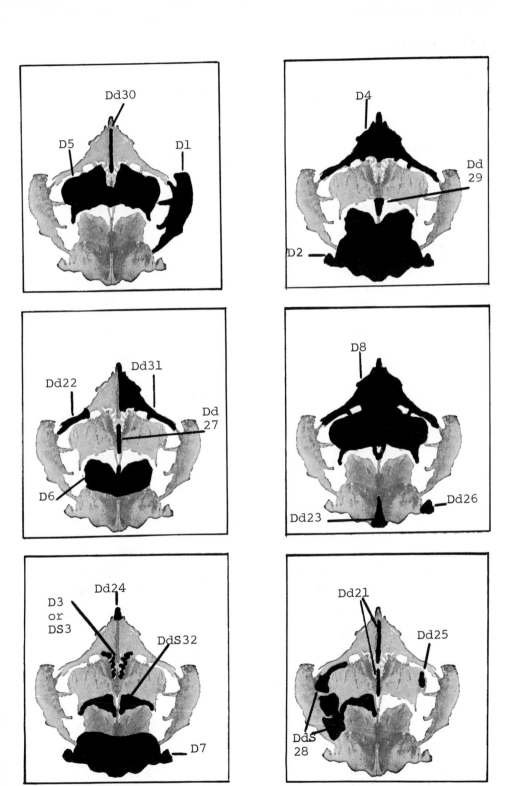

Figure 10. Common (*D*) and unusual (*Dd*) areas for Card VIII.

Table A (Continued)

Loca-tion	Form Quality	Category	Loca-tion	Form Quality	Category

CARD VIII

Loca-tion	Form Quality	Category	Loca-tion	Form Quality	Category
W	Good	Anatomy (nonspecific)		Good	Pagoda
	Good < ∨	Animal(s)		Poor ∨	Pelvis

(This class of response is good form when the D1 area is identified as the animal and other areas of the blot are reported as landscape. When the card is turned sideways, the scene is reported as a reflection)

				Poor	Pyramid
				Good	Rocket
				Poor	Rubbish
				Poor	Sea animal
				Good	Seashell
				Good	Ship (with sails, viewed from end)
	Good	Art (abstract)			
	Poor	Bat		Poor	Skeleton
	Poor	Bird		Poor	Skull (animal)
	Good	Bowl (ornamental)		Poor	Statue
	Poor	Butterfly		Poor	Stomach
	Poor	Cage		Poor ∨	Torch
	Good	Carousel		Good	Vegetation (tropical, or underwater)
	Good ∧ ∨	Chandelier			
	Good	Christmas tree		Good	Vase
	Good	Coat-of-arms		Good	Volcano (erupting)
	Poor	Clouds		Good	X-ray (chest)
	Poor	Crab		Poor	X-ray (unspecified)
	Good	Crown (ornamental)	D1	Good	Animal (four legged)
	Good	Design (abstract)			
	Good	Emblem			
	Poor	Face (animal, human, or insect)			

(This class of response includes a wide variety of species and also includes four legged prehistoric animals. The most common classes of animals reported are of the canine, feline, or rodent varieties, such as badger, bear, beaver, cat, dog, gopher, lion, mouse, possum, rat, and wolf)

	Poor	Fish			
	Poor	Flag			
	Good	Floral design			
	Good ∧ ∨	Flower			
	Good	Foliage			
	Good	Fountain		Poor	Bird
	Poor	Frog (opened)		Poor	Blood
	Poor	Head (animal, human, or insect)		Poor	Camel
				Poor	Dolphin
	Good	Headdress (ornamental)		Poor	Fish
	Good	Illustration (biological)		Poor	Flower
	Pocr	Insect		Poor	Frog
	Poor	Intestines		Poor	Insect
	Poor ∧ ∨	Jacket		Poor	Lung
	Poor	Jellyfish		Poor	Porpoise
	Good < ∧	Landscape (aerial view)		Poor	Reptile
	Good	Lantern (oriental)		Poor	Seal
	Poor	Leaf		Poor	Shrimp
	Poor	Lobster		Poor	Tree
	Poor	Map			
	Poor	Mask	D2	Poor	Anatomy
	Good	Monument		Poor	Animal (sea)
	Poor	Moth		Poor ∧ ∨	Bat
	Good	Mountains		Poor	Bug
	Good	Ornament (Christmas)		Good ∧ ∨	Butterfly

Table A (Continued)

Loca-tion	Form Quality	Category	Loca-tion	Form Quality	Category
	Poor	Buttocks		Poor	Crab
	Poor	Chest		Poor	Crawfish
	Good	∨ Coat		Poor	Crown
	Good	Coral		Poor	Fish
	Poor	∨ Crown		Good	Frog (leaping)
	Poor	∨ Dog		Poor	Hat
	Good	Fire		Poor	Head (animal)
	Poor	Flesh		Good	House
	Good	∧ ∨ Flower		Good	Iceberg
	Poor	∨ Hat		Good	Insect
	Good	∨ Head (animal, horned)		Poor	Lobster
	Poor	Head (human)		Good	Mountain
	Poor	Head (insect)		Poor	Octopus
	Good	Ice cream		Good	Rocket
	Poor	Insect		Good	Roots
	Good	∨ Jacket		Poor	Scorpion
	Good	Jello		Good	Shrubbery
	Good	Lava		Poor	Skull
	Poor	Leaf		Poor	Spider
	Poor	Meat		Good	Stump (tree)
	Good	Mountains		Good	Temple
	Poor	Pelvis		Good	Tree (fir)
	Good	Rock(s) (crystals)		Good	Waterfall
	Good	Slide (biological, stained)	D5	Good	Bat
	Poor	Spinal cord		Poor	Bird
	Poor	Vagina		Good	Butterfly
				Good	Cliffs
D3 /	Good	< Animal (reflected)		Good	Cloth (denim or velvet, torn)
DS3	Good	Bone structure			
	Poor	∨ Cave		Good	Flags
	Good	Corset		Poor	Flower
	Poor	Face (animal or human)		Poor	Heads (animals or birds)
	Poor	Funnel		Good	Ice
	Poor	Head (animal or human)		Good	Landscape (aerial view)
	Good	Mask		Poor	Leaves
	Good	Rib cage		Poor	Lungs
	Good	Skeleton		Poor	Map
	Good	Skull (steer)		Poor	Pelvis
	Good	∨ Teepee		Good	Pillows
	Good	∨ Tent		Good	Sails (ship)
	Good	Vertebrae		Poor	Sky
	Poor	Web		Good	Water
D4	Good	Airplane (jet)	D6	Poor	Anatomy
	Poor	Animal (sea)		Good	∧ ∨ Butterfly
	Poor	∨ Antlers		Poor	Face (animal or human)
	Poor	∧ ∨ Bat		Good	Flower(s)
	Poor	Boomerang		Poor	Frog
	Good	Bridge (natural)		Good-Poor	< ∧ Head (animal)
	Good	Butterfly			
	Good	Cliffs			
	Poor	Clouds			

(This class of response includes the heads of anthropoids, canines, and fe-

Table A (Continued)

Location	Form Quality		Category	Location	Form Quality		Category
			lines. All other animal heads are poor form)		Good		Humans (two)
					Poor	∨	Legs
	Good		Ice cream		Good	∨	Pincers
	Poor		Lungs		Good		Trees (fir)
	Good		Rocks	Dd25	Poor	<	Alligator
D7	Poor		Bird		Poor		Fish
	Good		Blood (dried)		Poor		Human
	Good	∧ ∨	Butterfly		Good		Island
	Poor		Buttocks		Good		Statue (carved)
	Poor		Coat	Dd26	Good	∨	Dog
	Poor		Face (animal or human)		Good	<	Head (animal)
	Poor		Head (animal or bird)		Poor	<	Head (bird)
	Good		Ice cream (sherbet)		Poor	<	Head (human)
	Poor		Leaf (autumn)		Good	∨	Lion
	Poor		Mountain		Good	<	Rock
	Good		Painted desert	Dd27	Good		Alligator
	Good	< ∨	Rocks		Poor		Needle
	Good	∨	Vest		Good		Pen (writing)
D8	Poor		Anatomy		Good		Spear
	Poor		Butterfly		Poor		Worm
	Good	∨	Chandelier	DdS28	Poor		Clouds
	Good	∨	Floral display		Good		Snow
	Poor		Insect		Poor		Water
	Good		Rocket	Dd29	Good	∨	Bottle (milk)
	Poor		Shell		Poor		Ghost
Dd21	Poor		Esophagus		Poor		Statue
	Poor		Human		Poor		Tooth
	Poor		Rocket		Good	∨	Triangle (musical)
	Good		Spinal cord	Dd30	Good	∨	Cane
Dd22	Good		Arm		Good		Gorge
	Good		Branch (tree)		Good		Spinal cord
	Good		Hand		Good		Stick
	Good	∨	Horn	Dd31	Poor	<	Ghost
	Good		Root		Poor		Insect
Dd23	Good		Anus		Good		Tree root (or stump)
	Poor		Flask	DdS32	Good		Albatross
	Good		Genitals (female)		Good		Bird
	Good	∨	Waterfall		Good		Butterfly
Dd24	Poor		Birds		Good		Seagull
	Good		Feelers		Good		Snow
	Good		Fingers				

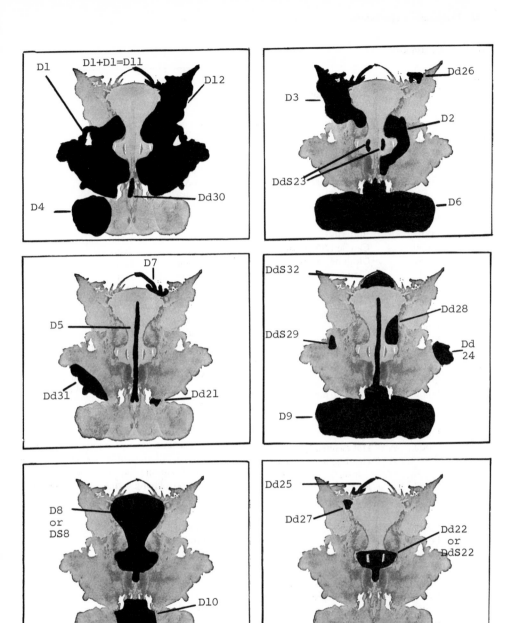

Figure 11. Common (*D*) and unusual (*Dd*) areas for Card IX.

Table A (Continued)

Loca-tion	Form Quality		Category	Loca-tion	Form Quality		Category
			CARD IX				
W	Poor		Anatomy	D1	Good	∧ ∨	Animal
	Good		Art (abstract)		Poor		Animal (sea)
	Poor	∧ ∨	Bird		Poor		Bird
	Good	∨	Birds (under tree, D3 as birds)		Poor		Butterfly
					Good		Cloud
	Good		Bowl (ornamental)		Poor	∧ ∨	Dog
	Poor		Bug		Poor		Elephant
	Poor	∧ ∨	Butterfly		Poor		Fish
	Good		Candle (D6 as base)		Poor		Frog
	Good	∨	Clothing (woman's)		Good		Grass
	Poor		Clouds		Poor		Hat
	Good		Coral		Good	∨	Head (animal)

(This class of response includes animal heads which have the snout at the D5 centerline or at Dd24. These responses are good form only when the card is inverted)

Loca-tion	Form Quality		Category
	Poor		Crab
	Good		Decoration
	Good		Emblem
	Good	∧ ∨	Explosion
	Poor	∧ ∨	Face (animal, human, or insect)
	Good	∧ ∨	Fire (with smoke)
	Good		Floral arrangement
	Good		Flower
	Good	∧ ∨	Fountain
	Good		Garden
	Good	∧ ∨	Hat (woman's)
	Poor	∧ ∨	Head (animal, human, or insect)
	Good	∨	Human
	Good		Illustration (biology)
	Poor		Insect
	Poor		Island
	Poor		Jellyfish
	Good	∨	Lamp (ornamental)
	Good	< ∧	Landscape

Good	Head (human, profile, with Dd24 as chin)
Poor	Heart
Poor ∧ ∨	Human
Good <	Human

(This class of response has several variations, all of which use Dd24 as the head. Among the most common are, a person playing a musical instrument, a person riding a cycle, or a woman chasing a child)

Loca-tion	Form Quality		Category
	Good	∨	Jacket
	Good	< ∧	Landscape
	Poor		Leaf
	Poor	∧ ∨	Lion
	Poor	∨	Lungs
	Poor		Map
	Good		Monster
	Poor	∨	Mushroom
	Good	∧ ∨	Pig
	Poor		Plant
	Poor	<	Rabbit
	Good		Shrub
	Good		Smoke
	Poor	<	Tree Stump
	Poor		Wings

(When the card is turned to the side, landscape is typically reported as a reflection)

Loca-tion	Form Quality		Category
	Poor		Leaf
	Poor		Map
	Good	∧ ∨	Mask
	Good		Paint
	Good		Pallet (artist)
	Good		Plant
	Poor		Sea animal
	Good		Seaweed
	Poor		Skull
	Poor	∨	Throat
	Poor		Tree
	Good	∨	Tree
	Good		Vase
	Good		Waterfall (in forest)
	Poor		X-ray

Loca-tion	Form Quality		Category
D2	Good		Alligator
	Poor		Carving (abstract)
	Good		Crocodile
	Good	<	Head (animal, antlered)
	Good		Head (animal, long snout)
	Poor		Head (human)

Table A (Continued)

Location	Form Quality		Category
	Good		Head (reptile)
	Good		Log
	Poor		Mountains
	Poor		Tree
D3	Poor		Anatomy
	Good		Animal (antlered or horned)
	Good	∧ ∨	Bird
	Good		Blood (stain)
	Poor		Carrot
	Good		Cliff
	Poor		Cloud
	Good		Clown
	Poor	∨	Club
	Good		Crab
	Good	< ∧	Deer
	Poor		Dog
	Good		Dragon
	Good		Fire
	Poor		Fish
	Good		Flower
	Poor		Footprint
	Good		Ghost
	Good		Head (animal, antlered)
	Good		Head (human)
	Good	<	Hill
	Good		Human
	Poor		Insect
	Good		Lava
	Poor	∧ ∨	Leg
	Good		Lobster
	Poor		Lungs
	Good		Map (topographic)
	Good	∨	Owl
	Good	∨	Parrot
	Good		Plant
	Poor		Rodent
	Good		Sand
	Poor		Sea animal
	Poor		Shrimp
	Good		Sun spot
	Good		Wing
	Good		Witch
D4	Poor		Anatomy
	Good		Apples
	Good		Balls
	Poor		Blood
	Poor		Head (animal)
	Good		Head (human)
	Poor		Eye
	Good		Flower

Location	Form Quality		Category
	Poor		Meat
	Poor		Pot
D5	Poor		Animal
	Poor		Arrow
	Good		Bone
	Good		Candle
	Good		Cane
	Poor		Esophagus
	Good		Fountain
	Good		Geyser
	Good		Gorge
	Good	<	Landscape (reflected)
	Poor		Peninsula
	Poor		Penis
	Good		River
	Good		Road
	Good	<	Shoreline
	Good		Skewer
	Good		Spinal cord
	Good		Stalactite
	Good		Stem
	Good		Sword
	Poor		Tree
	Good		Waterway
D6	Poor		Animal(s)
	Good		Apples
	Good		Babies (two)
	Good		Balloons
	Poor	∨	Bird
	Poor		Buttocks
	Good		Cloud
	Good		Embryo (two)
	Good	∨	Face (insect or science fiction)
	Good		Fire
	Good	∧ ∨	Flowers
	Poor	∧ ∨	Head (animal(s))
	Good	∧ ∨	Heads (human)
	Poor		Island
	Poor		Marshmallows
	Good	∨	Mushroom
	Poor		Pots
	Good		Powder puff
	Good		Sherbet (raspberry or strawberry)
	Good	∨	Shoulders (human)
	Poor		Skin
	Good		Smoke
	Poor		Vagina
	Poor		Wings

Table A (Continued)

Location	Form Quality	Category	Location	Form Quality	Category
D7	Poor	Animal		Poor	Furnace (coal)
	Good	Antlers		Poor	Lungs
	Good	Branches (tree)		Good	Rocks
	Poor	Cannons			
	Good	Claws	D11	Good	Bat
	Good	Drawbridge (opening)		Good	Butterfly
	Good	Fire		Poor	Carving
	Good	Horns		Good	Pelvis
	Poor	Human		Poor	Plant
	Poor	Lightning			
	Good	Roots	D12	Poor	< Dragon
	Good	Skeletal		Good	< Landscape
	Poor	Trees		Poor	∨ Tree
				Poor	X-ray
D8 /	Poor	Anatomy			
DS8	Poor	Animal	Dd21	Good	Claws
	Good	Bottle		Good	Fingers
	Good	Canyon		Poor	Icicles
	Good	Cave		Poor	Rake
	Good	Chandelier		Poor	Spears
	Poor	Chest (cavity)		Poor	Stalactites
	Good	∨ Dress			
	Poor	∧ ∨ Face (animal or human)	Dd22 /	Poor	Candles
	Poor	∧ ∨ Head (animal or human)	DdS22	Good	Cavern
	Good	Hourglass		Poor	Doors (swinging)
	Poor	Keyhole		Good	Eyes
	Good	Lamp		Poor	Face (animal)
	Poor	Mask		Good	Face (human)
	Good	∨ Salt shaker		Poor	Head (animal)
	Poor	Sky		Poor	Head (fish)
	Poor	Uterus		Poor	Jellyfish
	Good	Vase		Good	Lakes
	Good	Violin		Good	Mask
	Good	Waterfall		Good	Pumpkin (halloween)
				Poor	Skull
D9	Poor	Animal			
	Good	∧ ∨ Chandelier	DdS23	Good	Eyes
	Poor	Head (animal, human, or insect)		Good	Holes
				Poor	Islands
	Good	∨ Head (elephant)		Poor	Nostrils
	Good	∨ Heron (on one leg)		Poor	Pillows
	Poor	Human		Poor	Shells
	Good	∨ Flower			
	Good	Fountain	Dd24	Good	< ∨ Head (animal)
	Good	∨ Lamp		Good	< Head (human)
	Good	Spindle (office)			
	Good	∨ Tree	Dd25	Good	Archway
	Good	∨ Umbrella		Good	Claws
				Good	Feelers
D10	Poor	Animal		Good	Fingers
	Poor	Bird		Good	Roots
	Good	Buttocks		Good	Tentacles

Table A (Continued)

Location	Form Quality		Category	Location	Form Quality		Category
Dd26	Poor		Animal	DdS29	Poor		Bell
	Poor		Finger (pointing)		Poor		Face
	Poor		Foot		Good		Ghost
	Good		Gun		Poor		Human
	Good	<	Human		Good		Lake
	Poor		Key	Dd30	Good		Candlewax (dripping)
	Poor		Nose		Poor		Caterpillar
	Good		Trumpet		Poor		Intestine
Dd27	Poor		Animal		Poor		Penis
	Poor		Human	Dd31	Good	∨	Cover (pot)
	Poor	<	Top		Good		Face (animal)
Dd28	Poor		Blood		Good		Face (human)
	Good		Egg	DdS32	Poor		Shell
	Poor		Head		Poor		Sunspot
	Poor		Stomach		Good		Tent

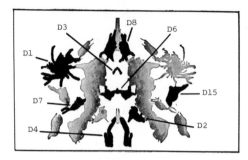
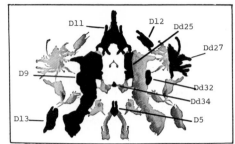
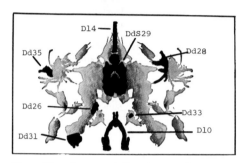

Figure 12. Common (*D*) and unusual (*Dd*) areas for Card X.

Table A (Continued)

Loca-tion	Form Quality	Category	Loca-tion	Form Quality	Category
		CARD X			
W	Poor	Anatomy		Good	Lobster
	Good	` Animals (marine)		Poor	Map
	Good	Art (abstract)		Poor	Mask
	Good	Aquarium		Good	Octopus
	Poor	Aviary		Poor <	Reindeer
	Good	Bacteria		Good	Roots
	Poor	Birds		Good	Scorpion
	Poor	Butterfly		Poor	Sea shell
	Good ∧ ∨	Chandelier		Good	Snowflake
	Poor ∧ ∨	Christmas tree		Good	Spider
	Poor	Clouds		Good	Water (drop)
	Good	Design (abstract)		Poor	Web
	Poor ∧ ∨	Face (human)		Good	Weed
	Poor ∧ ∨	Fireworks			
	Good ∧ ∨	Floral (design)	D2	Good	Amoeba
	Good ∨	Flowers (bouquet)		Poor	Animal (unspecified)
	Poor	Headdress		Good ∨	Bird (flying)
	Good	Insects		Good	Cell (biological)
	Good	Islands		Poor	Chicken
	Good	Kaleidoscope		Good	Dog
	Poor	Map		Good	Egg (fried)
	Poor	Mask		Poor ∧ ∨	Eye
	Good	Mobile (abstract)		Poor	Fish
	Poor	Pagoda		Good	Flower
	Good	Painting (modern)		Poor	Frog
	Good	Painting (finger)		Poor	Head
	Good	Pallet (artist's)		Good	Lion
	Good	Plants		Poor	Monkey
	Good	Poster (abstract)		Poor	Sea animal
	Good	Puzzle (pieces)		Good	Seal
	Good	Sea animal			
	Good	Underwater scene	D3	Poor	Airplane
D1	Good	Amoeba		Good ∨	Antennae (TV)
	Poor	Beetle		Good	Antennae (insect)
	Poor	Bird		Poor	Bird
	Good	Bug		Good	Buds
	Good	Cell (biological)		Poor	Bug
	Poor	Cockroach		Good	Cherry pits
	Good	Coral		Poor	Crab
	Good	Crab		Poor	Ear muffs
	Poor	Earring		Poor	Earphones
	Good	Fern		Poor ∧ ∨	Human
	Poor	Fish		Poor	Flowers
	Good	Flower		Good ∧ ∨	Governor (on motor)
	Poor	Head		Good	Instrument (for measuring wind velocity)
	Good	Insect		Poor	Instrument (medical)
	Poor	Island		Good	Knocker (door)
	Poor	Jellyfish		Good	Lights (electric)
	Poor	Landscape		Poor ∨	Necklace
	Poor	Leaf		Poor	Notes (musical)

Table A (Continued)

Location	Form Quality		Category	Location	Form Quality		Category
	Poor		Ovaries	D6	Good		Animals
	Good	∨	Parachutist		Good		Bagpipes
	Good		Pawnbrokers symbol		Poor		Bat(s)
	Poor		Scissors		Good	∧ ∨	Birds
	Good		Seed pod (maple)		Poor		Brassiere
	Poor		Stethoscope		Poor		Breasts
	Poor		Testicles		Good		Bridge (natural)
	Good		Tongs (ice)		Poor		Clouds
	Poor		Twig		Good		Coral
	Good		Wishbone		Good	∨	Dolls
	Poor	∨	"V"		Good		Ducks
					Poor		Eyeglasses
D4	Poor		Anatomy		Poor		Face(s)
	Poor		Animal		Poor		Flowers
	Poor		Arms		Good	∨	Ghosts
	Poor		Bug		Good	∨	Gorillas
	Good	∧ ∨	Caterpillar		Poor		Hands
	Poor		Cucumber		Good		Heads (animal)
	Poor	∨	Dinosaur		Good	∨	Humans
	Good		Eel		Poor		Insects
	Poor		Fish		Poor		Kidneys
	Poor	∨	Head (animal or human)		Poor		Lungs
	Good	∨	Head (Peacock or swan)		Poor		Ovaries
	Good		Horns		Poor		Pipes (smokers)
	Poor		Insect		Good		Skeletal
	Good		Plant		Poor		Water
	Good		Saxophone				
	Good	∨	Sea horse	D7	Good		Animal (leaping)
	Poor		Snail		Good		Bird
	Good		Snake		Poor		Clam
	Good		Tail (bird)		Good		Cocoon
	Poor	∨	Tree		Poor		Claw
	Poor		Wings		Good		Crab
					Good		Crayfish
D5	Good	∨	Angel		Good		Deer
	Poor		Clothespin		Poor		Dog
	Good	∨	Crucifix		Poor		Frog
	Good		Devil		Poor		Human
	Good		Head (animal, long eared)		Poor		Kidney
					Poor		Lobster
			(Good form responses included in this class are donkey, llama, and rabbit. Most other animal heads will be poor form)		Good	∧ ∨	Mouse
					Good		Nest (bird)
					Good		Rats
					Good		Roots
	Poor		Head (human)		Poor		Sea animal
	Poor		Head (insect)		Good		Seed pod
	Poor		Head (sea animal)		Poor		Spider
	Good	∨	Human	D8	Good		Animal (prehistoric)
	Poor		Insect		Poor		Ant
	Good		Mask		Good		Beetle
	Poor	∨	Tooth		Good		Bug
	Good		Tweezers		Poor		Chicken

Table A (Continued)

Loca-tion	Form Quality	Category	Loca-tion	Form Quality	Category
	Good	Chipmunk		Good	Sea Horse
	Poor	Crab		Good	Specimen (biological)
	Good	Dragon		Good	Worm
	Good	Dwarf	D10	Poor	Animal (marine)
	Good	Elf		Poor	Bird
	Good	Emblem		Good ∨	Comb (ornamental)
	Poor	Face		Good ∨	Door knocker
	Poor	Fish		Poor ∧ ∨	Flower
	Poor	Frog		Good	Fountain
	Good	Gnome		Poor ∨	Funnel
	Poor	Goat		Good ∨	Head (animal, horned)
	Good	Head (human)		Good ∨	Horns
	Poor	Head (insect)		Good ∨	Human (in swing)
	Good	Human-like		Poor	Insect
	Good	Insect		Good	Lyre
	Poor	Lizard		Good ∨	Parachutist
	Good	Martian		Poor	Praying mantis
	Good	Mask		Poor	Saddle
	Good	Mouse		Poor ∨	"U"
	Poor	Monkey		Good	Wishbone
	Poor	Parrot			
	Good	Rat	D11	Poor	Airplane
	Good	Roots		Good	Animals (on each side of a pole or stick)
	Poor	Sea animal			
	Poor	Shrimp		Good	Art (abstract)
	Poor	Skeletal		Good	Beavers (gnawing at a tree)
	Poor	Spider			
	Good	Unicorn		Poor	Broom
D9	Poor	Anatomy		Good	Castle
	Good	Animal (mythological)		Poor	Centipede
	Poor	Bacon		Good	Eiffel tower
	Good	Blood		Good ∨	Flower
	Poor	Bone		Good ∨	Funnel
	Poor	Bug		Good	Insects (with pole or stick)
	Good ∧ ∨	Caterpillar			
	Good	Coastline		Poor	Intestines
	Good	Coral		Good	Mistle toe
	Poor	Dolphin		Poor	Nervous system
	Good	Elf		Good	Plant
	Good	Fire		Good	Rocket
	Poor	Hair		Good	Roots
	Poor	Head (human)		Good ∨	Scarecrow
	Good	Human		Good	Skeletal

(This class of response ordinarily involves child-like or mythology figures)

Loca-tion	Form Quality	Category	Loca-tion	Form Quality	Category
				Poor	Skull
	Poor	Insect		Good	Statue
	Good	Island		Good ∨	Tree
	Good	Map (topographic)		Good	X-ray
	Good	Mountain (aerial view)	D12	Poor	Bean
	Good	Mummy		Poor	Bird
	Poor	Porpoise		Good	Buffalo
				Good	Bull

Table A (Continued)

Location	Form Quality		Category	Location	Form Quality		Category
	Poor		Claw	D15	Poor		Animal
	Poor		Dog		Good	∧ ∨	Bird
	Good		Fish		Good		Bud (flower)
	Poor		Goat		Good	∨	Butterfly
	Poor		Grasshopper		Good		Flower
	Good		Insect		Poor		Head
	Good		Lamb		Poor		Insect
	Good		Leaf		Poor		Jellyfish
	Poor		Plant		Good		Rose
	Good		Ram		Poor	∨	Seal
	Poor		Rodent		Good		Wings
	Poor		Seed				
	Good		Unicorn	Dd25	Poor		Head (animal)
	Good		Whale		Good		Head (human)
D13	Good	<	Animal		Good		Head (human-like, mythological)
	(This class of response is good form for bear, buffalo, cat, dog, lion, and similar varieties of animals)			Dd26	Good		Face (human)
				Dd27	Good		Insect
	Poor		Bird	(see also	Poor		Seaweed
	Poor		Bug	D1)	Poor		Vulture
	Poor		Cloud				
	Poor		Face	Dd28	Good		Clown
	Poor		Fish		Poor		Insect
	Poor		Flower		Good		Puppet
	Poor		Human				
	Poor		Insect	DdS29	Good		Buddha
	Good		Leaf		Good		Fan (with D11 as handle)
	Good		Potato chip		Good		Lantern (with D11 as handle)
	Poor		Seashell				
	Poor		Sponge (marine)		Good		Paddle (with D11 as handle)
D14	Poor		Artery				
	Good		Baton	DdS30	Good		Canyon
	Poor		Bone		Poor		Skeleton
	Good		Candle				
	Good		Chimney	Dd31	Good	∨	Head (animal)
	Good		Face (abstract, human)		Good	∨	Head (caterpillar)
	Poor		Finger		Good	∨	Head (human)
	Good		Handle (wooden)				
	Poor		Knife	Dd32	Good		Head (animal)
	Good		Log				
	Good		Missile	Dd33	Good		Acorn
	Good		Pencil		Poor		Eye
	Good		Penis		Poor		Head
	Good		Post		Good		Orange
	Poor		Root		Good		Walnut
	Good		Shotgun (barrels)	Dd34	Poor	∨	Basket
	Good		Spinal cord		Poor		Tooth
	Good		Statue		Poor		Skull
	Good		Stove pipe				
	Good		Test tube	Dd35	Good		People (on a cliff)
	Poor		Vase		Poor		Reptile

Table B. Scoring Examples, by Card, of Good and Poor Form Responses, Differentiated into the Four Categories of the Modified Mayman Scoring for Form Quality, $+$ = Plus, o = Ordinary, w = Weak, and $-$ = Minus. Material Relevant to the Scoring Decision Which is Taken from the Inquiry is Shown in Parenthesis

	Location	Response
CARD I, $+$ RESPONSES	W	Two witches dancing around a woman in the center
	W	A butterfly (It ll it might be a rare type with the very irregular wing formations, and the white markings in the center. The antennae, which are very small are up here and u can c the body contour easily)
		Note. Popular responses are commonly scored as ordinary; however, in this instance the specification and articulation level make the response extraordinary and thus scored plus for form quality.
	W	∨ A house in a nightmare (It almost looks as if it is moving with the wind. It has four windows and an unusual chimney, its like one of the houses u would conceive of in a fairy tale or something like that with the crude, irregular shape to it)
	D4	This ll a woman with her arms raised in supplication. (She has on a transparent skirt held together with a metal clasp here (points). Her head must be thrown back as u can't c it, like she were in some sort of dance movement. The outline of her body is quite clear)
	D4	Two people doing a dance, u get the impression that they have their arms around each other, they r in profile, as if they were spinning. (They each have an arm raised as if it were part of the dance, sort of a Slavic type movement)
	D2	< This ll a donkey, like the one in, well its a Christmas story but I don't remember the name of it. Anyhow the donkey is struggling with a heavy load and that's what I'm impressed with here (U can c the arched back as if he were carrying a load of wood or something and the ear is raised upward as if he were listening for something, and the little tail is tucked in, as if the load was really causing him to strain his muscles)
	DdS30	This ll the kids in the Fisk Tire ad, u kno, where u c the kid in a niteshirt and he's holding a candle, his hair is all ruffled in the front, it really has that impression
CARD I, o RESPONSES	W	A bat (It has wings and feelers like a bat)
	W	It ll s.s. of flying animal to me, c these r the wings and this is the body

Table B (Continued)

Location	Response
W	Its like a coat of arms (It has these thgs out on each side and a symbolic thing here in the middle, its the sort of thing u might c as a badge on a hat or an army patch or s.t. like that)
W	∨ It might be s.k. of hat, like a Russian fur hat, c these things would be the ear flaps
D1	A couple of claws
D1	It sorta ll mittens, u can c the thumb part
D2	It might be some kind of map, like a continent or s.t., I don't kno what tho (Well it has this irregular outline and this peninsula here)
D4	U kno it ll a woman with her hands in the air
D6	∨ This ll a bushy tree of s.s., maybe like a big Maple
D8	U kno, u can see a seal here if u look hard enuff (Yeah, its like he's got his nose pointing up in the air)
Dd24	This ll a bell, like the Liberty Bell (C, here is the clapper)
DdS30	This ll a ghost to me (It's all white and u can c the general outline of a human form, it ll its arms are outstretched)
CARD I, w RESPONSES W	It could be a wasp I think (Well it has wings and stingers)
W	It ll the base of an anchor (It's all rounded like that part of an anchor is and here (points) is where u hook the chain)
W	I think it's some kind of jellyfish (They have thse kinds of projections on the sides, like wings or s.t. and this center is the body) *Note.* Ordinarily the response of Jellyfish to Card I is scored minus, however, in this instance the subject has identified wings and a body which is consistent with the form of the blot)
WS	This ll an x-ray of s.s. of organ to me (Maybe its a person's lungs and the white cld be the TB spots)
D1	A couple of humans, no actually they ll bears now (They each have their paws extended like they were up on their hind legs)
D2	It ll s.k. of bug, see the big wing on it
D5	Maybe a rock (Well, I don't kno, I just thought it c.b. one because its pretty irregular) *Note.* This type of response is not listed for the D5 area as good or poor form. Since the form requirement is vague it is best scored as weak

Table B (Continued)

Location	Response
D7	< It might be a map, like of South America, it comes way down like this
Dd27	If u use this center line as a cable, it cld b a cable car going up or down it
Dd31	V It almost ll a hatchet if u hold it this way (This is the blade, its like those knights used to have

CARD I, − RESPONSES

Location	Response
W	It cld b an amoeba (It almost doesn't have any shape to it)
W	It's some sort of a body that is split open
W	It could be a frog I suppose with the legs extended out
D1	V These are like the roots of teeth
D4	This ll somebody's brain to me
D8	< Maybe this part is a triangle insect
Dd23	These are like telegraph signals
Dd24	This part is a bowel movement
DdS29	These are eyes
Dd31	This is a bomb, like an atomic bomb
DdS32	There are a couple of faces in there looking out toward you

CARD II, + RESPONSES

Location	Response
W	This ll two dancing bears in a circus, they are balancing a ball or s.t. between them and they'r wearing tall red clown-like hats
W	It ll two people toasting each other. It could be that they'r at a party, maybe a costume party the way they are dressed up
D1	< This ll a rabbit sliding along some ice, like the rabbit in Bambi, I think his name is Thumper, he has his legs stretched out like he was sliding along
D1	V This could be a couple of boxers, like they'r both leaning back looking for an opening to get a punch in. (They are very muscular looking, like a head to head boxing match from the old days
D4 + DS5	This looks like a temple off in the distance, across this lake (A temple or shrine, it looks like it has very high doors)
Dd22 + Dd23	V This looks like a person riding a horse (He has a jockey cap on, u can get a glimpse of the tail of his shirt sticking out and the horses ear is bent forward, like into the wind)

CARD II, o RESPONSES

Location	Response
W	V A butterfly (You see the wings and the divided tail like some of the more unusual butterflies have. It's very colorful too)

Table B (Continued)

	Location	Response
	W	∨ It could be an explosion, maybe like a volcano, the upper red part there could be the lava shooting up (This dark part would be the volcano itself and this other red is also some lava I guess)
	D1	Two dogs rubbing noses together, its just the upper parts of the dogs that are visible here
	D2	A stocking cap
	D2	∨ This looks like it could be a holster for a gun (It has that general shape)
	D3	This could be a very colorful butterfly (You can see the delicate features quite well)
	D3	A crab (It has that general form if u ask me)
	D4	This is like a bullet that just tore through something
	DS5	This could be a top spinning around (It looks like it is really balanced there)
	Dd26	A caterpillar (He's crawling along with his head raised up just a little)
	Dd31	This could be a statue of a man's head, like it was carved from rock (You get the impression of a strong jaw and this is the nose)
CARD II, w RESPONSES	W	∨ A bat (You can see the wings and the antennae and the slip tail like some bats have)
	W	∨ A pelvis
	D1	Rain clouds (They are all dark and billowy)
	D2	∨ If you hold it this way these things could be a couple of torches
	D3	This reminds me of a sea anemone (It has all the little pointed things on it like they have)
	D4	A sultan's hat (It's like they wear in India with the things that go around the middle)
	DS5	This part is shaped like a kite like a kid would fly
	Dd24	Right in the middle here it ll a bowling pin (Its got that curved shape to it like a bowling pin)
CARD II, − RESPONSES	W	∨ It looks like somebody's insides (This white part is the heart and the red parts are the stomach and kidneys)
	W	It ll a face screaming (Its like a cat's face to me with the mouth open. It must be hurt cause there is blood around the chin and on the ears)
	D1	A map of America
	D2	∨ A red shoe
	D2	This ll a fingerprint
	D3	An anal cavity (You can see the slit)
	D4	A candle of some sort

Table B (Continued)

	Location	Response
	DS5	This white part could be a bell (It has that shape like the Liberty Bell)
	DS5	A cold heart
	D6	Somebody's lungs
	Dd23	A frog (You get that impression from the nose of it)
	DdS30	These are eyes, very big eyes
CARD III, + RESPONSES	W	This ll a party of some sort (I can see two people, apparently men, they are bowing to each other, its very formal and these red things would be decorations at the party. The men seem to be wearing formal clothing, like tuxedos I guess)
	W	Two people are playing the drums in synchronization (These here are the drums and you can tell they are in sync because they are exactly the same, even to the body posture)
	D1	Two waiters or servants are carrying a large cauldron (They have on formal attire even with big bow ties and high neck collars. It is sort of like the 1800's by the way they are dressed, even to the wearing of spats)
		Note. This class of response is usually scored *o*, however, the extent of specification and articulation here warrants the scoring of +
	D11	∨ This ll a bird, like an eagle perched on a ball or s.t. (It cld b that its a carving or statue designed to give the impression of a bird standing in the wind. You can see the eye and the shape of the head gives the impression of standing in the wind)
CARD III, *o* RESPONSES	W	∨ A man with his arms raised up in the air
	D1	Two people picking something up (It seems as if it might be a basket or s.t., it looks heavy)
	D1	Two monkeys grappling for something down here
	D2	A couple of monkeys swinging by their tails
	D3	This could be a red bowtie
	D3	You know this part reminds me of the cross-section of the spinal cord
	D4	Mittens, yeah, they ll mittens
	D7	This ll an x-ray of some bones
	D10	This part could be a high-heeled shoe, it seems to be formed like one to me
	Dd22	∨ It ll a bird to me (Well you can see the wings and the body if you look closely)
	Dd26	This could be a penis if you stretch your thinking a little

Table B (Continued)

	Location		Response
CARD III, *w* RESPONSES	*W*		It ll parts of a skeleton to me with all different kinds of bones and things (These are red bones here)
	W	∨	It could all be a black widow spider with the red marks on it like they have (Here are the legs and this is the head part)
	D2		It's like a hook (It's abstract but it still has the general shape of a hook as I see it)
	D2		I think its a musical note (It has that shape to it, like you would see on music sheets)
	D4		This mite be a breastbone of some animal
	D7		It could be a crab with all those legs and things
	Dd28		Its like a corset (It has the lacing up the middle)
	Dd29	<	If you turn it, it could be a valentine, its all red like one and its shaped like a V
CARD III, − RESPONSES	*W*		Insides (It's all blood and bones)
	W		Its s.s. of map
	D1		An insect (You can see the head here)
	D2		A blood artery
	D3		This could be a bird
	D4		Eyes
	Dd22		Some kind of animal I don't know what though
	Dd25		Maybe its a root
	Dd30		An icicle (It just ll one to me)
CARD IV, + RESPONSES	*W*		A pair of boots hanging up on a post or tree trunk (It's as if they got wet and were hung to dry because of all the wrinkles in them)
	W	∨	This ll an anchor thats been on the bottom too long (It's got the form of an anchor but its all bumpy too like it had a lot of algae covering it)
	W		This is a caterpillar sticking his head out from in under a leaf (He got the antennae and the kind of rough body and this part up here looks like a leaf although I don't kno the tree)
	D1	∨	This is like an ancient oriental carving, a religious carving of s.s. (It has very fine gradations so that each of these minute projections has a separate meaning)
	D3		A photographic negative of a flower that is just in the process of opening up (You can see all of the folds in considerable detail, it looks very delicate because there are so many of them)
CARD IV, *o* RESPONSES	*W*		A gorilla sitting on a stump
	W	∨	A bat (it has its wings outstretched like it was gliding along. This is the big head like they have)
	W	∨	It could be a pelvis or an x-ray of a pelvis

Table B (Continued)

	Location	Response
	D2	< A dog sitting down
	D3	It could be a flower of some sort, maybe an orchid
	D5	A spinal cord (it certainly has the shape of a bony structure to me)
	Dd21	It ll a temple
	Dd26	It could be some fingers (Two of them)
	Dd30	∨ Maybe its a rocket taking off
CARD IV, W RESPONSES	W	It could be a candle with a lot of wax melted down around it
	D1	It could be an x-ray of part of the spine (It's all funny looking like bones)
	D3	It ll a seashell (It has all those grooves in it like some kinds of seashells have)
	D5	Some sort of crawling insect
	D8	Its pretty jagged like a rock
	Dd26	It ll a couple of fangs to me, like very sharp teeth
	Dd30	Its like an infected tooth that you would see in a dentist's x-ray of one
CARD IV, — RESPONSES	W	A dragon crab
	W	The whole thing ll a piece of flesh (It could be all burnt or else its a Negro's skin)
	D1	A fish (It's his head, the head of a flatfish)
	D2	A bone
	D6	A secret map, like the CIA has all the time
	D7	Maybe it's a tree, I guess it could ll one
	Dd22	An eye
	Dd30	A heart that has been cut out of somebody
CARD V, + RESPONSES	W	This could be a ballerina dressed up in some sort of bird costume (Yes, its like a Stravinsky or something, she is dressed to look like a bird with the wing coverings here and you can see her slender legs and the cap she has on with the antennae)
	W	This looks like two people laying back to back (They are in a resting position, each with the head nodded forward a bit. Here are the legs extended)
	W	Two deer in a mating struggle (They are banging head to head with the rear legs extended outward here to give them strength against each other)
	D7	This could be two seals peeking over a rock (You get a pretty good impression of the upper parts of their bodies and here is the rock)

Table B (Continued)

	Location	Response
	D9	∨ You know, this could be a couple of turkeys, they look like they are primping or something (The bodies have that long neck as if they were stretching)
CARD V, *o* RESPONSES	W	A butterfly (You can see the wings and the body)
	D1	This could be the head of the alligator here (It has that kind of shape to it)
	D4	This could be the profile of a bearded man (You can see most of the features of the face pretty well such as the eye here and the chin and the beard)
	D6	This could be a pair of pliers
	Dd22	This part could be an arrow
	Dd24	This looks like a nipple up here (Like on a breast or a babies bottle)
CARD V, *w* RESPONSES	W	∨ An x-ray of some kind of bone structure (It might be part of the hips or that region)
	W	It could be a wilted flower (The long petals are drooping downward like it has had too much sun)
	W	It could be a tent (Like a tent they use in the Arabian countries where you can see the poles up through the top of it)
	D3	< A witches finger pointing at you (You can tell it must be a witch because of the long fingernail)
	D5	A breast (A woman's breast, you can see the form of it)
	DdS28	∨ I5 has the general outline like a helmet (Its one of those kind like the Vikings use to wear)
CARD V, − RESPONSES	W	An animal that has been squashed
	W	It could be some sort of bacteria
	D2	This could be somebody's foot
	D6	Someone with their hands in the air (Its like they were lifting them up seeking salvation)
	Dd23	The head of a deer
	DdS27	A Greek letter (Like in their writing)
	DdS29	This part in here could be a snake
CARD VI, + RESPONSES	W	This is like a cartoon cat that just got run over with a steam roller (It's pretty unreal, the head is still in good shape with the bushy whiskers sticking out, but his body is all flattened so that each of his legs is completely extended. You see a lot of this in a cartoon about a cat that's always chasing a little bird)

Table B (Continued)

Location	Response
W	∨ Well this could be a coat, or at least the beginnings of a coat (It's like it was hung on a model so to add the different pelts as its created, you can only see the post that hold the model up and here around the base are some more pelts that haven't been used yet)
D1	< This could be a submarine cruising along in the night (It has a good outline with the conning tower and all and you can even get a differentiation of the waterline. It's all being reflected in the moonlight down here)
D4	This could be a silhouette of a person taking a bath (This (D9) is the person with the head turned up a little and the rest is the bathtub)
D5	This could be a landscape scene that you might see if you were off in a boat (The lighter area is probably a village or town, in fact you can see some of the outlines of buildings in the area right next to it where its darker again. Its all sort of being reflected as you can actually see the shoreline there)
CARD VI, *o* RESPONSES W	I guess it could be a bearskin
W	If you use all of this lower part as a mountain, this part up here could be some big monument (It might be some abstract religious monument with the winged effect to it)
W	Some sort of an unusual guitar (This end here is where the strings get tightened and the rest is where the sound comes from)
D1	It could be a leaf of s.s.
D2	This part is shaped like a bedpost (one of those you see on maple furniture)
D3	This could be a butterfly
D6	This part looks like some flames that are shooting out
D9	< This is a walrus (It has pretty much the shape of one)
CARD VI, *w* RESPONSES W	∨ A flag (Its on this pole, its almost like kids would use for a sail on a raft, like Huck Finn)
W	A frying pan (Not really a pan more like a griddle like you make pancakes on, this part is the handle)
D1	It looks like some skin (Its like off a snake with all the designs on it)
D2	This part could be a drill (The end of a drill like oil drillers use)
D3	A fly (You can see the wings here)
D5	This center thing could be a pole, like a barber's pole with the knob on top)

Table B (Continued)

	Location	Response
	D11	These things could be lungs I guess (They have that shape to them, just like a pair of lungs)
CARD VI, − RESPONSES	W	Its an airplane (It has great big wings like a jet)
	D1	An x-ray of something (Its just something in the body but I can't say what)
	D2	A fish
	D4	This part could be a map
	D7	These are eyes
	Dd21	A pair of hands here
	Dd31	This is the nose of a snake
CARD VII, + RESPONSES	W	∨ Two can-can dancers (Their heads are thrown back and apparently one leg is thrown outward like they were doing their kick)
	W	Looking down it could be one of those very contemporary seating arrangements you sometimes find in waiting rooms (Its a sectional, rather plush, with each of the sections arranged so that it touches the next but it is also somewhat separate, so that people can sit either way, facing inward or outward)
	D8	This could be a city or town in the distance (You get the impression of buildings and a spire here like a church steeple)
	D11 + D6	∨ This could be a parachute 'This part (D11) is the parachute itself and here (D6) is the man'
CARD VII, o RESPONSES	W	It could be two animals
	W	∨ It might be an entrance to a cave
	W	All of it could be clouds (They are billowy and touching each other)
	D1	Two kids playing indian
	D3	This part could be the head of a dog
	D2	< This could be a scotty dog
	DS7	∨ This could be a lamp (It has a big shade on it)
	Dd26	This part in here might be a river
CARD VII, w RESPONSES	W	∨ A fur cap with earlaps on it (Its like a big Russian snow hat and these would cover your ears)
	W	∨ It could be a wig (It looks like one they might have used in France during Napoleon's time)
	W	It could be an x-ray of some sort of bone structure
	D1	It could be a high backed chair except you can't see the legs
	D5	This looks like a goat's horn or something like that
	DS7	∨ This way the center part could be a mushroom
	Dd25	A seagull (His wings are spread out like he was just gliding along)

Table B (Continued)

	Location	Response
CARD VII, − RESPONSES	W	Some sort of ugly bug
	W	∨ This way it looks just like a frog with his legs out like he was jumping
	D1	∨ I guess I see a horse here
	D3	A sting ray
	D5	I see a snake in here
	D11	This looks like somebody's bottom (Their behind)
	Dd27	You get the impression of Christ here, like he is dying for all men
CARD VIII, + RESPONSES	W	A carousel (A toy one with two animals on the outer edges. Its like an abstract of one with a very colorful center. It's the sort of thing that a child might have as a toy)
	W	An animal carefully picking his way across some rocks and vegetation (It's a small animal, like a muskrat or something. You get the impression of him and the whole thing reflected below as if he were stepping on stones and pieces of wood trying to get across a stream)
	W	This looks like the rear view of a sailing ship (It has very colorful masts, like an old pirate ship with this part up here being the yardarms and the lower part is the hull)
	DS3	∨ This part is like an Indian teepee. You can see the different designs on it and the lacings are coming around it (The pole is coming through the top part)
	D4	This is like a frog seen from behind (Yes, he's leaping away from you. There are little horned projections from his head and you get the impression that his front legs are stretching outward while the back legs are pushing off)
CARD VIII, o RESPONSES	W	Some sort of sketch from a medical text (It shows a lot of different anatomy)
	W	A coat-of-arms (It has animals on each side like they do and the other parts each represent something of the family history)
	D2	A dish of ice cream sherbet (It looks like raspberry to me)
	D5	A couple of flags going out in different directions
	Dd21	This could be a spinal cord here
	Dd23	∨ This part might be a waterfall (it has that form to it)
	Dd29	∨ This is like a triangle that they use in a band
	DdS32	It looks like a seagull with its wings stretched out like it was gliding along

Table B (Continued)

	Location	Response
CARD VIII, *w* RESPONSES	*W*	It could be a very elaborate party mask representing the face of a mechanical man (It really doesn't ll a face but if you think of this top thing as a hat of metal and the bottom thing as a chin or mouth part, it could represent some mechanical man's face)
	*D*1	It could be dried blood spots (They are light pink and you can see where the blood ran down here in a few places, but now it's all dried
	*D*2	It might be a very colorful leaf (I don't know what leaf, like what tree it's from, maybe part of it is missing too)
	*D*4	It's some kind of sea animal, like a crab or crawfish (You see the long legs here)
	*Dd*23	That looks like a flask, sort of like and Arabian flask, like a jinni comes out of (It has that form)
	*Dd*26	It looks like the head of a cartoon character (Its a little man with a big mustache)
CARD VIII, − RESPONSES	*W*	A bat of some sort (it really looks that way)
	W	The skeleton of a fish
	*D*1	A frog
	*D*2	This could be a piece of flesh
	*D*5	Some sort of flower in here
	*D*8	This reminds me of the insides of an animal
	*Dd*25	It could be a shark
	*DdS*28	There are some clouds in this white part
	*Dd*31	There might be an insect in there (Its got a long arm)
CARD IX, + RESPONSES	*W*	A very elaborate bowl of some sort (It's ornamental with three different sections. This pink part is a base and the other two sections are intricately carved designs)
	W	A jungle waterfall (This part here would be the pool into which the water flows and the sides are rocks and vegetation. The waterfall itself is set back into the rocks)
	*D*1	< This is a woman chasing a child (Each have their arms stretched out)
	*D*12	< A very heavy guy on a bicycle or motorcycle going up this hill
	*D*3 + *D*8	This is two witches cooking something in a cauldron (You can see they have pointed hats on and each one is holding some sort of magic stick over the cauldron)
CARD IX, *o* RESPONSES	*W*	It could be some sort of abstract art (Its all symmetrical and it must have some meaning)
	W	∨ It could be an atomic explosion with the fire at the bottom and the clouds in the upper part
	*D*1	The head of some sort of animal

Table B (Continued)

Location	Response
D3	∨ On this side it looks like there is a parrot (it could really be two of them, leaning toward each other)
D4	It's the head of a person, right here (points)
D8	It looks like a vase to me
D9	This could be a spindle like you use in an office to stick notes on
Dd25	This looks like an archway of some kind

CARD IX, W RESPONSES	W	It could be a relief map with the different colors showing the different elevations (The green and white are at sea level, the pink is a plateau, and the orange are mountains)
	D1	∨ It could be a mushroom (It's all tilted like it didn't grow correctly)
	D3	∨ These are carrots (They are round at the one end and pointed at the other)
	D5	This center thing could be your windpipe
	D6	∨ This is like the head of an animal with great big ears
	D7	This is like a streak of lightning (It's jagged like you see lightning)
	Dd26	This is like the end of a key to a door

CARD IX, − RESPONSES	W	Somebody's insides
	W	∨ It all looks like a jellyfish
	D1	∨ It's a dog here
	D3	It's some kind of fish
	D5	A penis, I say it looks like one to me
	D10	It could be someone's lungs here
	D12	This whole part looks like some sort of x-ray
	Dd21	Icicles here
	Dd26	It's a finger that is pointing at someone
	Dd30	This is all gory like someone's insides

CARD X, + RESPONSES	W	It looks like what you see if you look inside an aquarium (There are different kinds of undersea life like crabs and crawfish and seahorses and a lot of vegetation and this pink stuff could be a coral piece)
	W	∨ A beautiful floral design here (The center part with these long pink leaves is some sort of hybrid flower and the rest is laid out to accent the hybrid in the center)
	D1 + D12	This is a spider that has caught a small insect and is holding on to it trying to bring it into its mouth
	D11 + DdS29	This is a paddle (its like a fraternity paddle, this is the handle and here is a little design on it)

Table B (Continued)

	Location	Response
CARD X, *o* RESPONSES	W	A lot of undersea animals (I don't know what most of them are but there are crabs in there. I guess the rest is just sea life)
	W	A chandelier (It has all different colored lights in it)
	D1	This looks like a spider very much because of all these long legs
	D2	A fried egg (There's two of them with yolks in the center)
	D4	It could be a caterpillar
	D6	It's like a couple of ducks here (It really looks like a duck on each side there)
	D10	∨ This could be a door knocker
	D14	This is like a stovepipe
	Dd23	This could be a walnut
CARD X, *w* RESPONSES	D1	These could be a couple of earrings (They are big ones like they wear nowadays)
	D2	This might be a frog sitting and croaking (You can see his front legs are pushed out like when they croak)
	D3	This looks like a set of earphones (They are like the kids wear today with their stereo radios)
	D4	∨ It could be a snail without his shell (they have this general shape to them)
	D5	∨ This looks like a tooth (You can see the long roots and this little white part would be the cavity)
	D7	Some sort of sea animal with long legs
	D13	It looks like a sponge (It has that irregular form to it and it's the right color)
	D15	It's some sort of long necked animal like a dinosaur
CARD X, − RESPONSES	W	It all looks like somebody's insides
	W	It could be a chinese headdress
	D1	A jellyfish
	D1	A spider here with an eye in it
	D2	An eye, see it here
	D3	Some kind of bug
	D3	Somebody's ovaries, not mine though
	D5	The face of a man
	D6	A pair of kidneys here, it looks just like them
	D9	Some bone, a dog has been eating at it
	D11	An airplane
	Dd27	A vulture
	Dd33	An eye in here
	Dd34	A tooth, that gives off evil in the mouth

Table C. Organizational (Z) Values for Each of the Ten Cards

| Card | W | Type of Organizational Activity | | |
		Adjacent Detail	Distant Detail	White Space With Detail
I	1.0	4.0	6.0	3.5
II	4.5	3.0	5.5	4.5
III	5.5	3.0	4.0	4.5
IV	2.0	4.0	3.5	5.0
V	1.0	2.5	5.0	4.0
VI	2.5	2.5	6.0	6.5
VII	2.5	1.0	3.0	4.0
VIII	4.5	3.0	3.0	4.0
IX	5.5	2.5	4.5	5.0
X	5.5	4.0	4.5	6.0

Table D. Best Weighted ZSum Prediction When Zf Is Known

Zf	Zest	Zf	Zest
1	*	26	88.0
2	2.5	27	91.5
3	6.0	28	95.0
4	10.0	29	98.5
5	13.5	30	102.5
6	17.0	31	105.5
7	20.5	32	109.0
8	24.0	33	112.5
9	27.5	34	116.5
10	31.0	35	120.0
11	34.5	36	123.5
12	38.0	37	127.0
13	41.5	38	130.5
14	45.5	39	134.0
15	49.0	40	137.5
16	52.5	41	141.0
17	56.0	42	144.5
18	59.5	43	148.0
19	63.0	44	152.0
20	66.5	45	155.5
21	70.0	46	159.0
22	73.5	47	162.5
23	77.0	48	166.0
24	81.0	49	169.5
25	84.5	50	173.0

Table E. Popular Responses Used in the Comprehensive System

Card	Location	Criterion
I	W	Bat or butterfly. The response always involves the whole blot and alterations in location or content have not been found to be Popular.
I	D4	Human figure, ordinarily reported as female. The figure is described as a whole human or headless human. No other variations are P, nor is the lower half of this area (D3) described as a part of a human found to be P. Where the percept to D4 is of a male figure, the scoring of (P) may be most appropriate.
II	D1	Animal forms, usually the heads of dogs or bears, however, the frequency of the whole animal to this area is sufficient to warrant the scoring of P also. If the content does not specify a dog or bear, the (P) score may be more appropriate. *Note.* The percept of whole humans or animals to the entire blot does not meet the P criterion but does approach that level and may be scored as (P).
III	D1 or D9	Two human figures, or representations thereof, such as dolls, caricatures, etc. The scoring of P is also applicable to the percept of a single human figure to area D9. Human movement is frequently associated with, but not necessary for the scoring of P.
III	D3	Butterfly, designated by reason of form, but sometimes involving the use of color as a determinant.
IV	W or W minus D1	Animal skin, or human figure dressed in animal skin or an appropriate variation thereof, such as "in a fur coat." This category of Popular also includes the large "furry" animal. The proof of P rests with the designation of the "furry" pelt or pelt-like covering.
IV	D6	Shoe or boot, seen separately or in association with an animal or human figure. The designation of the shoe or boot in the D2 area has not been discovered to be P.
V	W	Bat or butterfly, the apex of the card upright or inverted. Variations of the content, such as moth, vulture, eagle, etc. are probably best scored as (P).
VI	W or D1	Animal skin, hide, rug, or pelt.
VII	D1	Human heads or faces, ordinarily perceived as women or children. A W response involving the human percept typically notes the lower D4 portion of the blot as a content separate from the Hd, such as a rock, pedestal, bush, etc. Where D4 is reported as part of the human figure, the scoring might better be (P).
VIII	D1	Whole animal figure. This is the most frequently perceived common answer, the content varying considerably, such as bear, dog, rodent, fox, wolf, coyote, etc. All are scored P. The P is also scored when the animal figure is reported as part of a W percept as in, a family crest, seal, emblem, etc.
IX	D4	A human face or head, usually reported as male and frequently identified as T. Roosevelt, or perceived as an infant.
X	D1	Crab, lobster, or spider. In some instances the object has greater specificity as in sand crab, daddy long legs, crawfish, etc. Other variations of multi-legged animals are not P.

Table F. Group Means for Location Scores, Determinant Scores, Some Content Scores, Plus Various Summary Scores for Nonpsychiatric Subjects Plus Three Psychiatric Groups

Category	Non-Psychiatric (N = 200)	Out-Patient Non-Psychotic (N = 100)	In-Patient Non-Schizophrenic (N = 70)	In-Patient Schizophrenic (N = 125)
R	21.60	23.10	20.70	23.80
W	7.10	6.70	8.90	7.30
D	13.40	15.50	9.60	11.30
Dd	1.10	0.90	2.20	5.20
S	1.00	2.20	0.80	1.80
P	6.70	7.20	6.20	2.40
M	3.20	3.70	2.10	3.60
FM	2.80	3.50	1.70	2.90
m	0.80	1.10	0.60	1.40
FC	3.20	1.80	1.70	1.90
CF + C + Cn	1.20	2.90	1.90	3.80
C' + C'F + FC'	0.60	1.30	1.60	1.20
T + TF + FT	1.40	2.60	2.80	2.30
Y + YF + FY	1.30	2.50	2.60	1.90
V + VF + FV	0.40	0.90	1.30	0.70
FD	0.80	2.30	2.50	0.50
Fr + rF	0.20	0.70	0.90	1.20
(2)	7.30	9.60	7.10	10.80
F	9.20	7.30	9.90	7.10
Blends	3.90	5.80	4.10	4.60
Zf	7.30	9.20	6.30	7.20
Sum C	3.60	4.70	3.80	5.90
Lambda (L)	0.74	0.44	0.56	0.39
F + %	0.91	0.83	0.80	0.62
X + %	0.84	0.78	0.81	0.58
A%	0.39	0.41	0.53	0.31
H + Hd	4.20	3.90	4.80	3.10

PART THREE

Interpretation

CHAPTER 10

Introduction

The interpretation of Rorschach data is complex, but not nearly as complex as often implied. It does require considerable training, skill, and experience. It is time consuming, but probably no more so than is required for the interpretation of any other sophisticated clinical instrument. The clinical psychologist seems best equipped for this task as, through his training, he gains a reasonably good knowledge of personality and behavioral theories from which his interpretive postulates can be given "context." More importantly, he is trained as an expert in psychopathology, from which his interpretive postulates can be judged against the broad framework of human behaviors. The third element, which needs to be added to these skills for effective Rorschach interpretation, is a knowledge of the test itself, which includes the basic reference data plus an understanding of the general meaningfulness of different kinds of responses and response patterns.

Magical thinking or crystal ball operations have no place in Rorschach interpretations. Quite the contrary, it is a process of analysis and synthesis, drawn intelligently from the quantitative and qualitative material in the record. A Rorschach tester is not necessarily a Rorschach interpreter, for the skills required for the latter are considerably more comprehensive than are the skills of the other. A well trained clerk can be a good examiner, but a well trained clerk cannot be a good interpreter. Interpretation of the Rorschach is a product of the test plus the clinician, the latter investing his accumulated knowledge, skills, and experience to translate the varieties of Rorschach scores, configurations, and words into a meaningful understanding of the individual.

THE RORSCHACH DATA

The Rorschach is commonly identified as a "projective method," by reason of its unstructuredness and ambiguity, which, according to Frank's "projective hypothesis," (1939) provide the circumstances under which the subject conveys or projects in his response, his own needs, interests, conflicts, and so on. The validity of this phenomenon has been demonstrated numerous times in well designed research studies on the various projective techniques, including the Rorschach. But this does not mean that the data of the Rorschach are exclusively projective in nature, for that is not the case. Rapaport (1946) has probably given one of the best descriptions of the "birthing" of a response to the inkblots. He suggests that it represents a complex "cogwheeling" process in which the external stimulus (the blot) becomes perceptually internalized, various attempts mainly based on memory and structural similarities are made to identify the stimulus, and ultimately some identification is generated which represents a composite of what the person actually sees, and what the person is oriented, by his own needs, to see at that given moment. In other words, the response is a composite of a perceptual procedure and a projective process. The idiography of the Rorschach data frequently represents projection at its most exquisite level, but such projection almost always, except for the most extremely disoriented subjects, is combined with a perceptual component. When the interpreter approaches the Rorschach data, he must recognize that some of his interpretations will be based on the perceptual elements of the responses, and he will gauge this against nomothetic data available to him, such as reference norms. Concurrently, he will be alert to the projective features of the responses which will often add the "flesh" to the nomothetic skeleton. Both kinds of data are Rorschach data, and together they constitute that which is to be interpreted.

THE INTERPRETIVE PROCESS

Rorschach (1921) was very cautious about what kinds of conclusions might be drawn from the test data. He indicated that he did not know how to differentiate manifest from latent symptoms, and questioned the value of the test for studying "unconscious" characteristics of thinking. While it seems plausible that Rorschach would have accepted Frank's projective hypothesis as applicable to the test, Rorschach himself gave no indication that he considered such a process in the test. He was especially forceful in emphasizing that the test does not provoke a continuing "stream" of thought, but rather, is one requiring adaptation to external stimuli.

As the Rorschach has "matured," so too has the process of Rorschach interpretation. Each of the Rorschach systematizers, as well as other authorities of the test, has gone well beyond Rorschach's original position concerning interpretation. Most all have used the bulk of Rorschach's interpretive postulates as the nucleus of their own interpretive frameworks. Most of those postulates have ultimately gained solid empirical support. But Rorschach was far less concerned with the validity of specific test factors as applied to interpretation, as he was with stressing the necessity of approaching the test data in its totality. He very accurately perceived that similar test signs or features, such as a given number of M responses would, in different test configurations, be interpreted differently. For example, a preponderence of M answers in a protocol might indicate the existence of a strong tendency to use the inner life for gratification. Assuming that statement to be valid, it provides, at best, only a very limited understanding of the person. Important questions concerning the degree of adaptivity afforded by that inner life, or the extent to which the tendency to the inner life impairs interaction with the environment, cannot be answered simply by studying the number of M's in the protocol. In fact, if there is also a preponderence of color responses in the record, the statement itself *would not be valid*. Similarly, many other Rorschach features could alter, or negate, any statement taken from a single "sign."

Each of the Rorschach systematizers, while differing in their own approaches, have solidly agreed with Rorschach's recommendation that the totality of the test must be considered in interpretation. This has generally been referred to in the literature as the "global" approach, and, in effect, it requires that *all* Rorschach data be considered in the interpretive process in a manner which is concerned with the configuration of data, as opposed to the interpretation of pieces of data in isolation.

This process is essentially the same as occurs in any clinical interpretation, whether that interpretation be of data drawn from interviews, tests, or therapy sessions. Levy (1963) offers an excellent work on the subject of psychological interpretation which identifies the components of the process in more detail than is necessary here; however, extrapolating from Levy, Rorschach interpretation might best be described as a two-stage procedure. The first stage is a propositional one, while the second stage is one of integration.

THE PROPOSITIONAL STAGE

The onset of Rorschach intepretation begins with a careful review of each of the test components. These include the Structural Summary, with all of its frequencies, ratios, and percentages, the specific scorings of responses and their sequence of occurrence, the verbalizations given during the Free Association, and finally, the verbalizations given during the Inquiry. As the various component parts of each of these Rorschach units are surveyed, propositions or hypotheses are formulated. At this point it is important that no reasonable hypothesis be rejected simply because it does not seem compatible with other propositions generated from the review. It is also quite important that all of the components are studied, not simply those which are unusual or dramatic. It is true that the unusual or dramatic are probably more distinctly representative of the idiography of the subject, but the usual or commonplace are equally important in "getting at" the entire person.

The propositions are usually generated through a cross-checking of several features within a unit or across units. For example, it might be noted in the Structural Summary that a subject has given a below average number of responses, has an absence of color responses, and has a proportionally high frequency of Popular responses, and that most of the responses given are of good form quality. The composite of these features leads to at least one and possibly two hypotheses. First, because of the low R and absence of color, the possibility of constriction and/or defensiveness must be entertained. Second, the high frequency of P and the fact that most of the responses are of good form quality, suggest a capacity and/or willingness to approach the blots in a conventional or conforming manner. Numerous questions and additional hypotheses can be generated from these two propositions. For instance, does the tendency toward conventionality in percepts represent a defensive style? In a more serious context, does the absence of color plus the tendency toward giving conventional answers represent a defensive containment of emotion as is often found in the depressed person? Neither of these questions could be answered from the four bits of data given here, but the existence of these data does establish a propositional framework against which other data will be reviewed.

While the absolute use of single signs to form postulates is generally unwarranted, there are occasional exceptions. These are generally instances where the datum is very striking and unique. A response, such as "the remnants of a decayed penis", cannot help but warrant some hypothesizing by the interpreter. Similarly, the complete absence of good form quality leads to obvious speculation about the failures of reality contact. It is important to stress, however, that even when these strikingly unique single features do occur in a protocol, the interpreter should not neglect the remainder of the data on the assumption that "the case is solved." It is not uncommon to find protocols which contain an extremely unique, or even bizzare component, the interpretive significance of which will be tempered substantially by other data in the record.

The actual number of propositions which might be generated from a given protocol will vary with the "richness" of the protocol plus the deductive skills of the interpreter. The Roschach, as most projective instruments, is a *wideband procedure*, that is, one which may yield information relevant to many different decisions. Cronbach and Gleser (1957), in their discussion of decision theory, point to the fact that the wideband technique, although often condemned on the basis of validation research, renders information from which numerous hypotheses can be formulated, some of which, when they are confirmed, have great practical importance. They indicate that, although any single hypothesis may be questionable or undependable, the sequential accumulation of hypotheses will often draw attention to information which might otherwise be missed by the interpreter.

Each of the four major units of the protocol, the Structual Summary, the sequence of scores, the Free Association, and the Inquiry, contain data from which propositions are formulated. Ordinarily, the interpreter will begin with the Structural Summary in his review and proceed through the sequence analysis to the verbalizations. This procedure keeps the interpreter from "getting caught up" in the unique or sometimes dramatic verbalizations prematurely. Those kinds of verbalizations may be quite important in the interpretive process; however, they can also be very misleading, especially to the novice interpreter. As propositions accumulate throughout the procedure, the interpreter finds many which are related either directly or indirectly to each other. No terminal decisions are made prior to reviewing all data in the record. The ultimate weight given any Rorschach feature is determined during the second stage of interpretation, that of integration.

THE INTEGRATION STAGE

After the numerous propositions have been formulated by reviewing each of the four major units of the Rorschach data, the interpreter comes to the point of creating a meaningful description of the subject. This description is the product of a logical integration of the various postulates which have been formed. It is not simply a process of adding statements together, but instead, involves the clinical conceptualization of the psychology of a person. Some of the propositions previously formulated may be rejected, although more commonly they are modified or clarified by other propositions. It is here that the clinician goes beyond specific data, using his propositional statements as a base and adding to that base his own deductive logic and knowledge of human behavior and psychopathology. This is the output of the Rorschach clinician. The yield is essentially descriptive, designed to aid in understanding the subject. It is predicated on a matrix of data which has led to propositions and conceptions. It is not necessarily *predictive* at this point, nor does it ultimately need to be predictive. Predictions and recommendations, while clearly a function for the psychodiagnostician, accumulate from the total information available to the clinician regarding the subject. Rorschach interpretation may be only one element of that information. For example, a Rorschach description may include information to the effect that a subject is "quick" to display emotion under stressful conditions. Assuming that statement to be valid, it provides only a limited understanding of the person and the manner in which he handles emotion. A major unanswered question is whether he is able to use this proclivity adaptively, or whether it is a liability. Other Rorschach data may add some clarification to the issue. It may be determined that his contact with reality is reasonably effective, that he has a sufficient interest in people so as not to avoid them, that he is able to perceive things conventionally, and that he apparently does not experience overwhelming feelings of tension or anxiety. All of these factors might lead the interpreter to "predict" that the subject probably handles his emotions effectively, and that there is no need for concern that he will be dominated by these affective experiences. Such a recommendation or prediction, however, is not based on the Rorschach data, but on an intelligent hunch of the interpreter. If the same interpreter already knew that the subject had a history of temper outbursts plus some incidents of assaultiveness, it is highly unlikely that he would make the same recommendations or predictions. But that added information would not change the Rorschach derived conclusions. The description that the subject is quick to show emotion under stress, that his reality contact is reasonably effective, that he maintains a normal or average interest in people, and that he is able to perceive things conventionally remains true. The added behavioral information simply clarifies how the emotion is displayed. Naturally, this added clarification is critically important to the clinician who may be asked to speculate concerning future emotional displays and exemplifies how inputs from many sources, including the Rorschach contribute to the process of making recommendations or predictions. The focus of the integration stage, however, is not oriented toward prediction, except that it includes information which may ultimately contribute to predictions and/or recommendations. Sarbin (1941) has suggested that any diagnostic statement is meaningful only when it has reference to the future; that is, when it is predictive. Unfortunately, Sarbin's position tends to neglect the scientifically diagnostic importance of simply understanding a person. This position has been well defended by Holt (1970), and it is in the context of the Holt premise that the integrative stage of Rorschach interpretation renders its greatest yield.

BLIND INTERPRETATION

The matters of prediction and recommendation raise the specter of blind analysis or interpretation of the Rorschach data. This has been a controversial issue for the Rorschach, and one which has often been confusingly distorted. Blind interpretation implies that the interpreter works only with the test data, possibly also knowing the age, sex, and marital status of the subject. At times, the interpreter may also have a useful referral question which poses a specific question, but more commonly these questions are vague and/or overinclusive.

There has been considerable divergence among Rorschachers, especially among those who have researched the test, regarding the value and appropriateness of the blind method. Rorschach had suggested that the method would be useful to validate the test, and used it himself, apparently developing several of his more important postulates by keeping himself completely naive concerning the subject. He did not, however, suggest that final conclusions be drawn exclusively from Rorschach data interpreted in the blind. The Rorschach systematizers have all, to some extent, endorsed the usefulness of blind interpretation, but there has been considerable disagreement regarding how material developed through blind interpretation should be used. Beck (1960) and Piotrowski (1957, 1964) have been the most staunch supporters of blind interpretation. Each contends that the test should be interpreted completely before other information concerning the subject is available, and then integrate that interpretation with data from other tests and social history information, *without changing the Rorschach interpretation*. Beck's 1960 work demonstrates very neatly how this may be accomplished, and Piotrowski's entire approach to a computerized Rorschach interpretation has been based on the validity of this premise.

The Rapaport-Schafer approach offers only partial agreement with the position of Beck and Piotrowski. They are, of course, oriented toward the concept of the test battery; all data from which they suggest should be interpreted blindly, but in totality, so that postulates derived from Rorschach data might be altered by the total data pattern. The Klopfer position concerning blind analysis, which once strongly advocated this approach, changed gradually as his experience with the test increased. Klopfer (1954) recommends that interpretation should always begin with the Rorschach, and essentially in the blind, but cautions that some Rorschach derived conclusions may be modified or omitted if other data sources provide clearly different conclusions. The Hertz approach to the matter of blind interpretation probably differs most extensively from Beck and Piotrowski. While endorsing the blind approach for teaching purposes, Hertz advocates an "interactionist" approach to the clinical interpretation of the test. This method of interpretation calls for Rorschach interpretation to occur in conjunction with, and regard for, all other test data plus the complete socio-educational-developmental history. Hertz defends this approach on the premise that the varieties of data contribute to a more realistic and meaningful interpretation of any given data.

Table G. Summary of Blind Analysis Studies Concerning the Rorschach

Author	N	Design	Conclusions
Abel (1942)	1	Blind analysis versus case study	Agreement with case study by Margaret Mead
Bailick and Hamlin (1954)	25	Blind estimate of I.Q. versus Wechsler scores	Four judges made valid estimates of I.Q. showing correlations of .61, .64, .69, and .73
Benjamin and Brosin (1938)	36	Accuracy of Blind analyses versus extensive case analyses	The blind analyses were as "accurate" as the extensive case analyses
Benjamin and Ebaugh (1938)	55	Blind analysis versus final clinical diagnosis	84.7% correct
Chambers and Hamlin (1957)		Twenty clinicians were asked to identify each of five protocols according to five diagnostic groupings	Selections were correct in 58 of 100 attempts
Clapp (1938)	1	Blind analysis versus clinical case data	"High agreement"

Table G. Summary of Blind Analysis Studies Concerning the Rorschach—(continued)

Author	N	Design	Conclusions
Cummings (1954)	10	Blind analysis versus established diagnoses of 10 patients in five diagnostic groups using a single Rorschach card	"Analysis significant"
Grant, Ives, and Razoni (1952)	146	Blind ratings on a 4 point scale of normal subjects by three Rorschach "experts" and two inexperienced judges	Rorschach judges placed from between 61 and 71% of subjects on the maladjusted end of the continuum with a high correlation between judges
Hamlin and Newton (1938)	2	Blind ratings of adjustment versus established evaluation	Ratings were "reasonably accurate"
Hertz and Rubenstein (1938)	1	Blind analysis versus data collected in 14 interviews	"High agreement"
Kluckhohn and Rosenzweig (1949)	2	Blind analysis versus anthropological data	"High agreement"
Krugman (1942)	20	Comparisons by three blind judges in matching interpretations by two experienced examiners for 20 subjects	The three judges made a "perfect" score in matching the pairs of interpretations to the subjects
Lisansky (1956)	40	Blind judges versus judges using life history data	Rorschach judges did not show significantly better agreement than did the life history judges
Little and Shneidman (1959)	12	Blind analyses compared to previously existing assessment and with each other	Diagnostic agreement better than chance although wide variations occurred in the assignment of diagnostic categories
Monroe (1945)	1	Blind analysis versus teacher observations	"Satisfactory agreement"
Newton (1954)	5	Blind analysis versus comprehensive case material and psychiatric evaluation	Rorschach judgements did not correlate significantly with criteria
Oberholzer (1944)	37	Blind analysis versus data collected by ethnologist	"Considerable" congruency
Palmer (1949)	28	Blind analyses to be selected by patient's therapist	In 39% of the cases the selection of the therapist was correct
Schachtel (1942)	3	Blind analysis versus anthropological findings	"Close convergence"
Siegel (1948)	26	Blind analysis versus psychiatric evaluations	88.5% agreement
Silverman (1959)	10	Blind analysis versus evaluations of psychotherapists using 30 blind judges each analyzing protocols for seven variables	Blind analysis agreed with therapists judgements greater than chance although validity coefficients ranged from low to moderate
Swift (1944)	26	Blind analysis versus psychiatrist evaluations	88% agreement
Symonds (1955)	1	Blind analysis by seven judges versus comprehensive case study	65% agreement
Vernon (1936)	45	Blind analysis versus personality sketches by two psychologists	Correlation of .83

The issue of blind interpretation has probably been given more notoriety than may have been warranted. This was especially true for the period from 1935 to 1955 when the question of Rorschach validity was so fequently challenged and defended. Numerous studies using a blind methodology to evaluate the validity of the test were reported during this period. They generally fall into three design categories: (1) those using a blind interpretation to generate a *personality description* which was then compared for congruence with personality descriptions created by "expert" judges using methods other than the Rorschach, (2) those using blind analysis to derive a *diagnostic impression* versus diagnostic impressions rendered by "expert" judges, and (3) those using blind analysis versus some previously *established criteria*. A summary of 24 of these studies is shown in Table G. It will be noted from examination of Table G that the results are generally mixed, although a substantial majority do provide support for the Rorschach.

The issue of blind interpretation, as has been recommended by several of the Rorschach systematizers, and the approach to the issue of the test validity using blind interpretation, *are not the same issues*. The systematizers conceptualize blind interpretation as a clinical method designed to keep the interpreter free of any sets or biases. Beck, Klopfer, and Piotrowski all maintain that the best way to approach the test is free of any set. None suggests that the process of clinical interpretation or diagnosis necessarily ends with the Rorschach summary developed in the "blind," although each has demonstrated a phenomenal skill in being able to produce a thorough and highly accurate personality description from nothing other than a blind Rorschach interpretation. Even with this skill, however, all have remained clinical realists, recognizing the limitations of the Rorschach and the importance of other kinds of data. Each conceives of the Rorschach interpretation as a nuclear understanding of the subject, which is added to by inputs from other sources, thus providing a complete clinical evaluation. They differ only in terms of *how* additional data should be used, not *whether* they should be used.

The researchers have attempted to use the method of blind interpretation as a test of the test, as Rorschach himself had suggested. While these have been generally legitimate designs, the goal of the researcher in using the method is different than that of the clinician using the method. The researcher uses the blind interpretation as an end in itself, which becomes compared with other criteria. The interpretation is not extended or clarified by other inputs, as is the case in the clinical setting. Unfortunately, many critics of the Rorschach have frequently cited the sometimes limited findings derived from the blind interpretation research works as both a criticism of the test and of the procedure as useful with the test. Such a position, of course, neglects the manner in which blind interpretation is commonly used, that is, as a beginning rather than an end.

It is in keeping with the recommendations of Beck, Klopfer, and Piotrowski that interpreters of the comprehensive Rorschach system are encouraged to begin their interpretation *in the blind*. This means developing propositions only from the Rorschach data, and ultimately integrating these postulates into a meaningful description of the subject. This is a difficult challenge for many Rorschachers, as the interpreter is often the one responsible for administering the test, and will naturally be influenced to some extent by that event, and by the cursory review of the verbalizations which occurs during the process of scoring the test. The astute clinician is aware of this, and makes attempts to restrict his interpretive logic only to the basic Rorschach data. If he has been "turned on," or "turned off," by a subject, he attempts to make sure that his subjective "feel" for the person does not cause him to neglect any of the data. If he has also collected data from other tests prior to his Rorschach interpretation, he attempts to avoid being "overwhelmed" by this information. If he has prior access to socio-educational-developmental history information, he is alert to the fact that any of this information can create an unwanted set. As Levy (1970) has pointed out so well, very simple demographic information, such as socioeconomic status, can have a significant impact on the conclusions of the interpreter.

INTERPRETATION: SCIENCE VERSUS ART

Many clinicians and nonclinicians have concluded that the work of the Rorschach interpreter is more an art than a science. To some extent, that is, the extent to which the interpreter injects his own feelings, prejudices, biases, sets, and such into his interpretation, it is an art-form, based on considerable subjectivity. It does not have to be an art-form, however, especially where the interpreter is willing to consider all of the Rorschach data, and concurrently maintain a position of objectivity in the formulation of propositions and their ultimate integration. One need not be a Beck, a Klopfer, a Hertz, a Piotrowski, or a Rapaport to use the Rorschach wisely and scientifically. The superb skill in working with the Rorschach which they have often manifest is essentially a product of a thorough knowledge of the test plus a thorough knowledge of people and their peculiar kinds of maladjustment. Assuming that there really is a lawfulness to the behaviors of humans, any well trained clinician who has a thorough grasp of the test and a reasonably good understanding of people, will be able to be an expert Rorschach interpreter in his own right. A word of caution here seems appropriate. Much has been written concerning Rorschach interpretation. Some of the postulates which have been offered, and some of the procedures which have been recommended, are "system-specific"; that is, they are relevant only to the system which has been used in their formulation. All postulates concerning Rorschach interpretation are not viable, or valid, across all systems. Obviously, it behooves the interpreter to have a thorough understanding of the system which he is using, plus an allegiance to that particular approach. The Rorschacher, or Rorschach researcher, who intermixes systems is adding "apples and bananas," whether he knows it or not. The product of his interpretation can be disastrous to his subject. Similarly, the Rorschacher who ignores all of the components of the test, the scorings, scoring structure, and the verbalizations, is equally negligent in his work. He offers a less than complete service to his client and abuses the process of Rorschach assessment.

THE COOKBOOK APPROACH

Finally, it seems important to set forth some additional cautions concerning Rorschach interpretation. Some years ago, Meehl (1956) made an intelligent and intriguing appeal for a "cookbook" approach to diagnostics, which would simplify the task and provide more time for the clinician to perform other important functions such as intervention. While Meehl's position was clearly reasonable, especially for the very limited diagnostic task of "label hanging," it is not one which is applicable to the Rorschach. There is no simple checklist of Rorschach signs which automatically may be translated as representative of "dynamics" or behaviors. All together too often, the novice interpreter seeks out these simple equations from which his task will supposedly be made easier. This tendency of the novice is often encouraged by Rorschach authors who convey the impression that simplistic translations of scores, or classes of response contents, are useful procedures in interpretation. That supposition is "pure nonsense," and the unwitting interpreter who binds himself to that concept would do much better to select instruments other than the Rorschach for his work. The Rorschach cannot be approached with a cookbook. Interpretation of the test requires "full measure" of the interpreter, and only then, can an understanding and description of the subject, which recognizes the precious uniqueness of each human being, be expected.

INTERPRETIVE PREREQUISITES

The procedure of interpretation will usually begin with a careful review of the response scores, including the frequencies with which each occurs, and the sequential patterns of answers which they represent. Ultimately, a similarly careful review of the words takes place, as they have been generated in the Free Association, and elaborated in the Inquiry. This procedure does not represent the *quantitative versus qualitative* dichotomy which has often been mentioned concerning Rorschach interpretation. The scores, like the words, are a form of language, both of which are subject to quantitative *and* qualitative interpretation. The frequency of scores may be justly considered as quantified data, but the interpretation of these frequencies often takes on the more qualitative character, since so many score configurations require study and so many different propositions will be formed, modified, and ultimately accepted or rejected. The same holds true when dealing with the verbalizations, which will often be weighed heavily because of the frequencies of occurrence, and concurrently be evaluated for both symbolic and direct meaningfulness.

The flow of this process is made possible because the interpreter has an understanding of the various sorts of psychological activity which give rise to the different response features, regardless of whether those features are represented by scores or words. It has been noted that a knowledge of psychopathology, or more importantly, a knowledge of people, is prerequisite to successful Rorschach interpretation. The knowledge of the test is probably an even more important prerequisite to this process. Each response reflects a particular "psychology of the person" at the moment it occurs. Numerous factors, such as motives, affect, set, and experiences, are involved, and the interpretive task is to "sort out" as many of these elements as possible. When a substantial accumulation of response features, either words or scores, occurs, the data become "pregnant" by reason of frequency, but even where these significant frequencies do not occur, the response features continue to represent the psychologic action of the subject. Since the inception of the test there have been thousands of investigations concerning the significance of the various test elements. While many have offered only contradictory findings, a literature has been built regarding most of the major test features. Concurrently, numerous hypotheses have developed regarding the significance of the various test elements, some from a solid empirical base, others from strongly supported theoretical assumptions. Collectively, they represent an impressive body of interpretive postulates from which the interpreter can proceed with his work. The creation of the interpretive format for the comprehensive system is based largely on empirical findings. Where the empirical data have been inconclusive or contradictory, added research has been carried out. Many questions concerning the unique significance of some Rorschach elements remain unanswered; however, the bulk of data is such that the interpreter should feel reasonably confident that his propositions are based largely on scientifically derived findings.

The following chapters contain postulates regarding the various Rorschach scores, configurations, percentages, verbalizations, and so on. *None may be taken as an absolute*, for any may be modified by the presence of other test variables. They are offered as "a point from which to begin." Each is inconclusive to the extent that it is not integrated with the whole of the test. Each is conclusive where *other* data confirm the premise.

REFERENCES

Abel, T. M. The Rorschach test in a study of culture. *Journal of Projective Techniques*, 1948, **12,** 1–15.

Bailick, I., and Hamlin, R. The clinician as judge: Details of procedure in judging projective material. *Journal of Consulting Psychology*, 1954, **18,** 239–242.

Beck, S. J. *The Rorschach Experiment: Ventures in Blind Diagnosis*. New York: Grune and Stratton, 1960.

Benjamin, J. D., and Brosin, H. W. The reliability and validity of the Rorschach Test. In Benjamin, J. D. and Ebaugh, F. G., *The diagnostic validity of the Rorschach Test. American Journal of Psychiatry*, 1938, **94,** 1163–1168.

Benjamin, J. D., and Ebaugh, F. G. The diagnostic validity of the Rorschach test. *American Journal of Psychiatry*, 1938, **94,** 1163–1168.

Chambers, G. S., and Hamlin, R. The validity of judgements based on "blind" Rorschach records. *Journal of Consulting Psychology*, 1957, **21,** 105–109.

Clapp, H., Kaplan, A. H., and Miale, F. R. Clinical validation of Rorschach interpretations. *Rorschach Research Exchange*, 1938, **2,** 153–163.

Cronbach, L. J., and Gleser, G. C. *Psychological Tests and Personnel Decisions*. Urbana: University of Illinois Press, 1957.

Cummings, S. T. The clinician as judge: Judgements of adjustment from Rorschach single-card performance. *Journal of Consulting Psychology*, 1954, **18,** 243–247.

Frank, L. K. Projective methods for the study of personality. *Journal of Psychology*, 1939, **8,** 389–413.

Grant, M. Q., Ives, V., and Razoni, J. H. Reliability and validity of judges ratings of adjustment on the Rorschach. *Psychological Monographs*, 1952, **66,** No. 234.

Hamlin, R., and Newton, R. Comparisons of a schizophrenic and a normal subject, both rated by clinicians as well adjusted on the basis of "blind analysis." *Eastern Psychological Association*. Atlantic City, N.J., 1952.

Hertz, M. R., and Rubenstein, B. B. A comparison of three blind Rorschach cases. *American Journal of Orthopsychiatry*, 1949, **19,** 295–313.

Holt, R. R. Yet another look at clinical and statistical prediction: Or, is clinical psychology worthwhile. *American Psychologist*, 1970, **25**, 337–349.

Klopfer, B., Ainsworth, M. D., Klopfer, W., and Holt, R. *Developments in the Rorschach Technique*. Vol. 1. Yonkers-on-Hudson, N.Y.: World Book Company, 1954.

Kluckhohn, S., and Rosenzweig, S. Two Navajo children over a five year period. *American Journal of Orthopsychiatry*, 1949, **19**, 266–278.

Krugman, J. A clinical validation of the Rorschach with problem children. *Rorschach Research Exchange*, 1942, **5**, 61–70.

Levy, L. *Psychological Interpretation*. New York: Holt, Rinehart and Winston, 1963.

Levy, M. R. Issues in the personality assessment of lower class patients. *Journal of Projective Techniques*, 1970, **34**, 6–9.

Lisansky, E. S. The inter-examiner reliability of the Rorschach test. *Journal of Projective Techniques*, 1956, **20**, 310–317.

Little, K. B., and Shneidman, E. S. Congruencies among interpretations of psychological test and anamnestic data. *Psychological Monographs*, 1959, **27**, No. 476.

Meehl, P. E. Wanted—A good cookbook. *American Psychologist*, 1956, **11**, 263–272.

Monroe, R. L. Three diagnostic methods applied to Sally. *Journal of Abnormal Psychology*, 1945, **40**, 215–227.

Newton, R. The clinician as judge: Total Rorschach and clinical case material. *Journal of Consulting Psychology*, 1954, **18**, 248–250.

Oberholzer, E. Blind analysis of the people of Alor. In DuBois, C. *The People of Alor*. Minneapolis: University of Minnesota Press, 1944.

Palmer, J. O. Two approaches to Rorschach validation. *American Psychologist*, 1949, **4**, 270–271.

Piotrowski, Z. *Perceptanalysis*. New York: MacMillan, 1957.

Piotrowski, Z. Digital computer interpretation of ink-blot test data. *Psychiatric Quarterly*, 1964, **38**, 1–26.

Rorschach, H. *Psychodiagnostics*. Bern: Bircher, 1921.

Sarbin, T. R. Clinical psychology—Art or science. *Psychometrika*, 1941, **6**, 391–400.

Schachtel, A. H. Blind interpretation of six Pilaga Indian children. *American Journal of Orthopsychiatry*, 1942, **12**, 679–712.

Siegel, M. The diagnostic and prognostic validity of the Rorschach test in child guidance clinics. *American Journal of Orthopsychiatry*, 1948, **18**, 119–133.

Silverman, L. H. A Q-Sort study of the validity of evaluations made from projective techniques. *Psychological Monographs*, 1959, **27**, No. 477.

Swift, J. W. Matchings of teacher's descriptions and Rorschach analysis of pre-school children. *Child Development*, 1944, **15**, 217–244.

Symonds, P. M. A contribution to our knowledge of the validity of the Rorschach. *Journal of Projective Techniques*, 1955, **19**, 152–162.

Vernon, P. H. The evaluation of the matching method. *Journal of Educational Psychology*, 1936, **27**, 1–17.

CHAPTER 11

Structural Data: R, Location, Organization, Form Quality, and Populars

The interpretive approach to the structural data should be oriented toward creating the nucleus, or skeleton, of the final interpretation. Other elements, from the test, and from other data, will ultimately deliver the character of "flesh" to that nucleus. While the determinants, contents, and verbalizations probably comprise the most important data of the Rorschach, other variables, such as the R (record length), the location features, the organizational activity, the form quality, and the frequency of Popular answers provide a wealth of information for the interpreter. These data establish an intepretive framework from which the other data of the test may be studied more precisely.

NUMBER OF RESPONSES (R)

The R will naturally vary from subject to subject. Most adult subjects give between 17 and 27R under the instructions of the comprehensive system. Deviations from this range are not necessarily indicative of psychopathology, but they should be carefully considered. In some instances the examiner may provoke the longer or shorter record; however, this is the exception rather than the rule. A test of this postulate was completed using 16 student examiners, none of whom had prior Rorschach training. After three 2-hour training sessions in the mechanics of administration, including a demonstration plus role-playing, each collected two "familiarization" protocols which were discarded. Subsequently, each tested five subjects drawn randomly from a pool containing both psychiatric and nonpsychiatric subjects. Fifty-nine of the 80 protocols collected were of the expected length (17 to 27R), while the 21 records with R's above or below the expected range were reasonably distributed across examiners, so that in only three cases did an examiner obtain more than one record, the length of which deviated from the expected range. In those three instances, one examiner obtained four out of five records containing less than 17R, and in another instance, one examiner obtained four of five protocols containing more than 27R. Observation of these two examiners, each taking a sixth protocol, revealed that both were deviating from standard procedure, one manifesting rather abrupt tactics, while the second used considerable reinforcement, both verbal and nonverbal. These data seem especially useful in studying the expected length of records since none were informed, until after the study was completed, of the purpose of the study, nor were they given any specific information concerning expected length.

When the R falls below 17, the interpreter must consider the possibilities of intellectual limitations, defensiveness or constriction, organicity, depression, or attempts at malingering. None of these possibilities can be confirmed or rejected simply by reviewing the number of responses given. Other factors of the test, and possibly outside the test, will require careful review before any of these postulates, or others, can be supported with reasonable certainty. When the *R* is low, it is also important that the interpreter be especially alert to the limitations which may occur in reviewing the data in the Structural Summary. Some of the proportions and percentages can be sharply altered in the brief record by one or two responses. For example, seven Pure Form Responses in a 13*R* protocol will appear somewhat high if the Lambda Index is studied (1.16), whereas if the same length record contained only six Pure Form answers, the Lambda (0.85) would be within "normal" limits.

The long protocols also pose special problems for the interpreter working with the Structural Summary. This is especially true when the *R* exceeds 33, which falls three standard deviations above the mean for adults. Frequently, in these longer records, subjects tend to exhaust the *W* possibilities quickly, and thus give a proportionally higher number of *D* and *Dd* type answers. Pure Form responses also occur with a high frequency, usually in relation to the *Dd* response, and it is not uncommon to find an inordinately large number of *R* to Cards VIII and X, thereby elevating the Affective Ratio. While none of these data should be disregarded, each requires special attention in relation to the *R*.

All of the data in the Structural Summary are useful, regardless of the length of the protocol; however, where the record is unusually brief, or inordinately long, the interpreter must exercise caution in the development of some propositions. In brief records, the more unusual features of the summary may provide the "bulk" of the interpretive input, or greater weight may be placed on the sequence analysis and the content. In the longer records, a broad review of the total configuration of the structure may be the "key" to understanding the usefulness of a particular datum. It is most important that any interpretive propositions be developed within the framework of *R*, regardless of the actual length of the protocol. This is especially paramount as each of the different components of the quantitative Rorschach are studied.

LOCATION SCORES

The location scores tend to reveal the manner in which the subject approaches his world, and particularly, the ambiguities of it. They do not reveal why this approach is used, but simply indicate the manner of approach that has been employed. For example, someone who goes almost exclusively to the *Dd* type response, which is unusual, and generally involves small areas of the blots, is quite different than the subject who almost exclusively employs the *W* in his answers. Both may be creative, or conversely, both may be limited by their own psychological features in such a manner that they cannot perform easily in another mode of approach. In this context, it is important that the interpreter give careful review to the proportions of the different types of location scores which occur in the record, *and* be acutely aware of the developmental quality scoring distribution for these scores.

The *W* Response

Whole answers have been investigated more than any of the other types of location scores. Rorschach (1921) had postulated that *W* has a direct relationship to intellectual operations and to the ability to organize the components of one's environment into a meaningful concept. All of the Rorschach systematizers have included this postulate into their respective systems of interpretation, but with the caution that it can only be understood in relation to other scores in the record and in terms of the quality of the *W*.

As early as 1932, Beck demonstrated that *W* did have some relation to intellectual operations; however, the extent of that relation has been questioned consistently. The literature on this issue has been somewhat contradictory. Abrams (1955) reported a correlation of near .40 between the number of *W*'s and I.Q.'s. A substantially lower correlation was reported by Armitage (1955) between the same variables. Previously, McCandless (1949) had reported no significant findings in studying the *W* response as related to academic achievement, and Wittenborn (1950) found no relationship between several measures of mental ability and the frequency of *W*. Lotsoff (1953) reported that *W* has a relationship to verbal fluency but not necessarily to overall intelligence *per se*. Holzberg and Belmont (1952) and Wishner (1948) failed to find any significant relationship between *W* and the Similarities subtest of the Wechsler-Bellevue Scale. The developmental evidence concerning the frequency of *W* and intelligence is also nonsupporting. Ames (1971) reports that *W* occurs in greatest proportion in the 3 to 4 year old groups, with a gradual decline through childhood and adolescence until reaching the general adult proportion, which is between 25 and 35% of the record.

When the location scores, including the *W* answers, are studied with regard to *developmental quality*, the findings become much more consistent, and definitive relationships are found with different kinds of intellectual operations. Friedman (1952) has reported that "normal" adults produce more *W+* answers than do schizophrenics or children. Frank (1952) has shown the same to be true when normals and neurotics are compared. Blatt and Allison (1963) report a highly significant positive correlation between the higher developmental quality *W*'s and problem solving ability. The general quality of *W* answers is also reported as tending to increase through midadolescence (Ames, 1971).

In general then, while *W* appears to have some relationship to intellectual activity, the relationship can only be understood with reasonable clarity when the quality of the *W*'s are reviewed. There is at least one other factor which also requires study when evaluating the meaningfulness of the *W* answers in a protocol. This is the matter of which cards have produced *W* answers. Beck (1945) has reported that *W*'s occur in greatest frequency to Cards V, I, IV, and VI. He suggests that this is because these are solid, unbroken blots, which do not necessarily require the more complex synthesis activity for the *W* formation. A study of the 200 protocols collected from nonpyschiatric subjects using the methodology of the comprehensive system confirms Beck's findings. The greatest frequencies of *W*, by card, occur to Cards V, I, IV, and VI, in that order, with the lowest frequencies of *W* occurring to Cards X, IX, III, and VIII. Thus when a record contains an average number of *W*'s (approximately one-third), some indication of the psychological willingness of the subject to approach the more complex stimuli in a global manner, may be gleaned by studying both the developmental quality of the *W* plus the stimulus complexity which provoked the *W*. A *W+* response to one of the unbroken cards is probably among the more difficult challenges to the subject, since it requires "breaking the blot up" and then reintegrating it. Similarly, a *W+* or *Wo* answer to one of the broken blots is apparently also a challenging task, as it is much "easier" to give *D* answers to these cards.

The proportion of *W*'s in a protocol is also an important interpretive element. The *W*: *D* ratio found in using the comprehensive system with nonpsychiatric subjects is about 1 to 2 (see Table F). Psychiatric out-patients manifest a similar ratio of *W* to *D*, but in-patients, particularly nonschizophrenics, tend to show ratios which are closer to 1 to 1. The *W*% ranges, based on plus or minus one standard deviation from the mean, for each of the four reference groups shown in Table F, are 27 to 37% for nonpsychiatric subjects, 24 to 35% for out-patients, 36 to 51% for in-patient nonschizophrenics, and 26 to 36% for in-patient schizoprenics. When the *W*: *D* ratio deviates from the 1 to 2 standard in the average length protocol, the interpreter will find the developmental quality scores useful in determining whether this deviation is a function of the creative intellect at work, where *W+* and *D+* scores will appear in quantity, or is a manifestation of the more perfectionistic or withdrawing styles, where the proportion of + type answers will be noticeably low.

The frequency and quality of *W* can be increased by sets or training (Keyes, 1954), or decreased as a function of depression (Guirdham, 1936), or anxiety (Eichler, 1951). The quality of *W* appears to deteriorate with maladjustment, and the general quality of all responses will be somewhat mediocre in instances of organicity or where intellectual limitations are present.

The *D* Response

Rorschach hypothesized that the *D* answer represents the ability to perceive and react to the "obvious" characteristics of the environment. The systematizers have all incorporated this postulate into their own interpretive frameworks. This assumption appears logical in that the majority of responses, in most records, consist of *D* type answers. In the reference samples collected for use with this work, the mean percentage of *D* for nonpsychiatric subjects is 62%, for the out-patient sample 67%, for in-patient nonschizophrenics 46%, and for in-patient schizophrenics 47%.

It is not too surprising that there is lack of literature specific to the *D* response. Generally, it has been considered somewhat of a baseline from which the frequencies of *W* and *Dd* could be evaluated. Ames has demonstrated that the proportion of *D* responses gradually increases with age, but even at the age of 16 has not yet reached expected adult level. Card X, apparently because of its broken stimulus features, produces substantially more *D* than any of the other cards. When stress factors occur, the frequency of *D* often decreases, usually with a corresponding increase in *Dd* answers. The literature concerning the developmental quality of *D* responses suggest that *D+* type answers, especially to the broken blots, are generally indicative of higher levels of developmental functioning (Friedman, 1952). The more severely maladjusted subjects have been noted to give a somewhat higher proportion of *D* answers of lower developmental quality (*v* and −). Beck (1945) and Klopfer

(1954) both suggest that where D is overemphasized, the subject may be overly concerned with more practical, concrete interests, often at the expense of his full intellectual potential; that is, he is preoccupied with the obvious and reluctant to test-out his own resources. An examination of pre- and posttreatment protocols taken from chronic schizophrenics in a study of different treatment effects reveals a highly significant shift from a low mean $D\%$ prior to treatment (40%), to a high mean $D\%$ of 73% posttreatment (Exner and Murillo, 1973; Murillo and Exner, 1973). Other pre- and posttreatment data collected, including MMPI's, psychiatric ratings, behavioral ratings, and self-reports, tend to indicate that the remitted schizophrenic is cautious, conservative, and oriented toward making more socially desirable responses.

Generally, it would appear that the D answers are easier to give than either W or Dd and represent a psychological conservatism or efficiency. Like W, any interpretation of D answers must include reference to the developmental quality element. Some estimate of intellect is also important in understanding the appropriateness, or lack thereof, of a frequency or sequence of D answers.

The Dd Response

The frequency with which the Dd type response occurs is significantly less than either W or D. Ordinarily about 5% (one response in 20) can be expected to be Dd for nonhospitalized subjects. In the more severe disturbances this proportion will increase, sometimes to more than 25% of the protocol. This is especially true for the schizophrenic and for the severely impaired compulsive. For the latter, the Dd is often a manifestation of a "cognitive flight" through which he seeks a narrowed environment which can be made compatible with his own ideation. Conversely, the compulsive functions in a mode of "leaving no stone unturned" and is often caught-up in the importance of specific forms which avoid some of the bending of reality which is required in the W answer. The smaller the detail, the more precise the form may be. Kadinsky (1952) reports that the relationship between Dd and external adjustment is negative, but between Dd and internal adjustment is positive. Klebanoff (1949) has reported that male paretics give significantly more Dd than do normal males. Rabin et al. (1954), using a retest method, have found that Dd decreases significantly after the ingestion of substantial quantities of alcohol, and Schachter (1948) has reported a significantly higher percentage of Dd responses than expected in the protocols of female prostitutes shortly after their arrest.

Generally, the Dd might best be interpreted as a form of respite from the ambiguities of the larger or more common blot areas. Where the proportion of Dd is reasonably appropriate to W and D, it is probably a "healthy" sign showing both initiative and capacity to withdraw. When it occurs in disproportionate numbers, it is probably more indicative of flight, and if combined with any of the various types of movement, may well be indicative of an impairing ideational process.

The S Response

Rorschach postulated that the use of white space represents some form of oppositional or negative tendency. Both Beck (1945) and Rapaport (1946) tend to endorse this postulate but caution that it may simply represent a form of "contrariness" which may serve or accent the uniqueness of the subject. Piotrowski (1957) has added to this by suggesting that it may represent a striving for independence. Klopfer (1954) has suggested that it should be interpreted as a "constructive self-assertiveness" if it does not occur disproportionately in the record. All of the systematizers have emphasized that where *S* occurs with considerable frequency, it may be a form of negativism which can easily impinge upon reality contact and become overtly and/or covertly destructive.

The research literature is partially supportive of this position. Fonda (1951) and Bandura (1954) both report a significant positive relationship between *S* responses and "oppositional" tendencies. Murray (1957) has criticized these and similar findings because of a failure to control for *R*. Rosen (1952) reports that the frequency of *S* is not correlated with the diagnosis of psychopathy, but is significantly correlated with high *Pd* scores on the MMPI for nonpsychopathic subjects. Counts and Mensh (1950) showed a significant increase in *S* answers using a retest model with subjects after hypnotically inducing conflict. Rapaport (1946) reports the highest incidence of *S* answers among paranoid patients, and Molish (1955) suggests that where *S* occurs in the schizophrenic, it represents a mediational process through which a passive kind of resistance to the environment is maintained. Fonda (1960) in a review of the literature concerning *S*, concludes that the proportion of *S* gives some indication of the effort being devoted to the defense of autonomy. This conclusion seems consistent with earlier findings of Werner (1945) showing that organics tend to give proportionally more space answers than do defectives and nonbrain injured cases. There are essentially no empirical data to suggest that *S* responses are an indication of acting-out, or acting-out potential. In a study of egocentricity (Exner, 1973), it was noted that the protocols of successful suicides ($N = 18$) were generally marked by the occurrence of *S* responses, frequently combined with other blot areas. The sample size, however, is far too small to draw firm conclusions.

Thus it seems appropriate to approach the interpretation of *S* as indicative of some form of negativism or oppositional feature, which may be considered healthy or useful depending on the frequency of *S* plus the other configurational characteristics of the record. Where *S* is proportionally high, a caution should automatically be raised by the interpreter, and if combined with poor form quality and/or the more primative kinds of movement answers (*FM* or *m*), or the presence of responses not dominated by Form (*CF*, *TF*, etc.), the interpreter may do well to consider the "anger affect" and its potential consequences.

The *DW*, *DdW*, and *DdD* Responses

These are generally considered as "confabulatory" types of answers, which Rorschach generally interpreted as representing an intellectually limited, organic, or schizophrenic form of perception. Obviously, it is a highly unique form of response in which some of the more important cognitive controls fail, or are lacking. Rorschach considered these responses to be uniformly pathological. All of the systematizers, except Beck, have agreed with this premise. Beck, possibly because of a more liberal scoring of the confabulatory answer, has been prone to qualify this postulate by also noting that these kinds of responses may occur in the protocols of the very healthy adult, especially when the intellectual endowment is superior. The criterion for scoring a response as confabulatory in the comprehensive system is somewhat more stringent than provided by Beck, and thus it would logically seem that such a score would represent some form of psychological operation marked by pathological features.

The literature concerning the confabulatory response, as represented by the *DW*, *DdW*, *DdD* scorings, is very sparse, and, at best, provides very limited support for the interpretive postulates. It is important to note that the kind of confabulatory answer represented by these location scores *differs substantially* from the process of confabulation often found in the qualitative evaluation of verbalizations in some responses, especially common among schizophrenic subjects. The latter, which is discussed in detail in the chapter concerning qualitative interpretation, seems to clearly represent a form of autistic association, while this is not necessarily true of the *DW* type response. An examination of the 200 protocols collected from non-psychiatric subjects, and the 100 records obtained from out-patients used to form some of the reference data for the comprehensive system, yields a sum of *zero DW*, *DdW*, and *DdD* scorings. This sample does contain, however, numerous responses, representing about 4% of the records, which would be judged as confabulatory using the Rapaport (1946) criterion. Similarly, the 195 records collected from in-patients for the reference data sample contain only nine confabulatory location scorings, three of which are in the same record, and six of which are scored *DW*. Concurrently, approximately 35% of these protocols contain the Rapaport kind of confabulatory verbalizations. It is important to mention here that the reference sample of 495 protocols represent very few, if any, subjects who would be considered severely retarded intellectually, and possibly a sample of that sort might yield a greater frequency of the confabulatory location answers.

In general, it seems safe to suggest that the interpreter can consider the confabulatory location response as highly unique and a serious sign when it does occur. It may be indicative of gross intellectual dysfunction, or as Beck (1945) suggests, a kind of alogical cognition.

DEVELOPMENTAL QUALITY SCORES

The importance of the developmental quality scores has been mentioned several times in this chapter, and in Chapter 4. They contribute substantially to the interpretation of the location components, and to the interpretation of the structure of the protocol. They represent an area of the Rorschach which has been researched with considerable success in that the findings are very consistent. Goldfried, Stricker, and Weiner (1971) conclude that this approach differentiates children at the various age levels, and also provides a basis from which normals, neurotics, brain-damaged, and schizophrenics can be differentiated.

Generally, the higher *DQ* scores (+ and *o*) are found among the brighter and/or more psychologically "effective" subjects, while the lower *DQ* scores (*v* and −) are noted among very young children, intellectually limited subjects, brain-damaged, and the severely disturbed. Friedman (1952) demonstrated that the hebephrenic and catatonic schizophrenics manifest substantial quantities of lower *DQ* scores and suggested that this may be interpreted as characterizing a primative, rigid, diffuse sort of cognition. Siegel (1953) reports that the paranoid schizophrenic, while still manifesting high frequencies of low DQ scores, tends to function cognitively at a higher level than do catatonics or hebephrenics. Becker (1956) found process schizophrenics yielding greater numbers of lower DQ scores than do reactive schizophrenics. Wilensky (1959) obtained a similar finding when comparing "closed-ward" versus "open-ward" schizophrenics. Hurwitz (1954) and Misch (1954) both conclude that lower DQ scores are related to tendencies toward motoric expression of affect, and that subjects manifesting such scores have less "capacity" for delay of impulse. Kruger (1954) found more lower DQ scores among subjects actually attempting suicide than among those simply threatening suicide. Kruger also reports a similar differentiation between sexual "deviants" who act out impulses versus those who are preoccupied with sexual desires.

The interpreter should not tend to confuse the DQ scores with those derived from an evaluation of form quality. There is obviously some overlap in that each appears to represent some aspects of the cognitive operations. While there may be a very high positive correlation between these sets of scores for the very primative, severely disturbed schizophrenic, the correlation is substantially lower for most other types of adult subjects. It is not uncommon to find the subject whose functioning is marginally effective to manifest a significant proportion of poor form quality answers, but use location selections which are generally o or even $+$. The reverse can also be true. Similarly, the protocols of nonpsychiatric subjects frequently contain location selections which have DQ scores of v, and in some instances, even $-$. Where the low DQ scores are proportionally abundant, the interpreter must consider the possibility of a rigid, concrete, and somewhat immature kind of cognition. If this is confirmed by other data in the record, or from elsewhere, some of the recommendations which may be made concerning intervention possibilities will definitely be effected. At the opposite pole, when the record contains a preponderance of high DQ scores, the flexibility and seeming higher maturational level of the congitive operations, *if confirmed* by other data, warrant consideration of different intervention models.

The data concerning DQ scores entered in the Structural Summary show only the frequency with which each type of score has occurred in the record. Frequently, the interpreter will be able to glean additionally important information by reviewing the DQ for the different types of location scores, W, D, and Dd. Data taken from the $23R$ protocol of a 31 year old male serve as a good example.

$$
\begin{aligned}
W &= 5 & + &= 4 \\
D &= 15 & o &= 15 \\
Dd &= 3 & v &= 3 \\
 & & - &= 1
\end{aligned}
$$

Some speculations and propositions can be developed from these data as they are. First, the presence of one $DQ-$ is somewhat unusual in a record where more than one-sixth of the answers are $DQ+$. This is a warning sign or "flag," raising the question as to why this has occurred. It may be explained as an attempt at creativeness that did not succeed, or it may represent some other phenomena. Second, the relatively low proportion of W answers and the elevated number of Dd responses are important. Collectively, these data might be used to postulate that a somewhat conservative cognitive approach exists, which tends to avoid the totality of the stimulus environment (low W, high D), with possibly some preference to create or restructure the stimulus world in a more ideationally compatible manner (Dd), and where some instances occur in which the mediational process does not coincide with the cognitive capacities of the subject ($DQ+ = 4$, $DQv + DQ- = 4$). A further examination of the DQ scores reveals that the four low DQ scores all occur to W answers while three of the four $DQ+$ scores occur with Dd responses. These facts not only strengthen the basic proposition, but also serve to expand it considerably, raising more questions. The DQ distribution, by location selection, is such to suggest that the conservative cognitive approach may actually represent a "psychological inability" to deal with complex stimulus inputs effectively, and that the more highly developed cognitive elements tend to function best where the stimulus features of the environment are reorganized into more narrow and idiosyncratic patterns. In other words, the subject may experience considerable difficulty in responding to his real world and finds it easier to use his cognitive resources in a world which he creates. These postulates are, of course, tentative, and may be modified by many other features of the record, but they are justified in light of these small but distinct segments of the total data. Had the DQ distribution fallen more evenly among the location scores, a significantly different proposition would have probably evolved, thus emphasizing the importance of considering all of the data when evaluation of location components occurs. For instance, the $23R$ record obtained from a 27 year old female reveals the identical distribution of location and DQ scores in the Structural Summary. Examination of the distribution of the DQ scores, however, indicates that two of the $DQ+$ responses occur to W answers, and two occur to D responses. One of the DQv scorings is to a W answer, the second occurs in a Dd response, and the third plus the $DQ-$ scoring occur to D responses. In this instance, the proposition is that the subject has a more "fluid" kind of cognitive effectiveness, the variations of which may be related to specific kinds of ideation. A study of other components of the protocol, especially content scores and the verbalizations, should be useful in understanding these variations more specifically. Regardless of the final conclusions that might be drawn from the total record, there appears no evidence in this set of location scores to suggest remoteness or withdrawal from the world as seemed the case in the first protocol.

A study of the elements related to location is generally a good beginning point for the interpreter. They give some index of the cognitive-perceptual approach of the subject, which is the kind of information from a better understanding of other data can evolve.

THE ORGANIZATIONAL (Z) ACTIVITY

A review of the data concerning organizational activity should also contribute to the understanding of the perceptual-cognitive operations of the subject. Four basic scores pertaining to Z are available to the interpreter in the structural summary (Zf, ZSum, Zest, and Zd), and, of course, the weighted Z scores for specific responses are also frequently important in reviewing sequence and studying individual responses.

Most of the relevant literature concerning the Z score has already been mentioned in Chapter 6, the bulk of which pertains to the relation of Z to intellectual activity. Hertz (1960), in reviewing the work which has been reported concerning organizational activity, suggests that Z, as such, represents not only the ability to analyze and synthesize, but also offers information about conceptual activity, reflects a sort of cognitive energy or initiative, and tells something of how the cognitive complexity of the person is integrated with reality. In other words, it may be a composite representation of intellect, drive, creativeness, and efficiency. The obvious task of the interpreter is to sort some of these elements out so that they are used meaningfully to understand the subject.

The frequency of Z in the records of adult nonpsychiatric subjects is about one-third of the responses. The Z occurs in these records to W as compared with D answers at a ratio of about 2:1. This figure seems particularly interesting in that the expected W:D ratio is about 1:2. Thus it would appear that the occurrence of organizational activity in the D answer is somewhat unusual and should be given careful consideration. The most common D responses in which Z occurs are in Cards II, III, and VII. The appearance of Z in D responses to other cards should probably be considered as more idiographic and special consideration should be afforded those answers. There is a greater frequency of Z noted among the protocols of out-patients, and the occurrence of Z in the D answer is more common. The opposite is true for in-patients, especially nonschizophrenics, where the tendency to Z is somewhat lower than for the nonpsychiatric group.

As mentioned in Chapter 6, the ZSum for nonpsychiatric subjects has a high correlation with the prediction from the Wilson and Blake table estimating the sum from the frequency. This holds true in considerably fewer cases where the protocol is from a psychiatric subject. Although the data must be regarded as somewhat tentative, it seems reasonable to speculate that where the ZSum is 3.0 or more lower than the Zest, that is, Zd equals at least -3.0, there is some cognitive dysfunctioning, possibly created by excessive strivings for achievement which are not being realized, or more commonly, by some negative affect state such as anxiety and depression. The interpretive logic here is that the Zf represents the drive or initiative of the subject, probably based on some experienced intellectual capability, although that may not always be the case. In any event, the strivings of the subject to organize fall short, probably because of affective interference. The opposite is true where the Zd is substantially high; that is, the difference between ZSum and Zest is plus 3.0 or more. In these cases it would seem that the energy or initiative is aided by some experience of favorable affect so as to permit organization beyond the level which is normally expected or experienced. The high plus Zd score may also represent some form of cognitive style which the subject has developed as an asset or as a defense. For example, compulsives in the out-patient sample tend to yield plus Zd scores, although not always exceeding the critical level of 3.0. Conversely, hypomanic subjects, and patients diagnosed as psychopathic frequently exceed the plus 3.0 Zd level. In two of these three kinds of subjects, compulsives and psychopaths, it seems reasonable to suggest that overorganization is part of their style of life. In the third, the hypomanics the organizational activities may be more of a need than a style.

There are few data from which higher or lower than expected Z frequencies can be interpreted except in terms of intellect. Bright subjects tend to give more Z; dull subjects tend to give less Z. But any interpretation of the Zf, developed independently from the ZSum or Zest, is probably no more than a "shot in the dark" which will be wrong more times than right. Evaluation of the events of Z is quite important. In some protocols, Z is predominant among the responses which have poor form quality, suggesting that an ideational factor is responsible. This is most commonly found among the severely impaired schizophrenics. When Z occurs in a *Dd* type answer, it is a rare event and should be regarded as highly idiographic. Such responses appear to be more common among instances of psychopathology than among nonpsychiatric subjects. It is also important for the interpreter to note those instances in which the weighted Z score assigned to a response is higher than that afforded most frequently to the specific type of response for a given card. For instance, the *W* response to Card I automatically obtains a Z value of 1.0. When the *W* answer to Card I includes the use of adjacent detail, the higher value of 4.0 is assigned, thus revealing a different form of integration of the whole blot than is the case in the more ordinary 1.0 type *W*. When the form quality of these types of answers is good, or superior, it would appear to represent an efficiently organized, creative effort by the subject. Notations of these kinds of response are particularly important in the records of psychiatric subjects as they tend to orient the interpreter to consider a broader variety of intervention techniques than might be the case for the subject whose Z answers are more basic or bland.

It is very important that the organizational activity not be interpreted in "isolation," that is, separate from the other features of the record. Instances are noted in the reference samples collected for this work where Z occurs only in conjunction with blend answers, or other cases where Z is always accompanied by shading determinants.

FORM QUALITY

One of the most important elements among the structural data of the Rorschach is the form quality. Form is, of course, a basic ingredient to most all Rorschach answers. A substantial portion of the responses are Pure Form, and most of the remaining responses will be marked by a form component. Rorschach had postulated that the manner or quality in which form is used reflects the subject's ability to perceive things conventionally, or realistically. All of the systematizers have agreed with this proposition, and a substantial literature supports this notion.

Generally, the inclusion of form in a response has been considered as an "ego" or thinking operation. Rapaport (1946), for example, drawing from the concepts of ego psychology, suggests that the use of form denotes a process of formal reasoning, wherein the mediation of the stimulus calls attention to the contours of the stimulus areas. In other words, the use of form appears to represent the operations of perception and reasoning. It reflects the ability of the subject to direct his attention and ideation to the elements of control, discriminating judgment, and regard for the standards of the environment. Korchin (1960) has discussed this process in the framework that the subject "selectively organizes" that which is perceived. Beck (1945) holds that, where the quality of the form use is "good" (+ or *o*), the subject demonstrates a respect for reality, whereas the frequent use of "poor" form quality manifests a disregard for this element.

Baughman (1959), in his classic work on the stimulus features of the blots, has clearly demonstrated that form does play a dominant role in the formulation of most answers. His work and that of Exner (1959) can be viewed as offering evidence for the important role of form in Rorschach answers. In both works, the color and shading properties of the cards were altered, sometimes causing variations in the frequencies for the use of different determinants and/or the response contents; however, it appears that the proportion of responses, including form, remains relatively stable.

Three sets of data in the comprehensive system provide the interpreter with important information concerning the form quality. One is the $F+\%$, representing the proportion of Pure Form responses which have been scored either $+$ or o. The second is the $X+\%$, which is the proportion of $+$ and o answers for the total record. The third is the distribution of form quality scorings, both for Pure Form answers and for all of the responses. The literature concerning these data is reasonably rich, particularly for the $F+\%$, which had been originally suggested by Rorschach and which has been used by all of the systematizers except Klopfer.

As Molish (1967) has noted, the $F+\%$ will vary with both intellect and the affective state of the subject. Much early Rorschach research concerned the $F+\%$ as related to intellect. Beck (1930, 1932) demonstrated a relatively high correlation between the low $F+\%$ and limited intellectual endowment. Similar findings were reported later by Sloan (1947). Klopfer and Kelley (1942) also reported a significant relationship between the low $F+\%$ and retardation. Studies concerning the relation of the $F+\%$ to the I.Q.'s of nonretarded subjects have yielded much more contradictory findings. Several, such as Holzberg and Belmont (1952), Paulsen (1941), Abrams (1955), and Armitage et al. (1955), report the $F+\%$ to be significantly correlated with I.Q. or M.A. Another group of studies, such as that of Wishner (1948), Gibby (1951), and Taulbee (1955), have led to the general conclusion that no single Rorschach factor, or grouping of factors, manifests a consistently significant correlation with intelligence. The work of Ames (1971) indicates that while the $F+\%$ is generally low for the very young child, it typically exceeds 80% by the sixth year, and her adolescent groups routinely yield mean $F+\%$'s in excess of 90. Some types of brain-injured subjects also manifest significantly lower $F+\%$'s. A review of the studies with the brain-injured by Molish (1959) indicates that substantial variations exist among these types of subjects for the quality of form, which Molish interprets as a manifestation of the type of damage plus the adaptive functions of the ego to the impairment. The data concerning the $F+\%$ among geriatric subjects are somewhat mixed. Ames (1954) has found a tendency for the $F+\%$ to decline in senility. A similar decline in $F+$ among older subjects has been reported by Klopfer (1946), Davidson and Kruglov (1952), and Caldwell (1954). However, Prados and Fried (1943) and Chesrow et al. (1949) both report that older subjects do maintain a relatively high $F+\%$.

The most striking data concerning form quality have developed in studies of the more seriously disturbed psychiatric patients, schizophrenics in particular. As Weiner (1966) points out, "Virtually all studies of $F+\%$ in schizophrenia and control groups have replicated the findings presented by Beck and Rickers-Ovsiankina in their historically significant 1938 contributions." In each of those studies, schizophrenics showed a mean $F+\%$ in the 60's while controls yielded a mean $F+\%$ significantly higher, 87.3 for the Rickers group, 83.9 for the Beck group. Similar findings have been reported by Friedman (1952), Berkowitz and Levine (1953),

Knopf (1956), and Molish and Beck (1958). Some of these data have led Beck to establish as a *critical minimum*, a cut-off of 60% $F+$. In other words, where the good form quality, for Pure Form responses, is 60% or lower, Beck considers these findings as representative of severe psychopathology or serious intellectual limitations, or as an index of brain dysfunction. The Beck critical minimum may be somewhat conservative according to the sample collected for the reference data in the comprehensive system. A comparison of the nonpsychiatric ($N = 200$) and schizophrenic ($N = 125$) groups reveals a highly significant difference with nonpsychiatric subjects showing a mean $F+\%$ of 91 versus a mean $F+\%$ of 62 for the schizophrenic group. Using a "cut-off" of $F+\% = 75$, only 13 (6.5%) of the nonpsychiatric subjects fall at this point or lower, while 101 (80%) of the schizophrenics fall below this point. Thus it would seem safe to hypothesize that where the $F+\%$ falls below 70%, the interpreter must give careful consideration to the possibilities of severe psychopathology, organicity, or intellectual limitations. The differences between the Beck minimum and that recommended here are probably created by the differences which exist in the lengths of the records, where the Beck instructions breed more responses, a greater tendency toward D and Dd type answers, either of which could produce a better form quality response.

The low $F+\%$ should not always be interpreted as indicating the schizophrenic condition, for that is not the case. Weiner (1966) warns that subjects trying to impress the examiner with psychopathological signs may offer many poor form answers. This is an exceptionally difficult task for the untrained subject, however, as is demonstrated in another study completed for this work. Twenty-six subjects, 13 of whom were naive undergraduates, and 13 of whom were blue collar workers, none of who had graduated high school, were tested with specific instructions to present a record which would "typify" the hospitalized psychiatric patient. The mean $F+\%$ for this group was 77%. Subdivided, the undergraduates show a mean of $F+ = 73\%$, while the blue collar sample yields a mean of 80%. When the records were reviewed by two Diplomate clinicians, only three were considered to be "possibly schizophrenic." These data indicate that it is difficult for the malingering subject to distort the reality of the blots in a manner similar to that common among the schizophrenic population. This seems to be true even for the shorter records. Sherman (1952) divided a group of 71 normal subjects and 66 schizophrenic subjects into high and low responders. He reports that the $F+\%$ and the number of poor quality form answers discriminates the schizophrenics from the normals in both groups.

The $F+\%$ also seems to be a reasonable index of the capacity to deal more effectively with stresses. Goldberger (1961), using an isolation study design, found that subjects manifesting a greater "reality testing strength," as indicated by the adequacy of good form quality in the Rorschach, were more capable of handling "the primary process intrusions of sensory deprivations" than were subjects yielding a lower quality of form answers. Baker and Harris report similar results in a design using "speed quality" under stress. There have been some reports of an increase in the $F+\%$ as a result of therapeutic change (Piotrowski, 1939; Kisker, 1942; Beck, 1948); however, Zamansky and Goldman (1960) report, in a very well designed study of 96 hospitalized patients, no significant increase in $F+\%$ following intervention, although a "global" analysis of the pre- and posttreatment protocols was significantly differentiating. An examination of the pre- and posttreatment protocols of 53 schizophrenics studied by Exner and Murillo (1973) reveals about a 10% increase, which is not statistically significant, in the mean $F+\%$ for the posttreatment records ($F+\%$ at pretreatment $= 64\%$, at posttreatment $= 74\%$). Interestingly, when the protocols of nine subjects who relapsed during the first 6 months after discharge from the hospital are eliminated from the sample, the pre- and posttreatment mean $F+\%$'s both increase, to 69% at pretreatment, and 80% at posttreatment. While this difference does not reach a satisfactory level of statistical significance, it does seem worth noting, and becomes even more important when the data from the $X+\%$ is considered. The mean $X+\%$ for the entire sample was 56% at pretreatment and 75% at posttreatment, a difference significant at .01. When the nine relapsing subjects are eliminated, the pretreatment mean $X+\%$ remains essentially unchanged, at 55%, but the posttreatment mean increases to 80%. Thus it would seem that while the $F+\%$ by itself represents important data, the combination of the $F+\%$ and the $X+\%$ can yield a greater understanding of the reality oriented operations.

The Extended $+\%$ ($X+\%$), as mentioned in Chapter 8, is a derivation of the Extended $F+\%$, which had been recommended by Rapaport (1946) and elaborated on by Schafer (1954). As Weiner (1966) points out, this kind of index may be a more reliable representation of the reality testing of the subject in that it reflects a larger number of responses than does the $F+\%$. Weiner also mentions that, for the brief record, or those containing few Pure Form responses, it may be the only useful data concerning perceptual accuracy. In that the $X+\%$ includes the data from the $F+\%$, the correlation between the two is generally high. Feldman et al. (1954) report a correlation of approximately .80 between the $F+\%$ and the Extended $F+\%$ in both normal and neurotic groups. The correlation between the $F+\%$ and the $X+\%$ for the 200 nonpsychiatric subjects in the reference sample of the comprehensive system is .78. Interestingly, while the high correlation holds for the 125 in-patient schizophrenics included in the reference sample ($r = .73$), it is considerably lower for the in-patient nonschizophrenics ($r = .62$) even though the mean $F+$ and $X+$ percents are almost identical for that group, $F+\% = 80$, $X+\% = 81$. An examination of those 70 protocols seems to reveal a sizeable number of records where the $F+\%$ is extremely high (100%) and where the $X+\%$ is less than 50%. Since that group includes a large proportion of "affective" disturbances, this may represent an example of how affective dysfunction can interfere with the reality operations. Cass and McReynolds (1951) found that the Extended $F+\%$ to generally be higher than the $F+\%$ in normal adults; however, this is not generally the case for the $X+\%$. As may be noted in Table C, the mean $X+\%$ is lower than the mean $F+\%$ for the nonpsychiatric, out-patient, and schizophrenic groups in the reference sample. The difference between these data and that reported by Case and McReynolds is probably created by the fact that the $X+\%$ includes all of the responses in the protocol while the Extended $F+\%$ concerns only Pure Form and form dominated answers. In fact, a study of the 200 nonpsychiatric records from the reference sample shows that poor form quality appears among Pure Form and nonform dominant (CF, TF, etc.) answers at approximately 35% more frequently than among the form dominant answers (FC, FT, FY, etc.).

The general interpretive approach to the $X+\%$ should be essentially the same as that used with the $F+\%$ data, that is, as an index of the reality testing features in the record. When the $X+\%$ is low, less than the 70% level, consideration must be given to the limitations in perceptual accuracy or reality testing operations. It is also important to emphasize the importance of relating the $F+\%$ and the $X+\%$ in interpretation. As Schafer (1954) points out, an interpretation of "poor reality testing" in a protocol which has a $F+\%$ of 60 and an $X+\%$ of 85% is probably inappropriate. Conversely, where the $F+\%$ is within acceptable limits, for instance, 80%, and the $X+\%$ is much lower, 55%, the proposition that the reality oriented operations are impaired *under certain conditions* is a necessary postulate.

When the $F+\%$, or the $X+\%$ appear to be very high (near 100%), the interpreter should consider the possibility of an "undue" preoccupation with reality that may cause the subject some sacrifice of his own uniqueness. All of the systematizers have offered this caution. Ordinarily, some "bending" of the reality features of the cards is expected. An examination of the 200 nonpsychiatric records from the reference sample shows that 58 (29%) manifest an $F+\%$ of 100%, and only 26 (13%) yield an $X+\%$ of 100%. Where the record is very brief, a high $F+\%$ is more expected. Data provided by Fiske and Baughman suggest that a low $F+\%$ is particularly "deviant" in the brief record. The same would appear to hold true for the $X+\%$ in that the brief record often represents some form of constraint by the subject wherein he is more able to "pick and choose" his answers. If these more deliberately selected responses are of poor form quality, the judgement of the subject, as well as his reality testing, would seem to be questionable.

The distribution of the form quality scorings is especially useful for evaluating the meaningfulness of the $F+\%$ and the $X+\%$. Mayman (1970), using a set of cases drawn from an earlier work of Schafer, has neatly demonstrated how the differentiation of the form quality scorings adds an important interpretive dimension. For instance, the differentiation between the weak (w) and minus ($-$) answers is critically important to the diagnosis of schizophrenia. While the w answer does mark a shift away from reality, it generally does not reflect the gross distortion of reality found in the $-$ answer. Similarly, the $+$ response represents a significantly higher level of perceptual and cognitive accuracy and inventiveness than does the more common o answer. Thus in the protocol where the $F+$ and $X+$ percents are within acceptable limits, the presence or absence or the $+$ type responses will often yield data concerning the cognitive sophistication of the subject. In this same context, where the record contains $F+$ or $X+$ percents significantly lower than expected, the frequency of w versus $-$ responses will often yield information concerning the extent of detachment and cognitive disorganization. The frequency of $-$ answers is especially important because of the stringent criterion required for their scoring. Mayman has reviewed several validation studies which offer considerable support for his approach to scoring form quality. These include a study differentiating "process and reactive" schizophrenics (Zukowsky, 1961), one differentiating legally sane from legally insane murderers (Kahn, 1967), and one concerning improvement of 20 schizophrenic patients treated by chemotherapy (Saretsky, 1963). These works all employ the seven category scoring recommended by Mayman, which, as noted in Chapter 6, is somewhat more extensive than the four category method used in the comprehensive system. Thus it seemed important to research the four category scoring. Five such investigations have been completed.

The first is a review of the frequencies for each of the four form quality scorings as they occurred among the four groups of subjects in the reference sample. The mean percentages for each of the four form quality scores are shown, by group, in

Table 23. It will be noted from examination of Table 23 that the schizophrenic group clearly deviates from the other three for *o*, *w*, and − answers, while giving more + responses than do the in-patient nonschizophrenics. Interestingly, the out-patient sample gives the greatest percentage of + answers, more − answers than in-patient nonschizophrenics, and totally, slightly more poor form quality answers (*w* plus −) than the in-patient nonschizophrenics.

Table 23. Mean Percentages of +, *o*, *w*, and − Scorings in the Protocols of Four Reference Groups

Scoring	Nonpsychiatric (*N* = 200) (%)	Out-Patient (*N* = 100) (%)	In-Patient Nonschizophrenic (*N* = 70) (%)	In-Patient Schizophrenic (*N* = 125) (%)
+	26	31	16	21
o	58	47	65	37
w	12	14	15	24
−	4	8	4	19

The second study concerned changes in the form quality of responses in the pre- and posttreatment records of the 53 schizophrenics used in the Exner and Murillo investigation of treatment effects. The posttreatment records were collected 8 to 10 weeks after discharge from hospitalization and compared with the pretreatment records taken at admission. Each of the two protocols was taken by a different examiner, neither of whom were aware of the purpose of the testing other than that it was routine. A significant increase is found in the posttreatment protocols for both + (16 to 21%) and *o* (39 to 59%) answers. There was also a slight increase in the *w* responses (12 to 15%) and a significant decrease in − responses (23 to 5%). These data appear to support the hypothesis that the four category form quality scoring will differentiate between the seriously disturbed schizophrenic and those who have been treated somewhat successfully.

The third study concerned the comparison of the form quality scores in the records of 14 subjects, who later suicided (within 90 days) with the records of 33 subjects who were unsuccessful at suicide attempts. No significant differences were noted between these groups, nor do they differ substantially from the form quality scorings of the out-patient reference sample.

The fourth study has focused on 37 out-patients in psychoanalytically oriented psychotherapy. This group represents psychosomatics, hysterics, and obsessive-compulsive patients being treated by one of 11 therapists. None of the patients were considered psychotic or "prepsychotic." Protocols were collected shortly after the onset of treatment by one of four examiners, and 16 months later by a different examiner. All were still involved in psychotherapy at the second administration. There were no statistically significant differences for any of the four form quality scores; however, some apparent changes seem worth noting. First, there is a slight increase in the proportion of + responses (29 to 34%) while the *o* answers decrease slightly (53 to 49%). Second, there is a slight increase in the percentage of *w* answers (11 to 14%) and a slight decrease in the proportion of − responses (7 to 3%). It would seem that the general pattern of change is in the desired direction.

The final study is possibly the most interesting of the group. Protocols were collected from 77 nonschizophrenic patients at the time they were discharged from hospitalization. A second protocol was collected from the same subjects, by a different examiner, 7 months later *or when the patient relapsed*. Twenty-two of the subjects relapsed (seven during the second or third posthospitalization months, and 15 during the fourth, fifth, or sixth months out). There were no statistically significant differences for the form quality scores at discharge which would differentiate the relapsers from the nonrelapsers; however, the comparison of the second protocols does show considerable differentiation. The relapsers give significantly fewer + answers than do the nonrelapsers, and significantly more *w* answers. Interestingly, the proportion of − responses is about the same for both groups. In other words, neither the relapsers or nonrelapsers show a remarkable detachment from reality as is manifest in the − answer; however, the relapse group does show a greater willingness to "bend" reality as evidenced by the preponderence of *w* responses, and a considerably less effective contact with reality at the higher levels as is manifest in the + type answer. These findings seem consistent with many of the observed behavioral manifestations of the relapsing nonschizophrenic, especially the depressive type of disorder, where the discomfort of the depression appears to precipitate frequent disregard for, or distortion of, reality. The findings also seem to lend support to Mayman's argument that the weak (*w*) kind of response, although reflecting a kind of poor form quality, is different than the more gross distortions of reality as found in the minus answers, and probably represents a somewhat different set of perceptual-cognitive operations.

The findings from these five studies seem consistent with both the hypotheses and empirical supports of the Mayman method for scoring form quality, and appear to lend some justification to the use of the four category method in the comprehensive system. Regardless of which method the scorer may select, it seems obvious that a differentiation of form quality, beyond the traditional plus-minus categories, offers an important discrimination to the structural data.

THE POPULAR RESPONSE

The common or Popular answer was originally regarded by Rorschach as representing the ability to perceive the commonplace in the stimulus features of the blots. All of the systematizers have agreed with this postulate, although disagreeing on the criterion for the scoring of a Popular. The *P* has been found by Baughman (1954) to be one of the most stable features of the test, being least subject to interference by the examiner. Bourguinon and Nett (1955) and Hallowell (1956) have demonstrated that the listing of Populars also seems to hold well for other cultural groups, although several studies (Leighton and Kluckholm, 1947; Honigmann, 1948; Joseph and Murray, 1951) have reported on the unique Populars for special cultural groups. Beck (1932), Kerr (1934), and Hertz (1940) have all reported the incidence of *P* to be low among intellectually retarded subjects. Ames (1971) reports a gradual increase in the number of Populars given by children as they become older (based on a possible 16*P*) and finds that the majority of adolescents give between 5 and 8 Populars. She suggests that if an adolescent gives fewer than 5*P*, his record should be carefully examined. This probably also holds true for the adolescent examined using the comprehensive system.

In that P has a finite limit, as opposed to other kinds of Rorschach answers, it seems reasonable to assume that low and high P frequencies can be easily defined. Nonpsychiatric subjects in the reference sample give an average of about $6P$ responses. Out-patients and nonschizophrenic in-patients give about 7 P's per protocol, but the in-patient schizophrenic group gives an average of less than 3 P's per record. It is not only the schizophrenic who tends to avoid the P response, however. When the nonschizophrenic in-patient group is subdivided into "depressive" versus "characterological" disorders, the later group is note to give an average of 5.3 Populars while the depressive group manifests a mean P of 7.9. Thus it may be, as Guirdham (1936) reported, that depressives do tend to give a higher frequency of P, while the opposite may be true for the subject who tends to reject conformity or conventional thinking. Molish (1967) points out that neurotic subjects vary considerably in the frequency of P. He suggests, for example, that if P is low in the obvious obsessive compulsive, the possibilities of a latent schizophrenic condition need be explored. Molish indicates that most compulsive subjects will give a greater than usual number of Populars as they tend to exhaust the response possibilities.

The low P, or P failure, is of considerable importance to the interpreter. Popular answers are found to occur most frequently in the reference sample to Cards I, III, V, and VIII. Where the P is consistently absent to these cards, the interpreter must consider the possibilities of severe psychopathology or an intense form of "nonconformity." An evaluation of the P failure is often best accomplished by using the testing-of-limits technique. In some instances, especially with the very bright and possibly arrogant subject, the P is perceived but not reported because of the obvious "simplicity" of the percept. The response of, "Oh, sure I see that but I thought you wanted something more original," it not uncommon among this group. Where a low P is a reality, the interpreter should consider the aloofness from the environment, or the possibility of the inability to perceive that which others commonly report.

The appropriate interpretation of the P frequency must also give due consideration to other variables in the structure of the test. For example, a low P in the protocol of a subject manifesting a goodly number of high DQ scores, substantial organizational activity, and high $F+\%$ znd $X+\%$ is most likely the very unique, creative person who tends to shun conventionality in his response style. Where the other factors are not supportive, however, the low P may give evidence of a kind of psychopathological detachment from conventionality. Conversely, the high P may indicate an unusual tendency to conform to that which is obvious. In the rich record, the high P probably does no more than indicate that the subject gives attention to the obvious, whereas in the more limited record, the high P may represent a defensive clinging to conformity to escape revealing the more individualistic percepts.

The P must always be interpreted in terms of R, plus the Z activity and the form quality reflected in the protocol. These elements of the record are importantly interrelated. None can be interpreted adequately by itself, but the composite establishes a basic mode of understanding of the perceptual-cognitive approach to the blots which becomes critically important data for the interpretation of other test variables.

REFERENCES

Abrams, E. W. Predictions of intelligence from certain Rorschach factors. *Journal of Clinical Psychology*, 1955, **11**, 81–84.

Ames, L. B., Learned, J., Metraux, R. W., and Walker, R. N. *Rorschach Responses in Old Age*. New York: Hoeber, 1954.

Ames, L. B., Metraux, R. W., and Walker, R. N. *Adolescent Rorschach Responses*. New York: Brunner/Mazel, 1971.

Armitage, S. G., Greenberg, T. D., Pearl, D., Berger, D. G., and Daston, P. G. Predicting intelligence from the Rorschach. *Journal of Consulting Psychology*, 1955, **19**, 321–329.

Bandura, A. The Rorschach white space response and oppositional behavior. *Journal of Consulting Psychology*, 1954, **18**, 17–21.

Baughman, E. E. A comparative analysis of Rorschach forms with altered stimulus characteristics. *Journal of Projective Techniques*, 1954, **18**, 151–164.

Baughman, E. E. An experimental analysis of the relationship between stimulus structure and behavior in the Rorschach. *Journal of Projective Techniques*, 1959, **23**, 134–183.

Beck, S. J. The Rorschach Test and personality diagnosis: The feeble minded. *American Journal of Psychiatry*, 1930, **10**, 19–52.

Beck, S. J. The Rorschach Test as applied to a feeble-minded group. *Archives of Psychology*, 1932, **84**, 136.

Beck, S. J. *Rorschach's Test. II: A Variety of Personality Pictures*. New York: Grune and Stratton, 1945.

Beck, S. J. Rorschach F Plus and the Ego in treatment. *American Journal of Orthopsychiatry*, 1948, **18**, 395–401.

Beck, S. J., and Molish, H. B. *Rorschach's Test. II: A Variety of Personality Pictures*. (2nd ed.) New York: Grune and Stratton, 1967.

Becker, W. C. A genetic approach to the interpretation and evaluation of the process-reactive distinction in schizophrenia. *Journal of Abnormal and Social Psychology*, 1956, **53**, 229–236.

Berkowitz, M., and Levine, J. Rorschach scoring categories as diagnostic "signs." *Journal of Consulting Psychology*, 1953, **17**, 110–112.

Blatt, S. J., and Allison, J. Methodological considerations in Rorschach research: The *W* response as an expression of abstractive and integrated strivings. *Journal of Projective Techniques*, 1963, **27**, 269–278.

Bourguinon, E. E., and Nett, E. W. Rorschach Populars in a sample of Haitian protocols. *Journal of Projective Techniques*, 1955, **19**, 117–124.

Caldwell, B. M. The use of the Rorschach in personality research with the aged. *Journal of Gerontology*, 1954, **9**, 316–323.

Cass, W. A., and McReynolds, P. A contribution to the Rorschach norms. *Journal of Consulting Psychology*, 1951, **15**, 178–184.

Chesrow, E. J., Woiska, P. H., and Reinitz, A. H. A psychometric evaluation of aged white males. *Geriatrics*, 1949, **4**, 169–177.

Counts, R. M., and Mensh, I. N. Personality characteristics in hypnotically induced hostility. *Journal of Clinical Psychology*, 1950, **6**, 325–330.

Davidson, H. H., and Kruglov, L. Personality characteristics of the institutionalized aged. *Journal of Consulting Psychology*, 1952, **16**, 5–12.

Eichler, R. M. Experimental stress and alleged Rorschach indices of anxiety. *Journal of Abnormal and Social Psychology*, 1951, **46**, 344–355.

Exner, J. E. The influence of chromatic and achromatic color in the Rorschach. *Journal of Projective Techniques*, 1959, **23**, 418–425.

Exner, J. E. The Self Focus Sentence Completion: A study of egocentricity. *Journal of Personality Assessment*, 1973, **37**, 437–455.

Exner, J. E., and Murillo, L. G. Effectiveness of regressive ECT with process schizophrenics. *Diseases of the Nervous System*, 1973, **34**, 44–48.

Feldman, M. J., Gurrslin, C., Kaplan, M. L., and Sharlock, N. A preliminary study to develop a more discriminating F+ ratio. *Journal of Clinical Psychology*, 1954, **10**, 47–51.

Fiske, D. W., and Baughman, E. E. Relationships between Rorschach scoring categories and total number of responses. *Journal of Abnormal and Social Psychology*, 1953, **48**, 25–32.

Fonda, C. P. The nature and meaning of the Rorschach white space response. *Journal of Abnormal and Social Psychology*, 1951, **46**, 367–377.

Fonda, C. P. The white space response. In Rickers-Ovsiankina, M. (Ed.), *Rorschach Psychology*. New York: Wiley, 1960.

Frank, I. H. A genetic evaluation of perceptual structuralization in certain psychoneurotic disorders by means of the Rorschach Technique. Unpublished doctoral dissertation, Boston University, 1952.

Friedman, H. Perceptual regression in schizophrenia: An hypothesis suggested by use of the Rorschach Test. *Journal of Genetic Psychology*, 1952, **81**, 63–98.

Gibby, R. G. The stability of certain Rorschach variables under conditions of experimentally induced sets: The intellectual variables. *Journal of Projective Techniques*, 1951, **3**, 3–25.

Goldberger, L. Reactions to perceptual isolation and Rorschach manifestations of the primary process. *Journal of Projective Techniques*, 1961, **25**, 287–302.

Goldfried, M. R., Stricker, G., and Weiner, I. B. *Rorschach Handbook of Clinical and Research Applications*. Englewood Cliffs, N.J.: Prentice-Hall, 1971.

Guirdham, A. The diagnosis of depression by the Rorschach Test. *British Journal of Medical Psychology*, 1936, **16**, 130–145.

Hallowell, A. I. The Rorschach Technique in personality and culture studies. In Klopfer, B., et al. (Eds.), *Developments in the Rorschach Technique*. Vol. 2. Yonkers-on-Hudson, N.Y.: World Book Company, 1956.

Hertz, M. R. The shading response in the Rorschach inkblot test: A review of its scoring and interpretation. *Journal of General Psychology*, 1940, **23**, 123–167.

Hertz, M. R. The organization activity. In Rickers-Ovsiankina, M. (Ed.), *Rorschach Psychology*. New York: Wiley, 1960.

Holzberg, J. D., and Belmont, L. The relationship between factors on the Wechsler Bellevue and Rorschach having common psychological rationale. *Journal of Consulting Psychology*, 1952, **16**, 23–30.

Honigmann, J. J. *Culture and Ethos of Kaska Society*. Yale University Publications in Anthropology, No. 40, 1949.

Hurwitz, I. A developmental study of the relationship of motor activity and perceptual process as measured by the Rorschach Test. Unpublished doctoral dissertation, Clark University, 1954.

Joseph, A., and Murray, V. F. *Chamorros and Carolinians of Saipan: Personality Studies*. Howard University Press, 1951.

Kadinsky, D. Significance of depth psychology of apperceptive tendencies in the Rorschach Test. *Rorschachiana*, 1952, **4,** 36–37.

Kahn, M. W. Correlates of Rorschach reality adherence in the assessment of murderers who plead insanity. *Journal of Projective Techniques*, 1967, **31,** 44–47.

Kerr, M. The Rorschach Test applied to children. *British Journal of Psychology*, 1934, **25,** 170–185.

Keyes, E. J. An experimental investigation of some sources of variance in the whole response to the Rorschach inblots. *Journal of Clinical Psychology*, 1954, **10,** 155–160.

Kisker, G. W. A projective approach to personality patterns during insulin shock and metrazol convulsive therapy. *Journal of Abnormal and Social Psychology*, 1942, **37,** 120–124.

Klebanoff, S. G. The Rorschach Test in an analysis of personality in general paresis. *Journal of Personality*, 1949, **17,** 261–272.

Klopfer, B., and Kelley, D. *The Rorschach Technique*. Yonkers-on-Hudson, N.Y.: World Book Company, 1942.

Klopfer, B., Ainsworth, M., Klopfer, W., and Holt, R. *Developments in the Rorschach Technique*. Vol. 1. Yonkers-on-Hudson, N.Y.: World Book Company, 1954.

Klopfer, W. Rorschach patterns of old age. *Rorschach Research Exchange*, 1946, **10,** 145–166.

Knopf, I. J. Rorschach summary scores and differential diagnosis. *Journal of Consulting Psychology*, 1956, **20,** 99–104.

Korchin, S. J. Form perception and ego functioning. In Rickers-Ovsiankina, M. (Ed.), *Rorschach Psychology*. New York: Wiley, 1960.

Kruger, A. K. Direct and substitutive modes of tension-reduction in terms of developmental level: An experimental analysis by means of the Rorschach Test. Unpublished doctoral dissertation, Clark University, 1954.

Leighton, D., and Kluckholm, C. *Children of the People: The Navaho Individual and his Development*. Harvard University Press, 1947.

Lotsoff, E. Intelligence, verbal fluency and the Rorschach Test. *Journal of Consulting Psychology*, 1953, **17,** 21–24.

Mayman, M. Reality contact, defense effectiveness, and psychopathology in Rorschach Form-Level scores. In Klopfer, B., Meyer, M., and Brawer, F. (Eds.), *Developments in the Rorschach Technique*. Vol. 3. New York: Harcourt Brace Jovanovich, 1970.

McCandless, B. B. The Rorschach as a predictor of academic success. *Journal of Applied Psychology*, 1949, **33,** 43–50.

Misch, R. C. The relationship of motoric inhibition to developmental level and intellectual functioning: An analysis by means of the Rorschach Test. Unpublished doctoral dissertation, Clark University, 1954.

Molish, H. B. Schizophrenic reaction types in a Naval hospital population as evaluated by the Rorschach Test. Bureau of Medicine and Surgery, Navy Department, Washington, D.C., 1955.

Molish, H. B., and Beck, S. J. Further exploration of the six schizophrenias: Type S-3. *American Journal of Orthopsychiatry*, 1958, **28,** 483–505, 809–827.

Molish, H. B. Contributions of projective tests to psychological diagnosis in organic brain damage. In Beck, S. J., and Molish, H. B. (Eds.), *Reflexes to Intelligence*. Glencoe, Ill.: The Free Press, 1959.

Molish, H. B. Critique and Problems of Research. In Beck, S. J., and Molish, H. B. *Rorschach's Test. II: A Variety of Personality Pictures*. (2nd ed.) New York: Grune and Stratton, 1967.

Murillo, L. G., and Exner, J. E. The effects of regressive ECT with process schizophrenics. *American Journal of Psychiatry*, 1973, **130**, 269–273.

Murray, D. C. An investigation of the white space response in an extratensive experience balance as a measure of outwardly directed oppositions. *Journal of Projective Techniques*, 1957, **21**, 40–46.

Paulsen, A. Rorschachs of school beginners. *Rorschach Research Exchange*, 1941, **5**, 24–29.

Piotrowski, Z. Rorschach manifestations of improvement in insulin treated schizophrenics. *Psychosomatic Medicine*, 1939, **1**, 508–526.

Piotrowski, Z. *Perceptanalysis*. New York: MacMillan, 1957.

Prados, M., and Fried, E. Personality structure of the older aged groups. *Journal of Clinical Psychology*, 1943, **3**, 113–120.

Rabin, A., Papania, N., and McMichael, A. Some effects of alcohol on Rorschach performance. *Journal of Clinical Psychology*, 1954, **10**, 252–255.

Rapaport, D., Gill, M., and Schafer, R. *Psychological Diagnostic Testing*. Vol. 2. Chicago: Yearbook Publishers, 1946.

Rorschach, H. *Psychodiagnostics*. Bern: Bircher, 1921 (Transl. Hans Huber Verlag, 1942).

Rosen, E. MMPI and Rorschach correlates of the Rorschach white space response. *Journal of Clinical Psychology*, 1952, **8**, 283–288.

Saretsky, T. The effect of chlorapromazine on primary process thought manifestations. Unpublished doctoral dissertation, New York University, 1963.

Schachter, W., and Cotte, S. Prostitution and the Rorschach Test. *Archives of Neurology*, 1948, **67**, 123–138.

Schafer, R. *Psychoanalytic Interpretation in Rorschach Testing*. New York: Grune and Stratton, 1954.

Sherman, M. H. A comparison of formal and content factors in the diagnostic testing of schizophrenia. *Genetic Psychology Monographs*, 1952, **46**, 183–234.

Siegel, E. L. Genetic parallels of perceptual structuralization in paranoid schizophrenia: An analysis by means of the Rorschach Technique. *Journal of Projective Techniques*, 1953, **17**, 151–161.

Sloan, W. Mental deficiency as a symptom of personality disturbance. *American Journal of Mental Deficiency*, 1947, **52**, 31–36.

Taulbee, E. S. The use of the Rorschach Test in evaluating the intellectual levels of functioning in schizophrenia. *Journal of Projective Techniques*, 1955, **19**, 163–169.

Weiner, I. B. *Psychodiagnosis in Schizophrenia*. New York: Wiley, 1966.

Werner, H. Perceptual behavior of brain-injury mentally defective children: An experimental study by means of the Rorschach Technique. *Genetic Psychology Monographs*, 1945, **31**, 51–110.

Wilensky, H. Rorschach developmental level and social participation of chronic schizophrenics. *Journal of Projective Techniques*, 1959, **23**, 87–92.

Wishner, J. Rorschach intellectual indicators in neurotics. *American Journal of Orthopsychiatry*, 1948, **18**, 265–279.

Wittenborn, J. R. Statistical tests of certain Rorschach assumptions: The internal consistency of scoring categories. *Journal of Consulting Psychology*, 1950, **14**, 1–19.

Zamansky, H. J., and Goldman, A. E. A comparison of two methods of analyzing Rorschach data in assessing therapeutic change. *Journal of Projective Techniques*, 1960, **24**, 75–82.

Zukowsky, E. Measuring primary and secondary process thinking in schizophrenics and normals by means of the Rorschach. Unpublished doctoral dissertation, Michigan State University, 1961.

CHAPTER 12

Structural Data: Form, Form Dimension, and Movement

The determinants are generally considered as representing the "core" of the structural data. While location, organizational, and form-quality scorings illustrate some features of the perceptual-cognitive activity, the determinants specify that activity more precisely, and render a greater appreciation for the idiography of the subject. The determinants reflect the psychological action which has occurred during the formation of a response. It is frequently tempting, especially for the novice interpreter, to deal with the determinants as if each were independent from the others, such as assuming that form represents a kind of psychology which is completely different than is represented by color answers. This tendency has often been encouraged indirectly by research works which have focused exclusively on a single determinant. The reality of interpretation, however, is quite different. There is considerable overlap in the kinds of activities which are represented by the determinants, and the impact of any single activity will usually be influenced by the strength of other activities. Thus it is important to interpret determinants in the "configurational patterns" of the protocol rather than as discrete events. This procedure is described in detail in Chapter 15, but before that information can be introduced, it is necessary to review the general psychological significance of the determinants as separate classes of response. This chapter deals with three classes of determinants, which are configurationally related in that all consistently are based on the contour of the blots, but they are also related to other determinants. The interpretive postulates offered here are not "absolutes," but rather form the basis for beginning interpretation.

THE PURE FORM RESPONSE

The Pure Form answer has generally been regarded as "being created" under reasonably "affect-free" conditions or interference. This hypothesis is a derivative of Rorschach's (1921) suggestion that the Pure F is a good index of the attention-concentration features of the subject's thinking operations. Most of the systematizers have generalized from Rorschach's original postulate to describe the Pure Form answer as representing a form of affective delay or control. Rapaport (1946) goes slightly beyond this interpretation to suggest that the Pure F answer reflects a process of "formal reasoning," wherein mediation of the stimulus properties focus on the blot contours while deferring the impingements of emotional stimulation. Rapaport draws attention to the similarity between this concept and that offered by Hartmann (1939) concerning a "conflict-free-sphere" of ego functioning. Beck

(1945) and Klopfer (1954) seem considerably more conservative than Rapaport in their view of the psychologic activity associated with the Pure F answer. Both imply agreement with the notion of affect-delay, but both also emphasize that an excess of Pure F responses probably indicates some form of defense and/or constriction, neither of which would be considered "conflict-free," nor would there necessarily be an absence of affect. The Beck-Klopfer stance indicates that there may be affect and/or conflict present during the creation of the Pure F answer, but that it is somehow controlled by the more deliberate and probably conscious thought operations.

There is a variety of empirical data which lend some support to the Beck-Klopfer position concerning Pure Form. In the developmental studies of Ames et al. (1952, 1971), a relatively high proportion of Pure F responses are found in children and in adolescents. Klopfer (1956) has interpreted this as a form of rigidity, reflecting the inability of the youngster to manifest his affects without fear or reprisal. Beck (1932), Paulsen (1941), and Swift (1945) have all reported that the proportion of Pure F has a significant relation to intelligence; that is, the more retarded children give significantly lower frequencies of Pure F. Significantly lower proportions of Pure F have also been noted among epileptics (Arluck, 1940). Rabin et al. (1954) reports that the proportion of Pure F increases under intoxication but the quality of the responses decreases. Buhler, Charlotte, and LeFever (1947) report that alcoholics generally give a proportionally higher frequency of Pure F answers than do "psychopaths." Henry and Rotter (1956) found that more Pure F responses are produced by subjects who have a knowledge of the purpose of the test. Hafner (1958) reports that when subjects are instructed to respond as quickly as possible, a significantly lower proportion of Pure F answers occur. The composite of these data appear to indicate that when the subject is in the more defensive position, he is prone to increase the number of Pure Form answers that he gives. The data also suggest that when the subject is unable to promote the necessary delays required for the formulation of the Pure F answer (as in the organic or characterological style prone toward impulse display), the proportion of Pure F answers will be proportionally lowered.

These findings also gain some support from the studies of the more severe psychopathologies. Sherman (1955), for example, notes that the incidence of Pure F is relatively lower among the acute schizophrenics, a phenomenon which he interprets as experiencing much stress as well as struggling for some solution to the crisis state. Kelley, Margulies, and Barrera (1941) have reported a significant increase of the Pure F frequency after one ECT treatment. Rapaport (1946) has noted a significantly greater proportion of Pure F answers among paranoid schizophrenics than other types of schizophrenia. Goldman (1960) has found that recovering schizophrenics tend to give significantly higher proportions of Pure F than occurred prior to remission. A significantly higher Pure F is found among the 53 schizophrenics studied by Exner and Murillo (1973) at discharge than at admission. In another study completed for this work, 109 patients, approximately half of whom had been diagnosed as schizophrenic, were evaluated at admission and again 8 to 10 weeks after discharge of hospitalization. A significant increase in the proportion of Pure F is found at discharge.

The reference samples also give some credence to the notion that the Pure F answer is somehow related to the absence or delay of affect. The nonpsychiatric group gives significantly more Pure *F* than do any of the three psychiatric groups. Interestingly, the most seriously disabled group (in-patient schizophrenics) does not give a significantly different proportion of Pure *F* answers than out-patients. This finding may suggest that people in turmoil, regardless of the degree of debilitation, are prone to give greater numbers of responses which *are not* Pure Form, possibly manifesting their affective pressures more directly.

The Lambda ratio represents the proportion of Pure *F* responses in the record. It differs, as noted in Chapter 8, from the *F*% in that it reflects the proportion of Pure *F* to the proportion of non-Pure *F*. The range of Lambda for nonpsychiatric subjects extends from .33 to 3.08; however, when the mean (.74) plus or minus one standard deviation is considered, the range for the majority of protocols is .59 to .94. The range for the Lambda in the three psychiatric reference groups is also substantial, 0.5 to 2.5 for out-patients, 0 to 14.0 for in-patient nonschizophrenics, and 0 to 5.3 for schizophrenics. The plus or minus one standard deviation ranges are considerably more narrow, .22 to .78 for out-patients, .28 to .80 for nonschizophrenics, and .20 to .58 for schizophrenics. While the four groups do overlap, the psychiatric groups clearly tend to give both higher and lower proportions of *F* than do the nonpsychiatrics.

The interpretation of the Lambda datum should be approached with caution as the frequencies of the other kinds of determinants will usually provide important clarifying information. Generally, however, when the Lambda exceeds 1.0, the possibilities of affective constriction and/or guardedness must be considered. At the opposite extreme, when the Lambda falls below .50, the probability that emotion is making a significant impact on the cognitive operations is very high. As Lambda extends outward from either of these two "cut-off" points, the degree of emotional constriction or lability will be greater. It seems of interest to note that only the two in-patient groups give protocols in which there is a complete absence of Pure Form answers, and that only the in-patient nonschizophrenic group, comprised largely of depressive reactions, yields protocols which are exclusively Pure *F*. The high or low Lambda should not automatically be interpreted as an index of maladjustment or psychopathology, but rather as providing some information concerning the *style of response* to situations which have the potential to involve affect. Many "overly emotional" people can and do function very effectively by using their emotionality as an asset. Indeed, in some cultural situations they are very "socially desirable." Conversely, there are other cultural situations where the constraint of affect is the desirable phenomenon. In other words, Lambda will provide data concerning *how* the subject is prone to respond to the ambiguously stressful situation, but other elements of the test must be evaluated before the effectiveness of that sort of response can be judged.

THE FORM DIMENSIONAL RESPONSE (*FD*)

As noted in Chapter 5, the impetus for including a separate scoring for dimensional or perspective answers based exclusively on the form of the blot area came from the study of 60 protocols taken from subjects who, during a period of 90 days after testing, made a suicide attempt, 18 of which were successful. These records contained an average of 3.1 *FD* responses as contrasted with an average of 0.8 *FD* answers for the nonpsychiatric reference group. Thus, at first glance, it appeared that the *FD* response might be related to the depressive features common to the suicidal individual. This proved to be only partially correct, however, as an examination of the out-patient reference group revealed an average of 2.3*FD*'s per record. Interestingly, the schizophrenic reference group gives an average *FD* of only 0.5. These data led to the speculation that *FD* may be related to an introspective activity, the logic being that out-patients, by their therapeutic routine are encouraged to be introspective, while depressives are stimulated toward a form of introspection by their psychopathology. Three investigations were completed to evaluate this postulate. In the first, a computer sort of all of the protocols from the reference samples was accomplished using the number of *M* answers and the weighted Sum *C* as the sorting criterion. The 495 records were divided into three groups irrespective of reference group classification. The three groups are (1) Sum *M* is greater than Sum *C*, (2) Sum *M* equals Sum *C*, and (3) Sum *M* is less than Sum *C*. The rationale of this sort is that *M* is generally considered to be an internal responsiveness whereas color answers are generally conceived as a response involving affect. Logically, the introspective person should be more prone to "internalization" and less prone to affect display. The middle group (Sum M = Sum *C*) was discarded and the remaining two groups compared for mean *FD* answers using a *t* test. Where the Sum *M* exceeded Sum *C* (N = 187), the mean *FD* was 2.42, while the mean for the group in which Sum *C* exceeded Sum *M* (N = 206) was 0.93, the groups being significantly different at the .01 level. This finding supports the notion that the *FD* response is related to internalization and seems consistent with the data concerning *F* answers; that is, some element of "delay" is involved. The question concerning introspectiveness, *per se*, however, remained unanswered.

The second study was designed to evaluate introspectiveness as related to the *FD* response. Forty subjects were taken from a "waiting list" of a psychiatric facility and randomly assigned, 10 each to four different groups. They were informed that while waiting for the assignment of individual therapists they would be included in "holding" groups through which they might be able to initiate their treatment plans and goals. Each group met for 2 hours per week with the same group therapist who had agreed to conduct the sessions, but who had no knowledge of the Rorschach study. Three raters were trained to observe each of the four groups and to score each of the verbalizations of the subjects on a two-dimensional grid used to designate whether the verbalization was directed toward the "self" or others, and whether it pertained to the present, past, or future. It was assumed that the more introspective subjects would focus more on the self than others, and that the verbalizations would be more concerned with the present than with the past or future. Rorschachs were administered to all subjects, during a period of 10 days prior to the first group meetings, by four examiners who were naive to the purpose of the study. Verbalizations were scored for the first three group sessions. The 40 subjects were divided into two groups based on a median split of the numbers of *FD* answers for purposes of data analysis. The mean *FD* for the upper half was 2.83, and for the lower half 1.34. The upper half gave significantly more "self" verbalizations during the first three sessions than did the lower half, but there were no differences between the two groups for focus on the present versus past or future. It was noted, however, that the upper group gave more verbalizations centering on the past plus the present than did the lower half. In other words, subjects giving the greater frequency of *FD* answers tended to focus more on themselves in the context of the past and present than did those giving fewer *FD* answers. This finding appears to support the postulate that *FD* responses are somehow related to an introspective framework, although also raising the question regarding whether the self-oriented responses were simply a manifestation of egocentricity or were a manifestation of self-examination. The issue was evaluated using the scoring patterns of these subjects taken from the Self Focus Sentence Completion (Exner, 1973), which seems to provide useful information concerning egocentricity. This test had also been administered with the Rorschach prior to the formation of the groups. The data from the SFSC indicates that the upper *FD* group is slightly more oriented toward the external world than the lower *FD* group, which would appear to rule out the possibility that the "self" verbalizations in the group were simply manifestations of egocentricity.

The third investigation used a test–retest procedure with 15 nonpsychotic patients as subjects. Five males and 10 females were administered the Rorschach at the onset of individual psychotherapy with one of five therapists. They showed a mean *FD* of 2.06 with a range of 0 to 4. It was hypothesized that, if introspection is related to *FD*, the mean should increase during the early stages of treatment as a function of being "trained" to self-examination. The Rorschach was administered a second time after the 10th treatment session. The mean *FD* for the group in the second administration was 3.11 with the range also increasing to 1 to 6. The Rorschach was administered a third time to these subjects at the termination of psychotherapy. The timing of the third administration varied considerably among subjects. Three subjects terminated after 40 to 45 sessions (approximately 7 months), eight subjects terminated after 65 to 80 sessions (approximately 11 months), and four subjects terminated after more than 100 sessions (13 months or longer). The mean *FD* for the group at the third administration was 1.24 which is significantly lower than for the second administration, but not statistically different from the first administration. The range of *FD* scores in the third administration is 0 to 3, which is also similar to that noted in the first administration. These data seem to offer additional support for the proposition that *FD* is related to a psychological activity involving self-inspection or examination, or at least self-awareness.

If the *FD* is also interpreted as a type of Form response, it seems logical to assume that the affect-delay operations noted in the Pure *F* answers are also applicable to the *FD* activity. In other words, the self-examination may be a form of coping with affective urges, a process which delays the discharge of affect through a type of reasoning which centers of the self, its assets, and liabilities. The impact and/or effectiveness of this operation cannot be judged by a study of the *FD* answers alone. Rather, it is probably best understood in the context of all coping activities plus the manifestations of the affects.

THE HUMAN MOVEMENT RESPONSE (*M*)

The *M* response has probably been the subject of more investigation than any other Rorschach determinant. Rorschach offered the postulate that *M* represents an "internalization" phenomenon. His notion of introversiveness implies that *M* somehow manifests the more deliberate inner experience in a manner which is also affectively adaptive. Beck (1945, 1967) has used this Rorschach postulate as the nucleus of his own position. Beck regards M answers as indicating an awareness of the external world, wherein the vestiture of energy is used to develop a private fantasy through which a displacement of pent-up needs is permitted. Beck also identifies M as reflecting emotions which are in some way concealed from an overt display. Klopfer (1954) and Hertz (1951) have both suggested that M should be interpreted as a psychological process in which a functional relationship exists between the fantasy life of the individual and his external orientations to reality and object relationships. Thus Beck, Klopfer, and Hertz all tend to agree that M does represent some form of internalization, although neither Beck or Hertz would necessarily agree that M is a manifestation of the kind of introversiveness described by Jung, a position taken by Klopfer. Rapaport (1946) admits to only a partial acceptance of Rorschach's stance on M. He rejects the notion of introversion as such, but agrees with Beck that M does represent a readiness to make a response. Rapaport maintains that in some instances, this readiness will result in internalization, but in other instances, the product will be an overt gesture. For Rapaport, the M answer is much more indicative of a type of delay of response than a tendency toward internalization, the delay being provoked by the more sophisticated cognitive functions so as to permit a more consciously determined response to occur. In other words, M reflects a resistance to spontaneous behavior, the result of which may be either internalization or externalization. Piotrowski's position concerning M responses differs most significantly from Rorschach, and from the other systematizers. As early as 1937 he adopted the position that the correlation between M and overt behavior is positive: "The M indicates prototypal roles in life, i.e., definite tendencies, deeply embedded in the subject and not easily modified, to assume repeatedly the same attitude or attitudes in dealing with others when matters felt to be important and personal are involved." While Piotrowki's position is different from the other systematizers, it is not completely different. These is at least a segment of agreement between Klopfer, Hertz, and Piotrowski in that all regard M as bridging the inner resources with the external reality. The Piotrowski and Rapaport positions on M are also not completely different in that both concede, Rapaport directly and Piotrowski indirectly, that M may represent an internalization action by the subject. Both also agree that the type of internal reasoning manifest in the M response is a form of inhibition to impulse, which may be transient.

There are many problems in the researching of M, several of which have often been neglected by investigators. The most primary of these is that the category of M includes several different kinds of responses. For example, M's occurring to tiny areas appear to be different from M's occurring to W or D areas in the type of psychological activity involved. Similarly, M's including only one human figure are probably different in psychological activity than M's involving more than one human figure. The M's involving aggressive content are somewhat different than M's which convey a sense of cooperativeness, and so on. Nevertheless, the large quantity of research which has been completed concerning M does generally "knit" together so as to establish some understanding of the basic psychological process involved in the formation of the M answer.

It is quite well established that M has a direct relationship to intellectual operations. Numerous studies (Paulsen, 1941; Abrams, 1955; Altus, 1958; Somer, 1958; Tanaka, 1958; Ogdon and Allee, 1959) have demonstrated a positive correlation between I.Q., or some other direct measure of intelligence, and the frequency and/or quality of M responses. Schulman (1953) reports that M is positively correlated with abstract thinking and has demonstrated that the activity involved in both functions requires some delaying operations. Levine, Glass, and Meltzoff (1959) have also demonstrated that M and the higher levels of intellectual operation require delaying activities. Ames (1971) reports that the frequency of M is very low in the young child, and that a steady increase in M frequency occurs to about the 10th year. Ames (1960) has also reported that the frequency of M tends to decline in the elderly. Kallstedt (1952) found significantly less M in the protocols of adolescents than in those of adults. Ames implies this in her 1971 norms for adolescents.

The M has frequently been identified as an index of creativity, however, the empirical findings on this issue are somewhat equivocal. The different criteria that have been used for creativity appear to have clouded the problem considerably (Dana, 1968). Hersh (1962) has found a significant relationship between M and artistic talent. Richter and Winter (1966) report a positive relation between "intuition and perception" scores and M. Dudek (1968) has found that subjects giving a large number of M's show greater ease in expressing themselves "creatively" in TAT stories and Lowenfield Mosaic Designs. By most other criteria, however, M and creativity appear unrelated.

The results of work concerning M and fantasy have been much more definitive. Page (1957) reports a direct relationship between M and daydreaming. Loveland and Singer (1959), Palmer (1963), and Lerner (1966) have noted that increased M is related to sleep and/or dream deprivation. Orlinsky (1966) has also shown a significant relation between M and dream recall and total dream time. Dana (1968) has also demonstrated a positive relation between M and fantasy. He suggests that M answers can represent any/or all of six different psychologic actions, including fantasy, time sense, intellect, creativeness, delay, and some aspects of interpersonal relations. Cocking, Dana, and Dana (1969) report findings which appear to confirm the relationship between M and fantasy, time estimation, and intellect.

The relationship between M and motor inhibition has been the subject of numerous investigations, essentially because Rorschach postulated the occurrence of kinesthetic activity when M answers are formed. Singer, Meltzoff, and Goldman (1952) found that M increased after subjects were instructed to "freeze" in awkward positions. Similarly, an increased M has been noted after an enforced period of delay (Singer and Herman, 1954; Singer and Spohn, 1954). Bendick and Klopfer (1964) report a significant increase in both M and FM answers under conditions of motor inhibition, and significant increases in M, FM, and m under conditions of experimentally induced sensory deprivation. In an earlier work, Klein and Schlesinger (1951) presented data to suggest that a relationship may exist between motor inhibition and a variety of Rorschach responses, including movement answers. In a similar context, Steele and Kahn (1969) failed to find significant increases in muscle potential with the production of movement answers. They did note, however, a tendency of subjects who produced many M's to show increases in muscle potential. Possibly of greater interest is the fact that increases in muscle potential were noted accompanying almost all aggressive content answers, regardless of whether movement was involved. Motor expression has also been noted as precipitating an increase in the frequency of movement answers by Cooper and Caston (1970). They used two sets of Holtzman Ink Blots given before and after a 5 minute period of physical exercise. They suggest that their findings give support to

Piotrowski's concept of M. In general, the issue of kinesthetic activity in movement answers is, at best, only an indirect approach to the study of the psychological activity associated with their formulation, and the contribution of these works to the interpretation of M answers is still an open issue. Possibly, studies concerning the relationship between M and the delay of behavior have a more direct relevance to the interpretation of this kind of response.

Frankle (1953) and Mirin (1955) have both demonstrated that subjects who produce greater numbers of M tend to longer motor delays in their social adjustments. Bieri and Blacher (1956) have found that mean reaction times to the blots are significantly longer for subjects giving more M than Color responses. Levine and Spivack (1962) report a significant correlation between the productivity of M and an independent index of repression. Earlier, Hertzman, Orlansky, and Seitz (1944) noted that high M producers showed a greater tolerance for anorexia due to simulated high altitude conditions (18,500 feet), than did subjects giving low frequencies of M.

Some of the important data concerning the interpretation of M are derived from studies of various psychopathological groups. Guirdham (1936) noted that depressives tend to give lower frequencies of M. That finding is consistent with the mean frequency of M found in the nonschizophrenic in-patient reference sample which is significantly lower than any of the other three reference groups. In fact, when only protocols of depressive subjects are drawn from the in-patient nonschizophrenic sample ($N = 48$), the mean M is altered from 2.1 for the total group to 1.6 for only the depressives. Schmidt and Fonda (1954) report a high occurrence of M among manic patients. Gibby et al. (1955) found that hallucinatory patients give significantly more M than do delusional nonhallucinatory patients. Thomas (1955) offers similar findings. King (1960) has shown that paranoid schizophrenics who have interpersonal delusions produce significantly more M than do paranoid schizophrenics with somatic delusions.

When the form quality of M is poor, the likelihood of psychopathology appears to be high. This has been noted by Phillips and Smith (1953) in their study of 1500 records, and has also been found by Beck (1965) and Molish (1965). Weiner (1966) suggests that that the $M-$ type answer is probably related to deficient social skills and poor interpersonal relationships. He tends to agree with Phillips and Smith that any notable frequency of poor form quality M's is probably indicative of psychosis. The data from the reference samples seem to support this contention. Minus form quality M's occurred in only 6 of the 200 nonpsychiatric protocols, while appearing in 18 of the 100 out-patient records, 17 of the 70 non-schizophrenic records, and 48 of the 125 schizophrenic records. Brain-injured subjects have been found to give very few M's (Piotrowski, 1937, 1940; Evans and Marmorston, 1964). The presence of good quality M's has been regarded as a positive prognostic indicator, especially for the seriously disturbed patients. This factor is weighted heavily in both the Rorschach Prognostic Rating Scale (Klopfer, Kirkner, Wisham, and Baker, 1951) and the Piotrowski Prognostic Index (Piotrowski and Bricklin, 1958, 1961). Rees and Jones (1951), and Lipton, Tamerin, and Lotesta (1951) report good quality M's significantly differentiate schizophrenics who respond to somatic treatments. Piotrowski (1939), Halpern (1940), and Stotsky (1952) have all reported significant increases in the frequency of M among patients who show improvement versus those who are unimproved. A study of the admission and postdischarge

Rorschachs of 71 schizophrenics followed in a relapse study, completed for this work, does not reveal a significant increase in *M* frequency although the quality of the *M*'s is significantly greater. However, when the protocols of the 19 subjects who relapsed during the first year after discharge were compared with those of the 52 nonrelapsers, the latter group is noted to have given significantly more *M*'s in both their admission and postdischarge records.

Any attempt to summarize the full psychological meaning of *M* responses will probably fall short of describing the extremely complex activities which must be involved. Clearly, *M* has an intellectual base which includes a sort of reasoning, the components of imagination, and a form of higher level conceptualization. It is a form of delay from yielding to the more spontaneous impulses or responses, which depends on an active kind of ideation. It is an inner experience which appears to be "deliberate," and which manifests fantasies that are related to the external world. The fantasies, or inner experiences, apparently play an important role in formulating the response solution selected for a given stimulus constellation. Response tendencies may be thwarted and/or displaced into a continuing ideational activity, or they may be externalized, either directly or indirectly in behaviors which are interpersonally related. The *M* does not appear to be a "conscious" process, but rather a form of cautious defensiveness through which the world, and potential responses to it, are "sorted through."

The *M* cannot be interpreted very accurately without also giving consideration to the components of the response itself, or without also reviewing other variables of the test, especially the responsiveness to color. Rorschach, of course, recognized this in his differentiation of *M*'s into the flexion-extension categories, and the development of the Erlebnistypus (*EB*), representing the ratio of Sum *M* to weighted Sum *C*. The Erlebnistypus is discussed in more detail in Chapter 15, however, it is important to note here that the ratio of *M* to weighted *C* offers a considerably more precise index of the "tendencies to respond" than does an evaluation of *M* by itself. In a similar context, *M*'s occurring to an *Hd* content are generally regarded as much less adaptive or effective than are *M*'s occurring with *H* content. The role of *M* in the psychological activity of the subject is also better understood when the number and kinds of *M* are evaluated in relation to other kinds of movement answers in the protocol, and when the active-passive dimension, for which all movement responses are scored, is evaluated. These data provide an index concerning the extensiveness of the more sophisticated fantasy operations as manifest in *M*, as contrasted with the less sophisticated sorts of thought as represented in the other kind of movement answers, and provide information concerning the *style* of ideation involved. This understanding of the thinking operations forms a nucleus of information from which data regarding other aspects of the psychological activity, such as affects, cognitive approach, and reality operations, can be better understood.

THE ANIMAL MOVEMENT RESPONSE (*FM*)

As noted in Chapter 5, the scoring of *FM* for animals in animal-like movement is common only to the Klopfer, Hertz, and Piotrowski approaches to the Rorschach. Rorschach himself assumed that these types of answers did not involve kinesthesis, and therefore should not be included in a dimension seemingly related to M. Beck and Rapaport have followed that orientation, although Rapaport did take issue with Rorschach's notion that kinesthesis must somehow be involved in the formulation of the M answer. Logic, and the literature, however, argue in favor of the FM scoring. It is a discrete kind of response, different than either F or M answers.

The basic interpretation of FM offered by the three systematizers using it is that it represents a more "primitive" operation than is reflected in the M answer. It is purported to manifest a sense of urgency, in which the subject becomes psychologically aware of impulses striving for a more immediate gratification. Thus, unlike M, it is an operation less oriented to delay. Klopfer and Hertz both emphasize that FM may not be directly correlated with "immediate" discharge of impulse, and suggest instead that the ultimate responsiveness to these urges will be dependent on the total configuration of the personality. Piotrowski believes that FM may be related to subcortically controlled patterns of action. He describes the meaningfulness of this kind of response more positive than either Klopfer or Hertz, suggesting that it reflects something of the "vitality" of the person which is manifesting less well developed patterns of thought. All three of the systematizers agree that when the frequency of FM is substantially greater than the frequency of M, the probabilities of overt expression of impulses are higher than when the reverse is true. Thus a preponderance of FM may represent the individual who is more accustomed to being "ruled" by needs for immediate gain than by longer term goals.

The literature concerning FM generally tends to support these interpretive postulates. Ames (1971) finds a greater frequency of FM than M in the records of children. Klopfer (1956) reports that the same is true for the aged subject, while Meli-Dworetzki (1956) indicates that the records of adult subjects generally show more M than FM. The reference samples collected for the comprehensive system show that the mean frequency of M consistently exceeds FM for all four groups, although in none of the four is the mean M *significantly* greater than the mean FM. Some support for the concept that FM may represent a less sophisticated operation than M is found in the work of Warshaw et al. (1954) who noted a significant increase in FM answers under sodium amytal. Similarly, Piotrowski and Abrahamsen (1952) report that subjects who give more FM's tend to be much more aggressive in diminished states of consciousness, as under the influence of alcohol. Goldman and Herman (1961) report that FM answers increase significantly in frequency under conditions of physical immobilization. Thompson (1948) reports that FM is significantly correlated to MMPI measures of irresponsibility, aggressiveness, and distractability. Sommer and Sommer (1958) found that a significant correlation exists between aggressive FM answers and assaultiveness. Altus (1958) notes that college students scoring high on the MMPI Schizophrenia Scale give significantly more FM than do students scoring low on that scale. The FM answers also seem to be related to defensiveness. Haan (1964) reports a very interesting design in which 86 subjects were studied for defensiveness and coping features. She found that where the frequency of FM exceeds the frequency of M, a significantly high correlation exists with several measures of defensiveness, specifically, intellectualization, rationalization, regression, and substitution. Haan suggests that FM may represent either an overt behavioral expression of impulse, as in substitution, or an internalization behavior, oriented toward containment of the impulse, as in intellectualization, rationalization, or regression.

Piotrowski and Schreiber (1952) report that the quality of the *FM*'s tend to change during treatment, generally becoming more assertive and less passive, and that these changes correspond to behavioral changes in which the successfully treated subjects demonstrate more "vitality and liveliness" in their actions. Berryman (1961) reports that *FM* is related to the level of "productivity" in creative artists. Exner, Murillo, and Cannavo (1973) followed 105 nonschizophrenics for a 12 month period after hospitalization. Rorschachs were collected on all at the time of discharge. Twenty-four of these patients relapsed during the first year out. A review of the Rorschachs taken at discharge shows that 17 of the 24 relapsers gave more *FM* than *M* while only nine of the 81 nonrelapsers had more *FM* than *M* in their records. Other Rorschach variables, such as the *Erlebnistypus*, the *X+*, the frequency of *a/p* answers, the proportion of pair and reflection answers, and the proportion of shading answers also differentiate the two groups, making it difficult, if not impossible, to specify the role which the *FM* kind of activity may have played in contributing to the ultimate relapse. It is interesting to note, however, that most of the relapses appear related to interpersonal difficulties in the immediate family, and the preponderance of *FM* over *M* may indicate more limitations in being able to delay responsiveness in these stress situations.

THE INANIMATE MOVEMENT RESPONSE (*m*)

The scoring for *m* has also been used in only three of the Rorschach systems, Klopfer, Hertz, and Piotrowski, although the criterion for the use of the scoring differs among them. Klopfer (1954) has generally interpreted *m* as an index of forces or impulses which are beyond the control of the subject, thereby posing a threat to the overall stability and organization of the personality. Piotrowski (1957, 1960) and Hertz (1943) do not interpret *m* as threatening as does Klopfer, although they do agree that thoughts or drives not well integrated into the cognitive framework are reflected in these kinds of answers. They suggest that *m* answers represent a "wished-for" life role which the person feels is beyond him. All three of these systematizers indicate that *m* is probably associated with the experience of frustration, especially with regard to interpersonal activities.

The Rorschach literature is relatively sparse concerning *m*. Ames (1971) finds that it occurs very infrequently during the first 10 years, increasing in frequency during adolescence to an average of about 1*m* per record by the age of 16. The four reference samples collected for use with the comprehensive system reveal that outpatients and in-patient schizophrenics average slightly more than 1*m* per record while nonpsychiatric subjects average slightly less than 1*m* per record. Obviously, when *m* occurs in significant frequency, it should be regarded as a warning sign which may represent the impingement of excessive tension, frustration, and/or hostility on the personality integration. McArthur and King (1954) have found that the combination of high frequency *m* plus a preponderance of color responses differentiates unsuccessful college students, while Majumber and Roy (1962) report that *m* answers occur with significantly greater frequencies in the records of juvenile delinquents. Neel (1960), using different models of motoric and "idea" inhibition, found that *m* increases significantly as compared with controls. She interprets her findings as indicative of tension and conflict created by the inability to integrate needs with behavior. Piotrowski and Schreiber (1952) report that *m* answers "tend to disappear" in the posttreatment protocols of successfully treated patients. Shalit (1965) administered the Rorschach twice to 20 male subjects at intervals of about one year. The first testing was part of a selection routine used by the Israeli Navy while the second testing was done on board ship during severe storm conditions. Shalit reports that the frequencies of *M* and *FM* answers remained essentially unchanged; however, the frequency of *m* increased significantly. Shalit interprets this change as a function of the stressful conditions under which the second test was administered, postulating that the increased *m* activity reflects the sense of disruption and disintegrating forces at work.

It would appear that the kind of psychological activity associated with *m* has a more direct relation to *FM* than to *M*. Where *M* is a more deliberate inner experience related to the mediation of stimulus inputs, both *FM* and *m* represent considerably less sophisticated and less well organized activities. Both imply a sense of urgency in response to stressful conditions and both appear to *act on* the individual as a form of stimulation, whereas *M* appears to *act for* the individual as a form of responsiveness. While *FM* seems related to internal strivings, that is, the desire for a prompt gratification of basic needs, *m* appears more directly related to the interaction of the subject and his world. In this framework, the postulates of both Klopfer and Piotrowski concerning *m* seem correct, as the *m* activity does operate as an irritating force which is disequilibrating. This force apparently reflects the tension and discomfort experienced by the inability to attain a stabilizing relationship with the environment, and logically, if carried to excess, can be disruptive and disorganizing to the overall response patterns of the individual. In this context, the *FM* and *m* actions can be significantly useful to the individual by stimulating goal oriented behaviors. Naturally, the other elements of the personality will be extremely influential in determining whether the goal oriented behaviors will take a socially acceptable or desirable pattern, as in the "dynamic" businessman or the highly competitive athlete, or whether a more asocial or antisocial routine will evolve. For instance, if the level of affect is high, and the various forms of control and/or delay are low, there is a substantial probability that a more "spontaneous" pattern of behavior will be the picture. Thus to understand the effects of the composite force illustrated in the *FM* plus *m* answers, other elements, such as the frequency of *M*, the Sum *C*, the frequency of *P* and *S*, the distribution of *DQ* scores, and the levels of perceptual accuracy as represented by the $F+\%$ and $X+\%$ must be carefully evaluated. The active-passive dimension of the movement answers also takes on much importance in understanding the behavioral avenues which may be most "preferred" in response to this psychological action.

THE ACTIVE–PASSIVE DIMENSION OF MOVEMENT ANSWERS (*a*/*p*)

The use of the active–passive scoring for all movement answers is somewhat different than that suggested by Rorschach. He described the *M* answers as being marked by "flexion" or "extension," using the center axis of the blot area being used as the focal point from which these judgements of *M* would be made. Thus *M*'s which demonstrate an "inward effect" in the movement are flexor, while movements which indicate a "pulling away" from the center axis are extensor. Rorschach hypothesized that extensor M's generally represent "assertiveness," while flexor M's represent "submissiveness and/or compliance." The literature on the flexor–extensor M's is quite limited, but important to the decision to use the a/p scoring. Hammer and Jacks (1955), studying imprisoned sex offenders, report that extensor M's are significantly related to the more aggressive offenses, such as rape, while the flexor M's are prominent in the protocols of the offenders involved in the more passive activities, such as exhibitionism. Mirin (1955) found that schizophrenics giving predominantly extensor M's were resistive to contradictions in a memory task, while schizophrenics giving flexor M's were more willing to give in, to the contradictions. Wetherhorn (1956), using a series of special plates designed to evoke M answers, reports no relationship between the extensor–flexor responses and measures of ascendency–submissiveness, or masculinity–femininity. Both Beck (1961) and Piotrowski (1960) have warned about the limitations of approaching M interpretation simply on the basis of Rorschach's extensor–flexor concept. Beck has pointed out that some M's are "static" and therefore, cannot be judged by Rorschach's criterion. Piotrowski reports two studies in which the features of the M's were evaluated by other criteria. In the first, he evaluated 115 United States Army prisoners who had at least one M in their protocols. He judged the M as favorable if it was "free of restraint, in which two figures cooperated freely," or "unfavorable" if it contained only one figure or was characterized by "inhibition, doubt or inconsistency when two or more figures appeared in it." He then followed these subjects after they were paroled to determine the effectiveness of their conduct. Fifty-seven of the 69 subjects giving no "unfavorable" M's showed "good parole conduct," while 32 of the 46 subjects giving at least one unfavorable M showed "poor parole conduct." In the second study, Piotrowski evaluated the Rorschachs of 50 successful and unsuccessful business executives. He found that the successful group tended to give M's which were "self-assertive and confident postures," demonstrated cooperation, and/or manifest friendly, nonhostile interpersonal relationships. Conversely, the unsuccessful group gave significantly more M's characterized as blocked, or in circular movement, passively giving into the force of gravity, or manifesting hostility.

The Beck caution concerning the static M's, plus the Piotrowski findings, based on classifications of M's different than the Rorschach flexor–extensor evaluations, encouraged further investigation to determine if a scoring format could be developed to further differentiate M responses in an interpretively meaningful way. Four studies were completed concerning this question. The first focused on the flexor–extensor dimension. All M answers contained in the 835 protocols in the protocol pool were evaluated for the flexor–extensor qualities. The records were then subdivided into a variety of groupings, such as in-patient versus out-patient, patient versus nonpatient, schizophrenic versus nonschizophrenic, male versus female, and age groupings. The flexor–extensor scoring failed to differentiate any of the groupings at a significant level, although an obvious trend was noted in the protocols of subjects over age 60 ($N = 31$) to give predominantly flexor M's. A definite problem, as Beck had cautioned, was the fact that nearly 25% of the M's could not be scored as flexor or extensor, but even when these "static" M's were arbitrarily included into the frequencies as flexor types, no significant differentiations were found. Subsequently, all of the M's were rescored for three features derived from Piotrowski's findings. They are (1) active–passive, (2) hostile–nonhostile, and (3) cooperative–noncooperative. In addition, all FM's were scored for active–passive features and hostile–nonhostile characteristics, and all m's were scored as active or passive. The new scoring yielded more definitive results. First, when only the scorings of the M answers were analyzed, no differentiations occurred; however, when the hostility scorings for the M's and FM's were combined, two groups show a significantly higher mean score than any of the others. These two groups are (1) first admission reactive (acute) schizophrenics ($N = 47$), and (2) a general grouping of forensic cases which includes both psychotic and non-psychotic subjects ($N = 31$). Second, and more important, when the active–passive scorings were studied for *all* movement responses, the same differentiations occurred, plus two others. Passive scores occurred significantly more for neurotic out-patients, and a group of depressive in-patients, and active scores occurred significantly more for a grouping of out-patient "character disturbances." Several tentative conclusions were drawn from these results. First, it appeared as though any attempt to formally score flexor–extensor M's would not contribute to the Structural Summary of the record. Second, any scoring format restricted exclusively to the M responses could not be justified easily, if at all. Third, although the hostility scorings for M and FM did provide some differentiations, the active–passive scorings probably tended to score the same characteristic, and since the active–passive scorings offered the greatest differentiation, they should be the target of additional investigation.

The second study constituted a replication of the earlier work with the protocol pool, but using the records collected for the reference samples. While the N for this sample (495) is somewhat smaller than the protocol pool (835), all were collected using the methodology of the comprehensive system and more data were generally available on these subjects than those in the protocol pool. Thus all movement answers were scored as either active or passive, and the data were analyzed by the four basic groupings of nonpsychiatric, out-patients, in-patient nonschizophrenics, and in-patient schizophrenics. The only significant differentiation found was that in-patient nonschizophrenics give significantly more passive movement answers; however, when the three psychiatric groups were subdivided by diagnostic classification, and compared only to each other, the differentiations become clearer. Reactive (acute) schizophrenics, in-patient characterological disorders, and patients with a history of assaultiveness (regardless of diagnosis) give significantly greater numbers of active movements. Process (chronic) schizophrenics and depressives give significantly more passive movement answers. Interestingly, while these psychiatric subgroups can be differentiated from each other, only the depressives, giving high frequencies of passive movements, are significantly different from the nonpsychiatric group. This finding stimulated a reevaluation of the data, using a d score obtained by subtracting the number of passive movements from the number of active movements. This procedure yielded very interesting results, which offer some clarification to the manner in which the $FM + m$ activities effect the individual.

First, the nonpsychiatric subjects tend to show d scores of 3 or less. This is found in 138 of the 200 nonpsychiatric subjects. Conversely, psychiatric subjects tend to reveal d scores of 3 or more. This is found in 190 of the 295 psychiatric subjects (69%). While the d of 3 overlaps the groups considerably, the results warranted a closer examination of these differences. Instead of using an algebraically derived d, a proportional d was employed, representing the percentage constituted by the greater of the two scores, a or p. In other words, if the number of active movements equals 6 and the number of passive movements equals 2 (75 and 25%, respectively), the difference between the two is 50%, or stated somewhat differently, the active movements exceed the passive movements by 50%. Applying this *percentage d* score to the protocols of the nonpsychiatric group reveals that 132 of the 200 subjects have an $a/p\ d\%$ which is less than 50%. This same procedure applied to the records of the psychiatric groups shows that 207 of the 295 subjects have an $a/p\ d\%$ which is at the 50% level or greater. Thus while the majority of nonpsychiatric subjects tends to show a "mix" of a/p answers, the majority of psychiatric subjects tend to show a distinct preference for either the active or passive movement, but generally not the "balanced mix" found in the nonpsychiatric group.

The findings were then used as a guideline to examine whether the consistency of preferring either the active or passive kind of movement crossed all movement answers, or whether the less preferred kind of movement occurred to a specific type of answer, that is, all M's, FM's or m's. Protocols showing a $d\%$ of 50% or more were studied. This sample includes 207 psychiatric records and 68 nonpsychiatric records. Slightly more than half of the psychiatric records, 105, show the less preferred kind of movement occurring *exclusively* to either the M answers or the $FM + m$ combination. A similar pattern was noted in 24 of the 68 nonpsychiatric protocols. A very small number of the records, six psychiatric and two nonpsychiatric, showed the less preferred kind of movement occurring exclusively to m; however, in 21 psychiatric records and five nonpsychiatric records, the less preferred kind of answer occurred either to $M + m$, or exclusively to the FM answers.

These data appear to suggest that a definitive *style* of "inner experience" is common to people experiencing adjustment difficulties which is manifest by a preference for a given kind of ideation in response to stress experiences. Furthermore, it would appear that the preference or style of response is either common to all ideational activities, as in the instance of all movements taking on the same general a/p characteristics, or is discrete to a specific pattern of activity, such as all M answers or all $FM + m$ answers. The nonpatient is more generally characterized as showing a flexibility or balanced mix in his ideation activities, suggesting greater elasticity is his cognitive responsiveness to needs, fantasies, and stress situations. An evaluation of this hypothesis was accomplished using the pre- and posttreatment protocols of 38 adolescents followed in a study of egocentricity (Exner, 1973). All were between the ages of 15 and 17, and were entering treatment, for "behavioral problems." A variety of tests, including the Rorschach, were administered at the onset of intervention, and again at termination. Evaluation of treatment effects was accomplished using the Katz Adjustment Scales (Katz and Lyerly, 1963) which were completed prior to intervention, and again 4 to 6 weeks after termination by a close relative and a teacher who had frequent contact with the subject. After the posttreatment evaluation, the group was subdivided into two groups, "improved" and "unimproved," and compared. Data concerning the a/p characteristics of the movements responses in the Rorschach are shown in Table 24. It will be noted from examination of Table 24 that both groups give about the same number of movements answers in each of the testings, and the proportion of S's showing a 50% or greater $d\%$ is substantial for both groups at the first testing. The posttreatment patterns are quite different. The improved group contains significantly fewer records in which the movement answers are in the same direction while the unimproved group shows little change. The improved group shows only about 30% of the rec-

Table 24.   Proportional Differences of a/p Answers in the Pre- and Posttreatment Protocols of Two Groups of Adolescents

	Improved (N = 24)		Unimproved (N = 14)	
	Pre-	Post-	Pre-	Post-
Mean number movement R's	6.3	7.1	6.6	6.8
a/p Exclusively in one direction	13	3	7	6
a/p $d\%$ equals 50% or more	20	7	12	10

ords (7) with an a/p $d\%$ of 50% or more, while about 70% of the records in the unimproved group show this high $d\%$. In other words, the majority of subjects rated as behaviorally improved, by relative and teacher ratings, manifest a more balanced distribution of a/p movement answers than do those whose behaviors are not rated as improved. These data appear to lend support to the postulate that the a/p distribution may represent an index of flexibility of ideational coping activities.

A second study concerning the postulate that the a/p proportions may reflect an index of flexibility in ideational style was completed using two groups of female subjects. One group consisted of 17 women entering psychotherapy for psychosomatic complaints. The second group consisted of 17 women, with no psychiatric history, who were being medically treated for fractures and/or serious lacerations. The average age for each group is about 30, and approximately two-thirds of each group are married. Rorschachs were administered 10 to 15 days after the onset of treatment, and all subjects were paid, for 25 days thereafter, to create two "diaries." The first, designated as a "behavioral" diary, was a reconstruction of "important" behavioral events which had occurred for a period of 6 months prior to treatment. The second was an "imposed daydream" diary, which represented the *deliberate* 10 minute per day daydreams of the subjects. Each subject was instructed to select a relatively constant time period each day during which she would deliberately daydream for approximately 10 minutes, after which she would record the daydream in the diary. No instructions were given concerning repetitive or continuing daydreams. A practice daydream session was completed and recorded prior to the "paid" period. It had been anticipated that the psychosomatic group would give Rorschach movement answers tending to show a/p $d\%$'s at the 50% or greater levels and that the medical subjects would show a/p $d\%$'s consistently lower than the 50% level. These trends did occur, but the groups could not be statistically differentiated. Fourteen of the psychosomatics gave a/p $d\%$'s at 50% or greater, as did nine of the 17 medical subjects. Thus two arbitrary groups were created based on the movement a/p $d\%$, and disregarding psychiatric involvement. Using this method of differentiation, 23 subjects fall into the a/p "disproportionate" group ($d\%$ = 50% or more), and 14 subjects are in the "proportionate" group ($d\%$ = less than 50%). The daydreams were scored by one of three psychometrists using the activity of the central figure of the daydream as the guideline. Thus the daydream would be scored as "active," "passive," or marked by a shift from active to passive or *vice versa*. If a shift occurred, the last activity of the daydream (a/p) would be scored as the characteristic of the daydream so as to be able to have only one a/p score for each of the 25 daydreams. If more than one shift occurred in a daydream, only one scoring of shift was recorded. In that the number of daydreams scored for each subject is a constant (25), a simple difference score, derived by subtracting the passive scores from the active scores for each subject was obtained. t tests were then calculated for the mean difference scores for each of the groups, and for the mean number of shifts per group. These data are shown in Table 25 and reveal that the subjects giving the majority of Rorschach movement answers in a single direction also tend to give the majority of daydream scores in a single direction, and have relatively few shifts in the activity of the central figure in the daydreams. The opposite is true for subjects having Rorschach $d\%$'s lower than the 50% level. They tend to give daydreams which have an almost equal mix of active and passive characteristics for the central figure and show shifts from one kind of characteristic to the other in a substantial number of the daydreams.

Table 25.   Mean Difference Scores and Shift Scores for Daydreams of Two Groups of Female Subjects

Group	Mean Daydream d Scores	Mean Daydream Shifts
Rorschach $a/p\ d\%$ = 50% or more (N = 23)	11.3	3.4
Rorschach $a/p\ d\%$ = less than 50% (N = 14)	4.1[a]	10.3[a]

[a] Significantly different from higher $d\%$ group at .01.

It would be impractical to suggest that a high Rorschach $a/p\ d\%$ is always indicative of maladjustment, for that is obviously not the case. It does seem true, however, that the high $d\%$ is some index of consistency of ideation, which may represent a form of cognitive constriction, that can make effective adjustment patterns a more difficult achievement because of the lack of flexibility in coping behaviors.

A SUMMARY CONCERNING MOVEMENT ANSWERS

Any overview of the psychologic meaning of the various types of movement answers must focus mainly on the "coping" characteristics which seem to be illustrated in this array of responses. The M answers appear to involve a more sophisticated inner experience, marked by organization and reasoning, whereas the FM and m activities are less well organized and probably less controlled than M. The M answers provide a glimpse of the ideational style which develops with cognitive maturation, while the FM and m responses represent a more "primative" inner response pattern which often functions to precipitate behaviors as well as thoughts. Each of these three types of inner activity serve to defend and reorient the individual in situations of disequilibration. When these inner experiences can take on either an "active" or "passive" character, a dimension of *coping flexibility* is added to the behavioral patterns which are possible. Conversely, when the ideational characteristics are predominantly active or passive, this flexibility is diminished, and the possible patterns for defensive behavior are reduced in number and scope.

The constellation of movement responses offers the interpreter some insights concerning the specifics of ideation as related to needs. The product of that ideation, however, cannot be gleaned from a study of the movement answers alone. Quite the contrary, information concerning the manifestations of affect, especially as derived from an evaluation of the color and shading answers, becomes critical in determining the manner in which the ideation is experienced, and the consequences thereafter.

REFERENCES

Abrams, E. N. Prediction of intelligence from certain Rorschach factors. *Journal of Clinical Psychology*, 1955, **11**, 81–83.

Altus, W. D. Group Rorschach and Q-L discrepancies on the ACE. *Psychological Reports*, 1958, **4**, 469.

Ames, L. B., Learned, J., Metraux, R., and Walker, R. N. *Child Rorschach Responses*. New York: Hoeber-Harper, 1952.

Ames, L. B. Constancy of content in Rorschach responses. *Journal of Genetic Psychology*, 1960, **96**, 145–164.

Ames, L. B., Metraux, R. W., and Walker, R. N. *Adolescent Rorschach Responses*. New York: Brunner/Mazel, 1971.

Arluck, E. W. A study of some personality differences between epileptics and normals. *Rorschach Research Exchange*, 1940, **4**, 154–156.

Beck, S. J. The Rorschach test as applied to a feeble-minded group. *Archives of Psychology*, 1932, **84**, No. 136.

Beck, S. J. *Rorschach's Test. II: A Variety of Personality Pictures*. New York: Grune and Stratton, 1945.

Beck, S. J., Beck, A., Levitt, E. E., and Molish, H. B. *Rorschach's Test. I: Basic Processes*. (3rd ed.) New York: Grune and Stratton, 1961.

Beck, S. J. *Psychological Processes in the Schizophrenic Adaptation*. New York: Grune and Stratton, 1965.

Beck, S. J., and Molish, H. B. *Rorschach's Test. II: A Variety of Personality Pictures*. (2nd ed.) New York: Grune and Stratton, 1967.

Bendick, M. R., and Klopfer, W. G. The effects of sensory deprivation and motor inhibition on Rorschach movement responses. *Journal of Projective Techniques*, 1964, **28**, 261–264.

Berryman, E. Poets' responses to the Rorschach. *Journal of General Psychology*, 1961, **64**, 349–358.

Buhler, C., and Lefever, D. W. A Rorschach study on the psychological characteristics of alcoholics. *Quarterly Journal of Studies of Alcohol*, 1947, **8**, 197–260.

Beri, J., and Blacher, E. External and internal stimulus factors in Rorschach performance. *Journal of Consulting Psychology*, 1956, **20**, 1–7.

Cocking, R. R., Dana, J. M., and Dana, R. H. Six constructs to define Rorschach M: A response. *Journal of Projective Techniques and Personality Assessment*, 1969, **33**, 322–323.

Cooper, L., and Caston, J. Physical activity and increases in M response. *Journal of Projective Techniques and Personality Assessment*, 1970, **34**, 295–301.

Dana, R. H. Six constructs to define Rorschach M. *Journal of Projective Techniques and Personality Assessment*, 1968, **32**, 138–145.

Dudek, S. Z. M an active energy system correlating Rorschach M with ease of creative expression. *Journal of Projective Techniques and Personality Assessment*, 1968, **32**, 453–461.

Evans, R. B., and Marmorston, J. Rorschach signs of brain damage in cerebral thrombosis. *Perceptual Motor Skills*, 1964, **18**, 977–988.

Exner, J. E. The Self Focus Sentence Completion: A Study of Egocentricity. *Journal of Personality Assessment*, 1973, **37**, 437–455.

Exner, J. E., and Murillo, L. G. Effectiveness of regressive ECT with process schizophrenics. *Diseases of the Nervous System*, 1973, **34**, 44–48.

Exner, J. E., Murillo, L. G., and Cannavo, F. Disagreement between ex-patient and relative behavioral reports as related to relapse in non-schizophrenic patients. Eastern Psychological Association, 1973, Washington, D.C.

Frankle, A. H. Rorschach human movement and human content responses as indices of the adequacy of interpersonal relationships of social work students. Unpublished doctoral dissertation, University of Chicago, 1953.

Gibby, R. G., Stotsky, B. A., Harrington, R. L., and Thomas, R. W. Rorschach determinant shift among hallucinatory and delusional patients. *Journal of Consulting Psychology*, 1955, **19**, 44–46.

Goldman, R. Changes in Rorschach performance and clinical improvement in schizophrenia. *Journal of Consulting Psychology*, 1960, **24**, 403–407.

Goldman, A. E., and Herman, J. L. Studies in vicariousness: The effect of immobilization on Rorschach movement responses. *Journal of Projective Techniques*, 1961, **25**, 164–165.

Guirdham, A. The diagnosis of depression by the Rorschach Test. *British Journal of Medical Psychology*, 1936, **16**, 130–145.

Hafner, A. J. Response time and Rorschach behavior. *Journal of Clinical Psychology*, 1958, **14**, 154–155.

Haan, N. An investigation of the relationships of Rorschach scores, patterns and behaviors to coping and defense mechanisms. *Journal of Projective Techniques and Personality Assessment*, 1964, **28**, 429–441.

Halpern, F. Rorschach interpretation of the personality structure of schizophrenics who benefit from insulin therapy. *Psychiatric Quarterly*, 1940, **14**, 826–833.

Hammer, E. F., and Jacks, I. A study of Rorschach flexor and extensor human movement responses. *Journal of Clinical Psychology*, 1955, **11**, 63–67.

Hartmann, H. *Ego Psychology and the Problem of Adaptation.* New York: International Universities Press, 1939.

Henry, E. M., and Rotter, J. B. Situational influences on Rorschach responses. *Journal of Consulting Psychology*, 1956, **20**, 457–462.

Hersh, C. The cognitive functioning of the creative person: A developmental analysis. *Journal of Projective Techniques*, 1962, **26**, 193–200.

Hertz, M. R. Personality patterns in adolescence as portrayed by the Rorschach ink-blot method: IV The "Erlebnistypus." *Journal of General Psychology*, 1943, **29**, 3–45.

Hertz, M. R. Current problems in Rorschach theory and technique. *Journal of Projective Techniques*, 1951, **15**, 307–338.

Hertzman, M., Orlansky, D., and Seitz, C. P. Personality organization and anoxia tolerance. *Psychosomatic Medicine*, 1944, **6**, 317–331.

Kallstedt, F. E. A Rorschach study of sixty-six adolescents. *Journal of Clinical Psychology*, 1952, **8**, 129–132.

Katz, M., and Lyerly, S. Methods of measuring adjustment and social behavior in the community. *Psychological Reports*, 1963, **13**, 503–535.

Kelley, D., Margulies, H., and Barrera, S. The stability of the Rorschach method as demonstrated in electric convulsive therapy cases. *Rorschach Research Exchange*, 1941, **5**, 44–48.

King, G. F. Rorschach human movement and delusional content. *Journal of Projective Techniques*, 1960, **24**, 161–163.

Klein, G. S., and Schlesinger, H. G. Perceptual attitudes toward instability: Prediction of apparent movement experiences from Rorschach responses. *Journal of Personality*, 1951, **19**, 289–302.

Klopfer, B., Ainsworth, M. D., Klopfer, W. G., and Holt, R. R. *Developments in the Rorschach Technique. 1: Theory and Technique.* Yonker-on-Hudson, N.Y.: World Book Company, 1954.

Klopfer, B., et al. *Developments in the Rorschach Technique. II: Fields of Application.* Yonkers-on-Hudson, N.Y.: World Book Company, 1956.

Klopfer, B., Kirkner, F., Wisham, W., and Baker, G. Rorschach prognostic rating scale. *Journal of Projective Techniques*, 1951, **15**, 425–428.

Levine, M., and Spivack, G. Human movement responses and verbal expression in the Rorschach Test. *Journal of Projective Techniques*, 1962, **26**, 299–304.

Levine, M., Spivack, G., and Wight, B. The inhibition process, Rorschach movement responses and intelligence: Some further data. *Journal of Consulting Psychology*, 1959, **23**, 306–312.

Lerner, B. Rorschach movement and dreams: A validation study using drug-induced deprivation. *Journal of Abnormal Psychology*, 1966, **71**, 75–87.

Lipton, M. B., Tamarin, S., and Latesta, P. Test evidence of personality change and prognosis by means of the Rorschach and Wechsler-Bellevue tests on 17 insulin treated paranoid schizophrenics. *Psychiatric Quarterly*, 1951, **25**, 434–444.

Loveland, N. T., and Singer, M. T. Projective test assessment of the effects of sleep deprivation. *Journal of Projective Techniques*, 1959, **23**, 323–334.

Majumber, A. K., and Roy, A. B. Latent personality content of juvenile delinquents. *Journal of Psychological Research*, 1962, **1**, 4–8.

McArthur, C. C., and King, S. Rorschach configurations associated with college achievement. *Journal of Educational Psychology*, 1954, **45**, 492–498.

Meili-Dworetzki, G. The development of perception in the Rorschach. In Klopfer, B., et al. (Eds.), *Developments in the Rorschach Technique. II: Fields of Application.* Yonkers-on-Hudson, N.Y.: World Book Company, 1956.

Mirin, B. The Rorschach human movement response and role taking behavior. *Journal of Nervous and Mental Disorders*, 1955, **122**, 270–275.

Molish, H. B. Psychological structure in four groups of children. In Beck, S. J. (Ed.), *Psychological Processes in the Schizophrenic Adaptation.* New York: Grune and Stratton, 1965.

Murillo, L. G., and Exner, J. E. The effects of regressive ECT with process schizophrenics. *American Journal of Psychiatry*, 1973, **130**, 269–273.

Neel, F. A. Inhibition and perception of movement on the Rorschach. *Journal of Consulting Psychology*, 1960, **24**, 224–229.

Ogdon, D. P., and Allee, R. Rorschach relationships with intelligence among familial mental defectives. *American Journal of Mental Deficiency*, 1959, **63**, 889–896.

Orlinski, D. E. Rorschach test correlates of dreaming and dream recall. *Journal of Projective Techniques and Personality Assessment*, 1966, **30**, 250–253.

Page, H. A. Studies in fantasy-daydreaming frequency and Rorschach scoring categories. *Journal of Consulting Psychology*, 1957, **21**, 111–114.

Palmer, J. O. Alterations in Rorschach's experience balance under conditions of food and sleep deprivation: A construct validation study. *Journal of Projective Techniques*, 1963, **27**, 208–213.

Paulsen, A. Rorschachs of school beginners. *Rorschach Research Exchange*, 1941, **5**, 24–29.

Phillips, L., and Smith, J. G. *Rorschach Interpretation: Advanced Technique*. New York: Grune and Stratton, 1953.

Piotrowski, Z. The Rorschach ink-blot method in organic disturbances of the central nervous system. *Journal of Nervous and Mental Disorders*, 1937, **86**, 525–537.

Piotrowski, Z. Rorschach manifestations of improvement in insulin treated schizophrenics. *Psychosomatic Medicine*, 1939, **1**, 508–526.

Piotrowski, Z. Positive and negative Rorschach organic reactions. *Rorschach Research Exchange*, 1940, **4**, 147–151.

Piotrowski, Z. *Perceptanalysis*. New York: MacMillan, 1957.

Piotrowski, Z. The movement score. In Rickers-Ovsiankina, M. (Ed.), *Rorschach Psychology*. New York: Wiley, 1960.

Piotrowski, Z., and Abrahamsen, D. Sexual crime, alcohol, and the Rorschach Test. *Psychiatric Quarterly Supplement*, 1952, **26**, 248–260.

Piotrowski, Z., and Bricklin, B. A long-term prognostic criterion for schizophrenics based on Rorschach data. *Psychiatric Quarterly Supplement*, 1958, **32**, 315–329.

Piotrowski, Z., and Bricklin, B. A second validation of a long-term Rorschach prognostic index for schizophrenic patients. *Journal of Consulting Psychology*, 1961, **25**, 123–128.

Piotrowski, Z., and Schreiber, M. Rorschach perceptanalytic measurement of personality changes during and after intensive psychoanalytically oriented psychotherapy. In Bychowski, G., and Despert, J. L. (Eds.), *Specialized Techniques in Psychotherapy*. New York: Basic Books, 1952.

Rabin, A., Papania, N., and McMichael, A. Some effects of alcohol on Rorschach performance. *Journal of Clinical Psychology*, 1954, **10**, 252–255.

Rapaport, D., Gill, M., and Schafer, R. *Psychological Diagnostic Testing*. Vol. 2. Chicago: Yearbook Publishers, 1946.

Rees, W. L., and Jones, A. M. An evaluation of the Rorschach Test as a prognostic aid in the treatment of schizophrenics by insulin coma therapy, electronarcosis, electroconvulsive therapy, and leucotomy. *Journal of Mental Science*, 1951, **97**, 681–689.

Richter, R. H., and Winter, W. D. Holtzman ink-blot correlates of creative potential. *Journal of Projective Techniques and Personality Assessment*, 1966, **30**, 62–67.

Rorschach, H. *Psychodiagnostics*. Bern: Bircher, 1921 (Transl. Hans Huber Verlag, 1942).

Schmidt, H., and Fonda, C. Rorschach scores in the manic states. *Journal of Psychology*, 1954, **38**, 427–437.

Schulman, I. The relation between perception of movement on the Rorschach Test and levels of conceptualization. Unpublished doctoral dissertation, New York University, 1953.

Shalit, B. Effects of environmental stimulation on the M, FM, and m responses in the Rorschach. *Journal of Projective Techniques and Personality Assessment*, 1965, **29**, 228–231.

Sherman, M. H. A psychoanalytic definition of Rorschach determinants. *Psychoanalysis*, 1955, **3**, 68–76.

Singer, J. L., and Herman, J. Motor and fantasy correlates of Rorschach human movement responses. *Journal of Consulting Psychology*, 1954, **16**, 325–331.

Singer, J. L., and Spohn, H. E. Some behavioral correlates of Rorschach's experience type. *Journal of Consulting Psychology*, 1954, **18**, 1–9.

Singer, J. L., Meltzoff, J., and Goldman, G. D. Rorschach movement responses following motor inhibition and hyperactivity. *Journal of Consulting Psychology*, 1952, **16**, 359–364.

Sommer, R., and Sommer, D. Assaultiveness and two types of Rorschach color responses. *Journal of Consulting Psychology*, 1958, **22**, 57–62.

Steele, N. M., and Kahn, M. W. Kinesthesis and the Rorschach M response. *Journal of Projective Techniques and Personality Assessment*, 1969, **33**, 5–10.

Stotsky, B. A. A comparison of remitting and nonremitting schizophrenics on psychological tests. *Journal of Abnormal and Social Psychology*, 1952, **47**, 489–496.

Swift, J. W. Rorschach responses of eighty-two pre-school children. *Rorschach Research Exchange*, 1945, **7**, 74–84.

Tanaka, F. Rorschach movement responses in relation to intelligence. *Japanese Journal of Educational Psychology*, 1958, **6**, 85–91.

Thomas, H. F. The relationship of movement responses on the Rorschach Test to the defense mechanism of projection. *Journal of Abnormal and Social Psychology*, 1955, **50**, 41–44.

Thompson, G. M. MMPI correlates of movement responses on the Rorschach. *American Psychologist*, 1938, **3**, 348–349.

Warshaw, L., Leiser, R., Izner, S. M., and Sterne, S. B. The clinical significance and theory of sodium amytal Rorschach Testing. *Journal of Projective Techniques*, 1954, **18**, 248–251.

Weiner, I. B. *Psychodiagnosis in Schizophrenia*. New York: Wiley, 1966.

Wetherhorn, M. Flexor-extensor movement on the Rorschach. *Journal of Consulting Psychology*, 1956, **20**, 204.

CHAPTER 13

Structural Data: Color, Shading, Reflection, and Pairs

It has been noted in the preceding chapter that Form, Form Dimension, and Movement answers are primarily contingent on the contours of the blot or blot areas selected. This may also be true when color or shading features are involved in the answers, but the importance of the contour may vary from primary, as in the instance of *FC* or *FY* answers, to the point of being disregarded, as in the Pure *C* or Pure *Y* responses. In other words, answers which use either color or shading features of the blots represent a different organization of stimulus inputs than do those which are void of color or shading characteristics. Similarly, the formation of reflection and/or pair answers is not based simply on blot contours. Quite the contrary, these kinds of responses appear to depend on a cognitive recognition and responsiveness to the *symmetry* of the blot features, regardless of the form characteristics involved. The potentials for extensive variation in the use of form in color, shading, reflection, and pair responses make for an interesting challenge to the subject in the mental "cogwheeling" which takes place as the response is created. He may ignore the "formless" blot features, that is, color, shading, and symmetry, as in the instance of the Pure *F* answers; he may integrate his own ideation with the contours, as in the movement answers; or he may yield to the "formless" stimuli, and attempt to integrate them with the contour features. When the latter occurs, the effectiveness of the cognitive delays is usually indicated by the extent to which the form features maintain a dominant versus secondary role. When form is relegated to the secondary role, as in *CF* or *TF* answers, the subject is responding to the more ambiguous stimulus features of the blot, and in doing so, alters some of his coping tactics, and a more direct manifestation of his inner experience occurs. Conversely, when the form features are primary in the response, the inner experience is subject to greater mediation and control.

Obviously, the interpretation of any determinants which may include a composite of form plus other blot features must include special concern for the influence of the form. While some useful information can be derived by a simple review of the frequency by which any class of determinant occurs, that is, how many color or shading answers are in the record, a more meaningful understanding of the inner activities of the person is derived through examination of the frequencies for each of the types of response within a determinant class.

COLOR RESPONSES (*C, CF, FC, Cn*)

Rorschach (1921) proposed that responses involving the chromatic colors of the blots relate directly to affect. He argued that color answers represent an index of

277

emotional excitability *or lability*, and thus the extent to which the use of color is avoided or controlled reflects the "degree of stabilization" of affective urges. In this context, the *FC* response illustrates the process of affective adaptability, whereas the *CF* answers manifest affectivity which has little or no capability for adaptiveness, and Pure *C* responses are a product of the impulsive, labile discharge with no regard for adaptiveness. Rorschach emphasized that while the *CF* and *C* responses represent little or no adaptiveness, they are, nevertheless, important kinds of affective displays relating to the interaction between the subject and his world. He perceived this kind of affect as being involved in sensitivity, irritability, suggestiveness, empathy, and such, pointing out that the proportion of *FC* to *CF* + *C* would be the best index to evaluate the extent of control, or lack thereof, present in the affective state of the subject.

All of the Rorschach systematizers have incorporated Rorschach's color-affect hypothesis and suggest expected *FC*:*CF* + *C* ratios which vary from 3:1 to 4:1. This is generally consistent with the data for the nonpsychiatric reference group which reveals a ratio of approximately 3:1. Interestingly, the nonpsychiatric group is the only one of the four reference samples in which the mean *FC* exceeds the mean *CF* + *C* + *Cn*. The ratio for the out-patients is approximately 1:1.5, for the nonschizophrenics about 1:1, and for the schizophrenics about 1:2. This would seem compatible with Rorschach's notion that maladjusments are generally characterized by failures in affective adaptability.

The rationale for color answers has been considered somewhat extensively, and the color-affect hypothesis has been the subject of frequent disagreement. One of the earliest works on the rationale of the color answer was that of Schachtel (1943), who argued that the perception of color requires minimal activity by the subject and defines the color answers as a *passive process*. Concurrently, Rickers-Ovsiankina (1943) reviewed a significant number of research works concerning the perceptual process and concluded that color perception is a more immediate process than form perception, requiring less cognitive activity in the mediation of the stimulus input. Rapaport (1946) suggests that the response to color is essentially *affective*, and that the Pure *C* and *CF* answers represent "short-circuits" of the delaying functions. Shapiro (1956, 1960) reviews a variety of clinical and experimental literature in defining a "mode of perception" associated with the color experience. He agrees with Schachtel and Rickers-Ovsiankina that the color response involves a perceptual passivity, in which the more complex cognitive functions necessary for affective delay are temporarily relaxed. This relaxation permits the affective discharge, the impact of which will be proportional to the degree of relaxation. Piotrowski (1957) takes a slightly different view, suggesting that the *FC* answers involve considerable complexity of cognitive activity, in which both delay and affective need are weighed. He agrees that *CF* and Pure *C* types of responses represent situations in which the cognitive elements have been overly relaxed, or possibly overwhelmed by the affective state.

Much of the controversy concerning the color-affect hypothesis has centered on the concept of "color-shock," a concept introduced by Rorschach and defined as a startle reaction to the color figures. Extensive listings of indices of color-shock were developed between 1932 and 1950 which include elements such as longer reaction times, disruption of sequence, *P* failure, increase in weak form quality, increase in color dominated answers, and reduction in *R*. Numerous studies appear in the literature which have attempted to validate items in the various listings, but most have been unsuccessful. Keehn (1953) reviewed many of these studies and concluded that few, if any, of the signs were actually precipitated by the color features of the blots. Similarly, Siipola (1950), Barnett (1950), Canter (1951), York (1951), Swartz (1953), and Hamlin (1955) have all offered evidence challenging the validity of the color-shock hypothesis. Crumpton (1956) has noted that color shock signs occur as frequently to an experimentally created achromatic Rorschach series as to the standard cards. It is somewhat unfortunate that the substantial research energy which has been devoted to studies on color-shock has also been interpreted as a testing of the color-affect theory. While color-shock, as such, remains a confusing and complex issue, the impact of color itself, as a stimulant, seems less in doubt. Klatskin (1952) reports that content which involves both color and texture is more susceptible to stress than any other Rorschach variable. Brody has found that "neurotics" are more disturbed and disorganized by the color cards. Wallen (1948) notes that the "affective quality" of color has a facilitating effect on associations. Grayson (1956) has reported that the composite of color and form rather than color alone influences productivity. Crumpton (1956) has found that color cards tend to elicit more undesirable affect and more aggressive and passive contents than do achromatic cards. Forsyth (1959) reports that the color cards facilitate an anxiety score. Exner (1959) has found that both *R* and content scores are altered significantly when Card I is presented in a variety of chromatic colors as contrasted with the standard grey-black version. One of the most frequently cited studies, generally used to support arguments against the color-affect hypothesis, is that of Baugman (1959). He used eight groups of subjects, administering one the standard Rorschach series, a second an achromatic series, a third the standard Rorschach series with a modified inquiry, and the remaining five groups each one set of modified Rorschach cards. Although the Baughman analysis of data was quite thorough, he neglected a specific comparison of the standard and achromatic Rorschach groups for *R* to the chromatically colored cards (II, III, VIII, IX, and X). A review of his data suggest that the group responding to the standard series gave nearly 200 more answers than did those responding to the achromatic series, the majority of which were to Cards II, III, VIII, IX, and X.

Another controversial approach to the color-affect hypothesis is shown in studies concerning the proportional number of answers to Cards VIII, IX, and X of the test. Both Klopfer (1942) and Beck (1961) have postulated that the number of responses to the last three cards, as contrasted with the *R* to the remaining cards, gives some index of the "affective" responsiveness to one's world. Even though they have disagreed on the method for calculating this proportion (Klopfer using the 8-9-10%, and Beck using the Affective Ratio), they have agreed on this basic principle. When the proportion of *R* to Cards VIII, IX, and X is high, the subject is regarded as affectively responsive, and conversely, when the proportion is low, the subject is viewed as affectively guarded and/or withdrawn from affective stimulation. Several studies have investigated this postulate but have generally reported negative findings (Sapenfield and Buker, 1949; Dubrovner et al., 1950; Allen et al., 1951; Perlman, 1951; and Meyer, 1951). Unfortunately, most of these works are marked by flaws in experimental design, such as either using a group administration technique, or a test–retest method. Exner (1962) used a matched groups design, administering one group the standard Rorschach series and the second group an achromatic version.

The results clearly demonstrate that the colored cards of the standard series stimulate a greater productivity to each of the three cards. Reaction times were also generally longer to the standard chromatic series than to the achromatic versions. While these data lend no direct support to either the color-affect, or 8-9-10% hypotheses, they do indicate that color, as a stimulus, has a substantial impact on the formulation of answers.

The literature on developmental studies of the Rorschach appears to lend indirect support to the color-affect hypothesis. Several investigators (Halpern, 1940; Klopfer and Margolies, 1941; Ford, 1946; Rabin and Beck, 1950; and Ames, 1952, 1972) report that the Pure C response is predominant in very young children. Ford also notes that color naming is very common is this age group. Ames has found that CF becomes the predominant color answer after the second year and remains so through the 16th year, although a gradual increase in FC responses is noted with growth.

There are a number of studies on behavioral correlates of color responses, or their absence. Brennan (1943) reports that subjects giving a higher Sum C are more easily hypnotized, suggesting that the susceptibility to color is related to suggestibility. Similarly, both Steisel (1952) and Linton (1954) have noted that subjects with a higher Sum C are more likely to alter their judgments in accordance with the suggestions of a "confederate" examiner. Mann (1956) has found a significant relationship between the number of words related to the environment on a free association task and the Sum C. Gill (1967) reports that subjects who can delay responses in a problem solving task give significantly more FC answers, while those who cannot exercise delay give significantly more CF and Pure C answers. Several works also demonstrate the relationship between color answers and impulsive or aggressive behaviors. Gardner (1951) obtained significant correlations between Rorschach color scores and ratings of impulsiveness. Storment and Finney (1953) compared matched groups of assaultive and nonassaultive patients and found that poor quality color answers differentiated the groups. Finney (1955) used a similar design with assaultives and nonassaultives and found significantly higher CF and Sum C frequencies in the assaultive group. Sommer and Sommer (1958) report that the composite of Sum C and a high frequency of $FM + m$ answers differentiates assaultive from nonassaultive patients. Townsend (1967) finds that the presence of CF and the absence of M is significantly related to ratings of aggressiveness in adolescents. Fortier (1953) and Pruyser and Folsom (1955) report that the records of epileptics are notably void of color answers. Significantly fewer color answers are also found in the protocols of depressed patients (Fisher, 1951; Kobler and Steil, 1953; Costello, 1958).

The ratio of FC to $CF + C$ appears to change as a function of treatment. Stotsky (1952) reported that treatment "success" was achieved more frequently with schizophrenics whose pretreatment records were marked by fewer CF and C answers than with those whose records showed the reverse to be true. Examination of the pre- and posttreatment protocols of 105 nonschizophrenics studied by Exner, Murillo, and Cannavo (1973) indicates that the posttreatment records show a significant alteration in Sum C and in the $FC:CF + C$ ratio. Patients who had been diagnosed as a "depressive" disorder increased the Sum C at discharge, while the $FC:CF + C$ ratio showed a tendency to change from approximately 1:1 to 2:1. Patients who had been diagnosed as "characterological" disorders tended to maintain essentially the same Sum C, but the FC:CF + C ratio was distinctly altered from 1:2 to 2:1. Similarly, the records of 53 schizophrenics taken at posttreatment show a significant change in both Sum C (lower) and the FC:CF + C ratio which altered from 1:3 to 2:1 (Exner and Murillo, 1973).

The literature on color naming is quite sparse. Piotrowski (1937) considered it as one of the basic signs for organic involvement. Weigl (1941), Goldstein and Sheerer (1941), and Schilder (1953) have demonstrated that brain damaged subjects do tend to show an increase in color interest and have a "stimulus bound" characteristic in their color perception. Kral and Dorken (1950) found that color responses are rare among patients with diencephalic lesions. Shapiro (1960) considers color naming to be indicative of the concrete response to the sensory input which is not well conceptualized.

A SUMMARY CONCERNING COLOR ANSWERS

Color, as a stimulus property, is probably more ambiguous than contours. People respond to color, often without being aware of that responsiveness. In the Rorschach color answers may be delayed and organized, as in the instance of the FC response, or they may be more emotionally "rampant," as is the case with the CF, C, and Cn types of answers. The responses in which color dominates manifest a looseness or excessive relaxation of cognitive control, wherein the mental activity of the subject is overwhelmed and, at least temporarily, controlled by emotion. Color answers are not, however, related to all affects. They tend to disappear in depression, an obviously painful affect state. Thus color answers seem to be more related to responses which may be *external*, or externally related. Responses to color may be illustrated in ways other than articulation of color. For example, the Affective Ratio may be inordinately high but the protocol may show a relatively small number of color answers. In these circumstances, the affective output may still be high, but the concealment of it may be extensive. When the frequency of CF, C, or Cn responses approaches, or is greater than the frequency of FC answers, the potential for labile behaviors is great. Conversely, when the record is marked by an absence of CF or C answers, the question of excessive control must surely be raised. Nonpsychiatric subjects generally produce about 3 FC answers for each CF or Pure C response, although Pure C answers are extremely unusual in this group. Any attempt to interpret color answers without a careful review of other determinants will meet with little success. An evaluation of the movement answers is especially important to an understanding of the affect manifest in color answers.

ACHROMATIC COLOR RESPONSES (C', C'F, FC')

As noted in Chapter 5, Klopfer (1938) was the first to specifically provide a separate scoring for responses in which the white-grey-black features are used as color. Rapaport adopted the same scoring in his approach to the test, and Hertz and Piotrowski adopted different scoring symbols for the same purpose. Klopfer postulated that the C' type response illustrates some form of "toned-down" affective experience in which a "hesitancy" occurs regarding the more direct expression of affect. He suggested that, when the composite of C' types of answers plus texture determined responses exceeds the total frequency of color responses, the responsiveness to external stimuli has been "interferred with by some kind of traumatic experience, resulting in withdrawal." He also hypothesized that the C' response could take on a "euphoric" character, especially when space is used as white color, and if the protocol is marked by a substantial number of color answers. Rapaport (1946) has suggested that the C' answer represents some form of "conscious control or defense" against affective expression. In a broad sense, it is an anxious or cautious form of adaptation wherein the cognitive elements thwart affective expression. Piotrowski (1957) generally agrees with both Klopfer and Rapaport, although he emphasizes that the element of euphoria may be present when the responses are to the white or light grey areas of the blots. He cites the findings of Weber (1937) who noted a significant frequency of the use of white and grey, as color, among alcoholics. All three of these systematizers suggest that the C' response may be some index of depressive feelings, especially when the grey-black features of the blots are used.

The C' answer has been among those least studied in the literature. In part, this has been caused by a tendency to include these responses under the rubrics of "shading" or "light-dark" responses, and by the fact that investigators using a Beck scoring methodology have included these answers in the scoring of Y or its variations. Klopfer and Spiegelman (1956) report on a single case of a severely depressed male who gave only five responses to the test. Two of these answers were of the C' variety, leading them to conclude that the C' answer is related to depressive features. This postulate is not confirmed, however, if the suicide literature is used as a base. Studies on "single signs," which are related to suicide attempts, have focused mainly on the use of chromatic color and shading as a blend determinant (Applebaum and Holtzman, 1962; Applebaum, 1963; Applebaum and Colson, 1968; Colson and Hurwitz, 1973). The Colson and Hurwitz study is of special importance here as they created a series of stimuli designed to evoke a greater number of shading answers than is ordinarily the case from the Rorschach plates. They found that the color-shading answers did occur more significantly among patients who had attempted suicide than among controls. They also noted that this difference *did not* occur for responses to achromatic color. Similarly, a variety of studies—using a configuration of signs to predict suicide (Beck 1946; Rabin, 1946; Hertz, 1949; Martin, 1951; Sakheim, 1955; Daston and Sakheim, 1960; Neuringer, 1965; Cutter, Jorgensen, and Farberow, 1968) offers little information concerning the C' response. Most of these studies have followed a Beck scoring so that any C' answers would be subsumed in the Y scoring. A reasonably consistent finding, however, is that the relative absence of "shading" scores and a preponderance of chromatic color scores are more likely associated with suicidal acts. While these investigations appear to dispel the notion of a direct relationship between C' responses and depression, or at least the kind of affective state associated with suicide, the question remains open concerning a possible relationship between C' responses and "contained" affect.

The reference samples show an interesting distribution of C' responses, with only the nonpsychiatric group yielding an average of less than one per record (0.6). Out-patients average 1.3 C' answers per record, schizophrenics 1.2 per record, and nonschizophrenics give a mean of 1.6 per record. The latter group is of particular interest in that about 70% of that sample is comprised of patients diagnosed as "depressive" reactions, leading to the speculation that *C'* may indeed be related to a form of affective constraint. Two investigations were completed to evaluate this proposition. In the first, 64 protocols were collected at the onset of intervention from patients diagnosed as a form of affective disturbance (reactive depression, neurotic depression, involutional reaction, depressive psychosis), none of whom had any history of suicidal attempt. Sixteen of these patients made suicidal gestures within 55 days of the testing (only two of which were successful). The protocols of the attempters were compared with those of the nonattempters for a variety of Rorschach variables, including the frequency of *C'* answers. The mean *C'* score for the attempters is 0.7 and for the nonattempters is 1.8. A comparison of the number of protocols in which *C'* answers occurred is more striking. Thirty-four of the 48 records of nonattempters contain at least one *C'* type response (71%), while only five of the 16 records obtained from attempters (31%) show *C'* answers. Although these samples are very small, the findings do support a speculation that nonattempters do "contain" affect more, possibly contributing to the agony of depression, whereas attempters are more prone to "act-out" the affect, even though in a self-destructive manner. Some of the other findings of this investigation, which lend support to this postulate, are that attempters give more Sum *C* and *CF* answers, have fewer pair responses, and give more *FM* and *m* responses. In other words, the attempters apparently experience greater internal pressure, are more negative, and have less affective control.

The second study was designed to evaluate contained affect on a broader pathological spectrum. The protocols of 21 psychosomatics, 11 obsessive-compulsives, and 10 "schizoids" were used to create a "Constrained Affect" group, while the records of 29 "psychopaths" and 13 passive-aggressive subjects were used as a group of "Unconstrained Affect." A third group of 42 control subjects was drawn from the nonpsychiatric reference sample. Data concerning the *C'* types of responses in these three groups are shown in Table 26.

If it is true that the composite group of psychosomatics, obsessive-compulsives, and schizoids does represent types of subjects who ordinarily constrain affect, the data presented in Table 26 appear to support the conclusion that the *C'* type of response is related to that phenomenon. There were, of course, other differences

Table 26. Frequencies of *C'* Type Responses in Three Groups of Subjects

	Constrained Affect (N = 42)	Unconstrained Affect (N = 42)	Control (N = 42)
Total *R*	787	999	891
Number of *FC'* answers	34[a]	13	20
Number of *C'F* answers	7	1	2
Number of *C'* answers	3	0	0
Total *FC'* + *C'F* + *C'*	45[a]	14	22
Number of Protocols in which at least 1 *C'* type answer occurred	36[a]	9	21

[a] Significantly different from other two groups at .01.

in the protocols of these three groups, especially in the use of color and movement answers. Among the more interesting differences is that the "Constrained Affect" group gave significantly more *passive* movement answers than either of the other two groups, although the actual frequency of movement answers was approximately the same for all three groups.

Assuming that the C' answer does illustrate a form of affective constraint, it is important for the interpreter to evaluate the use of form in these responses. When form is dominant, as in the FC' answer, the operation of constraint is probably more cognitively controlled than when the reverse is true. When form plays a secondary role, or is completely absent, the impact of the affect on the cognitive operations is probably much more intense and potentially disruptive. It is also important that "constraint" is not confused with anxiety, although anxiety may accompany the experience. Constraint is probably best described as a form of internal expression of affect which is more direct than the displacements noted as accompanying the M answers, or the delay which is illustrated in both the Form and Form Dimension responses. In the C' answer, the affect is apparently released, but not exposed directly into the external world. Rather it is concealed and has behavioral consequences which are far less obvious than when affect is discharged in activities reflected by chromatic color answers. The experience associated with the C' kind of action is probably pain and/or tension, either or both of which can be very disequilibrating to the cognitive stability of the subject.

TEXTURE RESPONSES (T, TF, FT)

The texture answer is the most common of the shading responses as defined in the comprehensive system. The nonpsychiatric subjects in the reference sample give 1.4 texture answers per record while the psychiatric groups consistently average more than two texture answers per protocol. Klopfer (1936) was the first to establish a special scoring for texture answers (c). His scoring and criterion were included later by Hertz in her system, and ultimately Beck (1949) adopted the symbol T to represent these responses. The Piotrowski (1957) system does not include a separate scoring for texture answers, and Rapaport (1946) scores texture only when it is combined with the use of chromatic color. Klopfer (1954) hypothesized that the texture response is a manifestation of affective need, and suggested that the degree of form use in them relates to the "awareness and differentiation of the person's needs for affection and dependency." Beck (1945, 1967) agrees that the texture response indicates a painful affective experience, and suggests that it relates to the more infantile "erotic" needs of the subject. The importance of evaluating the use of form in the texture answer has been emphasized by both Klopfer and Beck, each suggesting that where form is the dominant characteristic, the affective need is controlled and possibly used to the subject's advantage. Conversely, when the use of form is secondary, or absent in the texture answer, the painful affective experience of the subject, created by an affective deprivation, is much more overwhelming and causes interference with the attempts of the individual to maintain useful and productive interpersonal contacts.

The literature concerning texture responses lends some support to the Klopfer postulate. Ames (1952, 1971) notes that the frequency of texture answers shows an increase through childhood, finally appearing as the most dominant kind of shading answer by the 15th year. McFate and Orr (1949) have found that texture answers, with form as secondary or absent, are common in early adolescence, but that these generally "give way" to the FT kind of response in later adolescence. Kallstedt (1952) suggests that this is because the young adolescent is more socially and sexually insecure. Montalto (1952) finds that children between the ages of 6 and 7 whose mothers are restrictive give significantly more texture answers than do children whose mothers are "democratic." Breecher (1956) found significantly more texture responses in the protocols of maternally overprotected patients as compared to patients who were maternally rejected. She suggests that maternal rejection leads to a reduction in "needs to be liked," thus accounting for the fewer T answers. Hertz (1948) finds that texture answers represent a cautious behavior, based on sensitivity and an attempt to come to grips with the outside world. She indicates that the texture response reflects a willingness to be more open with the environment. Brown et al. (1950) report that psychosomatic patients give significantly fewer texture answers than do patients being treated for other complaints. Brockway (1954) offers data which are consistent with that in the reference samples; that is, texture answers are given approximately twice as often by maladjusted individuals as compared with nonpatient controls. Steiner (1947) found that unsuccessful workers give significantly more texture answers than do successful workers. Ainsworth and Kuethe (1959) used a sorting task in which the objects to be sorted were rough, soft, smooth, and such. They found a significant correlation between sorting scores and texture answers for psychotic patients, but not for nonpsychotic patients or nonpatient controls. Allerhand (1954) reports that texture responses are significantly correlated with an index of anxiety in an experimentally created conflict situation. Waller (1960) found that the presence or absence of texture answers is not related to scores on either the Welsh or Taylor anxiety scales, but is related with the "overall" impression of anxiety.

The texture response is probably best interpreted as indicating needs for affective interpersonal contact. It is possibly more infantile, as Beck suggests, than adult. The literature suggests that it is the kind of response common among late adolescents and adults, occurring with greater frequencies among individuals with adjustment problems. People who are less successful in their adult lives tend to give more texture answers. According to Potanin (1959), individuals who acknowledge "dependency features" prefer geometric designs with textural details significantly more than those who describe themselves as "independent." Texture, as Hertz suggests, is a form of cautious reaching outward for affectively rewarding relationships. Obviously, the impact of this need will vary with the kinds of interpersonal security a person experiences. When the T answers appear in considerable frequency, or when they dominate form use, the needs are probably intense and disruptive to the conservative reality orientation of the cognitive process. Conversely, an absence of T answers may signal a more extreme affective impoverishment, early in life, so that the person no longer strives for deep or meaningful interpersonal experiences. The presence of T in most records is due mainly to the stimulus features on Cards IV and VI. Texture answers to these cards occur with a frequency of about 10 times greater than to any of the other cards. This seems to be a function of the internal contours of these blots rather than the grey-black features. Exner (1961) presented these cards in chromatic forms (blue, green, magenta, and pink), one card each to 40 subjects, while administering the standard achromatic version to 40 matched control subjects. The frequency of texture responses to both cards was approximately the same regardless of the chromatic version used. In the non-psychiatric reference sample, a T failure, or absence, occurred in only nine of the 200 protocols. A T failure occurred in 58 of the 295 psychiatric protocols even though the mean T for this group is substantially higher than for the nonpsychiatric group. Coan (1956), studying Rorschach determinants factorially, indicates that the composite of M with texture answers relates to an inner sensitivity or empathy. It seems probable that when the composite is of chromatic color and texture answers, the behaviors may be more direct and less "mature" in seeking the security of inter-personal contact.

VISTA RESPONSES (V, VF, FV)

Rorschach (1923) offered only a passing reference to the use of shading features to denote dimensionality, suggesting that "it appears to be correlated with the cautious and measured affectivity with depressive nuances." It was not until 1942 that Klopfer introduced a formal scoring for this kind of answer (FK), but un-fortunately, he did not offer a clear differentiation of FK answers from those in-volving the more diffuse use of shading (KF and K) and included the scoring of reflection answers in this category. Beck (1944), following Klopfer's lead, adopted the symbols V, VF, and FV to denote responses involving dimensionality based on the shading features of the blots, but also included reflections in this category as well as some "common" answers of dimensionality where shading is unarticulated. Interestingly, although Klopfer and Beck disagreed on the criterion for scoring these types of answers, they do agree on the general interpretation which should be applied to this kind of determinant. Klopfer suggests that FK answers illustrate an attempt by the person to handle his anxieties by "introspective efforts," that is, by distancing himself from his problems so as to view them more objectively. Klopfer cautioned that it is important to avoid confusing introspectiveness with insight, noting that the two are quite different. Beck regards the dimensional answer as more painful, but also involving self-appraisal. He perceives these answers as representing a "morose feeling tone," involving a depression of affect and feel-ings of inferiority.

The fact that vista answers are created by the grey-black features of the blots seems well established by Baughman's work (1959), in which vista type responses were given only to cards which were achromatic. Baughman also noted that the presence of chromatic color in the blots tends to "suppress" manifestations of V. The vista responses are the least frequently given kinds of shading answers, occur-ring in the nonpsychiatric reference sample on an average of 0.4 per record, a mean of 0.5 in schizophrenic records, 0.9 for out-patients, and 1.3 for nonschizophrenic in-patients, the majority of whom are depressives. Vista responses are rare in children according to Phillips and Smith (1953), although they occur in an almost adult-like frequency among adolescents. Klopfer (1946) has noted very few vista answers among aged subjects. Similar findings are reported by Light and Amick (1956).

Meltzer (1944) has shown that vista answers occur with significantly greater frequency among stutterers than nonstutterers. Bradway et al. (1946) report that vista answers are significantly related to "treatability" in delinquent adolescent females. Buhler and LeFever (1947) found that alcoholics give significantly more vista answers than do psychopaths. They interpret this finding to indicate that alcoholics are considerably more self-critical. Rabinovitch (1954) has shown that vista answers are significantly correlated with greater GSR deflections and perceptual thresholds, and interprets this as indicating an anxiety responsiveness, probably related to the attempted avoidance of unpleasant stimuli. Fiske and Baughman (1953) have noted that the incidence of vista answers increases among out-patients with the length of the record.

The limited literature concerning vista answers, plus the different criterion used in the comprehensive system, prompted three investigations to study these answers more specifically. In the first, previously mentioned in conjunction with the *C'* response, 64 protocols were collected at the onset of intervention from patients diagnosed as affective disturbances. None had any history of suicidal attempts prior to testing. Sixteen of these patients attempted suicide within 55 days of the testing, and this group gave significantly more *V* type answers than did the nonattempting group (2.36 versus 1.53). Both groups gave significantly more *V* type answers than did a randomly selected group of 50 out-patients (0.73), and a randomly selected group of 50 nonpatients (0.44). Fifteen of the 16 records of attempters showed at least one vista response, as did 36 of the 48 records of nonattempters. Conversely, only 21 of the 50 out-patient records contained at least one *V* type answer, and only 11 of the 50 nonpatient protocols had this feature. These data seem to suggest that the *V* answers are associated with depressive features, and may represent the sorts of painful introspection common to these kinds of patients. The second study concerning vista was mentioned in the preceding chapter regarding *FD* answers. Forty subjects were taken from a waiting list and randomly assigned to one of four "holding" groups. Each group met for 2 hours per week with the same therapist. Three raters were trained to observe each of the four groups and to score verbalizations on a two-dimensional grid used to designate whether the verbalizations were directed toward the self or toward others, and whether the verbalization pertained to the past, present, or future. It was assumed that the more introspective subjects would focus more on themselves and would be concerned more with the present than with the future or past. These subjects were divided, using a median split for the number of *FD* responses in their Rorschach taken prior to the formation of the groups. As previously noted, the group giving the greater number of *FD* answers also gave more self-focusing verbalizations and concentrated more on the present and past than did the low *FD* group. The high *FD* group also gave significantly more vista answers ($\bar{X} = 1.41$) than did the low *FD* group ($\bar{X} = 0.52$). Vista answers appear in 18 of the 20 high *FD* protocols and in only seven of the 20 low *FD* protocols. These findings appear to support the notion that the vista answer does relate to introspective activity.

The third investigation consisted of comparing the pre- and posttreatment records of 74 in-patients diagnosed as some form of affective disorder. At the onset of treatment this group showed at least one vista response in 62 of the protocols ($\bar{X} = 1.61$). The posttreatment records reveal vista answers in only 29 of the 74 cases ($\bar{X} = 0.59$). Interestingly, the number of *FD* answers for the group at discharge (2.1) differed very little from that given in the pretreatment records (2.3). This can be interpreted to suggest that the painful characteristics of introspection diminished, but the tendency to introspect remained somewhat prominent.

The composite of studies concerning the vista response tend to support the hypothesis that it does reflect an introspective process. They also appear to argue in favor of Beck's proposition that it is a painful process, rather than the Klopfer view that it represents a more dispassionate view of oneself. Vista answers should always be regarded carefully in the interpretive process as the frequency of their occurrence is quite low. Unlike the texture responses which are expected to appear in most records, the absence of vista answers is probably a favorable sign, especially if some *FD* answers appear in the record. A single *FV* response is an average length record may be merely an indication of self-examination, which although painful, can be productive. The appearance of *VF* or *V* answers is extremely rare and should be cause for concern, as is also the case when the frequency of *FV* responses is greater than 1. The presence of *V* type responses in a protocol marked by a substantial frequency of *FM* + *m*, a *C* + *CF* frequency which exceeds the *FC* total, and/or the presence of numerous poor form quality answers should provoke questions regarding the potential destructive nature of the introspective operations. While this should not be regarded as an *absolute* manifestation of suicidal potential, many of the basic ingredients, for a form of damage to the self, are evident.

DIFFUSE SHADING RESPONSES (*Y, YF, FY*)

Binder (1932) was the first to offer a detailed approach to shading. Following his lead, each of the Rorschach systematizers has included a variety of scores to denote the different types of shading answers. While there has been disagreement on some of the criteria for scoring shading, all have included a scoring for diffuse shading, and have identified it as one of the more important determinants in the test. Klopfer (1936, 1942) was the first, after Binder, to differentiate the scoring of shading, using the symbols *KF* and *K* to denote diffuse shading, and *k* and its variations to identify shading as used in a "toned down" manner. By 1944, Beck had differentiated the shading answers in a somewhat similar manner, using the *Y* symbol for diffuse shading responses, plus *V* and *T* for responses of a special variety. Hertz (1942) has used the symbols (*C*) and *Ch* to denote shading answers comparable to the Beck and Klopfer scorings for diffuse shading, and Rapaport (1946) has adopted essentially the same methodology. Piotrowski (1957) has preferred to use only two scorings for diffuse shading answers, *c* and *c'*, the differentiation being based on the extent to which the answer reflects a "dysphoric mood" or the degree of use of darker-black areas are associated with the content of the response.

It has generally been postulated that the use of diffuse shading is some manifestation of anxiety. Klopfer (1954) indicates that these responses manifest anxiety in a free-floating nature, revealing the experience of frustration against which the individual has not yet built a scheme of defenses. (Beck 1945) suggests that diffuse shading answers reveal a painful absence of action, through which the individual defends himself against unwanted intrusions. Beck (1967) perceives this psychological inactivity or paralysis as being both beneficial, as in the *FY* answer illustrating delay, to the more extreme experience of being unable to respond, as in the *YF* and Y responses. Whereas the former represents a tendency to mobilize energies, the latter manifests an inability to do so. Beck defines both as "unhappy" states wherein the idiographic ideas are harshly experienced. Rapaport (1946) tends to agree with both Beck and Klopfer, suggesting that diffuse shading does represent a form of anxiety which demands adaptation, regardless of the state of other needs.

The varieties of Y answers appear in the reference samples with almost the same frequency as texture responses. Out-patients and nonschizophrenics give almost twice as many diffuse shading responses as do nonpsychiatric subjects. Schizophrenics give more Y type responses than do nonpatients but fewer than either of the other two psychiatric groups. The Ames (1952, 1971) data show a gradual increase in the diffuse shading answers through childhood and adolescence, with a corresponding increase in the primacy of form in these responses. The literature concerning the diffuse shading responses is often difficult to interpret due to three factors. First, the scoring and criterion differences among the systems makes it difficult and sometimes impossible to compare studies. Second, some investigators have grouped all responses to the grey-black features of the blots together, that is, adding achromatic color, texture, vista, and diffuse shading answers to create a broad category of "shading" answers. While there may be some common features to responses involving the grey-black characteristics of the blots, the end product of these studies has limited usefulness as it is like adding "apples and bananas." Third, numerous studies have focused on the diffuse shading-anxiety hypothesis, but have approached this issue using a wide variety of test and behavioral criteria to denote anxiety, and little effort has been made to differentiate different types of anxiety. Nevertheless, there is support for both the shading-anxiety hypothesis and the shading-passivity hypothesis, although the latter is more consistently supported than is the former.

Buhler and LeFever (1947) were among the earliest to test the shading-anxiety postulate in their study of alcoholics. They assumed that alcoholics were more anxious than were nonalcoholics. They report a significantly greater use of diffuse shading among alcoholics. Eichler (1953) and Cox and Sarason (1954) both note significant increases in the use of diffuse shading under an experimentally induced stress situation. Similarly, Levitt and Grosz (1960) obtained significantly more Y responses after anxiety had been induced hypnotically. Lebo et al. (1960) treated 12 of 24 high anxiety subjects with CO_2 and found a significant decrease in Y answers as compared with the untreated group. While these studies tend to support the shading-anxiety hypothesis, numerous works contradict the hypothesis. Several studies have found no relationship between scores on the Taylor Manifest Anxiety Scale and diffuse shading answers (Goodstein, 1954; Holtzman et al., 1954; Goodstein and Goldberger, 1955; Levitt, 1957; and Waller, 1960). Schwartz and Kates (1957) used an experimentally induced stress model and found that stressed subjects gave significantly fewer Y variant answers than did controls. Berger (1953), Fisher (1958), and Schon and Bard (1958) each used designs in which the Rorschach was administered under "real life" stress situations and found no evidence that the Y variants were associated with the stressful situation. Neuringer has suggested that anxiety manifestations are probably better judged by a constellation of variables rather than by one variable such as the Y type answers. A similar position is implied by Goldfried, Stricker, and Weiner (1971) in their review of Elizur's Rorschach scoring for anxiety which focuses mainly on verbalizations in the test. The data concerning shading and anxiety are obviously equivocal, and at best, may be interpreted to indicate that Y answers represent *some types of anxiety at times*, but *cannot be routinely taken as a direct index of anxiety.*

Studies concerning the diffuse shading-passivity hypothesis are less numerous than those dealing with the anxiety issue, but the findings are clearly more consistent in favoring the Beck postulate. Klebanoff (1946) found that flyers experiencing "operational fatigue" give significantly greater numbers of Y variants. He also noted a tendency of these subject toward withdrawal and passivity. Elstein (1965) found the Y variants significantly related to passivity toward the environment. He noted that "high Y" subjects are more inhibited and resigned to their situation, and suggests that they attempt to seal themselves off from the world. Salmon et al. (1972) report the use of a factorial model to study various determinants. Unfortunately, they grouped all responses to grey-black features as "shading," but did find a striking correlation between "shading" and emotion and intellectual control, the composite of which could equal withdrawal behaviors. An examination of the 84 records from the "Constrained Affect" and "Unconstrained Affect" groups mentioned earlier regarding the C' answers (see Table 26), reveals that the Constrained Affect subjects gave significantly more Y variants than did the unconstrain's or the controls. These data appear especially relevant in that the Constrained Affect group also gave significantly more passive movement answers than did either of the other groups.

The diffuse shading answers are probably best interpreted as illustrating a form of psychological "helplessness" and/or withdrawal which may be accompanied by anxiety. These diffuse shading answers provide a hint of paralysis or resignation to stress. They are, like other responses to the grey-black features of the blots, painful affective experiences. The extent to which form is used in these responses probably conveys some indication of the cognitive coping which occurs in relation to the painful affect. When form is dominant, the experience is controlled and overt responses to it are probably delayed and organized. When form is secondary, or absent, there is a greater tendency for the affect to be expressed more directly as the subject tends to be overwhelmed by it. Some Y, particularly the FY variety, is expected in almost every record as the ambiguities of the blots should provoke some experience of insecurity. The absence of the Y variants may suggest an overly "loose" or unconcerned attitude toward ambiguity, caused either by naivete or disregard. The presence or absence of other coping indicators, especially Pure F, M and the Z activities should constitute a guide from which the overall impact of the process underlying the Y type answers can be better judged.

REFLECTION AND PAIR RESPONSES [rF, Fr, (2)]

The development of a special scoring for reflection responses, or a special designation for instances when the perceived object is reported as a "pair," have not been considered by any of the Rorschach systematizers. Klopfer (1954) scores the reflection answer based on blot symmetry as FK, if the midline is noted as a shading differentiation. Beck scores reflections as FV, assuming the same process is active in these answers as those involving depth and/or dimensionality. The separate scoring for reflection and pair answers included in the comprehensive system evolved somewhat accidentally in a study on acting-out. Four groups of 20 male subjects each were involved, representing overt homosexuals, character disorders diagnosed as psychopathic or sociopathic, depressives with a recent history of suicidal gesture, and nonpatients. An analysis of the Rorschachs taken from these subjects by 17 examiners showed that all gave a relatively high frequency of FV answers when scored by the Beck method. A closer inspection of these answers revealed that many, especially from the homosexual and character disorder groups, were reflections. When these responses were scored separately, as Fr or rF, a marked differentiation between the groups occurred. The homosexuals and character disorders gave significantly more reflections, averaging 1.85 and 1.45, respectively, while the depressives averaged 0.2 and the nonpatients averaged 0.6. Reflections occurred in 17 of the 20 homosexual protocols and 15 of the 20 character disorder records. Conversely, they appeared in only three of the 20 depressive records and seven of the 20 control records. In addition to scoring reflections separately, it was decided to also tally the frequency with which pairs of objects were reported, on the assumption that a pair type response might be a more subtle or controlled form of reflection answer. It was found that the homosexual group gave significantly more pairs than did the other groups and the depressives gave significantly fewer pairs than the other groups, although pairs occurred in almost all of the records (Exner, 1969).

Following that preliminary study, a sentence completion blank was devised, following a format similar to that used by Watson (1965) in her study of narcissism. The blank contained 50 stems, of which 34 contained personal pronouns (I, me, my), and was administered to 750 subjects selected from both college and noncollege populations. The 34 critical stems were scored for "self-focusing" answers on a simple yes–no basis and two groups of 40 subjects each were selected from the extremes of the distribution and administered the Rorschach by one of 14 graduate students taking their second Rorschach course. The examiners were familiar with the purpose of the study but did not know from which extreme their subjects had been selected. Reflection answers appeared in 37 of the 40 protocols taken from the "high narcissism" group with a frequency of more than twice that of the "low narcissism" subjects. Similarly, pair answers appeared nearly two and one-half times as often in the "high narcissism" group. This study was replicated after the sentence completion blank was revised so as to include only 30 stems and a more sophisticated approach to scoring developed (Exner, 1973). In the replication, two groups of 30 subjects each were selected from a nonpsychiatric population on the basis of their extremely high or extremely low self-focus scores. They were administered the Rorschach by 16 blind examiners. Reflection answers, and pair answers, occurred nearly twice as frequently in the self-centered group than in the other group.

It will be noted from the reference samples that reflections occur very infrequently in the records of nonpatients (0.2), while appearing most often in the protocols of schizophrenics (1.2). Out-patients average 0.7 reflections per record, while nonschizophrenic in-patients average 0.9. Approximately one-third of the responses from nonpatients are *pairs*, as is also the case for nonschizophrenics. Out-patients and schizophrenics tend to give a higher proportion of pair answers. When the nonschizophrenic sample is subdivided into depressive versus nondepressive, the number of reflections and pairs differentiates the groups sharply. Depressives average 0.3 reflections and 5.8 pairs, while nondepressives average 1.5 reflections and 10.4 pairs. The latter group is made up primarily of character disorders; thus these data are reasonably consistent with the findings of the earlier studies.

Raychaudhuri and Mukerji (1971) used four groups of 15 subjects each, taken from a prison population, to study reflections and pairs. The groups were comprised of active homosexuals, passive homosexuals, sociopaths, and controls. They report both homosexual groups as giving significantly more reflection answers than either of the other two groups, and sociopaths giving significantly more reflections than controls. They found the number of pair answers to be significantly high among both homosexual groups *and* the controls when contrasted with the sociopathic group.

Two studies were completed in conjunction with the development of the comprehensive system concerning reflection and pair answers. The first involved pre- and posttreatment testing of three psychiatric groups which includes 75 in-patient schizophrenics, 74 in-patient depressive reactions, and 31 in-patient character disorders. All subjects were evaluated prior to treatment by one of three psychiatrists or psychologists, working in "the blind," using the Inpatient Multidimensional Psychiatric Scale, and by the closest available relative or significant other using the Katz Adjustment Scale (form *R*). The same evaluations were completed 6 to 8 weeks after discharge from treatment, and the subjects were then divided into two groups, one representing subjects who had "changed" significantly according to the professional and relative ratings, and one which was essentially unchanged in the comparison of pre- and posttreatment ratings. The frequency and proportion of reflection and pair answers was analyzed by diagnostic groupings in terms of changed versus unchanged. These data are presented in Table 27. An examination of Table 27 reveals that those subjects rated as improved, altered the number of reflection responses significantly in the posttreatment records. The schizophrenics and character disorders decreased in the number of *rF* and *Fr* answers while the improved depressives increased in these kinds of responses. The unimproved groups stayed essentially unchanged for the number of reflection answers given. The pattern is somewhat similar for the pair answers. The improved schizophrenics gave significantly fewer pairs while the improved depressive gave more pairs. The improved character disorders gave slightly, but not significantly, fewer pair answers. These findings suggest that if reflection and pair answers represent a form of self-centeredness or *egocentricity*, too much or too little may accompany psychopathological states, and that improvement from these conditions is marked by a change toward a level of egocentricity which is more consistent with that found in nonpatient records.

A second study concerning reflections and pairs focused on the phenomenon of egocentricity itself. Twenty-one candidates for a junior engineering position were administered several psychological tests, including the Rorschach, by naive examiners. Subsequently, they were each interviewed by a member of the personnel staff of an industrial corporation concerning their employment applications. The interviews were all conducted in a 10 by 12 foot office which contained a two-way vision mirror. Each candidate was brought into the office by a receptionist where he was asked to wait for the arrival of the interviewer. Interviewers were instructed to arrive no sooner than 10 minutes after the candidate had entered the office. A video-tape unit was used to film each candidate during the 10 minute interval prior to the interviewer's arrival. The tapes were reviewed later and the amount of time each candidate spent viewing himself in the mirror was recorded. The range of mirror

Table 27.   Pre- and Posttreatment Reflection and Pair Responses for Three Psychiatric Groups, Subdivided on a Criterion of Changed Versus Unchanged Based on Two Behavioral Ratings

Group	Number of Reflections	$\overline{X}$	Number of Protocols	Number of Pairs	$\overline{X}$	Number of Protocols
Schizophrenic (Improved N = 53)						
Pretreatment	67	1.26	46	541	10.04	53
Posttreatment	23[a]	0.43	15[a]	386	7.31[a]	53
Schizophrenic (Unimproved N = 22)						
Pretreatment	28	1.25	17	201	9.14	22
Posttreatment	21	0.95	15	164	7.45	22
Depressive (Improved N = 55)						
Pretreatment	14	0.25	11	266	4.83	43
Posttreatment	39[a]	0.71	28[a]	427	7.76[a]	55
Depressive (Unimproved N = 19)						
Pretreatment	6	0.32	5	97	5.10	15
Posttreatment	6	0.32	5	117	6.16	18
Character Disorder (Improved N = 21)						
Pretreatment	29	1.38	20	198	9.01	21
Posttreatment	15[a]	0.71[a]	13[a]	167	8.00	21
Character Disorder (Unimproved N = 5)						
Pretreatment	9	1.80	5	48	9.60	5
Posttreatment	10	2.00	5	42	8.40	5

[a] Significantly different from pretreatment at .01.

viewing time was from 6″ to 104″, with a median time of 49″. The group was divided using a median split and eliminating the candidate at the median. The average mirror viewing time for the upper half is 68.5″, and 27.1″ for the lower half. A comparison of the Rorschach data for these two groups reveals that the 10 subjects in the upper half gave eight reflection answers (six protocols) and 103 pair answers. The 10 subjects in the lower half gave no reflection answers and only 68 pair responses. The groups are significantly different for both scorings.

The several studies cited here appear to support the hypothesis that reflection and pair answers are related to egocentricity. An excess of self-concern, *or* a lack of sufficient self-concern are both related to psychopathological states, In other words, egocentricity is a natural characteristic of the individual, which probably functions as an asset unless "overdone" or "underdeveloped." In this context, an experimental ratio of $3r + (2):R$ has been created to provide an index of self-concern. Using nonpatients as a baseline, it is noted that the calculation of this ratio yields a range of .25 to .40 for approximately 70% of the sample. In that non-patients rarely give reflection answers, these figures are based primarily on pair responses. Schizophrenics, out-patients, and character disorders tend to give a higher proportion of reflection and pair responses. The mean $3r + (2):R$ ratio for this group is .54, and a range of .40 to .65 encompasses about 70% of this sample. Depressive subjects show a mean ratio of .27, and a range of .10 to .30 represents about two-thirds of that group. The reflection answers are weighed heavily in the ratio because of the relative low frequency with which they occur in all groups, especially nonpatients. When a reflection answer does appear in a record, it should be regarded carefully, regardless of the $3r + (2):R$ ratio, in that it probably represents an intense self-focus which may contribute to reality distortions, especially in interpersonal situations. Information concerning the level of cognitive maturation, as evidenced by the DQ distribution, perceptual accuracy, as manifest in the $F+\%$ and $X+\%$, and the awareness of conventionality (P) are important variables in understanding the manner in which egocentricity prevails in the thinking and behavior of the subject.

REFERENCES

Ainsworth, M. D., and Kuethe, J. L. Texture responses in the Rorschach and a sorting test. *Journal of Projective Techniques*, 1959, **23**, 391–402.

Allen, R. M., Manne, S. H., and Stiff, M. The role of color in Rorschach's Test: A preliminary normative report on a college student population. *Journal of Projective Techniques*, 1951, **15**, 235–242.

Allerhand, M. E. Chiaroscuro determinants of the Rorschach Test as an indicator of manifest anxiety. *Journal of Projective Techniques*, 1954, **18**, 407–413.

Ames, L. B., Learned, J., Metraux, R., and Walker, R. N. *Child Rorschach Responses*. New York: Hoeber-Harper, 1952.

Ames, L. B., Metraux, R. W., and Walker, R. N. *Adolescent Rorschach Responses*. New York: Brunner/Mazel, 1971.

Applebaum, S. A. The problem-solving aspect of suicide. *Journal of Projective Techniques and Personality Assessment*, 1963, **27**, 259–268.

Applebaum, S. A., and Colson, D. B. A reexamination of the color-shading Rorschach Test response. *Journal of Projective Techniques and Personality Assessment*, 1968, **32**, 160–164.

Applebaum, S. A., and Holtzman, P. S. The color-shading response and suicide. *Journal of Projective Techniques*, 1962, **26**, 155–161.

Barnett, I. The influence of color and shading on the Rorschach Test. Unpublished Doctoral Dissertation, University of Pittsburgh, 1950.

Baughman, E. E. An experimental analysis of the relationship between stimulus structure and behavior in the Rorschach. *Journal of Projective Techniques*, 1959, **23**, 134–183.

Beck, S. J. *Rorschach's Test. I: Basic Processes*. New York: Grune and Stratton, 1944.

Beck, S. J. *Rorschach's Test. II: A Variety of Personality Pictures*. New York: Grune and Stratton, 1945.

Beck, S. J. *Rorschach's Test. I: Basic Processes*. (2nd ed.) New York: Grune and Stratton, 1949.

Beck, S. J., Beck, A., Levitt, E., and Molish, H. B. *Rorschach's Test. I: Basic Processes*. (3rd ed.) New York: Grune and Stratton, 1961.

Beck, S. J., and Molish, H. B. *Rorschach's Test. II: A Variety of Personality Pictures*. (2nd ed.) New York: Grune and Stratton, 1967.

Berger, D. The Rorschach as a measure of real life stress. *Journal of Consulting Psychology*, 1953, **17**, 355–358.

Binder, H. *Die Helldunkeldeutungen im psychodiagnostischem experiment von Rorschach.* Zurich: Urell Fussli, 1932.

Bradway, K., Lion, E., and Corrigan, H. The use of the Rorschach in a psychiatric study of promiscuous girls. *Rorschach Research Exchange*, 1946, **9**, 105–110.

Breecher, S. The Rorschach reaction patterns of maternally overprotected and rejected schizophrenics. *Journal of Nervous and Mental Disorders*, 1956, **123**, 41–52.

Brennen, M., and Reichard, S. Use of the Rorschach Test in predicting hypnotizability. *Bulletin of the Menninger Clinic*, 1943, **7**, 183–187.

Brockway, A. L. Rorschach concepts of normality. *Journal of Consulting Psychology*, 1954, **18**, 259–265.

Brown, M., Bresnoban, T. J., Chakie, F. R., Peters, B., Poser, E. G., and Tougas, R. V. Personality factors in duodenal ulcer: A Rorschach study. *Psychosomatic Medicine*, 1950, **12**, 1–5.

Buhler, C., and LeFever, D. A Rorschach study on the psychological characteristics of alcoholics. *Quarterly Journal of Studies on Alcoholism*, 1947, **8**, 197–260.

Canter, A. An investigation of the psychological significance of reaction to color on the Rorschach and other tests. Unpublished Doctoral Dissertation, University of Iowa, 1951.

Coan, R. A factor analysis of Rorschach determinants. *Journal of Projective Techniques*, 1956, **20**, 280–287.

Colson, D. B., and Hurwitz, B. A. A new experimental approach to the relationship between color-shading and suicide attempts. *Journal of Personality Assessment*, 1973, **37**, 237–241.

Costello, C. G. The Rorschach records of suicidal patients. *Journal of Projective Techniques*, 1958, **22**, 272–275.

Cox, F. N., and Sarason, S. B. Test anxiety and Rorschach performance. *Journal of Abnormal and Social Psychology*, 1954, **49**, 371–377.

Crumpton, E. The influence of color on the Rorschach Test. *Journal of Projective Techniques*, 1956, **20**, 150–158.

Cutter, F., Jorgensen, M., and Farberow, N. Replicability of Rorschach signs with known degrees of suicidal intent. *Journal of Projective Techniques and Personality Assessment*, 1968, **32**, 428–434.

Daston, P. G., and Sakheim, G. A. Prediction of successful suicide from the Rorschach Test, using a sign approach. *Journal of Projective Techniques*, 1960, **24**, 355–361.

Dubrovner, R. J., Von Lackum, W. J., and Jost, H. A. A study of the effect of color on productivity and reaction time in the Rorschach Test. *Journal of Clinical Psychology*, 1950, **6**, 331–336.

Eichler, R. M. Experimental stress and alleged Rorschach indices of anxiety. *Journal of Abnormal and Social Psychology*, 1951, **46**, 344–356.

Elstein, A. S. Behavioral correlates of the Rorschach shading determinant. *Journal of Consulting Psychology*, 1965, **29**, 231–236.

Exner, J. E. The influence of chromatic and achromatic color in the Rorschach. *Journal of Projective Techniques*, 1959, **23**, 418–425.

Exner, J. E. The influence of achromatic color in Card IV and VI of the Rorschach. *Journal of Projective Techniques*, 1961, **25**, 38–41.

Exner, J. E. The effect of color on productivity in Cards VIII, IX, X of the Rorschach. *Journal of Projective Techniques*, 1962, **26**, 30–33.

Exner, J. E. Rorschach responses as an index of narcissism. *Journal of Projective Techniques and Personality Assessment*, 1969, **33**, 324–330.

Exner, J. E. The Self Focus Sentence Completion: A Study of Egocentricity. *Journal of Personality Assessment*, 1973, **37**, 437–455.

Exner, J. E., and Murillo, L. G. The effectiveness of regressive ECT with process schizophrenics. *Diseases of the Nervous System*, 1973, **34**, 44–48.

Exner, J. E., Murillo, L. G., and Cannavo, F. *Disagreement Between Patient and Relative Behavioral Reports As Related to Relapse in Non-Schizophrenic Patients*. Eastern Psychological Association, Washington, D.C., 1973.

Finney, B. C. Rorschach Test correlates of assaultive behavior. *Journal of Projective Techniques*, 1955, **19**, 6–16.

Fisher, S. The value of the Rorschach for detecting suicidal trends. *Journal of Projective Techniques*, 1951, **15**, 250–254.

Fisher, R. L. The effects of a disturbing situation upon the stability of various projective tests. *Psychological Monographs*, 1958, **72**, 1–23.

Fiske, D. W., and Baughman, E. E. The relationship between Rorschach scoring categories and the total number of responses. *Journal of Abnormal and Social Psychology*, 1953, **48**, 25–30.

Ford, M. The application of the Rorschach Test to young children. *University of Minnesota Child Welfare Monographs*, 1946, No. 23.

Forsyth, R. P. The influence of color, shading and Welsh anxiety level on Elizur Rorschach content analyses of anxiety and hostility. *Journal of Projective Techniques*, 1959, **23**, 207–213.

Fortier, R. H. The response to color and ego functions. *Psychological Bulletin*, 1954, **51**, 41–63.

Gardner, R. W. Impulsivity as indicated by Rorschach Test factors. *Journal of Consulting Psychology*, 1951, **15**, 464–468.

Gill, H. S. Delay of response and reaction to color on the Rorschach. *Journal of Projective Techniques and Personality Assessment*, 1966, **30**, 545–552.

Goldfried, M. R., Stricker, G., and Weiner, I. B. *Rorschach Handbook of Clinical and Research Applications*. Englewood Cliffs, N.J.: Prentice-Hall, 1971.

Goldstein, K., and Sheerer, M. Abstract and concrete behavior. An experimental study with special tests. *Psychological Monographs*, 1941, **53**, No. 239.

Goodstein, L. D. Interrelationships among several measures of anxiety and hostility. *Journal of Consulting Psychology*, 1954, **18**, 35–39.

Goodstein, L. D., and Goldberger, L. Manifest anxiety and Rorschach performance in a chronic patient population. *Journal of Consulting Psychology*, 1955, **19**, 339–344.

Grayson, H. M. Rorschach productivity and card preferences as influenced by experimental variation of color and shading. *Journal of Projective Techniques*, 1956, **20**, 288–296.

Halpern, F. Rorschach interpretation of the personality structure of schizophrenics who benefit from insulin therapy. *Psychiatric Quarterly*, 1940, **14**, 826–833.

Hamlin, R. M., Stone, J. T., and Moskowitz, M. J. Rorschach color themes as reflected in simple card sorting tasks. *Journal of Projective Techniques*, 1955, **19**, 410–415.

Hertz, M. R. The scoring of the Rorschach ink-blot method as developed by the Brush Foundation. *Rorschach Research Exchange*, 1942, **6**, 16–27.

Hertz, M. R. Suicidal configurations in Rorschach records. *Rorschach Research Exchange*, 1948, **12**, 3–58.

Hertz, M. R. Further study of "suicidal" configurations in Rorschach records. *Rorschach Research Exchange*, 1949, **13**, 44–73.

Holtzman, W. H., Iscoe, I., and Calvin, A. D. Rorschach color responses and manifest anxiety in college women. *Journal of Consulting Psychology*, 1954, **18**, 317–324.

Kallstedt, F. E. A Rorschach study of 66 adolescents. *Journal of Clinical Psychology*, 1952, **8**, 129–132.

Keehn, J. D. The response to color and ego functions: A critique in light of recent experimental evidence. *Psychological Bulletin*, 1954, **51**, 65–67.

Klatskin, E. H. An analysis of the effect of the test situation upon the Rorschach record: Formal scoring characteristics. *Journal of Projective Techniques*, 1952, **16**, 193–199.

Klenanoff, S. A. Rorschach study of operational fatigue in Army Air Force Combat Personnel. *Rorschach Research Exchange*, 1946, **9**, 115–120.

Klopfer, B. The shading responses. *Rorschach Research Exchange*, 1938, **2**, 76–79.

Klopfer, B., Ainsworth, M., Klopfer, W., and Holt, R. *Developments in the Rorschach Technique. I: Technique and Theory*. Yonkers-on-Hudson, N.Y.: World Book Company, 1954.

Klopfer, B., and Kelley, D. *The Rorschach Technique*. Yonkers-on-Hudson, N.Y.: World Book Company, 1942.

Klopfer, B., and Margulies, H. Rorschach reactions in early childhood. *Rorschach Research Exchange*, 1941, **5**, 1–23.

Klopfer, B., and Sender, S. A system of refined scoring symbols. *Rorschach Research Exchange*, 1936, **1**, 19–22.

Klopfer, B., and Spiegelman, M. Differential diagnosis. In Klopfer, B. et al. (Eds.), *Developments in the Rorschach Technique. II: Fields of Application*. Yonkers-on-Hudson, N.Y.: World Book Company, 1956.

Kobler, F. J., and Stiel, A. The use of the Rorschach in involutional melancholia. *Journal of Consulting Psychology*, 1953, **17**, 365–370.

Kral, V. A., and Dorken, H. The influence of subcortical brain lesions on emotionality as reflected in the Rorschach color responses. *American Journal of Psychiatry*, 1951, **107**, 839–843.

Lebo, D., Toal, R., and Brick, H. Rorschach performances in the amelioration and continuation of observable anxiety. *Journal of General Psychology*, 1960, **63**, 75–80.

Levitt, E. E. Alleged Rorschach anxiety indices in children. *Journal of Projective Techniques*, 1957, **21**, 261–264.

Levitt, E. E., and Grosz, H. J. A comparison of quantifiable Rorschach anxiety indicators in hypnotically induced anxiety and normal states. *Journal of Consulting Psychology*, 1960, **24**, 31–34.

Light, B. H., and Amick, J. Rorschach responses of normal aged. *Journal of Projective Techniques*, 1956, **20**, 185–195.

Linton, H. B. Rorschach correlates of response to suggestion. *Journal of Abnormal and Social Psychology*, 1954, **49**, 75–83.

Mann, L. The relation of Rorschach indices of extratension and introversion to a measure of responsiveness to the immediate environment. *Journal of Consulting Psychology*, 1956, **20**, 114–118.

Martin, H. A Rorschach study of suicide. Unpublished Doctoral Dissertation, University of Kentucky, 1951.

McFate, M. Q., and Orr, F. G. Through adolescence with the Rorschach. *Rorschach Research Exchange*, 1949, **13**, 302–319.

Meltzer, H. Personality differences between stuttering and nonstuttering children as indicated by the Rorschach Test. *Journal of Psychology*, 1944, **17**, 39–59.

Meyer, B. T. An investigation of color shock in the Rorschach Test. *Journal of Clinical Psychology*, 1951, **7**, 367–370.

Montalto, F. D. Maternal behavior and child personality: A Rorschach study. *Journal of Projective Techniques*, 1952, **16**, 151–178.

Neuringer, C. The Rorschach Test as a research device for the identification, prediction and understanding of suicidal ideation and behavior. *Journal of Projective Techniques and Projective Techniques and Personality Assessment*, 1965, **29**, 71–82.

Perlman, J. A. Color and the validity of the Rorschach 8–9–10 per cent. *Journal of Consulting Psychology*, 1951, **15**, 122–126.

Phillips, L., and Smith, J. G. *Rorschach Interpretation: Advanced Technique*. New York: Grune and Stratton, 1953.

Piotrowski, Z. The Rorschach ink-blot method in organic disturbances of the central nervous system. *Journal of Nervous and Mental Disorders*, 1937, **86**, 525–537.

Piotrowski, Z. *Perceptanalysis*. New York: MacMillan, 1957.

Potanin, N. Perceptual preferences as a function of personality variables under normal and stressful conditions. *Journal of Abnormal and Social Psychology*, 1959, **55**, 108–113.

Pruyser, P. W., and Folsom, A. T. The Rorschach experience balance in epileptics. *Journal of Consulting Psychology*, 1955, **19**, 112–116.

Rabin, A. I. Homicide and attempted suicide. A Rorschach study. *American Journal of Orthopsychiatry*, 1946, **16**, 516–524.

Rabin, A. I., and Beck, S. J. Genetic aspects of some Rorschach factors. *American Journal of Orthopsychiatry*, 1950, **20**, 595–599.

Rabinovitch, S. Physiological response, perceptual threshold, and Rorschach Test anxiety indices. *Journal of Projective Techniques*, 1954, **18**, 379–386.

Rapaport, D., Gill, M., and Schafer, R. *Diagnostic Psychological Testing*. Vol. 2. Chicago: Yearbook Publishers, 1946.

Raychaudhuri, M., and Mukerji, K. Homosexual-narcissistic "reflections" in the Rorschach: An examination of Exner's diagnostic Rorschach signs. *Rorschachiana Japonica*, 1971, **12**, 119–126.

Rickers-Ovsiankina, M. Some theoretical considerations regarding the Rorschach method. *Rorschach Research Exchange*, 1943, **7**, 14–53.

Rorschach, H. *Psychodiagnostics*. Bern: Bircher, 1921 (Transl. Hans Huber, Verlag, 1942).

Rorschach, H. The application of the form interpretation test. *Zeitschrift fur die gesamte Neurologie und Psychiatrie*, 1923, **82.**

Sakheim, G. A. Suicidal responses on the Rorschach Test: A validation study. *Journal of Nervous and Mental Disease*, 1955, **122**, 332–344.

Salmon, P., Arnold, J. M., and Collyer, Y. M. What do the determinants determine: The internal validity of the Rorschach. *Journal of Personality Assessment*, 1972, **36**, 33–38.

Sapenfield, B., and Buker, S. L. Validity of the Rorschach 8–9–10 per cent as an indicator of responsiveness to color. *Journal of Consulting Psychology*, 1949, **13**, 268–271.

Schachtel, E. G. On color and affect. *Psychiatry*, 1943, **6**, 393–409.

Schilder, P. *Medical Psychology*. New York: International Universities Press, 1953.

Schon, M., and Bard, M. The effects of hypophysectomy on personality in women with metastatic breast cancer as revealed by the Rorschach Test. *Journal of Projective Techniques*, 1958, **22**, 440–445.

Schwartz, F., and Kates, S. L. Rorschach performance, anxiety level and stress. *Journal of Projective Techniques*, 1957, **21,** 154–160.

Shapiro, D. Color-response and perceptual passivity. *Journal of Projective Techniques*, 1956, **20,** 52–69.

Shapiro, D. A perceptual understanding of color response. In Rickers-Ovsiankina, M. (Ed.), *Rorschach Psychology*. New York: Wiley, 1960.

Siipola, E. M. The influence of color on reactions to ink blots. *Journal of Personality*, 1950, **18,** 358–382.

Sommer, R., and Sommer, D. T. Assaultiveness and two types of Rorschach color responses. *Journal of Consulting Psychology*, 1958, **22,** 57–62.

Steiner, M. E. The use of the Rorschach method in industry. *Rorschach Research Exchange*, 1947, **11,** 46–52.

Steisel, I. M. The Rorschach Test and suggestibility. *Journal of Abnormal and Social Psychology*, 1952, **47,** 607–614.

Storment, C. T., and Finney, B. C. Projection and behavior: A Rorschach study of assaultive mental hospital patients. *Journal of Projective Techniques*, 1953, **17,** 349–360.

Stotsky, B. A. A comparison of remitting and non-remitting schizophrenics on psychological tests. *Journal of Abnormal and Social Psychology*, 1952, **47,** 489–496.

Swartz, M. B. The role of color in response to the Rorschach Test. An experimental investigation of the consistency of stress tolerance and related Rorschach factors. Unpublished Doctoral Dissertation, Columbia University, 1953.

Townsend, J. K. The relation between Rorschach signs of aggression and behavioral aggression in emotionally disturbed boys. *Journal of Projective Techniques and Personality Assessment*, 1967, **31,** 13–21.

Wallen, R. The nature of color shock. *Journal of Abnormal and Social Psychology*, 1948, **43,** 346–356.

Waller, P. F. The relationship between the Rorschach shading response and other indices of anxiety. *Journal of Projective Techniques*, 1960, **24,** 211–216.

Watson, A. Objects and objectivity: A study in the relationship between narcissism and intellectual subjectivity. Unpublished Doctoral Dissertation, University of Chicago, 1965.

Weber, A. Delirium tremens und alkoholhalluzinose in Rorschachschen Formdeutversuch. *Zeitschrift fur die gesamte Neurologie und Psychiatrie*, 1937, **159.**

Weigl, E. On the psychology of so-called processes of abstraction. *Journal of Abnormal and Social Psychology*, 1941, **36,** 3–33.

York, R. H. The effect of color in the Rorschach Test and in selected intellectual tasks. Unpublished Doctoral Dissertation, Boston University, 1951.

CHAPTER 14

Structural Data: Content Categories and Reaction Time

Content scores and reaction time data provide two other important inputs to the Structural Summary. The content scorings offer information about needs, interests, and social interaction, and, at times, give clues regarding various preoccupations. Reaction time data give an index of the impact of the blots on the subject, and often provide a greater understanding of the importance of specific responses.

CONTENT CATEGORIES

The Animal and Human contents appear more frequently than do other content categories. Rorschach (1921) apparently saw little need to establish special scorings for other classes of answers, except landscape, preferring to group most additional contents in a general category of Object (Obj). As the Rorschach has developed, the number of content categories has increased significantly to provide for greater differentiation of special categories. Some of these, particularly the dramatic or unusual, add valuable information to the interpretive framework even when occurring with a low frequency.

Normative studies consistently agree that the Animal contents present the largest single class of response (Beck et al., 1950; Cass and McReynolds, 1951; Brockway et al., 1954; Neff and Glaser, 1954; Ulett, 1954; Wedemeyer, 1954). The means and/or medians in these studies fall between 38 and 48%. Beck (1961) reports that Animal contents occur in about 45% of the responses in adult protocols, and a slightly higher percentage for children. Ames (1952, 1971) finds that about half of the responses from children are *A* or *Ad*, and only slightly lower than that for adolescents. Klopfer notes that 25 to 35% of the responses in the adult record should consist of *A* or *Ad* answers. He agrees with Beck (1945) that an excess of animal content is a signal reflecting intellectual limitations or emotional disturbance, noting that the high frequency of *A* and *Ad* responses probably occurs because animals are easiest to see in the blots. The data in the reference samples tend to agree with other findings concerning animal content. Nonpsychiatric subjects average 39%, schizophrenics 31%, and out-patients 41%. The nonschizophrenic sample is considerably higher, 53%; however, a major proportion of that group consists of depressives, who have been noted by most of the systematizers to give substantially greater numbers of *A* and *Ad*. This has been demonstrated in studies by Buhler et al. (1949), Kobler and Stiel (1953), and Kuhn (1963). At the opposite pole, the *A*% has been found to be significantly low in manic subjects (Schmidt and Fonda, 1954; Kuhn, 1963). Buhler and LeFever (1947) have also found a relatively high $A\%$ among alcoholics, while Wishner (1953) has demonstrated a positive relation between $A\%$ and respiration rate. In an excellent review of the literature concerning content, Draguns, Haley, and Phillips (1967) conclude that the $A\%$ relates to the more "mundane" features of adaptiveness and is probably related to reality testing "in its more concrete sense." They indicate that a high $A\%$ reflects the ability to react in a routine and predictable manner, although it also illustrates a potential for confusion where the stimulus inputs from the environment are complex or varied frequently. They regard the low $A\%$ as indicative of a more idiographic person who perceives the world in a personal manner.

The literature concerning the Human contents is also reasonably extensive. Ames (1952) finds that the H and Hd answers increase steadily with age through childhood to a median of 16 to 18% by the age of 10, and remains essentially stable through adolescence. Beck (1961) reports a mean $H\%$ of approximately 17% for his adult subjects. The reference samples show that nonpatients average about 19% $H + Hd$, while out-patients and schizophrenics average only about 13%. The nonschizophrenic reference group gives the highest mean $H\%$ of 23%. It is important to note that these figures represent the combination of H and Hd answers, and therefore are somewhat misleading as the different groups vary considerably in the proportion of $H:Hd$ given. Nonpatients give slightly more than 3:1, while the schizophrenics and nonschizophrenics approximate a 1:1 ratio. The out-patient group gives about $2H$ for every $1Hd$. Molish (1967) suggests that when the balance of $H:Hd$ shifts in the Hd direction, it is indicative of a constrictive defense. Beck (1945) argues that the emphasis on Hd may point to anxiety, depression, or intellectual limitations. He finds that it occurs frequently among subjects who feel "hemmed in" by their world. Klopfer (1954) postulates that excessive use of Hd is related to intellectualization and/or compulsiveness. He feels that these are answers illustrating a critical approach in which self preoccupations interfere with effective interpersonal contacts. Duran et al. (1949) have found that the $H\%$ is generally lower in schizophrenics than in normals. Sherman (1952) has confirmed this, but warns that the differentiation is possible only when the record is reasonably brief. Sherman (1952) and Vinson (1960) also report that the preponderence of Hd is significantly greater in schizophrenics than in normals. A significantly low H frequency has been found in the records of adult criminals (Walters, 1953), and delinquents (Ray, 1963; Richardson, 1963). Several studies (Halpern, 1940; Morris, 1943; Stotsky, 1952; Goldman, 1960; Piotrowski and Bricklin, 1961) have found a positive relationship between the frequency of H and treatment effectiveness. Draguns, Haley, and Phillips (1967) suggest that H varies directly with cognitive development and the potential for social relations. They indicate that it is an effective index from which to differentiate subjects who have withdrawn from social contacts.

One of the ratios in the structural summary, $H + Hd:A + Ad$, is designed to emphasize the proportion of human and animal contents for the interpreter. Ordinarily, this ratio can be expected to fall in a range of 1:2 to 1:2.5; however, the second ratio of $H + A:Hd + Ad$ becomes important to the interpretation of the first ratio. The $H + A:Hd + Ad$ ratio should usually fall in a range of 3:1 to 4:1. When the $Hd + Ad$ side of the ratio is proportionally higher than expected, it will indicate an excessive concern for detail, which is possibly a critical and/or constrictive style. It is equally important that the frequency of (H), (Hd), (A), and (Ad) answers also be noted carefully. Molish (1967) suggests that these answers may indicate forms of denial. They may also indicate an undue detachment from the real world into one in which fantasy provides a major role. Obviously, a protocol in which the $H + A:Hd + Ad$ ratio is adequate, and the $H + Hd:A + Ad$ ratio is unremarkable will not cause undue concern by the interpreter. if, however, the H and Hd answers that contribute to those ratios are predominantly parenthesized contents, the tendency to conclude that the potential for effective social contacts does exist *would be very erroneous*. A similar error would exist if the animal contents of the protocol were predominantly parenthesized, a finding that would more likely indicate some impairment to the cognitive tendency to approach ambiguities in a concrete, easygoing manner. An examination of the reference samples indicates that parenthesized human and animal contents occur about twice as frequently in the protocols of the three psychiatric groups as in the nonpsychiatric sample. Interestingly, these kinds of responses occur with approximately the same proportional frequencies in the out-patient and schizophrenic groups.

A considerable literature is also available concerning anatomy responses. In part, this is probably because they appear with a notable frequency (Beck reports an average of 1.5 per record), and in part because they appear logically related to body concern. Shatin (1952) reports a significantly greater frequency of An answers occur in psychosomatics than is the case for neurotics. Zolliker (1943) reports a substantially high incidence of An responses in women suffering from psychiatric complications due to pregnancy. Rapaport (1946) found a high frequency of these answers among "neurasthenics." Draguns, Haley, and Phillips (1967) conclude from their literature review that the An responses reflect a degree of the person's "self absorption," indicating that this phenomenon can be a product of either autism or physiological changes such as pregnancy, pubescence, or physical illness. It follows from this conclusion that subjects giving high frequencies of An responses are probably withdrawn from significant interactions with the environment, and may be prone toward an "obsessive" cognitive style. One of the basic problems in researching the anatomy response is the matter of control for physical health as well as psychiatric health. Weiss and Winnik (1963) suggest that this is *not* necessarily a crucial issue, postulating than An responses can indicate a vacarious preoccupation with body concerns without directly experiencing physiological discomfort. An examination of the reference samples shows that the frequency of An responses is generally low among all of the groups; however, when combined with the x-ray category a significant differentiation occurs. The nonpsychiatric group gives a mean for the combined An-x-ray scores of 0.6, while the three psychiatric groups give means that are at least twice as large. The out-patient sample yields a mean of 1.6, the schizophrenic group averages 1.4, and the nonschizophrenic group has a mean of 1.8, which constitutes approximately 9% of the answers in an average length record for that group. Anatomy responses, as scored in the comprehensive system, occur most commonly to the chromatic colored cards, especially to Cards VIII and IX. The x-ray answers occur most frequently to Card I. X-ray responses occur almost twice as often among the out-patient group as either of the other two psychiatric groups, and appear more frequently in the protocols of nonschizophrenics than in the schizophrenic records. Schizophrenics give the largest number of Anatomy answers. Most Anatomy answers involve the use of chromatic color, frequently of a CF variety, whereas x-ray answers consistently involve the grey-black features and are scored as variations of C' or Y. The distinct differences in the use of determinants suggests that some of the research conclusions, which have been drawn from the general study of "anatomy" responses (including the x-ray answers), must be reviewed conservatively. The x-ray answers may represent a more painful form of preoccupation in which attempts are made to resist stress and/or conceal reactions to it. Conversely, the anatomy answer *per se* may be more of an index of a direct affect "release" through the preoccupation. Some support for this hypothesis is illustrated by a comparison of the protocols of three psychiatric groups consisting of 20 subjects each. One group represents hospitalized depressives, a second group consists of out-patient psychosomatics, and the third group is comprised of hospitalized schizophrenics. All protocols were taken at the onset of treatment. The depressives and psychosomatics give significantly more x-ray answers than do the schizophrenics, and conversely the schizophrenics give significantly more *An* responses than the other two groups. These data appear especially important when the fact is noted that all three groups give approximately the same number of "Anatomy" responses when the *An* and x-ray answers are combined.

The literature concerning other types of content scores is much more fragmentary than for the animal, human, and anatomy categories. Draguns, Haley, and Phillips indicate that there is some evidence to support the postulate that Botany, Geography, and Nature contents may be related to passivity and/or immaturity. They also note that Sex and Blood responses occur with greater frequency among subjects whose controls are impaired by psychosis, and those who have been apprehended for sexual and/or aggressive acts. Sexual answers have also been reported to occur with a higher frequency among subjects with a "newly found" autonomy. Food responses have been postulated to occur more often in the records of affectively deprived; however, the support for this postulate is, at best, limited. Griffith (1961) found that Water percepts occurred more frequently in alcoholics than nonalcoholics; however, Ackerman (1971) failed to confirm that finding in an extensive study of the Rorschach answers of alcoholics.

The number of different classes of content used by a subject may provide some clues concerning his interests and/or intellect. Ford (1946) found a significant correlation between the number of content categories and intelligence as did Pauker (1963). Klopfer, Allen, and Etter (1960) failed to find any relationship between number of contents and intellect or interest patterns. The number of content categories do appear to give some crude indications about cognitive flexibility, and when the number of contents is especially low, probably reflects constriction and/or preoccupation. An examination of the reference samples shows that the nonpsychiatric group averages 6.6 contents per record as compared to 7.1 for schizophrenics and 7.4 for out-patients. The nonschizophrenics yield the lowest average number of contents, 5.4 per record.

It is also important to note that the frequency of content use appears to vary with occupational interests. Several studies have demonstrated that subjects from the general medical field tend to give higher frequencies of anatomy answers (Schachter, 1948; Molish, Molish, and Thomas, 1950; Dorken, 1954; Hohn, 1959; Rossi and Neuman, 1961). Roe (1952) reports that significant content differences occur among the various science groupings, finding that *An* and *Na* answers occur more often in the records of physicists and biologists, while human percepts are more common among the protocols of psychologists and anthropologists. Caution, however, must be exercised in simply disregarding high frequencies of a given class of content merely because it seems related to occupation or occupational interests. Any excess of content should be regarded as a form of preoccupation, after which, the impact of that preoccupation should be judged. Anyone can become "too wrapped up" in his occupational world at the expense of other features in his environment. In some instances, as in the arts, this is almost expected of the person who is to be a success, but in other instances, the degree of preoccupation may preclude effective interactions which may be necessary for adequate adjustment. Thus the medical student who sees little other than anatomy answers may well be overly withdrawn and potentially maladjusted. Similarly, the artist who conveys nearly all of his responses as abstractions may well be disregarding the realities of the world at great expense.

The literature concerning content seems to convey the notion that no single content category can be regarded as having an absolute relationship to any personality variable and/or psychopathological state, nor should such relationships be inferred in interpretation. The overall configuration of content, however, will often provide guidelines from which other data in the Structural Summary can be understood with greater specificity. Emphasis on a constellation of similar contents such as Botany, Landscape, and Geography, or Blood, Fire, and Explosions, will usually convey useful information toward a better understanding of movement or color answers, or generate a better understanding of the use of form quality. These kinds of constellations often tend to reveal response styles and/or preoccupations.

The scorings of highly idiographic contents, such as grave, ink, shoehorn, guitar, and spear, serve to mark those answers as quite important because they represent a special mix of mediation and ideation. They should be studied carefully in the review of the Structural Summary, but they should not be overemphasized at that point of interpretation. Rather, they signal the fact that highly idiographic answers exist in the record which should be studied carefully in the sequence analysis and review of the verbalizations. The latter will often afford the opportunity to review content in a somewhat different manner, that is, separate from the scorings. Special awareness of responses such as those involving emphasis on orality, facial features, and aggressiveness, is vitally important to the total interpretation of the protocol. This phase of interpretation is described in detail in Chapter 16. It is sufficient at this point to note, that information derived from the content scores, as well as the rest of the Structural Summary, establishes the framework from which the more subjective mode of interpretation can proceed effectively.

REACTION TIME

Rorschach concerned himself mainly with the *average* reaction time per response throughout the record and with the total amount of time elapsed during the Free Association period. There is no indication that he recorded initial reaction times per card with any precision, although he obviously did note long pauses. The Rorschach systematizers have urged a more specific timing of the test, sometimes almost to an extreme. Beck (1944), for example, recommended that initial reaction times be recorded in a fifth of a second, and all of the systems include a reasonably precise timing on a per card basis. Beck (1961) has ultimately argued against attaching significance to the average initial reaction time, suggesting that the range is often too great to render meaningful information by use of a mean. Beck and Klopfer have both suggested that a comparison of the average reaction time to the chromatic cards, with that to the achromatic cards, may provide information concerning the "shock" experience of the subject to these different broad classes of stimulus situations.

The literature concerning reaction times is quite limited, most being devoted to studies of initial reaction time per card. The assumption has been that, unless a particular blot is particularly "threatening," the initial reaction times should be within a reasonable range of each other. A well done study by Meer (1955) shows that this is not the case. He studied the difficulty levels for each blot in terms of average initial reaction times plus difficulty of form level. His data are quite convincing in support of his conclusions that Cards VI, IX, and X are the most difficult, and Cards II, III, and V the least difficult. He finds that reaction times, taken alone, show the chromatic series of II, III, VIII, IX, and X ranks 4th, 2nd, 5th, 10th, and 8th, respectively. The achromatic series of I, IV, V, VI, and VII ranks 3rd, 6th, 1st, 9th, and 7th. Meer strongly criticizes the concept that the reaction times to the last three cards of the test, VIII, IX, and X, can be used as any index of color shock as they ordinarily yield the 5th, 8th, and 10th longest reaction times and have difficulty ratings of 6th, 9th, and 10th. Extrapolating from Meer's difficulty ratings for the chromatic versus the achromatic series, it is to be expected that slightly longer mean reaction times would appear more commonly to the chromatic series. Burstein (1961) offers a strong argument for using median reaction times to study variations in initial response times per card. He follows Beck's argument that means are often unusually deceptive because of one score in a short series, whereas a median in a short series that has most scores similar will not be affected by the extremes.

Most of the systematizers have noted that the shortest reaction times occur among children, manics, and impulsives. The long reaction times have been frequently noted among depressives, compulsives, and some organics. The variance within groups is, however, considerable. A comparison of the reference samples shows no substantial differences for either the mean or median initial reaction times. The shortest reaction times occur most commonly to Cards III and V and the longest reaction times most frequently to Cards VI and IX. When the test is split into the chromatic and achromatic series, some differences in the reference samples are noted. The nonschizophrenics give substantially longer reaction times to the achromatic series while the schizophrenic group gives markedly shorter reaction times to the chromatic series.

The mean initial reaction times for the chromatic and achromatic series are provided in the Structual Summary so as to call attention to any major differences. Usually, no less than a difference of 8″ to 10″ should be regarded as significant, especially if the larger mean value is to the chromatic series. A careful review of the initial reaction times per card is also important to detect instances of exceptionally long or exceptionally short periods between exposure and the response. In some records, a very long reaction time will occur only to a single card, a clue to the interpreter that the responses to that card may indicate some aspects of coping style. Extremely short reaction times often occur to the chromatic cards, suggesting that the subject has been "caught up" in the color features and has been unable to delay affect. This hypothesis is strengthened when the quickly given response *is not* form dominant or when the form quality is weak or poor.

It is quite important that the interpreter does not overemphasize reaction time, as these data simply serve to call attention to seemingly important events.

REFERENCES

Ackerman, M. J. Alcoholism and the Rorschach. *Journal of Personality Assessment*, 1971, **35**, 224–228.

Ames, L. B., Learned, J., Metraux, R., and Walker, R. N. *Child Rorschach Responses*. New York: Hoeber-Harper, 1952.

Ames, L. B., Metraux, R., and Walker, R. N. *Adolescent Rorschach Responses*. New York: Brunner/Mazel, 1971.

Beck, S. J. *Rorschach's Test. I: Basic Processes*. New York: Grune and Stratton, 1944.

Beck, S. J. *Rorschach's Test. II: A Variety of Personality Pictures*. New York: Grune and Stratton, 1945.

Beck, S. J., Beck, A., Levitt, E., and Molish, H. B. *Rorschach's Test. I: Basic Processes*. (3rd ed.) New York: Grune and Stratton, 1961.

Beck, S. J., Rabin, A. I., Thiesen, W. C., Molish, H. B., and Thetford, W. N. The normal personality as projected in the Rorschach Test. *Journal of Psychology*, 1950, **30**, 241–298.

Brockway, A. L., Gleser, G. C., and Utlett, G. A. Rorschach concepts of normality. *Journal of Consulting Psychology*, 1954, **18**, 259–265.

Buhler, C., and LeFever, D. W. A Rorschach study of the psychological characteristics of alcoholics. *Quarterly Journal of Studies in Alcoholism*, 1947, **8**, 107–260.

Buhler, C., Buhler, K., and LeFever, D. W. *Rorschach Standardization Study I. Development of the Basic Rorschach Score with Manual of Directions*. Los Angeles, 1949.

Burstein, A. G. A note on time of first responses in Rorschach protocols. *Journal of Consulting Psychology*, 1961, **25**, 549–550.

Cass, W. A., and McReynolds, P. A. A contribution to Rorschach norms. *Journal of Consulting Psychology*, 1951, **15**, 178–183.

Dorken, H. A psychometric evaluation of 68 medical interns. *Journal of the Canadian Medical Association*, 1954, **70**, 41–45.

Draguns, J. G., Haley, E. M., and Phillips, L. Studies of Rorschach content: A review of the research literature. Part 1: Traditional content categories. *Journal of Projective Techniques and Personality Assessment*, 1967, **31**, 3–32.

Duran, P., Pechoux, R., Escafit, M., and Davidou, P. Le contenu des responses dans le test de Rorschach chez les schizophrenes. *Annual of Medical Psychologie*, 1949, **107**, 198–200.

Ford, M. *The Application of the Rorschach Test to Young Children*. Minneapolis: University of Minnesota Press, 1946.

Goldman, R. Changes in Rorschach performance and clinical comparison in schizophrenia. *Journal of Consulting Psychology*, 1960, **24**, 403–407.

Griffith, R. M. Rorschach water percepts: A study in conflicting results. *American Psychologist*, 1961, **16**, 307–311.

Halpern, F. Rorschach interpretation of the personality structure of schizophrenics who benefit from insulin therapy. *Psychiatric Quarterly*, 1940, **14**, 826–833.

Hohn, E. Theoretische grundlagen der inhaltsanalyse projektiver tests. *Psychologie Forschrift*, 1959, **26**, 13–74.

Klopfer, B., Ainsworth, M., Klopfer, W., and Holt, R. *Developments in the Rorschach Technique. I: Technique and Theori*. Yonkers-on-Hudson, N.Y.: World Book Company, 1954.

Klopfer, W. G., Allen, B. V., and Etter, D. Content diversity on the Rorschach and "range of interests." *Journal of Projective Techniques*, 1960, **24,** 290–291.

Kobler, F. J., and Stiel, A. The use of the Rorschach in involutional melancholia. *Journal of Consulting Psychology*, 1953, **17,** 365–370.

Kuhn, R. Uber die kritische Rorschach-Forschung and einige ihrer Ergebnisse. *Rorschachiana*, 1963, **8,** 105–114.

Meer, B. The relative difficulty of the Rorschach cards. *Journal of Projective Techniques*, 1955, **19,** 43–53.

Molish, H. B. Critique and problems of the Rorschach. A survey. In Beck, S. J. and Molish, H. B. *Rorschach's Test. II: A Variety of Personality Pictures.* (2nd ed.) New York: Grune and Stratton, 1967.

Molish, H. B., Molish, E. E., and Thomas, C. B. A Rorschach study of a group of medical students. *Psychiatric Quarterly*, 1950, **24,** 744–774.

Morris, W. W. Prognostic possibilities of the Rorschach method in metrazol therapy. *American Journal of Psychiatry*, 1943, **100,** 222–230.

Neff, W. S., and Glaser, N. M. Normative data on the Rorschach. *Journal of Psychology*, 1954, **37,** 95–104.

Pauker, J. D. Relationship of Rorschach content categories to intelligence. *Journal of Projective Techniques and Personality Assessment*, 1963, **27,** 220–221.

Piotrowski, Z. A., and Bricklin, B. A second validation of a long term prognostic index for schizophrenic patients. *Journal of Consulting Psychology*, 1961, **25,** 123–128.

Rapaport, D., Gill, M., and Schafer, R. *Diagnostic Psychological Testing.* Vol. 2. Chicago: Yearbook Publishers, 1946.

Ray, A. B. Juvenile delinquency by Rorschach inkblots. *Psychologia*, 1963, **6,** 190–192.

Richardson, H. Rorschachs of adolescent approved school girls, compared with Ames normal adolescents. *Rorschach Newsletter*, 1963, **8,** 3–8.

Roe, A. Analysis of group Rorschachs of psychologists and anthropologists. *Journal of Projective Techniques*, 1952, **16,** 212–224.

Rorschach, H. *Psychodiagnostics.* Bern: Bircher, 1921 (Transl. Hans Huber Verlag, 1942).

Rossi, A. M., and Neuman, G. G. A comparative study of Rorschach norms: Medical students. *Journal of Projective Techniques*, 1961, **25,** 334–338.

Schachter, M. Vingt medecins etudies au test de Rorschach. *Acta Neurologie de Belgium*, 1948, **48,** 22–36.

Schmidt, H. O., and Fonda, C. P. Rorschach scores in the manic state. *Journal of Psychology*, 1954, **38,** 427–437.

Shatin, L. Psychoneurosis and psychosomatic reaction. A Rorschach study. *Journal of Consulting Psychology*, 1952, **16,** 220–223.

Sherman, M. A comparison of formal and content factors in the diagnostic testing of schizophrenia. *Genetic Psychology Monographs*, 1952, **46,** 183–234.

Stotsky, B. A. A comparison of remitting and non-remitting schizophrenics on psychological tests. *Journal of Abnormal and Social Psychology*, 1952, **47,** 489–496.

Vinson, D. B. Responses to the Rorschach Test that identify thinking, feelings, and behavior. *Journal of Clinical and Experimental Psychopathology*, 1960, **21,** 34–40.

Walters, R. H. A preliminary analysis of the Rorschach records of fifty prison inmates. *Journal of Projective Techniques*, 1950, **17,** 436–446.

Wedemeyer, B. Rorschach statistics on a group of 136 normal men. *Journal of Psychology*, 1954, **37,** 51–58.

Weiss, A. A., and Winnik, H. Z. A contribution to the meaning of anatomy responses on the Rorschach Test. *Israel Annual of Psychiatry*, 1963, **1,** 265–276.

Wishner, J. Neurosis and tension: An exploratory study of the relationship of physiological and Rorschach measures. *Journal of Abnormal and Social Psychology*, 1953, **48,** 253–260.

Zolliker, A. Schwangerschaftsdepression und Rorschach'scher formdeutversuch. *Schweiz Archeives Neurologie und Psychiatrie*, 1943, **53,** 62–78.

CHAPTER 15

The Structural Summary

An understanding of the psychologic significance of the Rorschach variables described in the preceding four chapters is prerequisite to any interpretation of the Structural Summary. It also permits a more extensive discussion of five variables that appear in the Summary which have been mentioned only casually in Chapters 11 through 14. They are the Erlebnistypus (*EB*), the Experience Actual (*EA*), the Experience Potential (*ep*), the Experience Base (*eb*), and the Blend response. Each illustrates a complex feature of the test, and taken as a group, they form an important base of information in the Structural Summary that relates to the preferences and potentials for response. These variables are often the most critical in establishing a nuclear understanding of the person from which other features of the Summary can be interpreted more specifically.

THE ERLEBNISTYPUS (*EB*)

Rorschach (1921) considered the *EB* as one of the most important characteristics of the test. He proposed that it reflects the underlying preferential response style of the individual. The *EB*, as briefly described in Chapter 8, represents the ratio of the Sum of the *M* answers to the Sum of the *weighted* chromatic color responses, using weights of 0.5 for *FC*, 1.0 for *CF*, and 1.5 for Pure *C* and *Cn*. The reason for this particular scheme of weights is not completely clear; however, it appears as though Rorschach noted that chromatic color answers occur with a greater frequency than *M* responses and believed the weights should represent some equalization of those average frequencies, and at the same time, include appropriate emphasis for the color answers that minimize or exclude the use of form.

Rorschach hypothesized that when the ratio is distinctly weighed in the *M* direction, the person is more prone to use his inner life for basic gratifications. He termed this introversiveness but was careful to note that it is not the same as the Jungian concept of introversion. Whereas the Jungian introvert is generally conceptualized as being distanciated from people and frequently perceived as isolated or withdrawn into himself, Rorschach's notion of introversiveness focuses on the manner in which the resources of the person are used, *but* does not necessarily imply direct overt behavioral correlates. Thus the introversive person may be regarded by others as outgoing in his social relationships, but internally, he is prone to use his inner life for the satisfaction of his important needs. At the opposite pole is the extratensive person, whose *EB* is markedly weighed on the color side of the ratio. The extratensive is prone to use the interactions between himself and his world for gratification of his more basic needs. It is the *depth* of affective exchange that often marks the extratensive person; that is, he manifests affect *to his world* more routinely than does the introversive individual. Rorschach also recognized the "ambiequal," that is, one whose *EB* is essentially the same on both sides of the ratio. He suggested that the ambiequal may be the most flexible of the three "types" with regard to resources for gratification. Rorschach postulated that the *EB* illustrates a constitutionally predisposed response tendency, emphasizing that the introversive and extratensive features are *not* opposites, but simply different psychological styles or preferences. He noted that when the *EB* displays low frequencies such as 0:1, or 1:0, there has been a coarctation in the development and/or functioning of these preferences for response, so that the individual has only limited organized resources from which to draw. In some instances of psychopathology, the coarcted *EB* will indicate a rigid defensive effort wherein an almost complete paralysis of affect forms the basis of the effort.

While perceiving the *EB* as an essentially stable index of style, Rorschach also noted that various conditions could alter the response preference, either temporarily, or permanently. For instance, unusual or prolonged stress conditions could elicit a transient alteration in the *EB*, while some treatment effects could alter the *EB* more permanently. The literature concerning the *EB* is varied, and sometimes confusing because of a tendency to equate introversiveness and extratensiveness with the behavioral expectations implied in the introversion–extraversion model of Jung. In fact, Bash (1953), Klopfer et al. (1954), and Mindness (1955) have each offered theoretical arguments to demonstrate that they are really the same. Beck, Piotrowski, Hertz, and Rapaport have been less prone than has Klopfer to equate the two concepts. Beck and Piotroswki have aligned themselves most definitively in support of the Rorschach postulate.

Numerous studies have been published concerning personality and behavioral variables of the two basic styles represented in the *EB*. Goldfarb (1945, 1949) has found that children raised from very early life under impersonal institution conditions show marked extratensive *EB*'s. Rabinovitch et al. (1955) report EEG differences among the extreme *EB* types and suggest that the extreme introversive subjects show greater indices of cortical "harmony." Singer and Spohn (1954), and Singer and Herman (1954) found evidence of the influence of the *M* to Sum *C* balance as related to increases in motor activity during a waiting period. Singer (1960), in reviewing the literature concerning the *EB*, suggests that support clearly exists for the postulate that two dimensions of "constitutional temperament" are represented in the ratio, one representing a "capacity for internal experience," the second reflecting activity or motility. Singer suggests that these are modifiable "to a degree" by learning and/or experience. Molish (1967) suggests, in his literature review, that the elements illustrated in the *EB* have a critical directing effect on most all personality "nuances and their related correlates of behavior." Both Singer and Molish cite studies which demonstrate that introversives respond differently from extratensives in a variety of behavioral situations, such as problem solving, stress situations, and environmental responsiveness. It is important to emphasize that while subjects at the extremes of the *EB do* appear to function differently there is no indication *that one is preferable to the other*.

Two studies were completed to investigate the general stability of the *EB* over reasonable time periods. In the first, 30 psychiatric subjects of varying diagnoses were tested at the onset of intervention. Approximately half were in-patients. These subjects, treated with an array of intervention techniques depending on the diagnosis and the orientation of their therapists, were retested 18 months later. A control group of nonpatients was also tested and retested at an 18 month interval. Forty-one of the 60 subjects, 24 controls and 17 patients, showed *EB*'s in the same direction, with the *proportion* of *M* to *C* remaining approximately the same as in the first testing. The actual numbers in the ratio changed much more often than not, but the proportion remained stable. Five of the remaining controls continued to show the *EB* in the same direction as in the first testing; however, the proportions between *M* and *C* did not remain approximately the same. A similar finding was noted in five of the remaining patient subjects. One control subject and eight of the psychiatric subjects did show a distinct change in the direction of the *EB*. Six of these nine subjects had substantially more Sum *C* than *M* in the pretest and showed the reverse in the posttesting. Two of the nine appeared as ambiequal in the second testing. These data seem to support the notion that the *EB* does remain relatively stable in the psychological operations of the individual, especially in the absence of psychopathological conditions and/or prolonged intervention.

In a second study, three groups of 15 subjects each were selected from a larger nonpatient sample on the basis of their *EB* ratios. One group illustrates marked introversive features (*M* more than twice weighted Sum *C*); the second is a markedly extratensive group (Sum *C* more than twice Sum *M*); and the third group is ambiequal by reason that their *M* and Sum *C* scores do not differ by more than 1.0. These subjects were paid to be retested twice during the next 18 months. In the first retest, at a 9 month interval, the introversives and extratensives gave *EB*'s which are essentially the same as in the original testing. The ambiequal group did show changes. Four of the 15 subjects showed marked introversive *EB*'s, and two yielded marked extratensive *EB*'s. In the second retest, at 18 months, 14 of the 15 introversives, all of the extratensives, and 10 of the 15 ambiequals gave *EB*'s essentially the same as in the first testing. The one introversive altered to ambiequal, and the five ambiequals split, three to the introversive side, two to the extratensive side of the ratio. In other words, during three administrations of the test, over a period of 18 months, 39 of 45 subjects continued to show an *EB* which was stable in the *M* to Sum *C* proportions and interpretively would be identified consistently for the same response style. Reviewing the six subjects showing change during this period, it is noted that only one had manifest a marked preference for one side of the ratio (introversive), the remaining five subjects all having been identified as ambiequal in the original testing.

The accumulation of data appears to support Rorschach's contention concerning the meaning and stability of the *EB*. It does provide an index of style or preference for response and illustrates whether the subject relies more on his inner life, and prefers the delays associated with that kind of activity, or whether he is prone toward an affective discharge toward his world. An additional understanding of the *EB* is provided through the Experience Actual.

THE EXPERIENCE ACTUAL (*EA*)

Beck (1960) first described the Experience Actual. He noted that the *EB* includes the dynamically organized affective experiences of the individual, and reasoned that a composite index of the elements in the *EB* would therefore convey information concerning the breadth of this experience in relation to other personality features. He drew from case material to illustrate that subjects completing treatment successfully usually give EB's in a retest that follows the same direction as in the pretreatment testing; however, the actual numbers in the ratio are ordinarily greater. In other words, the posttreatment subject has organized more inner life and affective experiences which are now available to him as components of his "life style." Findings by Bash (1955) and Piotrowski and Schreiber (1952) lend support to Beck's concept although neither conceptualized the process. Bash administered Card IX to 28 subjects 200 times in succession, using a 5 second exposure and a 15 second interval. He found that the $M:C$ ratio for 18 of these subjects gradually became nearly equal; that is, a numerical decline of one component and an increase in the other component occurred. While a change in this experimental EB was noted, the numerical values comprising the EB remained essentially stable. Piotrowski and Shreiber studied 13 patients before and after prolonged psychoanalytic treatment. They report that both sides of the EB ratio increased significantly after treatment although the directions of the ratio generally remained constant, a finding comparable with that reported by Beck. One other study (Erginel, 1972) appears to lend some support to the EA concept. Erginel used data from an earlier study (Kemalof, 1952) in which six series of inkblots, similar to the Rorschach, had been administered to 12 subjects on six consecutive days. Erginel illustrates that the $M + $ Sum C does fluctuate on a daily basis and interprets this as a function of mood shifts. Interestingly, the EB's generally appear to maintain a relatively constant direction, and the EA's fluctuate 4.0 or less in 50 (70 %) of the 72 observations. Beck (1972) has suggested that the EA permits an evaluation of the EB which goes beyond "type thinking." He indicates that it reflects the full volume of the organized activity available to the individual.

It seems quite important to emphasize that the sort of experience or activity expressed in the EA is *organized*, that is, available to the individual. The painful affects and the more unorganized needs, as represented in the responses to the grey-black features of the blots and in FM and m answers, are not "organized." On the contrary, they *work on the individual rather than for him*. Three studies were completed for this work to test Beck's EA concept. Two of these have been mentioned previously in the description of the EB. In the first, two groups of 30 each, patients and nonpatients, were retested after an 18 month interval. The mean EA for the 30 controls at the first administration of the test was 6.25, and 6.75 at the retest. The patient group was subdivided into two groups on the basis of independent ratings from both professionals, in the blind, and relatives regarding the effectiveness of treatment. Eighteen subjects were judged as improved and 12 as unimproved. The mean EA for the improved group was 3.75 at pretreatment and 7.25 at posttreatment. The mean EA's for the unimproved group were 3.50 at pretreatment and 4.25 at posttreatment. The difference between the groups at posttreatment is significant at the .05 level. The second study concerned the three groups of 15 subjects, each selected from a nonpatient sample and retested twice at 9 and 18 month interval. Correlations from the EA's of the three groups calculated between the first and second testings are .88, .91, and .81, and between the first and third testings are .92, .89, and .78. The lowest correlations at each of the retests occurs for the ambiequal group which did fluctuate over time more than did either of the other two groups.

In the third study, two groups of 12 patients each were tested prior to and after the termination of treatment. One group was treated with a dynamic, uncovering form of psychotherapy, averaging 131 sessions during a 20 month period. The second group was treated using supportive and directive methods plus various forms of environmental manipulation. Both groups received medication as appropriate, but the medication was not considered as a primary treatment method. These subjects were drawn from a larger patient sample under study from four out-patient and two in-patient facilities. All subjects were retested 10 weeks after treatment had terminated. The mean *EA*'s were essentially the same at the pretreatment testing, 4.50 for the uncovering treatment group, and 4.75 for the supportive group. The posttreatment *EA*'s are significantly different, showing a mean for the dynamic treatment group of 8.25, and 5.50 for the supportive group. These results are somewhat similar to those reported by Beck and by Piotrowski and Shreiber, and suggest that when some reconstructive impact occurs to the individual, he is able to organize more of his resources. The data also support the notion that the *EA* is relatively stable over time unless some dramatic alteration of the basic organization of affects and inner experience takes place.

Other data from two of the three *EB-EA* studies gave rise to the conceptualization of the Experience Potential, which is an index seemingly related to the *EA*.

THE EXPERIENCE POTENTIAL (*ep*)

The Experience Potential represents the summation of the frequencies of *FM*, *m*, and all of the responses including the grey-black features of the blots. It has been noted in Chapters 12 and 13 that these are response features illustrating needs and affects which *act on* the individual rather than being more controlled psychological activities. In other words, they represent actions which are not "organized" in the sense of *M* and *C* answers.

In the study using two groups of 30 subjects each, it was noted that 22 of the 30 controls had *ep*'s that were less than the *EA* in the first testing. In the 18 month retest, the *ep* was less than the *EA* for 23 of these 30 subjects. The *EA-ep* difference for the 30 psychiatric subjects at the first testing showed that 21 of the 30 had *ep*'s which were *greater* than the *EA*. It is also important to note that the mean *R* for the two groups was essentially the same at the first testing, 23.4 for controls, 22.7 for the patient group. In the 18 month posttesting the *EA-ep* difference had shifted for 15 subjects from a greater *ep* than *EA* to a greater *EA* than *ep*. When this group of 30 subjects was studied using the subdivision of "improved" versus "unimproved," it was found that 14 of the 18 subjects rated as improved had *ep*'s greater than the *EA* in the first test and less than the *EA* in the retest. Seven of the 12 unimproved subjects had *ep*'s greater than the *EA* in the first testing and nine of these 12, including the original seven, had *ep*'s greater than *EA* in the retest. A logical conclusion drawn from these data is that some, or all of the unorganized or uncontrolled activity, became organized and available to those subjects rated as improved, as the *EA*'s increased significantly while the *ep*'s decreased significantly. Conversely, those subjects who are rated as unimproved show no essential change in either *ep* or *EA* after treatment.

These findings provoked a review of the pre- and posttreatment protocols of the 24 subjects used in the third *EB-EA* study. It was noted that eight of the 12 subjects treated with dynamic therapy had *ep*'s greater than the *EA* in the pretreatment records, as did seven of the 12 subjects treated using supportive methods plus environmental manipulation. The posttreatment records show that *all* 12 of the subjects treated with dynamic therapy had *EA*'s greater than *ep*'s. In fact, in half of those cases the *EA* exceeded the *ep* by at least three times the frequency. The subjects treated with supportive and environmental methods did not show similar changes. Five of the 12 continued to show *ep*'s greater than the *EA*, and in one instance where the *ep* had been slightly greater than the *EA*, it was now nearly three times as great.

In light of the data from these two studies, a review of data from another "treatment effects" project was undertaken. In that project, which was a pilot study to test design methodology, 44 nonpsychotic out-patients were randomly assigned, 11 each, to one of four treatment groups. The subjects, 19 males and 25 females ranging in age from 20 to 38, were selected on the basis of complaints of depression, anxiety, and tension, and ideation including preoccupation with death and/or suicide, although none had made a suicidal gesture. They were treated in one of two clinic settings. Subjects in Group I were treated with dynamic psychotherapy at least twice weekly. Subjects in Group II were treated with weekly supportive interviews. Subjects in Group III were treated weekly in group therapy, supplemented by infrequent supportive interviews, and the Group IV subjects were treated using medication and occasional supportive interviews by the attending psychiatrist. Prior to the onset of treatment, all subjects were rated in the blind by one of four psychiatrists and psychologists using the Inpatient Multidimensional Psychiatric Scale after a 30 minute interview. Concurrently, a "significant other," usually a close relative, rated the patient using the Katz Adjustment Scales, Form *R*. Several tests, including the Rorschach, were also administered by one of six examiners. The professional and "significant other" ratings were repeated at 4 month intervals and testing was readministered after 12 months. Six subjects withdrew from treatment against advice during this time, one each from Groups I and IV, and two each from Groups II and III. After the 12 month ratings were complete, the groups were evaluated for improvement. A substantial number of subjects in three of the four groups were rated as improved by both professionals and significant others, eight of 10 in Group I, seven of nine in Group III, and seven of 10 in Group IV. Only three of the nine subjects remaining in Group II (supportive) were rated as improved in both ratings. An examination of the pretreatment Rorschachs reveals that 26 of the 38 subjects had *ep*'s greater than the *EA*. Twenty-one of these subjects were among the 25 who were rated as improved at 12 months. An examination of the 12 month protocols shows that 17 of the 21 reversed the *ep-EA* difference so that the *EA* was greater than the *ep*. Conversely, only four of the 13 subjects who had *EA*'s greater than the *ep* prior to treatment were rated as improved at 12 months, and 10 of those 13, including the four who improved, continued to show the *EA* greater than the *ep*.

It is tempting, although premature, to suggest that the psychological resources illustrated in the *ep* somehow become more organized and/or controlled, thus explaining previously noted increases in *EA*. But this is obviously not the case for all subjects in this study, as *EA*'s increased substantially in only 15 of the 25 improved subjects, and also increased in six of the 13 unimproved subjects. A more conservative conclusion is that many of those stresses giving rise to *FM*, *m*, and shading answers were alleviated during treatment, thus causing either reduction in *ep*, or an increase in *EA*, *or both*. In other words, an alteration appears to occur in the manner in which the psychologic resources are utilized. In some cases, for example, where Pure *F* increases with improvement, the resources are expended conservatively, in tactics of delay and affective control. In other instances, where the *EA* increases, it may be that more resources are organized and controlled at the higher levels of operation. In either event, however, it is apparently an alteration of the activities reflected in the *ep* that permits these changes to occur. Greater controls are developed to contend with the forces that *act on* the individual, either neutralizing them to a reasonable extent, or reorganizing them in such a manner that they *act for* the individual. These findings are not too surprising, as most of the components contributing to the *ep*, especially the *FM* and *m* answers, have been noted by others (Klopfer et al., 1951; Piotrowski and Bricklin, 1952) to be key elements in prognostic indices. Just as the Erlebnistypus contributes to an understanding of the Experience Actual, the Experience Base contributes to an understanding of the Experience Potential.

THE EXPERIENCE BASE (*eb*)

The *eb* is a derivation of a ratio orginally suggested by Klopfer. It illustrates a Sum *FM* + *m* as contrasted with the Sum of all *T*, *V*, *Y*, and *C'* responses, whereas the Klopfer ratio included only *Fc*, *c*, and *C'* on the right side of the entry. Klopfer (1954) suggested that the ratio reflects response tendencies "not fully accepted by or available to the subject" at a given time. He argued that the *FM* and *m* answers are introversive manifestations, while the *Fc*, *c*, and *C'* responses represent extratensive features. His conclusions go somewhat beyond the empirical findings concerning these determinants, but not completely so. The *FM* and *m* answers do reflect forms of inner activity, while the responses to the grey-black features of the blots appear to be related to painful affective experiences, *and* neither type of activity is readily controlled by the individual's higher cognitive actions. Rather, they work on the individual to provoke responses.

The decision to include all responses to the grey-black areas in the ratio was indirectly suggested by Beck, in personal communication (1972), who pointed out that all shading variables give some indications of the degree and intensity with which the individual withdraws from his world, as opposed to acting into it. He suggests that the composite of the grey-black responses sheds some light on the psychological economy of the person by indicating the extent to which painful affects relate to the overall affective life, that is, *EA*. Extending his logic to the *eb*, it is assumed that any ratio illustrating the less well organized or controlled forces should naturally include all shading answers.

A review of the records in the reference samples lends some support for Klopfer's hypothesis that the *eb* should generally follow the same direction as the *EB*. This occurs in 164 of the 200 nonpsychiatric samples, but is evident in only 161 of the the 295 psychiatirc cases. In other words, the preferential response style of the individual does apparently relate both to organized and to unorganized activities. Further support for this postulate is derived from an examination of the pre- and posttreatment protocols of 122 in-patients, the second record having been taken at the time of discharge from hospitalization. The pretreatment records show that 57 of the 122 *eb*'s are in a direction opposite of the *EB*. The posttreatment protocols reveal that this is true in only 18 of the 122 cases. The reference samples also reveal that only 11 of the 200 nonpatient records contain *eb*'s in which a frequency of zero occurs on one or both sides of the ratio. Conversely, 58 of the 295 psychiatric records show such frequencies, 43 of which occur in the protocols of in-patients. The examination of the pre- and posttreatment records of the 122 in-patients mentioned above reveals that 29 had zero frequencies on one or both sides of the ratio in the first testing, but only one subject yielded a zero frequency (*FM* + *m*) in the posttreatment testing.

The *eb* is possibly most useful in illustrating the component features of the *ep*; that is, it accentuates those psychological features than impinge on the individual. As noted in Chapters 12 and 13, these features are responses that prompt other responses. For example, the shading answers reflect pain, passivity, and disharmony. They are the product of unresolved stress situations, and in that context they are responses. But their existence serves as a stimulus to other actions that might alleviate this discomforting state.

As a group, or configuration, the *EB*, *EA*, *ep*, and *eb* provide data from which the response tendencies of the individual can be evaluated more extensively than is possible by focusing on these indices separately. The following configurations, selected from the records of two male subjects in their midtwenties who were referred for problems in concentration, serve to illustrate this point.

CASE A			CASE B	
R = 22			*R* = 21	
EB = 5/1.5	*EA* = 6.5		*EB* = 2/4.5	*EA* = 6.5
eb = 1/4	*ep* = 5		*eb* = 4/1	*ep* = 5

In both records the *EA* and *ep* are identical, the *EA* being slightly higher and suggesting, in respect to *R*, that a substantial organization of resources has occurred. The *EB*'s and *eb*'s are essentially reversed. In Case A the *EB* suggests a more introversive style wherein delay and fantasy activities probably play an important role. The *eb* illustrates a notable use of shading, suggesting pain and withdrawal. This composite leads to the speculation that the difficulties in concentration *may* be related to excessive delay and/or unpleasant fantasies which are creating a pain response, which in turn could lead to more delay, more fantasy, and so on. In Case B, the opposite appears. The subject is more prone to extratensiveness and is oriented toward affective discharge into his world. The *eb* indicates that he experiences the promptings of less organized needs and apparently, in light of his extratensive features, is prone to respond to them, probably through overt affective action since that is his more preferred style. Tentative hypotheses comparing the two cases would be that Case A may have concentration problems related to his inner experiences, while Case B may have concentration problems related to his affective displays. Of course, neither of these hypotheses has a firm base without the other data in the protocol. The *DQ* scores, the *F*+ and *X*+ percentages, the *FC/CF* +*C* ratio, and such all will offer necessary information to strengthen, alter, or reject these hypotheses. Another important element in the record yields information concerning the complexity of the psychological activity of the subject. This is the blend answer.

BLEND RESPONSES (.)

When a blend occurs, it is an indication of a complexity of activity at the time of the response. Such complexity may characterize the individual, or it may simply be a manifestation where a specific stimulus event gave rise to a complex operation. The fact that more than one determinant occurs in an answer does not alter the significance of either of the determinants involved. For example, an $M.FC$ response conveys both the inner experience associated with the M component and the more externally associated experience of the FC. As noted in Chapter 6, Blends occur in slightly more than 15% of the responses of subjects in the nonpsychiatric reference sample. This seems to indicate that most subjects will manifest this form of complexity in their responsiveness to complex and ambiguous stimulus situations. The psychiatric reference groups, especially the out-patient sample and the in-patient schizophrenics, give substantially more Blend answers than do the nonpatients. This suggests, as Beck has noted, that a significant proportion of Blends may illustrate the psychological complexities that occur in psychopathological states.

When the Blend includes both M and C features, it may reflect a form of ambivalence concerning the most appropriate response to the stimulus. When the Blend includes both M and shading features, it may illustrate a painful affective state accompanying the inner experience. A Blend involving both chromatic color and shading represents the concurrent experience of pleasure (C) and unpleasantness (shading) occurring to the same cognitive experience. Blends which include two or more types of shading are rare and probably reflect a more "tormented" affective experience.

A psychological complexity, as represented in the Blend answer, is by no means a "negative" characteristic. Blends do occur more frequently in higher levels of intelligence and, *in low proportions*, appear to be manifestations of the varieties of cortical activities that may occur to an ambiguous situation. At the extremes, too few or too many Blends may signify a complexity of the psychological activities, or lack thereof, associated with "runaway" thinking, or thinking which is overly constrictive.

The Structural Summary includes an entry which notes the number of Blend answers as contrasted with the total R. When the number of Blends equals more than one-fifth of the record, it may be excessive, giving rise to the speculation, that the psychological operations are overly complicated and may be provoking a state of disorganization in the person. Conversely, when the proportion of Blends is very low, in an average length record or longer, there may be undue constriction of the psychologic processes. Examination of pre- and posttreatment protocols of out-patients indicates that the number of Blend answers usually decreases, *but does not disappear*, when the treatment effects are judged as favorable.

A REVIEW OF THE STRUCTURAL SUMMARY

It seems appropriate at this point to review all of the features in the Structural Summary, demonstrating how each may be used in the formulation of preliminary hypotheses. The Summary of the protocol L. S., a 26 year old married high school teacher, previously included in Chapter 8 will possibly serve as a useful sample case. In addition to the information above concerning L.S. the interpreter would be aware of the fact that the testing is not for psychiatric reasons. Rather, it was completed as a part of a project in which volunteer nonpatients were solicited for testing to establish a control group for a treatment effects project. Mr. L. S. was a volunteer, paid for his time. In addition to the data shown above, Mr. L. S. completed a short biographical questionnaire from which some additional information may be gleaned. He is the oldest of three children and has two younger brothers. All three are college graduates although neither parent attended college. Both parents are living, and the father continues working as a skilled tradesman in a small northeastern United States community. Mr. L. S.'s wife is also a college graduate,

Table 28. Structural Summary for the Protocol of L.S.

$R = 25$ $Zf = 12$ $Z\text{Sum} = 38.5$ $P = 11$ $(2) = 7$

Location Features		Determinants	Contents	Contents (Idiographic)
W = 8	DQ	$FM.FT.FD$ = 1	H = 4	Bell = 1
		$FM.FD$ = 1	(H) = 3	
D = 16	+ = 8	$m.CF$ = 1	Hd = 1	Rocket = 1
		$m.FY$ = 1	(Hd) =	
Dd = 1	o = 17		A = 8	Ship = 1
		M = 4	(A) = 0,1	
S = 1	v = 0	FM = 3	Ad = 2	=
		m =	(Ad) =	
DW = 0	— = 0	C =	Ab =	=
		CF =	Al =	
		FC = 3	An =	=
FORM QUALITY		C' =	Art = 1	
		$C'F$ =	Ay = 1	=
FQx	FQf	FC' =	Bl =	
		T =	Bt = 2	=
+ = 5	+ = 0	TF =	Cg = 1	
		FT = 1	Cl =	
o = 20	o = 9	V =	Ex =	
		VF =	Fi = 0,1	
w = 0	w = 0	FV =	Fd =	
		Y =	Ge =	
— = 0	— = 0	YF =	Hh = 1	
		FY = 1	Ls =	
		rF =	Na =	
		Fr =	Sx =	
		FD =	Xy =	
		F = 9		

RATIOS, PERCENTAGES, AND DERIVATIONS

$Z\text{Sum}/Z\text{est} = 38.5/38.0$	$FC/CF + C = 3/1$	Afr	$= .56$
$Zd = +0.5$	$W/M = 8/4$	$3r + (2)/R$	$= 7/25 = .28$
$EB = 4/2.5$ $EA = 6.5$	$W/D = 8/16$	Cont/R	$= 10/25$
$eb = 7/4$ $ep = 11$	$L = .56$	$H + Hd/A + Ad = 6/10$	
$\text{Blends}/R = 4/25$	$F+\% = 100$	$H + A/Hd + Ad = 12/4$	
$a/p = 7/4$	$X+\% = 100$	XRT Achrom	$= 4.6''$
$M^a/M^p = 4/0$	$A\% = 40$	XRT Chrom	$= 9.0''$

having majored in elementary education, but has not worked since the time that their son, age one, was born. Mr. L. S. has no remarkable medical history, is interested in tennis and golf, watches TV approximately 8 hours per week, and would like to be a college teacher but is not currently working toward any advanced degree in his professional area, which is social science.

The approach to the Structural Summary should ordinarily begin by examination of three of the frequencies shown at the top of the Summary Sheet, R, Zf, and P. These data reveal something of the kind of record involved, its length, attempts at organization, and the orientation to conventional percepts. Subsequently, the ratios, percentages, and derivations entered in the lower portion of the Summary Sheet are reviewed, and finally, the specific frequencies for each of the components are studied. At times, specific frequencies will be noted to aid in understanding some of the ratios and percentages before reviewing all of the frequencies. This general procedure facilitates the development of working hypotheses and ensures that all data are considered before moving on to a study of the sequence of responses and the verbal material.

R: The range of R for most adults is 17 to 27. The L. S. protocol has $25R$ suggesting that data from the reference samples may be applicable, and that a sufficient R has occurred to make the ratios and percentages useful. If R were very low, the usefulness of most of the ratios and percentages would be questionable.

Zf: The reference sample for nonpatients indicates that most adult subjects give about seven organized responses for about $22R$. The L. S. record shows a Zf of 12 suggesting the possibility of higher level intelligence and/or a need to account for the details in his world. This datum alerts the interpreter to a special awareness of those features of the Summary which will clarify this, especially the Zd score and the frequency of W's in the record plus an evaluation of the DQ scores.

P: The P score is the only aspect of the record which is finite. There are 13 possible Popular responses, and L. S. has used 11 of them, considerably more than the 6.7 average shown in the reference sample for nonpatients. This is somewhat striking and leads to the first tentative proposition, that is, *excessive concern with conventionality*. This is especially important to what is known about the L. S. record thus far, in that "bright" people, as suggested from the Zf, do not generally confine themselves to conventional answers to this extent in an average length record. Throughout the remainder of the interpretation, this proposition requires continuing evaluation to determine if the P answers are typical, or whether they are included in more creative and well organized responses. Had the P score been excessively low, such as 2 or 3, a similar consideration would be manifest, but concerning the lack and/or or rejection of conventionality.

$ZSum/Zest$, Zd: The $ZSum$ is about the same as the estimated Z score, yielding a Zd of $+0.5$. These data imply that, although L. S. organizes more than most non-patient adults, he does so effectively so that the levels of organization involved are compatible with the attempts. If the Zd score had been excessively higher, it might be postulated that he "overincorporates." If the Zd had been substantially lower than zero, it might be hypothesized that he strives for integration at a level which exceeds his cognitive functioning. An evaluation of the $F+\%$ and the $X+\%$ is relevant here to determine any problems of perceptual accuracy which may have occurred in this organizational activity.

EB, EA, ep, eb: The *EB* is slightly introversive, but not markedly so, indicating some flexibility in basic response style. He is apparently more prone toward delay and inner experience, but is also capable of acting into his world when gratifications are sought. The *EA* reveals that he has considerable organized resources in relation to this style of response, but the *ep-eb* data indicate that he is also stimulated by elements which are not well organized, and leads to the formulation of two tentative propositions. First, since the *ep* is nearly twice as great as *EA*, it may be hypothesized that *he has considerable resources which are not organized or easily available to him.* Second, the *eb* indicates a preponderance of *FM + m*, suggesting that *he is often prompted to responses by needs which are more basic or elementary.* Had the *ep* been less than *EA*, the first hypothesis would have noted that his resources appear to be generally well organized. Had the *eb* shown smaller frequencies on each side of the ratio, the second hypothesis would have noted that his needs are generally well organized and that he experiences few painful affects concerning them. As is, it would seem that he is often uncomfortable, possibly because of the promptings of the less sophisticated need experiences. The needs and resources identified in the two hypotheses offered concerning the *EB, EA, ep,* and *eb* should also be considered in the framework of the earlier proposition derived from the high *P*. In other words, his orientation toward conformity may relate to these less well organized states in some way, and the interpreter should be alert for this possibility as the review of the record proceeds.

Blends/R: L. S. gives four Blends, a frequency which is in line with that expected. This seems to indicate that his psychological operations are not excessively complicated. A cursory glance at the actual Blend frequencies does note, however, that at least one of these, and possibly two (*FM.FT.FD,* and *m.FY*) are somewhat unusual and will require special attention as the interpretation progresses. They may not shed any new light on the cognitive workings of L. S.; however, they may be sufficiently idiographic to hint of the unique characteristics that relate to the tentative propositions offered thus far.

a/p, M^a/M^p: The *a/p* ratio for all movement answers in the L. S. record shows that active movements exceed passive movements by 3, an acceptable level as noted in Chapter 12, and suggesting that he has flexibility in his ideational activities. Had the ratio been around 9/2, the speculation that he is more constrictive in the style of his ideation would have been warranted. It is noted that his *M* answers are all of the active variety, which may indicate that his fantasy life *is* more restrictive and raises a question concerning his basic response style, as illustrated in the *EB, EA, ep, eb* data. It has been hypothesized that he is more prone to introversiveness and that he has considerable prompting from unorganized resources. An inner life which is consistently "active" may reflect the aspired for goals that are not represented in his behaviors, that is, something of a "Walter Mitty" existence, where fantasy is used as a substitute for routine and/or forced inhibition. The high *P* value again becomes important, as it could reflect the constraints that may provoke the active fantasies. This may be stated as another tentative proposition. *He has fantasy strivings which, possibly, are incompatible with his needs for conventionality.*

FC/CF + C: The L. S. data show a ratio of 3/1 indicating that he does have useful affect and that it is ordinarily controlled by reality operations. At the same time, he is capable of some responses wherein the emotion commands the response. Apparently, he can "let himself go" under some circumstances, and it will be of interest to attempt to determine what those circumstances might be as the interpretation progresses. Had the ratio shown no CF or C, there could be some concern for an excessive constriction which has already been postulated from other factors. Had the ratio been more heavily weighted to CF and/or C, the logical conclusion would be that, when he projects affect into his world, he has little control over the accuracy or reality of the response. Since neither of these are true for L. S., his affective capabilities are probably an asset to him.

W/M: Since W and M have both been demonstrated as related to intellectual functioning, and W is also illustrative of strivings to use all of the stimulus elements, this ratio is a crude but useful index of aspiration as contrasted with capability. Nonpatient records generally show a 2/1 to 3/1 W to M ratio. The L. S. record falls in this range. Had the W exceeded the M by more than 3/1 it would be reasonable to speculate that he has aspirations that exceed his functioning level. Conversely had the ratio fallen below 2/1, it could be hypothesized that his aspirations are lower than he is capable of striving for. Naturally, the DQ and Form Quality scores offer much necessary clarifying information concerning any of these propositions.

W/D: This is primarily a normative ratio that indicates the extent to which the subject has selected the "easier" D areas of the blots as compared with the generally more demanding W answers. The L. S. record shows a 1/2 ratio which coincides with that given by the majority of nonpatients. Had the D side of the ratio been unusually elevated, that is, more than 1/3, the conclusion could be that the subject selects the easiest perceptual-cognitive "way out" when faced with ambiguity. Had the ratio been weighed heavily toward the W side, in an average length record, the assumption might be that the subject strives to excess in attempting to organize ambiguous stimulus situations.

L: The Lambda index represents the proportion of Pure F responses that have occurred in the record. As noted in Chapter 12, the L generally falls between .59 and .94, with .50 having been identified as a low limit. The L. S. Lambda is .56 which tends toward this lower limit, and, while not necessarily remarkable, does suggest that he may be prone toward more affective responses than may be useful for him in the context of his introversive style and high P value. Had the L fell below .50, the possibilities of affective lability would be considered. If the Lambda exceeds 1.0, it is generally an indication of excessive affective constraint. While no specific postulate can be drawn from the L. S. Lambda, it is sufficiently close to the lower limit to warrant close examination of the manner in which affect is displayed in the component frequency tally. For instance, if any one variable, such as Y, appears in quantity, it may suggest that L. S. is in jeopardy of becoming more affectively dominated than is now the case.

$F+\%$, $X+\%$: The form quality percentages for the Pure F answers, and for the overall record have been described in some detail in Chapter 11. Ordinarily, it is expected that both of these proportions will show good form quality for at least 75% of the responses included in them, with a 70% level considered the lower limit. Conversely, it is not expected that either percentage, and especially the $X+\%$, will approach 100% in records of average length or longer as some "idiographic bending of reality" is compatible with cognitive flexibility. The L. S. protocol shows both the $F+\%$ and the $X+\%$ to be 100 giving rise to another proposition; namely, *that he is overly concerned with reality accuracy and may be sacrificing some of his own uniqueness and creativity to achieve this.* This postulate is also related to the high P value and may give some clue concerning the effects of the orientation toward conventionality. It may, in addition, reveal some of the reasons for the relatively high ep; that is, his concerns with "doing the appropriate or correct" interfere with the development of his own talents and resources. The high $F+$ and $X+$ also offer some clarity to the question raised earlier concerning the substantial Zf of 12 and the Zd of $+0.5$. Apparently, he is able to function at higher levels of organizational activity without scarificing perceptual accuracy. Stated more simply, *he is probably a pretty intelligent fellow who may not be using his intellect fully.*

$A\%$:   This proportion, described in Chapter 14, is basically a normative element. Animals are among the easiest objects to perceive in the blots and most nonpatient adult records contain between 35 and 45% A and Ad percepts. The L. S. record is in the range, and thus is unremarkable for this feature. Had the $A\%$ been substantially low, that is less than 30% in this length record, two other elements would be important to any interpretive postulate. If the content scores showed the use of many categories, with none showing high frequencies, the subject may be manifesting an extensive intellectual effort, the effectiveness of which must be judged from other sources in the record such as the $+\%$'s, the DQ, the Zd, and such. Conversely, if the $A\%$ is unusually high, 50% or more, it illustrates a form of cognitive contriction which may be due to limited intellect, or may be a manifestation of a defensive pattern based on guardedness.

Afr: The affective ratio represents the proportion of responses to the last three cards in the test as contrasted with the number of responses to the first seven cards. It provides some index of the extent to which the subject is affected by the colors and may give a clue to the impact of the external world on his behavior. The Afr is probably limited to usefulness in conjunction with the Lambda index, the $FC/CF + C$ ratio, and the EB, all of which convey some information regarding emotionality. The majority of nonpsychiatric subjects show an Afr falling between .55 and .75. When the ratio is lower than .55 it may indicate a tendency to withdraw from affective stimuli. At the opposite extreme, when the ratio exceeds .75 it may demonstrate tendencies to become "caught up" in affective stimuli. The L. S. record yields an Afr of .56 which approaches the lower limit. In and by itself, the .56 means little; however, in the context of other postulates concerning constrictive features, it probably offers some support for the premise that he attempts to avoid any loss of control over affect, and may not permit himself the "full measure" of interaction with his world.

$3r + (2)/R$:   This weighted ratio offers some indications concerning egocentricity or self-esteem. It is important, as noted in Chapter 13, to review the frequency tallies to determine if any reflection answers have been involved. Ordinarily, the proportion of weighted reflections plus the frequency of pairs should equal no more than 30 to 40% of the R. If the proportion is lower than 30% it reflects a low self-valuation, usually created in part by excess concern for others and the values of the external world. When the proportion is unusually high, more than 40% it represents an excessive value on the self, usually at the expense of others and the values of the external world. The L. S. protocol shows that there are no reflection answers, which is generally a good sign, but that the number of pair responses, seven, equals only 28% of *R*, or slightly less than the 30% lower limit. This may signify *a lower than appropriate self-evaluation*, and in the framework of the high *P* value, it would appear that his concern for conventionality has limited his own self-esteem. This tentative proposition is important because it gives more strength to the earlier speculations that he does not use his talents fully, and may be sacrificing his own uniqueness to conformity.

Cont/R: The number of contents appearing in the L. S. record exceed the expected number, about seven, for most adult nonpsychiatric subjects. This probably a reflection of his intellect and interests. Had the number of contents been significantly low, 4 or less, it would indicate a narrowness of ideation and probably some form of preoccupations. If it had been higher than is the case, 12 or more, it would have suggested that he is "living on his intellect" at the expense of his affect.

H + Hd/A + Ad: This ratio appears to provide some index about the extent to which the subject is concerned with people. It represents the accumulated frequency of human percepts as contrasted with the "easier to see" animal responses. The reference sample for nonpatients indicates that the ratio usually falls between 1:2 and 1:2.5. The L. S. protocol yields a ratio of less than 1:2, suggesting that *he is "well aware" of others, and possibly even preoccupied with them.* Had the emphasis been in the opposite direction, as in 1:4, it would be concluded that the subject avoids and/or disregards others in his thinking and behavior. The slightly exaggerated emphasis on human percepts in the L. S. record is probably related to his own low self-esteem and his strong emphasis on conformity, as illustrated by the large number of *P* answers. It may also reveal something about his tendencies toward constriction of affective displays, and could account, at least in part, for some of the painful affects evident in the *eb*.

H + A/Hd + Ad: As mentioned in Chapter 14, this is essentially a normative ratio that depicts the extent to which one is overly narrow and/or critical in his cognitive operations. Most adult nonpatients show this ratio in a range of 3:1 to 4:1, as does the L. S. protocol. Had the ratio been higher on the left side, such as 6:1 or greater, it could reflect a lackadaisical approach to details. If it is high on the right side, such as 1:1 or even 2:1, it would indicate an unusual preoccupation with details, and possibly an undue suspiciousness in the basic style.

XRT's: The L. S. record shows that the mean reaction time to the chromatic cards is almost twice as long as to the achromatic cards. As noted in Chapter 14, this information serves as a signal to carefully review the reaction times to the individual cards during the sequence analysis. A longer reaction time is generally expected to the chromatic series, and the difference in the L. S. Summary is not especially remarkable. Nevertheless, if *all, or most all,* of the times to the chromatic cards are longer than those to the achromatic cards, it may lend support to the earlier speculation that he attempts to keep close control over his affective responses and does not permit himself to become too "close" to his environment. It may also be that the difference in the means is created by one single long reaction time to a chromatic card. If this is the case, it may indicate difficulty in organizing a response to that card, and the response(s) may be of special significance.

Location features: An examination of the frequencies for types of location areas selected often adds clarification to previously formulated hypotheses. For instance, a substantial use of *Dd* areas may indicate an avoidance of the obvious and/or an unusual preoccupation with details. Similarly, an emphasis on the use of white space may convey a form of negativism and/or hostility. The frequencies for location areas in the L. S. protocol are unremarkable. The proportions of *W*, *D*, *Dd*, and *S* all coincide with the means from the nonpsychiatric reference sample. The distribution of the *DQ* scores does add some support for the previous speculation that L. S. is intellectually above average. Nearly one-third of his responses are "synthesis" answers suggesting a cognitive orientation toward integration. It is also important to note that none of the locations used by L. S. are of the "lower" developmental quality. If two or three of the *DQ* scorings had been vague or minus *in this record*, it would give rise to concern that his proneness to cling to perceptual accuracy may actually be a disorganizing influence.

Form quality: The distribution of form quality scorings, both for Pure F answers (*FQf*), and for the entire record (*FQx*), provides another view of the reality orientation of his cognitive operations. These data are especially important in many records where the $F+\%$ and $X+\%$ are less than 100% and they provide some indication of the extent to which perceptual accuracy has been "bent" and/or abandoned. They also provide a review of the circumstances under which perceptual inaccuracies occur; that is, when affect is constrained (Pure *F*) versus conditions where affect is included (non-Pure *F*). The L. S. record is quite conservative in this context. All of the responses use good form quality, and it has been hypothesized that he may be sacrificing some of his own unique and/or creative features in his commitment to perceptual accuracy. This conservatism is accented in the form quality scorings which reveal that all of the Pure *F* answers are ordinary, and that only five responses in the record have a superior form level, representing the unusually well developed response. The latter is slightly less than the mean of 26% plus answers in the protocols of the nonpsychiatric reference group (see Table 23), and seems particularly low for a subject who is apparently as "bright" as L. S. These data add support to the proposition that *he is not using his talents fully*, and are probably best explained at this point in terms of the unusually high frequency of Popular answers previously noted. The high frequency of *o* answers is particularly unusual is a record where the *Zf* and the *DQ* plus scores are higher than expected, and suggests undue caution in the formulation of answers.

Determinant frequencies: The distribution of determinants offers a closer inspection of many of the factors that contribute to the ratios, percentages, and derivations previously reviewed. Emphasis on a particular determinant is sometimes "highlighted," and the absence of some of the more commonly expected determinants can often clarify propositions that have been formulated. For instance, the L. S. record is void of *r*, *V*, and *C'* determinants. The absence of these determinants is probably an asset for L. S. in that *he is not experiencing the more painful affective states*, which could have accompanied his constrictiveness and/or his limited self-esteem. It has already been noted, from examination of the *EB*, *eb*, and *a/p* ratios, that the protocol includes a preponderance of movement answers, the frequency distribution shows 5 *FM*'s, 4 *M*'s, and 2 *m* responses. Interestingly, all of his blend answers contain either an *FM* or *m* determinant suggesting that it is the less sophisticated forces that do provoke a complexity to his cognitive functioning. It is also important to note that the only use of *FD* occurs in the blend answers. In other words, the presence of *his less well organized needs also gives rise to affective experience and/or causes a tendency toward introspectiveness.* The distribution also reveals that all but one of his answers (*m.CF*) are form dominant, indicating that he keeps close control on his affect and probably offers some clarification for the preponderence of ordinary responses. He is uncomfortable with some of his needs, and his lack of adequate self-value may be a product of his guarded control concerning his inner experiences. His response to the gray-black features of the blots occurs in the form of 2 *FT* and 2 *FY* responses, one each appearing in a blend. The frequency of these answers is only slightly higher than expected and appears to reconfirm the postulate that he is not experiencing unusual pain in his situation, but rather has some orientation toward a passive withdrawal. The high frequency of *FM* and *m* raises the issue of tension and, when combined with the evidence concerning the constrictiveness of affect and the conservative use of intellect, suggests *a behavioral pattern of cautious alertness.*

Content frequencies: An examination of the distribution of contents will often yield clues about preoccupations and/or conflicts. It has been previously speculated that L. S. was well aware of others and possibly preoccupied with them. This postulate now requires additional consideration in light of the distribution of human contents. If all these responses include a whole human figure, not parenthesized, it would illustrate a strong interest in people. The L. S. record shows that only half of the answers involving human content have this character. The remaining three responses that use human content include one that is parenthesized and two which use human detail. This finding is also supportive of the proposition that *he is constrictive and possibly feels his own limitations more sharply than implied by the distribution of determinants.* It also implies that L. S. *does have an interest in others, but based on a defensiveness rather than a desire for more interpersonal contact.* The remaining content categories show low frequencies, except the animal category where a substantial frequency is expected. There is no apparent pattern to the contents used that is detectable from the Structural Summary. The three idiographic contents, bell, rocket, and ship, offer no definitive clues, although each should be reviewed carefully in the analysis of sequence and verbalizations.

A PRELIMINARY SUMMARY OF L. S.

The interpretation of the Structural Summary represents *only a part* of the complete interpretation of the Rorschach. Analysis of the sequence of responses, and the verbalizations involved in the Free Association and Inquiry, will add new propositions and alter or clarify those derived to this point. Nonetheless, it seems worthwhile to summarize the propositions developed from the Structural Summary, to determine if there is a consistency evident, to consider possible contradictions that may exist, and to focus on important questions that may have been raised by the propositions. The Structural Summary of L. S. yields at least 10 propositions, several of which are obviously interrelated.

1. He has a marked concern with conventionality (High *P*).
2. He has considerable resources which are not well organized or easily available to him (high *ep* in relation to *EA*).
3. He is frequently prompted to respond by needs and/or stresses over which he has little control and experiences some discomfort because of this (*eb*).

4. He is prone to resort to his inner life to delay and/or organize his responses (*EB*).

5. He was a reasonably rich fantasy life which appears more oriented toward "action" (M^a/M^p), but is also oriented to a more "passive" response pattern by other forces (a/p, $FY = 2$).

6. He appears overly "bound" to reality accuracy and may be sacrificing some of his individuality as a result (high $F+$ and $X+\%$'s and FQ distribution).

7. He is quite intelligent (*Zf*, *Zd*, *DQ*) but apparently not using this talent fully (see Proposition 6).

8. His self-evaluation is somewhat lower than desirable ($3r + (2)/R$).

9. He is aware of others ($H + Hd/A + Ad$) but in a comparative way that causes some constriction and awareness of his perceived limitations so that his interest in others is a defense more than a "seeking" response [$H/(H) + Hd$ and marginal *Afr*].

10. He apparently does not have a direct experience of pain (absence of C' and V) but probably does experience tension ($FM + m$) that gives rise to affect and/or introspection (Blends).

These propositions convey both assets and liabilities, and precipitate several questions. L. S. is a bright person who can organize quite well. His ideation is somewhat flexible but he seems to be in some conflict which includes active fantasies versus a more passive behavioral orientation that is strongly oriented toward "doing the right thing." In other words, he is conflicted by that which he wants to do, or is prompted to do, versus that which he feels he should do, or is committed to do. He has good resources, although some appear less available to him than is desirable. He is overly committed to perceptual accuracy, which, in turn, limits the extent to which his full resources are utilized. He feels some tension from his unresolved needs and/or stresses and appears to have the resources to channel those pressures into constructive or intrapersonally profitable behaviors. Unfortunately, his low self-esteem and allegiance to reality provoke him into a more cautious and constrictive use of his resources, which in turn reaffirms his feelings of "insecurity" and forces him to be somewhat "on-guard" with his environment. He is defensive about others and is unwilling to interact at deeper levels even though he has good affective resources. The cause of the tension ($FM + m$) is not clear at this point, nor is the antecedent of the orientation toward conventionality. The latter may be a response to the former, as a defense, or the opposite relationship between these elements may be true. It seems important to emphasize that L. S. is not a patient, nor even a prospective patient, thus the liabilities evident in the Structural Summary cannot be given too much weight.

The analysis of the sequence and the verbalizations of L. S. is presented in the next chapter and a final summary of the protocol is included there. The propositions and speculations which have been developed from the Structural Summary form a nucleus of information on which the idiographic data, derived from the verbalizations, are built to yield a description of a unique person.

REFERENCES

Bash, K. W. Einstellungstypus and Erlebnistypus: C. G. Jung and Herman Rorschach. *Journal of Projective Techniques*, 1955, **19**, 236–242.

Beck, S. J. *The Rorschach Experiment: Ventures in Blind Diagnosis.* New York: Grune and Stratton, 1960.

Beck, S. J. Personal Communication, March, 1972.

Erginel, A. On the test-retest reliability of the Rorschach. *Journal of Personality Assessment*, 1972, **36**, 203–212.

Goldfarb, W. Psychological privation in infancy and subsequent adjustment. *American Journal of Orthopsychiatry*, 1945, **15**, 249–254.

Goldfarb, W. Rorschach test differences between family reared, institution reared, and schizophrenic children. *American Journal of Orthopsychiatry*, 1949, **19**, 624–633.

Kemalof, S. The effect of practice in the Rorschach Test. In Peters, W. (Ed.), *Studies in Psychology and Pedagogy*. Instanbul: University of Istanbul Press, 1952.

Klopfer, B., Ainsworth, M., Klopfer, W., and Holt, R. *Developments in the Rorschach Technique. I: Theory and Practice*. Yonkers-on-Hudson, N.Y.: World Book Company, 1954.

Klopfer, B., Kirkner, F., Wisham, W., and Baker, G. Rorschach prognostic rating scale. *Journal of Projective Techniques*, 1951, **15**, 425–428.

Mindness, A. Analytic psychology and the Rorschach Test. *Journal of Projective Techniques*, 1955, **19**, 243–253.

Molish, H. B. Critique and problems of the Rorschach. A survey. In Beck, S. J. and Molish, H. B. *Rorschach's Test. II: A Variety of Personality Pictures*. (2nd ed.) New York: Grune and Stratton, 1967.

Piotrowski, Z., and Bricklin, B. A second validation of a long term prognostic index for schizophrenic patients. *Journal of Consulting Psychology*, 1961, **25**, 123–128.

Piotrowski, Z., and Schreiber, M. Rorschach perceptanalytic measurement of personality changes during and after intensive psychoanalytically oriented psychotherapy. In Bychowski, G. and Despert, J. L. (Eds.), *Specialized Techniques in Psychotherapy*. New York: Basic Books, 1952.

Rabinovitch, M. S., Kennard, M. A., and Fister, W. P. Personality correlates of electroencephalographic findings. *Canadian Journal of Psychology*, 1955, **9**, 29–41.

Rorschach, H. *Psychodiagnostics*. Bern: Bircher, 1921 (Transl. Hans Huber Verlag, 1942).

Singer, J. L. The experience type: Some behavioral correlates and theoretical implications. In Rickers-Ovsiankina, M. (Ed.), *Rorschach Psychology*. New York: Wiley, 1960.

Singer, J. L., and Herman, J. Motor and fantasy correlates of Rorschach human movement responses. *Journal of Consulting Psychology*, 1954, **18**, 325–331.

Singer, J. L., and Spohn, H. Some behavioral correlates of Rorschach's experience-type. *Journal of Consulting Psychology*, 1954, **18**, 1–9.

CHAPTER 16

Analysis of the Sequence and Verbalizations

Propositions formulated from the review of sequence and the verbal material are sometimes more subjective than those derived from the Structural Summary. This is not to suggest that these data are any less valuable, for this is not the case, but it is a procedure that should be approached cautiously, and with clinical skill. There are two phases involved. One consists of a review of the sequence of scores, and the second involves a study of the sequence of answers. Together, these procedures often reveal much of the idiography of the subject, and render both a broader and more specific understanding of him. If the propositions developed from the Structural Summary can be conceived as creating the "skeleton" of the person, those generated from the sequence and verbal material can be construed as creating the "flesh." The patterning of scores and words creates a complex set of clues that often illustrates aspirations, conflicts, and such. Single units of these data should not be overemphasized, but viewed instead as a composite, just as the data in the Structural Summary are used. Where propositions derived from the sequence and verbal material are inconsistent with those generated from the Structural Summary, the more conservative approach is to "opt" in favor of the Structural material, if reconciliation is impossible.

SEQUENCE OF SCORES

A review, by card, of the scoring features provides information concerning the distribution of reaction times, the manner of approach in the use of location areas, and such. Elements such as the sequence of determinants, Populars, Z scores, and the placement of the idiographic contents are all of interest. The scoring sequence for the L. S. protocol is shown in Table 29 and can be used to demonstrate the usefulness of this information.

A study of the reaction times in the L. S. protocol clarifies a question raised in the review of the Structural Summary concerning the differences in mean reaction times. Obviously, the longer mean RT to the chromatic cards is mainly a product of the long RT to Card IX. In that Card IX is one of the most difficult of the cards, a longer than average RT is not necessarily meaningful; however, the 19″ RT is more than twice as long as RT's to any of the other cards and may signify that the verbal material to that card has special idiographic importance.

The sequence of location selections often provides a hint of the manner in which the cognitive organization of the blots has occurred. Most nonpatients either approach the blot with a W response and then move to D answers, or begin with D responses and ultimately give the W. Psychiatric subjects, especially schizophrenics, are prone to be quite inconsistent in this methodology. The L. S. approach cannot

Table 29. Sequence of Scores from the Protocol of L.S.

Card	RT	No.	Location	Determinant(s)		Content(s)	Pop	Z Score
I	4″	1	Wo	$FM^p o$		A	P	1.0
		2	W+	M^a+	(2)	H, A	P	4.0
		3	Ddo	Fo		Bell		
II	6″	4	D+	$FM^p o$	(2)	Ad	P	3.0
		5	DS+	$m^a.CFo$		Rocket, Fi		4.5
III	5″	6	D+	$M^a o$	(2)	H	P	3.0
		7	Do	FCo		Cg		
IV	7″	8	W+	$FM^p.FT.FDo$		A	P	4.0
		9	Do	FYo		Bt		
V	4″	10	Wo	Fo		A	P	1.0
VI	3″	11	Wo	FTo		Ad	P	2.5
		12	Do	$m^p.FY+$		Ship		
		13	Do	Fo		Ay		
VII	5″	14	Do	Fo	(2)	Hd	P	
		15	Do	Fo		A		
		16	W+	M^a+	(2)	H		3.0
VIII	7″	17	Wo	FCo		Art		4.5
		18	Do	Fo	(2)	A	P	
		19	Do	$FM^a.FDo$		A		
IX	19″	20	Do	Fo		Hd	P	
		21	Do	Fo		Hh		
		22	D+	M^a+		H		2.5
X	8″	23	Do	Fo	(2)	A	P	
		24	Do	$FM^a o$		A		
		25	W+	FC+		Bt		5.5

be considered erratic, but it does have some interesting features. In the first card, he uses the whole blot twice and then moves to a *Dd* area. The two *W*'s may indicate an achievement orientation; however, the *Dd* answer suggests a "backing off" from this. As he proceeds through Cards II, III, and IV, four of his six answers are of a synthesis variety, illustrating good intellectual operations. After Card IV, he gives 16 more responses, but only three of these involve a synthesis effort, and in all three instances the synthesis occurs only after two other answers have been given to the card. This seems to be a much more conservative approach than is evidenced in his earlier approach. It may reflect a sense of being "too revealing" or "too affective" in his original approach. Some support for this postulate is found in the examination of his determinant sequence which shows that only one of his first nine responses is Pure *F*, and that some form of movement occurs in six of those nine answers. Conversely, eight of his last 16 answers use only Pure *F*, and while he continues to give movement answers, one each on the last four cards, they never occur in the first response, and in two instances appear only after two Pure *F* answers have been given (Cards VII and IX). Similarly, seven of his first 10 answers involved organizational activity, whereas only five of his last 15 responses are of the *Z* variety. A major theme in the propositions developed from the Structural Summary is that he is guarded and somewhat constrictive in the use of his resources, and that one of the ways in which he deals with his apparently rich inner life is passiveness.

The sequence of his answers appears to give support for this proposition and indicates that the more revealing contents may have occurred in the earlier part of the record, while responses appearing later in the protocol were more cautiously developed. Interestingly, three of the five + form quality answers that he gives appear in the latter part of the record, on Cards VII, IX, and X, and as the last response to each of those cards. This may suggest that when he is cautious, he is able to organize his resources to a high level of productivity, or stated in a different hypothesis, *he is able to use his intellect more fully when he does not feel the pressures of ambiguity or lack of control.* The fact that he is able to restrict his affective displays, as in the earlier versus the latter part of the record, may be considered an asset, provided he uses this restriction deliberately rather than as a response to the feelings of loss of control. His Popular answers appear consistently to each card, reaffirming his strong committment to conventionality. There is no significant clustering of his blend answers, although the two which have been identified as possibly the most important ($m^a.CF$, and $FM^p.FT.FD$) do occur in the earlier portion of the protocol.

ANALYSIS OF THE VERBALIZATIONS

Interpretation of the verbal material and its sequence has developed as a major data source for most Rorschachers, especially since the 1940s. The results of the Exner and Exner survey of 395 practitioners reveals that about one in every five do not score at all, and instead rely exclusively on the verbal material for their analysis of the record. Similarly, more than 75% of those responding indicate that they weigh the verbal material at least as much as the data in the Structural Summary. Rorschach (1921) was very cautious in his estimate of the interpretive yield from the verbal material. He pointed to the fact that the test does not provoke a "free flow" of ideation but did state that if unconscious or subconscious ideation did occur in the test, it would be manifest in the content. It does seem highly plausible, in light of Rorschach's training and orientation, that he would have accepted Franks' *Projective Hypothesis* (1939) as relevant to the interpretation of the test.

Lindner (1943, 1944, 1946, 1947) was among the first to make a formal argument encouraging a greater emphasis on "content analysis" than had been the case previously. He cited instances in which the scoring configurations did not provide an accurate "diagnostic" picture of psychopaths but where sequence analysis of the verbalizations were successful. He also presented a series of classes of answers to different areas of the blots which could be interpreted as symbolically representative of different types of psychopathological ideation. Following from Lindner's lead, many works have focused on the analysis of content as related to diagnostic types, personality traits, and the "meaning" of specific classes of verbalizations. Some of these, especially those dealing with traits, have evolved special scorings for particular classes of contents (Elizur—anxiety, 1949; Elizur—hostility, 1949; Walker—aggression, 1951; Stone—aggression, 1953; Wheeler—homosexuality, 1949; Smith and Coleman—tension, 1956; Fisher and Cleveland—body image boundary, 1958; Holt—defense effectiveness, 1960, 1966). Unfortunately, with the possible exception of the Holt index of defense effectiveness, these scoring approaches have yielded equivocal findings. This does not negate the usefulness of verbalization analysis, but instead emphasizes the problems involved in attempting to "formalize" these data into specific categories. For example, a review of the research concerning the Wheeler 20 signs of homosexuality suggests that six of the 20 signs are "unquestionably poor," six other hold up "fairly well under empirical test," and the remaining 12 are ambiguous (Goldfried, Stricker, and Weiner, 1971). Studies attempting to equate specific classes of content with a *specific* "symbolic" meaning have been equally limited in success. Goldfarb (1945) and Goldfried (1963) both emphasize that animal contents are not universal in, their symbolic meaning. Several studies (Bochner and Halpern, 1945; Meer and Singer, 1950; Rosen, 1951; Phillips and Smith, 1953; Hirschstein and Rabin, 1955; Levy, 1958; Zelin and Sechrest, 1963) have explored the postulate that Cards IV and VII represent "father and mother," respectively. The findings of these studies are somewhat equivocal; however, it may be reasonable to assume that most subjects do equate the stimulus of Card IV with masculinity and/or authority, and that Card VII does frequently provoke associations with femininity. Other postulates concerning the "symbolic" significance of the blot stimuli, such as Cards III and X, represent interpersonal relations, or that Card VI represents sexuality have not been confirmed, and it is dangerous for an interpreter to make these assumptions without specific clues *in the record itself* to support these postulates for a given subject. Sexual contents do generally reflect specific kinds of preoccupations. Pascal et al. (1950) present evidence to indicate that genital contents do have a universal meaning. Molish (1967) points out that sexual contents are frequently useful to interpretation because they are usually more direct than symbolic, but cautions that they must be interpreted in the total context of the personality. Prandoni et al. (1973), for example, have found a slightly greater frequency of sex associations in the protocols of sex offenders, but like Molish, caution that these types of answers have little meaning when interpreted in "isolation."

The most common approach to the analysis of verbalizations is based on the "logical" grouping of responses that seem to have a common theme. Schafer (1954) has presented one of the most comprehensive approaches to the verbal material using this method. He cites 14 broad ranging categories, using psychoanalytic constructs, which include dependency, aggressiveness, conflicts, fears, and such, and provides illustrations of how different contents may relate to the same theme. Although some of these examples are useful only if applied in the psychoanalytic framework, such as the response of "mud" reflecting an "anal" orientation, most serve to represent a consistency of themes that can be useful regardless of theoretical orientation. For instance, Schafer suggests that answers that include references to God, police, Ku Klux Klan figures, family crests, castles, and riches may all be related to an authority orientation. Similarly, a clustering of answers involving jellyfish, badly skinned animals, a straw man, weak branches, and such can relate to feelings of inadequacy and/or impotency. Schafer's work is a classic of this kind and can be of use by an interpreter, regardless of orientation, for it tends to give emphasis to the "obvious" classes of response that might "fit together" to convey idiographic needs, preoccupations, and such. Schafer also points to the importance of studying the emotional tone that is often conveyed by the wording of a subject. For example, a dpressive tone may be represented by such adjectives as cold, crying, desolate, impoverished, mourning, ruined, and such.

One of the great "pitfalls" of analysis of verbalizations occurs when the interpreter becomes overly "caught-up" in a single answer or cluster of adjectives and fails to use these data in the total context of the record. The result can be a misleading and/or erroneously accentuated postulate and a neglect of other Structural and Verbal material that support contrary or modifying positions. Emphasis on data that occur with considerable frequency should alleviate this pitfall, but the interpreter should always be alert to its possibility. A second problem that often occurs in the analysis of the verbal material is the tendency of some interpreters to review the verbalizations in the Free Association and the Inquiry together, as if a single stream of ideation is represented. *This is not the case*, as the verbal material in the Free Association is the product of one set of conditions, and that material in the Inquiry results from a different set of conditions. In the Free Association, the subject has few guidelines on which to operate. His ideation occurs in a considerably ambiguous circumstance, and he is naive to the blots. His responses are not interspersed with feedback from the examiner, at least none that is deliberate. The Inquiry occurs under different circumstances. The subject is no longer naive to the blots. He operates under a given "set" provided by the examiner before the Inquiry, and he is prompted by the questions of the examiner, even though nondirective, as the Inquiry proceeds. Thus analysis of the verbal material in the Free Association should occur first, as it comes closer to representing a continuity of ideation, interrupted only by the changing visual stimuli. Subsequently, the verbalizations in the Inquiry are studied, both separately and with regard to interpretations formulated from the Free Association material. A card by card analysis of the verbalizations in the L. S. record, beginning with the Free Association material, may serve to illustrate this phase of interpretation.

CARD	RT	FREE ASSOCIATION
I	4″	1. ll a bat gliding along

         (Wo $FM^{p}o$ A P 1.0)

       2. It cld also b a modrn dance of s.s. w a wm in the cntr w her hands in the air & 2 creatures dancing around her
   ($W+$ $M^{a}+$ (2) H, (A) P 4.0)

       3. Say, ths lowr prt c.b. a bell
   (Ddo Fo Bell)

The first answer is conventional, approaching the entire blot, and selecting an aggressive animal, but describing it somewhat passively, "*gliding along.*" It is this description that makes the response idiographic and leads to the speculation that he may be oriented to contain his own aggressiveness. The second answer is more creative and well organized. He describes it as a *modern* dance in which two *creatures* are dancing around the static woman. They are *active* while she is not. The term creatures may represent an unknown or unidentifiable or concealed feature of L. S., active in relation to the female. The fact that they are creatures implies a more primitive form of ideation and/or impulse. This may be especially important in that it is associated with a female. The response may reflect some aspects of interpersonal orientation, or may represent some aspects of his sexual orientation. This latter speculation would be somewhat premature at this point, and subject to discard or modification. The third response, however, does focus on an unusual detail area (the lower half of the Popular woman figure used in #2). The prefacing remark "*say*" is of importance in that it is an alerting stimulus that also usually has a quizzical or surprised connotation. A bell is also an *alerting stimulus* and may in this instance carry some sexual implication because of the previous use of the area identified. *No specific postulates* can be drawn from only one card and three answers; however, a speculative "set" concerning aggressiveness, interpersonal relations, and possibly sexuality has been formed which will require added evaluation as the analysis proceeds.

CARD	RT	FREE ASSOCIATION
II	6''	4. It cld b a cpl of dogs touching noses
		($D+$ FM^po (2) *Ad* P 3.0)
		5. The cntr prt cld b a rocket ship takg off & ths red cld b the exhaust fire
		($DS+$ $m^a.CFo$ Rocket, Fi 4.5)

The first response to Card II is also conventional and involves an animal content in passive movement. Unlike the bat response to Card I, *a couple of dogs* represents a more domestic and less aggressive content. It is also *a more cautious or passive interpersonal* answer than the two creatures in modern dance given to Card I. The second response to Card II is much more *active* and less controlled. It contains the first blend of the record, and the only determinant used which is not form dominant. It is of interest to note that in both Cards I and II, the first answer has involved passive movement followed by an active movement response. This may indicate some problems in maintaining the more passive orientation, suggesting that his tendencies toward a constrictiveness are successful only over brief periods when faced with continuing ambiguity. The rocket itself is a forceful object, generally uncontrolled "after launch." It is also phallic-like and could possibly illustrate the forcefulness of his own sexuality. A psychoanalytic interpretation could not neglect the *CF* exhaust, possibly translated into "anal" aggressiveness, or stated somewhat more conservatively, a relationship may exist between aggression and sexuality, and this may be one of the underlying causes of the tension and constriction identified in L. S. from the Structural Summary. It is still premature to formulate specific propositions; however, the verbal data in both Cards I and II seem to orient the interpreter toward a closer examination of aggression, interpersonal relations, and sexuality.

CARD	RT	FREE ASSOCIATION
III	5''	6. A cpl of men bending over to lift s.t. up
		($D+$ M^ao (2) H P 3.0)
		7. The cntr red area cld b a bow tie
		(Do FCo Cg)

The responses to Card III are both somewhat less idiographic than are found in the previous cards. The first answer follows the pattern of being conventional, and while active movement is involved, it has no hints of aggressiveness. Quite the contrary, it is a cooperative interpersonal answer, bolder than two dogs rubbing noses and less ambiguous than the symbolic modern dance. It is a *controlled and healthy answer*, which may represent the manner in which L. S. handles his less well organized urges, that is, through a cooperative interpersonal effort. The bowtie is also a nonaggressive object used as a form of social attire. This is the first *controlled use of color* in the record and may signify a *desire for an emotional interpersonal exchange* with the external world.

CARD	RT		FREE ASSOCIATION
IV	7''	8.	It cld b a gorilla sitting on a stump

$(W+ \quad FM^p.FT.FDo \quad A \quad P \quad 4.0)$

9. A delicate flower

$(Do \quad FYo \quad Bt)$

For the fourth consecutive time, L. S. begins his response pattern to the cards with a movement answer. The gorilla, like the bat on Card I, is an aggressive animal, but also like the response to Card I, L. S. reports the animal in a passive activity. It is a somewhat incongruous percept, synthesizing the whole blot, and using perceptual accuracy as the basis for the incongruity. It is also a complex response, ultimately using both texture and dimensionality, the latter possibly related more to perceptual accuracy than introspectiveness. The second response, a *delicate* flower, is an unusual response for any subject, but especially males. The word delicate may reflect his own self-image, *or* may represent the struggle that he experiences concerning his own needs, that is, the continuing vacillation from active to passive, aggressive to nonaggressive. If he does perceive Card IV as representing masculinity and/or authority, the alteration from a gorilla to a flower illustrates *some form of conflict concerning his identity and role*. This is a good working proposition in that support for it is derived from his responses to the first four cards of the test. Some interpreters may also speculate that since the area selected as the delicate flower is sometimes identified as a female sex area, he may be experiencing some difficulties in his sexual relationship. Although a similar speculation was drawn from his responses to Cards I and II, it would still seem premature as a firm hypothesis at this point.

CARD	RT		FREE ASSOCIATION
V	4''	10.	It cld be a bat or butterfly, I thk more a bf now that I look at it bec I said bat before

$(Wo \quad Fo \quad A \quad P \quad 1.0)$

Again there is evidence of vacillation with the rejection of the .aggressive animal and a preference for the nonaggressive and "delicate" butterfly. It is interesting that he feels the need to justify his response, which may be a form of intellectualization, and illustrates the guardedness in his behavior which has been emphasized in some of the interpretive propositions. It is also of interest that this is the first card to which he gives only one answer, selecting a very conventional percept. This may illustrate a passivity which is the result of previous percepts, especially those to Card IV in which he felt compelled to "neutralize" the gorilla and then projected a "delicate" flower. Either or both of those percepts could have been somewhat stressful for him, *or* more likely the cognitive activity involved in the vacillation and control was fatiguing. Thus his conventional Pure *F* answer to the next card is a retreat or regrouping of forces, and easy to accomplish, as Card V is the easiest and least complicated of the 10 cards. Although this form of responsiveness ignores some of his previously defined talents, it must be judged as an asset in stress situations.

CARD	RT		FREE ASSOCIATION
VI	3″	11.	Would u believe an animal skin?
			(*Wo FTo Ad* P 2.5)
		<12.	Ths c.b. a submarine cruising along in the darkness
			(*Do m^p.FY+* Ship)
		13.	U kno, that c.b. a totem pole too
			(*Do Fo Ay*)

The first answer follows the consistent pattern of using conventionality first. The response itself is unremarkable; however, the manner in which it is presented, as a question, probably gives more evidence for his guarded interaction. He wants to be sure of himself and may use external cues as guidelines for his behaviors. His second answer is the most idiographic thus far in the record. A submarine, a phallic-like object, is a tool of war that often moves unseen from the surface of the water. L. S. guards even more against disclosure by perceiving it "in the darkness." The unique nature of this answer (i.e., it is the first in which the card has been turned, it combines the passive unorganized movement with a type of shading that usually represents passivity, and it has a very idiographic content) seems to *support previous speculations concerning sexual preoccupation*. It also seems to support an earlier speculation that L. S. has *some confusion about sexuality and aggression*, the latter evidenced by the fact that there is a growing accumulation of contents which have aggressive features but are "neutralized" in the responses. It is important for L. S. to avoid or conceal his own aggressiveness, probably because he does associate it with sexuality. His third response to the card is also interesting in the same context. He selects the upper phallic-like area of the card and perceives it as an "inanimate object" that also has a religious connotation. The sequence of giving a Pure *F* answer after the more affective and revealing answers, noted in the combination of responses to Cards IV and V, appears to be repeated here. This demonstrates his orientation to become "affectless" when in jeopardy of being too revealing.

CARD	RT		FREE ASSOCIATION
VII	5″	14.	A couple of kids
			(*Do Fo* (2) *Hd* P)
		<15.	This way the side ll a scotty dog
			(*Do Fo A*)
		∨16.	This way it ll a cpl of wm doing the can-can
			(*W+ M^a+* (2) *H* 3.0)

There is considerably less idiography in the answers to Card VII than was evident in Card VI. The first response, a Popular again, uses Pure *F* even though the possibility for movement to be perceived is very good. This probably reflects his "delaying" orientation which is also noted by his card turning from the next two answers. The content of "kids" may demonstrate some feeling of immaturity or insecurity and his effort to contain this may be represented in the *movement absence*. The second answer also relies on Pure *F* and involves a small domestic animal often known more for its "bark than its bite." It is a "house-pet" that often plays a role determined by others. The third answer is intelligent, creative, organized, and does use active M. It manifests both cooperation and entertainment. Dancers are a focus of attention and this response may illustrate that need in L. S., and could be related to the modern dance response given to Card I. The dancers in this response are doing the "can-can," a revealing and historically "naughty" routine. A previous postulate suggested some sexual preoccupation, and this response may evidence the nature of that preoccupation, that is, he *would like to be more open and active in his sexuality.*

CARD	RT		FREE ASSOCIATION
VIII	7''	17.	The whole thing c.b. an emblem
			(*Wo FCo Art* 4.5)
		18.	This thg on the side c.b. animals of some sort
			(*Do Fo* (2) *A P*)
		19.	U kno, this top part c.b. a sand crab, like it was leaping forward, going away from you
			(*Do FM^a.FDo A*)

This is the first card in which the first answer is not a Popular. It is an organized, colorful emblem, which probably demonstrates his status or authority orientation. It is followed by the conventional Pure F answer, which, again, seems to exemplify his orientation toward control and/or delay. The third response is of considerable interest as it involves a hint of incongruity, "leaping forward, going away from you." This seems to be more evidence for the need to control his less well organized promptings, and possibly represents containment of aggressiveness again. The implication that the crab *is not* leaping toward you, that is, there is no threat, is apparently important for L. S. to convey in his interpersonal relations, possibly as much for his own protection as for the reassurance of those around him.

CARD	RT		FREE ASSOCIATION
IX	19''	20.	This ll Teddy Roosevelt's head
			(*Do Fo Hd P*)
		21.	This cntr part c.b. a vase
			(*Do Fo Hh*)
	<22.		U kno, ths way it ll a person on a motorcycle or bike
			(*D+ M^a+ H 2.5*)

Although the first answer to Card IX is Popular, the identification of a significant historical figure may also lend itself as support for the speculation concerning his need for status and/or authority. The perception of Roosevelt in this area is very common; however, it is difficult to neglect the possible association of "walk softly but carry a big stick" as being applicable to L. S., either interpersonally or sexually. Similar implications may be derived from the second answer. A vase is a receptacle, ordinarily for flowers which are colorful and attractive. L. S. may see himself as *"wanting" a more attractive and affective exchange* with his world. The first two responses are both controlled, Pure F answers. The third response, like that on Card VIII, is creative and involves active movement. It is a more unique and thus a more idiographic answer. It is interesting that he vacillates between a "motorcycle or a bike," the one being motorized, speedy, and often associated with a more "reckless" life style, whereas the second is "self-propelled," more controlled, and associated with a more conventional life style. Again, the conflict between the more direct and affective expression of his promptings versus the more controlled and conventional behaviors appears. It is also important to note that these three responses *occurred after* the longest initial reaction time in the test. The absence of color use possibly gives some clue concerning the long *RT*, plus the fact that the first two answers are Pure *F* responses. L. S. wants control, and he feels that it is important to contain his affectiveness.

CARD	RT		FREE ASSOCIATION

X   8''   23. Ths blue ths ll crabs
                    (*Do Fo* (2) *A P*)

               24. This brown c.b. a deer jumping
                    (*Do FM^{a}o A*)

               25. Ths way it ll a floral scene, w a hugh flwr in the cntr & smaller flwrs around it
                    (*W+ FC+ Bt* 5.5)

He is consistent in giving a Popular as the first answer and avoiding the use of his full talent until the third answer. Even though the first two responses do not use color as a determinant, he is obviously aware of it by the manner that he identifies the locations used, "This blue . . . This brown . . .". This is the second time he has used "crab" as content (Response #19, Card VIII), a hard shelled, defensive animal. The deer is also a defensive animal, not generally known for aggressiveness, that often "jumps" when frightened. The last response in the record, a flower scene, is the second time that he has used this content (Response #9, Card IV), and the second time in the last three cards that he uses color as a determinant. It is an "attractive" and affectively "gentle" response, much like the delicate flower on Card IV and may convey the same implications as the vase response on Card IX. Namely, he *wants to experience affect, but in a nonthreatening way. He wants his affect to be perceived by others as nonthreatening and attractive.*

A SUMMARY OF THE FREE ASSOCIATIONS OF L. S.

The accumulated speculations and hypotheses derived from the analysis of the verbalizations of L. S. in the Free Association to the blots lead to approximately 10 propositions, which subsequently will be integrated with those generated from the Structural Summary and analysis of the verbal material in the Inquiry.

1. He has a conflict about an active, self-oriented style, versus a more passive and conforming role. He generally adopts the more passive, guarded role in his behaviors.

2. His role behaviors often rely on external cues for direction.

3. He is alert to, and possibly preoccupied with sexuality, having a reasonably strong sex drive, but possibly being confused by sexuality and aggression.

4. He would like to be more open and "honest" in his interpersonal relationships.

5. He is very cautious and controlled in his interpersonal relationships, but would like a greater affective exchange with his world.

6. He has confusion about his identity and role, the product of which is feelings of unsuredness and/or insecurity.

7. He is often "overly" gentle in his affective displays because of an orientation to hide his aggressive feelings. This "counter-phobic" type of responsiveness only serves to perpetuate his conflicted feelings.

8. He is strongly oriented toward a conservative style in the face of ambiguity and relies heavily on his intellect to "see him through."

9. He apparently does not know how to relate to people easily, often projecting to them his own fears and suspicions.

10. He has reasonably strong status needs, probably aligned with his "conformity" values and orientation.

Some, if not all, of these propositions will "overlap" with those developed from the Structural Summary, serving to provide added support for them. The analysis of the verbalizations in the Inquiry will add to these, and hopefully offer clarification regarding some of the issues raised. It is especially important to note that, with very few exceptions, the verbal material in the Inquiry should not be taken as an adequate substitute for data from the Structural Summary or from the Free Associations because of the manner under which it is collected. In other words, propositions derived from the Inquiry must be judged against the manner in which they were elicited, that is, under a more direct and guided situation. A card by card analysis of the Inquiry verbalizations of L. S. may offer some clarification to this phase of the interpretive process. The Free Associations and questions of the examiner, other than the introductory repeating of the subject's response, are italicized in parentheses, together with the scoring of the response, so that the Inquiry material can be studied apropos to them.

CARD	FREE ASSOCIATION AND INQUIRY
I	1. (*ll a bat gliding along—Wo FMᵖo A P 1.0*)

1. (*ll a bat gliding along—Wo   FM^{p}o   A   P   1.0*)
It has the outstretched wings and the small front feet and the center part would be the body

2. (*It cld also b a modern dance of s.s. w a wm in the cntr w her hands in air & 2 creatures dancing around her—W+   Mᵃ+   (2)   H,   A   P   4.0*)
Yes, it ll her hands r raised in sort of supplication & these creatures on the side represent something symbolic of whatever she's doing. (*E: Symbolic?*) The rem. me of the animals in Greek mythology. I can't rem the name.

3. (*Say, ths lower part c. b. a bell—Ddo   Fo   Bell*)
It has a pretty good shape of one with the clapper here.

The first answer is well delineated and somewhat unremarkable. The mention of *small* front feet may indicate something of his own identity, but is not striking enough to be emphasized at this point. The second response is quite different. In the Free Association the focal point is the creatures dancing, while the Inquiry focuses mainly on the woman figure. She is now seen in movement while having been static before, "hands are arised in sort of supplication," and the creatures are described as being "*symbolic of whatever she's doing.*" This seems to be a reversal of sorts that has the effect of neutralizing the creatures and their activity, or in other words, containing his initial ideation. Interestingly, he neatly avoids the examiner's question and offers no clarification of what they represent. The sexual interest, identified from evaluation of the Free Association in the third answer, also seems to exist in the Inquiry material, "It has a pretty good shape . . .".

CARD	FREE ASSOCIATION AND INQUIRY
II	4. (*It cld b a cpl of dogs touchg noses—D+ FM^{p}o (2) Ad P 3.0*) Its the darker areas, it ll the upper parts of dogs, their noses are touching, this would be the ear. (*E:* Upper Parts?) Its just the neck and the head, u can't c the rest of the body.
	5. (*The cntr cld b a rocket ship taking off & ths red c.b. the exhaust fire—DS+ m^a.CFo Rocket, Fi, 4.5*) It has a delta shape and the way the color is there u get the impression of firey exhaust and upward motion.

Both of these inquiries are unremarkable and add little to the previously developed information. He is cautious, relying on form accuracy in both, and each are "toned down" in contrast to the Free Association. The dogs are reduced to the "upper parts," and the exhaust fire is now reported as an "impression of." While guarded, these verbalizations do indicate that L. S. *can defend himself well through reality operations* when some structure is imposed. This is probably an asset in his everyday behaviors.

CARD	FREE ASSOCIATION AND INQUIRY
III	6. (*A cpl of men bendg ovr to lift s.t. up—D+ M^{a}o (2) H P 3.0*) U can c the general outlines of them, it ll thy'r about to lift s.t. up but I can't tell what it is.
	7. (*The cntr red area c.b. a bowtie—Do FCo Cg*) Well, the red attracted my attention to it, made me think of those big red bowties that clowns wear sometimes.

L. S. is again vague and guarded in the Inquiry to the first of these responses, relying on form accuracy and telling the examiner that he prefers not to be "forced" into speculation about what the men may be lifting, "but I can't tell what it is." The second answer may be more revealing as he identifies the bowtie as similar to ones "that clowns wear sometimes." This suggests that he feels awkward and the possible object of humor when he is affective, *or* that his affect is "put-on" for a show. Either or both of these feelings may be real for L. S. in light of other information developed and supports the earlier proposition that he is *uncomfortable handling his own affect and is oriented to contain it, especially his aggressive feelings.*

CARD	FREE ASSOCIATION AND INQUIRY
IV	8. (*It cld be a gorilla sitting on a stump—W+ FM^p.FT.FDo A P 4.0*) Yeah, it looks all furry like a big animal, like a gorilla w the feet here sorta like he's leaning backwards bec the feet r so much bigger (*E: U said it looks furry*) Yes, all of the color variation makes it ll that.

9. (*A delicate flower—Do   F Yo   Bt*)
   I don't kno the name, my wife grows them, they almost ll velvet w ths contour & coloring effect (*Coloring effect?*) Yes, all the different shades in there.

Again L. S. relies on form accuracy to "state his case." The gorilla is perceived as leaning backwards because of this and the shading variations cause the impression of furriness. The "leaning backwards" description is not uncommon but important as it reflects a drawing away concept. The "my wife grows them" comment implies something about his own status in relation to his wife (delicate) and raises the *question about the stability and/or security of his marriage.* If the marriage should be fragile, it could easily account for his feelings of insecurity and needs to constrict some of his affect. Even if the marriage is "solid," it apparently fails to meet his sexual needs appropriately and would be good material for study if L. S. were a prospective patient. The use of the word velvet is quite unique in most protocols, and, drawing from what is known of texture answers, could signify the needs for a more dependent affective relationship.

CARD	FREE ASSOCIATION AND INQUIRY

V   10. (*It cld b a bat or a bf, I thk more a bf now that I look at it bec I said bat before—Wo   Fo   A   P   1.0*)
       Well it has the wings and antennae & the split tail like some bf's have.

L. S. is consistent in drawing the form features "around him" as a guard against unwanted verbalizations. The "split tail" may have special significance; however, it seems useless to speculate on these words without additional interpretive guidelines.

CARD	FREE ASSOCIATION AND INQUIRY

VI   11. (*Wld u believe an animal skin?—Wo   FTo   Ad   P   2.5*)
       I don't kno what kind of animal, prob fr the cat family bec of the stuff around the head (*E: The stuff around the head?*) Well actually the *W* thg looks furry and spotted like from a tiger or s.t. and these r whiskers.

       12. (*This c.b. a submarine cruising along in the darkness—Do   m^p.FY+ Ship*)
       It has a pretty good shape of a sub, & the fact its all black makes me think of darkness, like at night, the blackness is like a shadowy effect, like a night. You get a good effect of the superstructure, the conning tower part here & the long bow.

       13. (*U kno, that c.b. a totem too—Do   Fo   Ay*)
       The general form of it rem me of the kind of carving u mite c on a totem, usually a wings effect, like this has to it.

The identification of the animal skin, in the first response, as possibly that of a tiger, hints of a willingness to acknowledge the contained aggressive features. It is qualified, "or something," and only the skin, not the whole animal. The fact that shading is used with the answer possibly signals the discomfort accompanying the ideation, but the fact that he does verbalize this material is probably a good sign.

The second response is quite striking because of the emphasis on the blackness which conveys a sense of gloominess and emphasizes his orientation toward concealment. The repetition of the word "night" appears to characterize both the sexual features of the response and the concealing aspects. As with the dogs on Card II, he describes only the upper portion, the superstructure, adding further speculation about his sexual preoccupation. He becomes considerably more cautious in the third answer, using the qualification, "u mite c on a totem,II and again, "usually a wings effect . . . ," implying they are not wings but convey that impression. These are intellectual defensive operations which avoid a definitive committment.

CARD	FREE ASSOCIATION AND INQUIRY

VII   14. (*A cpl of kids—Do   Fo* (2) *Hd   P*)
Just the heads like they have feathers in their hair (*E: I'm not sure why they ll that*) U can c the general features, chins, noses, foreheads, that sort of thing

15. (*This way the side ll a scotty dog—Do   Fo   A*)
It has the blunt nose, there r the short legs, & here's the tail

16. (*Ths way it ll a cpl of wm doing the can-can—W+   Ma+* (2) *H*   3.0)
They have big hairdos and r dancing on one leg, sort of throwing their heads backward

In all three of these responses, L. S. keeps the Inquiry somewhat brief and restricts himself mainly to form characteristics. The kids are not identified by sex nor does he take advantage of the movement possibilities even though the examiner provides an appropriate "opening" by the comment, "I'm not sure why they look like that." The *short* legs on the dog may carry an implication similar to that found in the small front feet description of the bat on Card I. The description of the women in the third response is almost entirely form accuracy except for the word "throwing," which like the "split tail" on Card V probably has some meaning which is impossible to detect without further clues.

CARD	FREE ASSOCIATION AND INQUIRY

VIII   17. (*The W thg c.b. an emblem—Wo   FCo   Art*   4.5)
Yes, its like a family crest of s.s., being symmetrical and quite colorful.

18. (*These things on the side c.b. animals of s.s.—Do   Fo* (2) *A   P*)
There's 2 of 'em one on each side (*Can u tell me how u c them?*) Well they c.b. mice or s.t. of the rodent family, c here are the legs and head and tail.

19. (*U kno, ths top part c.b. a sand crab, like it was leaping forward, going away from u—Do   FMa.FDo   A*)
The pincers r here and the area where the eyes r, and it has the legs extended lik it was leaping out, probably going away from u, the proportions give that effect.

Once again L. S. presents a well controlled, form based justification for his responses. The "family crest" appears to verify the speculation concerning status.

A direct reference to the symmetry may signify anxiety in some subjects; however, in this instance it appears more consistent with L. S.'s intellectual use of form. A similar approach is taken in the second response, with the more cautious, "could be mice or something of the rodent family." He obviously does not like to commit himself with "certainty" in ambiguous situations. The third response is somewhat more aggressive but qualified by the "going away from you" statement. The focus on the pincers and eyes reflect a guarded, somewhat suspicious orientation and the "going away" statement might well illustrate his need to escape the probing of the examiner.

CARD	FREE ASSOCIATION AND INQUIRY

IX　　20.　*(Ths ll T. Roosevelt's head—Do　Fo　Hd　P)*
Rite here in the pink, its got the mustache and the flat forehead, its just the head, it really ll that.

21.　*(That center part c.b. a vase—Do　Fo　Hh)*
Its just shaped lik a vase to me.

22.　*(U kno, ths way it ll a person on a motorcycle or a bike—D+　M^a+　H　2.5)*
Ths whole grn prt, most it it ll the person, I guess a heavy set man & he's holding the handlebars. The bike isn't too clear but the way his head is formed there u can get the impression of his hair flying back in the breeze.

The first two responses to Card IX are brief and form dominant. There is a hint of challenge to the examiner in the statement, ". . . it really looks like that." The second answer is also somewhat forceful by the response, "Its just shaped like a vase to me," implying a greater sense of taking a firm stand than was the case earlier in the record. The third answer is more elaborate although still using form to the utmost for justification, ". . . a heavy set man and he's holding the handlebars. The bike isn't too clear but . . .". It is a solid, well developed response to the examiner's promptings, and although it has been obvious that L.S. does not care to be scrutinized by others, he does take a reality based stand and "justified himself" when necessary. Interestingly, the description in the Inquiry suggests that the vehicle is a bicycle rather than the motorcycle, possibly reflecting more of an orientation toward "self-control" and avoidance of the more "wild" behaviors.

CARD	FREE ASSOCIATION AND INQUIRY

X　　23.　*(The blue things ll crabs—Do　Fo　(2)　A　P)*
They just give that impression with all the legs.

24.　*(This brown c.b. a deer jumping—Do　FM^ao　A)*
The legs are outstretched and u can c the antlers here.

25.　*(This way it ll a floral scene, w a huge flower in the cntr and smaller flowers around it—W+　FC+　Bt　5.5)*
Well, the cntr flower made me think of it and I stretched it abit about the other things *(E: I'm not sure what u were seeing)* It's very colorful, the pink c.b. a daffodil and the blue pom poms, but I can't really identify the rest. It's very pretty though, like a floral display.

The first two responses are very brief and to the point, almost assuming that the examiner would accept this brevity with question. The third answer is somewhat apologetic, ". . . and I stretched it abit about the other things." Here L. S. apparently finds that he cannot easily use the form accuracy approach, but even after the examiner's question he fares quite well in his description and possibly offers one of his most affective and "human" responses, "Its very pretty though . . . ". This seems to offer some support for an earlier postulate that he would prefer a greater affective exchange with his world than is ordinarily the case.

This particular Inquiry yields only a few propositions, most of which carry some clarifications for previously developed postulates.

1. He is guarded and somewhat unsure of himself. He wants self-control and generally defends himself well against ambiguous intrusions by relying on reality.

2. He has status needs which appear compatible with his talent but not necessarily with his more constrictive level of functioning.

3. He has a distinct sexual interest, which apparently involves some conflict. His unsuredness and orientation toward passivity seems to make the resolution of this conflict improbable.

4. He does not like to justify his ideation, preferring instead to keep his "thoughts to himself." He feels somewhat awkward with his affect and generally tries to control it, although he does want more affective exchange with his world than is-now the case.

5. A question is raised about the depth, stability, and/or security that exists in his relationship with his wife. This factor may contribute significantly to many of his response features.

It is important to note that, at least in part, many of the Inquiry responses given by L. S., that is, their brevity and strong reliance on form, were probably precipitated by the examiner's instructions and probing. As is often the case, subjects approach the Free Association with no awareness that they will be called on later to clarify and "justify" their percepts, and when this occurs their defensiveness is heightened. This is especially true for the person whose response style is basically one of guardedness, and thus the verbalizations in the Inquiry often reflect as much of a situational responsiveness as they represent the more idiographic projections of the subject. This seems the case for L. S., as the length of most of his Inquiry verbalizations is no longer than those of the Free Association. The interpreter must also be alert for the opposite to occur. Frequently, especially with the more suggestible and/or dependent subjects, a relief is created when the examiner begins to provide more structure for the task, and the verbal material can exceed the length of the Free Associations by tenfold, and it is not unusual for these kinds of subjects to inject new responses during the Inquiry. All Inquiry material has some use, but it is very important that the interpreter be aware of "how and why" the material was elicited so as to study it in the appropriate context and be able to "sort out" situationally provoked answers from those which are more representative of the basic personality.

Once the interpretation of each of the components of the test has been completed, the interpreter can integrate the propositions and speculations from the various sources, Structural Summary, Scoring Sequence, Free Association, and Inquiry, into a comprehensive description of the subject, separating questions and speculations from the more definitive and firmly based propositions. This description can, in turn, be integrated with other information available concerning the subject, from other test data or anamestic data, to form a broader understanding of the subject, and answers to questions posed in the referral. An integration of the propositions, speculations, and questions gleaned from the Rorschach of L. S. illustrates how data from this test might be used.

A SUMMARY OF L. S.

A first step in generating a final Rorschach description of a subject is to collate the various propositions and speculations, examining them for contradictions or agreements. This procedure is shown below with the source of each statement identified in parentheses.

1. He has a marked concern for conventionality (Structure), having developed strong status needs which are probably aligned with his conformity orientation (Free Association).

2. He is apparently quite intelligent but not using his talents fully (Structure). His status needs appear compatible with his talent, but not with his more constrictive level of functioning (Inquiry). He is able to use his intellect more fully when he does not feel the pressures of ambiguity or lack of control (Scoring Sequence).

3. He is frequently prompted to respond by needs and stresses over which he has little control and experiences discomfort because of this (Structure). His role behaviors rely on external cues for direction (Free Association), which probably causes him to be guarded and somewhat unsure of himself. He wants control and generally defends himself well against ambiguity by relying on reality (Inquiry).

4. He is prone to resort to his inner life to delay and/or organize his responses (Structure); however, he does have some conflict about his basic response style, although usually adopting a more passive and constrictive style under stress (Free Association). He appears overly bound to reality and is sacrificing some of his individuality as a result (Structure). His rich inner life is often oriented toward a more direct behavior (Structure), but he does not like to justify himself and is hesitant to respond emotionally to his world, preferring to use his intellect as the basis for his interactions with others (Inquiry).

5. He has many "unorganized" resources (Structure), which apparently cause some confusion about his identity and role and create feelings of unsuredness (Free Association). He would like to be more open in his interpersonal relationships, but his feelings of unsuredness prompt him to be " overly constrictive and gentle" in his affective displays, often hiding his more aggressive feelings (Free Association).

6. His self-evaluation is lower than desirable (Structure) and he frequently compares himself to others in a competitive and guarded manner (Structure). He does not know how to relate to people easily, and often projects to them his own values, fears, and suspicions (Free Association).

7. He has a distinct sexual preoccupation (Free Association and Inquiry), but does not attempt any resolution of this problem because of his unsuredness and orientation toward passivity (Inquiry). He appears to confuse sexuality and aggressiveness, and this may be a basic seed contributing to his difficulties in interpersonal relations and contributing to his lack of self-esteem (Free Association and Structure). Fortunately for him, this problem is not overt, and he experiences relatively

little direct pain from it, but does experience a frequent experience of tension and the feelings of a need to be dependent on others (Structure).

8. A question is raised about the depth, and/or stability of his relationship with his wife, a factor which may influence many of his response features (Free Association and Inquiry).

These eight summary propositions all seem firmly supported by the test data and can easily be developed into a personality description for most any type of report. Speculations formulated from the test can also be a source of *less firm* postulates, which might be useful in some, but not all descriptions and/or reports. For instance, there are several clues in the record that he is guarded and constricted because of his fragile sex role identification. There is also evidence to suggest that he will, at times, be unable to maintain a tight control on his affect, and consequently "act-out" more directly. It can also be speculated that he is considerably less mature than is often conveyed by his behaviors. These are not really "new" propositions, rather they are more specific elaborations related to the more firmly based propositions. Overall, however, L. S. must be considered as "essentially normal," as there is no evidence in the record, or from other sources, to suggest the contrary. From what little is known of him, the fact that he is married, has one child, is from a blue collar family, and now teaches high school, there are no obvious problems in his thinking and/or behavior. He is a volunteer subject rather than a referral. Like all human beings, he has liabilities, some of which appear to be of considerable significance, especially if one were predicting his future. He should use his intellect more, and learn to develop his affective interaction with the world in a style with which he would feel more comfortable and that would evoke more gratification for him. He has seemingly good motives and is clearly talented. His marriage may be a major source of concern; however, his continuing orientation to "do the right thing" will probably negate the possibility of serious disruption in the marriage, at least for a reasonable period of time. If L. S. were a referred patient, the marriage would be the obvious starting place for intervention.

In Part IV, a variety of protocols of subjects who are in more distinct difficulty than L. S. are presented. They provide a broader illustration of the Rorschach manifestations of "psychopathology" than is the case with L. S., and demonstrate how many of the features, which appear in a more subtle form in this record, stand out sharply to make the task of interpretation easier than is often the case with nonpatients.

REFERENCES

Bochner, R., and Halpern, F. *The Clinical Application of the Rorschach Test*. New York: Grune and Stratton, 1945.

Elizur, A. Content analysis of the Rorschach with regard to anxiety and hostility. *Journal of Projective Techniques*, 1949, **13**, 247–284.

Exner, J., and Exner, D. How clinicians use the Rorschach. *Journal of Personality Assessment*, 1972, **36**, 403–408.

Fisher, S., and Cleveland, S. *Body Image and Personality*. New York: Van Nostrand Reinhold, 1958.

Frank, L. K. Projective methods for the study of personality. *Journal of Personality*, 1939, **8**, 389–413.

Goldfarb, W. The animal symbol in the Rorschach Test and animal association test. *Rorschach Research Exchange*, 1945, **9**, 8–22.

Goldfried, M. The connotative meaning of some animals for college students. *Journal of Projective Techniques*, 1963, **27**, 60–67.

Goldfried, M., Stricker, G., and Weiner, I. *Rorschach Handbook of Clinical and Research Applications*. Englewood Cliffs, N.J.: Prentice Hall, 1971.

Hirschstein, R., and Rabin, A. I. Reactions to Rorschach cards IV and VII as a function of parental availability in childhood. *Journal of Consulting Psychology*, 1955, **19**, 473–474.

Holt, R. R. Cognitive controls and primary processes. *Journal of Psychoanalytic Research*, 1960, **4**, 105–112.

Holt, R. R. Measuring Libidinal and aggressive motives and their controls by means of the Rorschach Test. In Levine, D. (Ed.), *Nebraska Symposium on Motivation*, 1966. Lincoln: University of Nebraska Press, 1966.

Levy, E. Stimulus values of Rorschach cards for children. *Journal of Projective Techniques*, 1958, **22**, 293–295.

Lindner, R. M. The Rorschach Test and the diagnosis of psychopathic personality. *Journal of Criminal Psychopathology*, 1943, **1**, 69.

Lindner, R. M. Some significant Rorschach responses. *Journal of Criminal Psycholopathology*, 1944, **4**, 775.

Lindner, R. M. Content analysis in Rorschach work. *Rorschach Research Exchange*, 1946, **10**, 121–129.

Lindner, R. M. Analysis of Rorschach's Test by content. *Journal of Clinical Psychopathology*, 1947, **8**, 707–719.

Meer, B., and Singer, J. A note of the "father" and "mother" cards in the Rorschach inkblots. *Journal of Consulting Psychology*, 1950, **14**, 482–484.

Molish, H. B. Critique and problems of research: A survey. In Beck, S. J., and Molish, H. B. *Rorschach's Test. II: A Variety of Personality Pictures*. (2nd ed.) New York: Grune and Stratton, 1967.

Pascal, G., Ruesch, H., Devine, D., and Suttell, B. A study of genital symbols on the Rorschach Test: Presentation of method and results. *Journal of Abnormal and Social Psychology*, 1950, **45**, 285–289.

Phillips, L., and Smith, J. G. *Rorschach Interpretation: Advanced Technique*. New York: Grune and Stratton, 1953.

Prandoni, J., Matranga, J., Jensen, D., and Waison, M. Selected Rorschach characteristics of sex offenders. *Journal of Personality Assessment*, 1973, **37**, 334–336.

Rorschach, H. *Psychodiagnostics*. Bern: Bircher, 1921 (Transl. Hans Huber Verlag, 1942).

Rosen, E. Symbolic meanings in the Rorschach cards: A statistical study. *Journal of Clinical Psychology*, 1951, **7**, 239–244.

Schafer, R. *Psychoanalytic Interpretation in Rorschach Testing*. New York: Grune and Stratton, 1954.

Smith, J., and Coleman, J. The relationship between manifestation of hostility in projective techniques and overt behavior. *Journal of Projective Techniques*, 1956, **20**, 326–334.

Stone, H. Relationship of hostile aggressive behavior to aggressive content of the Rorschach and Thematic Apperception Test. Unpublished doctoral dissertation, University of California at Los Angeles, 1953.

Walker, R. G. A comparison of clinical manifestations of hostility with Rorschach and MAPS performance. *Journal of Projective Techniques*, 1951, **15**, 444–460.

Wheeler, W. M. An analysis of Rorschach indices of male homosexuality. *Journal of Projective Techniques*, 1949, **13**, 97–126.

Zelin, M., and Sechrest, L. The validity of the "mother" and "father" cards of the Rorschach. *Journal of Projective Techniques and Personality Assessment*, 1963, **27**, 114–121.

PART FOUR

Clinical Applications

CHAPTER 17

Faltering Response Styles

All people have preferred "styles" of response, that is, patterns of internal and external behaviors which they have developed to deal with their needs and interactions with their world. Some may have a constitutional base, while others result from a vast array of learning experiences that occur during the developmental years. These preferences usually characterize the individual, and orient him toward specific behaviors under given conditions. Typically, a person learns to maximize the use of those behaviors that are rewarding, and minimize those behaviors that have a less predictable outcome. Ordinarily, people select "routines" of behavior in environments that are compatible with their styles of response. The quiet, more internalized person often selects an occupation which is sedentary and permits an acceptable degree of isolation from others. The more externally oriented person will choose an environment in which considerable interaction occurs. Whatever the preferred style or response pattern, people generally seem to select "miniworlds" in which this style is most effective, at least those in which interference with the stylistic behaviors is minimized. Occasionally, however, these worlds change, or for other reasons, habitual response patterns are inhibited or are no longer effective. In these conditions, the individual is faced with the difficult task of altering his pattern of responses, or as often the case, perpetuating them in spite of the fact that they are no longer effective. The stresses resulting from either of these circumstances can, and does, frequently lead to the identification of a person as "maladaptive." Generally, the professional is prone to describe these persons as "characterological" disorders, implying a lack of flexibility and a pattern of responses that are inconsistent with the needs of the person and/or the demands of the world. These problems possibly represent the largest single kind of "psychopathology" seen by professionals in clinics and hospitals. They do not have long standing "symptoms" and they are not detached from reality in the extreme sense of the psychotic. But, they are people in trouble who cannot find the appropriate new pattern of behavior that will permit them to adapt with a lesser degree of stress.

The protocols in this chapter illustrate how some of these maladjustments are manifest in the Rorschach. They are not meant to reflect a normative standard, but merely how different kinds of people, each functioning in the context of their own preferred response patterns, can evidence symptoms which are often confusing to those who attempt to assist them.

PROTOCOL #1 H. V.—THE INTERNALIZER

Referral. H. V. was referred for psychological evaluation by a consulting psychiatrist to a large insurance firm who had examined him on the recommendation of the company physician after H. V. had made a request for sleeping medication. The psychiatrist's referral stated, "I would appreciate any information you may provide about the possibility of an underlying schizophrenic process. I am also interested in any information you can give about his personality structure."

History.   The referral was accompanied by the following history. H. V. is a slender, blonde, average looking 32 year old, who is currently employed as an office manager in our company. His office is responsible for processing policy lapses. He has 11 employees under his supervision, all female, with whom he seems to interact very well but with no remarkable closeness. He has held this position for 7 years, having served an apprenticeship as an assistant office manager in another office for 5 years. He completed 30 months of college at a technical institute, majoring in the Department of Commerce, and received an A. A. degree. He married another employee of the company, his own age, 2 years after having been here. There was a short courtship, and if his statements are to be believed, she was something of a "swinger" looking for someone with good prospects. The marriage lasted about 18 months during which time she began keeping company with another man and finally asked H. V. for a divorce. They mutually agreed to the divorce, although he says that he tried to get her interested in seeing a marriage counselor before the final decision was made. She would have none of it. H. V. feels that she was "too immature" for marriage, and then adds that he probably was too. He feels that she made too many emotional demands on him and that he was unprepared for this. He is an only child. The father is a successful minister in the protestant faith and has recently retired. The father is 67. The mother is 63 and described by H. V. as "a pillar of strength for my father." H. V. considered the ministry when he was in high school, but after talking "at length" with the father and another minister, he agreed that it might not be the appropriate thing for him. He does remain active in the church, collecting on Sundays, participating in a youth group as a leader, singing in the choir, and such. He maintains close contact with his parents although they live in another city.

He has an excellent work record and seems well liked in the firm, or at least respected. He has handled the company blood drive and the United Fund Campaign for the past 3 years. He is in the company bowling league, although not a very good bowler. His immediate supervisor regards him as one of the best office managers in this region, mainly because H. V. keeps a good communication flow between himself and his supervisor. He has been recently recommended for promotion to a higher level of supervision and seemed pleased by the recommendation. The company has a rather unfortunate policy of sending their midmanagement personnel on "retreat week-ends" to a fairly plush lodge. While there, they are lectured a bit on policy and the demands of their jobs, and all are expected to participate in at least two "growth sessions." The procedure is unclear but it sounds like a combination of group therapy, stress interviewing, and a Saturday night at the Elks club. H. V. was pretty well taken apart in these sessions, being "accused" (his words) of being too distant, overcontrolled, and probably responsible for his marital failure. It's probably all true but the way that it happened really seems to have set him off. He has lost faith in his supervisor, has become very anxious and depressed, and feels that "he is going crazy." About 2 weeks ago, he went to the company physician asking for sleeping medication and was referred for psychiatric evaluation.

In the initial contact he was well oriented, demonstrated a sound memory for both distant and recent events, has a clear sensorium, but is quite flattened in affect. He seems schizoid but there are some things about his affect that raise the question about an underlying schizophrenic process that may have been in a latent form for some time. He is cooperative and willing to have further examinations. He is now on a mild tranquilizer.

Protocol #1. H. V., 32 Year Old Divorced Male, No Children, Employed as Office Manager

Card	Free Association	Inquiry	Scoring
I	21″		
	1. ll a bat to me	E: (Rpts S's resp) S: Well, the W thg I guess altho its a little ragged	Wo Fo A P 1.0
	(E: Most peopl c more than one thg)		
	<2. Well if u turn it on its side it c.b. an A of s.s.	E: I'm not sure how u c it S: Here r the wgs (points) & ths is the body E: (Rpts S's resp) S: Mayb a donkey I suppose E: Can u tell me what makes it ll that? S: It has ths long ear & the body & the legs	Do Fo A
II	35″		
	3. It c.b. 2 animal heads, kind of like their touching	E: (Rpts S's resp) S: Its lik thy were playing a game of s.s., it ll the heads of 2 dogs rubbing noses I guess. U can c the ears & the noses & the general face, it ll a terrier of s.s.	$D+$ FM^vo (2) Ad P 3.0
III	10″		
	4. It ll 2 people dancing	E: (Rpts S's resp) S: It ll 2 natives doing s.s. of native dance I guess, they hav a dark skin lik Africans wld hav. I'd say they'r men altho its kind of sketchy bec there r many irregularities. E: Irregularities? S: They don't ll real men, and these red thgs don't fit here at all	$D+$ $M^a.FYo$ (2) H P 3.0
	5. Ths red prt in the cntr c.b. a bf	E: (Rpts S's resp) S: It has the shape of one w the wings out like ths, it just rem me of a bf	Do Fo A P
IV	25″		
	6. This ll a big giant of s.s. looming over u	E: (Rpts S's resp) S: It ll u lookg up at it like it was one of those big green giants on the TV E: I'm not sure I c it as u do	Do $M^a.FDo$ (H)

S: Well, it is a big hulk of a thg, this cntr part down here wouldn't b included. It's in a definite perspective, with the huge legs and small head, that's abt all I can say

$Wo \quad Fo \quad A \quad P \quad 1.0$

V — 27″

7. A bf

E: (Rpts S's resp)
S: It has wings and the body, its the whole thg, its just the general shape of it

$Do \quad Fo \quad A$

8. Ths cntr part ll a rabbit

E: (Rpts S's resp)
S: It has the big ears and the slender legs like one, it just ll that with the body & the ears mostly

$Do \quad FTo \quad Ad \quad P$

VI — 30″

9. Well it sort of ll a bear skin

E: (Rpts S's resp)
S: Just the lower part ll that
E: Can u tell me how u c it?
S: Well it is shaded like fur I guess, the legs here & the main part here (points)

$D+ \quad m^a.FYo \quad Torch \quad 2.5$

10. The top part there ll a torch

E: (Rpts S's resp)
S: It has flame coming out of the side, mayb not as much as lite, mayb its more lik a streetlite than a torch, yes that's better showing the light. The shape of it gives that impression but especially the radiating effect of the light makes it ll that

$D+ \quad M^ao \quad (2) \quad Hd \quad P \quad 3.0$

VII — 15″

11. Well I'd say the top prt ll 2 kids playing indian

E: (Rpts S's resp)
S: Thy hav feathers sticking up fr their heads, I don't include ths bottm part, altho I guess it clb be a rock, anyhow they'r just a cpl of kids, its the faces & the upper prt of the body that I saw

$Do \quad Fo \quad A$

<12. If u turn it like this it c.b. a dog, a scottie dog

E: (Rpts S's resp)
S: It has a flat nose & the short body & short legs & this is the tail

353

Protocol #1 (Continued)

Card		Free Association		Inquiry	Scoring
VIII	20″	13. I c 2 animals	E: S:	(Rpts S's resp) One on either side, thy ll rats or s.t. like that. Thy hav a rat lik face & here's the legs & the body	Do Fo (2) A P
		14. The W thg ll a coat of arms	E: S:	(Rpts S's resp) Well like a coat of arms I think, its equal on both sides & it has all these different colors, probably each part has some meaning, its like u might c on a shield	Wo FCo Art 4.5
IX	64″	V15. This way it ll an explos	E: S:	(Rpts S's resp) Like an atomic explosion, the mushroom cloud is pretty well outlined & the rest ll its shooting out in a big bunch of smoke and fire	W+ m''.CFo Explo 5.5
			E: S:	Smoke and fire? Well ths green stuff is all billowy lik smok & the orange part wld b the fire	
		16. U kno the cntr part rem me of a flower pot, like a vase	E: S:	(Rpts S's resp) Its lik an antique vase of s.s., u don't c them any more very much, but its like they use to use for long stemmed flowers, it has that curviness to it	Do Fo Hh
X	35″	17. Well it kind of ll something underwater to me	E: S:	(Rpts S's resp) Well it's lik a bunch of underwater animals and things, its all pretty colorful, like that pink cld b coral & the crabs here in the blue & the brwn c.b. lobsters & the green some other kind of animal in the water & the rest would be sort of weeds and stuff	W+ FCo A, Ls P 5.5

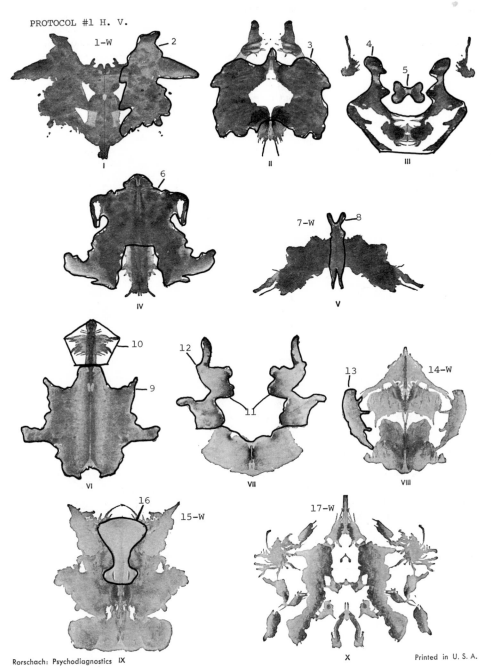

PROTOCOL #1 H. V.

Printed in U. S. A.

Protocol #1

Table 30. Structural Summary for Protocol #1—H. V.

$R = 17$ $Zf = 9$ $Z\text{Sum} = 29.0$ $P = 9$ $(2) = 4$

Location Features		Determinants	Contents	Contents (Idiographic)
$W = 5$	DQ	$M.FY = 1$	$H = 1$	$\underline{\text{Torch}} = 1$
		$M.FD = 1$	$(H) = 1$	
$D = 12$	$+ = 6$	$m.CF = 1$	$Hd = 1$	$\underline{\hspace{1cm}} =$
		$m.FY = 1$	$(Hd) =$	
$Dd = 0$	$o = 11$		$A = 8$	$\underline{\hspace{1cm}} =$
		$M = 1$	$(A) =$	
$S = 0$	$v = 0$	$FM = 1$	$Ad = 2$	$\underline{\hspace{1cm}} =$
		$m =$	$(Ad) =$	
$DW = 0$	$- = 0$	$C =$	$Ab =$	$\underline{\hspace{1cm}} =$
		$CF =$	$Al =$	
		$FC = 2$	$An =$	$\underline{\hspace{1cm}} =$
FORM QUALITY		$C' =$	$Art = 1$	
		$C'F =$	$Ay =$	$\underline{\hspace{1cm}} =$
FQx	FQf	$FC' =$	$Bl =$	
		$T =$	$Bt =$	
$+ = 0$	$+ = 0$	$TF =$	$Cg =$	
		$FT = 1$	$Cl =$	
$o = 17$	$o = 8$	$V =$	$Ex = 1$	
		$VF =$	$Fi =$	
$w = 0$	$w = 0$	$FV =$	$Fd =$	
		$Y =$	$Ge =$	
$- = 0$	$- = 0$	$YF =$	$Hh = 1$	
		$FY =$	$Ls = 0, 1$	
		$rF =$	$Na =$	
		$Fr =$	$Sx =$	
		$FD =$	$Xy =$	
		$F = 8$		

RATIOS, PERCENTAGES, AND DERIVATIONS

$Z\text{Sum}/Z\text{est} = 29.0/27.5$		$FC/CF + C = 2/1$		Afr	$= .42$
$Zd = +1.5$		$W/M = 5/3$		$3r + (2)/R$	$= 4/17 = .24$
$EB = 3/2.0$	$EA = 5.0$	$W/D = 5/12$		$Cont/R$	$= 6/17$
$eb = 3/3$	$ep = 6$	$L = .89$		$H + Hd/A + Ad = 3/10$	
$\text{Blends}/R = 4/17$		$F+\% = 100$		$H + A/Hd + Ad = 10/3$	
$a/p = 6/0$		$X+\% = 100$		$XRT \text{ Achrom}$	$= 23.6''$
$M^a/M^p = 3/0$		$A\% = 59$		$XRT \text{ Chrom}$	$= 32.8''$

Table 31.   Sequence of Scores for Protocol #1—H. V.

Card	RT	No.	Location	Determinant(s)	Content(s)	Pop	Z Score
I	21″	1.	Wo	Fo	A	P	1.0
		2.	Do	Fo	A		
II	35″	3.	D+	FMᵃo (2)	Ad	P	3.0
III	10″	4.	D+	Mᵃ.FYo (2)	H	P	3.0
		5.	Do	Fo	A	P	
IV	25″	6.	Do	Mᵃ.FDo	(H)		
V	27″	7.	Wo	Fo	A	P	1.0
		8.	Do	Fo	A		
VI	30″	9.	Do	FTo	Ad	P	
		10.	D+	mᵃ.FYo	Torch		2.5
VII	15″	11.	D+	Mᵃo (2)	Hd	P	3.0
		12.	Do	Fo	A		
VIII	20″	13.	Do	Fo (2)	A	P	
		14.	Wo	FCo	Art		4.5
IX	64″	15.	W+	mᵃ.CFo	Ex		5.5
		16.	Do	Fo	Hh		
X	35″	17.	W+	FCo	A, Ls	P	5.5

ANALYSIS OF THE STRUCTURE

Although the protocol is relatively short, $17R$, its length does fall within the average range, making most of the ratios and percentages useful. The Z frequency is "respectable," and the Zd score indicates that he is able to organize effectively. The number of P responses seems inordinately high, especially for a $17R$ protocol. Nearly 60% of his answers are Popular, suggesting a strong committment to conventionality, and probably reflects a strong value system. The EB indicates that he has some flexibility and is able to derive gratification either from within or without. The fact that the record is marked by six movement answers, however, implies that he uses his inner experiences as a means of coping with more stressful situations, such as that which he is now experiencing. The ep, which is slightly greater than the EA, reveals that he may have a substantial resource that is not readily available to him. It is also important to note that four of the six units that make up the ep are inanimate movement and diffuse shading answers, two each, hinting of an irritating stress experience responded to by a passive orientation. The frequency of blend answers is not remarkable but the fact that each contains some form of movement gives support for the notion that he uses an inner orientation in stressful circumstances. His movement answers are all active, implying an orientation to behaviors which are seemingly inconsistent with the tendencies toward passivity and what is known about his life style. His use of color appears commensurate with the expected, although the frequency of color answers is somewhat low. The Lambda is within normal limits and the $F+$ and $X+$ percents demonstrate a solid, although possibly overly rigid, capacity to work with reality. These features argue against the possibilities of an underlying schizophrenic state. The proportion of W answers to M is slightly less than expected suggesting that he does not set "high," or even adequate goals for himself. The $A\%$ is quite high, and the Affective Ratio quite low, giving evidence of a less mature, cognitively constricted functioning and a tendency to avoid affective interactions with the environment. These data appear to coincide with the high P, and may indicate that his excessive committment to a strong value orientation has a "binding effect" on any expression of affect and/or behaviors that exceed his value boundaries. The $3r + (2)/R$ derivation shows only four pair responses, yielding a proportion that is less than 25% of the record, and indicating a very low self-evaluation. The range of contents is unremarkable but the ratio of $H + Hd/A + Ad$ is noticeably high on the animal side, indicating a tendency to avoid others. This tendency is magnified by examination of the distribution of human percepts, only one of which is a whole human. The reaction times are somewhat long, but the difference between the means is unremarkable. The DQ scores reflect a more intelligent person than is noted in the other data, except the Z scores which also imply a good intellectual base. Conversely, the form quality scores convey the impression of someone bound to the more pedestrian aspects of perceptual accuracy, unable or unwilling to be creative or to bend reality to meet his own needs. The distribution of determinants is unremarkable except for the four movement blends, suggesting the possibility of "affective" arousal when the inner experience occurs. Similarly, the content distribution is unremarkable except for the explosion answer and the torch.

Specific propositions developed from the Structural Data are as follows:

1. There is no evidence of an underlying psychotic process, past or present in the record.

2. He is of at least average intelligence but is unwilling or unable to use this intelligence fully.

3. He is very "bound" to convention, and apparently has a very strongly developed and imposing value system.

4. He is able to use either his inner life or his interactions with his environment for gratification, but relies on the former under more stressful conditions.

5. He has some conflict between desires for a more "active" pattern of behaviors and his more passive life style.

6. He is overly committed to reality, being unwilling to use his own creative capabilities or to distort reality occasionally to meet his needs.

7. He manifests a constricted cognitive life, and generally avoids any deep interpersonal experiences. He seems withdrawn from his environment and prefers to interact with it on a more concrete level, probably selected on the basis that it is compatible with his rigid system of values.

8. His self-esteem is lower than desirable and probably serves to reinforce his committment to the behaviors aligned with his values.

9. He often experiences emotion during his inner experiences but usually does not display this without definitive controls.

ANALYSIS OF THE SCORING SEQUENCE

Two reaction times are worth noting, the shortest and the longest, both of which occur to cards containing color. All of the reaction times are consistently long, indicating a good deal of delay in the cognitive organization of the stimuli. The location sequence is generally unremarkable, with the distribution of synthesis answers occurring throughout the protocol. The approach is *D* oriented, with the *W* answers occurring first in four of five instances. Popular answers appear to all cards except IV and IX, each of which has a more idiographic type content—torch and explosion. The organizational activity also occurs consistently throughout the record, with only Card IV showing no *Z* score. There are no specific propositions that can be developed from the sequence of scores, except the postulate that he has approached the entire test with considerable caution (*RT*'s), and that the response contents to Cards III, IV, and IX may hold special significance.

ANALYSIS OF THE FREE ASSOCIATIONS

H. V.'s responses to the first card are brief and noncommittal, the second answer occurring only after the examiner's encouragement. His response to the second card is also vague and cautious, "kind of like they are touching," which probably illustrates his general orientation to interpersonal contact. His first answer to Card III is more encouraging, "people dancing," and occurs after the shortest *RT*, suggesting that when he does not delay excessively, he is oriented toward a healthy and cooperative interpersonal response. His next answer, "a butterfly," probably represents his own more fragile or delicate self-concept. He is apparently attracted by the color. "This red part . . . ," but does not use color as a determinant. His single response to Card IV is among the more idiographic in the record, "a big giant . . . looming over you." It conveys a sense of threat, and reflects his percept of authority, possibly his own value system which, in turn, probably represents his father's orientation, from what is known of the history. Both of his answers to Card V, a butterfly and a rabbit, illustrate more about his self-concept. They are passive, flighty, harmless creatures. The second response to Card VI, selected to a phallic-like area of the card, "a torch," gives evidence of sexual interest, but also conveys some experience of being unfulfilled in this respect. Both of his responses to Card VII use harmless, playful contents, and may illustrate his own lack of maturity, but also reflects his willingness for interpersonal contact. His first answer to Card VIII is defensive and unrevealing; however, the second answer does imply a status orientation. The "explosion" response to Card IX is given after a very long delay, and is the only answer with the card inverted. This may demonstrate his current reaction to the stress in which he finds himself; that is, under the emotional stimulation of the color of the card, his delaying tactics fail and he reveals his feelings of coming apart. Fortunately, it is a good form answer, frequently seen to this card, implying that even under the affective pressures from within, he is able to maintain good reality contact and does not become overly detached from his orientation toward convention. The next response, like that on Card VI, carries a sexual connotation, while his final answer, to Card X, suggests concealment.

Propositions developed from the Free Associations are as follows:

1. He is cautious in his interpersonal contacts, but does occasionally "let himself go" under affective provocation.

2. He perceives himself as delicate and fragile, and is threatened by authority, including his own system of values.

3. He is generally more comfortable in a passive role, and is somewhat less mature than males his own age.

4. He has a substantial sexual interest but apparently restricts himself, or is restricted, from frequent or meaningful sexual contacts.

5. He is status oriented, probably in line with his strong value orientation.

6. He currently experiences much turmoil, but is able to maintain good reality contact and reasonable affective control in spite of this. He prefers to conceal his feelings most of the time and does so quite well.

ANALYSIS OF THE INQUIRY

H. V. is considerably more verbal in the Inquiry than in the Free Association, mainly as a function of the examiner's promptings. He describes the bat on Card I, the only aggressive animal content of those given, as "a little ragged." which may represent his own image at this time. The second animal seen is a "donkey," which might be interpreted to illustrate himself also, the beast of burden, a hard working "ass." The next animal response, dogs, are "playing a game," as are the children on Card VII. This suggests that his own interpersonal relations are more "put-on" than real. His verbalizations concerning the two people dancing are especially interesting. He describes them as "natives," implying a more primitive activity than his own conventionality might accept. He also is very defensive about specifying the characteristics of the figures, "I'd say they are men although . . . there are many irregularities . . . they don't look like real men." Here he conveys his own lack of self-esteem and reveals some questioning about his masculinity. In Card IV he attempts to "tone down" the threat of the looming giant by describing him as "one of those big green giants on the TV" (the jolly green giant), suggesting that he attempts to view his own values in a positive, nonthreatening manner. He does the same with the "torch" response to Card VI, changing the flames to light and the torch itself to a streetlight, but it continues to give a "radiating effect." He apparently regards his status orientation as a defense, "its like you might see on a shield," in his description of the coat-of-arms on Card VIII. The vase response on Card IX also has an idiographic description, "Its like an antique vase . . . you don't see them any more very much . . . ." This provides added support for the postulate that although he is sexually interested, he has limited, if any, sex contact. He displays his most affective "warmth" in his description of the Card X response, ". . . its all pretty colorful . . ."; however, it is also all underwater, indicating that his own positive affects occur most in situations where he feels controlled and concealed. The Inquiry data generally strengthen and clarify some of the previous hypotheses, revealing the following:

1. He is somewhat immature and concerned about his masculinity.

2. He has an adequate sex interest but apparently very limited sex contact.

3. His self-image is somewhat passive, nonthreatening, and quite unlike the typical male stereotype.

4. He prefers to conceal his affect, and often "role plays" in interpersonal situations. Whenever possible he prefers to "tone down" affect so as to avoid its impact and/or ensure control of it.

A SUMMARY OF PROTOCOL #1

The psychiatrist is probably correct in his initial impression, that H. V. is a "schizoid." He does have these features, being more prone to internalization, constricted interpersonal relations, limited expression of affect, a very strong and seemingly rigid system of values, and a methodical clinging to reality. He is not creative or original, although apparently bright. He has a low self-concept but seems to have resigned himself to it. He has a natural sex interest but does not yield to it, probably because his values direct him away from such activity. Rather, he seems to displace his own needs to less direct but satisfying endeavors (work, blood drive, choir, etc.). He is in awe of authority, and this is possibly one of the factors that makes his such a productive worker. He is probably considered by those who know him "well," if anyone really does, as somewhat of an aloof and possibly eccentric person. He is not schizophrenic, nor will he be, provided that no additional stresses are placed on him before he can reconcile his present condition. The retreat incident appears to have temporarily "shaken him from his routine," and at the moment he needs support to reestablish his confidence and defenses. Although a promotion in his work can be satisfying to his needs for status, as well as rewarding to his value orientation, he probably will function best in a well structured, routine situation that minimizes ambiguity and/or stress. Left to the direction of his values and reality orientation, H. V. will probably rely mainly on his fantasies for more basic gratifications, establish superficial and nonthreatening interpersonal relations, and manifest a productive, although constrictive, style of living. He needs consolation and support for a brief period to reconstitute himself, beyond which further intervention should be unnecessary.

PROTOCOL #2   C. F.—THE EXTERNALIZER

Referral.   C. F. was referred by a psychologist who had seen her previously for about 5 months supportively, shortly after the "break-up" of her first marriage. He had not had any contact with her for approximately 2 years, during which time she had remarried and gave birth to a daughter. He had treated her, during their earlier contact with supportive methods, believing that her symptoms at that time, "nervousness and depression," were related to the divorce action. He now wonders if he may have been "remiss" in terminating her and states in the referral, "She currently complains again of tension and depression, plus occasional spells during which she looses her sense of time and place and feels overwhelmed by her emotions. She has not actually had lapses in memory but is very vague for events that occur during these periods. I would appreciate an independent evaluation of her personality and any guidance you may offer about the most appropriate treatment plans."

History.   C. F. was born and raised in a large metropolitan area. She graduated from high school with honors and completed one year of college in a local liberal arts school, on scholarship, before she married for the first time. She is a reasonably attractive, 25 year old blonde, slight in build, but conscientious in dress so as to maximize her physical assets. She is the oldest of four children, having three younger brothers, the oldest of whom is a recent college graduate, and the younger two who are still in high school. Both parents are living, the father, age 51, is an industrial salesman, the mother, age 50, a housewife. The parents expressed disappointment at C. F.'s early marriage; she was 19 at the time, and had just completed her first year at college. Her marriage lasted approximately 3 years and according to her statement, her husband, who was her own age, "just didn't want much from life. We were incompatible and I doubt that we would have married if I hadn't gotten all caught up in him being a football hero." She indicates that he demanded "too much of my time and didn't give me any freedom to do the things that I wanted." Shortly after her marriage C. F. began working as a receptionist in a law firm while her husband continued in college. She states, "There were always guys after me, you know, on the prowl, and I always felt funny about it cause some were really nice." Ultimately, she did have two extramarital affairs, the second of which precipitated the divorce. She remarried about 5 months after her divorce, during which time she had liaisons with several men, including her present husband who is a law clerk. She became pregnant approximately 4 months after her re-marriage, "it was a wonderful experience." Delivery was normal and "my husband has been a brick through the whole thing." She now has developed "feelings of being confined," complaining of increasing tension and frequent mood swings. She has taken a variety of mild tranquilizers, prescribed by her physician, but "they haven't helped much." She says that her sexual relationship with her husband is "just like always, you know, o.k.," but admits that she does not experience orgasm at each event. She has limited contact with her parents, "because they never really wanted me to marry in the first place and were really upset when I did it again" but writes frequently to her two oldest brothers. She suggests that her feelings of discomfort are created by "some unknown thing in my body, like some physical thing," but admits that several physicians have not detected any physiological problems. She is especially "tired" in the mornings, "I always wake up with a backache or something like that, like I couldn't sleep right," and yet she also has trouble going to sleep, "I lie awake some nights until two or three o'clock." Her menstrual cycle is normal although she does complain of "severe cramps, like a knife cutting into me" during the first day or two of menstruation. She does not want any more children "immediately," but speculates that she might have four or five more "if I can get myself straight."

Protocol #2. C. F., 25 Year Old, Married, One Child, Housewife

Card		Free Association		Inquiry	Scoring
I		1. Oh gee: it ll a bf	E:	(Rpts S's resp)	Wo Fo A P 1.0
			S:	The W thg ll that bec of the way the outside is w the wgs	
	S:	Do u want more?			
	E:	Most people c more than one thg			
		2. Well it cb. a cats face too, hissing	E:	(Rpts S's resp)	WSo FMᵃo Ad 1.0
			S:	These r the ears & the eyes & mouth r the white parts, it has puffy cheeks too lik it was hissing lik cats do	
		3. This cntr prt c.b. the body of a wm w.o. a head	E:	(Rpts S's resp)	Do Fo Hd P
			S:	I can c the body part here (points), c these r the legs & the breasts but there's no head	
II	3''	4. Wow, look at the color, it ll blood on these dogs, or mayb its paint, yes that's it they have been playing in the paint & got it all over them	E:	(Rpts S's resp)	D+ FMᵃ.CFo (2) A,Pnt P 3.0
			S:	I don't kno why I said bld at first cause it doesn't ll that but it does ll paint that these dogs, c thyr playg, touchg their noses & thyv got paint on their legs	
		5. Ths top red part might be a part of the body, lik inside, maybe a kidney, there's one on each side	E:	(Rpts S's resp)	Do F− (2) An
			S:	Well it ll a kidney, the way its shaped	
			E:	I'm not sure I c it as u do	
			S:	Kidneys just ll that, the roundness like that	
III	4''	6. It ll 2 cannibals & theyr carrying a pot up to this fire	E:	(Rpts S's resp)	D+ Mᵃ.CF.FC'.FD + (2) H, Fi P 4.0
			S:	The fire is back here & they r carrying ths pot	

363

Protocol #2 (Continued)

Card		Free Association	Inquiry	Scoring
			E: I'm not sure I c the cannibals S: Rite here, c, 2 black men, lik cannibals, they tall & lanky lik cannibals	
IV	12″	V7. If u turn it ths way the dark part ll an ugly bug	E: (Rpts S's resp) S: Well it might be a spider with the big eyes, sort of the bulging kind & the legs here	Do Fw A
		8. I'd have to say a monster man of s.s., all covered w fur	E: (Rpts S's resp) S: It's a great big monster lik in science fiction, all furry w big legs & a head that almost isn't even there, just a littl thing & a big tail too	Wo FTo (H) P 2.0
V	2″	9. Oh, a child dressed in a rabbit suit, standing to get her picture taken	E: (Rpts S's resp) S: Its lik a littl girl going to a party lik for halloween, she has a bunny hat & this fur suit lik a bunny, ths other stuff doesn't count	Do Mp.FT (H)
		10. It cld b another bf too	E: (Rpts S's resp) S: It has the wgs here & the bunny hat wld b the feelers	Wo Fo A P 1.0
		11. There r 2 legs too, one on each side	E: (Rpts S's resp) S: They just ll legs, lik u c in a stocking ad or s.t.	Do Fo (2) Hd
VI	23″	12. I'm not sure what ths top c.b. but the rest ll a piece of fur	E: (Rpts S's resp) S: It's lik an unfinished coat or fur jacket or s.t., it really hasn't taken shape yet altho these c.b. arm parts here, its just a piece of fur	Do TFo Cg (P)

364

VII

√13. If u turn it ths way ths part ll 2 birds in a nest, waiting to be fed, u just c the heads stickg up

E: (Rpts S's resp)
S: Its their heads (points) & this is the nest & they r just lik waiting for the mother bird

Dd+ FMᵖ (2) Ad, Nest 2.5

5″

14. Ths is a littl girl who just had her hair fixed & she's lookg at herslf in the mirror

E: (Rpts S's resp)
S: She has a pony tail that's probably held up w a comb or pins, she's really cute. I don't kno what the lower part is, it doesn't count

D+ Mᵖ.Fro Hd P 3.0

15. It c.b. rain clds too

E: (Rpts S's resp)
S: Oh, I d.k. why I said that, they just look all black lik rain clouds, there r 4 of them or mayb 6 I guess

Wv C'Fo Cl 2.5

VIII

16. Oh, ths is pretty, its lik a candy house

S: Well its all different kinds of candy put togthr to ll a house lik in fairy tales, the diffrnt colors r diffrnt candies & the white parts r frosting
E: I'm not sure I c it as u do
S: Here is the roof & the windows & the door, its not supposed to ll a real hous, but lik a fairy tale house

WS+ CF.C'F+ Candy House 4.5

3″

<17. If u turn it ths way it ll a beaver stepping over some stones & thgs seeing himself reflected in the water

E: (Rpts S's resp)
S: Its an A lik a beaver or s.t. but its funny all pink lik that, mayb it's a reflect fr the sun that gives that color Its lik in the forest, very colorful, & he's just walkg along, lik a crossing of the stream or pool of water

W+ FMᵃ.FC.Fr+ A, Ls P 4.5

18. There c.b. a skeleton in there too, lik a rib cage

E: (Rpts S's resp)
S: Rite here (points) u can see the spaces in it, it just ll s. bodies ribs

DSo Fo An

Protocol #2 (Continued)

366

Card		Free Association		Inquiry	Scoring
IX	5″	19. My God, more colors, I can c a waterfall in a canyon	E:	(Rpts S's resp)	$D+$ $m^p.CF.FD+$ Na, Ls 2.5
			S:	Its in the cntr, u can c the water falling, its set back in the jungle, all this green stuff, the pink part doesn't count tho, there is a cliff in front of it all colored by the sun & the water-fall in back in the distance	
		20. There are 2 unborn chil-dren here in the pink	E:	(Rpts S's resp)	Do FCo (2) (H) P
			S:	I said unborn bec they r pink thy hav the big heads & the littl bodies, lik twins	
		21. This thg in the cntr ll s.t. I hav on my desk to put papers on, its a sharp spike	E:	(Rpts S's resp)	Do Fo Spindle
			S:	I brought it home when I quit work-ing, it is s.t. u just poke the hole thru the paper & the pink wld b the base tht holds it	
X	5′	22. Wow, it ll s.b. thru paint all over the place, a mess	E:	(Rpts S's resp)	Wv C Paint
			S:	It just ll paint spattered all over when I first lookd at it, mayb its an artist's palate	
		23. Ths c.b. spiders here	E:	(Rpts S's resp)	Do Fo (2) A P
			S:	They hav all those legs that ll a spider to me, don't thy ll that to u?	
		24. These c.b. fried eggs 2 of 'em	E:	(Rpts S's resp)	Do FCo (2) Fd
			S:	Lik they were fried in butter cause thy'r yellow, ths is the yoke part & ths is the white only its yellow bec of the butter	
		25. Ths other yellow parts c.b. rose buds	E:	(Rpts S's resp)	Do FCo (2) Bt
			S:	Thyr pretty lik littl roses waiting to open, just the buds & the littl stem	

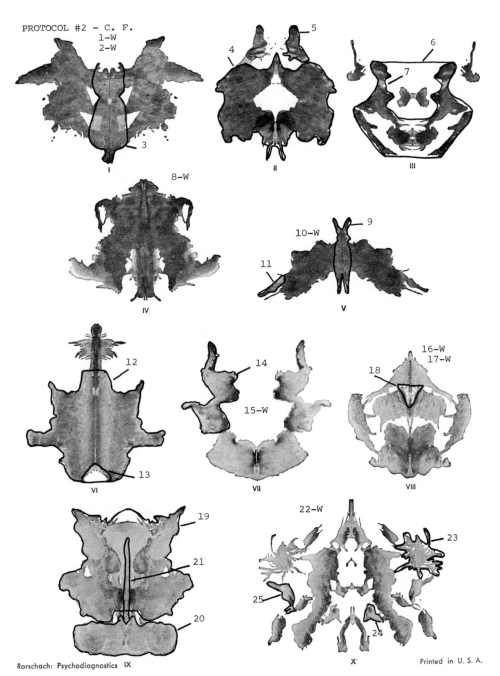

PROTOCOL #2 - C. F.
1-W
2-W

3

I

4

5

II

6

7

III

8-W

IV

10-W

9

11

V

12

13

VI

14

15-W

VII

16-W
17-W

18

VIII

19

21

20

IX

Rorschach: Psychodiagnostics

22-W

23

25

24

X

Printed in U. S. A.

Protocol #2

367

Table 32. Structural Summary for Protocol #2—C. F.

$R = 25$ $Zf = 12$ $Z\text{Sum} = 31.5$ $P = 10 + 1$ $(2) = 9$

Location Features	Determinants	Contents	Contents (Idiographic)
$W\ =\ 8$ **DQ**	$M.CF.FC'.FD = 1$	$H\ \ = 1$	Candy house $= 1$
	$M.FT\ \ \ \ \ = 1$	$(H)\ = 3$	
$D\ \ = 16$ $+\ =\ 7$	$M.Fr\ \ \ \ \ \ = 1$	$Hd\ = 3$	Nest $\ \ \ \ \ \ \ = 0, 1$
	$FM.FC.Fr\ = 1$	$(Hd)\ =$	
$Dd\ =\ 1$ $o\ = 16$	$FM.CF\ \ \ \ = 1$	$A\ \ \ = 6$	Paint $\ \ \ \ \ = 1, 1$
	$m.CF.FD\ = 1$	$(A)\ \ =$	
$S\ \ =\ 2$ $v\ =\ 2$	$CF.C'F\ \ \ = 1$	$Ad\ = 2$	Spindle $\ \ = 1$
	$M\ \ =$	$(Ad)\ =$	
$DW = 0$ $-\ =\ 0$	$FM = 2$	$Ab\ \ =$	$=$
	$m\ \ \ =$	$Al\ \ \ =$	
	$C\ \ \ = 1$	$An\ = 2$	$=$
FORM QUALITY	$CF\ =$	$Art\ =$	
	$FC\ = 3$	$Ay\ \ =$	$=$
$\ \ FQx$ FQf	$C'\ \ =$	$Bl\ \ \ =$	
	$C'F\ = 1$	$Bt\ \ \ = 1$	$=$
$+\ =\ 4$ $+\ =\ 0$	$FC'\ =$	$Cg\ = 1$	
	$T\ \ \ =$	$Cl\ \ = 1$	
$o\ = 18$ $o\ =\ 7$	$TF\ = 1$	$Ex\ \ =$	
	$FT\ = 1$	$Fi\ \ = 0, 1$	
$w\ =\ 1$ $w\ =\ 1$	$V\ \ \ =$	$Fd\ = 1$	
	$VF\ =$	$Ge\ \ =$	
$-\ =\ 1$ $-\ =\ 1$	$FV\ =$	$Hh\ \ =$	
	$Y\ \ \ =$	$Ls\ \ = 0, 2$	
	$YF\ =$	$Na\ = 1$	
	$FY\ =$	$Sx\ \ =$	
	$rF\ \ =$	$Xy\ \ =$	
	$Fr\ \ =$		
	$F\ \ = 9$		

RATIOS, PERCENTAGES, AND DERIVATIONS

$Z\text{Sum}/Z\text{est} = 31.5/38.0$	$FC/CF + C = 4/5$	$Afr\ \ \ \ \ \ \ \ \ \ \ = .67$
$Zd\ =\ -6.5$	$W/M\ \ \ \ \ \ \ \ \ = 8/3$	$3r + (2)/R\ \ \ = 15/25 = .60$
$EB = 3/7.5$ $EA = 10.5$	$W/D\ \ \ \ \ \ \ \ \ = 8/16$	$\text{Cont}/R\ \ \ \ \ = 11/25$
$eb\ = 5/6$ $ep\ = 11$	$L\ \ \ \ \ \ \ \ \ \ \ \ = .56$	$H + Hd/A + Ad = 7/8$
$\text{Blends}/R = 7/25$	$F+\%\ \ \ \ \ \ \ = 77$	$H + A/Hd + Ad = 10/5$
$a/p\ \ \ \ \ = 4/4$	$X+\%\ \ \ \ \ \ \ = 88$	$XRT\ \text{Achrom}\ = 9.6''$
$M^a/M^p\ \ = 1/2$	$A\%\ \ \ \ \ \ \ \ \ = 32$	$XRT\ \text{Chrom}\ \ = 4.0''$

368

Table 33. Sequence of Scores for Protocol #2—C. F.

Card	RT	No.	Location	Determinant(s)		Content(s)	Pop	Z Score
I	6″	1.	Wo	Fo		A	P	1.0
		2.	WSo	FMᵃo		Ad		1.0
		3.	Do	Fo		Hd	P	
II	3″	4.	D+	FMᵃ.CFo	(2)	A, Paint	P	3.0
		5.	Do	F−	(2)	An		
III	4″	6.	D+	Mᵃ.CF.FC′.FD+	(2)	H, Fi	P	4.0
		7.	Do	Fw		A		
IV	12″	8.	Wo	FTo		(H)	P	2.0
V	2″	9.	Do	Mᵖ.FTo		(H)		
		10.	Wo	Fo		A	P	1.0
		11.	Do	Fo	(2)	Hd		
VI	23″	12.	Do	TFo		Cg	(P)	
		13.	Dd+	FMᵖo	(2)	Ad, Nest		2.5
VII	5″	14.	D+	Mᵖ.Fro		Hd	P	3.0
		15.	Wv	C′Fo		Cl		2.5
VIII	3″	16.	WS+	CF.C′F+		Candy house		4.5
		17.	W+	FMᵃ.FC.Fr+		A, Ls	P	4.5
		18.	DSo	Fo		An		
IX	5″	19.	D+	mᵖ.CF.FD+		Na, Ls		2.5
		20.	Do	FCo	(2)	(H)	P	
		21.	Do	Fo		Spindle		
X	5″	22.	Wv	C		Paint		
		23.	Do	Fo	(2)	A	P	
		24.	Do	FCo	(2)	Fd		
		25.	Do	FCo	(2)	Bt		

ANALYSIS OF THE STRUCTURE

Many striking features in the Structural Summary identify C. F. as an unusual person. The record is of average length and the number of organized responses is not unusual; however, the level of organization, as evidenced by the Zd score, is considerably less than is expected for such an effort. Ordinarily this might indicate an "overachievement" motive, but there are other factors in the record that suggest that this may be a product of a "looseness" of affective control wherein the intellect becomes overwhelmed by impulse, thus reducing the effectiveness of the organizational effort. This is clearly an emotionally dominated protocol. The EB shows a definite orientation toward external interactions for the more basic gratifications, and the eb also shows a substantial affective input, consisting of C′ and T kinds of responses. While the EA indicates a rich affective and organized resource, the ep gives evidence that many resources are not well organized or controlled. The a/p ratios show flexibility to the inner life, but in this instance, it may be more a product of vacillation and indecision. There are seven blend answers in the protocol, suggesting a complex cognitive operation. The fact that the sum of CF + C is greater than the frequency of FC answers is evidence of a looseness of emotional control, and hints of lability. The Lambda is within normal limits but on the lower side of this range, also hinting of affective looseness. The F+ and X+ percentage are within normal limits indicating an adequate responsiveness to reality. The Affective Ratio is also within the average range, indicating that she is not "overly caught-up" by the emotionally toned stimuli from her environment. The $3r + (2)/R$ derivation is inordinately high, indicating a very strong egocentric orientation. Two reflection answers in the record strengthen this postulate. The breadth of content is quite good, although some of this is contributed by three very idiographic answers. Nevertheless, there is considerable evidence in the protocol to suggest that she is above average intellectually—the distribution of DQ scores, and especially the four superior form quality responses that she gives. The H to A ratio indicates an excessive preoccupation with people, but the distribution of human contents suggests that this may not be a "healthy" preoccupation. The longer mean RT to the achromatic cards implies some difficulties with the grey-black features, and may be an indirect suggestion of considerable anxiety. Some of her blends seem very unique, such as $M.CF.FC'.FD$, $m.CF.FD$, and $CF.C'F$. Two of these suggest a struggle between affective expression and affective constraint, while the third indicates some effort to control a stress reaction through introspection. She is obviously able to perceive conventionality, as evidenced by the sizable number of Popular answers, but the overall frequency of affective determinants, excluding movement answers, indicates that her "value" system is not a prime mover in determining her responses, except possibly to keep those responses in some "acceptable form." The two anatomy answers, while representing a low frequency, are probably indicative of some form of body preoccupation, which would be consistent with the high degree of egocentricity noted from the reflection and pair answers. Both types of grey-black responses appear with an above average frequency. The three texture answers may indicate strong feelings of affective deprivation, and a desire to return to a more dependent relationship. The C' responses indicate pain and restraint of affect and illustrate her discomfort, probably a result of her limited affective controls. The candy house, paint, and food answers all point to a less mature person and require special consideration during the analysis of the verbal material.

Specific propositions developed for the Structural Summary are as follows:

1. She is a very emotionally loose person, prone to seek her more basic gratification from interaction with her environment.

2. She seems to have considerable pain as a result of her affective looseness, or lability, but does not have the necessary assets to control her own impulses much of the time.

3. She is bright but unable to use her intellectual resources fully because of the affective problems.

4. Her reality testing is good, but she is extremely egocentric, and will often respond in accordance with that orientation rather than in accordance with her awareness of conventionality.

5. Currently, her cognitive operations appear overly complex, mainly as a result of the intense affect that she experiences.

6. She is quite preoccupied with people, but not in a healthy or mature manner. Possibly this preoccupation relates to her reasonably strong needs for dependency.

7. She has abundant resources which are not well organized or easily in her control, yet strives to organize her world much more than most people. Unfor-

tunately, because of the intellectual limitations, this organizational process is not fully successful, and at times may be misleading to her.

8. She is less mature than others her own age, a factor which probably causes difficulty in her interpersonal contacts.

ANALYSIS OF THE SCORING SEQUENCE

Her reaction times tend to be very short, especially to the chromatic cards, suggesting that she does become quickly attracted to affective inputs. Her *RT*'s to Cards IV and VI seem especially long and signal special attention to the responses on those cards. Her approach is generally unremarkable, being oriented to large detail areas most of the time. In most instances the *W* answer occurs first in the card, if it is to occur. Five of her seven blend responses appear to color cards, again offering evidence that she is attracted to, but also confused by affectively toned stimuli. She has Popular answers on every card and shows organizational activity on all but Card X, to which she gives her only "formless" and most labile response. Her Pure *F* answers, with the exception of the first response in the test, appear consistently after more complex determinants have been used. This may indicate an awareness of her tendencies to "overrespond" to ambiguity, and an attempt to constrain this responsiveness. This possibly relates to the large number of *P* answers, suggesting that her awareness of convention does prompt her to attempt more "restrained" behaviors.

There are two specific propositions that can be developed from the sequence of scores:

1. She becomes ambivalent under the pressures of emotionally toned stimuli, prompted to make an affective response but also prompted to constrained her affect.

2. Her displays of affect are usually followed by noticeable efforts for delay and containment, although her most creative activity ordinarily occurs under affectively charged conditions.

ANALYSIS OF THE FREE ASSOCIATION

The Free Association is reasonably rich in idiographic comments. Her use of "Oh gee, . . . , wow, oh, My God" all serve to illustrate one of the ways that her affect is displayed. They are ineffectual delays, signifying her own feelings and generally convey the notion of threat from the external world. She seeks guidance from others, "Do you want more?", but becomes defensively hostile, "hissing" when encouraged to go beyond that for which she is prepared. Her third answer in Card I, " a woman without a head," offers some evidence for her own lack of cognitive control. The impact of the colors is obvious throughout the protocol by her comments and by the manner in which it is often the focal point of her answer. Her constant struggle to inhibit these affective responses is exemplified in Card II where she quickly identifies the red as blood, but then in a counter-phobic move, alters the identification to paint and the dogs as playing. The association of cannibals may represent her own needs to "devour" others in her affect ("to this fire"), but if the affect is turned, as in the next response, she is an "ugly bug." Many of her percepts seem juvenile, or even infantile, "monster man . . . child dressed in a rabbit suit, standing to get her picture taken . . . a piece of fur . . . two birds waiting to be fed . . . a little girl looking at herself in the mirror . . . a candy house . . . unborn children." These illustrate her immature ideation and suggest a regressive orientation. She prefers to be "a child" or at least sees herself as one, and if her affective displays are a good index of her behaviors, she apparently acts "childishly" much of the time. The birds waiting in the nest to be fed reflects her dependency wants, and the monster in the fur coat may, in this instance, evidence her perception of male authority figures, that is, a threat but also a potential source of warmth. Her egocentricity is conveyed very directly by such responses as, the little girl waiting to have her picture taken, and the one who is looking in the mirror. The candy house and the fried eggs reveal an "oral" emphasis, giving further support for the notion of her immaturity. The "rain clouds" answer, following the mirror response on Card VII, seems to indicate some feelings of pain and the prospect of "bad weather ahead" as a result of her excessive concern with herself. It might be speculated that this sort of preoccupation led to the end of her first marriage and may be jeopardizing her current marriage. The waterfall in the canyon could illustrate this kind of apprehension, and the "unborn children" may reflect either her own regressive features *or* her fears of giving birth to other children. The "spindle" response on Card IX is probably quite idiographic and can have many meanings, probably all of which relate to some expression of aggression; that is, she has a "sharp spike" to put papers on. The paint responses are generally considered "anal" in nature by the analytic school, suggesting a willingness to display affect "all over the place" in this instance. She consistently identifies with "feminine" contents throughout the record, except for the "ugly bug," the "monster man," and the "beaver," indicating that she does have an appropriate, although primitive, sex role indentity.

Specific propositions developed from the Free Association material are as follows:

1. Her basic style of behavior is to externalize her feelings, often as a product of fear, but commonly because of a lack of cognitive control over her affect.

2. She is sometimes passively hostile but usually attempts to conceal this.

3. She is quite suggestible and readily gives way to the emotionally toned stimuli from her external world.

4. She is in a constant struggle to constrain her affect, but usually is unable to do this with any degree of effectiveness. At best, she is able to minimize the more aggressive features of her own emotional responsiveness.

5. She "feeds" on others for her more basic gratifications, usually in a dependent and immature manner.

6. She is very egocentric which, when combined with her basic immaturity, leads to behaviors that often cause regret and pain, and causes more efforts to "control" herself.

7. Her first marriage possibly failed because of her own excessive demands and labile outbursts. She currently fears a similar consequence for her second marriage and seems preoccupied with her newborn child, or yet to be born children, as a potential source of demand on her for which she is unprepared.

8. On those few occasions that she looks beneath her own egocentric orientation, she sees "ugliness and undesirability," prompting her to more regressiveness, dependency, and a view of her world generally based on denial and distortion; that is, everything will come out well in the end.

ANALYSIS OF THE INQUIRY

The verbalizations in the Inquiry add considerable support to the previously generated propositions. Her comment, "I don't know why I saw blood," to Card II typifies her attempts to minimize her more aggressive affective responses. Similarly, she suggests that the cannibals are "like you see on TV" rather than real figures. The monster is a "science fiction" character, and the "spattered paint" becomes an artist's palate. The egocentric answers are equally striking, "a little girl going to a party . . . she's really cute," both indicating an intense self-focus. The candy house is "like in fairy tales . . . it's not supposed to be a real house," illustrating the world of fantasy and denial that she is most aligned with. The jacket that "hasn't really taken shape" reflects her own lack of growth, as do the birds "just like waiting for the mother bird." Her emphasis on various body parts, "puffy cheeks . . . breasts . . . kidneys . . . ribs . . . bodies . . . a stocking ad . . . legs" and so on, suggest a reasonably strong preoccupation with her own body and may illustrate some of her own somatic complaints. A less direct but possibly more omnipotent form of egocentric ideation is hinted at in her references to things "colored by the sun" on Cards VIII and IX. Her attempts at form accuracy in the Inquiry frequently falter to a reliance on the coloring of the blots, giving more evidence of her limited capability to detach herself from emotion in her ideation and/or behaviors.

Most of the Inquiry data only serve to support other postulates, although one new proposition does become apparent:

1. She attempts to neutralize any aspects of aggression and/or hostility but resorts to less mature and juvenile forms of ideation.

A SUMMARY OF PROTOCOL #2

The attending psychologist was probably remiss during his first contact with C. F., not so much for early termination, but because he inappropriately identified the causes of her situation to be specifically "divorce related." Actually, the divorce was probably some form of relief for her from the trying demands of adult responsibility for which she has few, if any, resources. She is a child, operating in the body of an adult and, no doubt, frequently becomes confused, irritated, and experiences considerable pain when she cannot handle the demands of adulthood. She has but limited emotional control, being generally oriented to respond to her world as she "sees it," and quite often her perceptions of the world will be "colored" by her own narcissism and immaturity. She does not like anger, in herself or in others, and cannot handle it well, except to deny its existence. She is ambivalent about her limited controls and, at least in part, this ambivalence gives rise to periodic symptoms such as those about which she currently complains. She is bright and has a considerable unorganized resource which might make her a candidate for a reconstructive form of intervention; however, the extensiveness of her immaturity and suggestibility would make her a difficult patient with which to deal in an uncovering form of intervention. She relies on the cues from others for many of her behaviors, but her impulsiveness probably causes her to misinterpret those cues often. It is in this context that she is very preoccupied with others, but at the same time, her own concerns for herself prohibit the development of any deep or meaningful interpersonal relations. Her defensiveness "binds" her intellect so that she is not able to take full advantage of it, and causes her to be somewhat concrete in "affectless" situations. Her excessive demands for gratification and her tendencies to be overly dependent on others probably tend to make for difficulties in most interpersonal situations, and possibly led to the disorganization of her first marriage. These same features may now be threatening her current marriage, and no doubt the responsibilities of caring for a young infant add much stress to her world. One of the products of this situation is an overly complicated psychological activity, usually experienced as tension and/or confusion, and can lead to excessive somatic concerns among other things. She sees males as both threatening and protecting. She seems to need affiliations with them, but only if she can establish the limits and continually have her needs fulfilled. She is a primative hysteroid person who needs the world but who has not learned to interact with it in a mature or cognitively deliberate manner. Supportive intervention might "tide her through" her current round of symptoms, but the probability that they will reoccur is significantly high unless she can experience considerably more growth than has been the case. Intervention with a female therapist seems preferable because of her confusion and defensiveness with male figures. She would be less dependent on a female, as well as less threatened by one.

PROTOCOL #3 L. H.—THE IMPULSIVE

Referral. L. H. is a court referral, having been indicted for aggravated assault and attempted homocide. The consulting psychologist was asked to act as "amicus curiae" to the court in that L. H. claims to have no memory for the event and has a history of similar behaviors and a psychiatric discharge from military service. The specific referring question is whether he is "insane," or has some neurological or psychological impairment which would mitigate in favor of hospitalization rather than routine trial action.

History. L. H. is an impressive looking individual of medium height and weight. He stands out as well groomed and neat. He has a husky voice and a ready smile that seems to have "cooperativeness" written all over it. He picks his words carefully, and after a short while in the interview, it becomes obvious that he wants to make a good impression. Prior to psychological evaluation, he had a complete neurological examination which yielded negative findings. He is the third child, and oldest son, in a family of four. His father was an accountant and the mother a housewife. His older sisters, now ages 38 and 40, both married shortly after completing high school. Both parents are deceased, the father at age 58 of a coronary, the mother at age 59 from cancer. He does not know the whereabouts of his younger brother, age 29. L. H. is a high school graduate and has taken "a few" college courses "here and there." He has marked memory lapses for his various jobs but estimates that he has held "at least a dozen," all of which fall into the "blue collar" category except one as a salesman in an appliance store. He currently works as a fork lift operator in a storage warehouse, but claims to also make "a lot of extra money" gambling and "things like that." He describes his sex history with some rather grandiose claims of conquest, "I'd never get married with all the available women around . . . . Women just seem to want to fall into bed with me . . . No kidding doc, I haven't paid my own rent in two years . . . . I guess I'm lucky to have the natural talent that women go for." He claims his first sexual experience occurred at age 11 when he was seduced by "an older girl." He says that he may have fathered "a kid or two," but has no definite knowledge of any of his past loves giving birth. Most of his jobs have lasted less than one year, and he admits to being fired twice for fighting with supervisors. He freely admits to the attempted strangulation of the girl friend with whom he had been living for about 8 months, "I don't know what happened, one minute we were o.k. and the next minute I was like a wild man, I went crazy." He claims that this has happened at least twice before with other women. He also cites the fact that he could not control his temper "at all" during a 4 month stint in the Army after having been drafted. Military records indicated that he was discharged with a diagnosis of "Schizoid Personality with epileptoid features." He claims to be a heavy drinker but denies any use of drugs. He states, "Its about time I got myself some help because this temper is really bad and I can't control it."

Protocol #3. L. H., 32 Years Old, Single, Two Older Sisters, One Younger Brother, High School Graduate Plus a "Few" College Courses, Currently "Blue Collar," Employment

Card		Free Association	Inquiry	Scoring
I	37″	1. Holy Christ: I d.k. what ths is, mayb its a naked wm in the cntr w her hands up, like a model	E: (Rpts S's resp) S: Yeah, the more I look at it the more it ll that. Here's her hips & it ll the hands in the air, as if she's modeling s.t., but if she naked what's she modeling? That's a thought isn't it. E: Can u show me a bit more so that I c it the way u do? S: Well, c here is the outline, u can't c her head, mayb its back lik she was laughing, she looks pretty sexy to me doc.	Do M^{a}o H P
		E: (Most people c more than 1 thg) S: Gee, I don't c nothg else.		
II	41″	2. Oh u'r really kidding 'me aren't u? Am I supposed to tell u wht ths really ll to me? (E: Yes) Well doc ths is a good one, ths bttm prt ll some a-a- well I was gonna say pussy, but I'll say vagina to make it a littl better, how's that?	E: (Rpts S's resp) S: I heard somewhere if u c tht stuff u'r preoccup'd w it, is that right? E: Can u show me how u c it? S: Well it has the fuzzy look to it lik there was hair & u can c the slit, I'm tryg to b honest about it cause I hav a big responsibility to try & get bettr	Do FTo Sx
		3. Ths top prt ll a bldy thumb	E: (Rpts S's resp) S: Well it's all red lik bld, & its shaped lik a thumb, mite hav had an accident, there's really 2 of them, 1 on each side	D− CF− (2) Hd, Bl
III	21″	4. The ll 2 wm doing s. t. in ths pot, no wait a minute, its lik	E: (Rpts S's resp) S: Yeah, lik she's makin bad apples in her	W+ M^a.Fr+ (H) P 5.5

Card	Time	Response	Inquiry	Scoring
		a witch, lik in snow white & she's doing s.t., brewing s.t. in the pot & lookin in the mirror	den & thes red thgs r lik decorations, sort of symbols of her cult, lik trophies or s.t. E: Decorations? S: Just thgs on the wall, I d.k. what.	
IV	16″	V5. Ths is some old tattered & torn hide, mayb it was a jacket once but now its all ruined from being weathered	E: (Rpts S's resp) S: The W thg ll tht, altho the arms r gone I guess, it ll its all greasy & beat up E: Greasy & beat up? S: Yeah, c the drk splotches on it c.b. grease & its all ragged around the edges	Wv YFw Cg 2.0
V	7″	6. Ths ll a bat bearing down on a target w his feelrs stretch'd out ready to strike	E: (Rpts S's resp) S: It apparently sightd its prey & now its about to gobble it up E: Can u show me how u c it? S: Sure, c the wgs (points) & the body, it looks stiff, lik it's ready to strike	Wo $FM^{a}o$ A P 1.0
VI	71″	7. Well, I said I'd b honest, u'll prob lock me up & throw away the key, but ths top prt ll a man's—well—his sex organ, penis that is	E: (Rpts S's resp) S: Its ths top thg, I hav to admit these side thgs don't fit, at least I never saw one w feathers altho it wld b popular as hell I'll bet E: Can u tell me what maks it ll tht? S: Hell, if u don't c it u'd bettr lock me up & thro away the key, it just ll that 2 me damn it (Throws card down).	Do Fo Sx
VII	103″	8. ll a cpl of pieces of fried chicken to me	E: (Rpts S's resp) S: Well, thy'r sort of drumsticks altho the shape isn't really right, thy hav lik breading on them lik u get in chkn in a basket. E: Where is it that u c them? S: Ths bttm prt isn't included, altho I guess u can c it as anothr piece	Do TFo (2) Fd

Protocol #3 (Continued)

Card		Free Association	Inquiry	Scoring
	∨9.	If u turn it ths way it ll a cpl of can-can dancers going at it	E: U mentioned breading S: Thy look ruff & drk lik breadg, lik u kno, breadg is that way E: (Rpts S's resp) S: Thy hav thyr heads touchg lik thy were in a chorus line or s.s. of specialty dance, c the legs r kicking outward so u can't c it, u can c only one on each	W+ M^a+ (2) H 2.5
VIII	46″			
	∨10.	Ths prt ll sherbet, its got a glassy look to it, differnt from real ice cream	E: (Rpts S' resp) S: Yeah, its all colord like sherbet, orange & raspberry I guess & its kind of grainy lik sherbet	Dv C.T Fd
	<11.	ll a wolf, ready to spring at s.t., he's being reflected in a river or pond	E: (Rpts S's resp) S: C the legs here & the body & the wolf head, there's no tail tho, he's ready to spring, standg on some rocks or s.t. being reflectd dwn here I d.k. what ths (points to front prt) mite b, mayb a stump or s.t.	W+ FM^a.Fr+ A, Ls P 4.5
IX	16″			
	∨12.	ll the whole damn world is blowing up, u get the feelg of a lot of force	E: (Rpts S's resp) S: Lots of force, lik an atomic blast but it has so much color that it has 2 b the world or at least part of it, c all the fire here—I guess we'd b bettr off if it happened	Wv m^a.CFo Ex 5.5
	13.	If u turn it ths way the pink ll cotton candy, no stick but a couple of 'em, c one on each side	E: (Rpts S's resp) S: Well they'r pink & fluffy lookg, fuzzy lik cotton candy, u can't c the stick tho, just the round ball of cotton candy lik is on the stick like at a fair	Dv CF.TFw (2) Fd

	No.	Response	Inquiry	Scoring
X	14.	Well a cpl lady bugs at the top eatin on a weed	E: (Rpts S's resp) S: They hav legs & antennae, c (points) they look pretty good lik lady bugs	$D+$ FM^ao (2) A, Bt 4.0
32"	15.	The pink ll bld stains	E: (Rpts S's resp) S: Yeah, they ll bld stains to me, prob dried up cause the red isn't as dark as fresh bld, just a blob of dried bld	Dv C Bl
	16.	Ths up here ll a spider tht has caught a bug in its claws & is going to devour it	E: (Rpts S's resp) S: It has a lot of legs, I don't kno wht the grn thg is, s.k. of bug I guess, the ole spider has really got it tho	$D+$ FM^ao A P 4.0
	17.	Mayb a cpl dogs down here lik they were baying at the moon or s.t.	E: (Rpts S's resp) S: C here thy r, 1 on each side, the heads are tilted up lik thy were baying like dogs do	Do FM^ao (2) A
	18.	Ths blue thgs ll some sex thgs lik a cpl of ovaries or s.t., if there were a — penis there they cld b testicles but there isn't any so thy must b ovaries	E: (Rpts S's resp) S: They just rem me of that, I d.k. exactly why, I guess bec of the way they r formed there, I d.k. what that is between them tho, mayb a clitoris but that isn't where it's supposed to be	$D-$ $F-$ (2) Sx

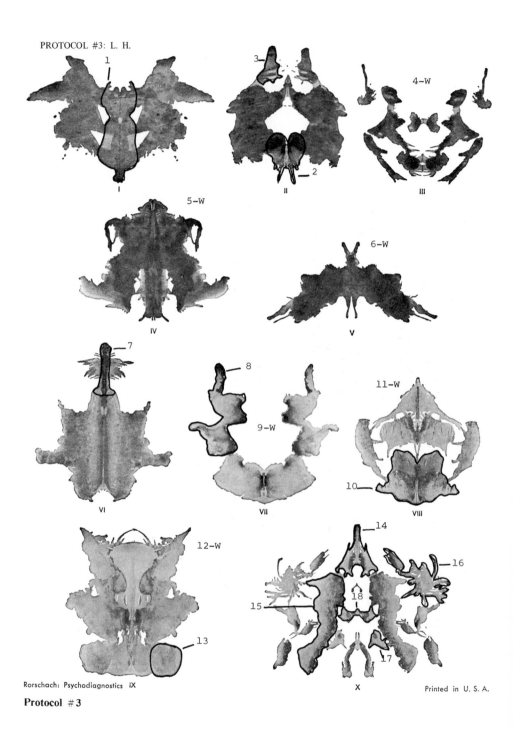

PROTOCOL #3: L. H.

I

II

III 4-W

5-W IV

6-W V

VI 7

8 9-W VII

11-W VIII 10

12-W IX 13

14 15 16 17 18 X

Rorschach: Psychodiagnostics

Protocol #3

Table 34. Structural Summary for Protocol #3—L. H.

$R = 18$ $\quad Zf = 8$ $\qquad Z\text{Sum} = 29.0$ $\quad P = 5$ $\quad (2) = 7$

Location Features		Determinants	Contents	Contents (Idiographic)
	DQ	$M.Fr = 1$	$H = 2$	_____ =
$W = 6$		$FM.Fr = 1$	$(H) = 1$	
$D = 12$	$+ = 5$	$m.CF = 1$	$Hd = 1$	_____ =
		$C.T = 1$	$(Hd) =$	
$Dd = 0$	$o = 6$	$CF.TF = 1$	$A = 5$	_____ =
			$(A) =$	
$S = 0$	$v = 5$	$M = 2$	$Ad =$	_____ =
		$FM = 4$	$(Ad) =$	
$DW = 0$	$- = 2$	$m =$	$Ab =$	_____ =
		$C = 1$	$Al =$	
		$CF = 1$	$An =$	_____ =
FORM QUALITY		$FC =$	$Art =$	
		$C' =$	$Ay =$	_____ =
FQx	FQf	$C'F =$	$Bl = 1, 1$	
		$FC' =$	$Bt = 0, 1$	_____ =
$+ = 3$	$+ = 0$	$T =$	$Cg = 1$	
		$TF = 1$	$Cl =$	
$o = 9$	$o = 1$	$FT = 1$	$Ex = 1$	
		$V =$	$Fi =$	
$w = 2$	$w = 0$	$VF =$	$Fd = 3$	
		$FV =$	$Ge =$	
$- = 2$	$- = 1$	$Y =$	$Hh =$	
		$YF = 1$	$Ls = 0, 1$	
		$FY =$	$Na =$	
		$rF =$	$Sx = 3$	
		$Fr =$	$Xy =$	
		$FD =$		
		$F = 2$		

RATIOS, PERCENTAGES, AND DERIVATIONS

$Z\text{Sum}/Z\text{est} = 29.0/24.0$ $\qquad FC/CF + C = 0/5$ $\qquad Afr = 1.0$

$Zd = +5.0$ $\qquad\qquad W/M = 6/3$ $\qquad 3r + (2)/R = 13/18 = .72$

$EB = 3/6.0 \quad EA = 9.0$ $\qquad W/D = 6/12$ $\qquad \text{Cont}/R = 7/18$

$eb = 6/5 \qquad ep = 11$ $\qquad L = .13$ $\qquad H + Hd/A + Ad = 4/5$

Blends$/R = 5/18$ $\qquad F+\% = 50$ $\qquad H + A/Hd + Ad = 8/1$

$a/p = 9/0$ $\qquad X+\% = 67$ $\qquad XRT$ Achrom $= 46.8''$

$M^a/M^p = 3/0$ $\qquad A\% = 28$ $\qquad XRT$ Chrom $= 31.2''$

Table 35.   Sequence of Scores for Protocol #3—L. H.

Card	RT	No.	Location	Determinant(s)		Content(s)	Pop	Z Score
I	37″	1.	Do	$M^a o$		H	P	
II	41″	2.	Do	FTo		Sx		
		3.	D−	CF−	(2)	Hd, Bl		
III	21″	4.	W+	$M^a.Fr+$		(H)	P	5.5
IV	16″	5.	Wv	YFw		Cg		2.0
V	7″	6.	Wo	FM^a		A	P	1.0
VI	71″	7.	Do	Fo		Sx		
VII	103″	8.	Do	TFo	(2)	Fd		
		9.	W+	M^a+	(2)	H		2.5
VIII	46″	10.	Dv	C.T		Fd		
		11.	W+	$FM^a.Fr+$		A, Ls	P	4.5
IX	16″	12.	Wv	$m^a.CFo$		Ex		5.5
		13.	Dv	CF.TFw	(2)	Fd		
X	32″	14.	D+	$FM^a o$	(2)	A, Bt		4.0
		15.	Dv	C		Bl		
		16.	D+	$FM^a o$		A	P	4.0
		17.	Do	$FM^a o$	(2)	A		
		18.	D−	F−	(2)	Sx		

ANALYSIS OF THE STRUCTURE

This 18 response record is sharply marked by indications of lability. All of the color responses are CF or Pure C; only two Pure F answers appear in the record, yielding a very low Lambda; the Affective Ratio is quite high, 1.0; and the EB shows a distinct preference for external action to gratify basic needs. All of his movement responses are active, and the composite of FM + m is twice the frequency of M. This configuration indicates the potentials for "acting-out" patterns, and when viewed with regard to the very limited emotional controls, makes such a pattern one of high expectancy. A very strong egocentric orientation, as illustrated by the reflection and pair answers, also contributes to this expectancy. The F+ % is of little use because of the very low frequency of Pure F answers; however, the X+ % gives evidence of limited reality testing. The number of minus form quality answers, two, is not substantial, indicating that he does not distort reality in a gross manner, as is the case in the more severe thought disorders. More likely, he is prone to "bend" reality to meet his own needs at a given time. The number of P responses is slightly below average, but not so much so to suggest that he is not aware of conventionality. Quite the contrary, he is probably very aware of it, but does not always respond to it because of his egocentricity and impulsiveness. He organizes quite well, showing a Zd score of +5.0. The H to A ratio suggests that he is also "people oriented," although the imbalance in the ratio may be more a function of relatively few animal responses (A% = 28), in favor of an emphasis on other contents. His mean RT's are both very long, indicating attempts at delay; however, the labile features and indications of impulsiveness prevail in the protocol in spite of this attempt. The distribution of *DQ* scores is quite unusual, with as many synthesis answers as vague selections. This can represent a lower developmental level, but may also reflect the disregard for perceptual accuracy associated with a more impulsive style. While these are not necessarily unrelated, they do imply different etiological factors. Four of the five shading determinants are texture answers, demonstrating an unusually strong affective deprivation, which is emphasized even more by the fact that one is Pure *T* and two others are *TF* responses. The content frequencies reveal three Food answers and three Sex answers, both being unusually high. The Food responses seem to support the notion of an "oral," more infantile orientation. The Sex responses signal a strong preoccupation, possibly related to the feelings of affective deprivation and the less mature kind of response style.

Specific propositions developed from the Structural Summary are as follows:

1. He is very labile, frequently commanded by affect rather than a more organized cognitive activity.
2. He experiences the "need to respond" quite often from less well organized inner forces, and when combined with his lability makes for a high probability of "acting-out."
3. He bends reality often, usually to meet his own needs.
4. He is very egocentric, an element sometimes causing him to disregard conventionality, and that also feeds into his impulsive life style.
5. He has very limited controls, and even when he does make attempts at organization and delay, his affect usually "breaks through" and dictates his response.
6. He has some features of immaturity, and may even be described as "infantile" at times. He has strong affective needs that frequently orient his behavior pattern.
7. He is noticeably preoccupied with sexuality, and this also probably contributes to his impulsive patterns of behavior.

ANALYSIS OF THE SCORING SEQUENCE

The reaction times have substantial variance, ranging from 7″ on Card V to 103″ on Card VII. They generally evidence attempts at delay, although the longest culminate in the more idiographic responses, a *TF* Food response after the 103″ delay, a *C.T* Food response after the 46″ delay, and an *FT* Sex response after the 41″ delay. All three involve texture and seems to indicate that when he does attempt delay, his inner needs intensify, and the resulting proccupations become overwhelming to his cognitive activity. His impulsiveness may well be a defense against this kind of experience. His approach to the test is somewhat erratic, selecting all *D* areas on the first two cards, then proceeding to *W* responses on the next three cards, and ending the test with six consecutive *D* answers. This inconsistency suggests that he often becomes "caught-up" by the stimulus rather than being able to function in a more routine perceptual manner. His blend answers all occur to color cards, again giving some evidence of the intense impact of affective stimuli on him.

A specific proposition evolving from these data is as follows:

1. His impulsive style serves a defensive purpose by creating a situation in which he avoids awareness of his very strong feelings of affective deprivation.

ANALYSIS OF THE FREE ASSOCIATIONS

The Free Associations of L. H. provide strong evidence of both impulsiveness and attempts at manipulation. His very first answer, coming after 37″ sets the tone of the record, "Holy Christ . . . a naked woman . . . ." The second response reveals the manipulative efforts, "Oh, you're really kidding me aren't you . . . . Well doc, this is a good one . . . I was gonna say pussy, but I'll say vagina to make it a little better, how's that?" The "bloody thumb" may indicate feelings of inadequacy concerning his own masculinity and could give some clue concerning his excessive sexual preoccupation. Another suggestion of this is noted by his response to Card IV, ". . . it was a jacket once but now its all ruined from being weathered." The manipulativeness is also evidenced in Card VI, "Well, I said I'd be honest, you'll probably lock me up and throw away the key . . . ." Some of his answers imply strong aggressive feelings, ". . . a bat bearing down on his target . . . a wolf ready to spring on something . . . the whole damn world is blowing up . . . a spider that has caught a bug in its claws and is going to devour it." None of his food answers are form dominant—"sherbet," "cotton candy," "fried chicken"— illustrating the intensity of his oral orientation. The explosion response to Card IX possibly typifies much of his own inner feelings, ". . . you get the feeling of a lot of force," and his last response may well illustrate his preoccupations with sexual adequacy, ". . . if there were a penis there they could be testicles, but there isn't any so they must be ovaries." All of the H and (H) answers are feminine—a woman modeling, a witch brewing something, and can-can dancers "going at it." This suggests that his own identity may be feminine rather than masculine, and that the aggressiveness and sexual concerns are attempts at concealment of this sex role problem.

Specific propositions generated from the Free Associations are as follows:

1. Attempts at delay fail to contain his impulsiveness.
2. He is quite manipulative of others.
3. Beneath a thin facade of "cooperativeness" is a strong aggressive orientation toward others.
4. He does not appear to have developed a masculine sex role identity, a factor which is probably responsible for the aggressiveness and his notable sexual preoccupation.
5. His emphasis on sexuality is a form of concealment and denial of his own role problems.
6. His feelings of affective deprivation are very strong and frequently overwhelming of his attempts to present an acceptable facade.

ANALYSIS OF THE INQUIRY

Much of the Inquiry material dramatizes the superficiality of his facade and the lack of control he is able to exert when confronted with challenge. The intensity of the sexual preoccupation is also firmly reinforced by his answers, ". . . but if she's naked what's she modeling? . . . like there was the hair and you can see the slit . . . . I have to admit these side things don't fit, at least I never saw one with feathers although it would be popular as hell I'll bet . . . . I don't know what that is between them though, maybe a clitoris, but that isn't where its supposed to be." His manipulative attempts seem overly obvious at times, "I'm trying to be honest about it cause I have a big responsibility to try and get better . . . . Hell, if you don't see it you'd better lock me up and throw away the key." A less direct view of his own self-image and valuation of his actions may be found in his description of the response to Card III, ". . . like she's making bad apples in her den and these red things are . . . sort of symbols of her cult, like trophies . . . ." This seems to indicate that he is aware of the negative features of his behaviors but also gains reinforcement from them.

The Inquiry material here, as in most protocols, serves to provide support for previously established propositions. One new hypothesis is developed from this segment of the test:

1. He is aware of his "nonconformity," but obtains significant reinforcement from it, a major factor serving to perpetuate it.

A SUMMARY OF L. H.

This is a 32 year old infant, oriented toward immediate discharge of his impulses, with little regard for the consequences. He is extremely labile, preferring to let his emotions command his behaviors than experience the pain that occurs when he attempts delay. He is extremely self-centered, a product of a reversal in sex role identity and a prolonged experience of affective deprivation. He has learned that ventilation of his impulses avoids discomfort, and also permits him to conceal his true inadequacies. He is quite aggressive and uses sexuality plus aggressiveness to create a superficial but reinforcing facade of supermasculinity, which in turn, defends against his own feelings of masculine impotency. His limited controls, and strong needs to thwart any awareness of inadequacy, breed an acting-out pattern in which his own perceptions supersede his awareness of conventionality and give direction to his behaviors. At a deeper level he has strong feelings of affective deprivation, possibly related to "overprotection" or severe rejection at a relatively early age. He is more intelligent than he prefers to convey to others and can organize quite well when not confronted with needs for immediate discharge of impulses. He bends reality as necessary and may often engage in behaviors which appear to others as "bizarre," but which to him have the special importance of providing immediate gratification. His lability, immaturity, and impulsiveness, combined with his strong needs to "prove himself in his sex role," establish the basic ingredients for frequent antisocial or asocial behaviors.

CHAPTER 18

Some Symptom Patterns

Whereas some people are identified because their styles of response are no longer effective to meet the demands of their situations, others develop more definitively inappropriate methods of handling stressful situations. These are usually identified as symptoms, and form an "overlay" to the basic styles of response. Some of these people are described an "neurotic," while others are characterized in terms of the symptom patterns that they present. All are in trouble, and none are able to function with any consistent degree of effectiveness. Instead, they maintain specific peculiarities in their behaviors that to others seem quite inappropriate, but to the individual are important techniques for defending themselves against known and/or unknown stresses. Most people with symptoms are able to continue in their environmental functions, although their overall levels of efficiency decrease substantially. The symptoms may be very specific, and thus requiring only a slight modification of prior behaviors, such as avoiding bridges, washing silverware twice, forgetting important events, and such, or they may take on a broader detachment from responsibility and a greater distortion of reality. In many instances, the alteration in behaviors requires a more methodical approach to tasks leaving less time to attend to seemingly extraneous stimuli.

The records presented in this chapter represent people who are still functioning, and not greatly detached from reality. They are in some disarray, but functional. They have not fled completely from their environments but have adopted unusual ways of combating the stresses that are frequently impinged upon them.

PROTOCOL #4 J. C.—AN OBSESSIVE WITH SOMATIC FEATURES

Referral. This 28 year old female was referred for psychological evaluation because of a reoccurring duodenal ulcer that had not been treated successfully over a period of 2 years, although a variety of medications and dietary regimens had been used. The condition became debilitating at approximately 4 month intervals, and in three instances required hospitalization for periods of from 7 to 24 days. Surgical intervention is currently being considered; however, the attending physician is concerned that the somatic complaint may represent a more chronic psychological problem, which treated surgically might lead to a more pronounced psychological disruption. His referral asks, "What dangers to her psychological state might be created by surgical interference with this symptom, and are there other methods of treatment that might yield greater *short term* success?"

History. J. C. is an attractive, short, dark haired registered nurse who currently has supervisory responsibility for six other nurses and 11 attendants on a large general medical ward. She holds a B.S. degree in Nursing from a well known university, and has worked at the same hospital for 7 years. Her work history is excellent. She manifests good patient relationships, accomplishes her own duties thoroughly and efficiently, and since being promoted to a "Head Nurse" position slightly more than 2 years ago, has set "commendable" standards for herself and those who work with her. She lives alone in a hospital apartment, dating irregularly. She was engaged during college to a resident physician, but "our interests didn't coincide, and so we called it off." She implies virginity but politely refuses to speak of sexual matters, "That is a personal matter that I'm not prepared to talk about now." She is the oldest of two daughters of parents who emigrated from a middle European country shortly after they married. Her family was poor during her developmental years, living in a "cold-water flat" in a large eastern city until she entered high school. By that time, her father had been able to establish himself as a skilled tradesman and purchased a small "duplex" house where the family still lives. J. C. entered college on a nursing scholarship and maintained a "Dean's list" average throughout her four years there. She dated frequently in high school and in college but "never for very long with one person." She is very thrifty in her spending habits, preferring to "save my money for a rainy day, or in the event that my parents ever need it." She attends a Protestant church each Sunday, "more to set an example than because I have a belief. In fact, I'm probably an agnostic although I don't go around telling everybody." Her younger sister, age 25, is now married, after having completed 2 years of college, to a businessman and is currently pregnant. J. C. describes both of her parents as the "salt of the earth." She indicates that both are very hard working, conservative, and "vigorously sincere." She says that she feels closer to her father than her mother but is uncomfortable in making any distinction between them. She verbalizes a feeling of contempt for many of her colleagues, "who work their eight to five and get out as quickly as they can. They just don't have much concern for those who they are suppose to be serving." She has great faith in "most doctors," but admits that she has seen some who she feels would fare better in other professions. She says that she sleeps well, has no appetite problems, exercises daily, likes horseback riding, tennis, and an occasional movie.

Protocol #4. J. C., 28 Years Old, Ulcer Patient, Single, College Graduate, Registered Nurse

Card		Free Association		Inquiry	Scoring
I	16″	1.	Two wm, prob witches dancing @ a fig. in the cntr, it seems to b a person, quite helpless, its a wm too bec u can c her breasts and hip & she has her hands up	E: (Rpts S's resp) S: Well, the witches r on each side, the hav big dark cloaks on & they'r doing a dance, I can't really tell if its a ritual or if theyr burng her at the stake. She is just there in the cntr w her hands up	$W+$ $M^a.FY+$ (2) $H, (H)$ P 4.0 (The scoring' of a-p is used as both features of M appear. Both are counted in the a/p ratio)
		2.	It cld b an x-ray of a pelvis too	E: (Rpts S's resp) S: Yes, the W thg ll one, its dark lik an x-ray & it has the general structure of a pelvic area, u c, u get the slant of the pelvic arch here	Wo FYo Xy 1.0
II	46″	3.	At the top ll 2 hens preparing to fite w e.o., these red areas	E: (Rpts S's resp) S: It ll 2 hens primping for a fite u can c the heads & feet & legs	$D+$ $F M^a w$ (2) A 5.5
		4.	The cntr ll a temple of worship w a tower of silver or platinum	E: (Rpts S's resp) S: Ths cntr white area is the temple & ths ll the tower, it clearly has the form of a towr & its colord like silver or platinum or some other valuable metal wld b colord, its the metal part that really attracts people to the temple bec its so valuable	$DS+$ $FC'o$ Temple 4.5
III	8″	5.	2 wm fiting over s.t. valuable, itll a basket that theyr fitg over, they must b angry the way theyr tugging so hard	E: (Rpts S's resp) S: Oh yes, these r the wm, u c the breast outline & the hi-heels, & theyr thin like wm & this is the basket, it must b full of goodies bec each wants it for her own, but neither seems able to get it	$D+$ $M^a o$ (2) H P 3.0

388

Card	Time	No.	Response	Inquiry	Scoring
IV	58″	V6.	Well, ths c.b. an x-ray too, I'm not sure of what, possbly a pelvic arch again & the sacral area of the cord	E: (Rpts S's resp) S: It's ths *W* thg, its kind of dark & it has a shape that conceivably cld b the pelvic area if u stretch u'r immag a littl. Ths prt wld b the part of the cord, & the rest the pelvis, it definitely has that kind of darknss to it like an x-ray	*Wo FYo Xy* 2.0
V	26″	7.	2 peopl leang against s.t., lying down w thr backs against ths thg in the cntr. I thnk thy'r wm, almost but not quite rstg back to back w thr legs stretchd out like thy wer relxg like they wer wrkd hard at s.t. & now theyr takg a break	S: Oh I rem ths one, I've sat lik that many times during the war when we'v had a surgery break. I use to hav a good friend who was killed in Seoul & most of the time when we couldn't rest for a long time we'd prop up like ths, u c her r the legs extendg outward	*W+ Mp+* (2) *H* 2.5
VI	77″	8.	A weapon, here at the top, lik an arrow that u would thrust at someone in battle, it has a spear type tip, s.t. u wld use to hurt or maim or kill	E: (Rpts S's resp) S: Yes, just ths top, it has a kind of dull tip lik it cld really do damage if it were misused, it just has the general characteristics of a weapon	*Do Fw* Weapon
		9.	U kno, ths cntr prt cld be a rivr or a road, far away, as if u were stdg on a mt or s.t. lookg down at it	S: Well, u hav to stretch u'r immag to c the next one, r u ready? E: Go rite ahead S: Well, it's just a straight line, as a road or river but its so small u'd hav to be far away to c it lik ths, c rite here (points)	*Do FDo Ls*
VII	12″	10.	2 wm arguing @ s.t. w.e.o., u just c their heads, it ll thy r disagreeg @ s.t.	E: (Rpts S's resp) S: Yes, just the head parts, mayb thy r the one's I saw earlier who were fitg ovr the basket of precious stuff, u	*D+ M^{a}o* (2) *Hd P* 3.0

Protocol #4 (Continued)

Card		Free Association	Inquiry	Scoring
			can c the facial features rather distinctly, especially the lips here, & ths wld b a hair piece of s.s.	
	<11.	If u turn it ths way it cld b a scottie dog w his flat snout & stubby legs here	E: (Rpts S's resp) S: Its a good liknss to one, ths is the tail & the snout & the funny littl legs	Do Fo A
VIII 9″	12.	There's a rib cage here, at the cntr	E: (Rpts S's resp) S: Its here (points), it has a pretty good formation lik a rib cage has	DSo Fo An
	13.	The W thg seems to be s.s. of anatomy chart but I can't identify the specific prts, oh!, bettr still, it cld b internal viscera & ths bttm prt cld b s.s. of internal viscera, it has a bloody mass effect there	E: (Rpts S's resp) S: Well not really a chart of An, it looks much more like the visceral organs & ths orag-pink prt here ll a wound, the organs r not clerly delineatd but it could b, the colorg is so strkg particulrly the effect of the wound but the other parts r also colord much like the visceral organs might b	Wv CFo An 4.5
IX 69″	14.	The orange ll 2 witches hovrg ovr a cauldron lik they r arggug @ wht to mix in it, thy hav peakd hats on	E: (Rpts S's resp) S: Rite here (points) thy r pointg to the cauldron here in the middle, I can't say what's goig on but thy r apparently arguing about what mixture shld go in it	Dd+ Mᵘo (2) (H) 2.5
	15.	U kno, ths cntr prt cld b a glass candl holder w a candle in it, lik u can c thru it	E: (Rpts S's resp) S: Well its rite here where the cauldron is except that it goes down further than the cauldron & u can c the candle inside it, u see thgs lik that in res-	DS+ mᵖ.FV+ Candle 5.0

X   13"

turants some times, it has a milky colrg about it as if the candle was givg off lite

16. 2 *A*'s tryg to do s.t. to ths pole lik thg, mayb thyr tryg to capture it or mayb thyr tryg to climb up it or mayb thyr not sure what to do w it

D+   FM^{a}o   (2)   (*A*)   4.0

E: (Rpts *S*'s resp)
S: Thy just look confused @ ths thg, thy r unknwn creatures w little legs & antennae, almst no legs at all, I can't decide what ths is, mayb its s.s. of food & thy r arguing about when to eat it, its difficult to decide

17. Ths cld b a seed fr a tree, a maple tree I believe, I'm not sure but there is s.s. of tree that has seeds shaped like ths & they turn brown after thy fall

Do   FCo   B*t*

S: The seed is easier to decrib, u c it is rite here (points) & its brwn as if it were ready for plantg or whatever when they fall so as to start a new tree

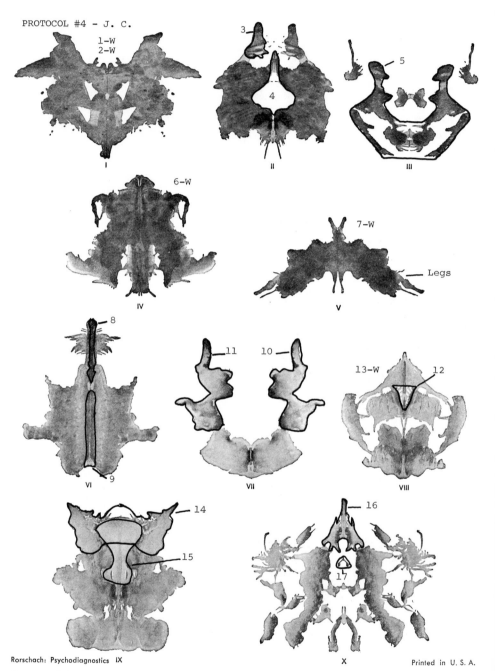

PROTOCOL #4 - J. C.

1-W
2-W

3

4

5

I II III

6-W

7-W

Legs

IV V

8

11 10 13-W 12

9

VI VII VIII

14

16

15 17

Rorschach: Psychodiagnostics IX X Printed in U. S. A.

Protocol #4

Table 36. Structural Summary for Protocol = 4—J. C.

$R = 17$ $Zf = 12$ $Z\text{Sum} = 41.5$ $P = 3$ $(2) = 7$

Location Features		Determinants	Contents	Contents (Idiographic)
$W = 5$	DQ	$M.FY = 1$	$H = 3$	Candle $= 1$
		$m.FV = 1$	$(H) = 1, 1$	
$D = 11$	$+ = 9$		$Hd = 1$	Temple $= 1$
		$M = 4$	$(Hd) =$	
$Dd = 1$	$o = 7$	$FM = 2$	$A = 2$	Weapon $= 1$
		$m =$	$(A) = 1$	
$S = 3$	$v = 1$	$C =$	$Ad =$	$\underline{} =$
		$CF = 1$	$(Ad) =$	
$DW = 0$	$- = 0$	$FC = 1$	Ab	$\underline{} =$
		$C' =$	$Al =$	
		$C'F =$	$An = 2$	$\underline{} =$
FORM QUALITY		$FC' = 1$	$Art =$	
		$T =$	$Ay =$	$\underline{} =$
FQx	FQf	$TF =$	$Bl =$	
		$FT =$	$Bt = 1$	$\underline{} =$
$+ = 3$	$+ = 0$	$V =$	$Cg =$	
		$VF =$	$Cl =$	
$o = 12$	$o = 2$	$FV =$	$Ex =$	
		$Y =$	$Fi =$	
$w = 2$	$w = 1$	$YF =$	$Fd =$	
		$FY = 2$	$Ge =$	
$- = 0$	$- = 0$	$rF =$	$Hh =$	
		$Fr =$	$Ls = 1$	
		$FD = 1$	$Na =$	
		$F = 3$	$Sx =$	
			$Xy = 2$	

RATIOS, PERCENTAGES, AND DERIVATIONS

$Z\text{Sum}/Z\text{est} = 41.5/38.0$	$FC/CF + C = 1/1$	Afr	$= .55$
$Zd = +3.5$	$W/M = 5/5$	$3r + (2)/R$	$= 7/17 = .41$
$EB = 5/1.5$ $EA = 6.5$	$W/D = 5/11$	Cont/R	$= 9/17$
$eb = 3/5$ $ep = 8$	$L = .21$	$H + Hd/A + Ad$	$= 5/3$
$\text{Blends}/R = 2/17$	$F+\% = 67$	$H + A/Hd + Ad$	$= 7/1$
$a/p = 6/3$	$X+\% = 88$	XRT Achrom	$= 37''$
$M^a/M^p = 4/2$	$A\% = 18$	XRT Chrom	$= 29''$

Table 37.   Scoring Sequence for Protocol #4—J. C.

Card	RT	No.	Location	Determinant(s)		Content(s)	Pop	Z Score
I	16″	1.	$W+$	$M^{a-p}.FY+$	(2)	$H, (H)$	P	4.0
		2.	Wo	FYo		Xy		1.0
II	46″	3.	$D+$	FM^aw	(2)	A		5.5
		4.	$DS+$	FC'		Temple		4.5
III	8″	5.	$D+$	M^ao	(2)	H	P	3.0
IV	58″	6.	Wo	FYo		Xy		2.0
V	26″	7.	$W+$	M^p+	(2)	H		2.5
VI	77″	8.	Do	Fw		Weapon		
		9.	Do	FDo		Ls		
VII	12″	10.	$D+$	M^ao	(2)	Hd	P	3.0
		11.	Do	Fo		A		
VIII	9″	12.	DSo	Fo		An		
		13.	Wv	CFo		An		4.5
IX	69″	14.	$Dd+$	M^ao	(2)	(H)		2.5
		15.	$DS+$	$m^p.FV+$		Candle		5.0
X	13″	16.	$D+$	FM^ao	(2)	(A)		4.0
		17.	Do	FCo		Bt		

ANALYSIS OF THE STRUCTURE

The *Zd* score, the substantial number of synthesis answers, and the proportionally high number of *M* responses present a configuration of a well above average intelligence. The preponderance of *M* answers, as represented in the *EB*, indicates that she prefers her inner life as the source for her more basic gratifications. The fact that the *eb* is in the opposite direction from the *Eb* may suggest that she is experiencing both discomfort and conflict concerning this response style. Her *ep* is slightly higher than the *EA*, indicating that she has resources still to be organized and hint that she may be subject to promptings from less sophisticated and uncontrolled drives in her everyday behaviors. The *a/p* and M^a/M^p ratios reveal that she is ordinarily prone toward a more active than passive behavior pattern; however, three of her five shading responses involve diffuse shading, which indicates a more passive constraint to her behaviors. This dichotomy suggests the possibility of conflict, that is, whether to be "active or passive" in stress situations. Her use of color is very modest, but the very low Lambda indicates the possibility that she is effected by emotion much of the time. The *F+%*, although low, is probably not a good index of perceptual accuracy because of the low number of Pure *F* answers. The *X+%* is a better index of this activity, and is within normal limits. There are no gross distortions of reality in the record, although she does give evidence that she will "bend" reality when her own needs call for this. The low *A%* demonstrates that she is more oriented toward "intellectual" ideation than toward a more simple and conventional activity. This is also indicated by the sizable range of contents. The affective ratio is within normal limits indicating that she is not overly attracted by affectively toned stimuli. Similarly, her egocentricity ratio is at the upper end of the normal range indicating neither excessive, or undervalued self-esteem. She has a slightly high number of human responses in relation to animal contents; however, this may be a function of the reduced use of animals rather than an inordinate preoccupation with others. The mean RT's are both quite long indicating some delay in her approach to the cards, and signals attention to individual reaction times. Her blends both involve shading, suggesting that she experiences pain as a result of some of her fantasy activity. She has only three Popular percepts, revealing some disregard for conventionality, or possibily the fact that she may be more "tuned into" her own idiographic needs. The composite of two An plus two Xy answers indicates considerable body concern and is probably related to her somatic condition. The three idiographic contents warrant special consideration during analysis of the verbal material.

Specific propositions developed from the Structural Summary are as follows:

1. She is prone to use her inner life for gratification more so than interactions with the external world.

2. There is some evidence to suggest that her fantasies are not always reinforcing, and instead, can create the experience of pain.

3. She is prompted by less well organized resources and needs, and generally prefers an active pattern of ideation and behavior; however, she is also oriented toward a passivity in behavior, a situation that seems to mark a definite conflict.

4. She is very intelligent, and relies greatly on her intellect in dealing with her world, and probably with her own needs.

5. Although she does not manifest affect easily in the record, there is evidence that she is subject to considerable affective experience, much of which is painfully discomforting.

6. She appears to set goals for herself that are considerably lower than she is capable of achieving.

7. Her reality testing is adequate, although she is willing to "bend" reality on those occasions when it will meet her own needs.

8. She is generally cautious in her approach to the world.

ANALYSIS OF THE SEQUENCE OF SCORES

The individual reaction times fluctuate considerably, ranging from 8″ to 77″, but with no specific pattern. Her approach is generally consistent with synthesis activity occurring on all but three cards. All three of her white space responses occur to colored cards, suggesting that affectively toned stimuli may give rise to discomfort resulting in a negative and possibly hostile response pattern. Further evidence for this is noted by the fact that there are no Popular answers to the last three cards, and only one P to the five color cards. Her organizational activity is consistent throughout the record except on Card VI, which gives special significance to the two answers on that card.

One proposition generated from the Scoring Sequence is as follows:

1. She is prone to react in a negative and/or hostile manner to affectively toned stimulus imputs.

ANALYSIS OF THE FREE ASSOCIATIONS

The verbal material in the Free Associations is quite rich in the idiographic descriptions. Many of the Free Associations are unusually long, giving evidence of a carefully "thought through," meticulous response, involving considerable projection. Her very first answer sets the tone for this, ". . . it seems to be a person, quite helpless . . . ," suggesting a conflicted state ending in a form of indecisiveness or psychological paralysis. The themes of her associations continually manifest conflict, "Two women fighting over something . . . . I think they're women, almost but not quite resting back to back . . . . Two women arguing about something . . . . Two witches . . . arguing about what to mix in it . . . .Two animals . . . not sure what to do with it." The sexual implications of many of her responses is also very striking, ". . . a temple of worship . . . an x-ray of a pelvis . . . an x-ray of . . . a pelvic arch again . . . it has spear type tip you would use to hurt or maim or kill . . . internal viscera and this bottom part could be some sort of internal wound . . . a glass candle holder with a candle in it . . . . Two animals trying to do something to this pole." None of these answers illustrate a direct sexual preoccupation, but all are very suggestive of a concealed sexual preoccupation. All of the conflict responses involve feminine characters, witches, women, hens, indicating that she does identify adequately in her sex role, but apparently has much confusion about how that role should be manifest behaviorally. One answer, two women lying back to back "almost touching" hints of a homosexual orientation, and many of the sexually symbolic answers are suggestive of ideation that heterosexual contact is painful and/or undesirable. This could indicate that she is in a quandary about the expression of her own sexuality, and might lead to the conclusion that her somatic problems are a direct manifestation of this confusion, that is, a form of delaying action until the conflict can be resolved satisfactorily. Her responses to Card VI seem especially important in this context. She perceives a phallic-like weapon that can "hurt, maim, or kill," and then reports a vaginal like "river or road," seeing it as far away as "if you were on a mountain or something looking down at it." This is also the only card in which no organizational activity occurs, as if her substantial intellect fails temporarily, giving rise to a more direct expression of her conflicted state. The detailed nature of many of her answers implies a "perfectionistic" obsessive like use of her intellect in dealing with ambiguities, and making sure that her projections are not overly "direct." Nevertheless, she seems to reveal her basic problem rather clearly.

Specific propositions developed from analysis of the Free Association material are as follows:

1. She currently experiences intense conflict concerning her sex role. This conflict is experienced as aggressive and painful.

2. She has adequate identification with a feminine sex role; however, she seems unable to determine how this role is "best played," and has substantial fears of direct heterosexual contact.

3. She apparently also gives thought to homosexuality as an appropriate manifestation of her sexuality.

4. She defends herself against the conflict state through a high level intellectual activity, organizing her world meticulously, but is often prone to "overprojection" of her own needs and feelings and thus this defense pattern can, and does, fail.

5. Her somatic features appear to be another form of defense against her con-flicted state.

6. She is perfectionistic and obsessive in her general approach to ambiguity, a characteristic that probably represents her basic style of response.

ANALYSIS OF THE INQUIRY

The Inquiry verbalizations lend considerable support to her obsessive-perfectionistic style of response, and "spell out", in more detail characteristics, her conflict concerning sexuality. Her attraction with male sexuality is typified in her answer to Card II, ". . . its the metal part that really attracts people to the temple because it's so valuable." There is a suggestion that here she would prefer a masculine role to that of the female, and this conflict is also exemplified by her description of the basket in the Card III answer, ". . . it must be full of goodies because each wants it for herself, but neither seems able to get it." Again, in her second response to Card VI, she seems to dramatize her own feeling of inadequacy in a female role, ". . . its so small you'd have to be far away to see it like this." She offers a direct perseveration of her conflict in her description to Card VII, ". . . maybe they are the one's I saw earlier fighting over the basket of precious stuff . . . ." Her fears concerning heterosexual contacts are magnified by the elaboration to the first response on Card VI, ". . . it has kind of a dull tip like it could really do damage if it were misused . . . ." Her last response seems to offer a good prognosis, ". . . as if it were ready for planting or whatever . . . ," concerning her tentative solution of her conflicted existence.

Specific proposition generated from the Inquiry data are as follows:

1. She has a distinct obsessive-perfectionistic response style.
2. Her attraction to heterosexual activities is, at least in part, thwarted by her "envy" of the male role.
3. She is frightened of heterosexual contact because of the potential "harm" it may do her.
4. She seems ready at this time for definitive sexual contact.

A SUMMARY OF J. C.

J. C. appears to have been "overly instilled" with notions of correct and proper behaviors. She may have also overly identified with her father's role in the family, the combination of which have led her to delay and/or disregard sexuality in its more direct manifestations for an excessively long period of time. She is currently in severe and painful conflict concerning her own sex role, and her interests in sexuality are becoming more "dictatorial" to her behaviors. She defends herself through an obsessive-perfectionistic kind of behavior; however, her somatic problem gives evidence that this is not wholly effective. She lives a cautious and constrained psychological life, relying heavily on her well above average intelligence to ward off affective threats from within and without. She becomes irritated and hostile when confronted with affectively laden stimuli, but generally does not manifest this hostility in a direct manner. There are hints of homosexual orientation;

however, her reasonably strong affective controls indicate that she is more prone toward an indirect, rather than direct, expression of this. Surgical intervention for her ulcer would seem unwise at this point, in that it would remove an important vestige of defense and containment. Internalization is, and will continue to be, a basic response style for her, and somatization illustrates one aspect of this broad response pattern. A more reconstructive form of intervention, beginning with a strong supportive approach, seems necessary to assist her in resolution of her most primary conflict state, that is, sex identity and sex role, so as to alter some of her modes of defense and reduce the importance of the somatic orientation as a form of constraint.

PROTOCOL #5   B. N. —A PHOBIC WITH DEPRESSIVE FEATURES

Referral.   This 24 year old single female was referred for psychological evaluation by her family physician. She had been examined by him after complaining that she was in jeopardy of loosing her job as a secretary because she was missing work frequently. She cited chest pains, insomnia, difficulty breathing especially on buses or in elevators, and increasing problems in concentration. The physical examination was negative, and he prescribed a mild tranquilizer, suggesting that her difficulties might be psychological. She reluctantly agreed to psychological evaluation, as a process to "rule out" that possibility. He asks in the referral if there is evidence to indicate psychopathology, and requests recommendations on appropriate treatment.

History.   B. N. is slightly taller than most adult women and looks somewhat older than her age. Her dress is conservative, made more so by somewhat unattractive glasses and a "bun" hairdo. She is a high school graduate, having also completed one year of business school before obtaining her present position as a "pool" secretary for a brokerage firm. She is the second of three children, having a brother 27 and a sister 21. The brother is married and lives in another city, the sister is engaged and will marry in approximately 3 months. B. N. lives with her parents, although she did share an apartment with a woman her own age for approximately 18 months, "I just didn't care for it very much and usually came home on weekends anyway." She dates occasionally but never for very long with one man, "We just never seem to have the same interests." She spends much of her free time caring for a horse which her parents gave her as a Christmas present 2 years ago. She has joined a riding club and has been learning to develop the skills necessary to "show" the horse. She admits to several heterosexual experiences but describes them as "uninteresting and unstimulating." She considers herself to be knowledgeable about sexuality, "I've read a lot of books about it," and implies that her interest will increase once she finds the "right man." She has several friends, "all female," with whom she often attends movies, horse shows, plays, and such. She regrets not having gone to college and has considered attending evening classes.

Protocol #5. B. N., 24 Year Old, Single, Employed as a Secretary

Card		Free Association		Inquiry	Scoring
I	14″	1. It c.b. a mask of s.s., it looks rather vicious with the teeth like that	E:	(Rpts S's resp)	WS+ Fo Mask 3.5
			S:	The white parts & the eyes & the teeth, they'r cut lik that to give a vicious impr. lik for halloween, its s.s. of weird animal mask w ears sticking out here	
		2. It c.b. an insect too like a moth	E:	(Rpts S's resp)	WS+ FC'+ A 3.5
			S:	Well it has the wings & ths is the body, the white marks & the grey color make it ll a moth, the white is lik the simple designs that moths have on them	
II	19″	3. I can make out two dogs here they seem to be touching noses	E:	(Rpts S's resp)	D+ FMᵖo (2) Ad P 3.0
			S:	U can't see all of them, just their heads, the snout & the ears r here (points) & this is the collar area	
		4. The center is like a light	E:	(Rpts S's resp)	DSo FC'o Light
			S:	Its lik a globe for an office light or s.t. like that, it just has that shape, & its white lik a globe	
III	24″	5. This is weird, its like a painting of some dancers I think, or, no, not dancers, more like two people trying to lift something	E:	(Rpts S's resp)	D+ Mᵖo (2) (H), P 3.0
			S:	Thy don't really ll people, at least I've never seen any like that, thy hav mittens on, thy r leaning over getting ready to lift s.t. up, but they don't look real	
			E:	I'm not sure what u mean	
			S:	Thy look half man & half woman, lik in fairy tales or s.t., c the breasts but the rest ll men	

399

Protocol #5 (Continued)

Card		Free Association	Inquiry	Scoring
		6. It c.b. a bf in the middle	E: (Rpts S's resp) S: It has the wings & body it just ll one	Do Fo A P
IV	8″	7. It ll a pair of boots there	S: There's one on each side, lik they r leaning up against s.t. in the back, like a post w the tongues hanging out up here at the top, thyr all muddy E: Muddy? S: All the lines there, dark & lighter ll mud splotches to me, & the post behind them has got mud on it too	W+ FY.FD+ (2) Cg, Mud, P 4.0
		V8. Ths way its really ugly, it ll s.s. of deformed insect	E: (Rpts S's resp) S: It has ths big head & incompl wgs to it, lik half a worm & half some-thg w wgs	Wo Fo (A) 2.0
V	16″	9. It ll 2 people laying dwn, resting back to back	E: (Rpts S's resp) S: Its 2 clowns, lik they'r resting w their legs out here E: Clowns? S: They hav these peaked caps on, it might be an advertisemnt for s.t.	W+ Mᵖ+ (2) H 2.5
		V10. Ths way it ll a vulture	E: (Rpts S's resp) S: Well the big parts here w.b. the wings, thy look all bushy lik feath-ers, & the beak is here (points) & ths bony thgs out here at the ends r lik vultures have E: U said bushy lik feathers S: Yes, the coloring gives that effect	Wo FTo A 1.0

VI 15" 11. Ugh, ths one isn't very easy, the top c.b. a club of s.s.
E: (Rpts S's resp)
S: Lik an indian war club, thy always put feathers on thm like ths one, here is the handle, & ths r the feathers

Do Fo Club

V12. If u turn it ths way, ths part ll a face, lik Cyrano w the great huge nose
E: (Rpts S's resp)
S: Its the profile, w the long nose & the beard

Do Fo Hd

VII 11" 13. This cntr part c.b. a harbor
E: (Rpts S's resp)
S: Just ths white part, well no not really bec the dark w.b. islands or s.t. too but the cntr part ll an inlet, lik a harbor

WSv Fo Ls 4.0

14. It c.b. 2 children too, just ths top
E: (Rpts S's resp)
S: 2 little girls, as if thy r lookg at e.o. thy mayb sisters bec thy look very much alike, u can only c them from the waist up

$D+$ $M^{v}o$ (2) Hd P 3.

15. It cld all be fried chicken
E: (Rpts S's resp)
S: It's not really fried yet but u can c the breading on it lik it was ready to be fried, it ll 2 legs & 2 breasts

Wo FTo Fd 2.5

V16. If u turn it ths prt ll an elephants head w the long trunk
E: (Rpts S's resp)
S: It just ll an elephants head to me w the big trunk

Do Fo Ad

VIII 21" 17. Ths ll s.t. from a biol book
E: (Rpts S's resp)
S: Well it is a colorful repr. of a lot of insides, like organs & thgs, thy put each in a diff. color so as to make it stand out, there's the chest w the ribs & the side thgs c.b. lungs, & the lower part c.b. the stomach & the upper part cld repre the neck & respiration things

Wo FCo An 4.5

Protocol #5 (Continued)

Card		Free Association		Inquiry	Scoring
IX	27″	18. This is a hard one, it c.b. a salad bowl I suppose w each layer being given a different color	E:	(Rpts S's resp)	
			S:	The pink is the base & the green & orange repres the layers of it, it has the form of a big bowl	*Wo FCo* Bowl 5.5
X	13″	19. Ths top part c.b. dead roots or branches	E:	(Rpts S's resp)	
			S:	It ll after u pull up a flower or s.t. thes r lik the roots look	*Do Fo Bt*
		∨20. These c.b. 2 seahorses	E:	(Rpts S's resp)	
			S:	Thy are shaped lik sea horses to me	*Do Fo* (2) *A*
		21. This c.b. a seed falling off a tree	E:	(Rpts S's resp)	
			S:	It ll a seed pod that is just floating in space	*Do m^p Bt*
		22. There's a Buddha here too, u can just c the outline in ths white part	E:	(Rpts S's resp)	
			S:	The seed part w.b. a design on his stomach, the outline is really good	*DdS+ Fo Ab* 6.0

402

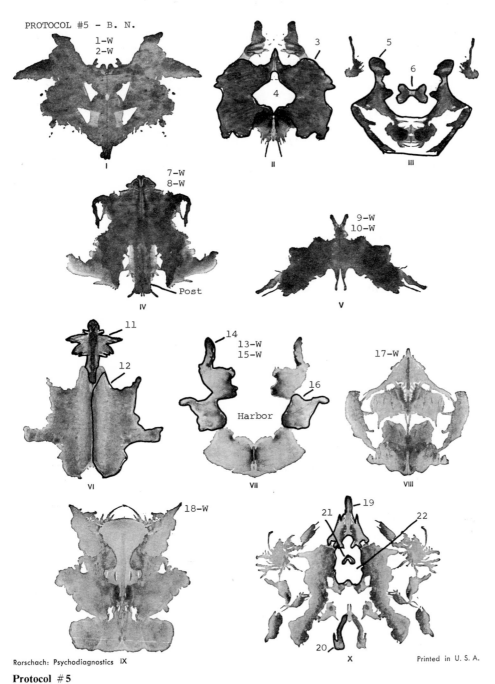

PROTOCOL #5 - B. N.

1-W
2-W

I

3

4

II

5

6

III

7-W
8-W

Post

IV

9-W
10-W

V

11

12

VI

14
13-W
15-W

16

Harbor

VII

17-W

VIII

18-W

IX

19
21
22
20

X

Protocol #5

Table 38. Structural Summary for Protocol #5—B. N.

$R = 22$ $Zf = 14$ $Z\text{Sum} = 48.0$ $P = 5$ $(2) = 6$

Location Features		Determinants	Contents	Contents (Idiographic)
W = 10	DQ	$FY.FD = 1$		
			H = 1	$\underline{Bowl}$ = 1
D = 11	+ = 8	M = 3	(H) = 1	
		FM = 1	Hd = 2	$\underline{Club}$ = 1
Dd = 1	o = 13	m = 1	(Hd) =	
		C =	A = 4	$\underline{Light}$ = 1
S = 5	v = 1	CF =	(A) = 1	
		FC = 2	Ad = 2	$\underline{Mask}$ = 1
DW = 0	− = 0	C' =	(Ad) =	
		$C'F$ =	Ab = 1	$\underline{Mud}$ = 0, 1
		FC' = 2	Al =	
FORM QUALITY		T =	An = 1	$\underline{\quad}$ =
		TF =	Art =	
FQx	FQf	FT = 2	Ay =	$\underline{\quad}$ =
		V =	Bl =	
+ = 3	+ = 0	VF =	Bt = 2	$\underline{\quad}$ =
		FV =	Cg = 1	
o = 19	o = 10	Y =	Cl =	
		YF =	Ex =	
w = 0	w = 0	FY =	Fi =	
		rF =	Fd = 1	
− = 0	− = 0	Fr =	Ge =	
		FD =	Hh =	
		F = 10	Na =	
			Ls =	
			Sx =	
			Xy	

RATIOS, PERCENTAGES, AND DERIVATIONS

$Z\text{Sum}/Z\text{est} = 48.0/45.5$	$FC/CF + C = 2/0$	Afr	$= .37$
$Zd = +2.5$	W/M = 10/3	$3r + (2)/R$	$= 6/22 = .27$
$EB = 3/1$ $EA = 4.0$	W/D = 10/12	$Cont/R$	$= 12/22$
$eb = 2/5$ $ep = 7$	L = .83	$H + Hd/A + Ad$	$= 4/7$
$Blends/R = 1/22$	$F+\%$ = 100	$H + A/Hd + Ad$	$= 7/4$
a/p $= 0/5$	$X+\%$ = 100	XRT Achrom	$= 12.8''$
M^a/M^p $= 0/3$	$A\%$ = 32	XRT Chrom	$= 20.8''$

Table 39.   Scoring Sequence for Protocol #5—B. N.

Card	RT	No.	Location	Determinant(s)		Content(s)	Pop	Z Score
I	14″	1.	$WS+$	Fo		Mask		3.5
		2.	$WS+$	FC'_t		A		3.5
II	19″	3.	$D+$	FM^po	(2)	Ad	P	3.0
		4.	DSo	$FC'o$		Light		
III	24″	5.	$D+$	M^po	(2)	(H)	P	3.0
		6.	Do	Fo		A	P	
IV	8″	7.	$W+$	$FY.FD+$	(2)	Cg, Mud	P	4.0
		8.	Wo	Fo		(A)		2.0
V	16″	9.	$W+$	M^p+	(2)	H		2.5
		10.	Wo	FTo		A		1.0
VI	15″	11.	Do	Fo		Club		
		12.	Do	Fo		Hd		
VII	11″	13.	WSv	Fo		Ls		4.0
		14.	$D+$	M^po	(2)	Hd	P	3.0
		15.	Wo	FTo		Fd		2.5
		16.	Do	Fo		Ad		
VIII	21″	17.	Wo	FCo		An		4.5
IX	27″	18.	Wo	FCo		Bowl		5.5
X	13″	19.	Do	Fo		Bt		
		20.	Do	Fo	(2)	A		
		21.	Do	m^po		Bt		
		22.	$DdS+$	Fo		Ab		6.0

ANALYSIS OF THE STRUCTURE

The configuration of the Zf, $ZSum$, and Zd, plus eight synthesis answers, suggests an above average intellectual functioning. The EA, however, leads to the conclusion that she has not organized many of her resources adequately, even though, as indicated by the EB, she is more oriented toward her inner life for basic gratifications. There is only one Blend in the record, demonstrating some lack of complexity to her psychological organization. Her five movement answers all have a passive character, and three of her five shading answers represented in the eb are C' and Y types, giving additional evidence of a passive, restrained style of response. She has a limited use of color, and seems strongly committed to perceptual accuracy, as indicated by her very high $F+\%$ and $X+\%$. She has a slightly greater proportion of W answers than M's and a considerably greater proportion of W's than D responses. This suggests that she may have aspirations which exceed her current functioning level. The relatively low number of Popular answers is somewhat unusual in the record of one using a continuous emphasis on form accuracy, and may represent some tendencies toward unconventionality. The Affective Ratio hints at withdrawal from the environment, and the Egocentricity Ratio indicates that her own self-valuation is slightly lower than desirable. There is a slight elevation in the proportion of H to A answers, and a slightly excessive use of Hd and Ad responses. In that only one of the human percepts is H, these features may indicate that she is guarded about others and has not established mature interpersonal contacts. Her mean RT to the Chromatic series is considerably longer than that to the Achromatic cards, suggesting some difficulties handling the more affectively toned stimuli. The most striking element is the Structural Summary is the emphasis on white space. She has five S answers, considerably more than is found in most records of average length. When considered in the context of the low P, the slight elevation in W, and the reasonably large proportion of Hd and Ad answers, this is probably best interpreted as evidence for a hostile and negative form of ideation, possibly related to her limited interactions with others and some degree of suspiciousness about them. Her broad range of contents, while indicating good intellectual aspects of her ideation, also seem to convey the impression that she may be attempting to use her intellect as a substitute for affect. The idiographic contents signal special forms of ideation that have been projected into the record and call for special attention during analysis of the Free Associations.

Specific postulates formulated from the Structural data are as follows:

1. She is intellectually talented but has not mobilized her resources fully, and thus functions at lower levels than which she is capable.

2. She has aspirations that exceed her current functioning level.

3. She is generally passive in her response pattern, possibly because of a low self-esteem and feelings of inadequacy when she compares herself to others.

4. She experiences considerable affective pain because of her constrictiveness, and would prefer a greater dependency relationship than she has at present.

5. She is guarded and withdrawn from her environment, and has developed an unusually negative perception of it and is somewhat suspicious of those around her.

6. She relies excessively on perceptual accuracy in selecting her response patterns and fails to give her own uniqueness appropriate "room to function."

7. She is essentially an internal person, and has failed to develop mature relationships with her environment, a factor which probably contributes to her negativism, her limited use of intellect, and her current symptomatology.

ANALYSIS OF THE SCORING SEQUENCE

Her longer reaction times occur mainly to the chromatic cards, reaffirming her attempts at restraint when faced with affectively laden stimulus situations. She gives the greatest number of answers to Cards VII and X. While the latter is not unusual, a large number of answers to Card VII is somewhat unique and warrants special consideration in the analysis of the Free Association material. The absence of Popular answers on IV, V, VI, VIII, and X is also striking and suggests that her percepts on those cards may be particularly revealing. Her approach, which is W oriented, is generally consistent except that she fails to organize the whole card on three of the five color cards, while not doing so on only one of the achromatic cards. This seems to be added support for the notion that she is troubled by more affectively loaded stimulus situations. No specific hypotheses are generated by the scoring sequence.

ANALYSIS OF THE FREE ASSOCIATIONS

Her first answer, "a mask," is possibly most indicative of her general response style. She prefers to conceal herself. The second response may convey some of her own feelings concerning herself, that is, as a moth, which is unattractive and undesirable. Her first attempt at movement is very cautious, "they seem to be touching noses," reflecting her guardedness in interpersonal contacts. The use of white space as a "light" is also possibly revealing; that is, her negative attitude permits a clearer evaluation of her situation in the world. Her answer to Card III, "this is weird . . . two people . . . ," may indicate her confusion about interpersonal situations. Namely, she is unaccustomed to them and feels "weird" in them. She is the butterfly in the middle, fragile, flightly, and not an object of human interest. Her second response to Card IV seems to illustrate her own picture of herself, ". . . really ugly . . . deformed insect." She can only approach people "back to back," an aggressive posture, and even then she is passive in her action. The "vulture" answer probably reveals more of how she feels, that is, feeding from the remains of others. The phallic-like area of Card VI is perceived as "a club," seeming to betray her true feelings about heterosexual relations. She feels like "Cyrano," the forelorned lover. This possibly illustrates her deeper fantasy life and her own estimates of her "chances" in life. Her varied responses to Card VII appear to represent her own confusion concerning the female role. It protects, as a harbor; it is childish but passive; it is something that others feed on; and it is a circus creature. In all, it is a sense of confusion and conflict. Her use of color on Cards VIII and IX appears to be forced, with each component neatly defined by color, with but no sense of direct responsiveness to the colored features of the cards. Her first answer to Card X indicates a sense of depression, dead roots, and later she adds "a seed falling," almost to imply a sense of helplessness in her world. She recovers a bit in her last answers, using white space and projecting an object of worship, as if at least she can be negative and hold less conventional responses in awe.

Specific proposition developed from the Free Association material are as follows:

1. She feels unattractive and immature and tries to conceal her feelings with a facade of negativism and hostility.

2. She is very guarded in interpersonal relations, feeling uncomfortable and "out of place" in them.

3. She feels fragile, unappealing, and "deformed," factors which contribute to her low self-esteem and avoidance of interpersonal contacts.

4. She is very passive in her response patterns, preferring to be dependent on the cues from others as a guide for her behaviors.

5. She has very negative feelings concerning sexuality, looking on heterosexual experiences as potentially damaging. At the same time she is prone to fantasize deep, but probably immature, male-female relationships.

6. She is confused about the feminine role, and this confusion leads to added withdrawal and containment of her affect.

7. She is depressed, feeling helpless in her situation, and is prone to cope with these difficulties with a less conventional form of response in which she "harbors" her unconventionality as a form of defense against a rejecting world.

ANALYSIS OF THE INQUIRY

The descriptions in the Inquiry offer considerable support to previously developed postulates. The mask becomes a halloween outfit whereas before the "vicious" features had been emphasized. This seems to illustrate her needs to keep her own angers "in check." Her confusion concerning sex role identity is quite evident in her answers concerning her first response to Card III, ". . . I've never seen any like that, they have mittens on . . . ," reflecting a "hands off" policy regarding interpersonal contact. The muddiness of the boots on Card IV may illustrate her immaturity and her inability to perceive things in a clear way. In psychoanalytic theory this would represent an "anal" orientation, consistent with her negative features. She describes the two people on Card V as "clowns," again reflecting her feelings about inter-personal contact. The Chicken on Card VII is "not really fried yet," implying a feeling of pending doom in her heterosexual relations. Her answer to the first re-sponse in Card X, ". . . after you pull up a flower . . . ," illustrates her feelings of being "squashed" and defeated by her world.

While the Inquiry data add support to other propositions, there is essentially no new postulate that might be developed from it.

A SUMMARY OF B. N.

B. N. is a helpless, withdrawn young woman, who has little faith in herself, and regards those around her as potentially threatening. She prefers an inner experience as a basic source of gratification, and has, in effect, shut out the world considerably. She attempts to control her affect stringently, although she experiences much internal pain as a result of her withdrawal. She is suspicious of others, and mani-fests negativism and hostility frequently to defend herself from the impact of the outer world. She appears to be bright but has failed to maximize the utilization of her resources. Consequently, she often sets goals that are beyond her current func-tioning level. She has considerable confusion about her own sex role, and no doubt her younger sisters' pending marriage has aggravated this condition. She feels un-attractive to others, and consequently guards herself against them. She has a low self-esteem, and clings to reality as a source of consolation. She is in much pain at the moment, and her Phobic-like symptoms probably represent a further attempt to defend herself against the unwanted intrusions of others. She is mildly depressed, a phenomenon that can become more pronounced if intervention is unsuccessful. The referring physician was correct in his conclusion that the problems are psycho-logical. She needs much support, for the moment, from a "caring" therapist. Prob-ably a female therapist would be more appropriate so as to avoid the potential threat from a male and to provide a new source of identification. A more realistic pattern of social interaction is ultimately essential.

PROTOCOL #6   H. J.—AN AGGITATED DEPRESSION

Referral. This 39 year old engineering executive was referred for psychological evaluation by his company physician. During a routine physical H. J. had admitted to an increasing "nervousness" and inability to concentrate. He denied moodiness but did reveal numerous instances of insomnia, loss of appetite, and periods when his work habits seemed "unable to get off the ground." The physical examination was entirely negative, except that H. J. is slightly underweight. The referral asks, "Is there anything seriously wrong, and if so what is the best method of treatment."

History. H. J. is a tall, slender, well groomed engineering division supervisor. He is responsible for the work of three groups of junior engineers in a manufacturing firm. He has been married for 17 years, and has no children. He and his wife did "try to have a child" about 10 years ago without success. Since that time they have considered adoption, but have not taken any definitive action about it. His wife is active in several civic groups, and worked as a teacher during their first 7 years of marriage. H. J. has aspirations for a vice-presidency, a position for which he was considered approximately 6 months ago, but another candidate was selected. He says, "I really didn't expect it now, I'm still too young, but I've got 15 or 20 more good years in me and I'll make it before then." He cannot account for his nervousness, except to say "There's been a lot of pressure lately on the job." He claims that his relationship with his wife is "fine," but reports a very low frequency of sexual activity and reveals that his wife usually determines when such activity will occur, "She's not always ready, I guess that's normal for our age."

Protocol #6. H. J., 39 Years Old, Married, No Children, Engineering Executive

Card		Free Association		Inquiry	Scoring
I	16″	1. A tattered moth		E: (Rpts S's resp)	Wo Fo A 1.0
				S: Its the whole thg, kind of re me of a moth that's dead, kinda decayg	
		(Returns card)		E: Decaying?	
		E: Mst peopl c more than 1 thg		S: It has ragged edges & it's pretty well	
		S: That's all it ll to me		beat up, c ths wgs out here (points) r	
				pretty rough	
II	23″	2. A coupl of bears fiting		E: (Rpts S's resp)	$D+$ $FM^a.CFo$ (2) A P 3.0
				S: Here r heads & bodies, it ll at least one of thm has a bldy foot	
				E: Bloody foot?	
				S: Yes, here (points) ths red ll bld, its like theyr in mortal combat, nose to nose & theyl fite until one will kill the other	
		3. It cld b an explos too altho not really		E: (Rpts S's resp)	DSv YFw Ex 4.5
				S: Not really an explos happeng, but rathr after its happnd w all the smok & stuff	
				E: I'm not sur I c it the way u do	
				S: Well its just the black part, it ll smok, all hazy-like & the cntr wld b the hole left by the blast	
III	46″	4. 2 wm' pickg s.t. apart		E: (Rpts S's resp)	$D+$ M^uo (2) H P 3.0
				S: It ll 2 wm leang over s.t., lik they were pickg it apart	
				E: Where do u c it there	
				S: Rite here (points) r the wm, thes red thgs aren't in it, it re me of a war scene w old wm pickg thru the garbage	

410

IV — 75″

5. An aerial view of a road

E: (Rpts S's resp)
S: It runs rite up the cntr here, the sides don't really mean a.t. except surroundg territory, it must be up high
E: Up high?
S: Well, the road is darkr so it must be down in, like in a ravine, its lower down than thes side areas

Do FVo Ls

6. 2 beat up old boots

E: (Rpts S's resp)
S: They ll 2 old boots that s.b. has thrown away—they ll theyv seen a lot of miles
E: A lot of miles?
S: The colorg makes them look all wrinkled lik an old pr of boots or shoes

Do FTo (2) Cg P

V — 18″

7. I guess it looks mostly lik a bf to me

E: (Rpts S's resp)
S: It has broad wgs lik a bf & a small body, ths end thg on the wgs (points) wouldnt b included, that spoils it

Ddo Fo A (P)

VI — 28″

8. Hum, a bear skin that's seen better days

E: (Rpts S's resp)
S: The top shouldn't b there, the rest ll a beat up old bear skin, its all furry like
E: Furry-like?
S: It ll that 2 me, all fuzzy like fur here around the middle especially, c thes side thgs would be the legs

Do FTo Ad P

VII — 8″

9. People's heads, like statues, the colorg makes it ll rock

S: Mayb statues of indians, they have feathers stickg up here, mayb they represent Cooper's book
E: What part of the blot r u using
S: Oh, all of it, ths bttm prt wld b the base & thes r the statues. The grey makes it ll rocks, like sculpture

Wo FC' (2) (Hd) P 2.5

Protocol #6 (Continued)

412

Card	Free Association	Inquiry	Scoring
VIII 6″	10. A coupl of *A*'s	*E*: (Rpts *S*'s resp) *S*: It cld b muskrats or s.t. like that they have clearly defined heads & bodies & legs, one on each side	*Do Fo* (2) *A P*
	11. Ths prt ll a rib cage u can c thru it, lik it was sticking out, rounded lik a rib cage	*E*: (Rpts *S*'s resp) *S*: It looks bony lik a rib cage looks *E*: I'm not positive that I c it as u do *S*: Rite here, its just shaped like a rib cage, c here & the white is spaces	*DSo FC′.FD An*
IX 39″	V12. This way its like an atomic explosion	*E*: (Rpts *S*'s resp) *S*: The pink is the mushroom cld effect & the green cld b smoke & the orange wld b the fire, u get the impression of force *E*: Force? *S*: Yeah, lik an explos & with ths orange fire & the mushroom I happend to thk of an atomic explos.	*Wo mᵃ.CFo Ex 5.5*
X 38″	13. A lot of mounted bugs in a design, a rather pretty design I'd say	*E*: (Rpts *S*'s resp) *S*: It ll a bug collection with a lot of kinds of bugs mounted in an attractive pattern *E*: I'm not sure how u r seeing it *S*: Well its all that way, part of it I don't know what kinds of bugs although I guess thes (blue) could b spiders or s.t., but the rest just hav a lot of vague bug-like shapes to me, its all very colorful & that's what made me thk of a deliber-ately mounted collection made into a pattern of s.s.	*W+ FC+ A P 5.5*

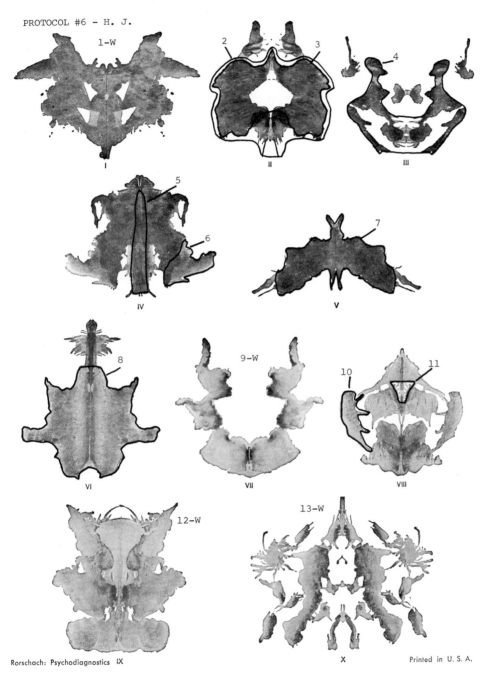

PROTOCOL #6 - H. J.

Printed in U. S. A.

Protocol #6

Table 40.   Structural Summary For Protocol #6—H. J.

$R = 13$	$Zf = 7$	$Z\text{Sum} = 25.0$	$P = 7 + 1$ (2) = 5

Location Features	Determinants	Contents	Contents (Idiographic)

Location Features	Determinants	Contents	Contents (Idiographic)
W = 4 DQ	$FM.CF$ = 1	H = 1	___ =
	$m.CF$ = 1	(H) =	
D = 8 + = 3	$FC'.FD$ = 1	Hd =	
		(Hd) = 1	___ =
Dd = 1 o = 9	M = 1	A = 5	
	FM =	(A) =	___ =
S = 2 v = 1	m =	Ad = 1	
	C =	(Ad) =	___ =
$DW = 0$ − = 0	CF =	Ab =	
	FC = 1	Al =	___ =
	C'	An = 1	
	$C'F$ =	Art =	___ =
FORM QUALITY	FC' = 1	Ay =	
	T =	Bl =	___ =
FQx FQf	TF =	Bt =	
	FT = 2	Cg = 1	___ =
+ = 1 + = 0	V =	Cl =	
	VF =	Ex = 2	
o = 11 o = 3	FV = 1	Fi	
	Y =	Fd =	
w = 1 w = 0	YF = 1	Ge =	
	FY =	Hh =	
− = 0 − = 0	rF =	Na =	
	Fr =	Ls = 1	
	FD =	Sx =	
	F = 3	Xy =	

RATIOS, PERCENTAGES, AND DERIVATIONS

$Z\text{Sum}/Z\text{est} = 25.0/20.5$	$FC/CF + C = 1/2$	Afr	= .44
$Zd = +4.5$	W/M = 4/1	$3r + (2)/R$	= 5/13 = .38
$EB = 1/2.5$ $EA = 3.5$	W/D = 4/8	Cont/R	= 6/13
$eb = 2/6$ ep = 8	L = .30	$H + Hd/A + Ad$ = 2/6	
$\text{Blends}/R = 3/13$	$F+\%$ = 100	$H + A/A + Ad$ = 6/2	
a/p = 3/0	$X+\%$ = 92	XRT Achrom	= 29.0″
M^a/M^p = 1/0	$A\%$ = 46	XRT Chrom	= 30.4″

414

Table 41. Sequence of Scores for Protocol #6—H. J.

Card	RT	No.	Location	Determinant(s)		Content(s)	Pop	Z Score
I	16″	1.	Wo	Fo		A		1.0
II	23″	2.	D+	FMᵃ.CFo (2)		A	P	3.0
		3.	DSv	YFw		Ex		4.5
III	46″	4.	D+	Mᵃo	(2)	H	P	3.0
IV	75″	5.	Do	FVo		Ls		
		6.	Do	FTo	(2)	Cg	P	
V	18″	7.	Ddo	Fo		A	(P)	
VI	28″	8.	Do	FTo		Ad	P	
VII	8″	9.	Wo	FC'o	(2)	(Hd)	P	2.5
VIII	6″	10.	Do	Fo	(2)	A	P	
		11.	DSo	FC'.FDo		An		
IX	39″	12.	Wo	mᵃ.CFo		Ex		5.5
X	38″	13.	W+	FC+		A	P	5.5

ANALYSIS OF THE STRUCTURE

The below average number of responses in this record limits the usefulness of some of the structural data as compared with expectancies for average length protocols. For instance, H. J. has a Zf of 7, which is average for records of normal length, but in this protocol of $13R$ it constitutes more than half of the responses. An attempt to prorate these data is tenuous, at best; however, it is known from other sources that he is a successful engineering executive, and thus it is probable that he does have the capability for a higher level of organizational activity than might be the case with an "average" subject. The Zd score of $+4.5$ offers some support for this speculation. Similarly, he has seven Popular answers plus one parenthesized Popular, which is an average number for a longer record. When compared to an R of 13, however, it seems proportionally high, leading to the speculation that he is strongly bound to conventionality and may have an influencial system of values orienting him toward conformity. Specific frequencies of determinants, though low for most records, take on special importance because they are unusual in proportion to R. The most striking example of this is one FV and one FD in this short record, both of which indicate forms of introspectiveness. Studied in proportion to R, they appear as highly important, suggesting an exaggerated focus on the self, accompanied by considerable pain. The fact that he is in much pain is evidenced by the shading emphasis in the record; that is, six of his 13 responses take this character. The frequency alone would illustrate strongly discomforting feelings in an average length protocol, a factor which is given added emphasis in this short record. The EB hints that he is more prone to seek gratification in his environment; however, the relatively low EA of 3.5 seems inappropriate for someone in a professional executive position. The much higher ep appears to indicate significant "disorganization"; that is, he is not able to control much of his psychological activity. This seems to be a function of his "runaway" affect illustrated by the six shading answers, 2 CF responses, and very low Lambda, and the fact that both CF answers occur in percepts marked by less sophisticated kinds of movement, *FM* and *m*. The low *R*, taken in this context, represents another form of containment, and probably illustrates the overall impact of his affective disruption on his psychological functioning. Nevertheless, his reality testing appears quite adequate, even though his intellectual talents may be penalized severely by this mode of operation. The limited number of human responses, one *H* plus one (*Hd*) answer, suggest a tendency to withdraw from others. The obvious pain, plus the fact that *FM* + *m* exceeds *M*, and *CF* exceeds *FC*, indicates a tormented person, prompted by uncontrolled forces, prone to a more impulsive action than is "healthy." The strong value system, plus the introspective orientation probably contributes to the pain, and could feasibly provoke suicidal ideation.

Specific postulates generated from the Structural data are as follows:

1. He is probably much brighter than his current level of functioning indicates.
2. He has an unusually strong orientation to convention, and is possibly dominated by a conformity oriented value system.
3. He is overly introspective, and appears to experience pain as a result of "what he sees."
4. He has limited control of his affect, and is trying somewhat desperately to contain this, however, the cost is more pain and disorganization.
5. His lability has caused him to constrict his overall functioning for fear of impulse dominated actions. His reality testing remains intact, but the cost to his intellect has been quite high.
6. He is withdrawing from people and from his environment in general, and his introspectiveness, when added to his disorganized psychological activity and affective lability, may precipitate forms of suicidal ideation.

ANALYSIS OF THE SCORING SEQUENCE

There is a very significant range of reaction times in the record, from 6'' to 75''. There is no obvious pattern involved although he does have particular difficulty with Card IV, which may provide some glimpse into his current estimate of his own authority and masculinity. His response to Card V, a *Dd* with a (*P*), indicates his attempts to narrow his world to more precise dimensions. The very short reaction time to Card VIII suggests that the answers to that card may be somewhat revealing of his response tendencies under more impulsive circumstances. The two explosion answers, in almost any length record, would be cause for concern. In this very brief protocol, they may indicate a feeling of loss of control over affect, and could dramatize his precarious state. One specific hypothesis is warranted from the scoring sequence data:

1. He is attempting to narrow his environment to a more precise level to deal with it more easily in the circumstances of his reduced intellectual functioning.

ANALYSIS OF THE FREE ASSOCIATIONS

The Free Associations lend considerable support to the notion that H. J. feels depressed and useless. He offers a "tattered moth," "beat up boots," a "bear skin that's seen better days," a "rib cage . . . like it was sticking out," and "A lot of mounted bugs . . . ." All of these convey depressive ideation. His internal struggles are noted by "bears fighting," "women picking something apart," and "peoples heads, like statues." His attempt at constraint is illustrated by his vacillation in the explosion response on Card II, ". . . an explosion too, although not really," and by the fact that he immobilizes the bugs on Card X, making them "mounted." The latter suggests his own state of psychological helplessness at this time. His long *RT* responses to Card IV, an aerial view of a road and beat up old boots, suggest that when he does "stand off" and review himself, the product is negative.

Specific propositions developed from the Free Associations are as follows:

1. He has a very low self-esteem which contributes to the formation of depressive feelings.
2. The struggle that he is going through is destructive, making him vulnerable to affective displays, and reduces his intellectual effectiveness.
3. When he attempts to "examine himself," he sees a person who is useless.
4. His affect is only contained when he makes a strong intellectual effort at reducing his cognitive activity.

ANALYSIS OF THE INQUIRY

The verbal material in the Inquiry underscores his gloomy attitude. The moth is "dead and decaying," the bears are in "mortal combat," the explosion has already happened and a "hole" has been left by the blast, the women are picking through "garbage," the boots have been "thrown away," the skin is a beat up old skin, the bones are sticking out, and the bugs are "deliberately mounted." These answers all convey a feeling of impending doom, a helplessness, and a psychological orientation that can only be destructive. He is not sure whether he will explode outward or inward, but either will lead to essentially the same consequences. These data lead to one additionally important hypothesis:

1. He feels propelled toward some form of destructiveness to his life style, either in ventilating his affect overtly in labile behaviors that would destroy his status, or in direct self-destructive behaviors.

A SUMMARY OF H. J.

This 39 year old man is in deep trouble. He feels helpless, worthless, and is gradually loosing control of his emotions. His self-esteem has depreciated substantially and his intellect has probably suffered markedly. He is in great pain, and although he is struggling to contain this destructive affect, he sees his effort as a "loosing" cause. He is withdrawing from people and becoming overly introspective. He is in jeopardy of overt, labile outbursts, or more likely a more covert labile gesture leading to self-destruction. Although his age might favor a label of "involutional reaction," the antecedents of the situation appear to be situational, in the composite of an unfulfilling marriage plus a sense of failure in his occupation. While he is able to verbally defend himself against recognition of either or both of these factors as "important causal elements," this defense must be very superficial and it seems likely that he would readily respond to external therapeutic support. Medication may be temporarily helpful, but he needs a much more direct level of support at this time which will ultimately lead to a reconstitution of his basic resources. His marriage should be examined closely and possibly a form of marital-sexual counseling may be in order. His value system also needs close but cautious scrutiny with the goal of reestablishing occupational targets that are realistic for him. His therapist should preferably be an older male who he can respect and with whom he can identify. Group therapy or an "uncovering" approach in individual therapy could be disastrous for him as they could serve to heighten his pain and further disorganize his precarious defenses.

PROTOCOL #7   L. Y.—MULTIPLE SUICIDE ATTEMPTS

Referral.   This 26 year old married female was referred by an in-patient psychiatric unit where she has been hospitalized for a period of 5 months. She has a history of four suicidal attempts during the past 14 months, the second of which led to hospitalization. Two more attempts have taken place while in the hospital. The psychiatric staff is divided about diagnosis and appropriate intervention methods. The majority feel that she is schizophrenic, mainly because of the nature of her suicidal attempts, the first by wrist slashing, the second by swallowing ammonia, the third by swallowing pieces of a broken lightbulb, and the fourth by stabbing in the neck with a table knife. During her first 3 months in the hosital she was treated using supportive and group methods, plus a mild tranquilizer. After her first suicide attempt in the hospital, she was treated with eight electroconvulsive treatments followed by more support and antidepressant medication. Her most recent attempt has occurred within 3 weeks and her neck wound is progressing satisfactorily. The majority of the psychiatric staff now feel that she should be treated as a schizophrenic, using heavy doses of antipsychotic medication plus psychotherapy, while a minority group challenge the diagnosis of schizophrenia and argue that antipsychotic medication may inhibit rather than enhance effective treatment. The referral question asks, "Is she schizophrenic and what recommendations can be made concerning treatment?"

History.   L. Y. is a high school graduate, having worked irregularly as a night telephone operator for approximately 7 years. She married at the age of 20, after learning that she was pregnant, and currently has three children, ages 5, 3, and 2. All are girls. Her husband works as an auto mechanic, drinks heavily, and has physically beaten L. Y. on several occasions. L. Y. has worked for a telephone company as a night shift long lines operator except for those periods when her pregnancies have required a "leave of absence." Her mother usually cares for the children while L. Y. is at work. L. Y. is the oldest daughter in a family of four children. Her two older brothers are both married and work in "blue collar" positions. Her younger sister is currently attending nursing school. L. Y. claims that everything "goes alright for a time and then I begin to feel sad and confused and the next thing I know I just want to die." She feels badly about her attempts because they "embarrass my family and go against my religion." She has several friends at work, "but I haven't had much contact with them since all this has begun." She likes to put puzzles together, and enjoys several TV programs. She misses her children but knows that "God will take care of them." She resists talking about sexuality, suggesting, "That's really not anybody's business but mine. It's not right to talk about it to strangers or doctors unless you've got something wrong, and I don't." She states the she doesn't know of any specific events that produced any of the suicidal attempts, "They just happened," and has only vague memory for the events themselves. She has a good memory for recent and remote events other than these, is generally alert and semi-cooperative during the testing, and does not present a noticeably "flattened" affective picture. She describes her husband as a "hard working man" and implies that her marriage is "alright," although she does not like to have to work to contribute to the support of the family, "I'd rather be with my children at night." She feels that those times when her husband has struck her have been, "Just accidents when he's had too much to drink and doesn't really know what he's doing. I know that he loves me and wouldn't hurt me on purpose." She predicts that it will not happen again, and feels that she should be released from the hospital as "I've learned my lesson and can get along o.k."

Protocol #7. L. Y., 26 Year Old Mother of Three Children, Having Made Four Suicide Attempts

Card	Free Association	Inquiry	Scoring
I 10″	1. A bf, some kids hav pulld it apart or s.t. (*E:* Most peopl c mor than one thg *S:* There's nothing else)	*E:* (Rpts *S*'s resp) *S:* Its got holes in it & the wgs r all brokn like, rippd arnd the edges	*WSo Fo A P* 1.0
II 3″	2. Two big animals, fiting w e.o., there's bld all over them	*E:* (Rpts *S*'s resp) *S:* Like big bears or s.t. thy hav bld all ovr their heads & feet, thyr on their bk legs lik really fiting fierce	*W+ FM^a.CFo* (2) *A, Bl P* 4.5
III 27″	V3. It ll 2 trees off on a hill in the winter	*E:* (Rpts *S*'s resp) *S:* Thy r way off in the dist, up a hill & there's snow all over too, ths white stuff	*DdS+ FD.FC'o* (2) *Bt, Na* 4.5
	4. There's a monkey falling thru the air	*E:* (Rpts *S*'s resp) *S:* It just ll a monkey w the long tail & he's falling	*Do FM^{p}vo A*
IV 15″	5. A big gorilla, lik he's leaning bkwrd puttg his big feet out	*E:* (Rpts *S*'s resp) *S:* Mayb he's jumping downward lik he was gonna land on the grnd & u can c him coming but u can't c his head too well *E:* I'm not sure how u c him as a gorilla *S:* He's just big & bulky lik one	*Wo FM^a.FDo A* 2.0
V 8″	6. A bf but there's s.t. wrong w the wings	*E:* (Rpts *S*'s resp) *S:* Its lik the ends of the wgs were brokn off or s.t., c here is the body & the feelers & ths is the brkn wgs	*Wo Fo A P* 1.0

VI 19″

7. Ths lik a bug tht's caught in s.t. sticky & its tryg to fly away

E: (Rpts S's resp)
S: Its caught back in ths glop or s.t., it all looks real sticky & its wgs r going a mile a minute tryg to get out
E: U said back in ths glop
S: Its back aways, it looks small & helpless tryg to get out of there

$W+ \quad FM^a.TF.FD+ \quad A, \text{Glop} \quad 2.5$

VII 35″

8. Its a big pit of s.s., part of the edge has fallen away & u can't c the bottom

E: (Rpts S's resp)
S: It just ll a hole here, lik a big pit & thes r the sides but ths prt has fallen into the pit so its not there anymore
E: I'm not sure how u c it
S: C the rounded edges here, lik it was going down

$WS- \quad VF- \quad \text{Pit} \quad 4.0$

9. It c.b. 2 littl girls too or mayb a littl girl lookg in the mirror

E: (Rpts S's resp)
S: She's lookg in the mirror after she just did her hair up, she's in back of ths table or whatever dwn here so u can't c all of her

$W+ \quad M^p.Fr.FDo \quad (2) \quad Hd \quad P \quad 2.5$

VIII 7″

10. It ll 2 A's tryg to climb ths tree

E: (Rpts S's resp)
S: There's one on each side, & thyr climb up ths tree in the middle, its lik an evergrn tree because its got all the colors on it

$W+ \quad FM^a.FCo \quad (2) \quad A, Bt \quad P \quad 4.5$

IX 5″

11. It ll a forest fire

E: (Rpts S's resp)
S: The flames r shooting up here & u can barely make out the trees anymore, here in the green & the pink part is like ashes still smoldering

$Wv \quad m^a.CFw \quad Fi, Ls \quad 5.5$

12. Ths white part in the cntr c.b. a hollow vase, u can c thru it

E: (Rpts S's resp)
S: The way the whiteness is there makes it look hollow, like u can c the back too, its hazy lik an empty vase is

$DSo \quad FVo \quad Hh$

Protocol #7 (Continued)

Card		Free Association	Inquiry	Scoring
X	2″	13. Oh, lik the 4th of July	E: (Rpts S's resp) S: Its just all colors bursting in a pattern lik some of the rockets thy shoot off on the 4th	Wv mᵃ.CFw Fi 5.5
		14. There's a decayd tooth in there too	E: (Rpts S's resp) S: Rite here in the cntr, it ll it has a cavity	Ddo Fw Tooth

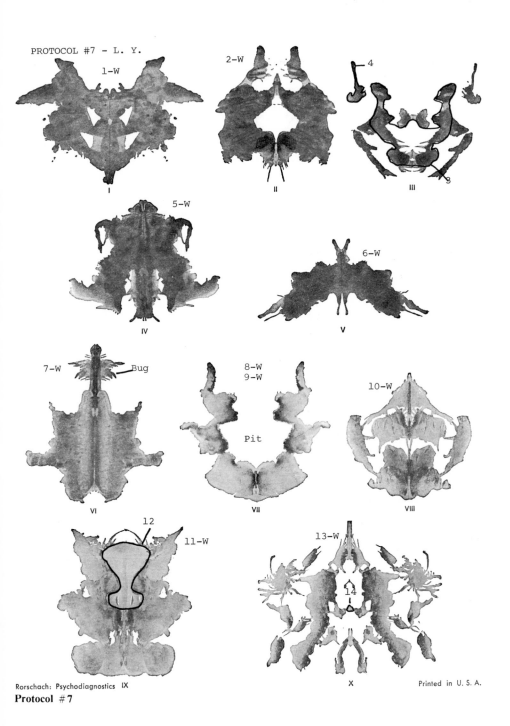

PROTOCOL #7 - L. Y.

1-W

I

2-W

II

4

3

III

5-W

IV

6-W

V

7-W   Bug

VI

8-W
9-W

Pit

VII

10-W

VIII

12

11-W

IX

13-W

14

X

Rorschach: Psychodiagnostics IX

Printed in U. S. A.

Protocol #7

423

Table 42. Structural Summary for Protocol #7—L. Y.

$R = 14$ $Zf = 11$ $Z\text{Sum} = 37.5$ $P = 5$ $(2) = 4$

Location Features		Determinants	Contents	Contents (Idiographic)
W = 10	DQ	$M.Fr.FD = 1$	H =	$\underline{Pit}$ = 1
		$FM.TF.FD$ = 1	(H) =	
D = 2	+ = 5	$FM.FC$ = 1	Hd = 1	$\underline{Tooth}$ = 1
		$FM.CF$ = 2	(Hd) =	
Dd = 2	o = 6	$m.CF$ = 2	A = 7	$\underline{Glop}$ = 0, 1
		$FD.FC'$ = 1	(A) =	
S = 4	v = 2		Ad =	$\underline{}$ =
		M =	(Ad) =	
DW = 0	− = 1	FM = 1	Ab =	$\underline{}$ =
		m =	Al =	
		C =	An =	$\underline{}$ =
		CF =	Art =	
FORM QUALITY		FC =	Ay =	$\underline{}$ =
		C' =	Bl = 0, 1	
FQx	FQf	$C'F$ =	Bt = 1, 1	$\underline{}$ =
		FC' =	Cg =	
+ = 1	+ = 0	T =	Ex =	
		TF =	Fi = 2	
o = 9	o = 2	FT =	Fd =	
		V =	Ge =	
w = 3	w = 1	VF = 1	Hh = 1	
		FV = 1	Na = 0, 1	
− = 1	− = 0	Y =	Ls =	
		YF =	Sx =	
		FY =	Xy =	
		rF =		
		Fr =		
		FD =		
		F = 3		

RATIOS, PERCENTAGES, AND DERIVATIONS

$Z\text{Sum}/Z\text{est} = 37.5/34.5$	$FC/CF + C = 1/3$	Afr	$= .56$
$Zd = +3.0$	W/M = 10/1	$3r + (2)/R$	$= 7/14 = .50$
$EB = 1/3.5$ $EA = 4.5$	W/D = 10/2	Cont/R	$= 7/14$
eb = 7/4 ep = 11	L = .27	$H + Hd/A + Ad = 7/1$	
Blends$/R$ = 8/14	$F+\%$ = 67	$H + A/Hd + Ad = 1/7$	
a/p = 6/2	$X+\%$ = 71	XRT Achrom	$= 17.4''$
M^a/M^p = 0/1	$A\%$ = 50	XRT Chrom	$= 8.8''$

424

Table 43. Sequence of Scores for Protocol #7—L. Y.

Card	RT	No.	Location	Determinant(s)		Content(s)	Pop	Z Score
I	10″	1.	WSo	Fo		A	P	1.0
II	3″	2.	W+	FMᵃ.CFo	(2)	A, Bl	P	4.5
III	27″	3.	DdS+	FD.FC′o	(2)	Bt, Na		4.5
		4.	Do	FMᵖo		A		
IV	15″	5.	Wo	FMᵃ.FDo		A		2.0
V	8″	6.	Wo	Fo		A	P	1.0
VI	19″	7.	W+	FMᵃ.TF.FD+		A, Glop		2.5
VII	35″	8.	WS−	VF−		Pit		4.0
		9.	W+	Mᵖ.Fr.FDo	(2)	Hd	P	2.5
VIII	7″	10.	W+	FMᵃ.FCo	(2)	A, Bt	P	4.5
IX	5″	11.	Wv	mᵃ.CFw		Fi		5.5
		12.	DSo	FVo		Hh		
X	2″	13.	Wv	mᵃ.CFw		Fi		5.5
		14.	Ddo	Fw		Tooth		

ANALYSIS OF THE STRUCTURE

This record, although brief, stands out because of its many unique features. The Zf is inordinately high for a 14 response protocol; however, the Zd score shows that the level of organization exceeds that which is expected. There are eight Blend answers, representing more than half of the responses and indicating a very complex psychological process. The EB suggests a style of going to the environment for satisfactions, but the EA is significantly lower than the ep, revealing that she is not in control of most of the psychological activity that she experiences, and illustrates a more primitive and unorganized individual. Seven of her 14 answers are marked by less sophisticated types of movement, and when she does use color, it is more often of the CF variety and is apparently stimulated by less sophisticated inner experiences. This composite illustrates a strong propensity for impulsive behavior, oriented toward immediate relief with little regard for the consequences. Her Lambda, which is quite low, provides added support for this postulate. Her W/M, W/D, and Zf all indicate levels of aspiration which usually exceed her current level of functioning. The $F+\%$ cannot be taken too seriously as it is based on only three Pure F responses. The $X+\%$, however, does approach a marginal level, and although not supporting a diagnosis of schizophrenia, does reveal that she has limited reality testing. For the most part, her poor form quality answers are weak rather than gross distortions or perceptual accuracy. Her high Egocentricity Ratio, the sizable $A\%$, the Affective Ratio, and the imbalanced H to A ratio all provide evidence to suggest that she is withdrawing from interaction with others and is focusing excessively on herself. This factor appears even more important when it is noted that the record contains two vista responses, and three FD answers, the composite of which reveal an unusually extreme and painful introspective orientation. She also uses white space with an unusual frequency, probably indicating negative and hostile feelings. These can only serve to heighten her tendencies toward an impulsive acting-out behavior pattern. Her five synthesis responses indicate a sound level of intellectual development; however, the three low developmental quality selections suggest an underlying immaturity and/or impairment to these operations.

Specific propositions developed from the Structural Summary are the following:

1. She is extremely labile and prone toward impulsive behaviors.

2. Although her style of response appears to be one that relies on environmental interaction for gratification, she is withdrawing from her world and has become excessively introspective.

3. Her introspectiveness leads to considerable discomfort and anger, and probably adds provocation to her tendencies toward acting out.

4. Her self-preoccupation and pain generate feelings of worthlessness and can lead to suicidal ideation.

5. Her emotional looseness and more primitive "unmet" needs tend to overwhelm any attempts at restraint.

6. She has aspirations that far exceed her current level of functioning, and probably serve as an added source of self-devaluation.

7. Her psychological life is quite disorganized and overly complex, generally leaving her defenseless in the face of threats from within or without.

8. There is no firm evidence of schizophrenia in the structure; however, her state of disorganization is such that she could begin to distort reality more severely if some relief is not experienced.

ANALYSIS OF THE SCORING SEQUENCE

Her reaction times are variable; however, she is prone to respond in shorter periods to the colored cards. This is probably indicative of her inability to thwart off affective stimuli. Her approach is predominantly W oriented; however, she has noticeable difficulty with four of the five colored cards and Card VII. Her poor quality form answers also occur in these cards. All of her affective determinants, except the vista answers, occur in combination with other determinants, the color always paired with a form of movement. Both of the vista answers occur in areas that include the use of white space, suggesting the possibility of self-directed anger. No new postulates are generated by the Scoring Sequence.

ANALYSIS OF THE FREE ASSOCIATIONS

Several of the Free Associations dramatize her feelings of worthlessness and the struggle that she is experiencing to maintain some form of adjustment. Both butterflys have something wrong with them, the first having been pulled apart by "kids." The trees are "off on a hill in the winter," the monkey is "falling," the bug is "stuck and trying to fly away," part of the edge has fallen away around the bottomless pit, the vase is "hollow," and the tooth is "decayed." These are grim descriptions, indicating the extreme feelings of disorganization that she has, and her more or less hopeless view of herself and her life. The fact that the bears are fighting and the animals are trying to climb the tree suggests that she has not completely given up in her life and death struggle; however, her affect comes on her like the "forest fire" in Card IX and with forcefulness of the "4th of July" in Card X, diminishing the effectiveness of her intellect, and in each instance causing impairment to her testing of reality. There is an implication in her very first answer in the test that much of her conflict is due to pressures created by the "burden" of motherhood. She may perceive her children as overly demanding on her, or may feel remorse for having others care for them while she works. On a more symbolic level, she may be suggesting that her own immaturity is at work. The implication of this postulate is that she is unprepared for adult responsibilities, especially those involving the role of a wife and the mother of three young children. Her response to Card IV may also convey some notions concerning her perception of authority and masculinity, that is, as threatening and overwhelming. The vase response on Card IX carries the suggestion that she now feels "hollow" and transparent to others as well as herself, and finally, the "decayed" tooth response ending the record may reflect the diminishing ability to contain her own hostility, as if the veneer of her own defenses is eroding away.

Specific hypotheses generated from the Free Association material are as follows:

1. She has strong feelings of unworthiness and is in constant struggle to maintain a minimal form of adjustment.

2. She is quite disorganized and currently manifests a rather hopeless view concerning her situation.

3. She feels unable to carry out an adult role, especially where responsibility for others is concerned.

4. She is continuously threatened by her own affect, which seems to easily diminish her intellectual effectiveness and dictate impulsive behaviors.

5. She feels "empty" and transparent, and views her defenses as faltering badly.

ANALYSIS OF THE INQUIRY

Most of the Inquiry material restates and emphasizes the features noted in the Structure and in the Free Association. She reiterates her damaged self-image in the butterfly responses, ". . . all broken like . . . ," and ". . . like the ends of the wings were broken off . . . ." She describes the bug as ". . . caught back in this glop . . . and its wings are going a mile a minute trying to get out." This possibly reveals more about the intensity of her inner struggle, as does the description of the bears, ". . . really fighting fierce." She is almost completely engulfed by affect, as portrayed by her elaboration of the forest fire response. "The flames are shooting up here and you can barely make out the trees anymore . . . ." There is a hint that her anger has contributed to her helpless state, ". . . the whiteness . . . makes it look hollow . . . hazzy like an empty vase . . . ." While the Inquiry material is very rich, it is not such to generate new propositions about her.

A SUMMARY OF L. Y.

This 26 year old woman is in serious disarray. She is extremely labile, being able to maintain only very limited controls over her emotions. Her withdrawal from her environment is increasingly extensive even though she has been oriented toward relying on her environment for support and satisfaction. She is impulsive, immature, and regressive. Her self-image is very poor, and she experiences feelings of worthlessness, anger, and pessimism. She is unable to carry out an adult role, especially one that assumes responsibility for others. The intensity of her affect and her own less sophisticated needs has led to much disorganization in both thinking and behavior. She looks on her prospects for the future with a sense of futility, and the frequent feelings of being overwhelmed by stresses from within and without have given rise to suicidal ideation as a reasonable method of resolution. Her intense experience of pain, plus her extremely limited affective controls, makes the probability of additional suicide gestures very high. She does distort reality in response to her needs and affects, but shows no firm evidence of schizophrenic thinking at this time. She does require immediate assistance in gaining a more definitive control of her affect, and in this context, the variety of medications available should be studied carefully. Such intervention, however, will be of little benefit without extensive psychotherapeutic inputs. She is reasonably bright, even though her intellect has suffered considerably under the stresses of her psychological disorganization. She needs, and would like, to be dependent on a nonthreatening adult who can offer strong supports to her faltering self-image, and who can assist in formulating viable planning for intervention with her family, and especially her husband. Her role in the family, with the husband and with her children, will be critically important to the achievement of any long term therapeutic goals.

CHAPTER 19

Schizophrenia

Schizophrenia is one of the most serious psychological disturbances. It is generally characterized as a "thinking" disturbance, marked by distortions and/or limitations in reality testing, poor judgment, difficulties in interpersonal relations, unstable patterns of control and/or defense, fluctuations in motivation, tendencies toward cognitive disorganization, and frequent impairment to the higher levels of intellectual operation. Although many schizophrenics are so debilitated by their cognitive disorganization that hospitalization is required, many others can maintain an ambulatory status in which they are able to function in their environments at marginal levels or better. Psychological evaluations are generally requested more often regarding patients in the latter group than in the former. The severely disorganized patient is usually identified quite easily by his behaviors. The "marginally effective" schizophrenic is often misidentified from his behaviors, or diagnoses are equivocal, and thus the added input from psychological evaluation is used for purposes of clarification of the syndrome, and planning for appropriate intervention methods. Behaviorally oriented therapists are often interested in early identification of "response–response" relationships. Psychiatrists will often rely on information from psychological studies to determine which types of medication might be most effective in maintaining the ambulatory status, and other therapists frequently use descriptive data such as derived from the Rorschach to plan more extensive treatment programs which might include family, group, milieu, or individual approaches. The protocols included here have been selected, because they represent "functioning" people about whom legitimate questions have been asked.

PROTOCOL #8 V. M. —A DISINTEGRATING ADOLESCENT

Referral. This 17 year old male, high school student, was admitted voluntarily, at the encouragement of his parents, to a private psychiatric unit. The parents felt that he had become overly withdrawn from his family and friends during the preceding year, an observation also made by school personnel, and that he seemed "detached and uninterested." Shortly before his admission he had been repairing a tire on his "prized" 10 speed bicycle and suddenly took a sledge hammer to it, ruining it completely. After 10 days of observation in the hospital, the staff consensus favored a diagnosis of "characterological problem," noting that he was quiet and cooperative. Psychological evaluation was requested to assist in treatment planning.

History. V. M. is the third child, and oldest son in a family of five children. His older sisters are ages 22 and 20, the older being married and living out of the home, the second a college student who lives at home. His younger two siblings are both male, ages 8 and 6. His father owns a construction firm. The mother does not work. V. M. has completed 11 years of school and had began his "senior" year in high school shortly before his admission. He describes himself as "getting more and more depressed lately. I lost all my interest in people and that's weird cause I used to enjoy getting into them." He states that he spent most of his recent time riding his bicycle and listening to music. He has dated but claims no sexual experience, "other than a little fooling around." He tried marijuana once but "didn't like it, that stuff is dumb." He feels that both his parents are "great," and that his siblings are "o.k. most of the time."

Protocol #8. V. M., 17 Years Old, 11th Grade Education, Parents Both Living, Two Older Female Siblings, Father Employed in White Collar Position

Card	Free Association	Inquiry	Scoring
I 3″	1. A face w 4 eyes	E: (Rpts S's resp) S: Ther's the top 2 eyes & thes r the bttm 2 eyes & ths is the nose. The way the bttm eyes get lighter ll a smile too. Ths r the ears & cheeks (points), its lik a face tht wld b carvd in a pumpkin	WS+ Fo (Hd) 3.5 InconComb
	E: Most peopl c mor thn 1 thg 2. They do? Well, it ll s.k. of flying object	E: (Rpts S's resp) S: I can't defin wht kind, but here r its wings & it ll its in flt. Its not wrkg too hard at it since its wgs r'nt fully spread. It mite b a bat E: I'm not sure I c it lik u do S: How can u tell if someone is sick or not from these, c its the W thg	Wo FMªo A P 1.0
II 4″	3. It ll a face & a wide open mouth	E: (Rpts S's resp) S: Hr r the eyes & ths r the eyebrows. The mouth is here & leads into the nose here. E: U mentioned a face S: Like s.o. is screaming & spitting up bld rite here r the spots	WS− Mª.CF− Hd 4.5
	4. It also ll a grave w a cross at the tombstne, a blk cross on top of the white tombstn	E: (Rpts S's resp) S: Ths prt here (white) is the dirt like u r lookg at it from a distance. Ths is the grave hr & up here is the cross. Ths line here (points) cuts the grave from the tombstn	DS+ FC'.FDw Grave 4.5

Protocol #8 (Continued)

Card		Free Association		Inquiry	Scoring
III	3″	5.	Ths ll to me lik 2 girls pulling on s.o.'s face	E: (Rpts S's resp) S: Ths is the girl, her head, breast & legs. Ths ll the face thyr pulling on, the eyes, nose & mouth. Its in the proc of being torn apart by ths 2 girls. The eyes r bulging out of the guy's face. The girls r pulling him w their arms	$D+$ M^a_w (2) H, Hd P 3.0 FabComb
		6.	Ths 2 thg here r broken guitars	E: (Rpts S's resp) S: On either side here, it ll s.o. has smashed them fr a side angle so the neck is hanging off, & the bttm is bent lik a boot, lik its guts r hanging out, lik the wire & other stuff, thts rite here (points)	$D-$ $F-$ (2) Guitar
IV	10″	7.	Tht ll, uh, ll one of thos guys from a "Keep on trucking" poster. Coming out of his body is a dragon	E: (Rpts S's resp) S: Its taken fr a vantage, horizon type drawing. Thes r his feet & hr r his arms & thy r a little deformed. His head has little shape but its ther. That's the dragon comg fr betwn his legs, or sk of monster E: I'm not clear abt the vantage, horizon type drawing S: Lik if u keep lookg at it, it gets thinner & thinner so tht u don't c it anymore.	$W+$ FDo $(H),(A)$ 4.0 FabComb
V	4″	8.	Tht ll a bf	E: (Rpts S's resp) S: Hr r its antlers & wgs & there r	Wo Fo A P 1.0

9. It also ll it cb a man w wgs & antlers. He's got a line running rite dwn the middle of him

the legs or whatevr u want to call them

E: (Rpts S's resp)
S: Yeah, her's his head & antlers & legs. Ths drk line running dwn him is from where they made the inkblot

Do Fo (H)

VI 11″

10. It ll s.k. of machine & its speared half the sun

E: (Rpts S's resp)
S: Yeah, ths is the machine, ths prt here. Ths line running dwn the middle is what u'd get in the machin to run it. Its s.k. of drill & its got half the sun. Thr r flames coming fr the sun so its got half the sun

$W+$ m^a_w Machine, Na 2.5 FabComb

11. Its also a plain inkblot

E: (Rpts S's resp)
S: It ll s.b. put ink on a pc of paper & folded it togthr. Thy prob fooled around a littl by pushg the ink around to get the shades, then they opned it up & said "wow, I've made s.t." but there's no real shape to it.

Wv Y Inkblot

VII 5″

12. It ll 2 Egyptian girls doing an Egyptial dance

E: (Rpts S's resp)
S: Yeah, here's their heads w their hair up. It comes over their forehead. Here's the chin, u can't c the mouth well. Thes r their arms out lik that, u can c them fr the head to the waist, ths dwn here is nothing

$D+$ M^a_o (2) Hd P 3.0

13. Or it c.b. 2 gals on rockng chairs

E: (Rpts S's resp)
S: Thes r rockg chairs balanced on the corner, mayb rockers lik blks of wood w a rounded bttm. The girls r the same as before & they just kinda rock on it.

$W+$ M^p_o (2) H P 2.5

Protocol #8 (Continued)

Card	Free Association	Inquiry	Scoring
VIII 6″	14. Ths ll 2 bears clmbg either side of a mt, 2 pink bears, or red, whtevr tht is	E: (Rpts S's resp) S: Here r the bears & thyr in motion, going up the side of the mt. Thy r on opposite sides of the mt.	W+ FMᵃ.FCo (2) A,Ls P 4.5
	15. In the mt is a face of an Eskimo, or Indian type ruler or god. It ll the bears hav their paws on his hair	E: (Rpts S's resp) S: Yeah, here r his eyes & his nose here. Ths green area is his mouth & he's got all the lines of his face, he's even got a littl paint on his face, lik littl green bits of paint on it here. Ths is his hair, its long hair, the bears hav opposite paws on his hair	D− FC.FMᵖ− (2) Hd,A 3.0 FabComb
IX 23″	16. It ll 2 profiles of Alfred Hitchcock	E: (Rpts S's resp) S: 2 bad profiles, rt here is the forehead & ths white part is his eye, ths is his nose & mouth is ths littl indentatn, he's got a pimple on his chin	DSo Fo (2) Hd
	17. Or, the head of a pig thy killed in Lord of the Flies	E: (Rpts S's resp) S: The same prt again, lik a profile of tht pig thy stuck on the stake & its drippg bld down here but evaporating up here E: Evaporating? S: Lik all the juice inside is evap up into the air	W− mᵖ.CF− (Ad),Bl 5.5
X 4″	18. Ths is just all kinds of bugs, yeah thts wht it is	E: Yeah, all kinds of bugs. Ths 2 blue ones r bugs & up hre ths 2 ll crawly brwn bugs. E.t. in the pic. gives more life to the bugs, u can detect their presence easier	W+ FCo (2) A 5.5

434

19. It's also got a face in it

E: (Rpts S's resp)
S: Hr r the eyes & the nose w a moustache like parts of the face & if u
turn it upsid dwn u get exactly the
same, c?, here r the nose, eyes &
moustache again

DdS – F – Hd 6.0

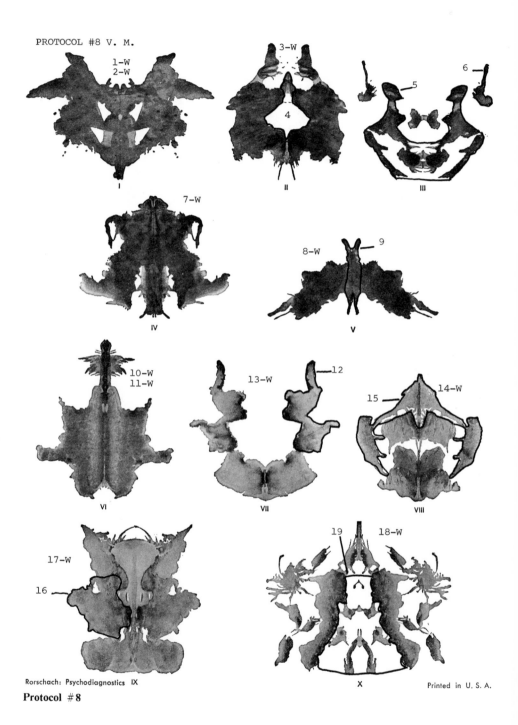

PROTOCOL #8 V. M.

Protocol #8

Table 44. Structural Summary for Protocol #8—V. M.

$R = 19$	$Zf = 15$	$Z\text{Sum} = 54.0$	$P = 6$	$(2) = 8$

Location Features	Determinants	Contents	Contents (Idiographic)

Location Features	DQ		Determinants		Contents		Contents (Idiographic)
W = 11			$M.CF$ = 1		H = 2		Grave = 1
			$FM.FC$ = 1		(H) = 2		
D = 7	+ = 9		$m.CF$ = 1		Hd = 5, 1		Guitar = 1
			$FC.FM$ = 1		(Hd) = 1		
Dd = 1	o = 4		$FC'.FD$ = 1		A = 4, 1		Inkblot = 1
					(A) = 0, 1		
S = 5	v = 1		M = 3		Ad =		Machine = 1
			FM = 1		(Ad) = 1		
DW = 0	– = 5		m = 1		Ab =		____ =
			C =		Al =		
			CF =		An =		____ =
			FC = 1		Art =		
FORM QUALITY			C' =		Ay =		____ =
			$C'F$ =		Bl = 0, 1		
FQx	FQf		FC' =		Bt =		____ =
			T =		Cg =		
+ = 0	+ = 0		TF =		Cl =		
			FT =		Ex =		
o = 10	o = 4		V =		Fi =		
			VF =		Fd =		
w = 3	w = 0		FV =		Ge =		
			Y = 1		Hh =		
– = 5	– = 2		YF =		Ls = 0, 1		
			FY =		Na = 0, 1		
			rF =		Sx =		
			Fr =		Xy =		
			FD = 1				
			F = 6				

RATIOS, PERCENTAGES, AND DERIVATIONS

$Z\text{Sum}/Z\text{est} = 54.0/49.0$	$FC/CF + C = 3/2$	Afr	$= .46$
$Zd = +5.0$	W/M = 11/4	$3r + (2)/R$	$= 8/19 = .42$
$EB = 4/3.5$ $EA = 7.5$	W/D = 11/7	Cont/R	$= 6/19$
$eb = 5/2$ $ep = 7$	L = .46	$H + Hd/A + Ad = 10/5$	
Blends/R = 5/19	$F+\%$ = 67	$H + A/Hd + Ad = 8/7$	
a/p = 6/3	$X+\%$ = 53	XRT Achrom	$= 6.6''$
M^a/M^p = 3/1	$A\%$ = 26	XRT Chrom	$= 8.0''$

Table 45.   Sequence of Scores for Protocol #8—V. M.

Card	RT	No.	Location	Determinant(s)		Content(s)	Pop	Z Score
I	3″	1.	WS+	Fo		(Hd)		3.5 InconComb
		2.	Wo	FMᵃo		A	P	1.0
II	4″	3.	WS−	Mᵃ.CF−		Hd		4.5
		4.	DS+	FC′.FDw		Grave		4.5
III	3″	5.	D+	Mᵃw	(2)	H, Hd	P	3.0 FabComb
		6.	D−	F−	(2)	Guitar		
IV	10″	7.	W+	FDo		(H), (A)		4.0 FabComb
V	4″	8.	Wo	Fo		A	P	1.0
		9.	Do	Fo		(H)		
VI	11″	10.	W+	mᵃw		Machine, Na		2.5 FabComb
		11.	Wv	Y		Inkblot		
VII	5″	12.	D+	Mᵃo	(2)	Hd	P	3.0
		13.	W+	Mᵖo	(2)	H	P	2.5
VIII	6″	14.	W+	FMᵃ.FCo	(2)	A, Ls	P	4.5
		15.	D−	FC.FMᵖ−	(2)	Hd, A		3.0 FabComb
IX	23″	16.	DSo	Fo	(2)	Hd		
		17.	W−	mᵖ.CF−		(Ad), Bl		5.5
X	4″	18.	W+	FCo	(2)	A		5.5
		19.	DdS−	F−		Hd		6.0

ANALYSIS OF THE STRUCTURE

The very high Zf and the excessive use of W locations suggests that he is strongly oriented to "incorporate" as much of his stimulus world as possible. The Zd score indicates that he has a tendency to overincorporate in this cognitive behavior; and, the significantly low $X+\%$ reveals that he is distorting reality far too much, leading to the postulate that his intellectual operations have become noticeably impaired. The EB and EA indicate considerable organization of his resources; however, the limited reality testing illustrates that these resources are not being used to his best advantage. The eb shows a substantial impact from less well organized drives, but this is not unusual for an adolescent who is still in development. The disproportionate $FC/CF + C$ ratio, plus the relatively low Lambda, suggests less affective control than is indicated in either the EB or the eb. The W/M ratio is slightly elevated to W, and the W/D ratio clearly reveals the orientation toward overincorporation. The low $A\%$ is probably representative of his tendency to give idiographic contents, and may reflect an "intellectualizing" orientation. The Affective Ratio denotes withdrawal from affective stimuli, and the inordinately imbalanced H to A Ratio signifies an unusual preoccupation with people. The Egocentricity ratio offers evidence of considerable "self-concern," and the $H+A$ to $Hd+Ad$ Ratio shows a considerable emphasis on human and animal details. The withdrawal, W orientation, lability, poor reality testing, self-focus, and detail emphasis represent a composite similar to that noted in patients with a "paranoid" form of ideation. The large number of synthesis answers, usually associated with higher levels of intellectual development, may, in this instance, reflect his need to incorporate his world, possibly to better defend himself against it. His percepts are essentially void of shading, except for a Pure Y answer, indicating that he operates essentially free of "pain"; however, the two FD answers give a hint of considerable "introspection," a phenomenon that may relate to his reported feelings of depression. The idiographic contents, especially "grave" and "machine," signal potentially important answers for analysis in the Free Associations. The general range of contents is within normal limits; however, the heavy emphasis on human and animal percepts seems quite unusual. The six Popular answers indicate an awareness of conventionality; however, the five white space answers imply a negative or hostile attitude which, when combined with the low $X+\%$, warns that he is often unwilling or unable to respond to his world in a conventional manner.

Specific propositions developed from the structural data are as follows:

1. He has substantial resources which are seemingly well organized; however, his reality testing is especially impaired under affective conditions and his overall intellectual functioning has suffered as a result of this.

2. He is potentially bright, but currently uses his intellect to "overincorporate" external stimuli, a process which may be detrimental to his adjustment patterns.

3. He is aware of convention, but is quite negative and/or hostile to his world, the product of which may be an impairment to perceptual accuracy and a tendency to use affect inappropriately.

4. He has loose emotional controls, and at times can be impulsive in his behaviors.

5. He is prone to withdraw from environmental interaction, but at the same time has developed an inordinate preoccupation with people.

6. He is focusing to some excess on himself, and appears suspicious of others in a paranoid form of ideation.

7. His thinking may be very personalized, and although he is able to "delay" behaviors under relatively affect-free situations, the composite of his lability, poor reality testing, preoccupation with people, and personalized ideation could lead to forms of acting-out behaviors detrimental to others.

ANALYSIS OF THE SCORING SEQUENCE

The reaction times are generally short, except those to the more difficult cards, IV, VI, and IX. The approach is mainly W oriented, and with one exception of a Wv on Card VI, he is able to give synthesis W's. Five of his nine movement answers, including two of the four M responses, are poor form quality, suggesting that his ideational process contributes to a distortion of reality. Three of his four color answers are also associated with movement, indicating that the ideation also tends to give rise to affect. Two of his four idiographic contents occur to Card VI, signaling for special attention to those Free Associations. Both of his answers to that card involve poor form quality. He gives at least four clear "Fabulized Combination" answers, which hint at a concreteness in his thinking, and a distortion in his organizational activities. Two specific hypotheses are generated by the Scoring Sequence:

1. His ideation frequently precipitates distortions in reality testing, and also stimulates less controlled affective states.

2. His thinking appears to be concrete and his orientation toward over-organization is probably seriously impaired by this.

ANALYSIS OF THE FREE ASSOCIATIONS

Many of his associations appear to illustrate his unique form of ideation. His first answer, "a face with four eyes," offers a clue to his "supersuspicious" style of functioning. The face and wide open mouth on Card II add support to this notion and seem to reflect a strong oral component. The "grave" response, also on Card II may represent his own feeling of impending doom, and may shed some light on his reported experience of depression. In Card III, he offers a Popular *M* answer, but then tends to contaminate it by perceiving part of the blot as someone's face being pulled apart. His second answer to Card III could be illustrative of the product of the "pulling," "broken guitars," phallic-like symbols which are used as instruments of affective exchange. The dragon, coming from the human form on Card IV, also appears to reveal a sense of fear and confusion concerning his own sexuality, and the phrase "keep on trucking" might hint of feelings of impotency. The concreteness of thinking is also represented in his description of a man with wings and antlers on Card V. His first response to Card VI is possibly the most symbolic and most revealing in the record, a "machine and its speared half the sun." Again, he concentrates on a phallic-like area, defining it as a machine, and identifies "half the sun" as its target. The implication here may be that his own sexuality, or at least his conceptualization of sexuality, is interferring with his role image, that of the "sun." It is also tempting to translate this response as reflecting his struggle between childhood and becoming an adult. Interestingly, his next answer is the most passively oriented in the record, using a crude form of denial as the base. His responses to Card VII vacillate from active to passive movement, possibly indicating more about his ideational struggles. His first answer to Card VIII is conventional and well organized, but his lack of cognitive control is evidenced in the fabulization that he offers next in a response involving a "ruler or god." Both responses to Card IX include heads, offering more evidence regarding the "seat" of his problem, that is, in his thinking. The second of these, that of a dead pig, provides an indication of his own self-image and, again, hints of a feeling of impending doom. His last response is quite unconventional and suggests his negative paranoid-like guardedness.

Specific propositions developed from the Free Association material are as follows:

1. He is very guarded and appears to manifest a paranoid style of ideation.

2. He is experiencing a significant conflict concerning his sexuality, apparently feeling that his own impulses are destructive to him and possibly to others.

3. His thinking is often concrete and he tends to confuse ideas very unrealistically.

4. In part, his conflicts stem from the experience of "leaving" childhood and assuming more "adult" responsibilities.

5. His confused thinking has created feelings of vulnerability and pending disaster.

6. He regards his sexuality as "uncontrollable" and appears to suspect that it will be, or is already, a force against which he can neither respond to effectively, nor defend himself adequately.

ANALYSIS OF THE INQUIRY

In several of his responses, he begins his description of human or animal contents by emphasizing the eyes and other facial features. Such an emphasis is very common among inordinately suspicious or paranoid individuals. His response to Card I, "Its not working too hard at it since its wings aren't fully spread," is probably indicative of his own passive style plus his feelings of not being "fully grown" yet. His characterization of the face on Card II as someone "screaming and spitting up blood" seems to dramatize his own agony and tenuous affective control. The elaboration that he gives to both responses on Card III offers some indication of his own "tattered" self-image and provides added support for the notion that conflicts about masculinity and sexuality have led to his disarray. This is also evidenced in his reaffirmation of the "dragon coming from between his legs or some kind of monster" on Card IV. His unique and concrete form of thinking is illustrated again by his answers to responses 10, 11, 15, 16, and 17, all of which contain very idiographic comments. The midline represents "what you'd get in the machine to run it," the profile has a "pimple on his chin," and "all the juice inside is evaporating up into the air." These sorts of comments illustrate a naive, almost childlike elaboration of form and color, and no doubt have special meaning in V. M.'s distorted ideation. For instance, the "juice evaporating" might represent some strange feelings of depersonalization or loss of sensation or diminution in affect. It would be precarious, however, to draw such specific conclusions without additional evidence. At best, this material can be taken as indicative of his disorganization, helplessness, and limited contact with reality.

Some complimentary postulates that are generated by the Inquiry data are as follows:

1. He is quite suspicious and uses a paranoid form of thinking.
2. He is immature and in considerable agony because of his emotions.
3. He is confused about masculinity and sexuality, factors which have been significant in the origins of his present state.
4. His thinking is very concrete and disorganized, and possibly marked by some form of "self-detachment."

A SUMMARY OF V. M.

A great bulk of Rorschach evidence argues against a diagnosis of characterological disorder, although definite signs of basic limitations in response style have predisposed the more serious schizophrenic episode that seems to be occurring. He is immature, and apparently has a reasonably long standing confusion concerning his own identity, especially regarding masculinity and sexuality. He has a substantial intellect, but this is faltering under the pressures of his confusion in thinking which focuses mainly on defending himself against unwanted "intrusions" from others. His reality testing has become impaired, and he has developed a sense of anger toward himself and his world. These features, when combined with his limited affective controls, set the stage for inappropriate actions that can be destructive to him or to others. He is attempting to withdraw from his world into a greater fantasy existence; however, his fantasy life often gives rise to distortions in reality and forces his thinking to a concrete level. He is both paranoid and disorganized, a combination that can only lead to more disorganization, withdrawal, and provides a great potential for "acting-out" behaviors. He is fearful of accepting adult roles and prefers a more juvenile existence. He feels vulnerable and probably anticipates impending disaster. Treatment planning should focus on containment of the schizophrenic decompensation. He needs to feel more comfortable in social relations, and much work is indicated in reorganizing his self-image in a realistic context. Direct supportive work with a "strong" male therapist is warranted, and investigation of the family as a potential source of intervention is worthwhile. Close supervision is necessary in the immediate future so as control for "acting-out" potentials.

PROTOCOL #9   D. C.—PARANOID SCHIZOPHRENIA

Referral.   This 48 year old married male high school janitor is a court referral. Approximately 3 weeks prior to examination his wife, age 30, told a next door neighbor that she was concerned because he husband had been "making vaginal inspections" on their 13 year old daughter each Sunday evening to ensure that "none of the high school boys had gotten to her." The neighbor reported this conversation to the police. It was confirmed by the wife, and subsequently, D. C. was arrested and charged with impairing the morals of a juvenile. The presiding jurist felt that the behavior of D. C. was bizzare and ordered a psychiatric evaluation, asking if the defendant could understand the charges against him or if he is "mentally limited" in some way as to believe that his actions were justifiable.

History.   D. C. has worked as a janitor in a high school for approximately 25 years. He obtained that position shortly after being discharged from military service, after spending 4 years as a motor vehicle mechanic. He is an only child, and both of his parents died while he was in high school. He lived with an uncle and aunt on a farm during his last 2 years of high school before entering the military. He enjoyed his two years of service in Europe after World War II, and admits to frequenting prostitutes, "it was just one of those things that a young boy does if he's given the chance." He married at the age of 34 after "having looked around." His wife was 16 at the time of the marriage. He likes his work but does not like the "attitudes" of the young boys in the high school about sex. He feels they are far too promiscuous and has vowed to protect his daughter "from those animals."

Protocol #9.   D. C., 48 Year Old Married, 1 Child (Age 13, Female), High School Graduate, Works as School Janitor

Card		Free Association		Inquiry	Scoring
I	116″	1. Well, I guess it ll a model, like a stage model, w.o. a head, we're at the bk of it, it isn't a good model but there's a distinction @ it	E: S: E: S:	(Rpts S's resp) The outline of a person's body, I d.k. whether it's man or wm, altho models r mostly wm, the arms & hands r up in the air U said we're at the back of it Yes, it ll the feet r going the opposite way	Do Mᵖ Hd P
		E: Most people c more than 1 thg			
		2. Well, I guess it cld b a fancy flower of s.s.	E: S: E: S:	(Rpts S's resp) Well it cld b one, altho I bet nobody ever saw one like this Cld u show me how u c it Well the leaves & petals r on the sides & the cntr is the stem, u can c thru part of it here where these holes r	WS− F− Bt 1.0
II	187″	3. U mite compare this to a puppet show where thy put puppets on their hands to represent what thyr talkg @ by demonstrating. Its blk magic of s.s., like to give a thrill, the white part mite b a lamp w fire comg out, & the puppets r operated from behind a screen, this dark part, that's the screen, it loks closer than they do	E: S:	(Rpts S's resp) The arms w the puppets r up here (points to upper red), its kind of a sawtoothed puppet behind ths curtain & the red is painted fire, like its not real, there's red on the puppets too so, well there's danger in red, it helps to build the thrill, I said blk magic bec. a.t. can be brought out by blk magic they say	WS+ Mᵃ.CF.FDw (2) H, Fi, Sym 4.5

443

Protocol #9 (Continued)

444

Card		Free Association		Inquiry	Scoring
III	65″	∨4. I'm going to compare ths to an hourglass, the picture represents time—it's nearing the time of turning over & starting over again	E: S:	(Rpts S's resp) It's rite here, the way I picture it's lik an hourglass shape & ths little white steak represents the stuff in it to represent time, its lik running thru	Ddo m^p- Hourglass
		5. Ths cld b some bloody stuff up at the top here	E: S:	(Rpts S's resp) Yes, it cld b s.t. bloody, I can't thk of what, mayb some piece of meat, it's all bloody, lik it was just cut or its painted to ll tht	Dv C Bl, Fd
IV	43″	6. Its a furry looking thg (feels card), lik the hide of a bear, sort of stretched out like a rug	E: S:	(Rpts S's resp) Well it has frt paws & there's an indication of the back here too & it has pretty good size to it too	Wo FTo Ad P 2.0
		7. It cld b a candle all melted out too, mayb its still burning at the top there but not much, most of it ll a heap of wax that melted off the candle	E: S: E: S:	(Rpts S's resp) Well, all those different colors make it ll wax from a candle & that cntr part is what's left of it but most of it has all melted into this here lump except the top where it's still burning a little Burning a little? The way it is there looks a little like its flame, just a low flame tho	$W+$ $m^a.YF_w$ Candle, Fi 4.0
V	38″	8. I'd say ths is a turtle opened out as if it were put back together it wld ll a turtle	E: S: E: S:	(Rpts S's resp) If the sides were brought together up under it, it wld ll a turtle I'm not certain how u c it The head is here (points to top) & the legs & paws r out here (end) so that it has the form of a turtle	$W-$ $F-$ A 1.0

VI	122″	9.	Ths c.b. an ornamental vase in which thy may hav used a fat or oil for a light. Thy put that in the littl top part vase & use it for lite, of course tht wld go way back before electric	*W*+ *m^a.FC'w* Vase, *Fi* 2.5

E: (Rpts *S*'s resp)
S: Yes, the *W* thg is lik a container of s.s., an oil container, with the lite prt on top, c ths littl streaks up here (points) r the lite it gives off, its lik a flame spreader, rather than shoot up it spreads it out lik w heat rays, u kno where there's fire there's heat & ths bttm prt is just a molding lik container & the oil container is at the top, its all made out of iron or s.t. lik that kind of metal, its all grey like iron wld b

VII	67″	V10.	I c a sort of road & a window & a model, I d.k. if she's a real model or a statue model, & there r steps leadg up each side, she's way back in there back of the steps, real tiny	*Dd*+ *FDw* (*H*), Steps 1.0

E: (Rpts *S*'s resp)
S: C in here there's the shape like a model & the window is right over her head (Points)
E: U mentioned a road & steps
S: The steps r here (points) for getting to the road I guess & she's way far off down the road
E: Far off
S: She's so tiny lik she's have to be far off

VIII	68″	V11.	Ths ll a land scene w mts, its an air view showg diffnt peaks & ravines w snow on them in the distance, these dots wld b trees	*DS_v* *CF.FV.CFo* *Ls* 4.0

E: (Rpts *S*'s resp)
S: Ths white prt wld b the snow, its a hi peak lik its rising upward & the green part is all belo the timberline & them dots & drk lines in the green all make it look pretty natural with trees and gullies

		12.	There's pliers here	*Ddo* *Fo* Pliers

E: (Rpts *S*'s resp)
S: C rite here (points), they ll a pair of tweezer pliers, needlenose pliers, to me, u can c the points real well & the handles must b here

Protocol #9 (Continued)

Card		Free Association	Inquiry	Scoring
IX 93"	<13.	Well if I turn it sideways it cld b an unusal water & land scene showg islands & vegetation & s.s. of an outlet leading thru the land to connect to the water on the other side, I cln't say whether its man made, but its all reflected down below here in the water	E: (Rpts S's resp) S: Ths green represents the island, the green maks it ll a lot of trees & the blue is the water & ths white part represents s.s. of outlet, its not too natural lookg so it must b man made & c its all the same dwn here lik a reflection	DdSv CF.rFo Ls 5.0
	14.	Ths prt ll s. bodies behind if u ask me, u don't c no legs r any other part, just a big behind	E: (Rpts S's resp) S: Yes, it just ll a big behind, a rear-end, lik of s.b. who's really fat, too fat	D− F− Hd
X 81"	V15.	Ths prt ll a connection across a sharp ravine w 2 persons reachg, handing s.t. to e.o., representing a sort of bridge of s.s.	E: (Rpts S's resp) S: It's an outline of 2 persons reachg across, both holdg s.t., lik handing s.t. across, it represents a connection E: Connection? S: Without them reachg across it wld just b a ravine of s.s. but w these men reachg out it illustrates a connection between them, not really handing s.t.. just a connection	D+ Mᵃo H, Sym 4.0
	16.	The launching of a missil, there's smoke at the base & the missil has fins on it	E: (Rpts S's resp) S: Its being launched now, c all the smoke @ it, that darkness there, its just takg off, lik a guided missil in war	Do mᵃ.YFo Missil
	<17.	Ths prt ll a dog, c his feet r out here, lik he is stretched out layg down lik dogs do	E: (Rpts S's resp) S: He's just stretched out there, c his feet & head & body, just restg	Do FMᵖo A

Note. Testing of limits failed to yield *P* responses on II, III, V, VII, VIII, or X.

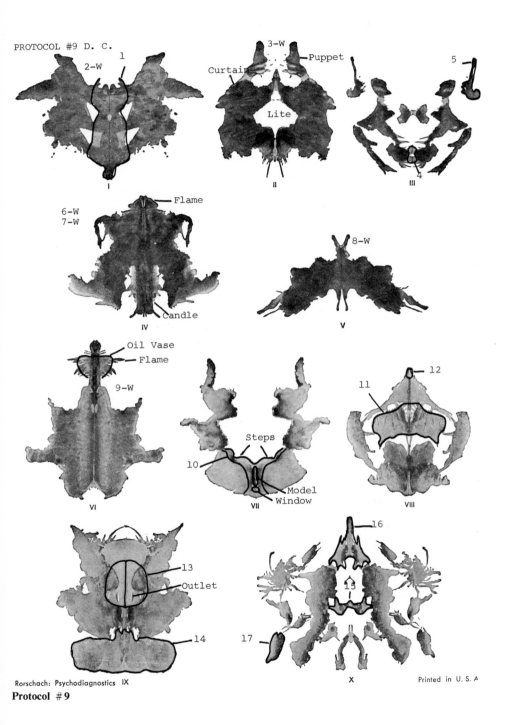

PROTOCOL #9 D. C.

I
2-W
1

II
3-W
Curtain
Puppet
Lite

III
5
4

IV
6-W
7-W
Flame
Candle

V
8-W

VI
Oil Vase
Flame
9-W

VII
Steps
10
Model
Window

VIII
11
12

IX
13
Outlet
14

X
16
15
17

Rorschach: Psychodiagnostics

Printed in U.S.A

Protocol #9

Table 46. Structural Summary for Protocol #9—D. C.

$R = 17$	$Zf = 10$	$Z\text{Sum} = 29.0$	$P = 2$	$(2) = 2$

Location Features	Determinants	Contents	Contents (Idiographic)

Location Features

$W = 6$	**DQ**
$D = 7$	$+ = 5$
$Dd = 4$	$o = 7$
$S = 4$	$v = 2$
$DW = 0$	$- = 3$

FORM QUALITY

FQx	FQf
$+ = 0$	$+ = 0$
$o = 8$	$o = 1$
$w = 4$	$w = 0$
$- = 4$	$- = 3$

Determinants

$M.CF.FD$	$= 1$
$m.YF$	$= 2$
$m.FC'$	$= 1$
$CF.FV.C'F$	$= 1$
$CF.rF$	$= 1$
M	$= 2$
FM	$= 1$
m	$= 1$
C	$= 1$
CF	$=$
FC	$=$
C'	$=$
$C'F$	$=$
FC'	$=$
T	$=$
TF	$=$
FT	$= 1$
V	$=$
VF	$=$
FV	$=$
Y	$=$
YF	$=$
FY	$=$
rF	
Fr	$=$
FD	$= 1$
F	$= 4$

Contents

H	$= 1$
(H)	$= 2$
Hd	$= 2$
(Hd)	$=$
A	$= 2$
(A)	$=$
Ad	$= 1$
(Ad)	$=$
Ab	$=$
Al	$=$
An	$=$
Art	$=$
Ay	$=$
Bl	$= 1$
Bt	$= 1$
Cg	$=$
Cl	$=$
Ex	$=$
Fi	$= 0, 3$
Fd	$= 0, 1$
Ge	$=$
Hh	$=$
Ls	$= 2$
Na	$=$
Sx	$=$
Xy	$=$

Contents (Idiographic)

Candle	$= 1$
Hourglass	$= 1$
Missil	$= 1$
Oil Vase	$= 1$
Pliers	$= 1$
Steps	$= 0, 1$
Symbolism	$= 0, 2$
	$=$

RATIOS, PERCENTAGES, AND DERIVATIONS

$Z\text{Sum}/Z\text{est} = 29.0/31.0$	$FC/CF + C = 0/4$	$Afr = .70$
$Zd = -2.0$	$W/M = 6/3$	$3r + (2)/R = 5/17 = .29$
$EB = 3/4.5 \quad EA = 7.5$	$W/D = 6/7$	$\text{Cont}/R = 10/17$
$eb = 5/6 \quad ep = 11$	$L = .31$	$H + Hd/A + Ad = 5/3$
$\text{Blends}/R = 6/17$	$F+\% = 25$	$H + A/Hd + Ad = 5/3$
$a/p = 5/3$	$X+\% = 47$	XRT Achrom $= 77.2''$
$M^a/M^p = 2/1$	$A\% = 18$	XRT Chrom $= 98.8''$

448

Table 47.   Sequence of Scores for Protocol # 9—D. C.

Card	RT	No.	Location	Determinant(s)		Content(s)	Pop	Z Score
I	116″	1.	*Do*	M^po		*Hd*	*P*	
		2.	*WS*−	*F*−		*Bt*		1.0
II	187″	3.	*WS*+	$M^a.CF.FDw$ (2)		(*H*), *Fi*, Sym		4.5
III	65″	4.	*Dd*−	m^p−		Hourglass		
		5.	*Dv*	*C*		*Bl, Fd*		
IV	43″	6.	*Wo*	*FTo*		*Ad*	*P*	2.0
		7.	*W*+	$m^a.YFw$		Candle, *Fi*		4.0
V	38″	8.	*W*−	*F*−		*A*		1.0
VI	122″	9.	*W*+	$m^a.FC'w$		Vase, *Fi*		2.5
VII	67″	10.	*Dd*+	*FDw*		(*H*), Steps		1.0
VIII	68″	11.	*DSo*	$CF.FV.C'Fo$		*Ls*		4.0
		12.	*Ddo*	*Fo*		Pliers		
IX	93″	13.	*DdSv*	*CF.rFo*		*Ls*		5.0
		14.	*Do*	*F*−		*Hd*		
X	81″	15.	*D*+	M^ao	(2)	*H*, Sym		4.0
		16.	*Do*	$m^a.YFo$		Missil		
		17.	*Do*	EM^po		*A*		

ANALYSIS OF THE STRUCTURE

The diagnosis of schizophrenia is readily apparent in the structure of the record. The *Zf* is elevated; however, the *P* frequency is very low, the *DQ* distribution quite variable, including three minus scores, the *F*+ % and *X*+ % are disastrously low, and the *FC/CF* + *C* ratio plus the low Lambda indicate extremely limited affective control. The *EB* suggests some flexibility in response style; however, the *ep* reveals considerable resources which are not controlled or well organized. The Affective Ratio indicates that he is prone to affective responsiveness and the *H* to *A* ratio signals the possibility of an unusual preoccupation with people. The wide range of content appears to reflect much idiographic thinking, and the emphasis on *Dd* and *S* in the record hints of a negative and obsessive form of ideation. The very long mean reaction times illustrate an attempt at delay; however, the very poor form quality, especially the three minus Pure *F* answers, reveals that this delaying tactic is generally ineffectual. There are four inanimate movement answers in the record, suggesting considerable stress at this time. The six shading answers give evidence of pain and reflect attempts to constrain his affect. His labile responsiveness to color, including a Pure *C* response, illustrates the failures of his defenses and offers indications of the futility of his attempts to organize and restrain himself. Four of the five human responses are parenthesized or human detail, also suggesting a paranoid form of thinking. This is also implied by the range of idiographic contents, especially the symbolism responses.

Specific propositions generated by the structural data are as follows:

1. He is schizophrenic.
2. He is unable to perceive, or at least is unable to respond to ambiguity in a conventional manner. His reality testing is very limited.

3. He is labile, and when affective responses occur, they are usually in command of his cognitive operations.

4. Much of his thinking is very idiographic, and a paranoid style of ideation appears to be present.

5. He is experiencing considerable stress and affective pain, and has attempted to control his thinking and affect by a passive, delaying response style; however, this is generally ineffective.

ANALYSIS OF THE SCORING SEQUENCE

His approach is quite variable, suggesting considerable fluctuation in his cognitive activity. One of his poorest responses occurs to Card V, generally the easiest card in the test. He manifests great difficulty with Cards II and III, being unable to use good form quality on either one. All of his *m* answers are marked by weak or minus form, betraying the substantial impact of stress on his reality operations. No new propositions are developed from the scoring sequence; however, these data do reaffirm a serious cognitive disruption.

ANALYSIS OF THE FREE ASSOCIATIONS

The Free Associations illustrate a classic study in paranoid symbolism. The model is facing away, "It isn't a good model," the puppets are involved in "black magic," a road and model and window are presented in Card VII, and part of Card IX is "somebody's behind." The anal preoccupation, the magical thinking, and the hint of voyeurism are all common features among paranoid schizophrenics. A substantial emphasis on sexual symbolism is also apparent in the record. The candle is "still burning at the top, but not much," the phallic-like area of Card VI is an ornamental vase which may have used a "fat or oil for light," there is "smoke at the base of the missile," and the hourglass is "nearing the time of turning over." Each of these answers contributes to the hypothesis that he is sexually preoccupied, probably as a result of his own feelings of impotency. His single interpersonal response, on Card X, keeps people distant and symbolic, but hints that he is interested in "re-establishing" some form of contact. He is the candle, "all melted out . . . still burning but not much." He is the turtle "opened out," his shell having been broken by stress, waiting to be put back together again. In this context, it seems likely that he has lived a "schizoid" life style for quite some time, a pattern that has gradually disintegrated because of his own sexual conflicts and frustrations.

Specific propositions developed from the Free Associations are as follows:

1. He has magical thinking in his paranoid ideation.

2. He has a pronounced sexual preoccupation, focusing on his own feelings of impotency.

3. He has apparently lived a detached existence for quite some time but current stresses have ruptured his defenses.

4. He is interested in forming some interpersonal contact but on a very cautious level.

ANALYSIS OF THE INQUIRY

Some sexual confusion may be evidenced in his difficulties in identifying the sex of the figure in Card I. His magical ideation is also evidenced in Card I by his statement, "nobody ever saw one like this," suggesting a kind of omnipotence in his voyeurism. He vacillates in his attempt to deny affective involvement on Card II, "the red is painted fire like its not real . . . anything can be brought out by black magic they say." The latter statement also implies a sense of power in his thinking. The weak attempt at affective denial is also noted in Card III, "its all bloody like it was just cut, or its painted to look like that." His lengthy elaboration concerning his response to Card VI is particularly interesting and seems to dramatize his sexual preoccupation. His feeling of omnipotence is again illustrated by his emphasis on the connection in his answer to Card X, "without them reaching across it would just be a ravine." This description also hints of a possible homosexual interest, as do the answers which include reference to "behinds" and "rear-ends."

Some clarifying hypotheses may be developed from this material:

1. There is some sexual confusion included in his preoccupation.
2. He is prone to deny his affect, but the product of this attempt is generally ineffective.
3. There is a sense of omnipotence in his thinking, as if he has some special power.
4. There is evidence of a homosexual interest and it seems reasonable to speculate that some of his heterosexual preoccupation is a form of defense against this.

A SUMMARY OF D. C.

This is a seriously disorganized individual whose thinking is often distorted, whose affect frequently commands his responses, who is in much pain, and who is no longer able to defend himself effectively. He has lost much of his ability to perceive things conventionally, and substitutes less realistic forms of cognitive interpretation which include magical thinking, feelings of omnipotence, and a paranoid style of ideation. He has a pronounced sexual preoccupation, seems confused regarding his own sex role, and exhibits some forms of homosexual interest, although the latter is probably not directly manifest in behavior. He feels old and impotent, and recent events appear to have broken his "shell" of defense. He is no doubt able to justify the vaginal inspections of his daughter and at the same time ventilate some of his own sexual needs. He is a rather pathetic man, old before his time, helpless in his world, and confused by his own thoughts. He would like contact with others but appears to have no realistic understanding of how this might be achieved. The fact that he married a much younger woman suggests that his feelings of sexual insecurity may have existed for a considerable time, and his activities with his daughter may be a "magical" reenactment of that marriage. Intervention should be oriented first toward the reestablishment of a more adequate level of reality testing, possibly through a well planned reinforcement routine. Once that is accomplished, a program of marital and social rehabilitation will be necessary. His age, and extent of confusion, argue against efforts at uncovering forms of therapy. A more direct supportive approach, supplemented by group techniques will probably have the best chances for success.

PROTOCOL #10 M. H.—A QUESTION OF REMISSION

Referral. This 40 year old married male has been hospitalized for a period of 7 months, with a diagnosis of "schizophrenia, undifferentiated." He has been treated with large doses of antipsychotic medication, plus supportive psychotherapy, plus group psychotherapy, plus a variety of other milieu accoutrements. During his first 2 months in the hospital he was actively hallucinating that others were accusing him of being homosexual. He also manifests a delusion that his wife had hospitalized him so that she could have an affair with a local minister. Beginning in the third month of hospitalization the hallucinatory experiences subsided, and by the fifth month had completely disappeared and the delusion concerning his wife was no longer mentioned. At that time his appetite improved, his medication level reduced substantially, and he began taking an active role in a variety of hospital routines such as occupational therapy, recreational events, and such. He is now being considered for discharge; however, some staff members believe that this may be premature, while others who are in favor of discharge are interested in developing a sound aftercare routine.

History. M. H. is a tall, slender, average looking high school graduate who has worked as a welder for nearly 20 years. He is the fourth of six children, having one older and one younger brother, and two older and one younger sisters. He married at the age of 19, shortly after graduating from high school to a young girl that he had been "going steady with" for 2 years. They have five children, ages 18, 15, 13, 11, and 10, all girls. He completed a 6 month apprentice welder's training shortly after his marriage and has been gainfully employed in that occupation ever since, except for a 4 month period about 5 years ago when he injured his back in an auto accident. He developed frequent headaches after returning to work and has been examined twice for them, but with negative findings in both instances. He describes his relationship with his wife as "o.k. except that she always wants things that we can't afford." His wife reports that he had been active in several hobbies such as fishing, hunting, and bowling, prior to his auto accident, but that his interest in these activities has diminished significantly since that time. She describes his "breakdown" as occurring gradually, beginning with accusations that she was no longer interested in him, and later, indicating that he was aware of a relationship between she and a local minister. She has been active in their church, but disclaims any close relationship with the pastor, "I've always loved my husband and I want him to get well." He was hospitalized shortly after accusing several co-workers of spreading rumors that he was homosexual, and threatening the life of one of them. At the time of admission he reported that "people come in the bedroom at night and say dirty things about me."

Protocol #10. M. H., 40 Year Old Schizophrenic In-Patient Being Considered for Discharge

Card		Free Association		Inquiry	Scoring
I	5″	1. Ths a bat	E:	(Rpts S's resp)	Wo Fo A P 1.0
			S:	There's his wgs & his body & his claws	
		2. A bee	E:	(Rpts S's resp)	Do Fw A
			S:	Just ths cntr body structure here, the framework ll the bee structure, here's the head	
		3. Also a child in the nude standing backwards	E:	(Rpts S's resp)	Do M^{p}o Hd
			S:	The lower part, the rump & the legs, its just the outline there's no head or a.t.	
II	3″	4. Two dogs kissing	E:	(Rpts S's resp)	D+ FM^{a}o (2) Ad P 3.0
			S:	There's the outline of the body structure, the ears & the nose. They'r attempting to kiss, c, like this (points)	
			E:	I'm not sure I c the dogs lik u do	
			S:	Just the tops of em, c, heads	
III	7″	5. I c 2 wm leaning ovr a table	E:	(Rpts S's resp)	D+ M^{p}o (2) H P 3.0
			S:	There's one & the other (points) excludg the red again, there's the legs & body & bust & face. That c.b. a table they'r ovr	
IV	18″	6. Its some form of head	E:	(Rpts S's resp)	Dd− F− Ad
			S:	I c s.t. lik a set of eyes here, it mayb lik an A or s.t., all I can c is the structure of a head or s.t. from here to here	
V	10″	∨7. It ll a deer that just got it, cut slashed thru the gut	E:	(Rpts S's resp)	W− F− A 1.0
			S:	There's the hindqurtrs, lik he's gutted lik for draining, his body's spread open	
			E:	Sprd open?	
			S:	Yeah, ths sides r the same & it ll he mite b split opn w his hindqurts lik that	

453

Protocol # 10 (Continued)

454

Card		Free Association	Inquiry	Scoring
VI	12″	8. It ll a bear rug on the floor	E: (Rpts S's resp) S: Its just an opn bear rug E: I'm not sure how u c it S: Lik a fur rug, lik the outlin repres a bear, lik a scatter rug on the floor	Do Fo Ad P
VII	23″	9. It ll features of *A*'s	E: (Rpts S's resp) S: Lik a cartoonish sort of an *A* with this one here & his mate, just the heads	Do Fo (2) (Ad)
		10. There r 2 girls kissg there	E: (Rpts S's resp) S: Kissing or looking at e.o. w.o. making contact. There's the pony tail in the air & the sillouettes of the faces	D+ M^{a}o (2) Hd P 3.0
VIII	12″	11. It ll the frame of a turkey	E: (Rpts S's resp) S: Its lik a turkey breast & the outer wgs & ths is his bone structure, its basically the outline & the bone structure re me of a turkey	W− F− Ad 4.5
IX	30″	12. It ll a skull in the cntr	E: (Rpts S's resp) S: The white outline cntr part w the eyes here, it ll a sillout of a skull, the white color makes it ll that	DdS− FC′− Skull
X	4″	13. Ths is very pretty, it ll a cpl of birds in the tree	E: (Rpts S's resp) S: Rite here on each side, these r little branches cause of the brownish color & thes r birds in them, sitting there	D+ FM^p.FCo (2) A,Bt 4.0
		14. A cpl of lobsters, thats about it	E: (Rpts S's resp) S: These thgs here, these blue thgs, just the silloutte of them	Do Fo (2) A P

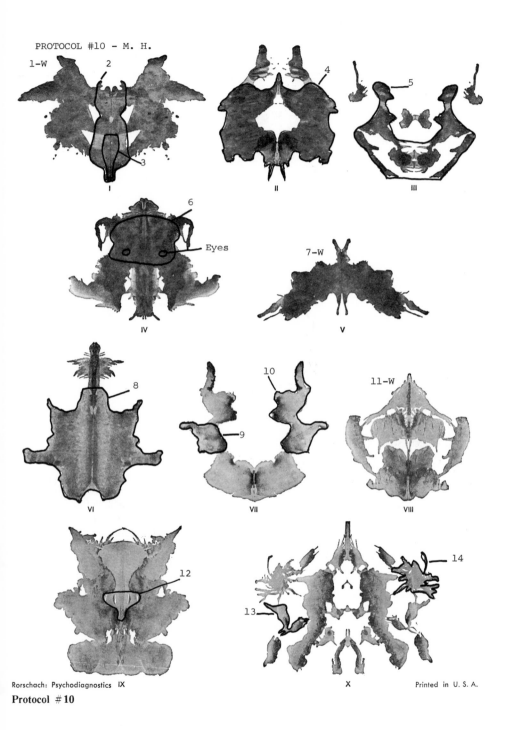

PROTOCOL #10 - M. H.

Protocol #10

Table 48. Structural Summary for Protocol #10—M. H.

$R = 14$ $Zf = 7$ $Z\text{Sum} = 19.5$ $P = 6$ $(2) = 6$

Location Features	Determinants	Contents	Contents (Idiographic)
W $= 3$ DQ	$FM.FC = 1$	H $= 1$	$\underline{\text{Skull}}$ $= 1$
		$(H) =$	
D $= 9$ $+ = 4$	M $= 3$	$Hd = 2$	$\underline{\hspace{1cm}}$ $=$
	$FM = 1$	$(Hd) =$	
$Dd = 2$ $o = 6$	m $=$	A $= 5$	$\underline{\hspace{1cm}}$ $=$
	C $=$	$(A) =$	
S $= 1$ $v = 0$	$CF =$	$Ad = 4$	$\underline{\hspace{1cm}}$ $=$
	$FC =$	$(Ad) = 1$	
$DW = 0$ $- = 4$	$C' =$	$Ab =$	$\underline{\hspace{1cm}}$ $=$
	$C'F =$	$Al =$	
	$FC' = 1$	$An =$	$\underline{\hspace{1cm}}$ $=$
	T $=$	$Art =$	
FORM QUALITY	$TF =$	$Ay =$	$\underline{\hspace{1cm}}$ $=$
	$FT =$	$Bl =$	
FQx FQf	V $=$	Bt $= 0, 1$	$\underline{\hspace{1cm}}$ $=$
	Y $=$	Cl	
$+ = 0$ $+ = 0$	$FV =$	Cg $=$	
	$VF =$	Ex $=$	
$o = 9$ $o = 4$	$YF =$	Fi $=$	
	$FY = 1$	Fd $=$	
$w = 1$ $w = 1$	$rF =$	Ge $=$	
	$Fr =$	Hh $=$	
$- = 4$ $- = 2$	$FD =$	Ls $=$	
	F $= 7$	Na $=$	
		Sx $=$	
		Xy $=$	

RATIOS, PERCENTAGES, AND DERIVATIONS

$Z\text{Sum}/Z\text{est} = 19.5/20.5$	$FC/CF + C = 1/0$	Afr $= .40$
$Zd = -1.0$	W/M $= 3/3$	$3r + (2)/R$ $= 6/14 = .43$
$EB = 3/0.5$ $EA = 3.5$	W/D $= 3/9$	Cont/R $= 3/14$
$eb = 2/2$ $ep = 4$	L $= 1.00$	$H + Hd/A + Ad = 3/10$
$\text{Blends}/R = 1/14$	$F+\%$ $= 57$	$H + A/Hd + Ad = 6/7$
a/p $= 2/3$	$X+\%$ $= 64$	XRT Achrom $= 13.6$
M^a/M^p $= 1/2$	$A\%$ $= 71$	XRT Chrom $= 11.2$

Table 49.   Sequence of Scores for Protocol #10—M. H.

Card	RT	No.	Location	Determinant(s)		Content(s)	Pop	Z Score
I	5''	1.	*Wo*	*Fo*		*A*	*P*	1.0
		2.	*Do*	*Fw*		*A*		
		3.	*Do*	*Mᵖo*		*Hd*		
II	3''	4.	*D+*	*FMᵃo*	(2)	*Ad*	*P*	3.0
III	7''	5.	*D+*	*Mᵖo*	(2)	*H*	*P*	3.0
IV	18''	6.	*Dd−*	*FY−*		*Ad*		
V	10''	7.	*W−*	*F−*		*A*		1.0
VI	12''	8.	*Do*	*Fo*		*Ad*	*P*	
VII	23''	9.	*Do*	*Fo*	(2)	*(Ad)*		
		10.	*D+*	*Mᵃo*	(2)	*Hd*	*P*	3.0
VIII	12''	11.	*W−*	*F−*		*Ad*		4.5
IX	30''	12.	*DdS−*	*FC'−*		Skull		
X	4''	13.	*D+*	*FMᵖ.FCo*	(2)	*A, Bt*		4.0
		14.	*Fo*	*Fo*	(2)	*A*	*P*	

ANALYSIS OF THE STRUCTURE

The brevity of the record signals caution to the usefulness of some ratios and percentages; however, several of those most important to the questions in the referral are obvious enough to provide a significant input. The *EB* indicates that he is basically oriented toward internalization as a source of gratification for his more fundamental needs. All of his *M* answers use satisfactory form quality, suggesting that his ideation is not overly distorted, even though his reality testing, as evidenced by the $F+\%$ and $X+\%$ is impaired. The very high Lambda and high $A\%$ present a constricted, somewhat stereotyped pattern of activity, and his a/p ratio indicates a generally passive orientation. There is little affect displayed in the record, suggesting that his passive and constrictive response style has contained, and possibly "flattened" his affect to some extent. The low Affective Ratio may indicate his withdrawal from the environment, although the low R in the record makes this conclusion somewhat tentative. The unusually high proportion of *Hd* and *Ad* contents hints of a continuation of a paranoid form of suspiciousness, and attempts to narrow his world to a more "workable" size. The restricted content range also suggests a narrow, stereotyped form of thinking and behavior.

Specific propositions generated by the structural data are as follows:

1. He is oriented toward internalization and has developed strong affective controls, so much so that his affect appears to be somewhat "flat" at this time.

2. Although his ideation does not appear to be grossly distorted, his reality testing is markedly limited and he is prone to gross distortions of reality in maintaining his rigid and containing patterns of thought.

3. His thinking and behavior are generally stereotyped in a defensive pattern of constriction. He is somewhat withdrawn from his world and continually attempts to narrow perceptual inputs so as to make them easier to deal with.

4. There is evidence of some paranoid forms of ideation.

ANALYSIS OF THE SCORING SEQUENCE

Although there is considerable variation in reaction times, no specific patterns of delay are obvious. His approach is essentially oriented toward more "easy to see" details, and he has difficulty in using the entire blot in two of his three attempts. This indicates that, unless he can control the breadth of stimulus inputs, he may be overwhelmed by a feeling of disorganization. The *P* failures on Cards V and VIII are also notable as they are among the more easily perceived. No new specific hypotheses are developed from the scoring sequence.

ANALYSIS OF THE FREE ASSOCIATIONS

A variety of clues suggesting a continuation of paranoid ideation are evident in the Free Associations. The child is nude and standing "backwards," a head is selected to an internal *Dd* area of Card IV, the deer just "got it, cut . . . through the gut." Kissing responses, one of dogs, the other of girls, reflect an oral, and possibly homosexual orientation. He is very cautious in many of his descriptions, such as "some form of head," "the features of an animal," and the "frame of a turkey." The turkey and skull answers appear to illustrate some feelings of "emptiness" and exposure to others.

Specific postulates developed from the Free Associations are as follows:

1. He is quite guarded and maintains an active form of paranoid ideation.
2. His sexual orientation appears somewhat juvenile and maybe homosexually oriented.
3. In part, his cautious and guarded approach relates to his own feelings of being exposed and vulnerable.

ANALYSIS OF THE INQUIRY

The Inquiry offers little more than a reaffirmation of previously developed postulates. The dogs and the girls are not quite kissing, the dogs attempting to, the girls possibly just looking at each other. The slashed deer answer on Card V illustrates his own feelings of exposure, as if he had been the "gutted" one. When he does display affect, as on Card X, it is a bird passively sitting on a limb. Many of his answers refer to "structures" or "silhouettes," both of which seem to convey his attempts at concealment and may represent an unclear form of body concern; that is, he does not want to be seen.

A SUMMARY OF M. H.

This is generally an impoverished record of an impoverished person. The distortions in reality operations, the flatness of affect, and the paranoid ideation, which apparently marked the condition at its onset are still present, but much more contained by a behavioral and ideational process of constriction and stereotypy. He is preoccupied with sexuality and appears to have some homosexual orientation; however, much of this is controlled, at least marginally, by his constricted pattern of responsiveness. He is not yet able to deal with complex stimulus inputs, and his reality testing sometimes fails dramatically under these conditions. For this reason it may be premature to release him from a controlled structured environment at this time, unless careful provisions are made to ensure no unusual stress situations, and to limit the breadth of the environment with which he will have to contend. It may be more appropriate to undertake a series of "trial visits" to his home or to place him in a "halfway house" routine wherein he might return to the hospital each evening after completing some planned, and reasonably well structured activities. Preparation of the family for his return also seems very important, especially with regard to the role that his wife may play in his new adjustment. Continuation of support through medication seems clearly warranted, and drastic alterations in the medical routine should be avoided until firm evidence exists for such changes.

CHAPTER 20

Children in Trouble

The Rorschach has a long history of usefulness with younger clients. Several important normative works, especially those of Ames et al., have contributed to a better understanding of the fact that Rorschach response patterns are often somewhat different in children than in adults. For instance, the appearance of M responses is less common in the protocols of very young children, than those of latency age, or of adolescents. Similarly, CF and C responses occur with greater frequency in the records of the very young, than do the more controlled FC answers. Children tend more to give W answers than to select D locations, and the use of animal contents is usually much greater than in adult records. Nevertheless, the psychological significance of each of the Rorschach features remains the same for clients of all ages, and in general, the same interpretive postulates can be derived from the series of scores, configurations, ratios, and such. It is quite important, however, that the interpretations be organized in the context of that which is known about children from the developmental literature. For example, children are usually expected to have less emotional control than adults. They are also not expected to manifest the well developed and "deeper" interpersonal relationships that characterize maturity, and they are expected to manifest more signs of dependency needs. In other words, Rorschach data collected from younger clients will only be as useful as the interpreters' understanding of the developmental process, and the common features of children at different age levels. No reference group has been assembled in the development of the comprehensive system that deals with children; however, as the protocols included here demonstrate, it is of use with younger clients.

PROTOCOL #11   R. J.—AN ISOLATE

Referral.   This 11 year old male was referred for evaluation by a concerned fifth grade teacher, with the reluctant consent of the parents. R. J.'s academic performance has fluctuated from "superior to disastrous," but with no particular pattern of interest being evident. On some days he approaches problems in a given area, such as math, with an "almost uncanny skill." On other days his work in math will be "totally incorrect, almost as if he were paying no attention at all to the task." He "daydreams" a great deal in school and appears to have no close friends. He often requests permission to "stay in" at recess, but rarely gives a reason for the request which "makes sense," except to say that he does not feel like going outside. His parents are unaware of any "disinterest" in things, citing the fact that he is outside of the house "almost continuously" when not in school. They admit that they do not know of close friends, but argue that he does play with neighborhood children frequently. The teacher's question asks whether there is anything seriously wrong with him, and she asks how, if at all, she may help. The parents believe that evaluation is a waste of time, but "want to do the right thing by him."

History.   R. J. is the older of two sons in an upper middle class family. His father is an executive in industrial sales, and "works long hours." The mother is socially active, but "I never neglect my children." R. J.'s birth and medical history are unremarkable. He is slightly short for his age but weight is normal. He is interested in radios and TV, but has no specific hobbies. He knows little about athletics, but does enjoy bicycle riding. He feels that his younger brother is a pest, and looks on the need for evaluation as a burden.

462

Protocol #11. R. J., 11 Years Old, One Younger Brother (Age 8), Currently in 5th Grade, Parents Both Living, Father Employed in Midmanagement position

Card		Free Association	Inquiry	Scoring
I	5″	1. Wow, that don't ll much 2 me, I guess it cld b a halloween mask	E: (Rpts S's resp) S: C the eyes & mouth (points) & it has big ears out here & its all black like a witches mask	WSo FC'o Mask 1.0
		E: Most people c more than 1 thg		
		2. I guess it cld b a bf too, no not a bf, more like a bat cause its all dark	E: (Rpts S's resp) S: Yeah, a bat, c its all black & its got these claws out in front like it was trying to grab s.t. E: Could u show me where u c it? S: Here r the wgs & ths is the body & the tail & the claws	Wo FM^a.FC' A P 1.0
II	11″	3. Ths ll 2 dogs rubbing their noses together	E: (Rpts S's resp) S: Rite here, just the head parts & their noses r touchg	D+ FM^{a}o (2) Ad P 3.0
		4. Hey, ths part cld b a rocket ship, its taking off like on a moon mission	E: (Rpts S's resp) S: Here is the nose cone, the capsule w the astronuts & ths is the rocket & ths is all the fire at blastoff	DS+ m^a.CF+ Rocket, Fi 4.5
III	6″	5. Ths is really weird, it ll 2 guys fiting over s.t.	E: (Rpts S's resp) S: They'r really pulling hard to get ths thg in the middle, it must b worth a lot E: Worth a lot? S: Well yeah, or thy wldn't b fiting over it	D+ M^{a}o (2) H P 3.0
		Can I turn ths? (E: If u want)		
		V6._ Ths way it ll a space creature that's tryg to catch ths bf	E: (Rpts S's resp) S: C the big claws & eyes, its like from outer space, you kno? Ths red part is a bf & ths thg is tryg to trap it & eat it up	D+ M^{a}o (H),A P 4.0

IV	23″	7.	Geez, ths ll s.s. of monster A lik from Mt Everest, I wldn't want to meet up w him	*E:*	(Rpts *S*'s resp)		
				S:	Yeah, wow, c he's got little scrawny arms hanging dwn there that probably get big when he reaches out, it really ll he's laying down cause his feet r so big, I dk wht ths thg is in the cntr, I don't thk that's part of him	*Do*	*Mp.FDo (H)*
		V8.	If I look ths way, that other part ll the head of a caterpillr	*E:*	(Rpts *S*'s resp)		
				S:	It's got those little feelers like I've seen in school & a flat end like a caterpillar	*Do Fo Ad*	
V	6″	9.	Holy geez, did u make these up, ths one ll one of those guys that comes up from the cemetery, uh, uh, vampire	*E:*	(Rpts *S*'s resp)		
				S:	He's got this big cloak w his arms spread out like he was getting ready to fly off	*Wo Mᵃ.FC'o (H) 1.0*	
				E:	Can u show me how u c it?		
				S:	C the wgs r here (points) & ths is his body w the skinny legs & he's all black like those guys		
		10.	Hey, ths ll an alligator's head	*E:*	(Rpts *S*'s resp)		
				S:	C, rite here, it ll an alligator to me, u can't c the rest of him	*Do Fo Ad*	
VI	3″	11.	Hah, I kno what ths is, it's like that coyote in the road runner cartoon after he's been run over by somethg	*E:*	(Rpts *S*'s resp)		
				S:	C he has a nose here (points) & here's his body all flattened out, u can tell that it's all furry by ths lines in it	*Wo FTo A P 2.5*	
		V12.	If u turn it ths way it ll some little birds in the nest waiting for their mother to feed them	*E:*	(Rpts *S*'s resp)		
				S:	C u can just make out their heads & ths is the nest part & they'r like waiting for food, like robins or s.t.	*Ddo FMᵖo (2) Ad*	
VII	3″	13.	Ths ll a cple of indians to me thy'r arguing about which way they should go	*S:*	I dk wht ths bottom thg is but the indians r up here & each one is pointing in a different direction, lik they were arguing about which way the rite trail was, I guess they'r behind ths rock, yeah that's what the bottm part must b	*W+ Mᵃ.FD (2) (H) P 2.5*	

463

Protocol #11 (Continued)

Card		Free Association		Inquiry	Scoring
	V14.	Here r a cple of elephant heads	E: S:	(Rpts S's resp) See the trunk here & the eye, it's just heads tho, no body that I can c	Do Fo (2) Ad
VIII	15.	6″ Hey, neat, ths ll a cpl of mt lions climbing up a mt	E: S:	(Rpts S's resp) It ll thy r tryg to get at ths thg at the top, some A I guess but I dk what, they'r crawling & climbg on some rocks or s.t., it ll in the forest cause all the colors r lik plants & trees & rocks	W+ FMª.FCo (2) A,Bt P 4.5
IX	16.	5″ It ll 2 witches up here & thyr lookg into ths cntr thg, lik a crystal ball of s.s., I dk what the rest is	E: S:	(Rpts S's resp) Yeah, lik thy'r leaning bk after thy lookd in ths ball thg in the middle, lik they didn't lik what thy saw, thy hav thos witch hats on & thos big robes lik witches wear	D+ Mªo (2) (H) 2.5
X	17.	12″ Boy, I dk what ths cld b, I guess these blue thgs cld b crabs	E: S:	(Rpts S's resp) Well, thy cld b, all the legs & all	Do Fo (2) A P
	18.	I c a rabbits head too	E: S:	(Rpts S's resp) Rite dwn here, c the ears & eyes, its just his head part	Do Fo Ad

464

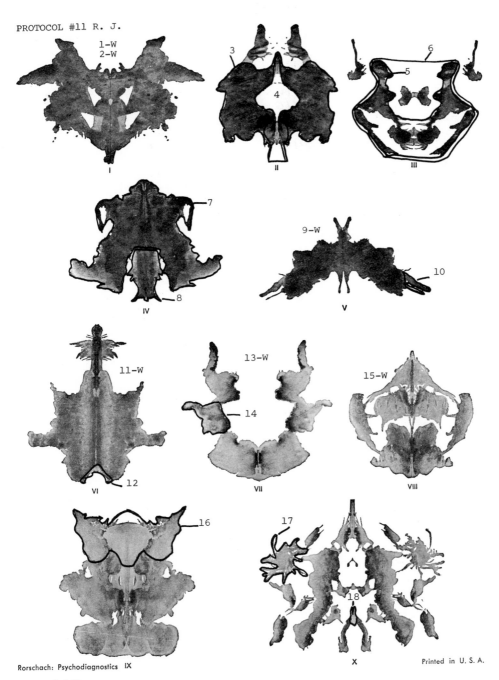

PROTOCOL #11 R. J.

1-W
2-W

I

3
4

II

6
5

III

7

8

IV

9-W
10

V

11-W
12

VI

13-W
14

VII

15-W

VIII

16

IX

17
18

X

Rorschach: Psychodiagnostics

Printed in U. S. A.

Protocol #11

465

Table 50. Structural Summary for Protocol #11—R. J.

$R = 18$　　　　$Zf = 11$　　　　　$Z\text{Sum} = 29.5$　　　$P = 8$　　$(2) = 8$

Location Features		Determinants	Contents	Contents (Idiographic)
$W = 6$	DQ	$M.FC' = 1$	$H = 1$	$\underline{\text{Mask}} = 1$
		$M.FD = 2$	$(H) = 5$	
$D = 11$	$+ = 7$	$FM.FC = 1$	$Hd =$	$\underline{\text{Rocket}} = 1$
		$FM.FC' = 1$	$(Hd) =$	
$Dd = 1$	$o = 11$	$m.CF = 1$	$A = 4, 1$	$\underline{\qquad} =$
		$M = 3$	$(A) =$	
$S = 2$	$v = 0$	$FM = 2$	$Ad = 6$	$\underline{\qquad} =$
		$m =$	$(Ad) =$	
$DW = 0$	$- = 0$	$C =$	$Ab =$	$\underline{\qquad} =$
		$CF =$	$Al =$	
		$FC =$	$An =$	$\underline{\qquad} =$
		$C' =$	$Art =$	
FORM QUALITY		$C'F =$	$Ay =$	$\underline{\qquad} =$
		$FC' = 1$	$Bl =$	
FQx	FQf	$T =$	$Bt = 0, 1$	$\underline{\qquad} =$
		$TF =$	$Cg =$	
$+ = 1$	$+ = 0$	$FT = 1$	$Cl =$	
		$V =$	$Ex =$	
$o = 17$	$o = 5$	$VF =$	$Fi = 0, 1$	
		$FV =$	$Fd =$	
$w = 0$	$w = 0$	$Y =$	$Ge =$	
		$YF =$	$Hh =$	
$- = 0$	$- = 0$	$FY =$	$Ls =$	
		$rF =$	$Na =$	
		$Fr =$	$Sx =$	
		$FD =$	$Xy =$	
		$F = 5$		

RATIOS, PERCENTAGES, AND DERIVATIONS

$Z\text{Sum}/Z\text{est} = 29.5/34.5$　　　$FC/CF + C = 1/1$　　　$Afr \qquad = .29$

$Zd = -5.0$　　　　　　　　　$W/M \qquad = 6/6$　　　$3r + (2)/R = 8/18 = .44$

$EB = 6/1.5$　　$EA = 7.5$　　$W/D \qquad = 6/11$　　$\text{Cont}/R \qquad = 4/18$

$eb = 5/4$　　　$ep = 9$　　　$L \qquad = .38$　　　$H + Hd/A + Ad = 6/10$

$\text{Blends}/R = 4/18$　　　　　$F+\% \qquad = 100$　　$H + A/Hd + Ad = 10/6$

$a/p \qquad = 9/2$　　　　　$X+\% \qquad = 100$　　$XRT \text{ Achrom} = 8.0''$

$M^a/M^p \qquad = 5/1$　　　　　$A\% \qquad = 55$　　　$XRT \text{ Chrom} = 8.0''$

Table 51. Sequence of Scores for Protocol #11—R. J.

Card	RT	No.	Location	Determinant(s)		Content(s)	Pop	Z Score
I	5″	1.	*WSo*	*FC′o*		Mask		1.0
		2.	*Wo*	*FM^a.FC′o*		*A*	*P*	1.0
II	11″	3.	*D+*	*FM^{a}o*	(2)	*Ad*	*P*	3.0
		4.	*DS+*	*m^a.CF+*		Rocket, *Fi*		4.5
III	6″	5.	*D+*	*M^{a}o*	(2)	*H*	*P*	3.0
		6.	*D+*	*M^{a}o*		*(H), A*	*P*	4.0
IV	23″	7.	*Do*	*M^p.FDo*		*(H)*		
		8.	*Do*	*Fo*		*Ad*		
V	6″	9.	*Wo*	*M^a.FC′o*		*(H)*		1.0
		10.	*Do*	*Fo*		*Ad*		
VI	3″	11.	*Wo*	*FTo*		*A*	*P*	2.5
		12.	*Ddo*	*FM^p*	(2)	*Ad*		
VII	3″	13.	*W+*	*M^a.FDo*	(2)	*(H)*	*P*	2.5
		14.	*Do*	*Fo*	(2)	*Ad*		
VIII	6″	15.	*W+*	*FM^a.FCo*	(2)	*A, Bt*	*P*	4.5
IX	5″	16.	*D+*	*M^{a}o*	(2)	*(H)*		2.5
X	12″	17.	*Do*	*Fo*	(2)	*A*	*P*	
		18.	*Do*	*Fo*		*Ad*		

ANALYSIS OF THE STRUCTURE

There are no obvious features in the Structural Summary, such as special contents, or a significant frequency of lower *DQ* scores, to suggest that this is the record of a child. Quite the contrary, the substantial *Zf*, the large number of synthesis *DQ* scores, a preponderance of *M* responses, and the significant *EA* all point to an intelligent, reasonably well organized, markedly introversive individual. The fact that the subject is only 11 years old leads to the postulate that he may be "psychologically old" for his years, and warns that he may be using his inner life too extensively. Some support for this is found in the large minus *Zd* score, indicating that his efforts at organizing his world often fall short of his aspirations. Conversely, the *W/M* ratio suggests that his goals are generally more limited than his talents might warrant. His thinking is complex, and his reality testing quite good, probably too much so for a youngster. A preponderence of *FC′* responses as contrasted with a limited use of color reveals a strong effort to suppress affect, and a corresponding experience of pain. The low Lambda betrays the facade of an "affectless" person, indicating that he is very responsive to affect. The high *M* frequency, the *FC′*, and the Affective Ratio all tend to illustrate the fact that he does not show affect easily, preferring instead to maintain it within himself. The *H* to *A* ratio indicates a reasonable interest in people; however, the large frequency of parenthesized human contents reveals that this interest is more fantasy than real, and may represent a "fearfulness" of others. This is not unusual, to some extent in children, but when judged in the context of the emotional constraint, the withdrawal from the environment, and the striving to organizational levels evidenced in the record, it may reflect a more serious failure to establish healthy interpersonal contacts. The *A%*

is slightly high, but not overly so for a child, especially one who may be retarded in his social growth.

Specific propositions developed from the structural data are as follows:

1. He is quite intelligent but seems to be using his intellect more defensively than in a healthy exploratory manner.

2. He is markedly introversive, relying heavily on his fantasy life for more basic gratifications.

3. He makes strong efforts to constrain his affect, the consequence of which is the experience of considerable pain.

4. He makes strong attempts to avoid affective stimulation from his environment. This probably accounts for his "overorganizing" efforts and his excessive reliance on perceptual accuracy.

5. He seems too "rigid" for a child, possibly a product of inadequately developed social skills and a general fearfulness of others.

ANALYSIS OF THE SCORING SEQUENCE

There is considerable variance in the reaction times, the longest occurring to Card IV and signaling special attention to those answers. His shortest reaction times occur on Cards VI and VII, both of which begin with Popular answers. This suggests that he does perceive conventionality with ease and is not reluctant to respond to it. His basic approach is W and a healthy distribution of synthesis answers appears throughout most of the test. Although his two responses to Card X are adequate, they are of a *Do Fo* variety, suggesting greater restraint of both his intellect and affect to this more disorganized stimulus figure. The P failure on Card V may be of some significance, and the first answer to that card requires special attention.

One specific hypothesis suggested by the scoring sequence is as follows:

1. His cognitive activity, although complex, is generally well controlled, and he is not easily disorganized by ambiguity or unfamiliar situations. He works easily with conventionality, and strives toward an integration of his world.

ANALYSIS OF THE FREE ASSOCIATIONS

The many prefacing comments that he uses, such as "Wow, Hey, Geez, Boy," are common among children, but also convey a defensiveness concerning the situation. Both of his answers to Card I indicate defensiveness and constraint, and the change of answer #2 from a butterfly to a bat, "cause its all dark," reflects his internalized affect and his tendencies to make his perceptual accuracy as "specific" as possible. His first interpersonal answer, "dogs rubbing their noses together," is appropriate and suggests a desire for contact with others. The second such response, on Card III, offers a more ominous portrayal of interpersonal contact, "fighting," that may illustrate his internal struggle concerning social contact, or may represent a broader attitude toward social relations in general. This is also suggested by his answer to Card VII, ". . . a couple of indians arguing about which way they should go." His view of masculinity and authority appears to have a fearful undertone as indicated in his comment to his percept on Card IV, ". . . I wouldn't want to meet up with him." His fantasy life apparently has some phobic features, as noted in the space creature trying to catch the butterfly, the vampire, the monster from Mt. Everest, the alligator's head, and the witches. Again, this is not unusual in children who do not yet feel comfortable with others, especially adults, but in this record the frequency of these answers may illustrate a greater fearfulness than is appropriate for good adjustment. His second response to Card VI, ". . . some little birds in the nest waiting for their mother to feed them," probably demonstrates his feelings of maternal rejection. This experience, when combined with a fearful, and probably confused, image of masculinity, leads to the postulate that neither parent has afforded adequate supports and role models for him. Consequently, he feels somewhat inadequate and guarded in his social growth.

Specific hypotheses developed from the Free Associations are as follows:

1. He appears to have a desire for contact with others, but is uncertain about how that role is best "played." He perceives a distinct possibility of agression from others.

2. He has a negative concept of masculinity and/or authority, probably the result of inadequate contact with his own father.

3. He seems more fearful of others than is appropriate to a healthy social adjustment, and appears to have developed several barriers to close relationships.

4. He has some experience of maternal rejection and would prefer a more dependent relationship with his mother than is now the case.

ANALYSIS OF THE INQUIRY

Much of the Inquiry material appears to reinforce the notion of an undue fearfulness of his environment. The bat has claws, "like it was trying to grab something," the space creature is trying to trap and eat the butterfly, the monster's arms "probably get big when he reaches out," the indians are behind a rock, and the vampire is "getting ready to fly off." His elaboration to Card III, "it must be worth a lot," may indicate some feelings of rivalry with his younger sibling concerning the mother. Many of his answers display a negative self-image. He sees things as skinny, ugly, flattened, and so on, any or all of which might represent his own feelings. Generally, however, his descriptions are precise and intelligent, suggesting a considerable creative potential for a youngster of his age. No new specific propositions are generated by the Inquiry material, although some possible clarification concerning his own limited and/or negative self-image is evidenced.

A SUMMARY OF R. J.

This is a very bright and psychologically complex youngster. He tests reality very well, and has developed an orientation to organize as much of his world as possible in a meaningful way. His emotions are overly controlled, and he has developed a marked style of internalizing. The resulting emotional constriction is often painful for him, but apparently that penalty is less costly than the potential response of others if affect is ventilated. He is quite fearful of others, especially authority figures, and has not developed social skills that are commensurate with his talents or needs. He feels somewhat awkward in interpersonal situations, and typically prefers to withdraw into his own inner life. He sees his mother as rejecting, or at least as not providing sufficient emotional supports. Neither of his parents have provided especially good role models for him, and there is a distinct possibility of a natural, but potentially harmful sibling rivalry. He is using his good intellect in a more defensive than healthy exploratory manner. He feels that emotional constraint and distanciation from his environment are more important than risk his "shaky" self-image in a more direct interaction with the world. He should be encouraged, possibly with a well developed system of reinforcements, to give a freer rein to his creative potentials in school. A much more important goal, however, is to assist him toward a more realistic level of social interaction. These goals may be combined in the classroom by requesting that he assist other children in certain types of work with which he feels comfortable, and then rewarding that effort. On a different level, a careful study of the family constellation is in order, with the end goal of providing R. J. with more effective role models and affective supports than is now the case. Both parents need to be involved, but special attention to his relationship with his father is vital.

PROTOCOL #12   A. L.—ACTING OUT

Referral.   This 11 year old male was referred by a psychiatrist to whom A. L. had been sent by a juvenile court after several acting-out incidents in school and at home. A. L. had established a reputation among his fifth grade classmates as a "toughy," willing to fight "at the drop of the hat." He degrades others quickly, including his teacher who he refers to as "that dyke." He has smashed windows in the school after being reprimanded for neglecting his work, and is suspected of starting a fire in a classroom wastebasket. At home he "just won't listen," according to his mother, and has stolen money from his 15 year old sister, and has threatened his younger brother with "stabbing" on several recent occasions. The psychiatrist has found him "uncooperative" and "detached" and asks, "Is he psychotic," and what might be the best method of intervention.

History.   A. L. is the second of three children, an older sister age 15, and a younger brother age 9, in a family where the father is a truck driver and the mother a housewife. His birth and medical history are unremarkable. He shares a bedroom with his brother but makes it known that "it's really my room, he's just there for awhile." A. L.'s performance in school has been slightly below average since the second grade but most of his teachers feel that he is above average in intelligence. His current teacher suggests that he has confronted her "from the first day," and consistently finds him a problem. His father thinks "he'll grow out of it," but his mother seems more concerned. A. L. rejected the first attempts at testing by an almost total uncooperativeness. During a second visit, however, he agreed to see the inkblots, "but I don't promise nothing."

Protocol #12. A. L., 11 Years Old, One Older Sister, One Younger Brother, Parents Both Living, Father Employed in Blue Collar Position, Subject Currently in 5th Grade

Card	Free Association	Inquiry	Scoring
I	12″		
	1. Hey, did u mak thes up, they'r really ugly, ths one ll a bat or s.t., zooming down on s.t.	E: (Rpts S's resp) S: C all the wg parts here & the body, like a rat, its flyg along ready to zoom at s.t.	Wo FMᵃo A P 1.0
	E: Most people c more than 1 thg		
	2. Yeah?, Well I don't c a.t. else except I guess that center prt cld b a bug of s.s.	E: (Rpts S's resp) S: Yeah, it ll a bug of s.s., it has thos feeler thgs in the ft & a squiggly body, lik a bug that wld hide in the grass	Do Fo A
II	3″		
	3. Wow, it ll a big big fite betwn ths 2 bears, they'r hurt bad, c the bld all over their heads & feet	E: (Rpts S's resp) S: They ll they'r really tearing at e.o. & thy r fiting it out E: U mentioned bld all over their heads & ft S: Sure, c it here, all ths red is bld lik thy'r really hurtg e.o.	W+ FMᵃ.CFo (2) A, Bl 4.5
	4. U kno there's a spade in here too, rite in the middle	E: (Rpts S's resp) S: U c this white part ll a spade like the ace of spades, it has the same shape to it	DSo Fo Spade
III	4″		
	5. Ths ll two black guys ftig over s.t., like thy was really pullg at it, a bag of s.t., probably s.t. thy stole	S: Well, u c thy got thm burry hair cuts like the blacks wear, there's a lot of 'em in my schl, & thy'r pullin on ths thg in the middl, lik a bag u kno?	D+ Mᵃo (2) H P 3.0
	6. Ther's some bld up here too but I don't kno if means a.t.	E: (Rpts S's resp) S: Yeah it ll bld to me, like on the wall or floor or s.t., just like it was running dwn, lik the flr was tilted, u kno?	Dv C.mᵖ Bl

471

Protocol #12 (Continued)

Card		Free Association	Inquiry	Scoring
IV	8″	7. Ths don't ll a.t. except mayb a big guy comg at u, he's got big muddy boots on	E: (Rpts S's resp) S: He's really big & c he's got mud all over his boots E: Mud? S: Yeah, its all yucky, lik mud & he's hangg his arms down lik he was really mad & ready to hit s.b.	Wo Mᵃ.TFo H Mud P 2.0
V	11″	8. Ths ll an old tree stump out here but I dk what the rest is	E: (Rpts S's resp) S: It just ll a tree part that was pulled out of the ground, c, rite here, a coupl of big roots (points)	Do Fo Bt
VI	18″	9. I never saw one like ths before, the top ll s.t. that the indians made lik to their God	E: (Rpts S's resp) S: One of them thgs lik we study in geography, a whatsiz name pole w the feathers carved in it	Do Fo Ay
		10. It mite be a piece of skin or s.t., mayb a piece of an old fur coat	E: Well u really can't tell what it is, but its got a lotta fur on it, c here (points), I thot it mite be a rug but nobody wld b so dumb to mak one lik ths so mayb its just a piece tht got rippd off a furry coat	Do FTo Ad P
VII	22″	11. It just ll a lot of islands to me	E: (Rpts S's resp) S: Well, lik in the ocean, just a ring of islands & ths (points to white) is a harbor that ships can come into	WSv Fo Ls 4.0
		12. Hey, u kno ths part cld b a knife	E: (Rpts S's resp) S: There's 2 of 'em, one here & here (points), u can't c the handle too well but it ll a blade, lik a knife blade to me, lik those arabs have with the slanted edge	Do Fo (2) Knife

472

VIII	3″	13.	Boy ths r nutty, ths one ll a bunch of insides to me, all bloody	E: (Rpts S's resp) S: It ll a dead horse or dog that it is all opened up & u can c the insides, lik it was run over by a truck or s.t. E: U said it was bloody? S: Well bly & all the other thgs that r inside, c bld & guts	Wv CFo An,Bl 4.5
		<14.	If u turn it lik ths it ll a rat	E: (Rpts S's resp) S: Yeah, c his legs & body & head, lik a rat	Do Fo A P
IX	5″	15.	Boy, ths sure r nutty lookin, ths one ll s.t. u wld buy at the vegetable stand	E: (Rpts S's resp) S: Yeah, lik cauliflower or s.t. w the big leaves on it E: I'm not sure how u c it S: Well if u ever went to a veg stand u'd kno what I mean, it has, I dk the name, it has big orge leaves just lik ths one & green leaves & the pink is the part u cook I thk, its really just lik ths here	W+ FCo Fd 5.5
		16.	Hey, I c an alligator in here	E: (Rpts S's resp) S: Its rite here (points), just the head mayb the rest is underwtr or st, anyhw u can only c the head w the long nose & the sharp teeth, c it?	Do Fo Ad
X	7″	17.	I can't mak much out of ths one except ths part ll a cpl of crabs	E: (Rpts S's resp) S: Yeah, c all the legs, lik crabs	Do Fo (2) A P
		18.	That's a horse jumpg over s.t.	E: (Rpts S's resp) S: One here & one over here, they have their legs stretchd out lik thy were jumping over s.t.	Do FM^{a}o (2) A
		19.	Like a gut out of s.t.	E: (Rpts S's resp) S: Well its all red lik bld & its squiggly lik a gut wld b if u ever saw in a meat market	Dv CF− An,Bl

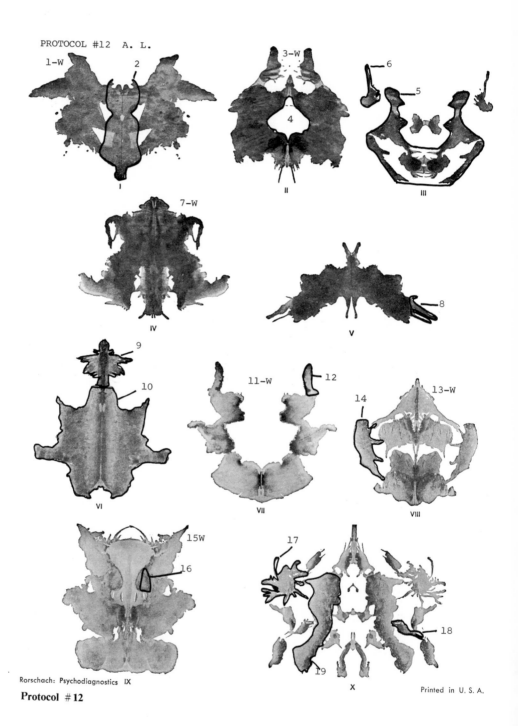

PROTOCOL #12   A. L.

Rorschach: Psychodiagnostics

Protocol #12

Table 52. Structural Summary for Protocol #12—A. L.

$R = 19$	$Zf = 7$	$Z\text{Sum} = 24.5$	$P = 6$	$(2) = 5$

Location Features	Determinants	Contents	Contents (Idiographic)
$W \ = \ 6$ DQ	$M.TF \ = 1$	$H \ = 2$	Knife $\ = 1$
	$FM.CF = 1$	$(H) \ =$	
$D \ = 13$ $+ \ = \ 3$	$C.m \ = 1$	$Hd \ =$	Spade $\ = 1$
		$(Hd) \ =$	
$Dd = 0$ $o \ = 12$		$A \ = 6$	Mud $\ = 0, 1$
	$M \ = 1$	$(A) \ =$	
$S \ = 2$ $v \ = \ 4$	$FM = 2$	$Ad \ = 2$	_____ $=$
	$m \ =$	$(Ad) \ =$	
$DW = 0$ $- \ = \ 0$	$C \ =$	$Ab \ =$	_____ $=$
	$CF \ = 2$	$Al \ =$	
	$FC \ = 1$	$An \ = 2$	_____ $=$
	$C' \ =$	$Art \ =$	
FORM QUALITY	$C'F =$	$Ay \ = 1$	_____ $=$
	$FC' =$	$Bl \ = 1, 3$	
FQx FQf	$T \ =$	$Bt \ = 1$	_____ $=$
	$TF \ =$	$Cg \ =$	
$+ \ = \ 0$ $+ \ = 0$	$FT \ = 1$	$Cl \ =$	
	$V \ =$	$Ex \ =$	
$o \ = 17$ $o \ = 9$	$VF \ =$	$Fi \ =$	
	$FV \ =$	$Fd \ = 1$	
$w \ = \ 0$ $w \ = 0$	$Y \ =$	$Ge \ =$	
	$YF \ =$	$Hh \ =$	
$- \ = \ 1$ $- \ = 0$	$FY \ =$	$Ls \ = 1$	
	$rF \ =$	$Na \ =$	
	$Fr \ =$	$Sx \ =$	
	$Fd \ =$	$Xy \ =$	
	$F \ = 9$		

RATIOS, PERCENTAGES, AND DERIVATIONS

$Z\text{Sum}/Z\text{est} = 24.5/20.5$	$FC/CF + C = 1/4$	Afr	$= .59$
$Zd \ = +4.0$	$W/M \ = 6/2$	$3r + (2)/R$	$= 5/19 = .26$
$EB \ = 2/5.0$ $EA = 7.0$	$W/D \ = 6/13$	Cont/R	$= 10/19$
$eb \ = 4/2$ $ep \ = 6$	$L \ = .90$	$H + Hd/A + Ad = 2/8$	
Blends$/R = 3/19$	$F+\% \ = 100$	$H + A/Hd + Ad = 8/2$	
$a/p \ = 5/1$	$X+\% \ = 95$	XRT Achrom	$= 14.2''$
$M^a/M^p \ = 2/0$	$A\% \ = 42$	XRT Chrom	$= 4.4''$

Table 53.   Sequence of Scores for Protocol #12—A. L.

Card	RT	No.	Location	Determinant(s)		Content(s)	Pop	Z Score
I	12″	1.	*Wo*	*FMᵃo*		*A*	*P*	1.0
		2.	*Do*	*Fo*		*A*		
II	3″	3.	*W+*	*FMᵃ.CFo* (2)		*A, Bl*		4.5
		4.	*DSo*	*Fo*		Spade		
III	4″	5.	*D+*	*Mᵃo*	(2)	*H*	*P*	3.0
		6.	*Dv*	*C.mᵖ*		*Bl*		
IV	8″	7.	*Wo*	*Mᵃ.TFo*		*H*, Mud	*P*	2.0
V	11″	8.	*Do*	*Fo*		*Bt*		
VI	18″	9.	*Do*	*Fo*		*Ay*		
		10.	*Do*	*FTo*		*Ad*	*P*	
VII	22″	11.	*WSv*	*Fo*		*Ls*		4.0
		12.	*Do*	*Fo*	(2)	Knife		
VIII	3″	13.	*Wv*	*CFo*		*An, Bl*		4.5
		14.	*Do*	*Fo*		*A*	*P*	
IX	5″	15.	*W+*	*FCo*		*Fd*		5.5
		16.	*Do*	*Fo*		*Ad*		
X	7″	17.	*Do*	*Fo*	(2)	*A*	*P*	
		18.	*Do*	*FMᵃo*	(2)	*A*		
		19.	*Dv*	*CF−*		*An, Bl*		

ANALYSIS OF THE STRUCTURE

The structural data in this record are much more compatible of the "stereotype" of an 11 year old than was noted in Protocol #11. A marked use of color is noted, with considerably more *CF* and *C* answers than the more controlled *FC* variety. The six Popular answers indicate that he is aware of, but by no means bound to, conventionality. He generally seeks his more basic gratifications from interaction with his world, rather than from his inner life. His reality testing is quite good, and, as probably should be the case for most children, he is often prompted by less well organized needs. He is active in his thinking, and probably in his behaviors. His Egocentricity Ratio reveals a relatively low self-valuation, and his broad range of contents appears to reflect some of the more juvenile preoccupations, several of which are more infantile than may be appropriate for his age. Although the Affective Ratio indicates no excessive attraction to the affective stimuli from his environment, the short mean *RT* to the chromatic cards hints of a more impulsive responsiveness to affect. The relatively long *RT* to the achromatic series may represent some attempt to avoid and/or control his reactions to painful stimuli. The distribution of *DQ* scores is not unusual for a youngster of this age, and the three synthesis responses give evidence that his intellect is developing satisfactorily. The two anatomy contents may reflect an unusual body concern, and the relatively low frequency of human contents appears to reveal some detachment from others.

Specific Propositions developed from the Structural Summary are as follows:

1. He is an extratensive youngster who ordinarily prefers to derive his more basic gratifications from interaction with his world.

2. He has limited affective controls, and can easily manifest labile behaviors.

3. His reality testing is quite adequate; however, his own self-esteem is inappropriately low.

4. He may have some preoccupation with his body, possibly as a technique to "offset" his limited self value.

5. While he is involved with his world, he is generally detached from any deep or involved interest in others.

6. Much of his thinking is appropriately juvenile, although in some instances it assumes a more infantile character, suggesting a limited maturation for his age.

ANALYSIS OF THE SCORING SEQUENCE

There is a marked variance in reaction times, with significantly longer *RT*'s occurring to Cards VI and VII. The *P* failure on Card V is of special interest, and suggests that although his reality testing and awareness of conventionality are adequate, he often discards them for a "safer" interpretation. His overall approach is detail oriented; however, all of his *W* answers occur first in a series. There are no specific hypotheses generated by the sequence of scores.

ANALYSIS OF THE FREE ASSOCIATIONS

Several of his responses are marked by common prefacing remarks, such as hey, wow, and boy, typical of children and defensive in nature. At least five of his answers convey an aggressive quality, a bat zooming, bears fighting, men fighting, a "big guy coming at you," and a knife. Conversely, at least two of his answers, ". . . an old tree stump," and "a piece of an old fur coat," have a depressive tone, quite uncommon among younger clients. The anatomy and blood contents are offered in a matter-of-fact, but very infantile manner, as if no sense of control existed at that moment. His response to Card VI conveys some elementary form of interest in sexuality, ". . . that the indians made to their God." Similarly, on Card IV, he implies a sense of domination by authority and/or masculinity, and on Card VII he ignores the Popular human percept in favor of an isolated grouping of islands. The use of the white area on Card VII as a harbor may provide a clue concerning of his own negativism that is a source of protection. That protection appears sorely needed if previous estimates of his low self-esteem are correct and if, in fact, he does perceive masculinity as a threat. Under those circumstances, his own hostility would be a modeling of that which he believes is both typical and expected. He sees both of his human percepts in aggressive acts, and is unable to report other human figures.

Specific postulates developed from the Free Associations are as follows:

1. Much of his thinking is marked by an infantile quality, and he is prone to respond quickly, without organizing his thoughts, to affective stimuli.

2. He apparently has learned to view the male role as commensurate with aggression, and although he is fearful of this, also models after it, possibly in terms of his relationship with his own father.

3. He uses hostility as a form of defense against his limited self esteem.

4. There is no evidence in the record that he has a meaningful relationship with either parent, and seems especially distant from his mother.

ANALYSIS OF THE INQUIRY

The material in the Inquiry varies from aggressive, "ready to zoom," to defensive and concealing, "like a bug that would hide in the grass." The extensiveness of his anger may be best illustrated by his description to Card IV, "like he was really mad and ready to hit somebody." He is often very critical in his percepts, "boy this sure is nutty," or "nobody would be so dumb to make one like this . . ." showing another dimension of his hostility. Most of his animal descriptions are either negative, hostile, or of animals that "travel alone" and tend to conceal themselves. He feels undesirable and attempts to hide this from the inspection of others.

Although the Inquiry material does not provoke new hypotheses, it does add clarifying dimensions to several of those generated from other data.

A SUMMARY OF A. L.

This 11 year old boy appears to be the product of inappropriate modeling effects. He is not psychotic, nor are there any traces of a thinking disturbance in the record. He is labile, but possibly no more so than many youngsters his own age. His thinking is often quite immature, and somehow, he has learned to use aggressiveness to demonstrate his own "maleness," and at the same time to protect him from exposing his own weak self-image to others. He functions on the premise that the "best defense is a good offense." Unfortunately, he is unable to contain that offense much of the time, and thus has apparently been rejected by others, including parents, siblings, and peers. He is especially fearful of his father and seems to have no substantial relationship whatsoever with his mother. Beneath his aggressive facade is a very immature, but potentially healthy youngster, who wants affection and companionship but does not know how or where to find it. He "hurts" as a result of this, a hurt which only serves to stimulate new aggressive feelings and displays. The most appropriate form of intervention might involve the entire family, but a careful evaluation of that constellation is in order before any firm decision might be made. On an individual basis he can profit enormously by acceptance and warmth, and truly needs an accepting male figure with which to identify. Behavioral control in the school might be gradually precipitated through a given schedule of positive reinforcements for specific actions, including social cooperativeness. A major reinforcer for this youngster, like many of his age range who are in trouble, is tolerance and love. These are often difficult to convey in the classroom but should be available in the home and in social relations.

Author Index

Abel, T. M., 226, 231
Abrahamsen, D., 264, 275
Abrams, E., 235, 244, 251, 260, 272
Abramson, L. S., 28, 38
Ackerman, M. J., 303, 306
Ainsworth, M. D., 18, 40, 51, 68, 105, 124,
    232, 253, 274, 285, 294, 297, 306, 327
Allee, R., 260, 274
Allen, B. V., 303, 307
Allen, R. M., 5, 17, 279, 294
Allerhand, M. E., 285, 294
Allison, J., 235, 251
Altus, W. D., 260, 264, 272
Ames, L. B., 3, 17, 235, 236, 244, 249, 251,
    256, 261, 264, 265, 272, 280, 284, 289, 294,
    300, 301, 306
Amick, J., 286, 297
Applebaum, S. A., 282, 294
Arluck, E. W., 256, 272
Armitage, S. G., 235, 244, 251
Arnold, J. M., 298

Baileck, I., 226, 231
Baker, E., 245
Baker, G., 262, 274, 327
Bandura, A., 238, 251
Bard, M., 289, 298
Barnett, I., 279, 294
Barrera, S., 256, 273
Bash, K. W., 310, 312, 326
Baughman, E. E., 6, 17, 25, 36, 38, 39, 91,
    104, 243, 247, 249, 251, 252, 279, 286, 287,
    294, 296
Beck, A., 67, 104, 124, 136, 272, 294, 306
Beck, S. J., 3, 7-14, 23, 24, 27, 32, 33, 35, 36,
    37, 39, 42, 45, 51, 53-56, 59, 60, 61, 63, 67,
    70, 73, 74, 78, 84, 87, 88, 93, 97, 101, 104,
    107, 108, 111, 112, 113, 117, 118, 119, 120,
    121, 123, 124, 126, 127, 130, 134, 135, 136,
    147, 148, 149, 153, 154, 226, 228, 231, 235-
    239, 243, 244, 245, 249, 251, 253, 256, 259,
    260, 262, 264, 267, 272, 279, 280, 282, 284,
    286, 288, 289, 290, 294, 298, 300, 301, 302,
    304, 306, 310, 311, 312, 313, 315, 317, 326, 327

Becker, W. C., 62, 67, 240, 251
Belmont, I., 235, 244, 252
Bendick, M. R., 261, 272
Benjamin, J. D., 226, 231
Berger, D., 289, 294
Berger, D. G., 251
Berkowitz, M., 244, 251
Berryman, E., 265, 272
Biederman, L., 15, 17
Bieri, J., 262, 272
Binder, H., 84, 86, 87, 88, 104, 288, 295
Blacher, E., 262, 272
Blake, R., 113, 125, 146, 150, 154, 242
Blatt, H., 112, 124
Blatt, S. J., 235, 251
Bloom, B. L., 130, 136
Bloom, B. S., 22, 41
Bochner, R., 331, 345
Booth, G., 149
Bourguinon, E. E., 249, 251
Bradway, K., 287, 295
Breecher, S., 285, 295
Brennan, M., 280, 295
Bresnoban, T. J., 295
Brick, H., 297
Bricklin, 262, 275, 301, 307, 315, 327
Brockway, A. L., 285, 295, 300, 306
Brosin, H. W., 226, 231
Brown, F., 21, 39
Brown, M., 285, 295
Browne, C. G., 3, 19
Buhler, C., 256, 272, 287, 289, 295, 300,
    306
Buhler, K., 306
Buker, S. D., 5, 19, 279, 298
Burchard, E., 149
Burstein, A. G., 305, 306

Caldwell, B. L., 244, 251
Calvin, A. D., 297
Campo, V., 84, 87, 104
Cannavo, F., 265, 273, 280, 296
Canter, A., 279, 295
Carp, A. L., 27, 39

246, 251, 300, 306
1, 271
5, 17, 18
15
. S., 226, 231
ow, E. J., 244, 251
Clapp, H., 226, 231
Cleveland, S. E., 135, 136, 330, 345
Coan, R., 286, 295
Cocking, R. R., 261, 272
Coffin, T. E., 24, 28, 39
Coleman, J., 330, 346
Collyer, Y. M., 298
Colson, D. B., 282, 294, 295
Cooper, L., 261, 272
Corrigan, H., 295
Costello, C. G., 280, 295
Cotte, S., 254
Counts, R. M., 238, 251
Cox, F. N., 28, 39, 289, 295
Cronbach, L. J., 6, 18, 44, 51, 224, 231
Crumpton, E. E., 279, 295
Cummings, S. T., 227, 231
Cutter, F., 282, 295

Dana, J. M., 261, 272
Dana, R. H., 261, 272
Daston, P. G., 251, 282, 295
Davidou, P., 306
Davidson, H. H., 40, 118, 124, 137, 244, 251
de de Santos, D. R., 84, 87, 104
Devine, D., 346
Dinoff, M., 31, 39
Dorken, H., 281, 297, 306
Draguns, J. G., 301, 302, 303, 306
Dubrovner, R. J., 5, 18, 279, 295
Dudek, S. Z., 261, 272
Duran, P., 301, 306

Ebaugh, F. G., 226, 231
Eichler, R. M., 236, 252, 289, 295
Elizur, A., 330, 345
Ellenberger, H., 86, 104
Elstein, A. S., 290, 295
Erginel, A., 312, 327
Eron, L., 4, 19, 52
Escafit, M., 306
Etter, D., 303, 307
Evans, R. B., 262, 273
Exner, D. E., 13, 16, 18, 26, 39, 48, 51, 56, 67, 73, 84, 88, 104, 107, 111, 118, 124, 330, 345
Exner, J. E., 5, 7, 9, 13, 16, 18, 24, 26, 37, 39, 43, 48, 51, 56, 67, 70, 73, 84, 88, 91, 99, 101, 104, 107, 111, 118, 124, 149, 237, 238, 244, 246, 252, 254, 256, 259, 265, 269, 273, 274, 279, 280, 281, 285, 291, 295, 296, 330, 345

Farberow, N., 282, 295
Feldman, M. J., 5, 18, 252
Finney, B. C., 280, 296, 299
Fisher, R. L., 289, 296
Fisher, S., 135, 136, 280, 296, 330, 345
Fiske, D. W., 21, 40, 247, 252, 287, 296
Fister, W. P., 327
Folsom, A. T., 280, 298
Fonda, C., 112, 124, 238, 252, 262, 275, 300, 307
Ford, M., 280, 296, 303, 306
Forsyth, R. P., 279, 296
Fortier, R. H., 280, 296
Fosberg, I. A., 27, 39
Foster, J. M., 28, 41
Frank, I. H., 62, 67, 235, 252
Frank, L. K., 221, 222, 231, 330, 345
Frankle, A. H., 262, 273
Fried, E., 244, 254
Friedman, H., 53, 61, 62, 63, 64, 67, 144, 149, 235, 236, 252

Gage, N. L., 21, 39
Gardner, R. W., 280, 296
Geidt, F. H., 21, 40
Gibby, R. G., 5, 18, 25, 28, 36, 39, 40, 244, 252, 262, 273
Gill, H. S., 280, 296
Gill, M., 19, 21, 41, 52, 68, 105, 124, 137, 150, 254, 275, 298, 307
Glaser, N. M., 300, 307
Gleser, G. C., 224, 231, 306
Goetcheus, G., 28, 40
Goldberger, L., 245, 252, 289, 296
Goldfarb, W., 310, 327, 331, 346
Goldfried, M. R., 7, 18, 62, 63, 67, 135, 136, 239, 252, 289, 296, 331, 346
Goldman, A. E., 245, 254, 264, 273
Goldman, G. D., 261, 275
Goldman, R., 256, 273, 301, 306
Goldstein, K., 281, 296
Goodstein, L. D., 289, 296
Gough, H. G., 3, 18
Graley, J., 5, 18
Grant, M. Q., 227, 231
Grayson, H. M., 279, 296
Greenberg, T. D., 251
Griffith, R. M., 303, 306
Grisso, J. T., 22, 40
Gross, L., 31, 40
Grosz, H. J., 289, 297
Guirdham, A., 236, 250, 252, 262, 273
Gurrslin, C., 252

Haan, N., 264, 273
Hafner, A. J., 256, 273
Haley, E. M., 301, 302, 303, 306
Hallowell, A. I., 249, 252

Halpern, F., 3, 18, 262, 280, 296, 301, 306, 331, 345
Hamlin, R., 226, 227, 231, 279, 296
Hammer, E. F., 267, 273
Harrington, R. L., 273
Harris, J. G., 6, 18, 245
Harrower, M., 21, 40
Hartmann, H., 255, 273
Hemmendinger, L., 62, 67
Henry, E. M., 28, 40, 256, 273
Herman, J., 261, 264, 273, 275, 310, 327
Herron, E. W., 51
Hersh, C., 261, 273
Hertz, M. R., 3, 7-14, 18, 23, 24, 27, 32, 33, 35, 40, 42, 45, 51, 54, 56, 57, 59, 60, 63, 67, 68, 70, 73, 74, 75, 76, 78, 80, 81, 84, 86, 87, 88, 101, 104, 107, 111, 112, 113, 117-121, 124, 130, 135, 136, 153, 226, 227, 231, 242, 249, 252, 260, 263, 264, 265, 273, 281, 282, 284, 285, 288, 296, 297, 310
Hertzman, M., 262, 273
Hirschstein, R., 331, 346
Hohn, E., 303, 306
Holt, R. R., 4, 18, 22, 40, 51, 68, 105, 124, 136, 225, 232, 253, 274, 297, 306, 327, 330, 346
Holtzman, P. S., 282, 294
Holtzman, W. H., 44, 51, 289, 297
Holzberg, J. D., 5, 18, 235, 244, 252
Honigmann, J. J., 249, 252
Hurwitz, B. A., 282, 295
Hurwitz, I. A., 240, 252
Hutt, M., 28, 40

Iscoe, I., 297
Ives, V., 227, 231
Izner, S. M., 276

Jacks, I., 267, 273
Jackson, C. W., 13, 18
Jensen, N. D., 346
Jolles, I., 112, 124
Jones, A. M., 262, 275
Jorgensen, M., 282, 295
Joseph, A., 249, 252
Jost, H. A., 5, 18, 295

Kadinsky, D., 237, 253
Kahn, M. W., 247, 253, 261, 276
Kallstedt, F. E., 261, 273, 285, 297
Kaplan, A. H., 231
Kaplan, M. L., 252
Kates, S. L., 289, 299
Katz, M., 269, 273
Keehn, J. D., 279, 297
Keeley, S., 15, 19
Kelley, D. M., 40, 51, 68, 105, 124, 136, 149, 244, 253, 256, 273, 297
Kelly, E. L., 21, 40
Kemalof, S., 312, 327
Kennard, M. A., 327
Kerr, F. J., 249, 253
Keyes, E. J., 236, 253
Kimble, G. A., 5, 18
King, G. F., 262, 274
King, S., 265, 274
Kirkner, F., 262, 274, 327
Kisker, G. W., 245, 253
Klatskin, E. H., 279, 297
Klebanoff, S. G., 237, 253, 290, 297
Klein, G. S., 261, 274
Klingensmith, S. W., 36, 40
Klopfer, B., 3, 7-14, 18, 23, 24, 27, 31, 33, 35, 37, 40, 42, 45, 48, 51, 54, 55, 56, 59, 68, 70, 73, 74, 75, 76, 78, 80, 81, 83, 84, 87, 97, 101, 104, 105, 106, 107, 111, 117, 118, 124, 126, 127, 130, 135, 136, 137, 147, 149, 226, 228, 232, 236, 238, 244, 256, 260, 262, 264, 265, 266, 274, 279, 280, 281, 282, 284, 286, 288, 289, 290, 297, 300, 301, 304, 306, 310, 315, 327
Klopfer, W. G., 18, 36, 40, 51, 68, 105, 124, 232, 244, 253, 261, 264, 272, 284, 297, 303, 306, 307, 327
Kluckhohn, S., 227, 232
Kluckholm, C., 249, 253
Knopf, I. J., 245, 253
Kobler, F. J., 280, 297, 300, 307
Korchin, S. J., 243, 253
Korman, A. K., 4, 18
Kostlan, A., 21, 40
Kral, V. A., 281, 297
Kropp, R., 112, 124
Kruger, A. K., 240, 253
Kruglov, I., 244, 251
Krugman, J., 227, 232
Kuethe, J. L., 285, 294
Kuhn, R., 300, 307

Learned, J., 17, 251, 272, 294, 306
Lebo, D., 289, 297
Lebowitz, A., 62, 68
LeFever, D. W., 256, 272, 287, 289, 295, 300, 306
Leighton, D., 249, 253
Leiser, R., 276
Lerner, B., 261, 274
Levin, M. M., 36, 40, 46, 52
Levine, J., 244, 251
Levine, M., 261, 262, 274
Levitt, E. E., 67, 104, 124, 136, 272, 289, 294, 297, 306
Levy, E., 331, 346
Levy, L., 223, 232
Levy, M. H., 229, 232

286, 297
1., 330, 346
280, 297

62, 274
27, 232
. b., 5, 19, 227, 232
oosli-Usteri, M., 34, 40
Lord, E., 25, 40
Lotesta, P., 262, 274
Lotsoff, E., 235, 253
Louttit, C. M., 3, 19
Loveland, N. T., 261, 274
Lubin, B., 15, 19
Luborsky, L., 22, 40
Luchins, A. S., 5, 19
Lyerly, S., 269, 273

Macfarlane, J. W., 5, 19
MacKinnon, D. W., 22, 40
Majumber, A. K., 265, 274
Mann, L., 280, 297
Manne, S. H., 5, 17, 294
Margulies, H., 256, 273, 280, 297
Marmorston, J., 262, 273
Martin, H., 282, 297
Masling, J., 25, 41
Matranga, J., 346
Mayman, M., 118, 119, 120, 122, 123, 124,
153, 247, 249, 253
McArthur, C. C., 265, 274
McCandless, B. B., 235, 253
McFate, M. Q., 285, 298
McMichael, A., 254, 275
McReynolds, P., 246, 251, 300, 306
Meadow, A., 22, 40
Meehl, P. E., 3, 15, 19, 229, 232
Meer, B., 305, 307, 331, 346
Meli-Dworetzki, G., 53, 60, 68, 264, 274
Meltzer, H., 286, 298
Meltzoff, J., 261, 275
Mensh, I. N., 238, 251
Metraux, R., 17, 251, 272, 294, 306
Meyer, B. T., 279, 298
Miale, F., 105, 149, 231
Miller, D. R., 25, 39
Milton, E. O., 28, 40
Mindness, A., 310, 327
Mirin, B., 262, 267, 274
Misch, R. C., 240, 253
Molish, E. E., 303, 307
Molish, H. B., 39, 51, 67, 104, 112, 123,
124, 136, 238, 244, 245, 250, 251, 253,
262, 272, 274, 294, 301, 303, 306, 307,
310, 327, 331, 436
Monroe, R. L., 227, 232
Montalto, F. D., 285, 298
Morris, W. W., 301, 307

Moskowitz, M. J., 296
Mukerji, K., 292, 298
Murillo, L. G., 237, 246, 252, 254, 256, 265,
273, 274, 280, 281, 296
Murray, D. C., 238, 254
Murray, V. F., 249, 252

Neel, F. A., 265, 274
Neff, W. S., 300, 307
Nett, E. W., 249, 251
Neuman, G. G., 303, 307
Neuringer, C., 282, 298
Newton, R., 227, 231, 232
Nichols, R., 4, 18

Oberholzer, E., 105, 137, 227, 232
Ogdon, D. P., 260, 274
Orlansky, D., 262, 273
Orlinsky, D. E., 261, 274
Orr, F. G., 285, 298

Page, H. A., 261, 274
Paine, C., 15, 19
Palmer, J. O., 227, 232, 261, 274
Papania, N., 254, 275
Pascal, G., 331, 346
Pauker, J. D., 307
Paulsen, A., 244, 254, 256, 260, 275
Pearl, D., 251
Pechoux, R., 306
Perlman, J., 5, 19, 279, 298
Peters, B., 295
Peterson, L. C., 28, 41
Phares, E. J., 28, 41
Phillips, L., 3, 19, 262, 275, 286, 298, 301,
302, 303, 306, 331, 346
Piaget, J., 61, 68
Piotrowski, Z., 3, 7-14, 19, 21, 23, 24, 27,
32, 33, 35, 41, 42, 52, 55, 56, 59, 68, 70,
73, 74, 75, 76, 78, 81, 84, 86, 88, 105, 107,
117, 124, 127, 130, 134, 137, 149, 150,
226, 228, 232, 238, 245, 254, 260, 262,
263, 264, 265, 266, 267, 275, 278, 281,
282, 284, 288, 298, 301, 307, 310, 312,
313, 315, 327
Poser, E. G., 295
Potanin, N., 285
Pottharst, K., 28, 40
Prados, M., 244, 254
Prandoni, J., 331, 346
Pruyser, P. W., 280, 298

Rabin, A. I., 237, 254, 256, 275, 280, 282,
298, 306, 331, 346
Rabinovitch, M. S., 310, 327
Rabinovitch, S., 287, 298
Rapaport, D., 3, 7-14, 19, 21, 24, 32, 33, 35,
41, 42, 46, 52, 53, 55, 61, 62, 63, 68, 74,

78, 81, 84, 86, 87, 88, 105, 107, 117, 118, 124, 127, 130, 134, 135, 137, 144, 150, 221, 226, 237, 238, 243, 246, 254, 255, 256, 260, 264, 275, 278, 281, 282, 284, 288, 289, 298, 302, 307, 310
Ray, A. B., 301, 307
Raychaudhuri, M., 292, 298
Razoni, J. H., 227, 231
Rees, W. L., 262, 275
Reichard, S., 295
Reintz, A. H., 251
Reisman, M., 36
Richardson, H., 301, 307
Richter, R. H., 261, 275
Rickers-Ovsiankina, M., 3, 19, 130, 137, 244, 278, 298
Roe, A., 303, 307
Rorschach, H., 3, 8, 11, 12, 19, 24, 30, 37, 42, 45, 48, 52, 54, 55, 57, 60, 69, 73, 74, 75, 76, 78, 81, 83, 84, 86, 96, 104, 105, 106, 107, 111, 124, 126, 127, 130, 134, 137, 146, 147, 148, 150, 222, 225, 232, 235, 254, 255, 259, 263, 266, 275, 277, 278, 286, 298, 300, 307, 309, 327, 330, 346
Rosen, E., 238, 254, 331, 346
Rosenzweig, S., 227, 232
Rossi, A. M., 303, 307
Rotter, J. B., 28, 40, 256, 273
Roy, A. B., 265, 274
Rubenstein, B. B., 227, 231
Ruesch, H., 346
Russell, E. W., 6, 19

Sakheim, G. A., 282, 295, 298
Salmon, P., 290, 298
Sapenfield, B. R., 5, 19, 279, 298
Sarason, S. B., 28, 39, 289, 295
Sarbin, T. R., 21, 41, 225, 232
Saretsky, T., 247, 254
Sawyer, J., 3, 4, 19
Schachtel, E. G., 24, 25, 41, 227, 232, 278, 298
Schachter, M., 303, 307
Schachter, W., 237, 254
Schafer, R., 3, 7, 8, 10-14, 19, 21, 23, 24, 25, 27, 32, 33, 35, 41, 42, 46, 52, 55, 68, 74, 105, 124, 136, 137, 148, 150, 226, 246, 247, 254, 275, 298, 307, 331, 346
Schilder, P., 281, 298
Schlesinger, H. G., 261, 274
Schmidt, H., 112, 124, 262, 275, 300, 307
Schon, M., 289, 298
Schreiber, M., 265, 266, 275, 312, 313, 327
Schulman, I., 261, 275
Schumer, F., 4, 19, 52
Schwartz, F., 289, 299
Sechrest, L., 331, 346

Seitz, C. P., 262, 273
Sender, S., 18, 68, 104, 297
Shalit, B., 266, 275
Shapiro, D., 278, 281, 299
Sharlock, N., 252
Shatin, L., 302, 307
Shavzin, A. R., 27, 39
Sheerer, M., 281, 296
Shemberg, K., 15, 19
Sherman, M. H., 245, 254, 256, 275, 301, 307
Shneidman, E. S., 5, 19, 227, 232
Siegel, E. L., 62, 68, 240, 254
Siegel, M., 227, 232
Siipola, E. M., 279, 299
Silverman, L. K., 227, 232
Singer, J. L., 261, 275, 310, 327, 331, 346
Singer, M. T., 261, 274
Sisson, B., 112, 124
Sloan, W., 254
Smith, J. G., 3, 19, 262, 275, 286, 298, 330, 331, 346
Sommer, D., 264, 275, 280, 299
Sommer, R., 260, 264, 275, 280, 299
Spiegelman, M., 282, 297
Spivack, G., 262, 274
Spohn, H. E., 261, 275, 310, 327
Steele, N. M., 261, 276
Stein, M. I., 22, 41
Steiner, M. E., 285, 299
Steisel, I. M., 280, 299
Stern, G. G., 22, 41
Sterne, S. B., 276
Stewart, L. M., 28, 41
Stiel, A., 280, 297, 300, 307
Stiff, M., 5, 17, 294
Stone, H., 330, 346
Stone, J. T., 296
Storment, C. T., 280, 299
Stotsky, B. A., 36, 39, 262, 273, 276, 280, 299, 301, 307
Stricker, G., 7, 18, 36, 38, 41, 62, 63, 67, 135, 136, 239, 252, 289, 296, 331, 346
Sundberg, N. D., 3, 15, 19
Suttell, B., 346
Swartz, M. B., 279, 299
Swarz, J. D., 51
Swift, J. W., 5, 19, 227, 232, 256, 276
Symonds, P. M., 227, 232

Tallman, G., 124
Tamarin, S., 262, 274
Tanaka, F., 260, 276
Taulbee, E., 112, 124, 244, 254
Thetford, W. N., 306
Thiesen, W. C., 306
Toal, R., 297
Thomas, C. B., 303, 307

262, 276
273
., 264, 276

..., 280, 299
...nam, R. D., 5, 19

Ulett, G. A., 300, 306

Van de Castle, R. L., 22, 41
Varvel, W., 112, 125
Vernon, P. E., 22, 41
Vernon, P. H., 227, 232
Vinson, D. B., 301, 307
Von Lackum, W. J., 5, 18, 295

Waison, M., 346
Walker, E. L., 25, 39
Walker, R. G., 330, 346
Walker, R. N., 17, 251, 272, 294, 306
Wallen, P., 279, 299
Waller, P. F., 285, 289, 299
Wallis, R. R., 15, 19
Walters, R. H., 301, 307
Warshaw, L., 264, 276
Watson, A., 99, 105, 291, 299
Weber, A., 282, 299
Wedemeyer, B., 300, 307
Weigl, E., 281, 299
Weiner, I. B., 7, 15, 18, 19, 23, 41, 62,

63, 67, 118, 125, 135, 136, 137, 239,
244, 245, 246, 252, 262, 276, 289, 296,
331, 346
Weiss, A. A., 302, 308
Werner, H., 61, 68, 238, 254
Wetherhorn, M., 267, 276
Wheeler, W. M., 330, 331, 346
Wickes, T. A., 31, 41
Wight, B., 274
Wilensky, H., 62, 68, 240, 254
Williams, M. H., 28, 41
Wilson, G., 113, 125, 146, 150, 154,
242
Winnik, H. Z., 302, 308
Winter, W. D., 261, 275
Wisham, W., 262, 274, 327
Wishner, J., 112, 125, 235, 244, 254,
301, 308
Wittenborn, J. R., 235, 254
Wohl, J., 13, 18
Woiska, P. H., 251
Wyatt, F., 6, 19

York, R. H., 279, 299

Zamansky, H. J., 245, 254
Zax, M., 36, 38, 41
Zelin, M., 331, 346
Zolliker, A., 302, 308
Zubin, J., 4, 14, 19, 43, 52
Zukowsky, E., 247, 254

Subject Index

Active-passive movement, examples, 77
  interpretation, 266-271
  scoring, 74
Administration, 23-38

Blend responses, 106-111, 317
  examples, 109-110
  intelligence, 107-108
  interpretation, 317
  main-additional scores, 106-107
Blind interpretation, 225-229
Body image boundary scores, 135

C, *see* Color responses, chromatic
C', *see* Color responses, achromatic
CF, *see* Color responses, chromatic
C'F, *see* Color responses, achromatic
Clinical method, 3-5
  Personality description, 4
  Versus statistical prediction, 3-5
Color responses, achromatic, 83-86, 281-284
    achromatic color-form responses (C'F), 85
    form-achromatic color responses (FC'), 85-86
    In experience base, 147
    In experience potential, 147
    Interpretation, 281-284
    Pure achromatic color responses (C'), 84-85
  chromatic, 76-83, 277-281
    color-form responses (CF), 80-81
    color naming (Cn), 81-82
    In Erlebnistypus, 147
    examples, 82-83
    in experience actual, 147
    interpretation, 277-281
    pure color responses (C), 78-80
Complex responses, 106-111. *See also* Blend responses
Confabulated detail responses (DdD), 60, 238-239
  interpretation, 238-239
Confabulated whole responses (DW), 57-60, 238-239

interpretation, 238-239
Content scores, 126-130, 304-305
  criteria and symbols, 128-130
  interpretation, 304-305

D, *see* Detail responses, common
Dd, *see* Detail responses, unusual
DdD, *see* Confabulated detail responses
Detail location areas, Card I, 155
  Card II, 161
  Card III, 166
  Card IV, 171
  Card V, 175
  Card VI, 178
  Card VII, 183
  Card VIII, 187
  Card IX, 191
  Card X, 196
Detail responses, common (D), 55-56, 236-237
  interpretation, 236-237
  unusual (Dd), 56-57, 237
  interpretation, 237
Determinant scoring, 69-105
  symbols and criteria, 71-72
  See also Specific scores
Developmental quality scores, 60-67, 239-241
  interpretation, 239-241
  See also Location scores
DW, *see* Confabulated whole responses

EA, *see* Experience actual
EB, *see* Erlebnistypus
eb, *see* Experience base
ep, *see* Experience potential
Erlebnistypus (EB), 147, 309-311
  interpretation, 309-311
Examiner influence, 24-26
Experience actual (EA), 147, 311-313
  interpretation, 311-313
Experience base (eb), 147, 315-316
  interpretation, 315-316
Experience potential (ep), 147, 313-315
  interpretation, 313-315

ct Index

sponses
esponses, chromatic
esponses, achromatic
nensional responses
t responses, animal
responses (FD), 97, 99, 100,
~59
~xamples, 100
interpretation, 257-259
Form quality, based on frequency, 117-118
  F+%, 148
  form level rating, 117-118
  good and poor form tables, 155-200
  interpretation, 243-249
  Mayman differentiation, 118-119
  modified Mayman differentiation, 120-123,
    201-214
  X+%, 148
Form responses (F), 71-73, 255-257
  interpretation, 255-257
Fr, see Reflection responses
Free association period, 31-33, 332-338
  encouragement, 31-32
  interpretation of verbalizations, 332-338
  questions, 31
  recording responses, 33-34
  timing, 33
Frequencies of scores, 138, 144-146
FT, see Shading responses, texture
FV, see Shading responses, dimensional
FY, see Shading responses, diffuse

Inquiry, 35-38, 46, 338-343
  analogy period, 38
  differences, inter-system, 35-36
  direct, 38
  interpretation of verbalizations, 338-343
  as separate test, 46
  testing limits, 38
Instructions, 26-31
  differences, inter-system, 27, 29
  sets, 28
Intelligence, 23, 107-108, 235, 244
  blend responses, 107-108
  location scores, 235
Interpretation, 221-346
  achromatic color responses, 281-284
  blind interpretation, 225-229
  color responses, 227-281
  content, 300-304
  form-dimension responses, 257-259
  form quality, 243-249
  form responses, 255-257
  integration stage, 224-225
  location scores, 234-241
  number of responses (R), 233-234
  organizational activity, 241-243
  popular responses, 249-250

propositional stage, 223-224
reaction time, 304-305
reflection and pair responses, 290-294
sequence, 328-330
shading responses, 284-290
structural summary, 309-327
verbalizations, 330-345

Lambda index (L), 148
Location scores, 53-67, 144-145, 234-241
  developmental quality, 60-64
  examples, 64-66
  interpretation, 234, 241
  symbols and criteria, 54
Location sheet, 53

M, see Movement responses, human
m, see Movement responses, inanimate
Modified Mayman form quality scoring, 120-
  123, 201-214
Movement responses, animal (FM), 75, 77,
  147, 263-265
  examples, 77
  in experience base, 147
  in experience potential, 147
  interpretation, 263-265
  human (M), 73-75, 77, 147, 259-263
    active versus passive, 74, 147
    examples, 77
    in Erlebnistypus, 147
    in experience actual, 147
    interpretation, 259-263
  inanimate (m), 75-77, 147, 265-266
    examples, 77
    in experience base, 147
    in experience potential, 147
    interpretation, 265-266
Multiple determinants, 106-111. See also
  Blend responses

Nonschizophrenics
  form quality, 246-249
  form responses, 256-257

Organizational activity (Z), 111-117, 215,
  146-147
  examples, 115-116
  intelligence, 112
  predicted Z sums, 146, 215
  weighted Z values, 114, 215
  Zd scores, 146-147
Original responses, 134-136
Out-patients, 217, 250, 257
  Reference sample means, 217

Pair responses (2), 102-103, 290-294
  examples, 102-103
  interpretation, 290-294

Popular responses (P), 127, 130-134
    criteria, 132-133, 216
    interpretation, 249-250
Projective hypothesis, 221-222
Protocols, aggitated depression, 408-418
    children, 460-478
    externalizer, 361-374
    impulsive, 374-385
    internalizer, 349-361
    obsessive, 386-398
    phobic, 398-408
    schizophrenia, 429-459
    suicide attempts, 418-428

Quantitative summary, 138-149
    frequencies of scores, 138, 144-146
    sequence of scores, 138, 144
    See also Structural summary

Reaction times, 33, 149, 304-305
    interpretation, 304-305
Reference group means, 217
Reflection responses, 99, 101-103, 290-294
    examples, 102-103
    form-reflection responses (Fr), 101-102
    interpretation, 290-294
    reflection-form responses (rF), 101
Response styles, 349-385
rF, see Reflection responses
Rorschach, contemporary use, 13-15, 48, 49,
        56
    criticisms, 3-7
    history, 3-14
    systems, 7-14
    teaching practices, 13

S, see White space responses
Schizophrenia, 217, 429-459
    protocols, 429-459
    reference group means, 217
Scoring, 42-51
    purpose, 42-45
    rationale, 45-51
    response complexity, 49-51
    statistical problems, 44
    See also Specific scoring categories
Seating, 24-26
Sequence of scores, 138, 144, 328-330
    interpretation, 328-330
Shading responses, 87-97, 147, 284-290
    See also Specific scoring categories
    diffuse, 96-98, 288-290
        examples, 98
        form shading responses (FY), 96-97
        interpretation, 288-290
        pure shading responses (Y), 96
        shading form responses (YF), 96-97
    dimensional, 92-95, 286-288

examples, 94-95
        form-vista responses (FV), 92-93
        interpretation, 286-288
        pure vista responses (V), 92
        vista-form responses (VF), 92
    interpretation, 284-290
    intersystem differences, 86-87
    texture, 88-91, 94-95, 284-286
        examples, 94-95
        form-texture responses (FT), 91
        interpretation, 284-286
        pure texture responses (T), 89
        texture-form responses (TF), 89-91
Special scorings, 134-136
    body image boundary scores, 135
    original responses, 134-135
    unusual verbalizations, 135-136
Structural data, interpretation, 233-327
    achromatic color responses, 281-284
    active-passive movement, 267-271
    blend responses, 317
    color responses, 277-281
    content categories, 300-304
    Erlebnistypus, 309-311
    experience actual, 311-313
    experience base, 315-316
    experience potential, 313-315
    form-dimensional responses, 257-259
    form quality, 243-249
    form responses, 255-257
    location scores, 234-241
    movement responses, 259-271
    number of responses, 233-234
    organizational activity, 241-243
    popular responses, 249-250
    ratios, percentages, and derivations, 319-
        325
    reaction time, 304-305
    reflection and pair responses, 290-294
    shading responses, 284-290
Structural summary, 145-149, 319-325
    form quality, 144-145
    location features, 144
    organizational activity, 145
    ratios, percentages, and derivations, 146-
        149, 319-325

T, see Shading responses, texture
Testing decisions, 20-23
TF, see Shading responses, texture

Unusual verbalizations, 135-136

V, see Shading responses, dimensional
Verbalizations, 328-346
    free association, 332-338
    inquiry, 338-343
VF, see Shading responses, dimensional

t Index

sponses
onses (S), 57, 237-238
(W), 54-55, 235-236

5-236

Working tables, 153-217

Y, *see* Shading responses, diffuse
YF, *see* Shading responses, diffuse

Z, *see* Organizational activity